D1591777

THE OXFORD HANDBOOK OF

CHURCH AND STATE
IN THE UNITED STATES

THE OXFORD HANDBOOK OF

CHURCH AND STATE IN THE UNITED STATES

Edited By

DEREK H. DAVIS

OXFORD

UNIVERSITY PRESS

2010

OXFORD
UNIVERSITY PRESS

Oxford University Press, Inc., publishes works that further
Oxford University's objective of excellence
in research, scholarship, and education.

Oxford   New York
Auckland   Cape Town   Dar es Salaam   Hong Kong   Karachi
Kuala Lumpur   Madrid   Melbourne   Mexico City   Nairobi
New Delhi   Shanghai   Taipei   Toronto

With offices in
Argentina   Austria   Brazil   Chile   Czech Republic   France   Greece
Guatemala   Hungary   Italy   Japan   Poland   Portugal   Singapore
South Korea   Switzerland   Thailand   Turkey   Ukraine   Vietnam

Copyright © 2010 by Oxford University Press, Inc.

Published by Oxford University Press, Inc.
198 Madison Avenue, New York, New York 10016
www.oup.com

Oxford is a registered trademark of Oxford University Press

All rights reserved. No part of this publication may be reproduced,
stored in a retrieval system, or transmitted, in any form or by any means,
electronic, mechanical, photocopying, recording, or otherwise,
without the prior permission of Oxford University Press.

Library of Congress Cataloging-in-Publication Data
The Oxford handbook of church and state in the United States / edited by Derek H. Davis.
p. cm.
Includes bibliographical references and index.
ISBN 978-0-19-532624-6
1. Church and state—United States. 2. United States—Church history. I. Davis, Derek, 1949–
BR516.O94   2010
322'.10973—dc22   2009045186

1 3 5 7 9 8 6 4 2
Printed in the United States of America
on acid-free paper

This volume is dedicated to my in-laws, Pat Jordan (deceased)
and Bob Jordan,
to whom I will always be grateful for their steady support
and encouragement shown in countless ways

Contents

CONTRIBUTORS

....

DEREK H. DAVIS is Dean of the College of Humanities and Dean of the Graduate School at University of Mary Hardin-Baylor, Belton, Texas, and Director of the UMHB Center for Religious Liberty. He was formerly Director of the J.M. Dawson Institute of Church-State Studies and Professor of Political Science, Baylor University, and Editor of *Journal of Church and State*. He is the author or editor of 17 books, including *Original Intent: Chief Justice Rehnquist & the Course of American Church-State Relations* (Prometheus, 1991), and *Religion and the Continental Congress, 1774–1789: Contributions to Original Intent* (Oxford, 2000). Dr. Davis has also published more than 150 articles in various journals and periodicals. He serves numerous organizations given to the protection of religious freedom in American and international contexts.

N.J. DEMERATH III is the Emile Durkheim Distinguished Professor of Sociology Emeritus at the University of Massachusetts, Amherst, where he has served since 1972. During that time, he has had visiting professorships at Harvard University, Jawaharlal Nehru University, the London School of Economics, and Yale University. He is a past-President of the Society for the Scientific Study of Religion, the Association for the Sociology of Religion, and the Eastern Sociological Society. Dr. Demerath's publications include such recent books as *A Bridging of Faiths: Religion and Politics in a New England City* (Princeton, 1992); *Sacred Companies: Organizational Aspects of Religion and Religious Aspects of Organizations, Crossing the Gods: World Religions and Worldly Politics* (Rutgers, 2001); *Sacred Circles and Public Squares: The Multi-Centering of American Religion* (Indiana, 2004); and the *Sage Handbook of the Sociology of Religion* (Sage, 2007).

DANIEL L. DREISBACH is Professor of Justice, Law and Society in the School of Public Affairs at American University, Washington, D.C. He received a Doctor of Philosophy degree from the University of Oxford and a Juris Doctor degree from the University of Virginia. He has authored or edited seven books, including *Thomas Jefferson and the Wall of Separation between Church and State* (2002) and *The Sacred Rights of Conscience: Selected Readings on Religious Liberty and Church-State Relations in the American Founding* (2009) (coeditor). Dr. Dreisbach has published numerous book chapters, reviews, and articles in scholarly journals, including *American Journal of Legal History, Constitutional Commentary, Emory Law Journal, Journal of Church and State, North Carolina Law Review*, and *William and Mary Quarterly*.

BETTE NOVIT EVANS is Professor *Emerita* of Political Science at Creighton University, Omaha, Nebraska, where she has taught since 1975. Her academic specializations include constitutional jurisprudence, political philosophy, and religion and politics in the United States. Dr. Evans has published articles on constitutional concepts of racial and ethnic equality, civil rights law and policy, and law and religion in the United States. During the past decade, Dr. Evans' work has been directed toward the First Amendment guarantees of religious freedom, and religious pluralism in the American context. Her book, *Interpreting the Free Exercise of Religion* was published in 1998 by the University of North Carolina Press, and in 2001 she received the *Alpha Sigma Nu* National Jesuit Book Award. She has published numerous articles on topics at the intersection of law and religion, and to relate religious pluralism to general theories of pluralism, both in the United States and internationally.

ROGER FINKE is Professor of Sociology and Religious Studies at the Pennsylvania State University, University Park, Pennsylvania and is Director of the Association of Religion Data Archives (www.theARDA.com). He has published in numerous social science journals and has coauthored two award-winning books with Rodney Stark: *Acts of Faith: Explaining the Human Side of Religion* (University of California Press, 2000) and *The Churching of America, 1776–1990: Winners and Losers in our Religious Economy* (Rutgers University Press, 1992; 2005). Dr. Finke's recent cross-national research on the relationship between government regulation of religion and religious persecution has appeared in the *American Sociological Review*. His newest book, *The Price of Freedom Denied: Religious Persecution and Violence*, coauthored with Brian J. Grim, will be published by Cambridge University Press.

RONALD B. FLOWERS is the John F. Weatherly Emeritus Professor of Religion at Texas Christian University, Fort Worth, Texas. He taught at TCU for 37 years and was chair of the Religion Department for 9 years. He is the author of several books, including *Toward Benevolent Neutrality: Church, State, and the Supreme Court* (coauthored with Robert T. Miller) which went through five revised and updated editions; *Religion in Strange Times: The 1960s and 1970s; That Godless Court?: Supreme Court Decisions on Church-State Relationships* (2nd edition 2005); and *To Defend the Constitution: Religion, Conscientious Objection, Naturalization, and the Supreme Court.* Dr. Flowers has also served as President of the American Academy of Religion/Southwest and is currently a member of the Editorial Council of the *Journal of Church and State.* He is still teaching at TCU part-time and recently completed a book, with Steven K. Green and Melissa Rogers, entitled *Religious Freedom and the Supreme Court.*

STEVEN K. GREEN is a Professor of Law, Adjunct Professor of History, and Director of the interdisciplinary Center for Religion, Law and Public Affairs at Willamette University in Salem, Oregon. Before joining the Willamette faculty in 2001, Green served for 10 years as Legal Director and Special Counsel for Americans United for Separation of Church and State in Washington, DC. Green has participated in many of the leading church-state cases before the U.S. Supreme Court, including serving as co-counsel in *Zelman v. Simmons-Harris*, the Cleveland voucher case. Green has testified in Congress and in several state legislatures on a variety of First Amendment issues. Since moving to Oregon, Dr. Green has filed friend of the court briefs in Supreme Court cases involving the Pledge of Allegiance and the Ten Commandments, among others. He is the author of the forthcoming book, *The Second Disestablishment: Church and State in the Nineteenth Century* (Oxford University Press, 2010), co-author of *Religious Freedom and the Supreme Court* (Baylor University Press, 2008), a casebook in church-state law, and author of more than 30 articles on religion and the law.

T. JEREMY GUNN is a professor of international relations at Al Akhawayn University in Morocco. He is also Senior Fellow for Religion and Human Rights at the Center for the Study of Law and Religion at Emory University School of Law and a member of the Advisory Council on Freedom of Religion and Belief of the Organization for Security and Cooperation in Europe (OSCE). His previous positions have included those of Director of the Program on Freedom of Religion and Belief at the American Civil Liberties Union, Director of Research for the U.S. Commission on International Religious Freedom, and Senior Fellow at the U.S. Institute of Peace. Dr. Gunn has taught at several universities, including the law faculties of the Université de Paris II (Panthéon-Assas), Université d'Aix-Marseille III, and the Universität Trier in Germany. He is the author of *A Standard for Repair: The Establishment Clause, Equality, and Natural Rights* (1992) and *Spiritual Weapons: The Cold War and the Forging of an American National Religion* (2009).

NIKOLAS K. GVOSDEV is a professor of national security studies at the U.S. Naval War College, Newport, Rhode Island. He was the Editor of *The National Interest* and a Senior Fellow of Strategic Studies at The Nixon Center. He is currently a senior editor at *The National Interest*. Dr. Gvosdev is a frequent commentator on U.S. foreign policy and international relations, Russian and Eurasian affairs, developments in the Middle East, and the role of religion in politics. He received his doctorate from St. Antony's College, Oxford University, where he studied on a Rhodes Scholarship. He was also associate director of the J.M. Dawson Institute of Church-State Studies at Baylor University. Dr. Gvosdev is the author or editor of six books, including the co-author of *The Receding Shadow of the Prophet: The Rise and Fall of Political Islam*.

ALLEN D. HERTZKE is Presidential Professor of Political Science and Director of Religious Studies at the University of Oklahoma, Norman, Oklahoma. He is author of *Representing God in Washington*, an award-winning analysis of religious lobbies, which has been issued in a Chinese language translation; *Echoes of Discontent*, an account of church-rooted populist movements; and coauthor of *Religion and Politics in America*, a comprehensive text now in its third edition. His latest book is entitled *Freeing God's Children: The Unlikely Alliance for Global Human Rights*.

A winner of numerous teaching awards, Dr. Hertzke has lectured at the National Press Club, the U.S. Holocaust Memorial Museum, the Council on Foreign Relations, the Carnegie Council on Ethics and International Affairs, and before numerous audiences in China. He has consulted with both the Pew Charitable Trusts and the John Templeton Foundation on global religious freedom.

TED G. JELEN is Professor of Political Science at the University of Nevada, Las Vegas. His main research interests are in public opinion, religion and politics, feminism, and the politics of abortion. He is a former editor of the *Journal for the Scientific Study of Religion,* and now serves as the coeditor of the journal *Politics and Religion.* Dr. Jelen has published extensively in the area of religion and politics, and in church-state relations. His publications include *To Serve God and Mammon: Church-State Relations in the United States,* 2nd ed. (Westview, 2010); *The Political World of the Clergy* (Praeger, 1993); and *The Political Mobilization of Religious Beliefs* (Praeger, 1991).

CAITLIN S. KERR graduated with honors from Christ College, the Honors College of Valparaiso University, Valparaiso, Indiana, in 2008. She is currently a Juris Doctor candidate at Indiana University Maurer School of Law-Bloomington, where she also serves as a teaching assistant in the Graduate Legal Studies office. While at Valparaiso, she served on the Honor Council, led an international student cultural conversation group through the University's Writing Center, and studied in Tuebingen, Germany. She is a member of Phi Beta Kappa.

ANDREW R. MURPHY is Associate Professor of Political Science at Rutgers University, New Brunswick, New Jersey. His interests focus on the intersections between religious and political thought and practice, focusing especially on the Anglo-American tradition, in both historical and contemporary contexts. Dr. Murphy is the author, most recently, of *Prodigal Nation: Moral Decline and Divine Punishment from New England to 9-11* (Oxford, 2008); as well as *Conscience and Community: Revisiting Toleration and Religious Dissent in Early Modern England and America* (Penn State, 2001). He has edited *The Political Writings of William Penn* (Liberty Fund, 2002); *Religion, Politics, and American Identity: New Directions, New Controversies,* with David S. Gutterman (Lexington, 2006); and *The Blackwell Companion to Religion and Violence* (forthcoming). He serves as a Book Review Editor for *Politics and Religion.*

RICHARD V. PIERARD is Professor of History Emeritus, Indiana State University, Terre Haute, Indiana. He served on the Indiana State University faculty from 1964 to 2000, and then spent 6 years at Gordon College, Wenham, Massachusetts as a scholar in residence and Stephen Phillips Professor of History. He is currently a visiting lecturer at the South Asia Institute of Advanced Christian Studies, Bangalore, India. He was a Fulbright Professor at the University of Frankfurt (1984–1985) and the University of Halle-Wittenberg (1989–1990), both in Germany, and a visiting lecturer at the University of Otago, New Zealand (2002). Among his many books are, *The Unequal Yoke: Evangelical Christianity and Political Conservatism* (1970, new edition, 2006), *Civil Religion and the Presidency* (with R. D. Linder, 1988), *The American Church Experience: A Concise History* (with T.A. Askew, 2004, new edition, 2008), and *Baptists Together in Christ: A Hundred-year History of the Baptist World Alliance* (2005). Dr. Pierard lives in Hendersonville, North Carolina.

SAM POTOLICCHIO is a doctoral candidate in the department of Government at Georgetown University, Washington, DC. He is a graduate of the Program in Religion and Secondary Education (PRSE) at Harvard University and the Christianity and Culture program where he earned a masters degree in Theological Studies. He frequently lectures on church–state issues for the American Councils for International Education at the Library of Congress. He teaches a course entitled "Religion and Politics" at Georgetown.

JAMES T. RICHARDSON is Professor of Sociology and Judicial Studies at the University of Nevada, Reno, Nevada, where he also directs the Judicial Studies graduate degree programs for trial judges, as well as the Grant Sawyer Center for Justice Studies, a research arm of the university. He has done research on minority religions for many years, focusing particularly on the relationship of law and the judicial system to such entities. He has produced a dozen books and over 250 articles and book chapters, mostly dealing with new or minority religions, but also with use of scientific evidence in court. Dr. Richardson has done research in a number of countries, particularly in Western, Eastern, and Central Europe. His most recent book is *Regulating Religion: Case Studies from Around the Globe* (Kluwer, 2004).

THOMAS ROBBINS is an independent scholar, living in Rochester, Minnesota, who taught at Queens College, The New School for Social Research, Yale University, and the Graduate Theological Union. A Harvard undergraduate, his Ph.D. in sociology is from the University of North Carolina. He is the author of numerous articles and books focusing on the social and theological elements of new religions. More recently, Dr. Robbins has focused on legal and church–state issues related to new religious movements. He has written extensively on the alleged use of mind control by religious groups and has been a vocal critic of the anti-cult movement's views on brainwashing.

MELISSA ROGERS serves as director of the Center for Religion and Public Affairs of the Wake Forest University Divinity School, Winston-Salem, North Carolina. She previously served as the executive director of the Pew Forum on Religion and Public Life and as general counsel of the Baptist Joint Committee on Religious Liberty. In 2008 Baylor University Press published a casebook coauthored by Rogers, *Religious Freedom and the Supreme Court*. She has written extensively on church–state issues, and particularly on the legal impact of the Religious Freedom Restoration Act. Rogers earned her law degree from the University of Pennsylvania Law School, where she was a member of the National Moot Court Team. She graduated Phi Beta Kappa from Baylor University.

ELIZABETH A. SEWELL is Associate Director of the BYU International Center for Law and Religion Studies, Provo, Utah, where she has been involved in recent years in sponsoring numerous church–state conferences, especially in Eastern Europe and Russia. She speaks English, Russian, Czech, and French. She graduated *summa cum laude* in 1997 from the J. Reuben Clark Law School, Brigham Young University, where she was Editor-in-Chief of the *BYU Law Review*. She is the associate editor of *Law and Religion in Post-Communist Europe* (Peeters, 2003), which has been translated and republished in Slovak, Greek, and Italian, and *Facilitating Freedom of Religion or Belief: A Deskbook* (Martinus Nijhoff, 2004), and the author of other publications on law and religion in various law journals and other periodicals.

BARRY ALAN SHAIN is Associate Professor of Political Science at Colgate University, Hamilton, New York. He earned B.A.s in industrial-arts education and philosophy from San Jose State and San Francisco State Universities, respectively, and a Ph.D. from Yale University in political science. In 1992, he was a National Endowment for the Humanities Fellow; in 1993, a John M. Olin Foundation Fellow in History; and in 2005, a National Endowment for the Humanities Fellow for the Understanding of American History and Culture. He has also won several awards for his teaching at Yale and Colgate Universities. His publications include: *The Myth of American Individualism: the Protestant Origins of American Political Thought*; *Man, God, and Society: An Interpretive History of Individualism*; *The Nature of Rights at the American Founding and Beyond*; and forthcoming, *The Declaration of Independence in Historical Context*. His teaching and research interests include British-American political thought and constitutionalism, Protestant political theology, Enlightenment thought, early-modern natural and international law, and American political culture and conservatism. Of particular interest to him are the changing late-eighteenth meanings of key political concepts: liberty and rights.

CLYDE WILCOX is professor of Government at Georgetown University, Washington, DC. He is the author of a number of books, chapters, and articles on religion and politics, gender politics, interest group politics, campaign finance, public opinion and electoral behavior, and the politics of social issues such as abortion, gay rights, and gun control. Dr. Wilcox has authored, coauthored, edited, or coedited more than 30 books. His books include *Public Attitudes on Church and State; Onward Christian Soldiers: The Christian Right in American Politics;* and *Religion and Politics in Comparative Perspective*. His latest books include *The Politics of Same-Sex Marriage,* coedited with Craig Rimmerman, and *The Values Campaign: The Christian Right in the 2004 Elections,* coedited with John Green and Mark Rozell.

JOHN F. WILSON was appointed to the Princeton University (Princeton, New Jersey) faculty in 1960 and became the Agate Brown and George L. Collord Professor of Religion in 1977. He served as Dean of the Graduate School from 1994–2002 and retired in 2003. His scholarly interests primarily concern American religious history. *Pulpit in Parliament* (1969) and *Public Religion in American Culture* (1979) were among his early publications while he also edited *The Study of Religion in American Colleges and Universities* (1970) with Paul Ramsey. Dr. Wilson later transcribed and published a critical edition of *A History of the Work of Redemption* (1989) in *The Works of Jonathan Edwards* (Yale Edition). A collection of readings and commentary on religion and American law, *Church and State in American History* (1965), has continued through several editions with Donald L. Drakeman (1987, 2003). Dr. Wilson directed a long-term project on "Church and State in American History" at Princeton that published two volumes (*Church and State in America: A Bibliographical Guide* 1986, 1987) and commissioned a number of specialized studies. He has also written essays exploring religion and the law in America about particular episodes and periods.

JOHN WITTE, JR. is Jonas Robitscher Professor of Law and Director of the Center for the Study of Law and Religion Center at Emory University, Atlanta, Georgia. A specialist in legal history, marriage law, and religious liberty, he has published 150 articles, 12 journal symposia, and 24 books, including recently *Religion and the American Constitutional Experiment* (2000, 2nd. ed. 2005); *Law and Protestantism: The Legal Teachings of the Lutheran Reformation* (2002); *Sex, Marriage and Family Life in John Calvin's Geneva* (2005); *Modern Christian Teachings on Law, Politics, and Human Nature*, 2 vols. (2006); *God's Joust, God's Justice: Law and Religion in the Western Tradition* (2006); *The Reformation of Rights: Law, Religion, and Human Rights in Early Modern Calvinism* (2007); *Christianity and Law: An Introduction* (2008); and *Sins of the Fathers: The Law and Theology of Illegitimacy Reconsidered* (2009). He has been selected 10 times by the Emory law students as the Most Outstanding Professor and has won many other awards and prizes for his teaching and research.

THE OXFORD HANDBOOK OF

CHURCH AND STATE
IN THE UNITED STATES

INTRODUCTION: RELIGIOUS PLURALISM AS THE ESSENTIAL FOUNDATION OF AMERICA'S QUEST FOR UNITY AND ORDER

DEREK H. DAVIS

THIS *Handbook* provides an overview of how church and state interact in the United States. The term *church–state,* a distinctively Western term that emerged in sixteenth-century Europe, remains useful because it is so commonly used, in the United States and elsewhere, to describe generally the interaction between religion and government. However, "church" connotes Christianity, of course, which is why it was an altogether appropriate term for how church and state interacted in Christian Europe in the sixteenth century. But things began to change, first in Europe, then more dramatically in the United States in the seventeenth and eighteenth centuries. The principal change was a broad experiment with separating church and state to maximize freedom, not only for Christian groups, but for other religious groups as well. The past persecution, torture, and even slaughter of human beings because of religious differences was thought to be largely a product

Portions of this Introduction were drawn from Derek H. Davis, "Religious Pluralism and the Quest for Unity in American Life." *Journal of Church and State* 36 (Spring 1994): 245–259.

of government having too much power to dictate conformity to one particular religion. The United States led the way in the experiment with the separation of church and state; a formal separation seemed the best way to keep government out of religion and ensure religious freedom for adherents of all religious traditions.

However, the experiment created a host of difficult problems. The United States was profoundly Christian at its founding. Would Christianity really be placed on equal footing with all other religious groups in receiving no favors from government? How could government function without some recognized set of underlying theological commitments that placed it under divine authority in a way that made sense to a majority of the American people? Was not some kind of theological foundation really necessary to ensure a stable government? The need of a common religion to ensure social and political solidarity had been a bedrock principle for millennia. Under the Constitution, how should the United States be characterized in terms of political theory? Was it a secular state, a religious state, some kind of semireligious state, or perhaps something else? What would be the role of religion in determining law and public policy? Would non-Christian traditions really enjoy the same access to government decision making as Christian groups? And, importantly, would religious pluralism actually become a positive value, something to embrace and celebrate, rather than something to be looked upon as a source of disorder and chaos?

All of these questions weighed heavily on the minds of the Founders, although the final one, pertaining to whether the nation would embrace religious pluralism as a positive matter of government policy, was especially important. As it turned out, the United States was serious about embracing religious pluralism, and the nation soon became a haven for all kinds of religious groups that immigrated to America in unimaginable numbers. The tensions created by this commitment to religious pluralism were many. These tensions are detailed throughout this volume, but suffice it to say that perhaps half of American society today still does not accept the notion that the Founding Fathers really sought to separate church and state—at least not in the way that the U.S. Supreme Court sometimes claims. The emergence of the Christian Right in the latter part of the twentieth century, a powerful political movement, is directly attributable to a deepening sense that America is turning away from its Christian roots and needs the power and influence of government to restore those roots before it is too late. The Christian Right frequently targets religious pluralism as the key problem.

Yes, religious pluralism *was* and *is* the problem; but it is *also* the solution. It is a *problem* if Christianity is to be the essential foundation of unity and order in the American setting; but it is also the *solution* if religious freedom and equal treatment under the law of all religious groups is to be the foundation of unity and order. The United States has wrestled with this tension since the founding era. It is still unresolved. It will likely remain unresolved, and perhaps that is as it should be. These two competing forces—legalized pluralism and Christian majoritarianism—still create dissension in America, but their coexistence also promotes harmony. There are many, many dimensions to church and state in the United States, and most of those dimensions are addressed in the chapters of this volume. In one way or another, all of the chapters address the underlying tension of America being culturally Christian, but constitutionally secular. Not all of the authors agree about how to find the proper balance in this ongoing tension; a presentation of different perspectives that in themselves illustrate this tension was a goal in the selection of contributors to this volume. To set the stage, I should say a bit more about this ongoing tension—the tension between Christianity as the culturally dominant religion in America and a constitutional order that treats all religions alike. Indeed, many of the church–state controversies in the United States really do center on religious pluralism and its accompanying problems.

Colonial Settlements

From the time of the earliest European settlements in the sixteenth century, America's face has been one of religious diversity. In the South and West, Spanish and French explorations resulted in the spread of the Roman Catholic faith. Along the eastern seaboard, English, German, Dutch, and Swedish settlements in the seventeenth century brought a diversity of Protestants, most of whom sought to escape the religious persecutions they had experienced in the Old World. By 1700, the colonies were dotted with Congregationalists, Separatists, Baptists, Quakers, Calvinists, Lutherans, Anglicans, Presbyterians, Moravians, Dunkers, Pietists, Huguenots, and Mennonites. Although Protestants commanded a majority in all of the colonies, Jews and Catholics increasingly made their presence felt, although by the time of Independence, neither represented more than 1% of the total colonial population.

Although religious pluralism was rampant in the colonies, peaceful relations among the various religious groups generally was not. Most of the colonists who departed from the Old World to escape religious persecution had no intention, once they arrived in the New World, of tolerating any religion other than their own. They had ventured to America not to experiment, but to practice and preserve already fully developed systems of belief. Consequently, most of the colonies established their own churches and persecuted, to one degree or another, those outside the approved form of worship. Notable exceptions to this pattern were Rhode Island, Pennsylvania, and Delaware, which never had formally established churches. However, in the New England colonies, Puritans persecuted and sometimes banished Quakers, Baptists, and Anglicans, whereas in many of the southern colonies, Anglicans harassed and persecuted Baptists and Puritans. Huguenots were banished from Florida, Jews from New York, and Catholics from almost everywhere but Maryland, where they had been the first settlers.

Thus, although religious pluralism was a social reality in the colonies, it was not always looked upon as something that was desirable. Religious hostilities were everywhere, and peace among the various religious groups was often thought to be impossible. Gradually, however, this perception changed. At first, peaceful coexistence was mandated by various acts of toleration. Maryland's Act of Toleration of 1649, for example, encouraged friendly relations among the multiplicity of religions by punishing anyone who would profane another by calling that person such horribles as Brownist, Calvinist, Roundhead, Papist, Puritan, Separatist, Presbyterian, heretic, or schismatic. The English Act of Toleration of 1689, widely enforced in the colonies from the time of its passage, forced the colonies to decriminalize various modes of religious behavior and remove civil disabilities against all but Catholics, Unitarians, and atheists. Later in the colonial period, religious pluralism was increasingly tolerated because it was widely recognized that its effects were not uniformly bad. Gradually, many came to believe that all religions produced character and integrity in their adherents, and that these elements contributed to the common good, especially since free and democratic government required a virtuous citizenry for its survival.

It was the movement for independence from the mother country, however, that more than any other single factor made peaceful allies of the ever-increasing multiplicity of religions in America. Despite doctrinal differences, most religious revolutionaries seemed to share three separate but interrelated commitments. First, they believed that the American independence movement was in keeping with eternal principles of nature, liberty, good government, and justice. All human affairs, they believed, are imbedded in the natural order conceived on the pattern of creation and creator. Thus, Thomas Jefferson, a deist, could say that "the God who gave us life gave us liberty at the same time."[1] Second, many American patriots from all religious persuasions believed that God controlled history and that the colonial cause against the British held God's favor. Oliver Wolcott, a Congregationalist and member of the Continental Congress from Connecticut, held firmly to his belief that the "God who takes care of and Protects Nations, will take care of this People."[2] Elbridge Gerry of Massachusetts apparently agreed. In a letter to Samuel Adams, he wrote that "history could hardly produce such a series of events as has taken place in favor of American opposition. The hand of Heaven seems to have directed every occurrence."[3] Third, Americans representing a great variety of faiths shared a commitment to republican government. Greatly simplified, republican government was understood to represent a constellation of political ideas: government by the people, separation of powers, limited government without jurisdiction to interfere with the people's natural rights, and a dependence upon public virtue. Thomas Paine exclaimed in 1776 that it was only common sense for Americans to become republicans.[4] And in the view of John Adams, "There is no good government but what is republican."[5] Republicanism was widely thought to embrace biblical ideals, and was therefore a uniting force among most Americans with religious commitments. These three factors, then, were instrumental in forging new bonds of unity among the nation's medley of peoples.[6]

Unity and Nationhood

Some of the nation's earliest official acts reflected the people's desire to subdue their differences in the interest of unity. The Declaration of Independence was itself a compromise of sorts, a coming together of 13 autonomous states that had always prized their individual sovereignty. The Declaration also seemed to mask the people's religious differences, using generic references to the "Creator," "Nature's God," and "Providence" in identifying the One whom they believed backed the colonies' revolutionary cause. On the same day that it adopted the Declaration, July 4, 1776, the Continental Congress appointed a committee of Thomas Jefferson, John Adams, and Benjamin Franklin to devise an official seal for the newly formed nation. One of the committee's recommendations, the motto *E Pluribus Unum* ("Out of many, one"), became a part of "the Great Seal" as finally adopted on June 20, 1782. Although the motto pointed primarily to the unity of the 13 states, it also was, and remains, a normative description of America as a pluralistic society, not merely religiously, but politically, ethnically, and socially as well.

The spirit of elation that came with victory over the British soon subsided as a host of problems plagued the new nation. The problems centered on the central government's inadequate taxing power, its inability to formulate binding foreign policy, and its feeble status as a mere creature of the states. A Constitutional Convention was called in 1787 to remedy these problems, and a new Constitution was the result. A matter of special concern for the framers in writing the Constitution was the protection of religious liberty, a concern generated by the diversity of religious opinion that spread across America. The framers virtually assured the continuance of America's religious pluralism by placing no restrictions on the free exercise of religion and by refraining from giving preferential status to any particular form of religion. Although the Constitution, as drafted and presented to the states in 1787 was silent on these matters, the 55 delegates to the Constitutional Convention unanimously understood the document in this way. The people, however, wanting explicit assurances that these ideals would be realized, made their ratification contingent on the adoption of a constitutional amendment to this effect, which in final form appeared as the first 16 words of the First Amendment: "Congress shall make no laws respecting an establishment of religion or prohibiting the free exercise thereof."

The religion clauses rendered the federal government incompetent to make judgments regarding the truth or falseness of any citizen's religious beliefs. In short, the framers created a secular, or neutral, state, one which was in no way hostile to religion, but which would be required to maintain some distance between it and religious matters. Religious belief was to be a matter of private right. As James Madison wrote, "The Religion then of every man must be left to the conviction and conscience of every man. . . . We maintain therefore that in matters of Religion, no man's right is [to be] abridged by the institution of Civil Society and that Religion is wholly exempt from its cognizance."[7] Moreover, Article VI of the Constitution made one's religious faith irrelevant in terms of one's right to hold federal office. The requirement that "no religious test shall ever be required as a qualification to any office or public trust under the United States," was not only a profound acknowledgment of the secular character of the American state, it also indirectly encouraged religious pluralism because no person would be legally disqualified from public service on account of one's religious opinions.

These ringing pronouncements for religious liberty in the federal Constitution mirrored a simultaneous movement for religious liberty in the various states. One by one, the states ended long-held religious establishments in which one or more preferred Protestant denominations were given monetary and other forms of support from the state. When independence from Great Britain was declared in 1776, only four states—Rhode Island, Pennsylvania, Delaware, and New Jersey—were without religious establishments. By the time the Constitution and Bill of Rights had been ratified, New York, Virginia, North Carolina, and South Carolina had joined the list, and by 1833, the remainder of the original 13 states—Georgia, Maryland, Connecticut, New Hampshire, and Massachusetts—had also ended their establishments. The decision of the last holdout, Massachusetts, to end its Congregational establishment proved wrong the prediction of John Adams that it would be easier to "change the movements of the heavenly bodies as [to] alter the religious laws of Massachusetts."[8] The Constitution's emphasis on the protection of the free exercise of religion, moreover, was reflected in a growing tendency in the states to decriminalize religious acts. For example, there were removed during the founding period laws in Virginia that provided for whippings for disrespect shown to an Anglican minister; the death penalty for blasphemy, impious reference to the Trinity, or habitual cursing; and the suppression of Quakers as "an unreasonable and turbulent sort of people . . . teaching and publishing lies, miracles, false visions, prophecies, and doctrines. . . ."[9] One by one, the religious tests for holding civil office in the various states likewise vanished. Most of these tests, such as Maryland's requirement that an officer "profess a belief in the Christian religion," North Carolina's exclusion from office any person who denied the "divine authority" of the Bible, or Pennsylvania's requirement that one "confess a belief in God," were eliminated during the 50-year period following independence.[10]

Although it is true that Protestants far outnumbered non-Protestants in the colonial and founding eras, there is good evidence that the new emphasis on freedom of religious belief was intended as more than a tolerance among the Protestant denominations. Even in Connecticut in 1784, in which the Puritan heritage was especially strong and the Congregationalist Church still established by law, Zephaniah Swift, a prominent Connecticut lawyer and politician, acknowledged that "Jews, Mahomedans, and others" enjoyed perfect religious freedom on the ground that they could practice their religion within the state—even if they had to pay for the support of the Christian one.[11] Thomas Jefferson clearly sought religious freedom even for nontheists. He wrote, for example, that his Virginia Statute for Religious Freedom, written in 1779, but not enacted until 1786, was "to comprehend within the mantle of its protection the Jew and Gentile, the Christian and

Mahometan, the Hindoo, and infidel of every denomination."[12] He later added that he did not care whether his neighbors believed in one or twenty gods, so long as they kept the civil peace.[13] On the strength of pronouncements such as these, religious pluralism in the new Republic seemed assured.

THE EXPANSION OF RELIGIOUS PLURALISM

Given the legal framework of disestablishment and religious free exercise that was well in place by the 1830s, one might have expected an immediate explosion of religious diversity. This is precisely what occurred. Hundreds, if not thousands, of new religious groups sprang up everywhere. Most failed to distinguish themselves and are now forgotten chapters in American religious history. Others, such as the Church of Jesus Christ of Latter-day Saints (Mormons), Jehovah's Witnesses, Seventh-day Adventists, Christian Scientists, and the Shakers gathered large followings and found their place in the religious landscape. The new standard of tolerance likewise became an agenda for the rise of Unitarians, transcendentalists, atheists, and philosophical pragmatists such as John Dewey and Horace Kallen. Catholics by the millions, and later Jewish and Eastern Orthodox peoples found their way to American shores. Meanwhile, in the midst of these rapid changes, Protestantism experienced growth patterns unparalleled in American history. Groups that had held the controlling positions in American religious life before independence—Episcopalians and Congregationalists in particular—began to take back seats to groups that previously had been religious minorities. The changes became evident in the Second Great Awakening, which witnessed the rise of the Methodists, Baptists, and Presbyterians as the dominant forces of American Protestantism. So powerful was the Awakening that it allowed Protestants to maintain their *de facto* establishment in American life, a state of affairs that lasted, according to Robert Handy, until after World War II, when Protestant ideals lost their ability to control America's political, social, and religious destiny.[14]

During this period of unprecedented growth in the diversity of American religion, unity, always the goal of *E Pluribus Unum,* more often than not was cast aside. The nineteenth century is replete with examples of widespread bigotry toward Catholics and Jews as well as the host of newly emerging religious groups. Catholics in particular, whose numbers increased more rapidly than all other immigrants combined, experienced widespread religious discrimination, reinforced in many instances by repressive state laws.[15] The Nativists, or "Know Nothing" party, seized control of a number of state legislatures and passed countless laws specifically directed against Catholic immigrants. Mormons were successively run out of New York, Ohio, Missouri, and Illinois before finding a somewhat more peaceful haven in the uninhabited regions of Utah. From their beginning in 1872, Jehovah's Witnesses were the object of ridicule and persecution for their hostile attitude toward a government they believed was controlled by Satan.

At the beginning of the twentieth century, approximately 35% of the American populous was affiliated with a church or religious group; as the twenty-first century opened, the figure was 65%.[16] In 1800 there were fewer than 40 identifiable religious groups in America; there are presently more than 1,500 communities of faith—churches, sects, temples, synagogues—each claiming to possess the truth on religious matters. If the constitutionally mandated framework of religious freedom can make any claim whatsoever, it is that it gave official sanction to a phenomenal growth in religious diversity. Even Benjamin Franklin, who at the Constitutional Convention remarked, "Finally, we're going to turn religion loose,"[17] could never have anticipated the growth of religion in so many directions.

The most remarkable development in the last 25 years has been the arrival of sizable numbers of adherents of Eastern and Middle Eastern religions, especially Muslims, Buddhists, and Hindus. The number of Muslims in the United States is disputed, but in 2009 the estimates ranged from 1.5 million to more than 7 million. However, even if the lower estimates are accurate, they still represent a sizable increase in Muslim presence in the last few decades.[18] More than 100 different Hindu denominations have been planted in America since 1965 and more than 75 forms of Buddhism currently exist; each of these two communities now claims from 3 to 5 million adherents, and their rate of growth continues to be among the highest in the country.[19] Islam, Buddhism, and Hinduism provide the most complete alternative on the most basic issues to Christianity. Dismissed for many decades as illegitimate in the American context, these groups are now forcing the encounter with non-Asian Americans at every level of society.

During the twentieth century, the New Thought metaphysical churches (Religious Science, Divine Science, and the Unity School of Christianity) became familiar sights on American street corners. Now with numbers in the hundreds of thousands, their influence has permeated the mainstream of American culture through the spread of their literature. Occult religions, among the least understood religious options, are also on the rise. Spiritualism, for example, often thought of as a nineteenth-century fad, has experienced a revival, especially in urban settings. Theosophy, based upon teachings received by Helena Blavatsky by what she claimed were ascended masters of wisdom, has spawned more than 100 organizations and several tens of thousands of members. Astrology and belief in reincarnation also now reach a growing segment of the American public.[20]

Not to be forgotten in the massive pluralism so evident in American contemporary life is the continuance and revival of Native American religious traditions. Native American themes of oneness with the sacred land, shamanism, and the transformative power of Indian rituals such as peyote ingestion, have caused dramatic increases in the number of Americans returning to ancient Native American practices so long suppressed during the days of American expansionism.

Those who are without religious faith also contribute to America's diversity. The Religious Identification Survey (ARIS) sponsored by Trinity College in Hartford, Connecticut, released in 2008, reveals some interesting facts about the rise of unbelief in the United States. The survey suggests that Americans claiming no religious ties have grown more than any other group surveyed. What the survey calls "Nones"—atheists, agnostics, humanists, secularists—now comprise 15% of the American public, up from 8.2% in 1990. Vermont is the state with the heaviest concentration of "Nones," 34% of its residents. The survey reveals that the religious landscape in the United States is changing dramatically in other ways as well. First, American citizens embracing Christianity are now only 76% of the population compared with 86.2% in 1990. Second, an increasing number of Christians identify with no particular denomination; rather than being Catholic, Baptist, Presbyterian or Lutheran, many Christians now want to be referred to more generally as "Christian" or "Believer." Third, the poll concludes what has already been generally stated: non-Christian religions such as Buddhism, Hinduism, Islam, Sikhism, Scientology, Daoism, Spiritualism, and other nontraditional religions have more adherents today than in 1990.[21]

Despite these interesting alterations to the religious landscape, the Christian community continues to dominate the American scene. Protestants now make up 55.2% of the total population, Catholics represent 28.6%; together they constitute a Christian majority—83.8% of the total U.S. population.[22] The number of Jews in America, about 6 million (2.4%), has remained roughly constant over the last 30 years. By all accounts, the spread of new and nontraditional religions in America is certain to influence the nation's future in a variety of ways. The reactions to these developments take many forms.

RESPONSES TO RELIGIOUS PLURALISM

One response to the rising religious pluralism of recent times has been the call for a return to "Christian America." Threatened by the loss of Christian hegemony and the realization that Christians are a shrinking culture group, there are movements today in America that actively seek to impose a particular theocracy on the rest of the nation. Theocracy, the direct rule of a nation by God through divinely selected spokesmen, has many exemplars in the modern world. Saudi Arabia and Iran are nations with obvious theocratic tendencies. In the United States, the Christian Reconstruction Movement proposes the purest form of theocracy. Reconstructionism, which claims 20 million members but probably is considerably smaller,[23] believes that the law given for the political and legal ordering of ancient Israel is intended for all people at all times; therefore, America is duty-bound to install a political system based entirely on biblical law. According to Rousas J. Rushdoony, the society that fails to do this "places itself on death row: it is marked for judgment."[24] The Reconstructionists' revamped polity would require capital punishment for adulterers, homosexuals, and incorrigible children.[25]

Installing a theocracy is one method of dealing with the problems associated with religious pluralism. Despite its commitment to bring America back to its senses, such a program fails in its efforts to unify America, however, because, as

Robert Booth Fowler has noted, it fails to deal with "the reality of pluralism in the modern United States."[26]

Meanwhile, others who have sensed that commonality among America's citizens is slipping have sought in a less particularistic way to find a set of core values around which all Americans can unite. In the 1960s, a group of social analysts and scholars, among them Sidney E. Mead, Robin Williams, Martin Marty, J. Paul Williams, and Robert Bellah, began a search for a common set of symbols to be transmitted across regions, generations, and peoples in America. The necessity for Benjamin Franklin's "public religion" came to be expressed in such terms as common faith, the religion of the republic, and the one that became most popular, civil religion. According to Bellah, the new search for a civil religion was caused by a crisis of meaning that produced a deepening cynicism among the American people, "and a good deal of anxiety about the future."[27] Moreover, the search became essential in a day of uncertainty about the nation's underpinnings, a condition exacerbated by a rapidly expanding religious pluralism. The search for the exact nature of America's civil religion continues until the present day. However, the reality of an American civil religion, albeit one that is imprecise in its dimensions, can hardly be denied.

The form of civil religion that exists today in the United States seems to embrace ideas from two distinct theological traditions. On the one hand, American civil religion consists of ideas derived from Puritanism such as the covenanted, millennial, and chosen nation. These ideas have been, and remain, inherently religious, and implicitly particularistic and coercive. On the other hand, ideas contributed from the American Enlightenment, such as the Declaration's affirmation that "all men are created equal," and are entitled to rights of "life, liberty, and the pursuit of happiness," are clearly more secular, and implicitly universalistic and persuasive in character. Both traditions have usually sought the aid of government for their advancement, which of course has created unique problems for the propagation of the more distinctly religious Puritan ideas because of the Constitution's church–state separation principle. Nevertheless, as Richard Hughes has rightly observed, most Christian patriots during the course of our nationhood have never perceived any tension between "the god of Puritan particularism and the god of universal liberties."[28] Even Bellah, the foremost scholar on the subject of American civil religion, uncritically fuses the two traditions in his description of that civil religion to which the nation should commit itself.

However, there are dangers in "constructing" any type of civil religion. Martin Marty noted more than 20 years ago that many seemed to be taking too seriously Robin Williams' assertion that "every functioning society has to an important degree a common religion," for Marty, an "observation that for many became an injunction: develop one."[29] If a civil religion must be developed, however, it should not intrude on, or offer itself as a substitute for, traditional religions. All religions should retain their autonomy and their freedom to proclaim their own understanding of truth. In short, any American civil religion should respect religious pluralism.

Religious pluralism, contrary to the assumption of many, does not threaten truth; in theory it only expands the possibilities of truth. A political framework that allows for religious pluralism is not committed to relativism, as it might seem. Rather, it is a policy fully open to truth, and entertains even the possibility of a final consensus on truth. What the Constitution does not permit is a governmental regulating and monitoring of the search for religious truth, or siding with any particular version of religious truth. This principle was clearly enunciated by the Supreme Court as early as 1872, in *Watson v. Jones,* when it declared, "The law knows no heresy, and is committed to the support of no dogma, the establishment of no sect." Supreme Court Justice Anthony Kennedy, in the case of *Lee v. Weisman* (1992), insightfully offered the view that civil religion, whatever its merits, is religion nonetheless and therefore as unqualified as any traditional sect or dogma to receive official governmental endorsement.

It should be noted that, although the church–state separation principle prohibits an official governmental endorsement of civil religion, the same principle in no way prevents the development of a cultural civil religion. It is civil religion as a *legal* institution rather than as a *cultural* institution that the Constitution prohibits. Bellah is surely correct in saying that "the fact that we have no established religion does not mean that our public life has no religious dimension nor that fundamental questions of our national existence are not civil religious questions."[30] Thus the prospect that a unifying civil religion might develop in America remains intact, although the precise elements of such a common faith remain uncertain.

For the present, the more important goal, and one that should never be disparaged, is building a healthy respect for religious pluralism—and for the related commitments that make it possible, religious liberty and the separation of church and state. Religious pluralism, for all of American history, has never been perceived as a major obstacle to unity. Thus, unity rightly remains a national goal, but it should never be achieved at the expense of limiting the people's constitutional right to believe in and practice their diverse religious traditions. Religious pluralism is one of America's best, not worst, traditions. Now and for America's future, religious pluralism is not something to be condemned, but something to be celebrated.

UNITY IN THE FACE OF DIVERSITY

Americans will never agree on a common religion; but this is not necessary for constructing a healthy society in which various religious traditions can live together in peace and with mutual respect. What is most necessary is that all faith communities in America have equal access to participation in public discourse. As long as every religious person and group in the nation knows with confidence that they can enter public dialogue, can be players in the making of law and public policy, and can have a real voice in influencing the course and direction of the nation, then unity in the face of diversity is possible. Although many in America are uncomfortable with this right of equal access to the public table, many are not and they accept it as principally the correct way to order American society, as central to religious freedom, and as a positive means to build mutual respect among the various religious traditions.

This framework of equal participation by all citizens and groups, religious and nonreligious alike, is central to the American political tradition. In theory and practice, religious arguments are as welcome and as potentially effective as any secular arguments that might be presented toward formulating public policy. This framework of equal respect accorded to all religious traditions in the public square is central to the very meaning of the separation of church and state. There are multiple dimensions to the separation of church and state, of course, and most of those dimensions are addressed in this volume. However, the separation of church and state in America has never been understood to exclude religious persons or groups from participating in public debate. This nondiscriminatory right to make genuine contributions toward the public weal, to have a bona fide voice in formulating policies that will affect all Americans, is a valuable tradition that forms a solid foundation for unity, respect, and tolerance among Americans in the face of their great diversity.

CONCLUSION

The American experiment in separating of church and state is, to say the least, highly controversial. The fundamental drive to merge church and state, to ground political life in the "other," a tendency feverishly characteristic of all societies throughout human history, continues to energize a large segment of the American population. Mostly conservative Christians, this segment of America has increasingly become a major political force in America since the 1970s. Often labeled the Christian Right, this sector of the U.S. citizenry frequently chafes at court rulings that restrict prayer in the public schools, limit public financial aid to religious institutions, permit abortions, allow homosexual couples to cohabit or marry, curb the display of religious symbols on public property, or otherwise challenge Christian hegemony in American culture. The Christian Right seeks merely to "unify" Americans around a common set of Christian beliefs and practices, but more liberal elements of the American population frequently criticize them for behavior that sometimes fails to respect and protect diversity. These more liberal critics also seek unity among American citizens, but they seek it under a different banner, under a different set of core beliefs that respects diversity of religious belief.

The "culture war," as it is sometimes called, is always at work, resulting in heated rhetoric and sometimes violent behavior. It is intense enough to draw as participants not just common citizens, but societal elites, including politicians, judges, and academicians. My own contention is that the culture war is fueled not simply by politicians and judges who pander to the Christian Right for political reasons, but by politicians and judges who fundamentally agree with many of the views of the Christian Right. They too feel the tensions created by competing world views, and thus find themselves contributing, however unwittingly, to the culture war by their legislative agenda or court rulings. It is not uncommon, for example, for judges, lawyers, and legal scholars to comment on the state of disarray in which U.S. Supreme Court decisions on church–state issues find themselves. This is mostly an accurate assessment, for almost anyone, save experts in the field, is certain to be frustrated when trying to discover logic and consistency in the Court's church–state decisions. The Court was very separationist in its rulings until the 1980s, when the Court began to make a more conservative turn after several conservative justices were appointed by Republican presidents. Church–state cases are now hotly contested and usually confusing in their outcomes to many American citizens. But however one analyzes the appointments to the Court, the anomalies, inconsistencies, and sometimes confusing rulings of the Court are mostly a reflection of disagreements among the justices generally about how religion, state, and law should interact, and specifically the extent to which Christian values and traditions should be legally protected.

This volume, in the final analysis, is a description of the many controversies pertaining to religion that make unity in American life seemingly impossible or at least improbable, but simultaneously, because of a Constitution that mandates equal respect for all religious traditions, eminently possible. Indeed, the contributors to this volume fall into different camps about how to resolve these controversies. However, vigorous debate is healthy. Controversy in any society is good, provided the discourse it engenders remains civil and free of violence. Democracy in America does not always succeed because agreement is reached on all points of controversy, but rather because peaceful disagreement, understood as essential to the system, is somehow usually achieved. A vibrant democracy never permanently enthrones a particular viewpoint; those who disagree remain hopeful that their ability to participate equally in pubic discourse might make them able to eventually champion a new perspective, a new law, a new policy. This is the beauty of a healthy democracy. It keeps citizens engaged, vigorously advocating change according to their own perspectives, believing that they can make a difference for good in their nation and in the world. If controversy over the merits of the separation of church and state helps fuel democracy, as I believe it does, then separation of church and state is a positive force in society.

ENDNOTES

1. Thomas Jefferson, "A Summary View of the Rights of British America," 1 August 1774, in *American Archives, ed. Peter Force* (Washington, DC: n.p., 1837-1846), 1: 690.

2. Oliver Wolcott to Laura Wolcott, 2 May 1778, in *Letters of Delegates to Congress, 1774–1789*, ed. Paul H. Smith (Washington, DC: Library of Congress, 1979), 9: 568.

3. Elbridge Gerry to Samuel Adams, 13 December 1775, quoted in Benjamin F. Morris, *Christian Life and Character of the Civil Institutions of the United States* (Philadelphia: George W. Childs, 1864), 119.

4. Thomas Paine, "Common Sense," in *Common Sense and the Crisis* (New York: Anchor Books, 1973), 21.

5. John Adams to J.H. Tiffany, 30 April 1819, in *The Works of John Adams, Second President of the United States*, ed. Charles F. Adams (Boston: Little, Brown & Co., 1856), 10: 378.

6. For an expansion on these three themes, see Derek H. Davis, *Religion and the Continental Congress, 1774–1789: Contributions to Original Intent* (Oxford, UK: Oxford University Press, 2000), 57–64.

7. James Madison, "A Memorial and Remonstrance against Religious Assessments," 1785.

8. John Adams (1774), in *Diary and Autobiography of John Adams*, ed. L.H. Butterfield (Cambridge, MA: The Belknap Press of Harvard University Press, 1961), 2: 152.

9. William W. Hening, *Statutes at Large* (Richmond, VA: n.p., 1810–1823), 1: 532.

10. Carl F.G. Zollman, *American Church Law* (St. Paul, MN: West Publishing, 1933), 5–7; William Addison Blakely, *American State Papers on Freedom of Religion*, 3rd rev. ed. (Washington, DC: Review and Herald, 1943), 395.

11. Thomas J. Curry, *The First Freedoms: Church and State in America to the Passage of the First Amendment* (New York: Oxford University Press, 1987), 184.

12. William Addison Blakely, *American State Papers on Sunday Legislation*, rev. ed. (Washington, DC: Review and Herald, 1911), 133, n.1.

13. Paul Leicester Ford, ed., *The Writings of Thomas Jefferson* (New York: n.p., 1892–1899), 1: 30.

14. Robert T. Handy, *A Christian America: Protestant Hopes and Historical Realities*, 2nd rev. ed. (New York: Oxford University Press, 1984).

15. William Warren Sweet, *The Story of Religion in America*, enlarged ed. (New York: Harper & Brothers, 1950), 334–335.

16. Ibid., 205–222.

17. Verner W. Crane, *Benjamin Franklin and a Rising People* (Boston: Little, Brown and Company, 1954), 200.

18. In a speech in Cairo, Egypt on June 4, 2009, President Obama referenced the "nearly 7 million American Muslims in our country today." A 2007 Pew Research Center study estimated the American Muslim population to be 2.35 million. See "Political Punch," http://blogs.abcnews.com/politicalpunch/2009/06.

19. Gordon Melton, ed., *The Encyclopedia of American Religions*, 3rd ed. (Detroit, Mich.: Gale Research, Inc., 1989), 174–176.

20. Ibid., 20.

21. Derek H. Davis, "Survey's Implications for Education," May 28, 2009, www.baptiststandard.com.

22. Derek H. Davis, "Christian Faith and Political Involvement in Today's Culture War," *Journal of Church and State* 38 (Summer 1996): 477.

23. Anson Shupe, "The Reconstructionist Movement on the New Christian Right," *Christian Century*, 4 October 1989, 881.

24. Rousas J. Rushdoony, *The Institutes of Biblical Law* (Philadelphia: The Presbyterian and Reformed Publishing Co., 1984), 4.

25. David A. Rausch and Douglas E. Chismar, "The New Puritans and Their Theonomic Paradise," *Christian Century*, 3 August 1983, 713.

26. Rob Boston, "The Christian Nation Debate," *Church and State* 46 (January 1993): 10.

27. Robert N. Bellah, *The Broken Covenant: American Civil Religion in Time of Trial*, 2nd ed. (Chicago: University of Chicago Press, 1993), preface.

28. Richard T. Hughes, "Civil Religion, the Theology of the Republic, and the Free Church Tradition," *Journal of Church and State* 22 (Winter 1980): 77–78.

29. Martin Marty, "A Nation of Behavers," *Worldview* 17 (May 1974): 11.

30. Bellah, *The Broken Covenant*, 169.

BIBLIOGRAPHY

Books

Adams, Charles R., ed. *The Works of John Adams, Second President of the United States.* Boston: Little, Brown & Co.,1856.

Bellah, Robert N. *The Broken Covenant: American Civil Religion in Time of Trial,* 2nd ed. Chicago: University of Chicago Press, 1993.

Blakely, William Addison. *American State Papers on Freedom of Religion.* 3rd rev. ed. Washington, DC: Review and Herald, 1943.

———. *American State Papers on Sunday Legislation*, rev. ed. Washington, DC: Review and Herald, 1911.

Butterfield, L.H., ed. *Diary and Autobiography of John Adams.* Cambridge, MA: The Belknap Press of Harvard University Press, 1961.

Crane, Verner W. *Benjamin Franklin and a Rising People.* Boston: Little, Brown, 1954.

Curry, Thomas J. *The First Freedoms: Church and State in America to the Passage of the First Amendment.* New York: Oxford University Press, 1987.

Davis, Derek H. *Religion and the Continental Congress, 1774–1789: Contributions to Original Intent.* Oxford: Oxford University Press, 2000.

Ford, Paul Leicester, ed., *The Writings of Thomas Jefferson.* New York: n.p., 1892–1899.

Handy, Robert T. *A Christian America: Protestant Hopes and Historical Realities*, 2nd rev. ed. New York: Oxford University Press, 1984.

Hening, William W. *Statutes at Large.* Richmond, VA: n.p., 1810–1823.

Information Please and Almanac: Atlas and Yearbook 1993, 46th ed. New York: Houghton Mifflin, 1993.

Melton, Gordon, ed. *The Encyclopedia of American Religions*, 3rd ed. Detroit, MI: Gale Research, 1989.

Morris, Benjamin J. *Christian Life and Character of the Civil Institutions of the United States.* Philadelphia: George W. Childs, 1864.

Rushdoony, Rousas J. *The Institutes of Biblical Law.* Philadelphia: The Presbyterian and Reformed Publishing Co., 1984.

Smith, Paul H., ed. *Letters of Delegates to Congress, 1774–1789.* Washington, DC: Library of Congress, 1979.

Sweet, William Warren. *The Story of Religion in America,* enlarged ed. New York: Harper & Brothers, 1950.

Zollman, Carl F.G. *American Church Law.* St. Paul, MN: West Publishing, 1933.

Articles/Chapters

Boston, Rob. "The Christian Nation Debate." *Church and State* 46 (January 1993): 10.

Davis, Derek H. "Christian Faith and Poliltical Involvement in Today's Culture War." *Journal of Church and State* 38 (Summer 1996): 477.

———— "Survey's Implications for Education." May 28, 2009, www.baptiststandard.com.

Hughes, Richard T. "Civil Religion, the Theology of the Republic, and the Free Church Tradition." *Journal of Church and State* 22 (Winter 1980): 77.

Jefferson, Thomas. "A Summary View of the Rights of British America." 1 August 1774, in *American Archives*, ed. Peter Force. Washington, DC: n.p., 1837.

Madison, James. "A Memorial and Remonstrance Against Religious Assessments," 1785.

Marty, Martin. "A Nation of Behavers." *Worldview* 17 (May 1974): 11.

Paine, Thomas, "Common Sense." In *Common Sense and the Crisis.* New York: Anchor Books, 1973.

Rausch, David A. and Douglas E. Chismar. "The New Puritans and Their Theonomic Paradise." *Christian Century*, 3 August 1983, 713.

Shupe, Anson. "The Reconstructionist Movement on the New Christian Right." *Christian Century*, 4 October 1989, 881.

PART I

HISTORICAL DIMENSIONS

CHAPTER 1

THE FOUNDING ERA (1774–1797) AND THE CONSTITUTIONAL PROVISION FOR RELIGION

JOHN F. WILSON

THE United States formed as a nation when the 13 colonies in North America that comprised it first rebelled against Great Britain and then secured their independence. Collaboration through a Continental Congress (1774) accompanied concerted military action. However tenuous their early prospects, they worked together through a weak Articles of Confederation (finally ratified in 1781). Its shortcomings stimulated pressure for a more centralized, if still limited, federal government. In the process of adopting that constitution (1789), many calls were made to strengthen it further. Amended in 1791 with a "Bill of Rights," the United States was fully "constituted" by the close of the eighteenth century. This period of rebellion, revolution, and nation-founding is central to understanding how it was initially configured, including the place accorded to religion. This chapter explores and explains how religious belief and practice related to governmental authority in founding the American nation.

The subject is framed in this way to establish a fundamental point, namely, that the founding generation necessarily confronted a range of daunting issues. Among the most pressing were how the former colonies would govern themselves and what kind(s) of relationship they would have with each other and external powers. Concrete issues such as regulation of overseas (as well as intercolonial) trade, taxation, and means of common defense necessarily trumped more abstract considerations, however important, such as definitions of citizenship or stipulation of legal rights and privileges. Accordingly, the provisions they made for what we loosely term "matters of church and state" were developed among powerful cross-currents of opinion and interest in a dynamic setting. Although many of its influential political leaders were exceptionally widely versed in history, and benefited from unusually broad experience, their sense of priorities was determined by the urgency of immediate tasks. Especially with respect to any policies and provisions having to do with religion, the founders' ability to improvise by crafting effective responses to challenges counted for as much as abstract principles and/or doctrines that they might (or might not) wish to promote. Searching for a singular intention concerning religion on the part of the founders, or assuming that they subscribed to fully enunciated principles about it, will obscure more than it discloses how the new United States dealt with the ancient problem of relating politics and religion. For those preoccupied with birthing the nation, settling church–state issues was necessarily secondary.

This chapter uses three focal points: (1) how separate colonies dealt with religion as they became states; (2) the minimalist provision crafted for the Constitution proper; and (3) the immediate amendment of the Constitution to include explicit assurances about religion among other concerns. Doubtless related subjects also merit extensive discussion, such as reviewing how independence affected separate American religious communions, noting their relationships to those of European lands and observing the range in claims of authority advanced by various religious groups. Nevertheless, although these and other related inquiries are interesting and fruitful, it concentrates on the preceding topics.

First, as the colonies moved into rebellion against British rule, they were faced with the necessity of self-rule; each colony became a "state." Although two took the expedient step of projecting their existing royal charters into the era of independence, most were very explicit in forming their governments through new constitutions. Whatever the path, one question each faced was the status that should be accorded to religion—necessarily addressing it if only by omission. In some respects the experience of colonies turning themselves into states anticipated the effort that would be required to craft an effective constitutional basis for the nation. Reviewing how the various colonies provided for religion introduces the issues that would inevitably challenge the nation. One advantage of this starting point is that it highlights both the range and variety of religious life in the colonies as they became independent while also indicating some common elements among them.

Next attention turns to the topic of the religious policy that was embedded in the draft constitution. In conceiving of a national government adequate to secure the nation's independence, the framers necessarily faced a challenge about what (if any) provision should be made for religion—in terms of both its practice among citizens and its existence as the source and sanction for movements and institutions. The Constitution as drafted devoted virtually no attention to religion. The Philadelphia Convention operated without public scrutiny and with few records about its deliberations. Participants' occasional reflections or reminiscences about exchanges in the Convention provide limited access to their thinking about religion. We are better served with respect to understanding opinions in the individual states as in turn they considered whether to ratify the proposed document. Numerous opinions were expressed in these conventions about the place that should be given to religion.

The concluding section discusses the steps taken, once the Constitution became effective, to amend it in response to the wide-ranging recommendations that had been offered, especially in certain states. The eventual "Bill of Rights" (i.e., the first 10 amendments) is so closely linked to the Constitution proper that its provisions are typically considered integral to it. Especially this may be the case with respect to the provision(s) relating to religion. However, if in law the First Amendment properly operates as wholly "constitutional," in the perspective of writing critical history these clauses stand apart and are markedly distinguished from the text of the original document.

THE COLONIES BECOME STATES

The Continental Congress, meeting in several sessions, received inquiries from the collaborating states about instituting their own governments. Actually some thought was given to recommending a model state constitution that each might adapt. In the end, however, individual states acted independently. New Hampshire effectively led the way in 1776 followed soon by South Carolina and New Jersey. Over that summer and fall, Virginia, Delaware, Pennsylvania, Maryland, and North Carolina followed suit, whereas Georgia and New York ratified their instruments in the spring of 1777. (Vermont, which comprised another potential state, separated itself from New York and New Hampshire, ratifying its constitution in the summer of 1778.)[1] Although Massachusetts had turned to the project early in this span of years, it succeeded in ratifying its constitution only in 1780. Connecticut and Rhode Island took the different approach of converting their existing royal charters into republican constitutions. (They adopted new constitutions in 1818 and 1842, respectively.[2]) In this process, self-governing and independent former colonies collaborating in the Continental Congress became states that completed ratifying the Articles of Confederation in 1781.[3]

Each of the states adopted provisions for religion that varied as widely as their separate paths to independent constitutions. Their courses of action reflect the complex status of religion in the revolutionary period. The most noteworthy developments with respect to religion took place in Virginia and Massachusetts; fuller attention will be given to them while noting the provisions made by others.[4] South Carolina's 1778 constitution effectively "established" Christianity, restricting legal incorporation to those bodies that subscribed to broadly Protestant beliefs. Although support for religion was not mandated, office-holding was restricted to "Protestants." With its second constitution (1790), only clergy were barred from holding office and the "free exercise and enjoyment of religious profession and worship" was extended to all.[5] When it had been a colony North Carolina favored the Church of England—however marginal its actual presence. With its 1776 constitution, nonetheless, no church was preferred, nor was any religious requirement placed on citizens—but office-holding was at least nominally limited to Protestant Christians.[6] Georgia's constitution of 1777 took a generally similar course—although it did permit assessment of citizens for the support of their own ministers. Successive Georgia constitutions (1789, 1798) eliminated the religious restrictions on office-holding and authorized assessments for support of religion.[7]

If this southern-most group of states manifested little apparent conflict about the status of religion, Virginia presented a contrasting picture. Wide-ranging religious revivals (often identified with the "Great Awakening") roiled relatively prominent Church of England parishes in the settled regions. Religion was contentious because it displayed deeper "fault-lines" in the society.[8] With Baptist preachers and Presbyterian clergy widely active, and proving to be effective in gathering new congregations, conflict with established prerogatives (such as the authority to issue preaching licenses) became virtually inevitable. For much of the decade after 1776, the religious situation in Virginia operated essentially within the old framework of a privileged body (namely, the former Church of England) having authority to license "dissent" on terms it set. Under these circumstances the central issue was whether there should be a general assessment to support religion and if so what that implied about freedom in its practice. Numerous petitions, chiefly from aggrieved dissenters of several stripes, explored the many dimensions of a larger question: What should the religious policy of Virginia look like? This was the context in which Thomas Jefferson proposed a bill for "Establishing Religious Freedom."[9]

The conclusion of the War of Independence (1783) leant urgency to resolution of the basic issue: How should Virginia support organized religion (primarily the former Church of England)? The obvious answer seemed to entail one among several versions of assessment. At this point James Madison crafted a "Memorial and Remonstrance" that rallied opposition to any government support for religion because that necessarily would entail subordinating religion to political ends.[10] The outcome in 1786 was adoption by the Assembly of the substance of Jefferson's earlier draft bill *including* explicit repudiation of all links between religion and office-holding and *excluding* any public responsibility for supporting religious institutions. One mark of the degree of separation between religion and government in Virginia is that legal incorporation was not extended to religious groups. In effect, religious bodies were denied recognition by the state.[11]

Precisely because this extended, extensive, and contested consideration of many issues involved in delineating a policy toward religion took place in Virginia, its political history has become a conventional reference point for interpreting "the American way in Church and State."[12] However, it is misleading to assume that Virginia's course of action was necessarily paradigmatic for the nation because it was only one among a number of states confronting these issues, no matter how extensively it did so.

Other colonies-becoming-states had their own, different, struggles with these issues, and they also contributed to constitutionalizing religion in the United States. Among settlements situated along the mid-Atlantic coast, Maryland went through the most direct—if confused—recasting of its provisions for religious life. At the outset of the Revolutionary period it was the most explicit among all of the colonies in sanctioning the Church of England as the established body. Nevertheless, with independence the remedy it took moved in directions that, although not necessarily coherent, flowed from an impulse to subordinate the religious life of the colony to political control—an approach technically termed "Erastian."[13] Office-holding was restricted to Christians—a provision formally repudiated only in the mid-twentieth century. Declaring it a civic duty to worship God in a manner individuals deemed "most acceptable," even though no one was compelled to practice it, religious liberty was assured to Christians. This raised the specter of requiring general assessments for support of Christian institutions. In the next years the legislature several times prescribed how the now-Protestant Episcopal Church should be organized.[14] At least in retrospect there are at least two reasons the Maryland experience is noteworthy. For one, in spite of giving explicit attention to religious affairs, there was little intellectual clarity about the basic issues that might be involved (such as was manifest in Virginia and Massachusetts). For another, of all the colonies Maryland was the traditional home to significant numbers of Roman Catholics. This posed the question of what status non-Protestant Christians would hold in the states' political charters.

The nearby colonies-becoming-states of Delaware, Pennsylvania, and New Jersey enacted comparatively few provisions relating to religion.[15] None of them supported an established church or required tax support of religion or religious ministries. All restricted office-holding to Christians who were effectively Protestants—although in Pennsylvania (and under Benjamin Franklin's influence) the 1790 constitution included a formula that made Catholic and Jewish citizens eligible for office-holding.[16] For its part New York presented no consistent pattern in addressing provisions for religion. At least in some counties the Church of England had held a favored position; any such privileges were lost in this period. Anti-Catholicism was more explicitly present in New York than in other middle-Atlantic states, and the young John Jay led a movement to deny Catholics religious liberty. In spite of its strongly Protestant ethos, however, and although it explicitly endorsed public support for religion, New York as a state did not legislate tax assessments to support ecclesiastical institutions.[17]

Among the New England colonies Massachusetts most directly addressed issues entailed in the relations between religion and government.[18] Congregationalists effectively comprised a privileged religious body that benefited from various forms of public support such as mandated tax support for ministers—although exemptions were permitted. Especially Baptists formed a phalanx of dissenters intent on embarrassing—and eventually seeking to overturn—this ecclesiastical system. After failing to gain approval from the towns in 1778 for a constitution (that did not include specified rights or guarantee free exercise of religion), a special convention produced a new constitution in 1780. Two articles provided for religion.

One stipulated the "right as well as the duty of all men in society" to worship a "supreme being," while guaranteeing the "free exercise of religion" to all who did not "disturb the peace" or "obstruct others." Another addressed support for religion and, in the interest of the common good, empowered the legislature to require citizens to attend services. It also assured religious liberty to Christians while effectively excluding Roman Catholics from office-holding.[19] Not surprisingly, this system failed to assuage those like the Baptists who did not accept its premises. One scholar captures the irony that the 1780 constitution "stood . . . Puritan ancestors on their heads" by proposing that religion should be used to support "good government" rather than receiving the protection the latter should afford.[20] Although these provisions engendered widespread discussion, and not a little continuing dissension, they effectively comprised the legal framework governing religion in the Bay State until 1833.

Although many of the same elements were present, none of the other New England states displayed such contentious exploration of religious policy.[21] Although ideally New Hampshire might share commitment to public support of religion with Massachusetts, Congregationalists never held a dominant position there. Located on the frontier, the colonial government was not as tightly knit, and increasingly Baptists, Quakers, and Presbyterians populated many of the settlements. Early state instruments did not mention religion. The 1784 constitution assured freedom of worship to its citizens, but failed to require the towns to provide support for religion, an arrangement that was central to the Massachusetts constitution. The state finally dropped this limited religious system in 1819 without the fanfare that accompanied its demise a year earlier in Connecticut or later in Massachusetts (1833). Vermont asserted self-government in a 1777 constitution that addressed many of the issues about religion agitating other states. For example, office-holders were required to affirm Protestant beliefs, and Protestants could not be deprived of civil rights. However, it did not include any thoroughgoing mandate for support of local religious institutions. Like New Hampshire this sparsely settled region lacked sufficient density of population for an ecclesiastical system to be feasible, and in any case as towns grew the percentage of Congregational adherents dropped. The revised 1786 constitution retained a religious test for office-holders and legal incorporation of worshipping religious communities was permitted in the next year.[22]

Connecticut—which shared general presumptions about religious matters with Massachusetts—converted its royal charter into a continuing instrument of government. Because no new constitution was drafted, none was subject to ratification. Here early opposition took the form of "Separates" who distanced themselves from the settled Congregational churches. Continuing resistance led to growing Baptist presence and influence. This system formally remained in place until 1818. Rhode Island was the other colony that became independent through reinterpreting its existing charter. However, the old charter's explicit commitment to religious liberty and the absence of any governmental provision for religious practice made this transition unproblematic.[23]

These independent and diverse paths from colonial status to independent state-hood are the critical back story to how the United States formed as a new nation under a constitution. A summary of the religious significance of these separate strands of this first period will prove useful. Taking markedly different routes the different colonies/states developed their own provisions, and as independent units they arrived at charters that incorporated elements that varied significantly. However, these struggles over how to provide for religion suggest the salient challenges that would face the new nation as it sought to secure a constitution. Certain issues entailing religion were contentious, whatever specific resolution each received in the separate states or would receive in the nation.

First, were there to be guarantees for a broad religious liberty—including freedom for those wishing *not* to be religious? Second, were there to be any links between citizenship and religious profession, and specifically would religion be a factor in eligibility for public office? Third, would public support for religious ministries be required? If so, were there limitations with respect to eligible groups? Were exemptions to be granted for individuals and groups, and if so, on what grounds? Fourth, would a new national government guarantee rights relating to religion against possible violations by constituent states? Finally, would there be explicit religious sanction for the new American nation? And by extension, would there be collective religious observances?

The experience of the colonies in providing for religion as they became independent states suggests the conjecture that at least some of these possible elements might well have been incorporated into a new constitution for the United States of America.

A Constitution for the New Nation

In September 1786 commissioners from five states—Virginia, Delaware, Pennsylvania, New Jersey, and New York—assembled in Annapolis. They were charged with recommending a federal plan to improve regulation of commerce under the Articles of Confederation. Missing representation from the other states, the commissioners proposed that the Continental Congress call for a convention of delegates from all 13 states (Vermont was not included) to address a broader range of shortcomings in the Articles. In mid-May 1787 the Constitutional Convention assembled in Philadelphia (without representation from Rhode Island). Its serious work began at the end of that month, and by mid-September it completed a draft constitution that it transmitted to the Continental Congress. This document was then sent to the various state legislatures with instructions that it be submitted for ratification to special conventions of delegates representing the people of each state.[24]

The sessions of the Philadelphia Convention had been closed to observers and remarkably little information about its deliberations leaked out—although James

Madison did publish his notes half a century later.[25] However, the larger (some might say intentionally subversive) strategy was to present a carefully constructed and complete instrument of government—a wholly new constitution—for the United States rather than to propose adjustments to the existing Articles of Confederation; and it was a meticulously crafted document. Beginning with a preface that located the foundation of government in "the people . . . ," seven "articles" addressed in turn the composition of the new venture in three branches of government, implications for the constituent states, provisions relating to its adoption and subsequent amendment, including ratification by at least nine of the states. Article I stipulated a bicameral legislature and in relatively detailed sections delineated the respective procedures and powers of the two "houses." Article II vested executive power in a president and specified the conditions and terms of office as well as means of selection. Article III proposed that judicial power rest in a Supreme Court augmented by "such inferior courts as the Congress may from time to time ordain and establish." Article IV addressed relations among the existing states and the possibility of adding new states as well as federal authority over new territory. Article V set the terms for amendment of the document, while Article VI explicitly stipulated that the authority of this government would be supreme, assuming responsibility for the nation's debts and "engagements" made under the Articles. Finally, Article VII provided that the Constitution would take effect following its ratification by at least nine of the states.[26]

What role did the Constitution delineate for religion? The remarkable conclusion is that, for all of the controversy with regard to religion that had attended constitution-making in the colonies as they became states, the Philadelphia Convention seems largely to have passed over this subject in silence. One very specific provision is embedded in Article VI. Its third paragraph specifies that all officers of the new federal government, as well as those in the several states, "shall be bound by oath or affirmation to support this constitution." Coupled with this requirement, the article declares that "no religious test shall ever be required as a qualification to any office or public trust under the United States." Such a blanket prohibition dramatically contrasts with the struggles that took place in many of the states, especially to retain religiously based restrictions on office-holding. In brief, the document crafted in Philadelphia entailed a strong premise that religion should not be a factor in constitutionalizing the new nation. There is no evidence that this position was thought to be an attack on religion any more than that—through silence—it might in some convoluted sense indicate support for it. Rather, the meaning seems to have been that the new nation's government was to be independent of religion, including any institutions expressing it and/or associated with it. Contemporary testimony from the first Treaty with Tripoli (1797) sustains this view, for it represented the United States as "not founded on the Christian religion," a clause actually omitted in the 1805 revision.[27]

Several associated points call for comment. One is the confluence of interests that led the "conspirators" in the Philadelphia Convention to proceed in this fashion with respect to religion. Taking their construction of the Constitution as a whole, it is evident that they sought to be as "economical" as possible, especially with respect to contentious issues. They understood that the new nation was in a critical passage with possibly only one clear chance to "get it right" in terms of a government for the United States that would prove to be adequate— as the Confederation under the Articles had failed to be. *With unrelieved focus on what they believed to be necessary provisions, they strategically ignored any divisive issues that had the potential to frustrate their objective.* A dramatic example is how they assiduously avoided taking a stand on slavery, a subject that had sufficient potential to forestall ratification of any constitution. This approach was manifested in Article I, where the apportionment of representatives included the notorious provision that their number would be based on considering any who were not free to count as "three fifths of all other persons." Article IV, concerning reciprocal rights and privileges among the citizens of the several states, also stipulated that anyone "held to service or labor in one state" who escaped to another should be returned. Within several generations Amendments XIV and XIII, respectively, replaced these provisions, but only following the North's victory in a bloody civil war. It may help moderns to comprehend why the framers passed over religion as a contentious topic if they recognize that it held the potential to engender divisions that would decisively frustrate their larger objective.

A second point relates to modern interpreters who have occasionally claimed to discover secondary or even hidden allusions to religion in the text of the Constitution, a point that might serve to prove that the United States was formally based on the Christian religion. One such reference is in Article VII, where the concluding paragraph dates the completion of the Philadelphia Convention and transmittal of its work to the Congress as "the seventeenth day of September in the year of our Lord one thousand seven hundred and eighty seven. . . ." That the framers used the conventional (Gregorian) calendar (itself a product of the sixteenth century) hardly seems to comprise evidence that they understood their work to be founded on Christianity, especially because the document also immediately dates their work in the "twelfth" year of the independence of the United States of America. This observation does suggest, however, that any claims about the new nation's place in the scope of world history should be grounded not so much in the Constitution as a manifestly practical document, but in the Declaration of Independence that had inaugurated and framed the preceding course of events.

Another point at which some have argued that a Christian commitment underlay the Constitution is in the stipulation (already noted) that federal as well as state office-holders were to be bound by an "oath"—which would implicitly invoke a higher power. However, alternatively the delegates were permitted to "affirm" their support in place of taking an oath. Affirmations entailed no reference to a higher power and thus addressed sensibilities such as those of the Quakers. In any case the next following clause explicitly declares that "no religious test shall ever be required as a qualification" for federal or state office holding.[28]

RELIGION AS AN ISSUE IN RATIFICATION OF THE CONSTITUTION BY THE STATES

As the states reviewed the Constitution to ratify it (or withhold support), the question of provision for religion's formal relationship to the new government was discussed and criticized, eliciting numerous suggestions.[29] Each of the states devised its own procedures for review of the proposed Constitution. Some chose to use largely self-contained conventions that entailed little or no outside consultation or influence. In other states, however, it is clear that substantial "intelligences," or reports about the reviews taking place elsewhere, were shared among them. Individuals supporting ratification were united by the conviction that the proposed Constitution was the "last, best hope" for the new nation. An influential set of essays arguing that case in compelling terms was written by Alexander Hamilton, John Jay, and James Madison; they are known as *The Federalist Papers*.[30] Following the draft Constitution these essays passed over the subject of religion in virtual silence. One exception is a passing observation by Madison in the tenth of the papers that sectarian religion was a leading source of faction comparable to other divisive passions such as a rage for paper money.[31] That point is entirely consistent with the Philadelphia Convention's effective silence about religion.

Those who opposed ratification of the Constitution are usually labeled Antifederalists.[32] As a disparate group of critics of the proposed government they were united by a deep distrust of the powers they thought the draft document would invest in the new national government. Many believed that this untried regime would necessarily limit the newly independent and constituent states. Numerous suggestions to improve the draft constitution (probably at least several hundred) were offered in the course of the states' reviews. Many concerned explicit guarantees about citizens' rights against the enlarged powers of the proposed central government. The Antifederalists argued that enumerating explicit rights over against the government would comprise one effective means to limit its reach and secure both the states and their citizens from possible abuse of its powers. Anti-federalism has come to be appreciated less as obstructionist by design and more as genuinely motivated by deep concerns about the balance of the proposed Constitution. A central contention was the document's failure to make more extensive provision for guaranteeing citizens' rights under the regime. Their intense interest in these rights was rooted in skepticism about the adequacy of the proposed mechanisms for separating powers and creating checks and balances, provisions that lay at the heart of the framers' design for a federal system. Ironically, its supporters' confidence in this frame for the new government was one basis for their conviction that an explicit enumeration of rights would be superfluous.

Among specific criticisms of the proposed draft Constitution that were voiced in the state conventions, concerns repeatedly emerged that inadequate attention was given to religion. This point was not necessarily made in consistent ways and several chief themes regarding it may even seem to be contradictory. As an example, the explicit prohibition of a test oath (Article VI, Section 3) apparently seemed ill advised to some who would have preferred that religious loyalties be positively mobilized to support the new regime. On the other hand, numerous concerns were voiced about the absence of a guarantee concerning the rights of conscience. These were not necessarily mutually exclusive positions, but in the main they do suggest that critics' concerns diverged markedly about how religion references might be incorporated into the Constitution. Those who were involved in ratifying it did not necessarily accept the position that had been taken by the Convention, and codified in the Constitution, namely, that formally defining provision for religion would be detrimental to creating an effective government for the United States.

Among concerns identified by critics of the draft Constitution, a number relating to religion were frequently formulated in terms of rights that it would be desirable to secure. Antifederalist critics especially insisted that religious liberty should be guaranteed against federal abuse. They also sought more explicit assurances that the new national government could not *either* privilege one church or religious body *or* deny such an arrangement to the states in which it might already exist. These concerns among many others (including the desirability of guaranteeing rights to free speech, unhindered assembly, etc.) were strongly advanced. Increasingly, proponents of the Constitution became obliged to promise enactment of some such "rights" if ratification of the draft Constitution was to be achieved. Thus a major driving force behind the religion clauses eventually incorporated in the First Amendment was a broad and deep—but not necessarily well-focused—consensus that limitations ought to be placed upon the proposed federal government to protect citizens against possible abuses of its powers. Most emphatically, however, it was generally thought that any such provisions should be designed primarily to limit the reach of federal authority and power rather than to protect the people against abuses at the hands of the state governments.

Pennsylvania held the initial state convention (in Harrisburg) to consider endorsing the proposed federal Constitution. The primary concern about religion expressed in it centered on the draft Constitution's failure to offer a guarantee regarding liberty of conscience. The overriding importance of "bills of rights" was to secure the authority of the people as the foundation of the government. Religious liberty was construed as one among these desirable basic rights. However, in this convention it certainly did stand alone, separated for example from protection for freedom of assembly and the press. James Wilson had been a central figure in the Convention proper and he forcefully argued that the proposed new federal government had no power to diminish the rights of citizens in the states.[33] His assurance proved insufficient, however, to persuade the delegates. The Harrisburg ratifying convention did eventually call for including liberty of conscience among the rights that should be protected under the new government of the United States. Another less prominent theme in the Pennsylvania convention was failure of the Constitution to provide for those who might be "conscientiously scrupulous of bearing arms." This issue arose, not surprisingly, in a state profoundly shaped and infused by traditions of the Society of Friends.

Massachusetts' review of the draft Constitution began in January 1788. Here concerns about religion centered on the provision that there was to be no religious test for federal office-holding. Not surprisingly, strong opinions were expressed on both sides of this issue. Only a very limited report exists about the debates in the Connecticut ratifying convention, also held in January 1788. Like Massachusetts, the concern about religion in Connecticut seems to have focused on the single relevant provision in Article VI. South Carolina's review also took place in January but gave relatively minor attention to religion.

Maryland's convention met in late April 1788 and explicitly considered proposing amendments to the Constitution. It is noteworthy that one relating to religion was compound—like the eventual text of the First Amendment. It included both a barrier to any national religion (i.e., a nonestablishment clause) and support for religious liberty (a guarantee of free exercise). However, none of the proposals finally endorsed by this convention pertained to religion. New York's convention met in Poughkeepsie in June at mid-month and effectively completed its work in 4 weeks, recommending that a bill of rights be appended to the Constitution but directing little attention to religion.

Virginia's convention met throughout the month of June 1788 and included well-known participants: Patrick Henry (who resolutely opposed it), James Madison, Governor Randolph, John Marshall, and James Monroe. At least in the setting of the ratifying conventions, Randolph likely provided the most sustained discussion of any conceptual basis for relating religion and regime that underlay the general absence of religious provisions in the draft Constitution.[34] Virginia's convention eventually ratified the Constitution while recommending a series of amendments that should be considered by the first Congress that might assemble under its authority. Twenty draft provisions addressed specific sections of the document, or subjects implicit in them. The Virginia convention additionally proposed that "there be a declaration or bill of rights. . . ." Among the 20 lengthy provisions that might be included in this "bill of rights"—most stipulated rights to be granted to freemen—only the last two explicitly concerned religion. At least with respect religion, the extensive discussion that took place in the Virginia convention effectively carried over into North Carolina's deliberations about ratification.[35]

North Carolina's delegates assembled toward the end of July 1788. This gathering seems to have debated questions raised by religion at least as widely as any of the conventions. Richard D. Spaight had been a delegate in Philadelphia and delineated the point of view taken at the Constitutional Convention: "As to the subject of religion. . . . No power is given to the general government to interfere with it all. Any act of Congress on this subject would be a usurpation."[36] In the end North Carolina declined to ratify the Constitution, but its discussion did lend impetus to the strategy of asking that any government formed under it should propose appropriate amendments to the original document. Indeed, virtually identical proposals were introduced in North Carolina—both for a "declaration of rights" and separate "amendments"— that had been proposed by Virginia's convention. Although not part of an endorsement of the Constitution, the recommendations from North Carolina did add weight to those coming forward to the First Congress from the other states.

Do any conclusions follow about the proposed place of religion in the new United States in light of the ratifying conventions? In the ratification process overwhelming attention centered on the perceived necessity to construct an effective alternative to the inadequacies the Articles of Confederation manifested. Taking the reports of the Philadelphia gathering at face value it had been a "conspiracy" to seek only the authority or power absolutely necessary to address the perceived failures of the Articles of Confederation; and the states essentially received it in these terms. From this point of view, what we would term cultural subjects, such as making provision for religion under the new government (or providing for education, which was not mentioned), were systematically avoided. Most emphatically, however, failure to make provisions for religion did not mean they thought the issue was insignificant. Rather, any attention given to such a matter was capable of generating deep divisions *among* the states not to speak of *within* many of them. Had sustained consideration been given to such issues that could be so divisive the likely effect would have been entirely to subvert their fundamental and overriding objective. Simply, this had been to achieve an effective framework for the government of the nation. *Stating the point most directly, had the framers of the draft Constitution chosen to stipulate more fully the role(s) to be accorded to religion, it is altogether likely that their entire effort to supersede the Articles of Confederation would have collapsed.* Effectively the judgment seems to have been that aggressive attention to provisions about religion, however desirable some might think it, would frustrate their basic objective. Indeed, those disparate and opposed ideas that were voiced in the ratifying conventions about how religion and regime might be related reflected the different and not necessarily coherent provisions operating in various states.

This analysis and discussion makes much of the diversity of both convictions and practices relating to religion in the several states. The relatively "advanced" ideas voiced in Virginia were as unlikely to gain assent in New England (except on the part of Rhode Island) as the practices of the latter in privileging particular bodies would prove acceptable within the middle or southern states. An additional factor rendering the situation even more complex was the rapidly changing distribution of religious "proto-denominations" across the states and regions. Furthermore, many religious bodies were undergoing far-reaching transformations, and in turn they were struggling with the new condition of national independence. Moreover, many religious prophets and leaders were generating new religious groups. In this dynamic situation, no principle or set of principles other than a resolve to leave such matters entirely to the states had any realistic chance of securing the loyalty and allegiance of "the people" for the federal government; and the people were, in the end, its reference point and ultimate ground.

FRAMING A FEDERAL BILL OF RIGHTS

The Constitution was declared formally ratified by the necessary three fourths of the states on July 2, 1788. Although adding a "bill of rights" had not been strictly a condition of approval, the First Congress lay under a moral obligation to consider that step. Bills of rights had been recommended in several state conventions. James Madison again took the lead, even as he had played a critical role in preparation for the Philadelphia Convention. He may not have personally thought that a federal bill of rights was required, but he had promised to work for one when standing for election to the House of Representatives. To this end he digested the recommendations from the state conventions and consolidated as many as 200 possible provisions into 19 proposals organized into nine possible amendments.[37] These were submitted to a select committee of the House. Two considerations should be highlighted.

First, Antifederalists, fearing that the new national government would claim more power than necessary, had issued calls for specification of rights. They thought inclusion of rights would comprise an additional limit on powers ceded by the states to the federal regime. The reservations shared by Madison and some other framers derived from the conviction that the new government was one of delegated powers only. In this perspective stipulating rights seemed contradictory to the basic division of labor that underlay the document—for specifying federal rights might appear to reduce further the power of the constituent states.

Second, although providing for its own amendment, the Constitution did not specify the form for that eventuality. Madison envisioned that its amendment would entail inserting newly ratified provisions at appropriate locations in the original text. Because the Constitution's organization was self-evidently federal, adding provisions at definite locations would manifestly reinforce rather than potentially compromise the structure of the new national government. Thus in form Madison's draft proposals underscored the fundamental objective of creating a limited national government rather than possibly seeming to set up rights against an already existing "state."[38]

Particulars of the legislative account pertaining to the provisions concerning religion in the First Amendment became insignificant when its final text was ratified. However, charting the stages of its evolving composition is critical for understanding how that text came to be. Certain key details should not be obscured in abridging a long story. Madison's initial draft included four distinguishable elements relating to religious interests, three to be embedded in Article I, Section 9 that detailed limitations on legislative power in the new nation. It stipulated that Congress had no authority to deal with certain subjects—such as importation of slaves (at least for two decades), bills of attainder, direct taxation, preferential relations among the states, and titles of nobility. These potential areas of action had simply been placed "off limits" to legislation. Madison thought further notice of, and protection for, religion should be located here; his proposed draft reads: "The civil rights of none shall be abridged on account of religious belief or worship, nor shall any national religion be established, nor shall the full and equal rights of conscience be in any manner, or on any pretext, infringed."[39] (He also offered parallel but independent sets of clauses concerning speech, press, assembly—really the substance of rights enumerated primarily in the First Amendment.)

First, these provisions would be limitations on the legislative power of Congress only—so there was no implication that they pertained to the several states. As such they would not apply to either the executive or judicial branches of the federal government—in which the exclusion of religious tests was assured. However, for substance this formulation entailed three quite separate provisions with respect to religion, that: (1) religious practices (including both belief and worship) would not entail adverse civil consequences; (2) no national religion could be "established"; and (3) "the full and equal rights of conscience" would not be "infringed." Such an explicit set of limits on legislative action indicates that in Madison's thinking the federal government would have nothing to do with religion. This position accorded with his conviction that for *idealistic* reasons religion should be free and unhindered. However, as important, these clauses also directly expressed his theoretical understanding of the nature of the republican experiment that entailed a *realistic* view of religion. These provisions would prove to be an additional means to stabilize the polity because religion was a classic source of "faction"—which he most feared as threat to any republican regime (the argument he set out in *Federalist 10*).[40] The complete and entire independence of religion from the federal regime would assure that no action of the government—however well-intentioned—could reduce the possibility for counterbalancing factions to arise. Thus Madison had gathered proposals from the Antifederalist critique of the draft Constitution to craft a set of limitations on the Congress that embodied both explicit protection for religion and an opportunity to strengthen the "constitutional system" on the federal model.

Madison's formulation also envisioned a fourth provision about religion that would be located in another part of Article I, where Section 10 addressed the "other side" of the division of duties between the new federal government and the states. This section prohibited states from making treaties or alliances (presumably with other states as well as foreign nations), the coining of money, granting titles of nobility, etc. These provisions enumerated limitations on their sovereignty that the states must accept for the federal regime to succeed where the government under the Articles had proved to be inadequate. Madison proposed that a new clause be inserted immediately after the initial statement of limitations upon the states. It would read: "No State shall violate the equal rights of conscience, or the freedom of the press, or the trial by jury in criminal cases."[41] So in Madison's original proposal, the "rights of conscience" would also have been protected against conceivable actions by the states, as would freedom of the press and trial by jury.

Madison's proposal thus incorporated language that responded to the concerns that had been voiced in the Antifederalist critique of the draft Constitution. The texts he devised indicate that he had brought together four separate concerns that, although standing independently of each other, also reinforced each other. First, the assurance that no civil rights be abridged on account of religion enlarged the previously ratified provision that excluded religious tests for those holding federal offices. Madison's phrasing "because of religious belief or worship" may suggest that for him worship was the form taken by religious action. Second, excluding any national religion likely implied there would be *neither* direct support by the federal government for one church, *nor* indirect support by means of the federal government *requiring* state or local governments to provide for a church or churches. The third provision, that rights of conscience would not be infringed or limited, was a constraint on the federal government. Fourth, the states would also have been forbidden from violating "equal rights of conscience." This set of four separate guarantees is markedly broader and more sweeping than the religion clauses that were eventually ratified in the First Amendment, and beyond limiting the federal regime, the states necessarily would have accepted constraints. Although the select committee of the House made some changes in Madison's language, its work largely endorsed both the conceptual framework and substantive elements he had introduced.

The House itself began its review in mid-August 1789. Here several members proposed numerous changes, and the interests of their states were often evident. Throughout the discussion, Madison appears to have graciously accepted many verbal adjustments and even substantive changes. Most significant may be his passing comment that he thought the proposed limitation on the states with respect to treatment of religion was more "valuable" even than guarantees against federal action.[42] The House proposed that any ratified rights should be grouped at the end of the Constitution rather than inserted into the existing text. Their repositioning has likely been more significant for modern generations after the serial legal "incorporation" of specific "rights" began because it has led them to imagining the "bill of rights" as *a set of separate claims against the government* rather than as itself *an expression of its federal structure*. For its part, the Senate completed its work on the proposed amendments expeditiously, reducing 17 articles in the House's version to the 12 eventually sent out to the states for ratification.[43] The hallmarks of its work were essentially the rearrangement and consolidation of the proposed elements.

The committee of conference—on which Madison sat—did significantly revise the amendments. In this final revision, language of the proposed Amendment 3 assumed the form in which it was eventually ratified: "Congress shall make no law respecting an establishment of religion, or prohibiting the free exercise thereof. . . ."[44] Specific shifts in terminology have occasioned extensive discussions; one example concerns the significance "respecting" should carry. More important is that the explicit federal reference remained; this was only a limitation on Congressional power to legislate; thus no provision remained that in any respect touched on state prerogatives. (This observation also applies to the associated provisions relating to speech, the press, etc.) With respect to religion, the evident interests of the New England states in preserving a privileged position for their churches seems to have gained most from the work of the Congress. Finally, the "First Amendment" as ratified was actually the third that was proposed to the states. It emerged as primordial in the constitutional fabric of the nation only by the contingency that the proposed First and Second Amendments failed to be ratified. They concerned the distribution of Congressional seats and adjusting payments to the members of Congress.[45]

Conclusion

The foregoing account traces several stages through which formal provisions regarding religion in the new nation eventually became the constitutional framework governing "Church and State" in subsequent American history. In the founding era, regulation of religion and its practice varied widely among the states and included elements such as respect for individuals' liberty of conscience, restrictions on office-holding, privileged positions for particular groups, and mandated support for one or more religious bodies. Such provisions would continue to operate among the states without check or supervision. This was because the framers of the original Constitution—which was immediately amended by the Congress (and ratified by the states)—opted that the national regime should be independent of religion. They took this position because their overriding concern was to secure an effective national government. This path directly contrasts with that taken by France in its contemporaneous revolution, in which the essential effort was to abolish traditional religion because it was integral to the old order. By contrast, the United States was committed to permit religion to develop freely at the state level where incremental adjustments did take place and new religious groups and movements soon flourished. Permeating society, religious ideas and practices necessarily proved important in shaping culture and influencing politics—locally, regionally, and nationally. In turn, this meant that religious institutions might well be employed to serve federal purposes—such as educating native peoples. It meant that the Houses of Congress could and did appoint chaplains, and that religious language would be appropriated by national leaders—occasionally even for highly partisan purposes. Actions such as these, whether advisable or not, were possible because in designing a federal regime to be independent of religion, religious impulses and institutions were left unconstrained in working directly among the people.[46] And insofar as the people of the United States were manifestly religious (and with increasing variability in its expression) they assumed that their government could not be antithetical to their practices.

Through two intervening centuries, Americans have not understood very well the contingent origin of the Constitutional provisions for making religion and government independent. They have too readily used Thomas Jefferson's overly simplistic characterization of the national ideal as a "wall of separation between church and state."[47] Madison's phrasing would have been preferable; he thought that the burden of "tracing a line of separation between the rights of religion and the Civil authority" would be more appropriate.[48] A more exact—if wholly awkward—description might have been better still, something like the "independence of religion and government in the U.S. combined with their continuing interaction and interdependence among its people."

The basic significance of both the minimal attention to religion in the Constitution and the convoluted reference to it in the First Amendment, however, is to be located in a broader imperative. This was to form a limited federal government grounded in separate branches, which through their balancing actions would check the exercise of power. Thus the provision to make religion independent from government derived from the ideal that the latter should be radically limited. Who among the framers could have imagined that within two centuries the United States would become a global superpower with an internally pluralistic culture? Or with such a transformation could any have conceived of the complex constitutional issues entailing religion that might arise? Through the intervening centuries unanticipated challenges have been explored—and legal determinations extrapolated—without seeming to satisfy either specialists in the law or religious partisans. If we recognize the contingent origin of these constitutional provisions, however, it is difficult to think that any other outcome was possible. In this perspective the religion policy of the American nation has been a work in progress from its outset and two centuries later it appears fated to continue as such.

ENDNOTES

1. Vermont eventually joined the United States in 1791 as the 14th state. See Willi Paul Adams, *The First American Constitutions*, trans. Rita and Robert Kimber (Chapel Hill, NC: University of North Carolina Press, 1980), 93–94.

2. On these states, see Adams, *The First American Constitutions*, 66–68.

3. Although the Articles of Confederation was sent to the states for consideration by the Continental Congress in November 1777, Maryland finally ratified it only in March 1781. See Adams, 280–283.

4. Adams' account includes very little attention to provisions for religion in the state constitutions. The most useful summary is Thomas J. Curry, *The First Freedoms: Church and State in America to the Passage of the First Amendment* (Oxford: Oxford University Press, 1987), Chapters 6 and 7.

5. Ibid., 148–151.

6. Ibid., 151–152.

7. Ibid., 152–153.

8. Virginia has deservedly received a great deal of attention with respect to the development of church–state issues as it made the transition from colony to state. See the account by Thomas E. Buckley, *Church and State in Revolutionary Virginia, 1776–1787* (Charlottesville, VA: University of Virginia Press, 1977). Also see Curry's summary, 134–148. Modern scholarship has explored these interfaces between religion and social divisions, beginning notably with the work of Rhys Isaac, *The Transformation of Virginia, 1740–1790* (Chapel Hill, NC: University of North Carolina Press, 1982).

9. See Curry, 139.

10. Ibid., 142–146.

11. Jefferson's draft may be consulted in Philip B. Kurland and Ralph Lerner, eds., *The Founders' Constitution*, 5 vols. (Chicago: University of Chicago Press, 1987), 5: 77. An echo of the controversy surrounding incorporation of religious groups in Virginia may be found in Madison's 1811 interchange with the House of Representatives concerning a bill to incorporate the Protestant Episcopal Church in Alexandria. See 99–101.

12. See Donald L. Drakeman, "The Church Historians Who Made the First Amendment What It Is Today," *Religion and American Culture* 17 (Winter 2007): 1, in which he explores the role played by religious historians whose work critically informed the Supreme Court about Virginia's extensive and public disagreements over the place of religion in the years before the new nation was founded.

13. Thomas Erastus, a sixteenth-century Swiss theologian, argued that civil authorities should supervise ecclesiastical affairs.

14. See Curry, 153–158.

15. Ibid., Chapter 7, 159 ff.

16. Ibid., 160–161.

17. Ibid., 161–162.

18. Ibid., 163–177.

19. Ibid., 163 ff.

20. Ibid., 165.

21. Ibid., 179–188.

22. Ibid., 188 f.

23. From its earliest years the course taken with respect to religion by Rhode Island and Providence Plantations placed it at odds, especially with other colonies in New England. One of its earliest leaders, Roger Williams, became a legendary figure for his opposition to "the New England Way." There is a large literature on his thought, his influence on the colony, and its place in the larger American story. In the revolutionary period Rhode Island's major role (beyond exemplifying religious liberty as the basis for public policy) was to serve as critic of and goad to Massachusetts, especially since it retained traditional attitudes and continued institutionalized religious privileges until 1833.

24. See Max Farrand, *The Framing of the Constitution of the United States* (New Haven, CT: Yale University Press, 1927). Farrand also edited and published *The Records of the Federal Convention*, 3 Vols. (New Haven, CT: Yale University Press, 1911).

25. See James Madison, *Notes of Debates in the Federal Convention of 1787*. Adrienne Koch issued a Norton paperback edition in 1987 based on a 1966 hardcover edition from Ohio University Press. *Notes* was initially published in volumes 2 and 3 of *The Papers of James Madison* (Washington, DC, 1840).

26. Kurland and Lerner, *The Founders' Constitution*. These volumes reproduce extensive materials about the various sections of the Constitution gathered from numerous sources and provide ready references to many relevant documents and sources. It is organized by section of the Constitution and the initial amendments.

27. See Anson Phelps Stokes, *Church and State in the United States*, 3 vols. (New York: Harper, 1950). Volume one of this collection includes materials relating to the nation's founding. On this treaty, see Stokes, 1: 497–499.

28. Development of the U.S. legal tradition has largely rested on the interpretation of individual clauses of the Constitution. Any critical historical interpretation of the document must attend to its overall structure. This is one factor differentiating the Bill of Rights (the text of which was set in passing by the conference committee) from the carefully constructed and edited original document.

29. *The Debates in the Several State Conventions on the Adoption of the Federal Constitution*, collected and revised by Jonathan Elliot, were originally published in 1836 and subsequently reissued. References that follow use the five-volume edition issued in Philadelphia by the J.B. Lippincott Co., 1901.

30. A recent and readily available edition is Isaac Kramnick, ed. *The Federalist Papers* (New York: Penguin Books, 1987).

31. See *The Federalist Papers*, Number 10, in which Madison uses sectarian religion as one example of faction that can threaten a nation: "A religious sect may degenerate into a political faction in a part of the Confederacy; but the variety of sects dispersed over the entire face of it must secure the national councils against any danger from that source." See page 128 of the Kramnick edition.

32. The term "Antifederalist" may confuse modern readers because it may seem to suggest opposition to a more powerful national government. In this period it designated those specifically opposed to the proposed constitution for a range of reasons, but who did agree and argue that it should be augmented in one or another respect.

33. James Wilson's speech was addressed to the Pennsylvania Convention on December 4, 1787 and is reported in Elliot's *Debates*, II: 453 ff.

34. Although Governor Randolph did not act as a participant in the Philadelphia Convention and sign the Constitution, he did discuss it in great detail in the Virginia ratifying convention. His discussion of freedom of religion is reported in Elliot's *Debates*, III: 204–205.

35. See Elliot's *Debates*, III: 659–661 for the 20 amendments Virginia proposed.

36. Richard Spaight's speech is available in Elliot's *Debates*, IV: 208, as well as in *The Founders' Constitution*, 5: 92.

37. See Edward Dumbauld, *The Bill of Rights and What It Means Today* (Norman, OK: University of Oklahoma Press, 1957), 32, in which Dumbauld reports that Madison gathered 186 separate items from the various conventions in the states, reducible to 80 or so substantive proposals. A good biographically oriented study has traced Madison's critical involvement in the founding of the nation, especially his central role in achieving passage of the "Bill of Rights." See Richard Labunski, *James Madison and the Struggle for the Bill of Rights* (New York: Oxford University Press, 2006). For summary reports of the various stages through which it passed, see Dumbauld, *The Bill of Rights*.

38. This is a point that may be overlooked in modern discussions because constitutional provisions are typically considered in relative isolation and consequently interpreted and applied apart from the overarching design of the document.

39. See Dumbauld, 206–209, in which he reproduces the set of amendments Madison offered in Congress on June 8, 1789.

40. See *The Federalist Papers*, Number 10, cited in note 32.

41. See Dumbauld, 208.

42. Available in *The Founders' Constitution*, 5: 94.

43. See Dumbauld, 44–48, in which he summarizes changes to the proposed amendments that originated in the Senate's review of them. He reproduces the text of the Senate version on pages 217–219.

44. See Dumbauld, 48–49, in which he discusses the outcome of the conference committee. He gives the text of the proposed 12 amendments sent to the states for ratification at 220–222.

45. Amendment I concerned adjusting the number of members of the House; Amendment II addressed compensation for the members of Congress and specifically provided that any change should not take effect until the body's next sitting following the subsequent election.

46. See, as an example, Madison's concerns about presidential proclamations entailing religion in *The Founders' Constitution*, 5: 102–103, 105–106.

47. Jefferson's phrase came from an 1802 letter addressed to the Danbury Baptist Association in Connecticut. Key paragraphs of the letter are reproduced in *The Founders'*

Constitution, 5: 96; see also Jefferson's letter to Samuel Miller in 1808 concerning his opposition to proclaiming a day of "fasting & prayer," 88–89.

    48. Madison's characterization was included in an exchange of letters with the Rev. Jasper Adams, President of the College of Charlestown. Reproduced in *The Founders' Constitution*, 5: 107–108.

BIBLIOGRAPHY

Books

Adams, Willi Paul. *The First American Constitutions.* trans. By Rita and Robert Kimber, Chapel Hill, NC: University of North Carolina Press, 1980.

Buckley, Thomas E. *Church and State in Revolutionary Virginia, 1776–1787.* Charlottesville, Va.: University of Virginia Press, 1977.

Curry, Thomas J. *The First Freedoms: Church and State in America to the Passage of The First Amendment.* New York: Oxford University Press, 1986.

Dumbauld, Edward. *The Bill of Rights and What It Means Today.* Norman, OK: University of Oklahoma Press, 1957.

Elliot, Jonathan. *The Debates of the Several State Conventions on the Adoption of the Federal Constitution* (collected and revised by John Elliot, 1836), cited in the edition issued by J.B. Lippincott Co., Philadelphia, 1901.

Farrand, Max. *The Framing of the Constitution of the United States.* New Haven, CT:Yale University Press, 1927.

Isaac, Rhys. *The Transformation of Virginia, 1740–1790.* Chapel Hill, NC: University of North Carolina Press, 1982.

Kramnick, Isaac, ed. *The Federalist Papers.* New York: Penguin Books, 1987.

Kurland, Philip and Ralph Lerner, eds. *The Founders' Constitution.* 5 vols.Chicago: University of Chicago Press, 1987.

Labunski, Richard. *James Madison and the Struggle for the Bill of Rights.* New York:Oxford University Press, 2006.

Madison, James. *Notes of Debates in the Federal Convention of 1787* (from the *Papers of James Madison*, Volumes 2–3, Washington, DC, 1840) edited by Adrienne Koch. Columbus, Ohio: Ohio University Press, 1966.

Stokes, Anson Phelps, ed. *Church and State in the United States.* 3 Vols. New York: Harper, 1950.

Articles/Chapters

Drakeman, Donald L. "The Church Historians who made the First Amendment what it is Today." *Religion and American Culture* (Winter 2007): Volume 17/1.

CHAPTER 2

EIGHTEENTH-CENTURY RELIGIOUS LIBERTY: THE FOUNDING GENERATION'S PROTESTANT-DERIVED UNDERSTANDING

BARRY ALAN SHAIN

IN eighteenth-century America, religious liberty, like almost every other understanding of liberty, enjoyed multiple, contested, and evolving meanings. When asked for definitions of liberty and a republic, Jefferson responded that these words "have been so multifariously applied as to convey no precise idea to the mind."[1] Even into the mid-nineteenth century, such confusion continued, for it was Lincoln who declared that "we all declare for liberty; but in using the same word we do not all mean the same thing."[2] This lack of clarity, though, did not prevent religious and civil liberty from being the twin and linked goals reported by Americans as having led them into and out of their war for independence. As Washington reported, "the establishment of Civil and Religious Liberty was the Motive which induced me to the Field."[3]

Although the eighteenth century is marked by a massive transformation in the declared goals served by the public support of Christianity—from serving God and openly soteriological ends, to serving man and unabashedly communal civil ones—the evolving sense of religious liberty for those in dissent, from toleration to equality, remained closely linked with two Christian concepts, logically dependent on the first and interchangeable with the latter.[4] The first is spiritual or Christian liberty, the liberty with which Christ freed all of his reborn followers from absolute servitude to sin and the necessity of following the dictates of Mosaic law (Halakha). This liberty (or, among a few progressive thinkers, a secular equivalent),[5] made freedom, as liberty—political, religious, civil— possible and different from license. The second concept, still more difficult to specify and more emphatically dissenting Protestant in origin, is the freedom of religious conscience. As the Westminster Confession explained, "God alone is Lord of the conscience, and hath left it free from the doctrines and commandments of men which are in any thing contrary to his Word, or beside it in matters of faith or worship. . . . [so that] the requiring of an implicit faith, and an absolute and blind obedience, is to destroy liberty of conscience, and reason also."[6] These two Christian concepts, along with contending schools of scriptural exegesis, importantly shaped how religious liberty was understood in eighteenth-century America.

Of course, on the political level, the invocation of equal religious liberty was most often made late in the century, not by the orthodox of a colony or state, but by dissenting Protestants seeking equal legal standing with other Protestant denominations and, as well, by a small but influential group of Christian humanists and deists who sought, in previously unheard of ways, to separate the intertwined functions of church and state.[7] Accordingly, in eighteenth-century America, equal religious liberty was the product of powerful currents in Protestant thought, which followed centuries-old pietistic and evangelical traditions, and supportive streams of what might be called secular thought.[8]

In ways difficult to keep in mind, let alone fully recover, these intertwined developments took place in, and were shaped by a world that was outwardly, openly, politically, and overwhelmingly Protestant.[9] Too often contemporary commentators fail to give this feature of the world of the founders its due.[10] Indeed, it is so essential a component of that world that it is even hard to imagine how Americans might have responded and what they might have thought if their world had been either less diverse in its range of Protestant denominations,[11] or less uniformly Protestant. The influx of Catholics and the rise of Mormonism in the nineteenth century and the repressive response they elicited, though, is usefully suggestive.[12]

After outlining, in brief, the remarkably Protestant background of the American social and political landscape in which religious liberty was necessarily understood, this essay will then consider the component parts of religious liberty. That is, *liberty* and its restrictive and objective rather than open-ended and subjective character is examined before looking at those concepts that undergirded the *religious* elements of religious liberty: the relatively constant understanding of spiritual or Christian liberty, and the evolving and expanding senses of freedom of religious conscience that, after the War for Independence, made equal religious liberty so different from the more narrowly "spiritual" goals that it had served earlier in the eighteenth century.

EIGHTEENTH-CENTURY PROTESTANT AMERICA

Americans were a Protestant rather than a secular people whose absolutist teleological patterns of thought, either rationalist or Christian (keeping in mind that then, those who subscribed to a theory of the universe as intelligently designed but not Christocentric were at the far edge of the progressive range, but today such thinkers are viewed as theologically conservative),[13] can be used accurately by contemporary secular elites only with difficulty, if honestly at all.[14] Almost all historians today, in fact, now agree that eighteenth-century Americans were a predominantly Protestant,[15] even if variegated and changing, people who wished to be guided not by reason alone, but rather by reason disproportionately informed by revelation and/or inner illumination. Indeed, Henry May, the preeminent student of the Enlightenment in America, believes that this religious description accurately captures "most people who lived in America in the eighteenth and nineteenth centuries."[16] Nor were they Protestant Christians in name only, for "the majority of inhabitants continued to go to church . . . [and] the preaching colonists heard most of the time—remained consistently otherworldly."[17] Critical legal theorist Mark Tushnet further observes "it was not 'religion in general' that the framers saw as the basis of secular order. Rather, it was Christianity and, more specifically, Protestant Christianity."[18] The very dominance of Protestantism in this time and place, in fact, makes it hard to imagine how a defense of religious liberty, irrespective of the author's personal beliefs or motivation,[19] might have been mounted without recourse to the soteriologically essential concept of religious conscience; that is, to one of several essential Protestant categories of thought with which religious liberty was often confused.[20]

For eighteenth-century Americans, as it had been for Christians for almost two millennia, it was not a perfected society, as counseled by European adherents of the late Enlightenment, which was necessary for individual and political well-being, but the intercession of Christ and the Holy Spirit, because only they were essential in freeing people from sin—above all our disfiguring selfishness, lusts, and passions. Very few in America, outside of a handful of unusually progressive liberal elite, thought that men and women,[21] without divine intercession and the social support that religion provided in shaping an individual's will, could lead a life of liberty (of various kinds), the kind of life necessary for a republic to flourish.[22]

As Benjamin Rush famously commented:

> The only foundation for a useful education in a republic is to be laid in RELI-
> GION. Without this there can be no virtue, and without virtue there can be no
> liberty, and liberty is the object and life of all republican governments. Such is my
> veneration for every religion that reveals . . . a future state of rewards and
> punishments, that I had rather see the opinions of Confucius or Mohammed
> inculcated . . . than see them [youth] grow up wholly devoid of a system of
> religious principles. But the religion I mean to recommend in this place is the
> religion of JESUS CHRIST.[23]

Possibly following William Warburton, the Anglican bishop of Gloucester and the author, among a number of important works, of the important *Alliance between Church and State; or the Necessity and Equity of an Established Religion* (1736), such an emphasis on the civil ends of religion were, by late in the eighteenth century, now to be expected. Still, though, it was religion and, if possible, the work of the Holy Spirit, that a life of liberty demanded.

Protestant-shaped goals, contrary to the claims of those who would relegate Christianity to the backwaters of American life,[24] are readily discoverable, with the possible exception of the Federal Constitution,[25] in all manner of American legal codes and social practices of the period. For example, only one of the 13 states, Virginia, failed to require a religious test for those wishing to hold public office.[26] All other states required that state office-holders, including federal Senatorial electors, be Protestant (Connecticut, Rhode Island, Georgia, Massachusetts, New Hampshire, New Jersey, North and South Carolina, and Vermont), Trinitarian Christian (Delaware), accepting of the truthfulness of Scripture (Pennsylvania and Vermont), Christian (Maryland), or non-Catholic (New York). Moreover, Delaware's constitution demanded of office-holders that they "profess faith in God the Father, and in Jesus Christ His only Son, and in the Holy Ghost." And, at the time of the Revolution:

> Only three colonies allowed Catholics to vote. They were banned from holding public office in all New England colonies save Rhode Island. New Hampshire law called for the imprisonment of all persons who refused to repudiate the pope, the mass, and transubstantiation. New York held the death penalty over priests who entered the colony, Virginia boasted that it would only arrest them. Georgia did not permit Catholics to reside within its boundaries; the Carolinas merely barred them from office.[27]

And, even among dissenters, the public role of government officials acting as "nursing fathers" (following Isaiah 49:23) in advancing the goals of Christianity was never questioned. Indeed, once the issue of the state's role in taxing its citizens in support of religious institutions was largely settled, such denominations were free to become still more supportive of such goals.[28]

During the War for Independence, therefore, we should not be surprised by the "deeply religious men in positions of national legislative leadership." For example, the Secretary of the Congress, Charles Thomson, "retired from public life to translate the Scriptures from Greek to English" and the famous pamphleteer, John Dickinson, "also retired from public life to devote himself to religious scholarship." Much the same was true of three of the Congress' presidents: Elias Boudinot, Henry Laurens, and John Jay.[29] Under their leadership, 13 times Congress unapologeti, via proclamations for days of fasting and humiliation, sought on behalf of the young nation the intervention of God, Jesus Christ, and, at other times, that of the Holy Ghost. Indeed, the Continental Congress on March 14, 1781 even appointed James Madison to serve on a committee of three "to prepare a recommendation to the states for setting apart a day of humiliation, fasting and prayer" for May 2, 1781. Like

Jefferson in Virginia in the 1770s and 1780s,[30] Madison too was involved in the linked workings of church and state in America. Thus, even the two men whose private views are often viewed today as representative or authoritative on eighteenth-century American church–state matters[31] publicly acted in ways that accurately reflected the deeply Protestant nature of the country.[32]

Not surprisingly, then, this same Congress readily supported Protestantism in its daily prayers, its appointment of military chaplaincies, its collective attendance at worship services as a body, its ordering that an American bible either be published or imported, and its persistent efforts to bring American Indians to Christ.[33] Such actions comport well with John Adams' assessment, in a letter to his fellow Deist Thomas Jefferson, that when looking back on the Revolutionary period, he was forced to admit that "the *general Principles*, on which the Fathers Atchieved [sic] Independence, were . . . the Principles of Christianity, in which all" were united.[34] All of this had occurred, too, while America's first national government was frantically trying to help organize new state governments, negotiate various foreign treaties, and manage a war against the world's greatest naval power.

Yet, in still other ways the early national and state governments boldly displayed the Protestant character of eighteenth-century America. Thus, "officials donated land and personalty for the building of churches, religious schools, and charities. They collected taxes and tithes to support ministers and missionaries. They exempted church property from taxation. They incorporated religious bodies. They outlawed blasphemy and sacrilege, [and] unnecessary labor on the Sabbath and on religious holidays."[35] Well into the nineteenth century, states and localities were comfortable in "endorsing religious symbols and ceremonies": crosses were common on statehouse grounds, holy days were official holidays, chaplains continued to be "appointed to state legislatures, military groups, and state prisons," thanksgiving prayers were offered by governors, subsidies were given to Christian missionaries, the costs of bibles were underwritten, tax exemptions were provided to Christian schools, "public schools and state universities had mandatory courses in the Bible and religion and compulsory attendance in daily chapel and Sunday worship services . . . [and] polygamy, prostitution, pornography, and other sexual offenses . . . were prohibited. Blasphemy and sacrilege were still prosecuted. . . . and other activities that depended on fate or magic were forbidden."[36]

These descriptions of the religious features of eighteenth-century American civic life are best understood when framed by the words of Justice Story, a respected jurist, Harvard professor of law, and Supreme Court justice, who argued that "it is impossible for those who believe in the truth of Christianity as a divine revelation to doubt that it is the especial duty of [this] government to foster and encourage it among all the citizens and subjects,"[37] or those of Chief Justice James Kent, "one of the fathers of American jurisprudence . . . [who] declared that . . . 'to revile with malicious and blasphemous contempt the religion professed by the whole community is an abuse of that right [to freedom of religious opinion] . . . We are a Christian people, and the morality of the country is deeply ingrafted upon Christianity'."[38] Protestant Christianity was simply an accepted part of American life and law and only a very few, and often only in private correspondence, believed that the hallowed rights of religious conscience and the expanding goals of equal religious liberty, most particularly among the dissenters who fought so doggedly for those rights, demanded anything other than a publicly endorsed world of protected Protestant practices, beliefs, and governmental institutions.[39]

Nonetheless, by the century's end, the heretofore dominant Reformed theology of Puritans and Presbyterians no longer provided "the moral and religious background of fully 75 per cent of the people who [had] declared their independence in 1776,"[40] as "evangelicalism emerged from the Awakening as the force of the future in American religion; those groups on the wrong side of it were driven to the sidelines."[41] However, in recognizing the late-eighteenth-century decline of Reformed denominations and the epochal rise of Baptists and Methodists, and that Socinians, Arians, and Arminians also give vent to legitimate expressions of Protestantism, the universe of Protestant-inspired thought and practices in eighteenth-century America is not diminished but broadened and made even more fully coextensive with eighteenth-century American culture, politics, and norms.

LIBERTY, NOT LICENSE

In this land of largely autonomous Protestant village communities, townships, and counties in the Middle and Southern colonies, the secular individualism of Hobbes with his collapsing of liberty into procedural freedom was, at least in speech and writing, accorded little standing. Indeed, amid overlapping Western traditions that can be teased out of American sermons, pamphlets, and newspapers, publicly defined limitations on the individual's subjective liberty are found consistently.[42] Eighteenth-century Americans' understanding of liberty, in ways foreign to us, did not describe autonomous individual freedom, but rather, in all but one of its various forms, a traditional Western understanding of a voluntary submission to a life of righteousness shaped by Christian moral standards and the authoritative interpretive capacity of congregation and community—if you will, an ordered and communal sense of liberty.[43]

Liberty in the eighteenth century, whether civil or religious or any one of 12 or more different varieties or meanings,[44] as it had been in the seventeenth century, continued to be more about making the right choices than simply the freedom to choose. Indeed, in one of the most famous speeches in American history, John Winthrop early in the seventeenth century set the tone for subsequent discourse concerning liberty.[45] For the sake of his auditors, who to his mind were confused (already) over the proper meaning of liberty, he followed traditional Christian categories of thought and discriminated between the "natural" (post-Fall or relative) liberty of man, one held in common "with beasts and other creatures," and true moral liberty, natural or absolute in a classic ontological sense. He unashamedly joined, as Americans have long continued to do, Christian and communal civil liberty, and instructed the General Court in 1645 that "the other kind of liberty I call civil or federal . . . is the proper end and object of authority, and cannot subsist without it; and it is a liberty to that only which is good, just, and honest . . . it is the same kind of liberty wherewith Christ hath made us free."[46] John Adams, a century later, when quizzed late in life, on the meaning of liberty, still counseled that "I would define liberty to be a power to do as we would be done by. The definition of liberty to be the power of doing whatever the laws permit, meaning the civil laws, does not appear to be satisfactory."[47] Unlike freedom, or even that which is merely legal, liberty carried with its high valuation, inherent constraints shaped by essential Christian and rational ends.[48]

In a particularly revealing manner, Peter Powers, in Vermont's second election sermon in 1778, explained that men and women were born free and rational but, as a result of their inherently sinful natures, to live well, they must be bound by societally reinforced constraints (and for almost all, this necessitated religion and, thus, for Americans, Protestantism). Accordingly, he began by describing man's natural freedom, that is, his rights and liberty before the Fall and, then, as had Winthrop over a century earlier, went on to make clear the need not only for communal oversight, but also the freedom that came only with rebirth in Christ. He held that "all men, indeed, are by nature equal: and all have, most certainly, an equal right to freedom and liberty by the great law of nature. No man or number of men, *has* or *can* have a right to infringe the natural rights, liberties or privileges of others." He did not stop there, but continued that

> It is a very plain case that many people of the present day, have very absurd
> notions of Liberty, as if it consisted in a right for every one to believe, do, or act
> as he pleases in all things civil and religious. This is a *Libertine* principle. No man
> has any right, before God, to believe or practice contrary to scripture. And
> Liberty consists in a freedom to do that which is right.[49]

This sermon, as one of dozens and dozens of similar examples, helps illustrate that for eighteenth-century Americans liberty was only rarely understood as unconstrained freedom but, rather, far more often as freedom rightly employed in the service of the common good.[50] Indeed, freedom improperly used, was not liberty at all, but instead license.

The freedom to live a life directed by lusts and passions, a life of sin free of the moral constraints offered by religion, was almost universally condemned both by orthodox Protestants and, possibly less expected, by rationalists as well.[51] Men such as Jeremiah Atwater, the first president of Middlebury College, found that "liberty, if considered as a blessing, must be taken in a qualified sense" in which "unbounded liberty" was nothing "other than the liberty of sinning, the liberty of indulging lawless passions."[52] With the goal of preventing such transgressions, most of the New England supporters of the new Federal Constitution, men such as Oliver Ellsworth, continued to argue that "the civil power has a right . . . to prohibit and punish gross immoralities and impieties . . . For this reason, I heartily approve of our laws against

drunkenness, profane swearing, blasphemy, and professed atheism."[53] This understanding was not a minority Federalist belief, but one held by dissenters and antifederalists too;[54] in short, "the vast majority of Americans" agreed that the "government
should enforce the sabbath and respect for the scriptures, limit office to Christians
or Protestants, and generally support the Christian Protestant mores that entwined
both state and society."[55] A life of liberty demanded moral restraint, and moral
restraint demanded religion.

From the perspective of eighteenth-century American Reformed Protestants,
however, the purely civil constraints defended by almost all elite rationalists for overcoming the sinful self were simply inadequate. Like their forebears in the Reformation,
pietistic and Reformed Americans staked out an unequivocal position in opposition to
such relative optimism concerning man's natural abilities, even when they were
shaped by well-designed social institutions resting on religious foundations, to follow
his reason and will moral behavior.[56] For men such as Hugh Alison of South Carolina, fallen men needed, above all, to be freed by Christ's righteousness; that is, by
"the operation of the blessed spirit! Their bondage is at an end, and their obedience
is a *perfect freedom*."[57] Before the provincial Congress of Georgia, John Zubly warned
the legislators in an often-reprinted sermon that "no external enemy can so completely tyrannize over a conquered enemy as sin does over all those who yield themselves its servants . . . till the grace of GOD brings salvation, when he would do good,
evil is present with him: in short, instead of being under a law of liberty, he is under
the law of sin and death."[58] In sermon after sermon, this transformation from license
to liberty demanded first the intercession of Christ and the Holy Spirit.

Baptist ministers too, and even some of the more humanistic Anglicans,
repeated the same message of people's unaided inability to fend off the wages of
original sin in trying to live a life of true liberty. Radical political activists such as the
Baptist Isaac Backus held that the "definition of true liberty was premised much
more on human depravity than on rationality or inalienable rights, and reflected
John Winthrop's sermon on Christian Liberty and Jonathan Edward's definition of
true virtue."[59] Even as progressive a minister as the Unitarian Simeon Howard
maintained humans' woeful inadequacy, through individual effort, to overcome
our inherent sinfulness and live within the contours of true liberty. In 1780 he asked
his audience "to reflect with shame upon the selfishness and corruption of our spe-
cies, who, with all their rational and moral powers, cannot otherwise be kept from
injuring and destroying one another," before going on to argue that "this is a very
humiliating consideration; and, so far as we know, there is no other order of creatures throughout the boundless universe who, if left to their natural liberty, would
be so mischievous to one another as man."[60] For most Protestants, living a life of
liberty demanded not only the efforts of the feeble individual but, more importantly, the action of the Holy Spirit in making spiritual liberty possible and, then,
the continuing work of brethren joined together in civil community and voluntary
congregations of the faithful.

Even at the end of the century when advocates of the French Revolution in
America had begun to champion bold ideas of human perfectibility and subjective

liberty,[61] the moderate pillars of American provincial society continued to distance themselves from any notion of unfettered secular liberty. Thus, in 1798, Israel Woodward compared the respective French and American understandings of liberty, secular and Christian, and found that:

> The *liberties* of the American and French nations, are grounded upon totally different and opposite principles. In their matters of civil government, they adopt this general maxim, that mankind are virtuous enough to need no restraint; which idea is most justly reprobated by the more enlightened inhabitants of the United States, who denominate such liberty, licentiousness.[62]

The American rejection of secular optimism in human perfectibility and unconstrained liberty rested on an understanding of humanity as fundamentally deformed by original sin,[63] a perspective that demanded that if people were properly to enjoy liberty, they needed Christ's intercession to achieve spiritual liberty. Even for the humanists among them, moral instruction resting on an essentially religious foundation.

SPIRITUAL LIBERTY

As an overwhelmingly Protestant people, eighteenth-century Americans regularly claimed that the most important form of liberty was not the instrumentally critical civil liberty of communal self-government or, until the end of the century, not even that of equal religious liberty, but instead the liberty offered by rebirth in Christ; that is, Christian or spiritual liberty. Phillips Payson, a scholar in the natural sciences and a member of the American Academy of Sciences as well a Congregational minister at Chelsea, Massachusetts, explained that "next to the liberty of heaven," the chosen possess spiritual liberty "in which they are freed from the bondage of corruption, the tyranny of evil lusts and passion." And this spiritual liberty was to be accounted as "the greatest happiness of man, considered in a private capacity."[64] Jonas Clark, the politically active minister who hid John Hancock and Samuel Adams on the night of Paul Revere's ride, further clarified that "the gospel of *Jesus Christ*, is the source of liberty, the soul of government and the life of a people."[65] Spiritual liberty was the ground, both at the individual and corporate level, that made possible for believing Christians a life of liberty—in both civil and religious forms—rather than license.

Christian or spiritual liberty, like other prevalent eighteenth-century understandings of liberty but to an even greater degree given its divine nature, defended a conception of liberty defined by its reflection of an objective set of Christian ethical standards.[66] As George Haskins explains, "this was not liberty in the modern sense, a freedom to pursue individual wishes or inclinations; it was a freedom from any external restraint 'to [do] that only which is good, just and honest.' Christ had been born to set men free, but the liberty so given was a freedom to walk in the faith of the gospel and to serve God through righteousness."[67] In the florid language of a Baptist minister in Virginia, David Thomas, "sin and Satan, and the world, and the flesh have an absolute dominion over" men, so much so that no man has the "power to deliver himself out of this woeful condition. . . . The dead as soon might leave their tombs, or dry bones, awake and live, as natural men by any virtue in them, repent and turn to GOD. . . . For without faith it is impossible to please him. And that faith . . . is to be obtained but by the operation of the HOLY-GHOST."[68] This form of liberty, then, was rather unlike the contemporary "negative" sense of liberty in that it was "freedom from the rule of Satan, sin, and death; from the compulsions of obedience to superpersonal forces of evil; from domination by self-interest and the passions . . . freedom for faith and hope and goodness, rather than a negative liberty from external control."[69]

The Christian essence of spiritual liberty looked backward to the values and hopes traditionally found in Protestantism and earlier forms of Christianity, where the believer was "freely" bound to order himself in accord with the commandments of Christ.[70] As explained by Augustine in his *Confessions*, Christian liberty was such that "'whenever God converts a sinner, and translates him into the state of grace, he freeth him from his natural bondage under sin, and by His grace alone inables him freely to will and to do that which is spiritually good.'"[71] Martin Luther succinctly captured this profound yet puzzling relationship when he wrote that "a Christian is a perfectly free lord of all, subject to none. A Christian is a perfectly dutiful servant of all, subject to all."[72] Some 250 years later, this peculiar antinomy in Protestant thought had changed little. It was described aptly by Hugh Alison, a South Carolinian pastor, who wrote in 1769 that spiritual liberty:

> frees us from the yoke of the ceremonial [Mosaic] law . . . from the dominion of lust and passion; and restores the soul to a religious self-government, and to the rational life of a Christian . . . [and] brings every thought into the obedience of Christ; nor does the soul ever act with greater liberty than when it acts under a divine command . . . those are the men of freest thought, whose thoughts are captivated and brought unto obedience to Christ.[73]

Americans, thus, continued to be reminded by a well-respected cultural, religious, and intellectual elite, as had earlier generations of Christians, that spiritual liberty was the key to true liberty.

Some Anglican Loyalist pastors during the Revolutionary crisis tried, unsuccessfully, to animate in America an opposing, possibly still more venerable, Christian tradition that distinguishes between corporate civil (political) liberty and the spiritual liberty of the individual.[74] The most articulate among them, Jonathan Boucher, also argued that "every sinner is, literally, a slave . . . and the only true liberty is the liberty of being the servant of God; for *his service is perfect freedom*," but then continued, noting that "the passage cannot, without infinite perversion and torture, be made to refer to any other kind of liberty . . . the word *liberty*, as meaning civil liberty, does not, I believe, occur in all the Scriptures."[75] His remarks made little impression on most of America's Reformed and pietistic Protestants. Thus, in the critical year of 1776, Judah Champion held in his election sermon of that year that "our civil liberties and privileges are nearly connected with, and greatly promotive of our religious (on which account they are chiefly to be esteemed)."[76] From the beginning of European settlement and most emphatically during the Imperial Crisis that led to the 13 mainland colonies separating from Britain, Americans regularly held, even if somewhat perversely, that the enabling conditions of Christian liberty were and should be intimately connected with communal political liberty.[77]

Not unusual, then, were the remarks of the Revolutionary New Divinity polymath Nathaniel Niles who, in 1774, amid the supercharged atmosphere created by the imposition of the "Intolerable Acts," argued in the second of his two discourses on liberty that:

> if we refuse spiritual liberty, that of the civil kind will be no otherwise agreeable than as it tends to advance our own private interests . . . Thus, by neglecting to embrace the gospel, we convert civil liberty, which is in itself, a delicious kind of food, into a slow poison which will render our death vastly more terrible than otherwise it would have been.[78]

From 1765 onward, it became common to argue that "while our civil liberties were openly threatened, our religious [liberties] shook; [and] after taking away the liberty of taxing ourselves, and breaking in upon our charters, they [the colonists] feared the breaking in upon the act of toleration, the taking away of liberty to choose our own ministers, and then imposing whom they [the Parliament and British imperial officials] pleased upon us."[79] The sanctity of Christian liberty, once attached to concerns for civil (political) liberty, made the latter nearly unrenounceable. For late-eighteenth-century Americans, "the cause of liberty thus became a sacred one." In particular, "political [civil] liberty" had become for them "a fundamental article of [Christian] faith."[80] But in a nod to Christian orthodoxy, "the traditional order of sin-salvation-service prevailed" and "ministers carefully avoided celebrations of civil liberties for their own sake. Rather, they were presented as necessary instruments for the preservation of the gospel."[81]

More successfully, eighteenth-century American pastors and congregations struggled to maintain Protestant orthodoxy against the desires of some in their flock to subjectivize spiritual liberty. This was sought by individuals so that they could "legitimately" escape the boundaries of socially mediated liberty as understood and enforced by political community and pastoral congregation.[82] As John Calvin had warned "some, under the pretext of this liberty, cast off all obedience to God, and precipitate themselves into the most unbridled licentiousness."[83] Delivering the Connecticut election sermon of 1749, Jonathan Todd, like many other American ministers, continued to warn against those who "under a *Pretence* of Liberty, *falsely so called*, they would *put down all Rule, & all Authority, & Power* among Men: Pleading in Defence of their licentiousness Doctrine, that CHRIST *hath made all his People Kings: and they shall reign on Earth*. This, they pretend is the *Liberty where with Christ have made them free.*"[84] Although a continuing tension in the eighteenth century, this battle against the subjectivizing of Christian liberty, or indeed of liberty more generally, would seemingly be lost only later in American history.

Nonetheless, quite probably the most revolutionary fallout of the War for Independence was the way in which Christian liberty, following the war's termination, would be secularized on the world stage.[85] In fact, Ernst Troeltsch, when asked "whence comes the idea of the rights of the individual?" answered that "it is derived from the Constitutions of the North American States . . . from their Puritan religious principles . . . It was only in virtue of being thus put on a religious basis that these demands became absolute, and consequently admitted of and required a theoretical legal exposition."[86] Similarly, for Carl Schmitt, "that the freedom of religion represents the first of all the fundamental rights, without regard to any historical details of development, is in a systematic sense unconditionally correct."[87] Elsewhere, Schmitt built upon this claim and argued that "all significant concepts of the modern theory of the state are secularized theological concepts . . . [and that] only by being aware of this analogy can we appreciate the manner in which the philosophical ideas of the state developed in the last centuries."[88] What, then, American pastors could only little anticipate was that spiritual liberty, along with the right of religious conscience, both defended so powerfully during the Revolutionary era, would soon create the foundation on which a new class of secular claims, both in America and elsewhere, would be constructed.[89] However, such a recognition does nothing to diminish the distinctly religious character of these, ultimately, protean concepts.

FREEDOM OF RELIGIOUS CONSCIENCE

Possibly of still greater importance than spiritual liberty to this epoch-making transformation is the freedom of religious conscience. Under its protective umbrella, the right of the individual to choose how to interpret Holy Scripture (and, later, under the "full" rights of conscience and equal religious liberty, how best to serve God publicly), could not be legitimately denied. However, as understood in America for most of two centuries, the right of religious conscience did not limit the community's exercise of its corporate civic responsibilities. Such responsibilities included fostering the individual's religious and rational capacities to live with liberty, publicly enforcing that respect be paid to God, and protecting the community from subversive religious ideas and practices. In typical fashion, then, Abraham Williams explained that:

> Human Laws can't controul the Mind.—The Rights of Conscience, are unalienable; inseparable from our Nature;—they ought not—they cannot possibly be given up to Society. . . . Yet civil Societies have a Right, it is their Duty, to encourage and maintain social public Worship of the Deity, and Instructions in Righteousness; for without *Social Vertues, Societies can't subsist; and these Vertues*

can't be expected, or depended on, without a belief in, and regard to, the supreme Being, and a future World.[90]

Again, powerful changes in this long-established relationship were slow to come and little anticipated by the eighteenth-century American defenders of the freedom of religious conscience.[91]

Additionally, as in most of Western Christendom,[92] the freedom of religious conscience in many of the North American British colonies in the seventeenth century was not applauded. According to one of that century's most celebrated students of Puritan New England, Perry Miller, "the Puritans were not rugged individualists . . . [and] they abhorred freedom of conscience."[93] It was only toward the end of the seventeenth century, outside of an anomalous Rhode Island, that New England colonial leaders began reluctantly to embrace the freedom of religious conscience. In 1673, Urian Oakes, the president of Harvard, without great enthusiasm for either, argued for an extremely narrow understanding of the freedom of conscience and even less for the merits of religious toleration when he held that religious liberty gives

> men liberty to destroy themselves. Such is the liberty of Conscience, even a liberty of Perdition, that some men so unconscionably clamor for. But remember, that as long as you have liberty to walk in the Faith and Order of the Gospel, and may *lead quiet and peaceable lives in all Godliness and Honesty*, you have as much Liberty of Conscience as *Paul* desired under any Government.[94]

Yet as a consequence, among other causes, of the colonies' loss of political autonomy under the Dominion of New England (1686) and the aggressive commercial goals of the British imperial administration,[95] a gradual movement began that led to full freedom of religious conscience and, ultimately by the end of the eighteenth century, equality of religious liberty.

Only after the close of the seventeenth century, then, did leaders in New England "embrace the doctrine of toleration as a defensive weapon" and become increasingly sympathetic to freedom of religious conscience and a new liberty, "religious liberty—not the [Christian] liberty they had understood, which was the liberty to do God's will and to require that all others in their midst conform, but the liberty John Locke suggested was the natural right of men."[96] It would only be, however, toward mid-century in his aptly titled *The Essential Rights and Liberty of Protestants* that the socially prominent minister, Connecticut Supreme Court justice, legislator, and former president of Yale, Elisha Williams, boldly followed Locke and defended the dissenting Protestant understanding of the predominantly religious purposes served by the freedom of conscience.[97] Williams wrote that nothing of equivalent value, not even life itself, could be offered in place of the freedom of religious conscience because of its centrality in deciding (or for the Reformed, clarifying) matters of everlasting life and death. He wrote that:

> the Rights of Conscience are sacred and equal in all, and strictly speaking unalienable. This *Right of judging every one for himself in Matters of Religion*

results from the Nature of Man . . . A Man may alienate some Branches of his property and give up his Right in them to others; but he cannot transfer the *Rights of Conscience*, unless he could . . . substitute some other to be judged for him at the Tribunal of God.[98]

For the next half century and beyond, there would be no logic that could directly challenge this hallowed Protestant claim.

Thus, writing a few years later in 1748 in the *Pennsylvania Journal*, an anonymous author similarly held that "private judgment was 'one of those sacred and original rights of human nature which the Gospel had revived and re-established'. . . . Thus the rights of conscience were sacred and equal in all men."[99] The future president of Yale too, Ezra Stiles, in an unusually ecumenical stance for 1761 Connecticut, argued that "the right of conscience and private judgment is unalienable; and it is truly in the interest of all mankind to unite themselves into one body, for the liberty, free exercise, and unmolested enjoyment of this right."[100] The American rationalist and future Loyalist, William Smith, Jr., in the *Occasional Reverberator*, similarly defended the immeasurable worth of this freedom, which could not be exchanged for any other social value.[101]

Some of the most vociferous claims defending the freedom of conscience, however, are not found in pastors' sermons,[102] but rather in the returns to the Massachusetts constitutional convention of 1780. In these, one discovers that in almost all cases the religiously essential right of conscience was the only individual right defended as unalienable. When it was not the only one, it was invariably still held to be the most important.[103] The town of Stoughton, for example, instructed its delegates to endeavor that "a Bill of Rights be in the first place compiled, wherein the inherent and unalienable Rights of Conscience and all those aleinable [sic] rights ar [sic] not necessary to be given up in to the hands of government together with the equivalent individuals ought undoubtedly to Recive [sic] from Government for their relinquishing a part of their natural and alienable rights for the necessary Support of the Same."[104] After having had one constitution rejected 2 years earlier, perhaps the members of the 1780 Massachusetts convention were more attentive than usual to the wishes of their constituents.

In an opening address, the members of the convention explained to their constituents that "we have, with as much Precision as we were capable of, provided for the free exercise of the *Rights of Conscience:* We are very sensible that our Constituents hold those Rights infinitely more valuable than all others."[105] However, many of their constituents rejected the third article (concerning religious taxation) of the introductory Declaration of Rights of the Constitution because they held that it infringed on their right of religious conscience and religious liberty (i.e., their desire to separate the financing of their religious life from state taxing powers). The residents of the town of Westford, accordingly, offered an alternative to the third article, one by which their "religious Freedom and the Unalienable Rights of Conscience may be better secured and established."[106]

By the 1770s, freedom of religious conscience had become a well-accepted understanding of liberty, frequently still viewed as the only truly individual right.[107]

Accordingly, Delaware's "Declaration of Rights" begins by holding that "all govern-ment of right originates from the people, is founded by compact only, and [is] instituted solely for the good of the whole." Only the right of conscience is then described as a possession of "all men." The Maryland "Declaration" follows that of Delaware and begins with the exact same communal language, but in its description of the right of religious conscience, it is more restrictive still. Only those "professing the Christian religion, are equally entitled to protection in their religious liberty." Not only atheists are excluded from enjoying this most basic right, but all non-Christians as well. Clearly, then, the right of religious conscience enjoyed an unparalleled status in the minds of eighteenth-century Americans in being the only individual right that could and must not be surrendered as one moved from a state of "nature" to one of civil society.[108] This right, deeply concerned with the most pressing personal religious matters and legitimated by that character, made a closely connected and evolving sense of equal religious liberty difficult if not impossible to oppose in post-Revolutionary America.[109]

CONCLUSION

Yet, in the decades immediately following the close of the War for Independence, Americans continued to disagree concerning the degree of religious liberty that was to accompany the freedom of religious conscience.[110] In accord with a relatively common understanding, Jefferson explained that he too believed that "religion is a matter which lies solely between man and his God, that he owes account to none other for this faith." He then went on to suggest, however, in ways almost never embraced by American pietistic and Reformed Protestants, that the First Amend-ment to the national Constitution had effectively built "a wall of separation between Church and State."[111] This was a position at variance with almost every recorded eighteenth-century statement that, while defending the hallowed right of religious conscience and a more robust form of religious liberty, had continued to defend the necessity—even if now for civil rather than soteriological ends—of a close working relation between church and state.

Indeed, the Baptists of Virginia who on several occasions helped elect Jefferson and Madison, most certainly did not conceive of religious liberty as a wall of sepa-ration, as did Jefferson.[112] Instead, they understood that the:

> struggle for religious freedom meant that all churches were now able to compete on a completely equal basis. *They were eager to do so, especially against the forces of deism and irreligion* . . . [and] the years ahead would see one move after another to embody evangelical values in the laws of Virginia, the other states, and ultimately the Union.[113]

Gregory Nobles, indeed, reminds us that it was the greater religious strictness and purity of the evangelicals that had led them to reject state establishments.[114]

From their perspective, then, it would have been more appropriate to describe the "wall" as a one-way permeable membrane, i.e., no state interference in religion was countenanced (that is the opposite perspective from that held by their more secular allies), whereas Protestant interference in the state was sought and encouraged during much of the next two centuries.[115]

Opposing both were the social and religious conservatives who wrote as if the support given to the freedom of conscience had gone too far and was already beginning to serve the forces of infidelity. Moses Hemmenway enunciated a central theme of the 1780s when he warned that "we should take heed that *Liberty of thinking* for ourselves, or the right of private judgment become not an occasion of infidelity, or skepticism . . . *Liberty of conscience* must not be abused into a pretence for neglecting religious worship, prophaning God's sabbath and ordinances, or refusing to do our part for the support of government and the means of religious instruction."[116] Five years later in Connecticut, Cyprian Strong emphatically asserted that "it is impossible, therefore, that civil government should take a neutral position, respecting religion or a kingdom of holiness. It must aid and countenance it, or it will discourage and bring it into contempt."[117] Such pillars of traditional Protestant America were trying to recreate accepted limits to contain the freedom of religious conscience and practice and, thus, prevent a feared loss of religiosity, morality, and civil responsibility that they were confident would follow.

Like Jefferson and Madison on the opposing side, such men now stood outside the mainstream of an American society that had accepted that full freedom of religious conscience and equal religious liberty were supportive of republican government, Protestant religiosity, and individual morality. A few in America had come to such beliefs for predominantly libertarian reasons, but the vast majority had done so for preeminently Protestant ones that included, for the expanding population of evangelical Protestants, their centuries-old defense of freedom of religious conscience and religious liberty, and their linked confidence that such a life of liberty was only possible because of Christ's saving grace and the spiritual liberty that followed. When such beliefs are joined to the overwhelming Protestant nature of their world and the institutions that did so much to maintain it, it seems hard to conceive, except possibly in a creative act of historical imagination, how religious liberty in eighteenth-century America could have been anything other than the product of this Protestant world, particularly one that was being newly populated by ever-increasing numbers of Baptists and Methodists.

The world, then, of nineteenth-century American religiosity, I imagine, would have been readily comprehensible, even if in many cases not at all congenial, to the varying populations of eighteenth-century American Protestants who we might today, broadly understood, view as founders of the American republic. The most religiously conservative among them would have found much to appall them in the decline of their own more or less state-centered denominations. Progressive Unitarians would have been similarly troubled by the growing strength of heartfelt, rather than ever more rationalistic, religiosity among their co-citizens; and the pietistic sects might, even while experiencing enormously rapid rates of growth, have complained of the lack of a commensurable change in the moral behavior of their co-religionists. All, though, would have been able to join together in opposition to the rise of Mormonism and resisting the ever-increasing numbers and strength of the Church of Rome.

The twentieth century, however, would have been less understandable to many of them. The transformation of many evangelical sects, at the beginning of the century, from progressively focused on world transformation, and staunchly protective of the rights of conscience, to becoming predominantly conservative and world-withdrawing and, later still in the century, surprisingly comfortable with some form of alliance between church and state, would have been something that few would have predicted. Likely still more surprising to eighteenth-century Americans would have been the increased diversity of the American population with large numbers of Catholics, and even a small but influential number of Jews and Muslims. Still more unexpected, though, would have been the number and cultural prominence of nonbelievers actively and openly hostile to publicly endorsed displays of Protestant religiosity. With the possible exception of a literal handful of prominent political actors, almost all the members of the eighteenth-century founding generation believed that religion (and this almost always meant some form of Protestantism) needed to publicly support dominant moral and civic norms and, in turn, in some form or other, to be supported publicly by civic institutions. In short, the contemporary world in which almost all the functions of church and state, including most importantly those at the local and state level, are truly to be kept separate and fully distinct, is a world that the founding generation of Americans would have little anticipated, understood, or desired.

ENDNOTES
....

1. Thomas Jefferson, "To Isaac H. Tiffany, April 4, 1819," in *The Political Writings of Thomas Jefferson*, ed. Edward Dumbauld (New York: The Liberal Arts Press, 1955), 55.

2. Cited by William Linn Westerman, "Between Slavery and Freedom," in *American Historical Review* 50 (January 1945): 213–217.

3. George Washington, "To the Ministers . . . of the Reformed German Congregation of New York, November 27, 1783," in *George Washington: A Collection*, ed. W.B. Allen (Indianapolis: Liberty Fund, Inc., 1988), 271.

4. See James H. Hutson, *Church and State in America: The First Two Centuries* (Cambridge, UK: Cambridge University Press, 2007), 54–55, who writes that pivotal in this transformation was "William Warburton, later Bishop of Gloucester . . . [who in 1736 explained] that 'THE TRUE END FOR WHICH RELIGION IS ESTABLISHED IS NOT TO PROVIDE FOR THE TRUE FAITH, BUT FOR CIVIL UTILITY'. . . . Warburton redefined the church's primary mission as being service to the state not the salvation of souls."

5. This secular understanding is often described as "inner" or "metaphysical" freedom. See F. A. Hayek, *The Constitution of Liberty* (Chicago: The University of Chicago

Press, 2007), 15, who notes that "it refers to the extent to which a person is guided in his actions by his own considered will, by his reason . . . the opposite of 'inner freedom' is not coercion by others but the influence of temporary emotions, or moral or intellectual weakness," for Christians, the product of original sin.

6. Chapter XX, "Of Christian Liberty, and Liberty of Conscience, Westminster Confession of Faith (1646)," in *Creeds of the Churches*, ed. John H. Leith (3rd ed., Louisville, KY: John Knox Press, 1982), 214–215.

7. See Hutson, *Church and State in America*, 92–93, and Ibid., 24–25, where he distinguishes the foundations of such views from those of Roger Williams; see too, Philip A. Hamburger, *Separation of Church and State* (Cambridge, MA: Harvard University Press, 2002), 39, 51, and 63–64, where he adds that "it is difficult to find dissenting denominations or even many individuals in America prior to 1800 who clearly advocated the separation of church and state."

8. Cf. Leroy Moore, "Religious Liberty: Roger Williams and the Revolutionary Era," in *Church History* 34 (March 1965): 67, who argues that the two major groups, the deists and the evangelicals, sought the same end but, for the former "the issue" and "the field of battle" rest on anthropocentric premises whereas for the latter, on theocentric ones. More accurately, Hutson, Ibid., 120, concludes that "the politicians hoped for a republic of reason in which future generations of Americans would profess some version of 'liberal' Christianity. The pietists wanted a born-again nation, convicted by the Holy Spirit and redeemed by the blood of Jesus Christ."

9. See Carl Bridenbaugh, *Mitre and Sceptre: Transatlantic Faiths, Ideas, Personalities, and Politics* (New York: Oxford University Press, 1955), xi, who writes that "no understanding of the eighteenth century is possible if we unconsciously omit, or consciously jam out, the religious themes just because our own milieu is secular . . . in England's American colonies the most enduring and absorbing public question from 1689 to 1777 was religion."

10. See, for example, Frank Lambert, *The Founding Fathers and the Place of Religion in America* (Princeton, NJ: Princeton University Press, 2003).

11. See Hutson, *Church and State in America*, 41.

12. See A. Gregg Roeber, "The Limited Horizons of Whig Religious Rights," in *The Nature of Rights at the American Founding and Beyond*, ed. Barry Alan Shain (Charlottesville, VA: University of Virginia Press, 2007), 206, who writes that "among the issues that demonstrated the restrictive features of the Founders' understanding of religious rights were the federal funding of Protestant missionaries among Native Americans; the response to the unnerving rise of a Roman Catholic presence and hierarchy; a reinvigorated anti-Semitism that began to take shape in the 1790s; the manner in which the challenges raised by African Americans . . . were treated; and the repressive response to the rise of Mormonism."

13. The respective theological statuses of those who defend intelligent design in the two cultures, as well as anything else, demonstrates the great distance between the two worlds.

14. See Jeremy Waldron, *God, Locke, and Equality: Christian Foundations in Locke's Political Thought* (Cambridge, MA: Cambridge University Press, 2002), 12–15, for his discussion of the difficulties of appropriating the thought of men still shaped by the contours of a purposeful universe; and Mark Tushnet, "Should Historians Accept the Supreme Court's Invitation?," in *Organization of American Historians Newsletter* (November 1987): 13, who concludes that the "normative understanding of the establishment clause cannot be translated directly into contemporary constitutional law without a substantial shift in our current intellectual universe, a shift that would somehow have to retrieve the assumption that this is a Protestant nation in a normatively attractive form."

15. See Stanley N. Katz, "The Legal and Religious Context of Natural Rights Theory: A Comment," in *Party and Political Opposition in Revolutionary America*, ed. Patricia U. Bonomi (Tarrytown, NY: Sleepy Hollow Press, 1980), 36–37, who observes that "curiously, however, neither the 1920's nor the 1960's interpretations took *religious* ideas seriously as a component of American opposition ideology . . . in what was, after all, still an intensely religious society"; and Norman Hampson, *The Enlightenment: An Evaluation of its Assumptions, Attitudes, and Values* (1968; reprint ed., New York: Penguin Books, 1986), 131, who writes of the eighteenth century that "it is something of an historical impertinence to consider the century as the age of Enlightenment since religion exercised a far greater hold over most sections of every society than it does today."

16. Henry F. May, *The Enlightenment in America* (New York: Oxford University Press, 1978), xiv, and see 45–46, in which he continues that "for most inhabitants of the American colonies in the eighteenth century, Calvinism was . . . in the position of laissez-faire in mid-nineteenth-century England or democracy in twentieth-century America."

17. Harry S. Stout, *The New England Soul: Preaching and Religious Culture in Colonial New England* (New York: Oxford University Press, 1986), 6.

18. Mark Tushnet, "The Origins of the Establishment Clause," *Georgetown Law Journal* 75 (April 1987): 1515.

19. See, for example, James Madison, "Memorial and Remonstrance," in *James Madison: Writings: Writings 1772–1836*, ed. Jack N. Rakove (New York: Library of America, 1999), 29–36; commenting on the same, see Hamburger, *Separation of Church and State*, 105; and see as well the curiously evasive language of Vincent Phillip Munoz, "James Madison's Principles of Religious Liberty," *American Political Science Review* 97 (February 2003): 28.

20. One might defend religious liberty on purely economic and libertarian grounds or, still more likely, by arguing that all men are innately religious (and contentious) and, thus, civil peace requires it. It is impossible, though, to find in a Protestant world like America, such arguments offered without patently religious ones and impossible to imagine that they would have gained much traction.

21. See Hutson, *Church and State in America*, 181, who argues that Madison "was the only politician in the nation who denied that religion had any 'public utility.' He was the only politician who opposed the appointments of legislative and military chaplains."

22. See May, *Enlightenment in America*, xv, xviii, who cautions that "a great many people believed throughout the period that the religion of the Bible, understood best by simple people, was the safest foundation for all essential truths . . . the Enlightenment developed among the middle and upper classes of European cities, spread mainly among similar groups in America, and failed to reach the agrarian majority. On the whole, various forms of Protestant Christianity served the emotional needs of most Americans better."

23. Benjamin Rush, "Thoughts Upon the Mode of Education," in *American Political Writing During the Founding Era, 1760–1805*, eds. Charles S. Hyneman and Donald S. Lutz (Indianapolis, Liberty Fund, Inc., 1983), 681.

24. See E. C. Ladd, "205 and Going Strong," *Public Opinion* 4 (June–July 1981): 11; and J. David Greenstone, "Political Culture and American Political Development: Liberty, Union, and the Liberal Bipolarity," in *Studies in American Political Development*, ed. Steven Skowronek 1 (New Haven, CT: Yale University Press, 1987): 2, 4, 17.

25. See Hutson, *Church and State in America*, 144, who concludes that "Washington, Hamilton, and other like-minded delegates, who in principle had no objections to funding and employing religion to produce virtuous citizens, were certain that injecting religion in

any form into the Constitution would antagonize voters who might already be dubious about the document for other reasons. Religion, therefore, was banished from the Constitution for political considerations"; Roeber, "Limited Horizons," in *Nature of Right at the American Founding and Beyond*, ed. Barry Alan Shain, 200, who describes that "what we know with confidence regarding what the Founders thought about the 'rights' of religion is that they, along with the Protestant majority, were determined that the new republic would not have a national religious establishment. We also know that they accepted the demands emanating from various states that religious liberty must be protected. . . . [so we must] avoid the temptation to attribute their determination to protect religious liberty to either religious indifference or hostility to Christianity"; and see John Adams, "Letter to B. Rush, June 12, 1812," in *The Spur of Fame: Dialogues of John Adams and Benjamin Rush*, ed. John A. Schutz and Douglass Adair (San Marino, CA: Huntington Library Publications, 1966), 224, who writes that his loss of office resulted from his having recommended a fast at the national level. "The secret whisper ran through all the sects, 'Let us have Jefferson, Madison, Burr, anybody, whether they be philosophers, Deists, or even atheists, rather than a Presbyterian President'. . . Nothing is more dreaded than the national government meddling with religion."

26. See Sydney E. Ahlstrom, *A Religious History of the American People* (New Haven, CT: Yale University Press, 1972): 380; and Edwin S. Gaustad, *Proclaim Liberty Throughout All the Land: A History of Church and State in America* (New York: Oxford University Press, 2003), 52, who reminds us that Maryland's "test act" lasted until 1961.

27. Derek H. Davis, *Religion and the Continental Congress, 1774–1789: Contributions to Original Intent* (New York: Oxford University Press, 2000), 153.

28. See Hamburger, *Separation of Church and State*, 107.

29. James H. Hutson, *Religion and the Founding of the American Republic* (Washington, DC: Library of Congress, 1998), 49.

30. See Daniel L. Dreisbach, "Another Look at Jefferson's Wall of Separation: A Jurisdictional Interpretation of the 'Wall' Metaphor," Witherspoon Fellowship Lectures, Family Research Council, August 2000, 5; and Hutson, *Church and State in America*, 185, who describes how Jefferson, so as to exonerate himself from the charge of being an atheist, began attending highly public worship services that offered "proof that he used the wall metaphor in the restrictive sense just described;" that is, to explain why he didn't proclaim days of Thanksgiving and fasting as President of the Nation—as he had done in proclaiming a "Day of Solemn Thanksgiving and Prayer" as governor of Virginia in November 1779.

31. See Daniel L. Dreisbach, "Founders Famous and Forgotten," *Intercollegiate Review* 42 (Fall 2007): 11, who describes that "the focus on these two Virginians is odd, if not counter-historical," and Hutson, Ibid., 181, who goes further and writes that "to claim that Madison's opinions on this subject [church/state relations] represented those of his fellow citizens across the new republic is as farfetched as to assert that Voltaire's views on religion represented those of the Catholic hierarchy in France."

32. See Kevin R. Hardwick, "Religion and Morality in the Political Thought of Edmund Randolph," Religion and the Founders, George Fox University, March 2, 2007, 17, who cites Edmund Randolph recalling that Madison's "'opinions against restraints on conscience ingratiated him with the enemies of the establishment, who did not stop to inquire how far those opinions might border on skepticism and infidelity'. As Randolph acidly noted, 'parties in religion and politics rarely scan with nicety the peculiar private opinions of their adherents'."

33. See, for example, Worthington Chauncey Ford, ed., *Journals of the Continental Congress, 1774–1789* (Washington, DC: Government Printing Office, 1904), November 11, 1775, 3: 351.

34. John Adams, "Letter to Thomas Jefferson," in *The Adams-Jefferson Letters*, ed. Lester J. Cappon (Chapel Hill: University of North Carolina Press, 1988), 339–340; and see John Adams, "Discourse XIII on Davila," in *The Works of John Adams, Second President of the United States: With A Life of the Author, Notes and Illustrations*, ed. Charles Francis Adams (Boston: Little, Brown, and Company, 1865), 6: 277, in which he describes the rights that Americans went to war to protect as those of men, Christians, and subjects.

35. John Witte, Jr., *Religion and the American Constitutional Experiment: Essential Rights and Liberties* (Boulder, CO: Westview Press, 2000), 53.

36. Ibid., 97–98.

37. Joseph Story, *Commentaries on the Constitution of the United States With a Preliminary Review of the Constitutional History of the Colonies and States Before the Adoption of the Constitution* (Boston: Hilliard, Gray and Company, 1833), 2: 603, and see Ibid., 2: 603–609, in which he writes that "the right of a society or government to interfere in matters of religion will hardly be contested," for "the great doctrines of religion . . . never can be a matter of indifference in any well-ordered community." Indeed, "the real object of the First Amendment was not to countenance, much less to advance, Mahometanism, Judaism, or infidelity, by prostrating Christianity; but to exclude rivalry among Christian sects." In making this point clearer, see James McClellan, *Joseph Story and the American Constitution: A Study in Political and Legal Thought* (Norman, OK: University of Oklahoma Press, 1990), 118–159.

38. Philip Schaff, "Church and State in the United States," in *Papers of the American Historical Association* (New York: Knickerbocker Press, 1890), 60.

39. See Hamburger, *Separation of Church and State*, 10–11 and 78, in which he writes that "like most Americans, Baptists . . . vigorously protested that their religious liberty was no threat to government, to Christian morality, or to the laws enforcing such morality . . . Committed to a vision of society in which their religion permeated their lives, and struggling to overcome the prejudice of their fellow citizens who feared religious dissent as a threat to morality and law, these dissenters had every reason to seek religious liberty and no reason to demand the disconnection of religion and government."

40. Ahlstrom, *Religious History of the American People*, 124; and see George Lee Haskins, *Law and Authority in Early Massachusetts: A Study in Tradition and Design* (Lanham, MD: University Press of America, 1960), 223–224; Patricia U. Bonomi, *Under the Cope of Heaven: Religion, Society and Politics in Colonial America* (New York: Oxford University Press, 1986), 3; and David Hackett Fischer, *Albion's Seed: Four British Folkways in America* (New York: Oxford University Press, 1989), 1: 423, who reports that of approximately 3000 congregations in 1775, only 500 or 18% were Anglican (Episcopal) and the vast remainder were Reformed.

41. Hutson, *Religion and the Founding of the American Republic*, 35.

42. See Roeber, "Limited Horizons," in *Nature of Rights at the American Founding and Beyond*, ed. Barry Alan Shain, 213, who writes that it is hard believe that any of "the Founders subscribe[d] 'literally' to this understanding of conscience as wholly subjective."

43. See Stout, *The New England Soul*, 259, who writes that in "the terms New Englanders continued to hear most of the time—liberty had changed little. In 1776 as in 1630, it remained the liberty to submit to God's word—and only God's Word—in all aspects of life and faith"; and Edmund S. Morgan, "The American Revolution Considered as an Intellectual Movement," in *Essays on the American Revolution*, ed. David L. Jacobson, (New York: Holt, Rinehart and Winston, Inc., 1970), 29, who writes that "the intellectual center of the colonies was New England, and the intellectual leaders of New England were the clergy, who preached and wrote indefatigably of human depravity and divine perfection."

44. See Barry Alan Shain "Liberty and License: The American Founding and the Western Conception of Freedom," in *Vital Remnants: America's Founding and the Western Tradition*, ed. Gary L. Gregg II (Wilmington, DE: Intercollegiate Studies Institute Books, 1999), 211–242.

45. Even as late as 1938, public speakers continued to affirm the general outlines of Winthrop's understanding of liberty. See Dr. Thompson who argued before the graduates of University of North Carolina in that year that "there are really just two kinds of freedom: the false, where a man is free to do what he likes; the true freedom, where a man is free to do what he ought." Cited by Dorothy Fosdick, *What is Liberty?: A Study in Political Theory* (New York: Harper and Brothers Publishers, 1939), 109.

46. John Winthrop, "Speech to the General Court," in *The Puritans: A Sourcebook of Their Writings*, ed. Perry Miller and Thomas H. Johnson (New York: Harper & Row, 1963), 206–207. The necessary voluntarism of Protestantism demanded freedom, but valued it only when exercised as liberty not as license.

47. Adams, *Works*, 10: 377.

48. See Hanna Fenichel Pitkin, "Are Freedom and Liberty Twins?" Paper presented at the Yale Legal Theory Workshop. Published in *Political Theory* 16 (November 1988). In the paper, 28, she writes that liberty has traditionally been viewed as "something more formal, rational, and limited than freedom; it concerns rules, and exceptions within a system of rules." Most importantly, liberty has connoted "firm, rational control of those mysterious depths and of the dangerous passions found there."

49. Peter Powers, *Jesus Christ the True King and Head of the Government* (Newbury-Port, MA: John Mycall, 1778), 10, 40.

50. Clearly, as indicated in both Winthrop's and Power's remarks, there were others whom they believed had begun to challenge this traditional Christian understanding of liberty.

51. See Gordon S. Wood, *The Creation of the American Republic, 1776–1787* (Chapel Hill, NC: University of North Carolina Press, 1969), 115–116, who notes that "everywhere the clergy saw 'Sins and Iniquities'. . . . And the sins were the same vices feared by a political scientist—infidelity, intemperance, profaneness, and particularly 'pride and luxury in dress'"; and Eric Foner, *Tom Paine and Revolutionary America* (New York: Oxford University Press, 1976), 90–91, who writes that "inherent in the Commonwealth ideology which shaped the American Whig mind was a view of human nature as susceptible to corruption, basically self-interested and dominated by passion rather than reason. It was because of this natural 'depravity' of human nature that democracy was inexpedient."

52. Jeremiah Atwater, "Vermont Election Sermon," in *American Political Writing*, ed. Charles S. Hyneman and Donald S. Lutz, 1172.

53. Oliver Ellsworth, writing under the pseudonym of "A Landholder," in *Essays on the Constitution of the United States: Published During Its Discussion by the People, 1787–1788*, ed. Paul Leicester Ford (1892, reprint ed., New York: Burt Franklin, 1971), 171; and see Josiah Whitney, *The Essential Requisites to Form the Good Ruler's Character* (Hartford, CT: Elisha Babcock, 1788), 11.

54. See Hamburger, *Separation of Church and State*, 76–77; and Hutson, *Church and State in America*, 132ff.

55. Thomas J. Curry, *The First Freedoms: Church and State in America to the Passage of the First Amendment* (New York: Oxford University Press, 1986), 190.

56. To gauge better the differences between the more and less rationalist, consider Philip Greven's, *The Protestant Temperament: Patterns of Child-Rearing, Religious Experience, and the Self in Early America* (New York: New American Library, 1977), 65–66,

description of the centrality of "the doctrine of original sin and of innate depravity" to eighteenth-century American evangelicals and that for them "human nature was corrupt, not in part but totally. Sinful men, said Jonathan Edwards, 'are totally corrupt, in every part, in all their faculties . . . There is nothing but sin, no good at all'."

57. Hugh Alison, *Spiritual Liberty: A Sermon* (Charleston: Hugh Alison, 1769), 14–16, who began by holding that "all men, being by nature the children of wrath and disobedience, lie exposed to the penalty of a broken law . . . But believers in Christ are already freed from the condemning sentence of the law, and delivered from the guilt of sin." This claim of sanctification remains today, in a certain sense, still difficult to control.

58. John Joachim Zubly, *The Law of Liberty . . . Preached at the Opening of the Provincial Congress of Georgia* (Philadelphia: J. Almon, 1775), 27, who continues "but whenever he feels the happy influence of the grace of the gospel, then this 'law of liberty makes him free from the law of sin and death'. Rom viii. 2."

59. Nathan O. Hatch, "In Pursuit of Religious Freedom: Church, State, and People in the New Republic," in *The American Revolution: Its Character and Limits*, ed. Jack P. Greene (New York: New York University Press, 1987), 393.

60. Simeon Howard, "A Sermon Preached . . . May 31, 1780," in *Pulpit of the American Revolution: or, the Political Sermons of the Period of 1776*, ed. John Wingate Thornton (Boston: Gould and Lincoln, 1860), 382–383.

61. See May, *Enlightenment in America*, 231, who discusses the few radical deists in America, like the blind Elihu Palmer, who adhered to the belief that man was perfectible and that "this great truth, the new deists tirelessly explained, had been hidden from mankind by the sinister alliance of priests and kings, whose chief reliance had always been the absurd doctrine of original sin"; and Carl L. Becker, *The Heavenly City of the Eighteenth-Century Philosophers* (New Haven, CT: Yale University Press, 1932), 102–103, who writes that "the essential articles of the religion of the Enlightenment may be stated thus: (1) man is not natively depraved . . . [and] (3) man is capable, guided *solely* [emphasis added] by the light of reason and experience, of perfecting the good life on earth."

62. Israel B. Woodward, *American Liberty and Independence: A Discourse* (Litchfield, CT: T. Collier, 1798), 8; and see also Benjamin Hale, *Liberty and Law: A Lecture* (Geneva, NY: Ira Merrell, 1838), 23, who emphasized how different the irreligiosity of men believed to be infidels like Paine were from the "true founders of our national independence [who] were religious men."

63. See Barry Alan Shain, "Religious Conscience and Original Sin," in *Liberty and American Experience in the Eighteenth Century*, ed. David Womersley (Indianapolis, IN: Liberty Fund, Inc., 2006), 153-208.

64. Phillips Payson, *Massachusetts Election Sermon*, in *American Political Writing*, ed. Charles S. Hyneman and Donald S. Lutz, 524.

65. Jonas Clark, *Massachusetts Election Day Sermon: A Sermon Preached Before His Excellency* (Boston: J. Gill and S. 1781), 37.

66. See Chapter XX, "Of Christian Liberty, and Liberty of Conscience, Westminster Confession Faith (1646)," in *Creeds of the Churches*, ed. John H. Leith, 215, in which it is explained that "they who, upon pretense of Christian liberty, do practice any sin, or cherish any lust, do thereby destroy the end of Christian liberty; which is, that, being delivered out of the hands of our enemies, we might serve the Lord without fear, in holiness and righteousness before him, all the days of our life."

67. Haskins, *Law and Authority in Early Massachusetts*, 17.

68. David Thomas, *The Virginian Baptist; or, A View and Defence of the Christian Religion as It Is Professed by the Baptists of Virginia* (Baltimore: Enoch Story, 1774), 9–10.

69. H. R. Niebuhr, "The Protestant Movement and Democracy in the United States," in *The Shaping of American Religion*, eds. James Ward Smith and A. Leland Jamison (Princeton, NJ: Princeton University Press, 1961), 31, 33, 36.

70. See Romans 6:15–23.

71. Cited by Perry Miller, *The New England Mind: From Colony to Province* (Cambridge, MA: Harvard University Press, 1953), 2: 69; and see Augustine, "On Grace and Free Will," 771, and "On the Predestination of Saints," 779–785, in *Basic Writings of Saint Augustine*, ed. Whitney J. Oates (New York: Random House, 1948).

72. Martin Luther, "The Freedom of a Christian," in *Martin Luther: Selections From His Writings*, ed. John Dillenberger (New York: Doubleday, 1962), 53; and see David B. Davis, "Slavery and Sin: The Cultural Background," in *The Antislavery Vanguard: New Essays on the Abolitionists*, ed. Martin Duberman (Princeton: Princeton University Press, 1965), 26–27, who writes that "perfect liberty, as theologians were long to maintain, lay in absolute conformity to God's will . . . [and] if a man were called to be a slave, he should not try to become free: 'For he that was called in the Lord being a bondservant, is the Lord's freeman: likewise he that was called being free, is Christ's bondservant'" [I Cor. 7:20–22; 12:13].

73. Alison, *Spiritual Liberty: A Sermon*, 19.

74. See Karl Holl, *The Cultural Significance of the Reformation* (1911, reprint ed., New York: Meridian Books, Inc., 1959), 72, who argues that the attempt to join political liberty surreptitiously to the legitimacy of spiritual freedom was a problem that had plagued the leaders of the Reformation from the beginning. He writes that "just like Luther, Calvin absolutely rejected the possibility of deriving consequences for political life from religious freedom."

75. Jonathan Boucher, "On Civil Liberty, Passive Obedience, and Non-resistance," in *A View of the Causes and Consequences of the American Revolution: In Thirteen Discourses, 1763–1775* (reprint ed., New York: Russell and Russell, 1967), 504–505.

76. Judah Champion, *Christian and Civil Liberty and Freedom Considered and Recommended* (Hartford, CT: E. Watson, 1776), 8, 10. There is an implicit assumption here that the freedom of religious conscience and one's achieving a state of spiritual liberty are in some manner connected and that both are jeopardized by a lack of political liberty.

77. See Nathan O. Hatch, *The Sacred Cause of Liberty: Republican Thought and the Millennium in Revolutionary New England* (New Haven: Yale University Press, 1977), 53. Hatch, however, also reminds us that the followers of Edwards and his purer brand of Calvinism, like some Anglicans, rejected this traditional American politicization of sacred concerns. He quotes Edwards' most devoted student, Joseph Bellamy, ibid., 35, who in a letter to his son in 1775 made clear his priorities, "'my desire and prayer to God is, that you my son Jonathan may be saved. And then, whatever happens to America or to you, this year or next, you will be happy forever'." Hatch attributes this citation to Mark Noll who, as a spokesman for contemporary evangelical Christianity, continues to warn his fellow Christians against politicization of what is essentially a soteriological concern.

78. Nathaniel Niles, "Second Discourse," in *Two Discourses on Liberty* (Newburyport, MA: I Thomas and H. W. Tinges, 1774), 56–57.

79. Joseph Emerson, *A Thanksgiving Sermon, Preached at Pepperrell* (Boston: Edes and Gill, 1766), 12.

80. Hatch, *The Sacred Cause of Liberty*, 157; and see Bonomi, *Under the Cope of Heaven*, 216, who holds that "religious doctrine and rhetoric, then, contributed in a fundamental way to the coming of the American Revolution . . . patriotic clergymen told their congregations that failure to oppose British tyranny would be an offense in the sight

of Heaven . . . By turning colonial resistance into a righteous cause . . . ministers did the work of secular radicalism and did it better."

81. Stout, *The New England Soul*, 270–271.

82. See Niebuhr, "The Protestant Movement and Democracy in the United States," 29, who writes that "the process of anti-authoritarian revolt cannot be stopped within the person himself. The individual who has set up his conscience in rivalry to the God-given law of the church discovers that conscience, subject to no sovereign, becomes prey to rebellious desires within him."

83. John Calvin, "Of Christian Liberty," in *The Institutes of the Christian Religion*, trans. John Allen (6th American ed., Philadelphia: Presbyterian Board of Publication, 1813), 2: 63.

84. Jonathan Todd, *Civil Rulers the Ministers of God* (New London: Timothy Green, 1749), 2.

85. See Sheldon S. Wolin, *Politics and Vision: Continuity and Innovation in Western Political Thought* (Boston: Little, Brown and Co, 1960), 338, who writes that "the great transformation was effected whereby 'individual interest' was substituted for individual conscience . . . It was invested with many of the same sanctities and immunities, for, like conscience, it symbolized what was most valued by the individual and what was to be defended against the group or society."

86. Ernst Troeltsch, *Protestantism and Progress: A Historical Study of the Relation of Protestantism to the Modern World* (1912, reprint ed., trans. W. Montgomery, Boston: Beacon Hill Press, 1958), 119–120; and see Holl, *Cultural Significance of the Reformation*, 72, who writes that individual rights "achieved world significance through the Constitution of the United States and the French Revolution."

87. Carl Schmitt, *Verfassungslehre* (München and Leipzig, 1928), 158–159, my translation. And see Roland Bainton, "The Appeal to Reason and the American Constitution," in *The Constitution Reconsidered*, ed. Conyers Read (New York: Columbia University Press, 1938), 127, from which the German original citation was taken, who describes the preceding as "the best commentary on the whole controversy" concerning the origin, secular or religious, of individual universal natural rights. Curiously it was early twentieth-century German scholars who showed a remarkable interest in exploring this late-eighteenth-century American- and French-inspired transformation.

88. Carl Schmitt, *Political Theology: Four Chapters on the Concept of Sovereignty*, trans. George Schwab (reprint ed., Cambridge, MA: MIT Press, 1985), 36.

89. See Miller, *New England Mind: From Colony to Province*, 171, who argues that this had been a gradual process in which "Protestantism was imperceptibly carried over into the new order . . . by translating Christian liberty into those liberties guaranteed by statute."

90. Abraham Williams, *A Sermon Preach'd at Boston, Before the Great and General Court* (Boston: S. Kneeland, 1762), 10.

91. See Georg Jellinek, *The Declaration of the Rights of Man and of Citizens: A Contribution to Modern Constitutional History*, trans. Max Farrand (1901, reprint ed., Westport, CT: Hyperion Press, Inc., 1979), 80, who writes that "with the conviction that there existed a right of conscience independent of the State was found the starting-point for the determination of the inalienable rights of the individual."

92. See Troeltsch, *Protestantism and Progress*, 66–67, who reminds us that in classic Protestant thought, "the modern problem of the relation of Church and State simply did not as yet exist . . . the applicability of religious standards to the whole body, the exclusion or, at least, the disenfranchisement of unbelievers and heretics, the principle of intolerance and infallibility, are for it also self-evident necessities."

93. Perry Miller, "Jonathan Edwards and the Great Awakening," in *Errand into the Wilderness* (Cambridge: Harvard University Press, 1956), 160–161.

94. Urian Oakes, *New-England Pleaded With* (Cambridge, 1673), 53, and 54–55, he continued, "I look upon an unbounded Toleration as the first born of all *Abominations* . . . it belongs to the *Magistrate* to judge what is *tolerable in his Dominions* in this respect. And the Eye of the *Civil Magistrate* is to be to the securing of the way of God that is duly established."

95. See Christine Leigh Heyrman, *Commerce and Culture: The Maritime Communities of Colonial Massachusetts, 1690–1750* (New York: W.W. Norton, 1984), 118; Hutson, *Church and State in America*, 28–39; and Isaac, *The Transformation of Virginia*, 151–152, who recounts how the British Board of Trade had advised the Virginian government that "'a free Exercise of Religion is so valuable a branch of true liberty, and so essential to the enrichening and improving of a Trading Nation, it should ever be held sacred in His Majesty's Colonies'"; and Rossiter, *Seedtime*, 78, who notes that the Board had "disallowed two Maryland anti-Catholic laws as tending 'to depopulate that profitable colony'."

96. Wesley Frank Craven, *The Legend of the Founding Fathers* (Ithaca, NY: Cornell University Press, 1956), 25.

97. See Thomas J. Curry, *The First Freedoms: Church and State in America to the Passage of the First Amendment* (New York: Oxford University Press, 1986), 97, who writes that this "pamphlet was the only eighteenth-century pamphlet—until the eve of the American Revolution—that addressed itself specifically to the question of liberty of conscience"; and John Dunn, *The Political Thought of John Locke* (Cambridge: Cambridge University Press, 1982), 264, who writes that "freedom of thought was required not because of any exuberant taste for the Promethean delights of unrestrained speculation, a matter at best of licence rather than liberty, but because it was a necessary condition for the pursuit of religious truth. . . . The human mind was to be made free in order that men might grasp more clearly their ineluctable confinement in the harness in which, ever since the delinquencies of their first ancestor, God had set human beings in the world."

98. Elisha Williams, *Essential Rights and Liberty of Protestants . . . Being a Letter from a Gentleman in the Massachusetts-Bay to his Friends in Connecticut* (Boston: Kneeland & Green, 1744), 8; and see John Locke, "A Letter Concerning Toleration," in *Treatise on Civil Government and A Letter Concerning Toleration* (1937, reprint ed., New York: Irvington Publishers, Inc., 1979), 173, who earlier had written that "no man can so far abandon the care of his own salvation as blindly to leave to the choice of any other, whether prince or subject, to prescribe to him what faith or worship he shall embrace." Certainly, Americans were Lockean, then, in their following his lead in legitimating individual rights by exploiting Protestant categories of thought and, too, in defending the majoritarian right of legislative self-government.

99. Lawrence H. Leder, *Liberty and Authority: Early American Political Ideology, 1689–1763* (Chicago: Quadrangle Books, 1968), 68–69. He is here citing from the "The Right of Private Judgment," in the *Pennsylvania Journal*, January 5, 1748.

100. Ezra Stiles, *A Discourse on the Christian Union* (Boston: Edes and Gill, 1761), 28.

101. See William Smith, Jr., *The Occasional Reverberator*, 5 October 1753 (the last of four issues).

102. See Carl L. Becker, *The Declaration of Independence: A Study in the History of Political Ideas* (1922, reprint ed., New York: Random House, 1958), 78, who holds that the mixture of "God, Nature, and Reason" had "crept into the mind of the average man" via the "later Massachusetts election sermons, from 1768 to 1773."

103. At the more articulate level, the highly popular Dr. Price had argued that the three principles on which English liberty was based were, "first, the right to liberty of conscience in religious matters. Secondly, the right to resist power when abused.—And Thirdly, the right to choose our own governors, to cashier them for misconduct, and to frame a government for ourselves." Taken from William Morgan, *Memoirs of the Life of the Rev. Richard Price* (London: R. Hunter, 1815), 165–166.

104. Reported by Oscar and Mary Handlin, ed., *The Popular Sources of Political Authority: Documents on the Massachusetts Constitution of 1780* (Cambridge, MA: Harvard University Press, 1966), 410–411, 423. Compare this to "The Bill Of Rights" of the New Hampshire Constitution of 1784 that held that "among the natural rights, some are in their very nature unalienable, because no equivalent can be given or received for them. Of this kind are the RIGHTS OF CONSCIENCE," in Benjamin Perley Poore, ed., *The Federal and State Constitutions, Colonial Charters, and Other Organic Laws of the United States* (2nd ed., Washington, DC, 1878, reprint ed., New York: Burt Franklin Publishing, 1972), 2: 1280–1281. However, New Hampshire then continues, without any sense of tension, in Article VI to sustain (for the next 30 years) its taxation "for the support and maintenance of public protestant teachers of piety, religion and morality."

105. Handlin, ibid., 436, and see articles I–II of the proposed constitution, and the highly controversial third article, 442–443.

106. Ibid., 683, but see 32, where Handlin writes that, for most, "general professions of belief in religious liberty therefore were not incompatible with demands for guarantees of a Protestant Christian state."

107. See the Federal Farmer, "Letter VI," in *The Anti-Federalist: Writings by the Opponents of the Constitution*, selected by Murray Dry from *The Complete Anti-Federalist*, ed. Herbert J. Storing (Chicago: University of Chicago Press, 1985), 70, who writes that "of rights, some are natural and unalienable, of which even the people cannot deprive individuals: Some are constitutional or fundamental; these cannot be altered or abolished by the ordinary laws; but the people, by express acts, may alter or abolish them—These, such as the trial by jury, the benefits of the writ of habeas corpus, etc. . . . and some are common or mere legal rights, that is, such as individuals claim under laws which the ordinary legislature may alter or abolish at pleasure."

108. See Barry Alan Shain, "Rights Natural and Civil in the Declaration of Independence," in *The Nature of Rights at the American Founding and Beyond*, ed. Barry Alan Shain, 116–162.

109. In 1795, in speech if not always in practice, religious liberty had come to mean, according to John Mellen, *The Great and Happy Doctrine of Liberty* (Boston: Samuel Hall, 1795), 17, "a freedom and exemption from human impositions, and legal restraints, in matters of religion and conscience."

110. See Philip A. Hamburger, "A Constitutional Right of Religious Exemption: An Historical Perspective," *George Washington Law Review* 60 (April 1992); and Hutson, *Church and State in America*, 126–137.

111. Thomas Jefferson, "Letter to Nehemiah Dodge and Others," in *The Portable Thomas Jefferson*, ed. Merrill Peterson (New York: Penguin Books, 1975), 303.

112. See James Madison, "James Madison's Autobiography," ed. Douglass Adair, in *William and Mary Quarterly* 2 (April 1945): 198–199, who writes of the Baptists that "notwithstanding the enthusiasm which contributed to render them obnoxious to sober opinion . . . he [Madison] spared no exertion to save them from imprisonment . . . This interposition tho' a mere duty prescribed by his conscience, obtained for him a lasting place in the favour of that particular sect."

113. Thomas E. Buckley, "Evangelicals Triumphant: The Baptists' Assault on the Virginia Glebes, 1786–1801," *William and Mary Quarterly* 45 (January 1988): 68–69, emphasis added.

114. See Gregory H. Nobles, *Divisions Throughout the Whole: Politics and Society in Hampshire County, Massachusetts, 1740–1775* (New York: Cambridge University Press, 1983), 84, 87.

115. See Hamburger, *Separation of Church and State*, 94–95; and Hutson, *Church and State in America*, 132ff.

116. Moses Hemmenway, *Massachusetts Election Sermon* (Boston: Benjamin Edes and Sons, 1784), 33–34.

117. Cyprian Strong, *The Kingdom is the Lord's* (Hartford: Hudson and Goodwin, 1799), 16–17, and see [John Mitchell Mason], *The Voice of Warning to Christians, on the Ensuing Election of a President* (New York: G. F. Hopkins, 1800), 18–19, who ties the cause of infidelity to Jefferson and asks if "no injury" will result from his election and the consequent undoing of "all the chords which bind you to the God of heaven."

BIBLIOGRAPHY

Books

Adams, John. *The Works of John Adams, Second President of the United States: With A Life of the Author, Notes and Illustrations*, ed. Charles Francis Adams, 10 vols. Boston: Little, Brown, and Company, 1865.

Adams, John and Thomas Jefferson. *The Adams-Jefferson Letters*, ed. Lester J. Cappon. 1959, reprint ed. Chapel Hill: University of North Carolina Press, 1987.

Adams, John and Benjamin Rush. *The Spur of Fame: Dialogues of John Adams and Benjamin Rush, 1805–1813*, ed. John A. Schutz and Douglass Adair. San Marino, CA: Huntington Library Publications, 1966.

Ahlstrom, Sydney E. *A Religious History of the American People*. New Haven, CT: Yale University Press, 1972.

Alison, Hugh. *Spiritual Liberty: A Sermon*. Charleston, SC: Hugh Alison, 1769.

Augustine, Saint. *Basic Writings of Saint Augustine*, ed. Whitney J. Oates. New York: Random House, 1948.

Becker, Carl L. *The Heavenly City of the Eighteenth-Century Philosophers*. New Haven, CT: Yale University Press, 1932.

———. *The Declaration of Independence: A Study in the History of Political Ideas*. 1922. Reprint, New York: Random House, 1958.

Bonomi, Patricia U. *Under the Cope of Heaven: Religion, Society and Politics in Colonial America*. New York: Oxford University Press, 1986.

Bridenbaugh, Carl. *Mitre and Sceptre: Transatlantic Faiths, Ideas, Personalities, and Politics, 1689–1775*. New York: Oxford University Press, 1962.

Calvin, John. *The Institutes of the Christian Religion*. Trans. John Allen. 2 vols. 6th American ed. Philadelphia: Presbyterian Board of Publication, 1813.

Champion, Judah. *Christian and Civil Liberty and Freedom Considered and Recommended*. Hartford, CT: E. Watson, 1776.

Clark, Jonas. *Massachusetts Election Day Sermon: A Sermon Preached Before His Excellency*. Boston: J. Gill and S. Edes, 1781.

Craven, Wesley Frank. *The Legend of the Founding Fathers*. Ithaca, NY: Cornell University Press, 1956.

Curry, Thomas J. *The First Freedoms: Church and State in America to the Passage of the First Amendment*. New York: Oxford University Press, 1986.

Davis, Derek H. *Religion and the Continental Congress, 1774–1789: Contributions to Original Intent*. New York: Oxford University Press, 2000.

Dunn, John. *The Political Thought of John Locke*. Cambridge, MA: Cambridge University Press, 1982.

Emerson, Joseph. *A Thanksgiving Sermon, Preached at Pepperrell*. Boston: Edes and Gill, 1766.

Fischer, David Hackett. *Albion's Seed: Four British Folkways in America*. New York: Oxford University Press, 1989.

Foner, Eric. *Tom Paine and Revolutionary America*. New York: Oxford University Press, 1976.

Ford, Worthington Chauncey, ed. *Journals of the Continental Congress, 1774–1789*. Washington, D.C.: Government Printing Office, 1904.

Fosdick, Dorothy. *What is Liberty?: A Study in Political Theory*. New York: Harper and Brothers Publishers, 1939.

Gaustad, Edwin S. *Proclaim Liberty Throughout All the Land: A History of Church and State in America*. New York: Oxford University Press, 2003.

Greven, Philip. *The Protestant Temperament: Patterns of Child-Rearing, Religious Experience, and the Self in Early America*. New York: New American Library, 1977.

Hale, Benjamin. *Liberty and Law: A Lecture*. Geneva, NY: Ira Merrell, 1838.

Hamburger, Philip A. *Separation of Church and State*. Cambridge, MA: Harvard University Press, 2002.

Hampson, Norman. *The Enlightenment: An Evaluation of its Assumptions, Attitudes, and Values*. 1968. Reprint, New York: Penguin Books, 1986.

Handlin, Oscar and Mary, ed. *The Popular Sources of Political Authority: Documents on the Massachusetts Constitution of 1780*. Cambridge: Harvard University Press, 1966.

Haskins, George Lee. *Law and Authority in Early Massachusetts: A Study in Tradition and Design*. Lanham, MD: University Press of America, 1960.

Hatch, Nathan O. *The Sacred Cause of Liberty: Republican Thought and the Millennium in Revolutionary New England*. New Haven, CT: Yale University Press, 1977.

Hayek, F. A. *The Constitution of Liberty*. Chicago: The University of Chicago Press, 2007.

Hemmenway, Moses. *Massachusetts Election Sermon*. Boston: Benjamin Edes and Sons, 1784.

Heyrman, Christine Leigh. *Commerce and Culture: The Maritime Communities of Colonial Massachusetts, 1690–1750*. New York: W.W. Norton, 1984.

Holl, Karl. *The Cultural Significance of the Reformation*. 1911. Reprint, New York: Meridian Books, Inc., 1959.

Hutson, James H. *Religion and the Founding of the American Republic*. Washington, DC: Library of Congress, 1998.

——— *Church and State in America: The First Two Centuries*. Cambridge: Cambridge University Press, 2007.

Isaac, Rhys. *The Transformation of Virginia, 1740–1790*. Chapel Hill: University of North Carolina Press, 1982.

Jefferson, Thomas. *The Political Writings of Thomas Jefferson: Representative Selections*, ed. Edward Dumbauld. New York: The Liberal Arts Press, 1955.

————. *The Portable Thomas Jefferson*, ed. Merrill Peterson. New York: Penguin Books, 1975.

Jellinek, Georg. *The Declaration of the Rights of Man and of Citizens: A Contribution to Modern Constitutional History*. Trans. Max Farrand. 1901. Reprint, Westport, CT: Hyperion Press, Inc., 1979.

Lambert, Frank. *The Founding Fathers and the Place of Religion in America*. Princeton, NJ: Princeton University Press, 2003.

Leder, Lawrence H. *Liberty and Authority: Early American Political Ideology, 1689–1763*. Chicago: Quadrangle Books, 1968.

Leith, John H., ed. *Creeds of the Churches*. 3rd ed. Louisville, KY: John Knox Press, 1982.

Locke, John. *Treatise of Civil Government and A Letter Concerning Toleration*. 1937. Reprint, New York: Irvington Publishers, Inc., 1979.

Luther, Martin. *Martin Luther: Selections From His Writings*, ed. John Dillenberger. New York: Doubleday, 1962.

McClellan, James. *Joseph Story and the American Constitution: A Study in Political and Legal Thought*. Norman, OK: University of Oklahoma Press, 1990.

Madison, James. *James Madison: Writings: Writings 1772–1836*, ed. Jack N. Rakove. New York: Library of America, 1999.

[Mason, John Mitchell]. *The Voice of Warning to Christians, on the Ensuing Election of a President*. New York: G.F. Hopkins, 1800.

May, Henry F. *The Enlightenment in America*. New York: Oxford University Press, 1978.

Mellen, John. *The Great and Happy Doctrine of Liberty*. Boston: Samuel Hall, 1795.

Miller, Perry. *The New England Mind*. Vol.2, *From Colony to Province*. Cambridge, MA: Harvard University Press, 1953.

————. *Errand into the Wilderness*. Cambridge: Harvard University Press, 1956.

Morgan, William. *Memoirs of the Life of the Rev. Richard Price*. London: R. Hunter, 1815.

Niles, Nathaniel. *Two Discourses on Liberty*. Newburyport, MA: I. Thomas and H.W. Tinges, 1774.

Nobles, Gregory H. *Divisions Throughout the Whole: Politics and Society in Hampshire County, Massachusetts, 1740–1775*. New York: Cambridge University Press, 1983.

Oakes, Urian. *New-England Pleaded With*. Cambridge [Massachusetts-Bay], 1673.

Poore, Benjamin Perley, ed. *The Federal and State Constitutions, Colonial Charters, and Other Organic Laws of the United States*. 2nd ed. 2 vols. 1878. Reprint, New York: Burt Franklin Publishing, 1972.

Powers, Peter. *Jesus Christ the True King and Head of the Government*. Newbury-Port, MA: John Mycall, 1778.

Rossiter, Clinton. *Seedtime of the Republic: The Origin of the American Tradition of Political Liberty*. New York: Harcourt, Brace, and World, 1953.

Schmitt, Carl. *Political Theology: Four Chapters on the Concept of Sovereignty*, trans. George Schwab. Reprint, Cambridge, MA: MIT Press, 1985.

Shain, Barry Alan, ed. *The Nature of Rights at the American Founding and Beyond*. Charlottesville: University of Virginia Press, 2007.

Smith, William, Jr. *The Occasional Reverberator*, 5 October 1753.

Stiles, Ezra. *A Discourse on the Christian Union*. Boston: Edes and Gill, 1761.

Storing, Herbert J., ed. *The Anti-Federalist: Writings by the Opponents of the Constitution*, selected by Murray Dry from *The Complete Anti-Federalist*. Chicago: University of Chicago Press, 1985.

Story, Joseph. *Commentaries on the Constitution of the United States With a Preliminary Review of the Constitutional History of the Colonies and States Before the Adoption of the Constitution*. Boston: Hilliard, Gray and Company, 1833.

Stout, Harry S. *The New England Soul: Preaching and Religious Culture in Colonial New England*. New York: Oxford University Press, 1986.

Strong, Cyprian. *The Kingdom is the Lord's*. Hartford, CT: Hudson and Goodwin, 1799.

Thomas, David. *The Virginian Baptist; or, A View and Defence of the Christian Religion as It Is Professed by the Baptists of Virginia*. Baltimore: Enoch Story, 1774.

Todd, Jonathan. *Civil Rulers the Ministers of God*. New London, CT: Timothy Green, 1749.

Troeltsch, Ernst. *Protestantism and Progress: A Historical Study of the Relation of Protestantism to the Modern World*. 1912. Reprint, trans. W. Montgomery, Boston: Beacon Hill Press, 1958.

Waldron, Jeremy. *God, Locke, and Equality: Christian Foundations in Locke's Political Thought*. Cambridge, MA: Cambridge University Press, 2002.

Washington, George. *George Washington: A Collection*, ed. W. B. Allen. Indianapolis: Liberty Fund, Inc., 1988.

Whitney, Josiah. *The Essential Requisites to Form the Good Ruler's Character*. Hartford, CT: Elisha Babcock, 1788.

Williams, Abraham. *A Sermon Preach'd at Boston, Before the Great and General Court*. Boston: S. Kneeland, 1762.

Williams, Elisha. *Essential Rights and Liberty of Protestants . . . Being a Letter from a Gentleman in the Massachusetts-Bay to his Friends in Connecticut*. Boston: Kneeland & Green, 1744.

Witte, John, Jr. *Religion and the American Constitutional Experiment: Essential Rights and Liberties*. Boulder: Westview Press, 2000.

Wolin, Sheldon S. *Politics and Vision: Continuity and Innovation in Western Political Thought*. Boston: Little, Brown and Co., 1960.

Wood, Gordon S. *The Creation of the American Republic, 1776–1787*. Chapel Hill, NC: University of North Carolina Press, 1969.

Woodward, Israel B. *American Liberty and Independence: A Discourse*. Litchfield, CT: T. Collier, 1798.

Zubly, John Joachim. *The Law of Liberty . . . Preached at the Opening of the Provincial Congress of Georgia*. Philadelphia: J. Almon, 1775.

Articles/Chapters

Atwater, Jeremiah. "Vermont Election Sermon," in *American Political Writing During the Founding Era, 1760–1805*, ed. Charles S. Hyneman and Donald S. Lutz, 1170–1188. Indianapolis: Liberty Fund, Inc., 1983.

Bainton, Roland. "The Appeal to Reason and the American Constitution," in *The Constitution Reconsidered*, ed. Conyers Read. New York: Columbia University Press, 1938.

Boucher, Jonathan. "On Civil Liberty, Passive Obedience, and Non-resistance," in *A View of the Causes and Consequences of the American Revolution: In Thirteen Discourses, 1763–1775*, 495–560. 1797. Reprint, New York: Russell and Russell, 1967.

Buckley, Thomas E. "Evangelicals Triumphant: The Baptists' Assault on the Virginia Glebes, 1786–1801." *William and Mary Quarterly* 45 (January 1988): 33.

Davis, David B. "Slavery and Sin: The Cultural Background," in *The Antislavery Vanguard: New Essays on the Abolitionists*, ed. Martin Duberman. Princeton, NJ: Princeton University Press, 1965.

Dreisbach, Daniel L. "Another Look at Jefferson's Wall of Separation: A Jurisdictional Interpretation of the 'Wall' Metaphor," *Witherspoon Fellowship Lectures*, Family Research Council, August 2000.

———. "Founders Famous and Forgotten." *Intercollegiate Review* 42 (Fall 2007): 3.

[Ellsworth, Oliver]. "The Letters of a Landholder," in *Essays on the Constitution of the United States: Published During Its Discussion by the People, 1787–1788*, ed. Paul Leicester Ford. 1892. Reprint, New York: Burt Franklin, 1971.

Greenstone, J. David. "Political Culture and American Political Development: Liberty, Union, and the Liberal Bipolarity," in *Studies in American Political Development*, ed. Steven Skowrownek. New Haven, CT: Yale University Press, 1987.

Hamburger, Philip A. "A Constitutional Right of Religious Exemption: An Historical Perspective." *George Washington Law Review* 60 (April 1992): 915.

Hardwick, Kevin R. "Religion and Morality in the Political Thought of Edmund Randolph," Religion and the Founders, George Fox University, 2 March 2007, 1.

Hatch, Nathan O. "In Pursuit of Religious Freedom: Church, State, and People in the New Republic," in *The American Revolution: Its Character and Limits*, ed. Jack P. Greene. New York: New York University Press, 1987.

Howard, Simeon. "A Sermon Preached . . . May 31, 1780," in *Pulpit of the American Revolution: or, the Political Sermons of the Period of 1776*, ed. John Wingate Thornton. Boston: Gould and Lincoln, 1860.

Katz, Stanley N. "The Legal and Religious Context of Natural Rights Theory: A Comment," in *Party and Political Opposition in Revolutionary America*, ed. Patricia U. Bonomi. Tarrytown, NY: Sleepy Hollow Press, 1980.

Ladd, E.C. "205 and Going Strong." *Public Opinion* 4 (June–July 1981): 7.

Madison, James. "James Madison's Autobiography," ed. Douglass Adair. *William and Mary Quarterly* 2 (April 1945): 191.

Moore, Leroy. "Religious Liberty: Roger Williams and the Revolutionary Era." *Church History* 34 (March 1965): 57.

Morgan, Edmund S. "The American Revolution Considered as an Intellectual Movement," in *Essays on the American Revolution*, ed. David L. Jacobson. New York: Holt, Rinehart and Winston, Inc., 1970.

Munoz, Vincent Phillip. "James Madison's Principles of Religious Liberty." *American Political Science Review* 97 (February 2003): 17.

Niebuhr, H. R. "The Protestant Movement and Democracy in the United States," in *The Shaping of American Religion*, ed. James Ward Smith and A. Leland Jamison. Princeton: Princeton University Press, 1961.

Payson, Phillips. "Massachusetts Election Sermon," in *American Political Writing During the Founding Era, 1760–1805*, ed. Charles S. Hyneman and Donald S. Lutz. Indianapolis: Liberty Fund, Inc., 1983.

Pitkin, Hanna Fenichel. "Are Freedom and Liberty Twins?" Paper presented at the Yale Legal Theory Workshop. Published in *Political Theory* 16 (November 1988): 523.

Roeber, A. Gregg. "The Limited Horizons of Whig Religious Rights," in *The Nature of Rights at the American Founding and Beyond*, ed. Barry Alan Shain. Charlottesville, VA: University of Virginia Press, 2007.

Rush, Benjamin. "Thoughts Upon the Mode of Education," in *American Political Writing During the Founding Era, 1760–1805*, ed. Charles S. Hyneman and Donald S. Lutz. Indianapolis: Liberty Fund, Inc., 1983.

Schaff, Philip. "Church and State in the United States," in *Papers of the American Historical Association*. New York: Knickerbocker Press, 1890.

Shain, Barry Alan. "Liberty and License: The American Founding and the Western Conception of Freedom," in *Vital Remnants: America's Founding and the Western Tradition*, ed. Gary L. Gregg II. Wilmington, DE: Intercollegiate Studies Institute Books, 1999.

————. "Religious Conscience and Original Sin," in *Liberty and American Experience in the Eighteenth Century*, ed. David Womersley. Indianapolis: Liberty Fund, Inc., 2006.

Tushnet, Mark. "The Origins of the Establishment Clause." *Georgetown Law Journal 75* (April 1987): 1509.

———— "Should Historians Accept the Supreme Court's Invitation?" *Organization of American Historians Newsletter* (November 1987): 12.

Westermann, William Linn. "Between Slavery and Freedom." *American Historical Review* 50 (January 1945): 213.

Winthrop, John. "Speech to the General Court," in *The Puritans: A Sourcebook of Their Writings*, eds. Perry Miller and Thomas H. Johnson. New York: Harper and Row, 1963.

CHAPTER 3

CHURCH AND STATE IN NINETEENTH-CENTURY AMERICA

STEVEN K. GREEN

THE nineteenth century is the "forgotten century" for traditional reviews of American church–state relations. Until recently, most legal case books and historical studies of church and state in America have given only cursory coverage to the period between ratification of the Bill of Rights and the beginnings of modern Supreme Court jurisprudence in the 1940s. Histories have commonly focused on the Puritan theocratic experiment in New England, jumped to the 1780s struggle for religious freedom in Virginia and the drafting of the First Amendment, and then fast-forwarded to the early incorporation cases of the twentieth century: *Cantwell v. Connecticut* (1940) and *Everson v. Board of Education* (1947). Along the way, mention is sometimes made of a handful of late-1800s Supreme Court rulings on church property disputes and the regulation of Mormon polygamy, as if these decisions represent the sum total of church–state development for more than a century.[1]

This state of affairs is surprising, and unfortunate, given the rich legacy of the period. Between 1791 and 1900, America underwent tremendous ideological, cultural, and demographic change. Many factors and events of the period influenced church–state relations and popular attitudes toward the same, helping flesh out those nascent principles espoused by the early founders. The legal principles and popular attitudes that developed in the nineteenth century laid the foundation for the church–state holdings of the twentieth century.[2] Rather than being a forgotten period in church–state development, the nineteenth century is indispensable to understanding modern approaches to this issue.

Between the 1790s and 1900, several events—some anticipated but most not—affected and modified the church–state template that the founders had installed in the First Amendment and its counterparts in the state constitutions. First, most of the founders had likely envisioned that the principles of religious free exercise and nonestablishment would work their magic within a nation overwhelmingly populated by Protestants, whose institutions would continue to reflect Protestant values. Although the religious diversity in the new republic was unmatched by any other nation, that pluralism was generally limited to a complement of Protestant sects and denominations. In 1800, America had approximately 50,000 Catholics and 2,000 Jews out of a total population of less than 5 million. Before the new century would draw to a close, the nation would experience unparalleled religious diversification, brought about by home-grown religious experimentation and foreign immigration, the latter adding millions of Catholics, Jews, Orthodox-rite Christians, and Buddhists, among others, to the American religious milieu.[3] Expanding religious pluralism, more than any other factor, would cause nineteenth-century Americans to reevaluate their understandings of religious equality, liberty, and separation, and affect both the law and public policy in dramatic ways.

A second change to church–state attitudes took place in the early years of the nineteenth century. Although Americans were overwhelmingly Protestant in 1800, religious piety and church attendance were at their lowest levels in the 200-year history of the settlements. Deism had flourished among the founding elite as well as among artisans and skilled workers in many east coast cities until it was discredited by the anti-clericalism of the French Revolution.[4] Also during the closing decades of the eighteenth century the momentum supporting legal disestablishment in the states had appeared unstoppable; whereas in 1785 only 6 (of 14) states had prohibited religious establishments, within 15 years that number had grown to 11 states. States also were following the lead of the national constitution by abolishing or liberalizing religious disabilities for public office-holding and participation in civic affairs.[5] Thomas Jefferson's model of a "wall of separation between church and state," a phrase he advanced in an 1802 letter to a group of Connecticut Baptists,[6] appeared to be an achievable reality.

This early secularizing trend, if it can be characterized as such, was brought to an abrupt halt in the initial decades of the century. As the nation was installing its "atheist President" in Thomas Jefferson, it was undergoing an upsurge in religious piety and enthusiasm—frequently called the "Second Great Awakening"—that would quadruple church membership and lead to the establishment and growth of many new denominations, mostly evangelical. Contemporaries and later scholars have referred to the century as the "Protestant Empire," one in which evangelical Protestant practices and attitudes came to dominate the culture and civic institutions. A leading church historian of the era, Robert Baird, estimated that by 1844, 2½ million Americans were in active communion with an evangelical church, with another 12 million under the influence of an evangelical body, out of a total national population of 17½ million. Importantly, evangelicals were united in basic doctrine and could be viewed "as branches of one great body, even (as) the entire visible church of Christ in this land," wrote Baird, which he saw as a sign of God's "election" of America's role in leading the world into the coming millennium.[7] Although modern-day scholars believe such estimates were highly inflated—regular church attendance at its height rarely exceeded 30% of the nation's population—the actual numbers were less important than the perception. The evangelical perspective quickly became a dominant force in the antebellum culture and helped define peoples' conceptions of themselves, their communities, and their government.[8] In his assessment of the period, religious historian Robert Handy has written that "[i]n many ways, the middle third of the nineteenth century was more of a 'Protestant Age' than was the colonial period with its established churches."[9]

One of the interesting ironies of the period is that this informal Protestant establishment was emerging at the same time the last three New England states were undergoing institutional disestablishment (Massachusetts being the last in 1833). Fueled by the religious revivals and the rise of religious reform societies that pushed a variety of moral causes ranging from Biblical literacy, Sabbath attendance, and temperance to the abolition of slavery and women's suffrage, an evangelical ethos enveloped the nation, one that through persuasion was more effective in regulating social customs and behavior than New Haven's infamous "Blue laws" had ever been. For evangelicals, institutional disestablishment did not mean that religion could no longer mold the culture or influence government actions that promoted morality and virtue. Lyman Beecher, leader of the evangelical reform movement, maintained that voluntary societies would supplement government efforts to combat vice and disorder by serving as "a sort of moral militia, prepared to act upon every emergency, and repel every encroachment upon the liberties and morals of the State. . . . [I]n a free government, moral suasion and coercion must be united." Following on the lead of Beecher and others, evangelicals formed a number of voluntary societies during the antebellum period, including the American Bible Society (1816), the American Sunday School Union (1824), the American Tract Society (1825), the American Temperance Society (1826), and the General Union for the Promotion of the Christian Sabbath (1828), all with the goal of perfecting and preserving the nation's status as a Christian nation while encouraging increased enforcement of laws promoting morality and public virtue.[10]

Evangelicals did not believe their effort to mold America into a Christian nation were at tension with disestablishment; on the contrary, "it was widely asserted that now that civilization in America had been freed of the corruptions of established ecclesiasticism, it would become more Christian than it had ever been. Churches had been disestablished and separated from the state, but the idea of a Christian society had not disappeared."[11] The "voluntary" system of church membership under disestablishment would reinforce religious freedom while it allowed religion to flourish. Evangelical enthusiasm would wax and wane throughout the century depending on location and event, but at no time did evangelical Protestantism lose its grip on culture and its civil establishments.

Protestantism's efforts to make America into a Christian nation reflected not only an invigorated theological vision, but also a reaction to the disaggregated forces of change during the century. The same "antebellum spiritual hothouse" that gave rise to evangelicalism, to use historian Jon Butler's rich phrase, incubated competing religious movements in Shakerism, Universalism, Mormonism, Adventism, Transcendentalism, and utopian societies.[12] Also, beginning in the 1830s and accelerating in subsequent decades, America experienced an onslaught of Catholic immigration, initially from Ireland and later from Germany and Italy. Finally, later in the century, Protestant America would face challenges from Darwinism, religious skepticism, and Biblical criticism, not to mention the disquieting social pressures produced by urbanization, industrialization, and labor unionization. Protestant leaders reacted to these challenges to their hegemony by doubling their efforts at moral suasion and seeking enforcement of Sabbath and blasphemy laws while fiercely holding onto the Protestant character of the public schools. One group even sought to have Congress adopt an acknowledgment of God and Jesus in the Constitution, as if that would stall the demographic forces. That the Protestant majority felt continually under siege indicates that church–state relations were dynamic throughout the century.[13]

An early episode that spurred debate over the proper relation between church and state involved a controversy over mail delivery on Sundays. Even though the majority of states had laws limiting "worldly behavior" on Sundays as a way of promoting religious piety and quiet respect for churchgoers, Sabbath laws were poorly enforced. Evangelical leaders such as Lyman Beecher viewed the "profanation of the sabbath" as evidence of the nation's spiritual waywardness and an impediment to achieving a culture in which Christianity could thrive. In 1810, however, U.S. Postmaster General Gideon Granger secured passage of a law requiring all postmasters to open their offices to the public on every day that mail arrived, Sundays included. Beecher and other evangelical leaders mounted a petition drive to Congress to have the law repealed, but it lost steam during the ensuing war with Great Britain. The matter continued to fester, and in 1828 Beecher organized the General Union for the Promotion of the Christian Sabbath (GUPCS). The GUPCS undertook a massive petition drive—likely the first example of a religious interest group organizing a direct mail, grassroots campaign. The drive took on greater consequence than simply the repeal of the law; it became a referendum on the religious character of the nation. As one petition asked rhetorically, if America was truly "a Christian nation, then our Government is a Christian Government, a Government formed and established by Christians, and therefore bound by the word of God, [and] not at liberty to contravene his laws."[14]

A sizeable number of Americans objected to the repeal drive and what they viewed as an attempt by evangelicals to enforce a religious custom through the law. One group of memorialists from New York responded that the repeal would favor a "religious duty," and was "contrary to the letter and spirit of the constitution, which guarantees freedom of opinions to every citizen." Viewing the repeal in constitutional terms, these memorialists argued it was "fraught with the most pernicious and dangerous consequences to our civil and religious liberties, and calculated to prepare the way for the final establishment of a national religion."[15]

Their arguments caught the attention of Congress, which in two reports rejected efforts to change the law to prohibit Sunday mail delivery. Both reports were written by Richard M. Johnson, a future vice president under Martin Van Buren. "Our Constitution recognizes in every person the right to choose his own religion, and to enjoy it freely without molestation," Johnson wrote. Thus, as he reiterated in the second report, "The framers of the constitution recognized the eternal principle that man's relation with his God is above human legislation, and his rights of conscience inalienable."[16] Because "a variety of sentiment exists . . . on the subject of the Sabbath day," Johnson insisted, Congress could not "determine for any whether they shall esteem one day above another."[17] Johnson argued the repeal of the delivery law would be the first step toward a religious establishment.

> If a solemn act of legislation shall, in one point, define the law of God, or point out to the citizen one religious duty, it may, with equal propriety, proceed to define every part of divine revelation, and enforce every religious obligation, even to the forms and ceremonies of worship, the endowment of the church, and the support of the clergy.[18]

Sunday mail delivery would remain a thorn in the side of evangelicals throughout the century; not until 1912 did Congress finally repeal the law at the request of a coalition of ministers and postal clerks.[19] The Sunday mail controversy demonstrates the competing views about the relationship between religion and government in antebellum society. The evangelical vision of a Christian nation, practically and symbolically, was on the rise, but it still encountered resistance by followers of the Jeffersonian model.

An interesting paradox is that as the culture was becoming more religious, a transformation was taking place in one of its central institutions—the law—one that was moving in the opposite direction. In the early part of the century, it was not uncommon for judges and lawyers to express the view that the law was based on religious principles. This belief was based in part on vague notions of higher law foundations, but also on more particular understandings that Christianity formed part of the common law. British jurists such as William Blackstone had written how the common law—which had been transferred to the colonies and adopted by the states—integrated Christian doctrine and principles, meaning that civil judges were obligated to interpret the law consistent with those doctrines and principles. Many early American jurists viewed the Christian underpinnings of the law only in abstract terms, but others understood it as an obligation to enforce Christian customs and behavioral norms through the civil law. Although the number of cases was never that great, during the first third of the century it was not uncommon for judges to uphold convictions for blasphemy or Sabbath violations or to issue rulings in domestic and probate cases by citing religious rationales.[20] In upholding a blasphemy conviction of a defendant for stating "the Holy Scriptures were a mere fable," the Pennsylvania Supreme Court in 1824 asserted that the charge was supported entirely by the maxim that Christianity was "part of the common law of Pennsylvania."

It is impossible to administer the laws, without taking the religion which the
defendant in error has scoffed at, that scripture which he has reviled, as their
basis; to lay aside these is, at least, to weaken the confidence in human veracity, so
essential to the purposes of society.[21]

By mid-century a noticeable shift was underway. Prosecutions for blasphemy
disappeared, replaced (if at all) by charges of public swearing or disorderly conduct.
Requirements that the taking of a legal oath be made on an affirmation of a belief in
God and in the certainty of eternal damnation for lying—a prerequisite to serve as
a witness or juror, execute a will, or sign most legal documents—liberalized considerably as the century progressed. By century's end, most states required that an
affirmant only profess some belief in a higher sanction for testifying falsely, thus
opening the privilege to Jews, Universalists, Buddhists, and members of other non-
conforming faiths; and the enforcement of Sunday laws was no longer justified as
preventing "the *desecration* of the *Sabbath* . . . which is set apart by Divine appointment." Rather, Sunday laws became public health–welfare regulations, supported
by secular rationales. Overall, the function of the law during the nineteenth century
shifted from reinforcing static "higher" norms to being an amoral instrument supporting economic development.[22]

This "secularization" of the law and adjustment of jurist attitudes continued
throughout the remainder of the century. Some scholars and judges resisted the
trend, or at least sought to retain some reference to the law's normative basis. Influential treatise writer Thomas M. Cooley wrote that Christianity remained part of
the law in the sense its ethical precepts influenced legal areas such as domestic
relations and charity law. "But," he noted, "the law does not attempt to enforce the
precepts of Christianity on the ground of their sacred character or divine origin."[23]
Resistance to the overall secularizing trend would find its way into an 1892 opinion
by the U.S. Supreme Court that declared "this is a Christian nation."[24] However,
generally, the growing professionalization of the law and the pressure to make it
adaptable to economic change meant that it had no role in enforcing religious precepts. Although Protestantism still retained great influence on the culture in the
final decades of the century, developments in the law would help lead the nation
into a more secular twentieth century.

NINETEENTH-CENTURY CONTROVERSIES

Three controversies in particular defined church–state relations during the nineteenth century: the controversy over Protestant religious exercises in the nation's
public schools and the ancillary issue of public funding of Catholic parochial schools
(otherwise known as the "School Question"); the government-sponsored Chris-
tianization of American Indians; and the government's attempt to eradicate
Mormon polygamy. The remainder of this chapter is devoted to these issues.

The "School Question"

American public schooling arose in the early years of the century. Before that time, most education of children took place through tutors, in denominational schools or those run by towns in conjunction with a local church, with the minister serving as the teacher. Education, by and large, focused on reading religious texts and involved the inculcation of religious doctrine. Several of the nation's founders, including Benjamin Franklin, Thomas Jefferson, Benjamin Rush, and Noah Webster, agitated for universal public schooling, believing that the success of the new nation depended on the teaching of republican values to future generations of children. These reformers also criticized the reliance on religious doctrine common in early schooling. In his 1779 proposal for public elementary schools in Virginia, Thomas Jefferson wrote that "instead of putting the Bible and Testament in the hands of children at an age when their judgments are not sufficiently matured for religious inquiries, their minds may here be stored with the most useful facts from Grecian, Roman, European and American History."[25] Most education reformers believed, however, that public schools should continue to teach moral precepts and religious values alongside liberal courses in mathematics, history, and science.

The early public or "common" schools that developed in cities along the eastern seaboard quickly instituted what became known as a "nonsectarian" curriculum in which universal religious doctrines and values were taught along with daily exercises in prayer, Bible reading, and hymn singing. Leaders of the early common school movements believed they could distill and teach religious values that all Protestants shared without reverting to denominationalism. The goal of nonsectarianism was not to indoctrinate, but to ensure that children were instructed in morals and religious values that served as the foundation of republican society. Although educator Horace Mann would later deemphasize the teaching of common religious doctrine—allowing the Bible "to speak for itself"—he never questioned the responsibility of public schooling to instill religious devotion among school children.[26]

Despite their characterization as "nonsectarian," many early programs were highly Calvinist or Protestant in character. Initially, and extended periods in some religiously homogeneous communities, such nonsectarian exercises elicited little opposition. With the influx of Catholic immigration in the 1830s and 1840s, however, Catholic leaders and parents began to object to the Protestant-oriented exercises, particularly when they disparaged Catholic doctrine. Catholic complaints intensified as their numbers grew, and Protestants frequently dug in. Anti-Catholic nativist groups picked up the mantel, particularly when Catholic leaders began requesting a share of the public school funds for their developing parochial schools. Tensions mounted, spurring religious hatred and violence. A Catholic convent was burned in Massachusetts and in 1844 Catholics and Protestants engaged in armed exchanges on the streets of Philadelphia, resulting in many deaths. Other communities sought common ground. School officials in Cincinnati, Ohio, with its large

German Catholic community, allowed separate instruction of Catholic children through the reading of the Douay Bible, whereas St. Louis school officials prohibited all religious exercises from the beginning. However, in most places Catholic children and parents were on the losing end of the conflict; objecting children were punished or expelled, with sanctions being upheld by courts. As the century progressed, however, devotional use of the Bible and other religious exercises became less common as school districts grew more aware of the conscientious scruples of non-Protestant children.[27]

Throughout the nineteenth century, Catholics were rarely more successful in obtaining a pro rata share of the public school funds for the education of children in parochial schools. Even before the rise in immigration, states began enacting laws and constitutional provisions that prohibited the transfer of public monies to religious institutions and schools. Although the primary motivation for these provisions was to ensure accountability and the financial stability of the nascent public schools, advocates of these early "no-aid" laws also saw their basis as originating in constitutional principles. As the New York City Council wrote in 1831 in rejecting an application by a Baptist school for a share of the common school fund, "to raise a fund by taxation, for the support of a particular sect, or every sect of Christians, . . . would unhesitatingly be declared an infringement of the Constitution, and a violation of our chartered rights."[28] To be sure, the passage of several later laws may also have been motivated by anti-Catholic animus, particularly the 1854 enactment of a constitutional provision in Massachusetts by a Know-Nothing controlled legislature.[29] However, the no-funding principle, which traces its roots back to James Madison's "three pence" argument, pre-dated and stood independent of how some used it in mid-century to ensure Protestant dominance over the public schools and American culture.[30]

The controversy over parochial school funding and the religious character of American public schooling came to a climax in the years after the Civil War. In 1869, the Cincinnati school board voted to abolish prayer and Bible reading exercises in its schools as a result of renewed complaints by Catholic, Jewish, and freethinking parents. Bible reading supporters sued the school board to have the practices reinstated. The ensuing controversy became known as the "Cincinnati Bible War," and it evolved into a national test case on the future of Bible reading. A state superior court overturned the school district's action in a 2-1 decision, with Judge Bellamy Storer writing that "[w]ithout the teachings of the Holy Scripture there is, we believe, no unvarying standard of moral duty [and] no code of ethics which inculcates willing obedience to law."[31] Judge Alphonso Taft, father of the future president and chief justice, wrote a memorable dissent that denied that Protestantism or any religion was entitled to preference under the law. Bible reading, even without note or comment, "was and is sectarian," Taft wrote. "It is Protestant worship. And its use is a symbol of Protestant supremacy in the schools, and as such offensive to Catholics and Jews."

> To hold . . . that Protestant Christians are entitled to any control in the schools,
> to which other sects are not equally entitled, or that they are entitled to have their

mode of worship and their Bible used in the common schools . . . is to hold to a
union of Church and State, however we may repudiate and reproach the name.[32]

The Cincinnati school board appealed the ruling to the Ohio Supreme Court
which, 3 years later, unanimously reversed the superior court decision, with the
justices adopting Judge Taft's reasoning.[33]

The Cincinnati Bible case reignited the controversy over religious exercises in
public schools and the public funding of religious schools. Several city school districts followed Cincinnati's lead by eliminating or further restricting prayer and
Bible reading, raising the ire of Protestant leaders who viewed the actions as an
attack on the Bible and a culture that equated Protestantism with republican values.
During the same period, the early 1870s, reports emerged that Catholic schools and
orphanages were secretly receiving public funding through sympathetic local politicians and ward bosses who desired the support of Catholic and immigrant voters.
The issues of religious exercises and funding were closely intertwined; for many
Protestant leaders, Catholic objections to Bible reading were chiefly ploys to obtain
wholesale funding of their parochial schools. Opposition to "Catholic designs"
grew, coinciding with renewed concern about foreign immigration, which was on
the upsurge.[34]

In September 1875, President Ulysses S. Grant recommended that Congress
adopt an amendment to the U.S. Constitution to resolve the School Question by
prohibiting states or local governments from appropriating funds for religious
schools. (At this time, the First Amendment to the federal Constitution restricted
the actions of the national government only, not those of the states.) Representative
James G. Blaine, a Republican Congressman and then Senator from Maine, picked
up Grant's proposal, introducing what became known as the Blaine Amendment of
1876. The proposed amendment, which went through several permutations, would
have applied the First Amendment's religion clauses to the actions of state and local
governments while expressly forbidding the appropriation of public funds for religious schools. Support for the amendment broke down largely along party lines.
Republicans supported the amendment in part to divert attention away from the
failures of Reconstruction and the corruptions of the Grant Administration. The
amendment also allowed Republicans to appear in favor of common schools, which
helped resolidify their relationship with their Protestant base. Democrats generally
opposed the amendment out of concern that it might mandate universal public
education in the South and offend their Catholic-immigrant base. Debate over the
proposed amendment, both in Congress and the public arena, was acrimonious,
with many believing that the future of universal public education was at stake. At
times, the debate devolved into anti-Catholicism; it is likely that both Blaine and
Grant supported the amendment in part as a way of appealing to anti-Catholic
voters in their respective efforts to secure the Republican nomination for president.
The proposed amendment passed the House of Representatives but failed by two
votes in the Senate to garner the necessary two thirds needed for passage and likely
ratification by the states.[35]

Even though the Blaine Amendment failed, the trends it highlighted were irreversible. In the 35 years after the failed Blaine Amendment, 21 states adopted express provisions in their respective constitutions prohibiting the appropriation of public funds to religious schools and institutions. Likely the Blaine Amendment served as a model or inspiration for several of these state provisions (although similar provisions already existed in 17 other state constitutions). Also, the trend toward de-emphasizing a devotional aspect of Bible reading continued in the latter quarter of the century, with many school districts abolishing all use of the Bible. U.S. Commissioner of Education William Torrey Harris reported in 1895 that:

> [outside] New England there is no considerable area where [the Bible's] use can be said to be uniform. This condition has come about as much by indifference as by opposition. . . . There has been a change in public sentiment gradually growing toward complete secularization of the Government and its institutions. . . . Secularization of the schools is accepted or urged by many devout people who deem that safer than to trust others with the interpretation of the laws of conscience.[36]

In fact, the dismal state of Bible reading and devotional training in the latter decades of the century would lead to an upsurge in state legislation in the early twentieth century authorizing the reading of the Bible without note or comment and to the creation of "release-time" programs for devotional instruction led by nonschool persons.[37] Clearly, the nineteenth-century School Question did not resolve the interrelated controversies of religious education in public schools and public funding of religious schools, issues that remain unresolved to this day to a certain extent. However, the School Question reveals the dynamic nature of these issues throughout the century and the way that educators, politicians, and judges approached these issues laid the foundation for future resolution by the U.S. Supreme Court.

THE CHRISTIANIZATION OF
AMERICAN INDIANS

By the time America entered the nineteenth century, attitudes toward American Indians and their religious beliefs already had a long history. For most European Americans, Native American customs and religious practices were heathen and barbaric, worthy of little regard. All of the British colonies instituted policies encouraging settlers to Christianize the local Native peoples. Most colonists had other priorities, however, so missionary efforts were sporadic and varied widely depending on time, location, funding, and denominational commitment. Of all religious groups, Moravians were the most committed and effective in evangelizing Indians.[38]

Early on, the new national government undertook policies to convert Indians to Christianity. The Second Continental Congress directed that Indian agents should "instruct [Natives] in the Christian religion" and, in 1785, provided a land grant to Moravians for the purpose of "civilizing the Indians and promoting Christianity." During George Washington's first administration, Secretary of War Henry Knox proposed appointing missionaries "of excellent moral character" to instruct Indians in matters of religion, farming, and husbandry. And in 1796, Congress enacted a law providing a land grant to the Moravians for the purpose of "propagating the Gospel among the Heathen." As can be seen, the federal government, small in size and unwilling to commit substantial resources, relied primarily on awarding grants to existing religious missions among the various tribes. The primary goal of the government was to civilize Native peoples rather than to proselytize them; however, throughout much of the nineteenth century the idea of civilizing presumed that Indians would first abandon their primitive and heathen beliefs and adopt Christian values.[39] No one would have disputed the assumptions underlying President John Quincy Adams' 1828 statement that it "was our policy and our duty to use our influence in converting [Indians] to Christianity and in bringing [them] within the pale of civilization."[40] Civilizing and Christianizing went hand in hand.

In 1819, Congress created the "Civilization Fund" to support the efforts of benevolent associations in the education of Indians. In addition to Moravians and Catholics, Baptist, Methodist, and Presbyterian missionaries shortly established mission schools among various tribes and received money from the Civilization Fund. One such group was American Board of Commissions of Foreign Missions, established in 1810 by Presbyterian and Congregationalist leaders, which by mid-century expended half of its funds, procured in part from Congress, on evangelism and education of American Indians. Conversion to Christianity was the primary goal of these agencies, goals that were inseparable from education and the instruction in those habits and skills "so essential to civilized life." Although the Civilization Fund and other Congressional appropriations uniformly made no mention of converting Indians to Christianity, language about instilling industry, morality, and civilization left no doubt that conversion would be a primary tool in achieving those goals. By 1826, 36 religious mission schools were supported by the Fund, with a total appropriation of $13,550. The Fund continued until 1873 and served as a financial link between the government and its religious allies.[41]

By mid-century, with the advent of reservations with government agents, federal Indian policy became increasingly inept and corrupt. Religious missions also suffered from government neglect and profiteering by federal agents. Following the Civil War, attention turned to resolving the "Indian Problem"—not only addressing the government corruption and Indian poverty and degradation, but also assimilating Indians into Western society. In 1867 Congress authorized a commission to investigate the condition of the Indian tribes and the policies of the military, which exercised oversight of the reservations. At the same time, delegations of Quakers and Episcopalians approached the newly elected President Grant to use religious mission boards and organizations in the reform efforts. The "Peace Commission's" 1868 report advocated a new policy of civilization (i.e., assimilation)—one that would teach Indians "the principles of Christianity" and "elevate them to the rights of citizenship." Based on the report, President Grant instituted the "Peace Policy" in 1869 to reform the system. Grant dismissed all military and civilian super-intendents and agents, replacing them with missionaries and religious officials who were authorized to formulate and administer federal Indian policy. In a later address to Congress, Grant stated that he "determined to give all the agencies to such religious denominations as had heretofore established missionaries among the Indians, and perhaps to some other denominations who would undertake the work on the same terms—i.e., as a missionary work." The societies were allowed "to name their own agents, subject to the approval of the Executive," and were expected "to watch over them and aid them as missionaries, to Christianize and civilize the Indian, and to train him in the arts of peace."[42]

As part of the Peace Policy, Congress created the Board of Indian Commis-sioners to oversee procurements for the Indian agencies and serve as a liaison between the tribes and the government. Again, the statute was silent on this matter, but the understanding was that the President would appoint representatives from various religious denominations to serve as commissioners. The Board quickly became known as the "Church Board." It coordinated activities with missionary societies, gathered information and issued reports on the conditions of Indians and their progress toward becoming "civilized." Its primary function, however, was to allot the Indian agencies among the various denominations. Initially, Catholics were not represented on the Board and received the short shrift in the denomina-tional allotment of Indian agencies. In time, Catholic missions would receive an increasing share of the allotments and supporting public funds.[43]

By the late 1880s, Catholic mission schools were receiving approximately two thirds of the federal funds under the Peace Policy. This led Protestant leaders to criticize the Catholic missions' share of the funding and the perceived sectarian character of their services. Protestant criticism caught the attention of the Commis-sioner of Indian Affairs Thomas J. Morgan, who in 1889 proposed creating a system of government-run schools to supplement and eventually replace the mission schools, the ostensible purpose being to provide education to the 50% of Native children who still received no formal schooling. Morgan proposed that the govern-ment Indian schools should model themselves after the "common-school system," in that they "should be non-partisan [and] nonsectarian." By 1892, most Protestant groups, acknowledging the trend, withdrew from participating in the Peace Policy, ending the funding of most Protestant missions. Catholic missions hung on, but in 1896 and 1897, Congress attached provisions to the appropriations bills prohibiting future contracts with religious mission schools. The funding of religious schools for Indians ceased in 1899.[44]

A footnote to the funding question arose in the 1908 Supreme Court case of *Quick Bear v. Leupp*. The issue was whether Indian treaty or trust funds, managed by the Bureau of Indian Affairs, could be used as an alternative to finance religious mission schools. The Supreme Court ruled that the contract between the B.I.A. and the Bureau of Catholic Indian Missions did not violate the Establishment Clause or the statutory appropriations ban. Payments derived from tribal funds or pursuant to treaty obligations were distinct from Congressional appropriations, Chief Justice Melville Fuller held. On the Establishment Clause claim, Fuller wrote that the Court could not "concede the proposition that Indians cannot be allowed to use their own money to educate their children in the schools of their own choice because the government is necessarily undenominational, as it cannot make any law respecting an establishment of religion or prohibiting the free exercise thereof."[45]

Catholic and Protestant missions continued after the demise of the Peace Policy, operating chiefly with private funds. The ban on government funding of religious missions did not mean that the assumptions about the importance of Christianity for civilizing had changed, however. Federal superintendents and agents still cooperated with missionaries and supported their goals of conversion. Within the government-run Indian schools, Native children were instructed in Christian principles. The government's own rules for Indian schools required Native children to attend church or Sunday schools and receive other nonsectarian instruction.[46]

Outside of the school context, the federal government instituted policies to eradicate Indian ceremonies that officials acknowledged had religious significance. Ceremonies such as the Ghost and Sun dances were viewed as impediments to civilizing and inconsistent with Christian values. In 1883, the Commissioner of Indian Affairs issued rules or "Courts of Indian Offenses" directed at prohibiting dances, mourning rituals, and other ceremonies on reservations. Punishments for participating in dances and ceremonies included fines, imprisonment at hard labor, and loss of rations.[47] The government efforts to suppress Indian religious practices came to a terrible climax in the 1890 Wounded Knee Massacre on the Pine Ridge Reservation in South Dakota, where more than 200 Indians, including women and children, were killed by Army troops who were ordered to quell a disturbance associated with the Lakota Ghost dance. Government suppression of Indian religious practices would continue until the late 1920s, even after Congress' award of citizenship to American Indians in 1923.[48]

By any account, the actions of the government toward Indian religion and culture during the nineteenth century constituted the most profound violation of church–state principles in the nation's history. Throughout the century, the government sought to eradicate the religious practices and traditions of a people while it actively supported—through funding and coercion—the conversion of those people to Christianity. These policies and actions reached their apex through the adoption of the Peace Policy and the creation of the religiously controlled Board of Indian Commissioners. The Peace Policy professed unabashedly religious objectives, expended large sums of public dollars to accomplish those objectives, instituted religious tests for office-holders and grant recipients, and delegated significant governmental authority to cooperating religious bodies. While it functioned, the Peace Policy represented the most thorough and indisputable religious establishment in the history of the nation.

THE "MORMON PROBLEM"

The effort of the federal government to eradicate Mormon polygamy and subdue the authority of the Church of Jesus Christ of Latter-day Saints is another sad episode in nineteenth-century church–state relations. The government's actions toward the Mormon Church between 1850 and 1895 share some parallels to those policies toward American Indians. In both instances, the government adopted official positions of hostility toward the religious beliefs and practices of identifiable groups of people. In both instances, the government sought to eradicate "barbarian" religious practices and dismantle the social structures that supported the respective faith communities. And in each instance, rights of citizenship and membership in the American political community turned on one's willingness to renounce his religious tradition and be "Christianized."

The federal government's actions toward the Mormons were unique in some respects, however. Government policies supporting the conversion of American Indians arose from relatively benign motives, albeit motives based on paternalism and prejudice. The official actions against the Mormon Church reflect no such well-meaning paternalism; rather, the actions bristled with hostility toward polygamy and the church itself. Unlike Native religious customs, Mormon beliefs and practices challenged core aspects of Protestant theology and their conception of an ordered Christian society. The Mormon polygamy, patriarchy, and theocracy represented threats to American culture in ways that the Lakota Ghost dance could. Making matters more complicated, Mormons were of European stock and professed to be Christian (in fact, Mormons shared elements with Protestant "restorationist" groups such as the Disciples of Christ). Thus Mormonism possessed the same presumption of legitimacy and entitlement to constitutional protections of religious liberty as other antebellum religious movements. Unlike the policies toward American Indians, officials and legislators were consciously aware of the constitutional implications of their actions toward the Mormon Church.[49]

Mormons had experienced run-ins with government authority long before they formally announced their revealed practice of polygamy in 1852. Mormon notions of cosmology, ongoing revelation, sacred texts, and their hierarchical communalism distinguished their religion from most religious movements that spread throughout the Midwest. Mormon separatist practices engendered animosity from non-Mormon "gentiles" as the church moved from Ohio to Missouri, and then to Illinois. Armed conflict erupted in Missouri with both Mormons and Gentiles being killed, leading the Missouri governor to issue an extermination order authorizing the killing of Mormons, likely (and thankfully) the only example of an American government ordering a religious genocide. The church squandered whatever sympathy it acquired after moving to Nauvoo, Illinois, where its prophet, Joseph Smith, assumed the mantel of spiritual, political, and military leader, raising accusations of theocracy. At Nauvoo the first rumors of polygamy among Smith and Mormon leaders would also arise. The Nauvoo episode would end tragically with the murder of Smith and his brother and the expulsion of the Mormons from the Midwest. However, the theocratic specter of Nauvoo and later Deseret (Utah) would haunt Mormons for another half-century, serving to complicate the church–state issue and neutralize accusations of repressive actions by the federal government.[50]

The 1852 church acknowledgment of polygamy confirmed what government reports and rumor had been asserting for several years. Still, the public reaction to the announcement was swift and hostile. For Mormons, plural marriage was a central religious tenet, a practice that helped a man achieve a higher level of spiritual fulfillment in heaven. From the very beginning, Mormons defended the practice on freedom of religion grounds found in the Constitution. For non-Mormons, however, polygamy was a barbaric and dehumanizing practice, one that challenged the fundamental structure of the family that had underlain Christian civilization for 1800 years. As the U.S. Supreme Court would remark in one of its many cases upholding the government's prosecution of polygamists, monogamous marriage was "the sure foundation of all that is stable and noble in our civilization; [it was] the best guarantee of that reverent morality which is the source of all beneficent progress in social and political improvement."[51] Additionally, critics viewed polygamy as promoting the sexual gratification of men while it debased womanhood, resulting in their effective enslavement. In the 1856 party platform of the newly formed Republican Party, Mormon polygamy was condemned along with slavery as being one of the "twin relics of barbarism."[52]

Distance from Washington to the Great Basin and opposition of Southern legislators to increasing federal authority over the territories meant that the national government did little to address the Mormon Problem until the Civil War. (In 1857 President James Buchanan authorized an unsuccessful military expedition to Utah, purportedly to quell an armed uprising against the federal government, though the action was urged on by public disdain for polygamy.) Finally, in 1862 with Southern Democrats absent, Congress enacted the first legislation prohibiting polygamy, the Morrill Act. The Morrill Act imposed a punishment of up to 5 years in prison for any act of polygamy, religiously based or not. However, additional sections of the law revealed where the true problem lay. The Act also invalidated the territorial incorporation of the Mormon Church and any territorial laws that established or supported polygamy while it prohibited the Mormon Church from acquiring or holding real property in excess of $50,000.[53] Although the Act disclaimed any animosity toward the Mormon Church, the legislative debate revealed disdain and revulsion for the church and polygamy. Of particular concern was the "theocratic" authority the church exercised over every aspect of life in Utah. As the House committee report explained:

> [t]he very attempt to incorporate the Church of Jesus Christ of Latter Day Saints, is an effort to accomplish in Utah, what has nowhere else has been effected by our authority upon this continent—the establishment of one form of religious worship to the exclusion of all others.[54]

The Morrill Act was rarely enforced because of the difficulty of prosecutors obtaining indictments or convictions from Mormon-dominated grand and petit juries. Finally, in 1874 church leaders put forward George Reynolds, the private secretary for Brigham Young, as a test challenge to the constitutionality of the Act. Reynolds was convicted after a second trial and appealed to the U.S. Supreme Court claiming that the Act's polygamy provision was an unconstitutional violation of freedom of religion. The Court rejected Reynold's free exercise claim. Chief Justice Morrison R. Waite wrote that although '[r]eligious freedom is guaranteed everywhere throughout the United States," that right was not unlimited.

> Congress was deprived of all legislative power over mere opinion, but was left free
> to reach actions which were in violation of social duties or subversive of good
> order. . . . Laws are made for the government of actions, and while they cannot
> interfere with mere religious belief and opinions, they may with practices.[55]

Despite having the Morrill Act as a tool to prosecute polygamy, other impediments stood in the way of effective enforcement. Mormon-controlled juries still refused to indict or convict, and wives regularly refused to testify against their husbands (prosecutors also encountered problems with using second wives to prove a first marriage—or vice versa—because the testifying wife was entitled to spousal privilege against testifying until the subsequent (or earlier) marriage could be proved independently. Also, Utah had no marriage law or registry, so the only proof of plural marriages existed in secret church documents or from testimony of Mormons in attendance at the private ceremonies.

Congress responded to this public and prosecutorial frustration by passing two draconian laws, the Edmunds Act (1882) and the Edmunds-Tucker Act (1887). The Edmunds Act prohibited not only polygamy, but also unlawful cohabitation between a man and a woman that could not be proved by marriage. An additional section clarified that prosecutors could exclude potential jurors from jury service for not merely practicing polygamy (or cohabiting) but also on grounds they "believe[d] it right for a man to have more than one living and undivorced wife at the same time, or to live in the practice of cohabiting with more than one woman." This latter provision disqualified not just practicing polygamists but also all faithful members of the Mormon Church based on their religious beliefs. Another section denied the right to vote or hold public office—elected or appointed—to any "polygamist, bigamist, or any person cohabiting with more than one woman," and to any woman in a polygamist marriage or cohabiting relationship. Finally, to ensure that Mormon political power was broken along with the power to resist federal enforcement, the Edmunds Act declared all elected territorial offices vacant and set up an electoral commission to oversee voter registration and election.[56]

The breadth of the Act—effectively disenfranchising many Mormons and disqualifying them from office or serving on juries—and the anti-Mormon rhetoric that accompanied the legislative debate, left no doubt that Congress intended not simply to eradicate polygamy, but also to subdue the Mormon Church. A handful of legislators voiced concerns that the Act persecuted Mormons for their beliefs while its disqualifying provisions established religious tests for office-holding and civic franchise. However, resolving the Mormon Problem had become a national obsession in the 1880s, and the Edmunds Act introduced a 12-year period of aggressive prosecutions in Utah referred to as "the Raid." Mormon officials and other polygamists fled into hiding, whereas more than 1,000 served time on chain gangs. Even though only approximately 2,500 Mormon men ever engaged in polygamy, all of Utah became an occupied territory where most residents possessed few rights.

The 1887 Edmunds-Tucker Act increased the penalties of several earlier offenses and abolished the spousal privilege against testifying. However, most significantly, the Act dissolved the incorporation of the Mormon Church and ordered the seizure and disposal of its assets. Supporters of the law insisted this latter action was necessitated by the ongoing intransigence of the Mormon Church and, as one representative stated, "to cut up by the roots this church establishment."[57] Any hope that the Supreme Court would intervene to limit the enforcement of the two Acts was dashed by a pair of important decisions in 1890. In the first case, *Davis v. Beason*, the Court upheld an Idaho territorial law that denied the vote not only to practicing polygamists but also to anyone who belonged to an organization that "teaches, advises, counsels, or encourages its members" to practice polygamy "or plural or celestial marriage as a doctrinal rite." Even though the law disqualified many voters only for their religious beliefs, not their actions, Justice Stephen Field reaffirmed the distinction from *Reynolds* between protected religious belief and unprotected conduct motivated by religious belief: "Laws are made for the government of actions, and while they cannot interfere with mere religious belief and opinions, they may with practices." The law merely regulated Davis's ability to vote. "To call [his] advocacy a tenet of religion is to offend the common sense of mankind," Field wrote.[58]

In the second case, *Late Corporation of Church of Jesus Christ of Latter-day Saints v. United States*, the Court upheld the seizure and liquidation of church property on the ground its assets had been used to evangelize and advocate the tenet of polygamy. Despite the best efforts of federal officials "to suppress this barbarous practice," wrote Justice Joseph Bradley, the Mormon Church "perseveres, in defiance of law, in preaching, upholding, promoting and defending . . . this nefarious doctrine," thus necessitating Congress' action.[59] With these two holdings and the ongoing prosecutions in Utah, the Mormon leadership quickly capitulated, with President Wilford Woodruff declaring in 1890 that nothing in the church teachings should be construed to "encourage polygamy." With the issuance of that manifesto, Congress finally authorized the admission of Utah as a state in 1896, reinstating the civil and political rights to Mormons. As with the actions against Native Americans, the federal government had undertaken actions that can only be viewed as transgressing rights of free exercise and nonestablishment. In the case of the Mormon Church, those actions were apparently justified to prevent the existence of Mormon theocracy considered incompatible with American values.

CONCLUSION

Church–state relations during the nineteenth century present an interesting paradox. On one hand, religious affiliation was unparalleled, and Protestantism exercised a dominating influence on the culture and its institutions. On the other hand, growing religious diversity and social, economic, and demographic forces placed tremendous secularizing pressures on American institutions. Understandings of religious liberty and separation of church and state expanded during the century, although they were tested by the nation's actions toward Native Americans and Mormons.

America entered the twentieth century still predominantly a Protestant country. However, it was a vastly different nation from 100 years earlier, one that had been changed forever by religious voluntaryism, pluralism, immigration, industrialization, and a growing secularism. The experiences and lessons of the nineteenth century would set the stage for the constitutional development during the next century.

ENDNOTES

1. See for example, Robert S. Alley, ed., *The Constitution and Religion* (Amherst, NY: Prometheus Books, 1999).

2. See generally, Philip Hamburger, *Separation of Church and State* (Cambridge, MA: Harvard University Press, 2002); John Witte, Jr., *Religion and the American Constitutional Experiment*, 2d ed. (Boulder, CO: Westview Press, 2005).

3. Edwin Scott Gaustad and Philip L. Barlow, *New Historical Atlas of Religion in America* (New York: Oxford University Press 2001), 157, 209–210.

4. Isaac Kramnick and R. Laurence Moore, *The Godless Constitution: The Case Against Religious Correctness* (New York: W.W. Norton & Co., 1996), 17, 88–109; Edwin S. Gaustad, *Faith of the Founders: Religion and the New Nation, 1776–1826*, 2d ed. (Waco, TX: Baylor University Press, 2004), 36–109.

5. Thomas J. Curry, *The First Freedoms: Church and State in America to the Passage of the First Amendment* (New York: Oxford University Press, 1986), 134–222.

6. Reprinted in John F. Wilson and Donald L. Drakeman, eds., *Church and State in American History*, 3rd ed. (Boulder, CO: Westview Press, 2003), 74.

7. Robert Baird, *Religion in the United States of America* (Glasgow: Blackie & Son, 1844), 602–603, 606.

8. Edwin Scott Gaustad, *Historical Atlas of American Religion*, rev. ed. (New York: Harper & Row, Pub., 1976), 37–57; Jon Butler, *Awash in a Sea of Faith: Christianizing the American People* (Cambridge: Harvard University Press, 1990), 283; Roger Finke and Rodney Stark, *The Churching of America 1776–1990* (New Brunswick, NJ: Rutgers University Press, 1992), 15–16.

9. Robert T. Handy, "The Protestant Quest for a Christian America, 1830–1930," 22 *Church History* (1953), 8–20, 12.

10. Lyman Beecher, "A Reformation of Morals Practicable and Indispensable" (1812), in *Lyman Beecher and the Reform of Society: Four Sermons, 1804–1828*, ed. Edwin S. Gaustad (New York: Arno Press, 1972), 17–19; Robert H. Abzug, *Cosmos Crumbling: American Reform and the Religious Imagination* (New York: Oxford University Press, 1994), 30–56; Robert T. Handy, *A Christian America: Protestant Hopes and Historical Realities*, 2d ed. (New York: Oxford University Press, 1984), 37–47; Butler, *Awash in a Sea of Faith*, 284–287.

11. Handy, *A Christian America*, 27.

12. Butler, *Awash in a Sea of Faith*, 225.

13. Gary Scott Smith, *The Seeds of Secularization: Calvinism, Culture, and Pluralism in America 1870–1915* (Grand Rapids, MI: Christian University Press, 1985), 53–73.

14. See Richard R. John, "Taking Sabbatarianism Seriously: The Postal System, the Sabbath, and the Transformation of American Political Culture," *Journal of the Early Republic* 10 (Winter 1990): 517; William Addison Blakely, ed., *American State Papers Bearing on Sunday Legislation* (Washington, DC: The Religious Liberty Association, 1911), 232–233.

15. "Preamble and Resolutions, Adopted at a Meeting of the Citizens of New York, Against the Passage of Any Law Prohibiting the Transportation and Opening of the Mail on the Sabbath," February 9, 1829, 20th Cong., 2d sess., Senate Document 64.

16. See "Senate Report on Sunday Mails," Committee on the Post Office and Post Roads, January 19, 1829, 20th Cong., 2nd sess., and "House Report on Sunday Mails," Committee on the Post Office and Post Roads, March 4 and 5, 1830, 21st Cong., 1st sess., in Blakely, *American State Papers*, 233–270.

17. Senate Report, 234–235.

18. House Report, 255.

19. John, "Taking Sabbatarianism Seriously," 563.

20. See Steven K. Green, *The Second Disestablishment: Church and State in the Nineteenth Century* (New York: Oxford University Press, 2010).

21. *Updegraph v. Commonwealth*, 11 Serg. & Rawl. 394, 407 (Pa. 1824).

22. *State v. Fearson*, 2 Md. 310 (1852), 313; Morton J. Horwitz, *The Transformation of American Law 1780–1860* (Cambridge, MA: Harvard University Press, 1977), 6–30.

23. Thomas M. Cooley, *A Treatise on the Constitutional Limitations*, 7th ed. (Boston: Little, Brown and Co., 1903), 670.

24. *Church of the Holy Trinity v. United States*, 143 U.S. 457 (1892), 471.

25. Jefferson, "A Bill for the More General Diffusion of Knowledge," in *The Essence of Jefferson*, ed. Martin A. Larson (Washington, DC: Joseph J. Binns, Pub., 1977), 150.

26. See generally, Noah Feldman, "Non-Sectarianism Reconsidered," *Journal of Law and Politics* 18 (2002): 65.

27. See *Donahoe v. Richards*, 38 Me. 379 (1854); *Commonwealth v. Cooke*, 7 Am. L. Reg. 417 (Ma. Police Ct.1859); Ray Allen Billington, *The Protestant Crusade, 1800–1860, A Study of the Origins of American Nativism* (New York: The MacMillan Co., 1938), 142–65, 220-37. See also R. Laurence Moore, "Bible Reading and Nonsectarian Schooling: The Failure of Religious Instruction in Nineteenth-Century Public Education," *Journal of American History* 86 (2000): 1581–1599.

28. William Oland Bourne, ed., *History of the Public School Society of the City of New York* (New York: William Wood & Co., 1870), 139.

29. See John R. Mulkern, *The Know-Nothing Party in Massachusetts* (1990), 76, 94–103; Lloyd P. Jorgenson, *The State and the Non-Public School, 1825-1925* (Columbia, MO: University of Missouri Press, 1987), 85–93.

30. James Madison, "Memorial and Remonstrance Against Religious Assessments, 20 June 1785," in *The Founders' Constitution*, eds. Philip B. Kurland and Ralph Lerner (Chicago: University of Chicago Press, 1987), 82.

31. Harold M. Helfman, "The Cincinnati 'Bible War,' 1869–1870," *Ohio State Archaeological and Historical Quarterly* 60 (1951): 369–386; Robert G. McCloskey, ed., *The Bible in the Public Schools—Arguments in the Case of John D. Minor, et al., versus The Board of Education of the City of Cincinnati, et al.* (New York: Da Capo Press Reprint, 1967), 380.

32. McCloskey, *The Bible in the Public Schools*, 408, 415.

33. *Board of Education v. Minor*, 23 Ohio St. 211 (1872).

34. See Steven K. Green, "The Blaine Amendment Reconsidered," *Journal of Legal History* 36 (1992): 38.

35. Ibid.

36. William T. Harris, *Report of the Commissioner of Education for the Year 1894–1895* (Washington, DC: Government Printing Office, 1896): II, 1656. See also Moore, "Bible Reading and Nonsectarian Schooling," 1581–1599.

37. See Jerome K. Jackson and Constance F. Malmberg, *Religious Education and the State* (Garden City, NY: Doubleday, Doran & Co., 1928), 1 (discussing a post-1900 "trend very definitely in the direction of giving Bible reading more place in the public schools.").

38. Henry Warner Bowden, *American Indians and Christian Missions* (Chicago: University of Chicago Press, 1981), 96–163.

39. R. Pierce Beaver, *Church, State, and the American Indians* (St. Louis, MO: Concordia Pub. House, 1966), 63–65; Robert F. Berkhofer, Jr., *Salvation and the Savage: An Analysis of Protestant Missions and American Indian Response, 1787–1862* (Lexington, KY: University of Kentucky Press, 1965), 2–4.

40. "Fourth Annual Message to Congress," December 2, 1828, in James D. Richardson, *A Compilation of the Messages and Papers of the Presidents, 1789–1897*, Vol. 2 (Washington: Bureau of National Literature and Art, 1901), 415.

41. Bowden, *American Indians and Christian Missions*, 167–169; Francis Paul Prucha, *American Indian Policy in the Formative Years* (Cambridge, MA: Harvard University Press, 1962), 213–227; Beaver, *Church, State, and the American Indian*, 61–80.

42. "Report of the Indian Peace Commission," January 7, 1868, "Report of the Board of Indian Commissioners," November 23, 1869, "The President's Second Annual Message to Congress," December 5, 1870, reprinted in Francis Paul Prucha, ed., *Documents of United States Indian Policy*, 2d ed. (Lincoln: University of Nebraska Press, 1990), 106–110, 131–34, 135; Robert H. Keller, Jr., *American Protestantism and United States Indian Policy, 1869–1882* (Lincoln, NE: University of Nebraska Press,1983), 17–30; Beaver, *Church, State, and the American Indian*, 124–130.

43. Francis Paul Prucha, *American Indian Policy in Crisis: Christian Reformers and the Indian, 1865–1900* (Norman, OK: University of Oklahoma Press, 1976), 52–60; Keller, *American Protestantism*, 32–36; Beaver, *Church, State, and the American Indian*, 134–138; "Instructions to the Board of Indian Commissioners," 1869, "Assignment of Indian Agencies to Religious Societies," November 1, 1872, in Prucha, *Documents*, 128–129, 141–143.

44. "Supplemental Report on Indian Education," December 1, 1889, in Prucha, *Documents*, 178–180; Prucha, *American Indian Policy*, 318–319; Beaver, *Church, State, and the American Indian*, 162–168.

45. *Ruben Quick Bear v. Leupp*, 210 U.S. 50 (1908).

46. Prucha, *The Churches and the Indian Schools*, 161–178.

47. "Courts of Indian Offenses," November 1, 1883, "Rules for Indian Court," August 27, 1892, in Prucha, *Documents*, pp. 160–162, 186–189.

48. Prucha, *American Indian Policy in Crisis*, 362–364; Robert M. Utley, *The Indian Frontier of the American West 1846–1890* (Albuquerque, NM: University of New Mexico Press, 1984), 253–257; Lawrence C. Kelly, *The Assault on Assimilation: John Collier and the Origins of Indian Policy Reform* (Albuquerque, NM: University of New Mexico Press, 1983), 295–348.

49. Sarah Barringer Gordon, *The Mormon Question: Polygamy and Constitutional Conflict in Nineteenth-Century America* (Chapel Hill, NC: The University of North Carolina Press, 2002), 19–54.

50 Leonard J. Arrington and Davis Bitton, *The Mormon Experience: A History of the Latter-day Saints* (New York: Vintage Books, 1979), 68–82; Gordon, *The Mormon Question*, 23; Edwin Brown Firmage and Richard Collin Mangrum, *Zion in the Courts: A Legal History of the Church of Jesus Christ of Latter-day Saints, 1830–1900* (Urbana, IL: University of Illinois Press, 1988), 83–113.

51. Murphy v. Ramsey, 114 U.S. 15 (1885), 45.

52. Gordon, *The Mormon Question*, 19–54.

53. 12 Stat. 501 (1862); Firmage and Mangrum, *Zion in the Courts*, 131–133; Orma Linford, "The Mormons and the Law: The Polygamy Cases, Part I," *Utah Law Review* 9 (1964): 308, 314–316.

54. H.R. Rep. No. 83, 36th Cong., 1st sess. (1860).

55. *Reynolds v. United States*, 98 U.S. at 162 (1878). 164.

56. Firmage and Mangrum, *Zion in the Courts*, 161–166; Linford, "Mormons and the Law," 317–319.

57. H.R. Rep. No. 2735, 49th Cong., 1st sess. 5–8 (1886); Linford, "Mormons and the Law," 326.

58. *Davis v. Beason*, 133 U.S. 333, 341–344 (1890).

59. The Late Corporation of the Church of Jesus Christ of Latter-day Saints v. Untied States, 136 U.S.1 (1890), 49–50.

BIBLIOGRAPHY

Books

Abzug, Robert H. *Cosmos Crumbling: American Reform and the Religious Imagination*. New York: Oxford University Press, 1994.

Adams, Jasper. *The Relation of Christianity to Civil Government in the United States*. Charleston: A.E. Miller, 1833.

Arrington, Leonard J. and Davis Bitton. *The Mormon Experience: A History of the Latter-day Saints*. New York: Vintage Books, 1979.

Baird, Robert. *Religion in the United States of America*. Glasgow: Blackie & Son, 1844.

Beaver, R. Pierce. *Church, State, and the American Indians*. St. Louis, MO: Concordia Pub. House, 1966.

Berkhofer, Robert F., Jr. *Salvation and the Savage: An Analysis of Protestant Missions and American Indian Response, 1787–1862*. Lexington, KY: University of Kentucky Press, 1965.

Billington, Ray Allen. *The Protestant Crusade, 1800–1860, A Study of the Origins of American Nativism*. New York: The MacMillan Co., 1938.

Borden, Morton. *Jews, Turks, and Infidels*. Chapel Hill, NC: University of North Carolina Press, 1984.

Bourne, William Oland, ed. *History of the Public School Society of the City of New York*. New York: William Wood & Co., 1870.

Bowden, Henry Warner. *American Indians and Christian Missions*. Chicago: University of Chicago Press, 1981.

Butler, Jon. *Awash in a Sea of Faith: Christianizing the American People*. Cambridge, MA: Harvard University Press, 1990.

Carwardine, Richard J. *Evangelicals and Politics in Antebellum America*. New Haven, CT: Yale University Press, 1993.

Colwell, Stephen. *The Position of Christianity in the United States*. Philadelphia: Lippincott, Grambo & Co., 1854.

Curry, Thomas J. *The First Freedoms: Church and State in America to the Passage of the First Amendment*. New York: Oxford University Press, 1986.

Dreisbach, Daniel L. *Religion and Politics in the Early Republic*. Lexington, KY: University of Kentucky Press, 1996.

Finke, Roger and Rodney Stark. *The Churching of America 1776–1990*. New Brunswick, NJ: Rutgers University Press, 1992.

Firmage, Edwin Brown and Richard Collin Mangrum. *Zion in the Courts: A Legal History of the Church of Jesus Christ of Latter-day Saints, 1830–1900*. Urbana, IL: University of Illinois Press, 1988.

Gaustad, Edwin S. *Dissent in American Religion*. Chicago: University of Chicago Press, 1973.

——— *Faith of the Founders: Religion and the New Nation 1776–1826*. 2d ed. Waco, TX: Baylor University Press, 2004.

Gaustad, Edwin S., ed. *Lyman Beecher and the Reform of Society: Four Sermons, 1804–1828*. New York: Arno Press, 1972.

Gaustad, Edwin Scott and Philip L. Barlow. *New Historical Atlas of Religion in America*. New York: Oxford University Press, 2001.

Gordon, Sarah Barringer, *The Mormon Question: Polygamy and Constitutional Conflict in Nineteenth-Century America*. Chapel Hill, NC: The University of North Carolina Press, 2002.

Green, Steven K. *The Second Disestablishment: Church and State in the Nineteenth Century*. New York: Oxford University Press, 2009.

Hamburger, Philip. *Separation of Church and State*. Cambridge: Harvard University Press, 2002.

Handy, Robert T. *A Christian America*, 2d ed. New York: Oxford University Press, 1984.

——— *Undermined Establishment: Church-State Relations in America, 1880–1920*. Princeton: Princeton University Press, 1991.

Harris, William T. *Report of the Commissioner of Education for the Year 1894–1895*. Washington: Government Printing Office, 1896.

Hatch, Nathan O. *The Democratization of American Christianity*. New Haven: Yale University Press, 1989.

Jackson, Jerome K. and Constance F. Malmberg. *Religious Education and the State*. Garden City, NY: Doubleday, Doran & Co., 1928.

Jorgenson, Lloyd P. *The State and the Non-Public School, 1825–1925*. Columbia, MO: University of Missouri Press, 1987.

Robert H. Keller, Jr. *American Protestantism and United States Indian Policy, 1869–1882.* Lincoln, NE: University of Nebraska Press, 1983.

Kramnick, Isaac and R. Laurence Moore. *The Godless Constitution: The Case Against Religious Correctness.* New York: W.W. Norton & Co., 1996.

McAfee, Ward M. *Religion, Race, and Reconstruction: The Public School in the Politics of the 1870s.* Albany, NY: State University of New York Press, 1998.

McCloskey, Robert G., ed. *The Bible in the Public Schools—Arguments in the Case of John D. Minor, et al., versus The Board of Education of the City of Cincinnati, et al.* New York: Da Capo Press Reprint, 1967.

Moore, R. Laurence. *Religious Outsiders and the Making of Americans.* New York: Oxford University Press, 1986.

Morris, B.F. *Christian Life and Character of the Civil Institutions of the United States,* Philadelphia: George W. Childs, 1864.

Noll, Mark A. *One Nation Under God? Christian Faith and Political Action in America.* San Francisco: Harper & Row, 1988.

Noll, Mark A. ed. *Religion & American Politics: From the Colonial Period to the 1980s.* New York: Oxford University Press, 1990.

Prucha, Francis Paul. *American Indian Policy in Crisis: Christian Reformers and the Indian, 1865–1900.* Norman, OK: University of Oklahoma Press, 1976.

Prucha, Francis Paul. *American Indian Policy in the Formative* Years. Cambridge, MA: Harvard University Press, 1962.

Prucha, Francis Paul, ed. *Documents of United States Indian Policy,* 2d ed. Lincoln, NE: University of Nebraska Press, 1990.

Smith, Gary Scott. *The Seeds of Secularization: Calvinism, Culture, and Pluralism in America 1870–1915.* Grand Rapids, MI: Christian University Press, 1985.

Turner, James. *Without God, Without Creed: The Origins of Unbelief in America.* Baltimore: The Johns Hopkins University Press, 1985.

Wilson, John F., and Donald L. Drakeman, eds. *Church and State in American History,* 3rd ed. Boulder, CO: Westview Press, 2003.

Witte, Jr., John. *Religion and the American Constitutional Experiment,* 2d ed. Boulder, CO: Westview Press, 2005.

Articles/Chapters

Esbeck, Carl H. "Dissent and Disestablishment: The Church-State Settlement in the Early Republic." *B.Y.U. Law Review* (2004): 1385.

Feldman, Noah. "The Intellectual Origins of the Establishment Clause." *New York University Law Review* 77 (2002): 346.

Feldman, Noah. "Non-Sectarianism Reconsidered." *Journal of Law and Politics* 18 (2002): 65.

Green, Steven K. "'Blaiming Blaine': Understanding the Blaine Amendment and the 'No-Funding' Principle." *First Amendment Law Review* 2 (2003): 107.

——— "The Blaine Amendment Reconsidered." *Journal of Legal History* 36 (1992): 38.

——— "The Insignificance of the Blaine Amendment." *B.Y.U. Law Review* (2008): 295.

———. "Justice David Josiah Brewer and the 'Christian Nation' Maxim." *Albany Law Review* 63 (1999): 427.

———. "A 'Spacious Conception': Separatism as an Idea." *Oregon Law Review* 85 (2006): 443.

Hamburger, Philip A. "Constitutional Right of Religious Exemption: An Historical Perspective." *George Washington Law Review* 60 (1992): 915.

Handy, Robert T. "The Protestant Quest for a Christian America, 1830–1930," *Church History* 22 (1953): 8.

Helfman, Harold M. "The Cincinnati "Bible War," 1869–1870." *Ohio State Archaeological and Historical Quarterly* 60 (1951): 369.

Jeffries, John C., Jr. and James E. Ryan. "A Political History of the Establishment Clause." *Michigan Law Review* 100 (2001): 279.

John, Richard R. "Taking Sabbatarianism Seriously: The Postal System, the Sabbath, and the Transformation of American Political Culture." *Journal of the Early Republic* 10 (Winter 1990): 517.

Lash, Kurt. "The Second Adoption of the Establishment Clause: The Rise of the Nonestablishment Principle." *Arizona State Law Journal* 27 (1995): 1085.

Linford, Orma. "The Mormons and the Law: The Polygamy Cases, Part I." *Utah Law Review* 9 (1964): 308.

Moore, R. Laurence. "Bible Reading and Nonsectarian Schooling: The Failure of Religious Instruction in Nineteenth-Century Public Education." *Journal of American History* 86 (2000): 1581.

CHAPTER 4

....

RELIGIOUS ADVOCACY
BY AMERICAN RELIGIOUS
INSTITUTIONS:
A HISTORY

....

MELISSA ROGERS

THE First Amendment to the United States Constitution prohibits the government from promoting or endorsing religion. At the same time, it recognizes the right of religious people and organizations to play active roles in the debate of public issues. The Supreme Court of the United States has said: "Adherents of particular faiths and individual churches frequently take strong positions on public issues including . . . vigorous advocacy of legal or constitutional positions. Of course, churches as much as secular bodies and private citizens have that right."[1] As this statement suggests, religious Americans of many different theological and political stripes have long exercised this right, and they have often exercised it in concert with like-minded believers through religious organizations.

This chapter traces some of the ways in which political advocacy by certain religious communities became institutionalized in the United States during the twentieth century. More specifically, it focuses on the formation of a handful of national religious groups and the positions they took on some key religious liberty issues, principally certain church–state cases heard by the U.S. Supreme Court. The chapter is divided into five parts that proceed chronologically.

The Old Guard: The Emergence of the Federal Council of Churches, the National Catholic War Conference, and a Trio of Jewish Advocacy Groups

A set of challenges that prompted religious people to organize in the early twentieth century were problems associated with the growing concentration of the extreme poor in the nation's cities. Two factors that contributed to this crisis were the industrial revolution and waves of poor immigrants that swept into the nation. The industrial revolution had begun before the commencement of the Civil War, but the pace of that revolution accelerated dramatically in the years following the war.[2] Particularly in New England, Sidney Ahlstrom has said,"[t]he result was a new kind of city, in which low wages, exhausting hours, and crowded living conditions became everyday facts of life."[3] Those who suffered under these conditions included many new immigrants who were destitute.[4] They came to the cities to find whatever work they could.[5]

Some Americans developed a spiritual way of thinking about and responding to these problems, an approach that came to be known as the "Social Gospel." The Social Gospel calls on Christians to work to change unjust structures of society as part of their religious discipleship.[6] During this era, proponents of the Social Gospel sought to stamp out specific practices and conditions such as child labor, sweatshops, miserable housing, and inadequate wages.[7]

The organization most prominently associated with the Social Gospel was the Federal Council of Churches, later known as the National Council of Churches of Christ in the USA.[8] The Federal Council was a federation of more than 30 denominations that was officially established in 1908.[9] Among other things, the Federal Council sought to "secure a larger combined influence for the churches of Christ in all matters affecting the moral and social condition of the people, so as to promote the application of the law of Christ in every relation of human life."[10] In its first year of operation, the Federal Council of Churches called for, among other things, protection of workers' rights "against the hardships often resulting form the swift crises of industrial change," a living wage as a minimum requirement, an end to child labor, "suitable provision" for elderly and injured workers, and the reduction of poverty.[11]

The Council did not focus solely on issues of social and economic justice, however. For example, an historian of the council, John Hutchison, has said: "The American system of separation of church and state was variously celebrated" at early meetings of the Council, with some leaders expressing an appreciation for the fact that, under this system, "no vested ecclesiastical interest might develop."[12] Hutchison added: "There seems to have been little or no recognition of the problems of church and state as they were to emerge in such a different world less than three decades later."[13]

The Protestant community was not the only religious community that responded to the struggles of working people during this era. American Catholics also were galvanized by these issues, in part because many Catholics were among the working poor.[14] Mark Massa has said that "[a] conservative, European-based social philosophy put American Catholics out of step with liberal industrial reform efforts in the pre-1880 period, but during the last decade of the century a distinctive Catholic social gospel took shape in response to radically new social and industrial conditions."[15]

The context of the First World War provided even more energy and urgency to the effort to organize American Catholic leaders to speak to public issues. Catholic bishops in the United States formed the National Catholic War Council (NCWC) in August 1917 to contribute to national mobilization.[16] Among other things, the council recruited about 1,000 military chaplains.[17] According to Sidney Ahlstrom, however, "[p]robably the most important side effect of the council's many activities was that it ended the neutrality or abstention of the bishops on specific questions of public policy."[18]

After the war, the National Catholic War Council became the National Catholic Welfare Conference, a body charged with coordinating the national aspects of the work of the Catholic Church in the United States.[19] (In later years, this body became known as the United States Conference of Catholic Bishops.)[20] In February 1919, the Welfare Conference developed what it called the "Program of Social Reconstruction."[21] The foreword to the statement said: "The ending of the Great War has brought peace. But the only safeguard of peace is social justice and a contented people."[22] The program included calls for the right of workers to organize, a living wage, abolition of child labor, a national housing program; and "comprehensive provision for insurance against illness, invalidity, unemployment and old age."[23] In addition to calling on the government to do its part on these issues, the Catholic Church developed an array of social service and educational institutions to serve Catholics and others, and it sometimes sought government funds to help operate those institutions.[24] Later in the century, the issue of whether the state could or should provide such aid gave rise to some hot debates.

Like the American Catholic community, the American Jewish community was heavily affected by immigration during this period, and it too sought to find its public voice.[25] Various sectors of the Jewish community formed three organizations to speak to public issues on their behalf—the American Jewish Committee, the Anti-Defamation League, and the American Jewish Congress.[26] All three organizations share a dedication to religious liberty and church–state separation, and their work overlaps in some other ways, but each reflect a particular sensibility and focus in part because of their historical origins.

Prominent Jewish leaders of German descent founded the American Jewish Committee in 1906.[27] These leaders initially came together to address pogroms against Russian Jews.[28] After several meetings, the Committee undertook an agenda that included engaging lawmakers on policy issues, performing research, and organizing diplomatic efforts on behalf of European and American Jews.[29] One of its early successes was convincing the U.S. Senate to abrogate a Russia–U.S. trade treaty as a rebuke for Moscow's anti-Semitic policies.[30] Today the American Jewish Committee continues to work to advance human rights at home and abroad through advocacy, research, and diplomacy.

The Anti-Defamation League was founded in 1913 as an affiliate of the B'nai B'rith, a network of fraternal associations for Jews that was formed in the mid-nineteenth century because Jews were rejected from fraternal lodges such as the Elks.[31] Some years later, a member of a local B'nai B'rith, Sigmund Livingston, established a "Publicity Committee" under the auspices of his local B'nai B'rith and wrote letters to newspapers taking issue with discrimination and bigotry against Jews.[32] Livingston's idea caught on—many B'nai B'rith lodges took similar steps, and in 1913 the top leadership of B'nai B'rith asked him to establish and run a national office, which became the Anti-Defamation League of B'nai B'rith (ADL).[33] During the rise of organized racism in the 1920s, the ADL began drafting antidiscrimination statutes and developing in-depth research on American-based hate groups, emphases that continue for the group today.[34]

In 1918, the American Jewish Congress formed to establish, as its name suggests, an elected congress of American Jews.[35] The founders of the Congress, most of whom were of European or Russian descent, were motivated to organize the body in part as a reaction against perceived elitism of other Jewish institutions.[36] The original aims of the Congress were to provide relief for European Jews who were victims of World War I and to restore the state of Israel.[37] As described in more detail later in this essay, after World War II the American Jewish Congress spearheaded a dogged, innovative, and controversial battle for separation of church and state and religious freedom through the nation's courts.[38]

PROTESTANT ALTERNATIVES: FUNDAMENTALISTS, EVANGELICALS, AND PACIFISTS

Like the Jewish community, the Protestant community was not content to speak through just one religious advocacy body. In other words, the Federal Council of Churches spoke for many Protestants, but it certainly did not speak for them all. For example, some Protestants distanced themselves from the Federal Council, partially because they associated the Social Gospel with theological liberalism, which they adamantly opposed.[39] This wing of Protestantism "regarded the Social Gospel and the Federal Council as dangerous enemies," Sidney Ahlstrom has said.[40]

Some of these Christians were known as "fundamentalists." The term "fundamentalist" is drawn from an influential series of booklets titled *The Fundamentals*, which were published between 1910 and 1915.[41] Those who wrote these booklets were concerned about what they perceived as increasing ignorance of and lack of adherence to biblical teaching as well as a corruption of the moral fiber of many Americans.[42] However, as Thomas Askew and Richard Pierard have noted, over time the term "fundamentalism" that "originally had referred to an orthodox ministerial effort to oppose theological liberalism in the northern denominations came to connote hostility to modern culture and social change."[43]

In the 1920s, these fundamentalists undertook a campaign to pass legislation that would prevent public schools from teaching about evolution.[44] Whereas some Christians believed that their faith was compatible with evolution, fundamentalists believed people must choose between the two.[45] When John Scopes, a Tennessee high-school biology teacher, violated his state's ban against teaching evolution, the famous Scopes trial followed.[46] At this trial, William Jennings Bryan, an economic populist, former Democratic presidential candidate, and a Christian who rejected evolution, appeared for the prosecution, whereas legendary lawyer Clarence Darrow handled the case for the defense.[47] Scopes was convicted, although the decision was later reversed on a technicality.[48] However, as John Green has noted, "the trial was a public relations disaster for the movement."[49] Bryan and his associates were seen as lacking knowledge and sophistication as well as candor.[50] At the same time, simply because the antievolution forces lost in court and were widely ridiculed did not mean that they lost everything in the court of public opinion. In the wake of the Scopes trial, many textbook publishers deleted references to evolution from science books to avoid controversy.[51]

In addition to the embarrassment at the Scopes trial, another low point for many Christians during the period between the world wars was the failure of Prohibition, which was repealed in 1933.[52] These and other developments caused Christian fundamentalists and some evangelicals to largely withdraw from political activism for a time.[53] However, many were ready to re-engage in public debate in the 1940s, and some did so through new groups like the American Council of Christian Churches (ACCC).[54] The emergence after World War II of the Soviet Union as the world's only other superpower provided fuel for the fundamentalists' fire.[55] As John Green has explained, anticommunism became a "master frame" for fundamentalists in that it "brought together many of the things fundamentalists opposed," including modernism and government social programs.[56] The fact that the Soviet Union was an officially atheistic state provided another reason for fundamentalists to rally against communism. The ACCC took an extremely confrontational approach, even accusing certain leaders of other Christian denominations of having ties to communists.[57]

A larger group of Protestants had some of the same concerns, but they wanted to set a more positive tone. This group formed the National Association of Evangelicals (NAE) in 1943.[58] Allen Hertzke has described the niche evangelicals occupied at this time:

> While most Protestants in the nineteenth century would have described themselves as evangelicals, by the 1940s the term came to characterize those who had split both from the mainline Protestant churches [such as those associated with the Federal Council] and from the fundamentalists. Thus, the leaders of

[NAE], created in 1943, saw themselves as representing a distinct religious minority. They rejected the liberal theology that dominated the seminaries of the mainline Protestant denominations and embraced the "fundamentals" of the faith, yet they did not share the separatist cultural movement of the fundamentalists, desiring instead to "transform" the culture rather than separate from it.[59]

In sum, the NAE sought to serve as an alternative both to the Federal Council and the ACCC.[60] It opened an office in Washington, DC in 1943 to help advance and protect its interests in areas such as religious freedom, religious broadcasting, and the military chaplaincy, among other things.[61]

In that same year, the Religious Society of Friends (Quakers) also opened an office in Washington, DC, on behalf of a group it called the Friends Committee on National Legislation (FCNL).[62]Part of what drew this pacifist group to the nation's capital was the need to deal with the federal government regarding conscientious objection to the military draft, which was instituted in 1940.[63] An early version of the selective service bill provided exemptions from military service only for pacifists who belonged to historic peace churches.[64] Quakers and others argued that people who were not members of historic peace churches also should be permitted to serve as conscientious objectors if they met other relevant standards.[65] Congress accommodated this objection, and a statute with revised language took effect in September 1940.[66]

World War II also played a role in the establishment of other religious offices in Washington, DC. For example, after the war the Southern Baptist Convention converted its committee on chaplains into a permanent entity and broadened its jurisdiction.[67]This entity then partnered with similar committees of the Northern Baptist Convention and the National Baptist Convention, Incorporated (a traditionally African American body). These bodies jointly establish an office in the nation's capital in 1946 under the name of the Joint Conference Committee on Public Relations.[68]Claiming a Baptist tradition pre-dating the nation's founding, the Joint Committee supported disestablishment of religion and robust protection for the free exercise of every faith.[69] During its early years, the Joint Committee fought against religious persecution in Rumania and the establishment of official relations between the United States and the Vatican, while it spoke in favor of including protection of religious liberty and other human rights in the charter of the United Nations.[70] The first director of the office, J.M. Dawson, also led in the founding in 1947 of Protestants and Other Americans United for the Separation of Church and State, now Americans United for Separation of Church and State.[71]

Yet another Protestant body that was founded in the first half of the twentieth century and came to play an important role in church–state battles is the General Conference of Seventh-day Adventists. Born in the midst of a turn-of-the century revival movement, the General Conference has traditionally drawn a hard line against government funding or sponsorship of religion as harmful for both the government and religion.[72] It also has enthusiastically supported the free exercise of religion and accommodation of religion in employment, a concern prompted partially by the needs of its members for workplace flexibility given their observance of a Saturday Sabbath.[73]

EARLY ESTABLISHMENT CLAUSE BATTLES

From the 1940s forward, the United States Supreme Court became increasingly engaged in church–state matters. There are several reasons for this trend. The most important is that, during the 1940s, the Court determined that the religious liberty clauses of the First Amendment—the Establishment and Free Exercise Clauses— applied to states and localities as well as to the federal government by virtue of the Fourteenth Amendment to the United States Constitution. This, among other factors, triggered a rising tide of religious liberty litigation for the Supreme Court to address.

Supreme Court battles over the First Amendment's Establishment Clause, which prohibits the government from promoting or endorsing religion, began in earnest in 1947 with the case of *Everson v. Board of Education*.[74] The *Everson* case involved the question of whether a state could reimburse parents for the costs of bus transportation for their children to and from Catholic schools as well as other private and public schools.[75]

Along with the General Conference of Seventh-day Adventists, the Joint Conference Committee filed a friend-of-the-court brief, known also as an "amicus curiae" or "amicus" brief, in this landmark case.[76] Amicus curiae briefs provide a way for persons interested in particular litigation but not parties to it to submit their views for the Court's consideration. The Joint Committee argued that "the use of tax moneys for the purpose of furnishing transportation of children attending sectarian schools is legislation respecting the establishment of religion and gives effective aid to such organizations in the teaching of their religious tenets and the extension of their religious ministrations" and thus contravenes the First and the Fourteenth Amendments.[77] This brief rebutted the argument that the aid only benefited the children, not the religious schools, a notion known as the "child benefit" theory. The Joint Committee characterized this theory as "an ingenious effort to escape constitutional limitations rather than a sound construction of their essential content and purpose."[78]

Another religious group filed an amicus brief on the other side of this case. The National Council of Catholic Men and the National Council of Catholic Women said that religious schools fulfill "a public function" and that the state did not violate the Constitution when it distributed aid to them on a nondiscriminatory basis to advance educational interests.[79] Father William McManus of the National Catholic Welfare Conference expounded on this position in a Congressional hearing on federal aid to nonpublic schools in 1947.[80]He explained that Catholics believed that the key question the government should ask in these situations was, "Does the particular school prepare boys and girls for their duties as American citizens?"[81] If the school did so, then the government should fund it, whether it was public or private, religious or nonreligious.[82]

In the *Everson* case, the Court gave both sides something to praise and something to bemoan. It upheld the specific aid at issue, but it described the reach of the Establishment Clause in very broad terms.[83] Beyond its particular context, this decision is significant because it recognized the application of the Establishment Clause to states and localities, and this helped open the courthouse doors to a wider range of church–state litigation.[84]

Another factor in the rising profile of Establishment Clause litigation was a decision by some Jewish leaders to launch a broad campaign against discrimination and bigotry during the post-war years.[85] Part of this plan involved the development of a litigation strategy against state subsidies for and other government sponsorship of religion.[86] Leo Pfeffer of the American Jewish Congress' Commission on Law and Social Action conceived and directed this plan.[87] In the past, the dominant impulse among American Jews had been to pull their punches, fearing the consequences of doing otherwise.[88] There was a shift in the wake of World War II. Amidst heightened awareness of the dangers of religious bigotry, the optimistic spirit and good economy of the 1950s, and the birth of the state of Israel,[89] the prevailing postwar attitude was that the time was right for an aggressive push for change.[90]

An early part of this campaign included the filing of an amicus brief on behalf of Jewish groups with the U.S. Supreme Court challenging an Illinois "released-time" program.[91] This program involved religious teachers coming into the public schools each week to offer a period of religious instruction as part of the school day. Students could be excused from such instruction, but it was clear that at least some felt pressured by their schools to participate in it.[92] The case was *McCollum v. Board of Education.*

The Synagogue Council of America, a body representing the rabbinical and synagogue associations of the three branches of Judaism, filed an amicus brief arguing that this governmental policy was unconstitutional under the First Amendment's Establishment Clause.[93] Joining with the Synagogue Council was the National Community Relations Advisory Council, an organization established in 1944 to coordinate the workings of the national Jewish agencies (including the American Jewish Committee, American Jewish Congress, and the Anti-Defamation League) and local Jewish community relations councils.[94] In their brief, these groups noted that "this [was] the first instance in which practically all American Jewish organizations, religious and lay, have joined in submitting a brief."[95] They argued that "[e]very phase of the released time program . . . serves to involve the authority and facilities of the public school system and to place the authority of the latter behind the religious instruction as behind other classes," serving to make released time "an integral part of the general education provided by the public school system."[96] The groups were careful to note that "American Jewry . . . places as high a value as any group on a well-planned and well-directed program of religious education."[97] But public schools should not promote or sponsor such devotional instruction, they said. The Joint Conference Committee on Public Relations and the General Conference of Seventh-day Adventists each filed amicus briefs in the case making similar arguments.[98]

The Protestant Council of the City of New York, a sponsor of a released-time program in New York City, filed an amicus brief arguing the other side of the *McCollum* case.[99] Among other things, this body argued that parents of schoolchildren "have the right to believe that a total exclusion from public education of recognition of religion may amount in the minds of their children to indoctrination in irreligion."[100] The Court, however, struck down the released-time program in 1948.[101]

Just a few years later, the Supreme Court took up a case involving a different released-time program. The case was *Zorach v. Clauson*.[102] In this program, public schools released the students to religious institutions for a period of instruction during the school day. The Federal Council of Churches, now known as the National Council of Churches of Christ in the USA (NCC), staunchly defended this program.[103] In its filings with the Court, the NCC noted that its International Council of Religious Education "ha[d] been in the forefront of the national movement for religious education on released time since its inception."[104] It claimed that the NCC (and the Federal Council before it) had developed released-time programs in virtually every state.[105] It argued that "[t]he growing secularization of education in publicly-supported schools ha[d] resulted in the gradual elimination of the religious element which was once an important part of all education."[106] Leo Pfeffer and Kent Greenawalt served as counsel for the plaintiff in this case. In their brief, they said that the Court's earlier decision in *McCollum* required it to reject the released-time program at issue in *Zorach*.[107] The Court, however, upheld this particular program in 1952, finding that it accommodated the spiritual needs of students and parents without enlisting the state in advancing religion.[108]

Civil Rights and Liberties Take Center Stage

From the mid-1950s through the 1970s, a prominent part of the national dialogue focused on civil rights and liberties. The U.S. Congress passed landmark civil rights legislation, and the U.S. Supreme Court played a leading role in defining these and other rights and liberties. A set of religious organizations played an active role in the debate over these matters.

One of the Jewish groups that played a leading role in the civil rights struggle was the Religious Action Center for Reform Judaism (RAC), a body officially founded in Washington, DC, in 1962.[109] The RAC is an outgrowth of the Reform movement's Commission on Social Action, an entity dating back to 1949.[110] Like other Jewish groups, the RAC considers church–state separation and religious liberty a priority, and it often associates itself with various Supreme Court amicus briefs under the auspices of affiliated Reform organizations such as the Union of American Hebrew Congregations and the Central Conference of American Rabbis. Another priority for the RAC during the 1960s was drafting and then advocating for the adoption of the 1964 Civil Rights Act, which prohibits racial discrimination in places of public accommodation and employment, among other things.[111] As President Lyndon B. Johnson reportedly said, this Act "could not have been passed without the backing it received from the churches and synagogues."[112]

Title VII of the Civil Rights Act of 1964 not only prohibits employment discrimination on the basis of race, it also prohibits discrimination on the basis of religion (among other characteristics), while exempting certain employee positions within religious organizations from this prohibition.[113] In 1972, Congress amended Title VII to broaden that exemption to include all employee positions within religious organizations.[114] During 1972, Congress also added to this statute an explicit obligation for employers to accommodate the religious practices of their employees unless doing so would cause undue hardship for them.[115] These provisions would be addressed by the Supreme Court in later years.

The 1960s era not only brought about changes in the law of religious freedom, it also brought about change in some religious communities' understanding of that concept. Most notable among these changes was the 1963 Declaration of Religious Freedom, written by John Courtney Murray, a prominent Catholic American priest and theologian.[116] In earlier years, Murray had attempted to soften the official Catholic position on religion and the state. As Jay Dolan has written, that position basically "advocated a union of church and state, where erroneous religions, i.e., those that were not Catholic, had no rights."[117] To say the least, this view was in obvious tension with the American constitutional tradition of religious freedom, which includes the principle that the government must protect the free exercise of all faiths while promoting none of them. Murray believed that Catholic teaching and the American tradition could and should be reconciled. Catholics should seek to influence the state for good, Murray said, but they also should recognize pluralism as an unavoidable fact of human society, and that no government should be permitted to impose a religion on its citizens or judge religious truth.[118] In the 1950s, Rome silenced Murray.[119] However, the release of the Declaration of Religious Freedom as part of Vatican II vindicated Murray's work.[120] An additional change that affected the American Catholic community during this era was the splitting in 1966 of the venerable National Catholic Welfare Council into two new bodies: the National Council of Catholic Bishops (NCCB) and the United States Catholic Conference (USCC).[121]

The turbulent early 1960s also was the time during which the Court released its rulings prohibiting school-sponsored prayer and Bible reading in *Engel v. Vitale* (1962) and *Abingdon Township v. Schempp* (1963).[122] In the *Engel* case, the Synagogue Council of America and the National Community Relations Advisory Council filed an amicus brief written by Leo Pfeffer arguing that school-sponsored prayer was unconstitutional.[123]Although the state asserted that it had written a nonsectarian prayer for school children, these groups said that "no prayer can be truly non-sectarian."[124] Further, even if the school did not require the student to participate in these prayers, the government still crossed the line when it promoted religion, they said.[125] These Jewish groups emphasized that their opposition to government-sponsored religion was not and should not be equated with hostility to faith.[126] The American Jewish Committee and the Anti-Defamation League jointly filed an amicus brief in this case making similar arguments.[127]

In the *Schempp* case, the American Jewish Committee and the Anti-Defamation League jointly filed another amicus brief. Among other things, they noted that it was important to distinguish between devotional reading of the Bible as part of public school classroom activity, which was unconstitutional, and the use of the Bible "as a source or reference book in the teaching of secular subjects such as literature, history, and social studies," which was constitutional.[128] Pfeffer also filed an amicus brief for the Synagogue Council of America and the National Community Relations Advisory Council in this case, arguing that school-sponsored Bible readings and recitation of the Lord's Prayer violated the First Amendment.[129]

Just a few years later the Supreme Court waded into controversial waters yet again when it held that public schools could not tailor their curricula so as to satisfy religious objections. The Court did so in case a 1968 case, *Epperson v. Arkansas*, involving an Arkansas statute prohibiting the teaching of evolution in public schools.[130] Along with the American Civil Liberties Union, the American Jewish Congress filed an amicus brief in the case.[131] These amici noted that there might be a free exercise right for certain students to be excused from lessons that contradicted their religious beliefs, and they noted that any law or policy that required or authorized a public school teacher to teach students that their religious beliefs were false would be unconstitutional.[132] However, they said, "a penal statute forbidding teachers of a secular subject from informing their students that a widely-held scientific theory exists, solely because some may consider the theory inconsistent with the Biblical account of the creation, is not an act of neutrality but a specific aid to a particular religion and therefore a violation of the Establishment Clause of the First Amendment."[133] The Supreme Court struck down the statute.[134]

Other Establishment Clause litigation of note during this period included a series of skirmishes over government aid for religious bodies, including elementary and secondary schools and institutions of higher learning. An important backdrop for some of these debates was the enactment of the Elementary and Secondary Education Act (ESEA) in 1965, which has been called "the most comprehensive federal legislation ever conceived to bolster the financial resources of state and local schools."[135] The basic purpose of the bill was to provide supplementary federal funds for public schools in poorer school districts.[136] Beyond its scale, an important distinguishing mark of ESEA was that, "[f]or the first time, the federal government made private schools eligible for [government] funds . . . and in so doing it did not exempt religious schools from receiving these benefits," Gregg Ivers has said.[137]

Protestant groups like the National Council of Churches normally would have been expected to take issue with the inclusion of private (including religious) schools in the program, but they were not willing to speak out against this aspect of the legislation because they feared doing so would doom the overall bill, which they supported.[138] Ivers has explained the context in which ESEA was considered:

> Congress passed the ESEA and President [Lyndon B.] Johnson signed it during the same legislative session that the major Jewish organizations, with [Leo] Pfeffer in the lead role, had assembled a broad-based and ecumenical coalition of religious and secular organizations to defeat the Becker Amendment, a constitutional amendment named for Congressman Frank Becker (D-NY) and intended to overturn *Engel* and *Schempp*. But when it came to the ESEA, the Jewish organizations were not able to hold together their traditional alliance with the major public education and teachers lobbies—such as the National Education Association and the United Parents Association, and the mainline Protestant bodies, such as the National Council of Churches—all of which had played a crucial role in defeating the Becker Amendment. Apart from a sole companion, the ACLU, the major American Jewish organizations stood alone.[139]

Apparently, President Johnson had picked up Catholic support for the bill by designing it to include religious schools, and he did not intend to lose that support by changing the bill.[140] Thus, rather than oppose this aspect of the bill, these Protestant bodies pushed instead for regulations that would mandate government control over all funds connected with the program.[141]

In addition to its general significance as a church–state landmark, the struggle over ESEA also was significant because it marked something of a debut for another voice on the religious liberty battlefield. As Gregg Ivers has explained, "Orthodox Jewish agencies, heretofore an unspoken voice in church–state politics and litigation, emerged as enthusiastic supporters of the ESEA, since their own fragile network of religious day schools stood to benefit from the act."[142] These Orthodox Jewish groups included Agudath Israel of America and the Union of Orthodox Jewish Congregations of America, which later established the Washington-based Institute for Public Affairs to speak on its behalf.[143]

Further, these and other Orthodox Jewish groups came together in 1965 to found the National Jewish Commission on Law and Public Affairs (COLPA), an organization that became active in filing amicus briefs with the Supreme Court on a wide range of church–state issues.[144] Previously groups such as the Union of Orthodox Jewish Congregations of America had been content to participate in a number of the amicus briefs as a member body of the Synagogue Council of America.[145] However, after 1965, they routinely joined briefs authored by COLPA, which often put them on the opposite side of other Jewish groups in Establishment Clause cases. For example, in a 1970 Supreme Court case involving religious schools and government aid, COLPA basically advanced a two-pronged argument: first, the government certainly did not violate the Establishment Clause when it allowed religious institutions to seek and receive state aid that was generally available to other nongovernmental institutions and clearly marked off from religious use; and second, any refusal by the government to include religious organizations in such programs "would raise serious questions under the Free Exercise Clause."[146] COLPA took similar positions in these sorts of cases over the next 30 years, making it a strong ally of the United States Catholic Conference.[147] Other Jewish advocacy groups, the Baptist Joint Committee, and Americans United for Separation of Church and State were among the organizations usually filing amicus briefs on the other side of such cases.[148]

Although litigation over Establishment Clause issues tended to create sharp divisions both within and among religious communities, litigation involving free exercise issues and Title VII religious accommodation issues often was a source of great unity for religious organizations of all stripes during this period. For example, when the U.S. Supreme Court confronted a challenge to the right of the Amish to refuse to send their children to school after those children completed the eighth grade, the Amish litigants received support in the form of amicus briefs from a diverse set of religious organizations.[149] In its amicus brief in this case, for example, the National Council of Churches said that "the entire Christian movement would be poorer if the Amish were forced to conform to the environing society, and that society itself would be poorer if the Amish were compelled to emigrate, as they have often done in preference to conforming."[150] COLPA urged the Court to vindicate the rights of "religious nonconformists."[151] The Synagogue Council of America and the American Jewish Congress registered their strong support for public education, religious freedom, and "a religiously and culturally pluralistic America."[152] The Supreme Court ruled in favor of the Amish in 1972.[153]

In a similar vein, when an employee of Trans World Airlines cited Title VII's religious accommodation requirements in his quest to take time off work to observe the Sabbath, those filing amicus briefs with the Supreme Court on his behalf included the General Conference of Seventh-day Adventists, COLPA, and the Central Conference of American Rabbis.[154] In 1977, the Supreme Court rejected the worker's claim, and seriously weakened the statutory requirements of religious accommodation in the process.[155] This and other Supreme Court cases provided the trigger for the formation of a diverse coalition of religious and civil rights groups, led by the American Jewish Committee and the General Conference of Seventh-day Adventists, that calls for amending Title VII to strengthen this accommodation requirement.[156]

For the most part, however, cases like these were greatly overshadowed by others that created deep fault lines between and within religious communities. These rulings including the Court's landmark 1973 decision in *Roe v. Wade*, in which it struck down many state laws restricting abortion.[157] The Catholic community, among others, reacted with horror at this decision, and marshaled its Office for Pro-life Activities within the United States Catholic Conference to lead the fight against abortion in the wake of *Roe*, a fight that included a drive for a constitutional amendment that would ban abortion nationwide.[158] Other religious groups differed. Indeed, the American Jewish Congress, the New York State Council of Churches, the Union of American Hebrew Congregations, and the Board of Christian

Social Concerns of the United Methodist Church, among others, jointly filed an amicus brief in *Roe* noting that, although they "d[id] not advocate abortion," they believed that the state laws at issue "unjustifiably restrict[ed] the reserved constitutional liberty of all persons to conduct their private lives without unwarranted governmental interference."[159]

Another case that drew close attention from religious communities in the 1970s was a lower court's decision to prohibit the Internal Revenue Service from recognizing the tax-exempt status of private schools in Mississippi that had race-based admissions policies.[160] This resulted in a new IRS policy to deny tax-exempt status under Section 501(c)(3) to nongovernmental schools that discriminated on the basis of race.[161] Ultimately, these issues made their way to the Supreme Court. In 1980 the Court upheld the IRS' denial of tax-exempt status to two schools, Bob Jones University and Goldsboro Christian Schools, because of their racially discriminatory policies.[162] Some religious groups agreed with the result. For example, the American Jewish Committee argued in its amicus brief that, even assuming for the sake of argument that the IRS policy burdened religious exercise, it was justified by the "compelling, constitutionally mandated national interest in eliminating government-supported race discrimination in education."[163]

On the other hand, other religious groups, including some that unequivocally condemned racial discrimination, were concerned about the degree to which the government could intervene in the policies and practices of religious schools by virtue of their tax-exempt status.[164] For example, the Center for Law and Religious Freedom of the Christian Legal Society (CLS), an association of Christian lawyers, judges, and law students founded in 1961, took this position.[165] In the *Bob Jones* case, CLS noted that it neither "subscribe[d] to [n]or condone[d] the University beliefs" regarding racial discrimination.[166] However, it argued that the Court should reject the IRS judgment because upholding it would "expand the range of governmental interests that can override a religious conviction, by making an ill-defined concept of 'public policy' paramount over religious liberty."[167]

MOBILIZATION OF THE CHRISTIAN RIGHT AND BEYOND

As suggested, some of these Supreme Court decisions were bitter pills for certain Christians to swallow.[168] The decisions triggered a series of "culture wars" during the 1970s, as did some local matters, including certain gay rights legislation, debates over the ratification of the Equal Rights Amendment, and the use of particular textbooks in public schools.[169] Some conservative political leaders saw potential in these uprisings, and they eventually helped mold them into much more than the sum of their parts.[170] These political leaders sought out Reverend Jerry Falwell and others with the idea of creating a broad movement of economic and social conservatives.[171]One result of these meetings was the formation of the Moral Majority in 1979 as well as like-minded groups.[172] Groups such as the Moral Majority advocated agendas such as the "Christian Bill of Rights," which included opposition to abortion, support for school-sponsored prayer, and noninterference with Christian schools.[173]

The Moral Majority certainly was not a regular presence at the U.S. Supreme Court, but it did file an amicus brief in 1984 urging the Court to uphold an Alabama law authorizing a period of silence "for meditation or voluntary prayer."[174] The Moral Majority's brief includes a lengthy quote by Rev. Falwell, in which he asked: "[W]hen will [American leaders] realize that a good society comes only from good people—people who feel bound by the moral principles given in the Bible and tied to recognition of God as our Creator and Judge?"[175] Falwell also asserted that he had "never met or heard of a child who was hurt by being exposed to voluntary school prayer."[176] The Jewish community begged to differ. In a brief jointly filed in this case, the American Jewish Committee, the American Jewish Congress, the ADL, and the Union of American Hebrew Congregations, among others, voiced concerns about situations in which school officials might assert a right to pray with their students, noting that "impressionable children prefer conformity to standing out."[177] These groups also noted that "[a]s a small religious minority in an overwhelmingly Christian country, commitment to the separation principle serves to help maintain the Jewish community's status as political and civic equals in a religiously alien society."[178] The Court ruled that the statute was unconstitutional, not because every moment-of-silence law was constitutionally defective, but because this one was enacted for "the sole purpose of expressing the State's endorsement of prayer activities for one minute at the beginning of each schoolday."[179]

As this example suggests, groups such as the Moral Majority did not have much success in terms of swaying the Supreme Court to adopt their agenda on church–state issues; and although this movement clearly had a major impact on electoral politics, it did not have much success in pushing its agenda through the United States Congress either.[180] For example, although it was able to convince President Ronald Reagan to attempt to amend the Constitution to reinstate school-sponsored prayer, the amendment failed in 1984.[181] The amendment was opposed by all three of the oldest Jewish advocacy groups as well as the Baptist Joint Committee, National Council of Churches, and General Conference of Seventh-day Adventists, among others.[182] The federal executive and legislative branches subsequently enacted some church–state legislation the Moral Majority favored, such as the 1984 Equal Access Act, a law that allows religious as well as other non-curriculum–related student clubs to meet on the campus of public secondary schools.[183] However, the key to that measure's success was the fact that it was driven by more centrist groups such as the Baptist Joint Committee and the Christian Legal Society.[184]

Indeed, the tide of the Moral Majority's movement ebbed as the 1980s progressed and the Moral Majority itself folded in 1989.[185] The movement, however, found unity and purpose once again in the early 1990s, partially because of opposition to Bill Clinton's presidency.[186] During these years, Pat Robertson used the infrastructure left over from his failed 1988 presidential bid to organize the Christian Coalition, which was founded in 1991.[187]

The Christian Coalition, like the Moral Majority, was not designed to be an active presence in the courts; but in the 1990s a set of new organizations was created for exactly that purpose. Pat Robertson launched the American Center for Law and Justice in the 1990s, intentionally playing off the name of the American Civil Liberties Union (ACLU) to signal that this new group would serve as a counterweight to the ACLU in litigation matters.[188] James Dobson and allies formed the Alliance Defense Fund in 1993 to carry out litigation on causes of concern to them and other Dobson-affiliated entities, including Focus on the Family and the Family Research Council.[189] Jerry Falwell supported the formation of Liberty Counsel in 1989, another legal advocacy group that regularly litigates church–state cases and files friend-of-the-court briefs in U.S. Supreme Court cases.[190]

Other religious entities that emerged during this time included a body supported by the Southern Baptist Convention. In 1991 the Southern Baptist Convention de-funded the old Joint Conference Committee, known as the Baptist Joint Committee on Public Affairs at the time, and formed its own public policy agency, first known as the Christian Life Commission and later as the Ethics and Religious Liberty Commission of the Southern Baptist Convention (ERLC).[191] This split occurred principally because new leaders in the Southern Baptist Convention read the Establishment Clause in a significantly more narrow fashion than the BJC historically had done.

For example, whereas the Southern Baptist Convention filed an amicus brief with the Supreme Court in the 1995 case of *Lee v. Weisman* urging it to uphold the practice school-sponsored prayer at the graduation of a public middle school in the early 1990s, the Baptist Joint Committee called on the Court to strike it down.[192]In its brief, Southern Baptists argued that "[t]raditional invocations and benedictions at public ceremonies do not violate the Establishment Clause, because they are non-coercive accommodations of the religious needs of the community and its student population."[193] The BJC, along with its co-amici, argued that when public schools sponsored prayer in this way, it not only violated the consciences of students, it also corrupted religion and "promote[d] least-common denominator faith and liturgy."[194] By a vote of 5-4, the Court ruled the school's practice unconstitutional.[195]

A glance at the list of amici in the *Lee v. Weisman* case demonstrates the way things had changed by the mid-1990s. Whereas no religious groups had filed amicus briefs favoring school-sponsored religious exercises in cases like *Engel* and *Schempp*, a long list did so in *Lee v Weisman*. Other than the Southern Baptist Convention, that list includes the Christian Legal Society, National Association of Evangelicals and the Fellowship of Legislative Chaplains, Inc.;[196] Concerned Women for America (founded in 1979 by Christian activist Beverly LaHaye);[197] Focus on the Family and the Family Research Council;[198] Liberty Counsel;[199] the Rutherford Institute (a legal institute created by lawyer John Whitehead in 1982 to "encourage Christians to play a more active role in the courts");[200] and the United

States Catholic Conference.[201] In addition to the Baptist Joint Committee, those filing jointly on the other side of this case were the American Jewish Congress, ADL, General Conference of Seventh-day Adventists, National Council of Churches, National Jewish Community Relations Advisory Council, and the Stated Clerk of the General Assembly of the Presbyterian Church (U.S.A.).[202]

Thus, although religious groups favoring a broad reading of the Establishment Clause had dominated the amicus process at the Supreme Court until the 1980s,[203] by the end of the twentieth century, activism by religious groups favoring a narrower reading of that clause certainly had caught up. Nonetheless, as the *Lee v. Weisman* ruling suggests, groups that sought to relax the Establishment Clause's prohibition on state-sponsored religious expression continued to fight an uphill battle.

Many of these groups were on the winning side, however, in a string of "equal access" cases. These were cases in which the Court basically held that, once the government decided to open its property for a wide range of uses by nongovernmental groups, religious groups had to the right to "equal access" to that property. Indeed, the head of the American Center for Law and Justice, Jay Sekulow, successful argued the 1993 case of *Lamb's Chapel v. Center Moriches Union Free School District* case, a key ruling in this line of cases.[204] It is important to note, however, that the equal-access concept was grounded in the Free Speech Clause and embraced by some who opposed efforts to narrow the interpretation of the Establishment Clause, including some religious groups, such as the Baptist Joint Committee, and some U.S. Supreme Court justices, such as Justices William Brennan, Thurgood Marshall, and Harry Blackmun.[205] Thus, at least in their eyes, these cases did not represent a break with separationist decisions of the past.

Nevertheless, by the end of the twentieth century, it was evident that there had been a clear break with the Court's separationist past when it came to Establishment Clause rules regarding government funding and religious institutions and activities. Indeed, in 1997 the Supreme Court announced that its "Establishment Clause jurisprudence [in this area] ha[d] changed significantly" since the mid-1980s, allowing many more types of government aid to flow to more kinds of religious institutions.[206] This development greatly pleased some religious groups and deeply disappointed others.

Although the Establishment Clause continued to divide religious communities toward the end of the twentieth century, issues related to the Free Exercise Clause still tended to be more unifying. For example, when the U.S. Supreme Court considered whether an Orthodox Jewish navy chaplain could wear his yarmulke while on the job, the American Jewish Committee and the Christian Legal Society jointly filed an amicus brief on his behalf.[207] After the Supreme Court ruled against the chaplain in 1986,[208] a diverse group of religious organizations supported the enactment of a law providing greater protection for the rights of service members to wear religious apparel.[209]

Further, when the Supreme Court dramatically reduced the protection it gave religious practice under the First Amendment's Free Exercise Clause in its 1990 decision in *Employment Division v. Smith*, religious groups ranging from the ADL to the American Center for Law and Justice—with the other Jewish groups, the Baptist Joint Committee, Christian Legal Society, and NAE, among others, in between—led the charge to push the Court to reconsider its actions.[210] When the Court refused to do so, these organizations urged the United States Congress to act, and their advocacy was instrumental in achieving the enactment of the Religious Freedom Restoration Act of 1993.[211] Although the Supreme Court struck down that Act in 1997 terms of its application to states and localities, it continues to require the federal government to demonstrate a narrowly tailored compelling interest when it substantially burdens religious exercise.[212]

Even unity on free exercise issues, however, became increasingly difficult to achieve in the waning years of the twentieth century. At the heart of the difficulties were clashes between the principle of nondiscrimination on the basis of sexual orientation and the principle of religious autonomy, including the freedom of religious groups to discriminate against homosexuals or homosexual activity. Conflicts over these issues doomed legislation known as the Religious Liberty Protection Act in 1999.[213] Diverse interests ultimately were able to unify around a narrower piece of legislation, the Religious Land Use and Institutionalized Persons Act, which was enacted in 2000.[214] This act provides heightened protection for the religious exercise of persons confined in governmental institutions, including prisons, and strong protection for religious bodies from burdensome and unnecessary land use regulation.[215]

It is impossible to predict how alliances and causes in this area may shift in the next century. One prediction seems safe, however: Religious groups of all theological and political stripes are likely to continue to try to shape American law and policy at least as much in the new century as they did in the last.

ENDNOTES

1. *Walz v. Tax Comm'n*, 397 U.S. 664 (1970), 670.

2. Thomas A. Askew and Richard V. Pierard, *The American Church Experience* (Grand Rapids, MI: Baker Academic, 2004), 141.

3. Sidney E. Ahlstrom, *A Religious History of the American People* (New Haven, CT: Yale University Press, 1972), 639.

4. Ibid., 851.

5. Ibid.

6. Paul Rauschenbusch, ed., *Christianity and the Social Crisis in the 21st Century* (New York City: HarperCollins, 2007), xi–xvii.

7. James A. Reichley, *Faith in Politics* (Washington, DC: Brookings Institution Press, 2002), 197.

8. John A. Hutchison, *We Are Not Divided: A Critical and Historical Study of the Federal Council of the Churches of Christ in America* (New York: Round Table Press, 1941),

55. Hutchison said, 99: "[T]he Federal Council may be said, except for the Presbyterian Department of Church and Labor, to have given the Social Gospel its first official and recognized ecclesiastical form. . . ."

9. Ibid., 55.

10. Ibid., 36 quoting the "Plan of Federation."

11. Ibid., 46–47, quoting the "Social Creed of the Churches." Hutchison suggests that the Council's focus on the working poor had both a theological and a practical basis. For example, an early leader in the Federal Council, Frank Mason North, called for "a greater interest on the part of the church in industrial problems . . . based upon a claim for Christ's sovereignty over social as well as individual life," according to Hutchison. Ibid., 41 The churches also were well aware that they were losing working people and that "labor had become militant and impatient of what it conceived to be the reactionism and other-worldliness of prevailing religion." Ibid., 39. Thus, "[b]y means of the Social Gospel the churches sought to win back the allegiance of laboring people." Ibid.

12. Ibid., 50.

13. Ibid.

14. Ahlstrom, *A Religious History of the American People*, 541. The fact that a large number of Catholics were poverty-stricken at this time is explained in part by the waves of Irish Catholic immigrants that came to America in the nineteenth century because of severe famine and economic hardships in their native land. Once these immigrants arrived, they often had to cope not only with appalling job conditions and other economic struggles, but also with religious and ethnic bigotry. Ibid., 555–568.

15. Mark S. Massa, "Social Justice in an Industrial Society," in *Church and State in America: A Bibliographical Guide: The Civil War to the Present Day*, ed. John F. Wilson (New York: Greenwood Press, 1987), 73. A key element in this change was the publication in 1891 of the papal encyclical *Rerum Novarum*. Ibid.

16. Ahlstrom, *A Religious History of the American People*, 891.

17. Ibid.

18. Ibid. In the period leading up and during the war, Protestants and Jewish Americans also established special bodies or initiatives to deal with wartime issues. For example, the Federal Council of Churches organized a General War-time Commission of the Churches in May 1917. Ibid., 889. This Commission "was a vast organization representing all the Protestant churches except the pacifist sects, and embracing every kind of war-time activity from pulpit appeals for Liberty Bonds, Red Cross, and prune pits to the moral welfare of soldiers and the comforting of grieving families," John Hutchison has explained. Hutchison, *We Are Not Divided*, 63.

Some churches went far beyond the tasks of recruiting chaplains and engaging in war-related social ministries; they incorporated pro-war, government-generated talking points into their sermons. Ahlstrom, *A Religious History of the American People*, 892. For that and other reasons, Sidney Ahlstrom concluded, "All in all, the judgment of W.W. Sweet will stand: 'At least for the period of World War I the separation of church and state was suspended.'" Ibid., quoting William Warren Sweet, *The Story of Religion in America* (New York: Harper & Brothers, 1950), 402. The actual experience of the horrors of that war, however, had a profoundly disillusioning effect on many Americans, including many religious Americans, and led to the formation of a powerful peace movement in the 1930s. James D. Beumler, "Church and State at the Turn of the Century: Missions and Imperialism, Bureaucratization, and War, 1898–1920" in *Church and State in America: A Bibliographical Guide: The Civil War to the Present Day*, ed. John F. Wilson (New York: Greenwood Press, 1987), 165.

19. Reichley, *Faith in Politics*, 208. The word "conference" was substituted for the word "council," however, as a way of "underlining the fact that the body was consultative rather than legislative." United States Catholic Conference of Catholic Bishops, "About Us: Brief History" http://www.usccb.org/whoweare.shtml. The National Catholic War Council was officially dissolved in 1931. Ibid.

20. United States Conference of Catholic Bishops, "About Us," http://www.usccb.org/whoweare.shtml.

21. Ahlstrom, *A Religious History of the American People*, 1005; Program of Social Reconstruction, National Catholic War Council (February 12, 1919) website of the Office of Social Justice of the Archdiocese of St. Paul and Minneapolis. http://www.osjspm.org/majordoc_us_bishops_statements_program_of_social_reconstruction.aspx. The Federal Council took on a similar task. In the wake of the war, it released a statement entitled, *The Church and Social Reconstruction*. Hutchison, *We Are Not Divided*, 183.

22. Program of Social Reconstruction, National Catholic War Council (February 12, 1919), website of the Office of Social Justice of the Archdiocese of St. Paul and Minneapolis. http://www.osjspm.org/majordoc_us_bishops_statements_program_of_social_recon-struction.aspx.

23. Ibid.; Reichley, *Faith in Politics*, 209; Ahlstrom, *A Religious History of the American People*, 1005.

24. One of the national bodies that organized these Catholic service groups was the Catholic Education Association, later known as the National Catholic Education Association (NCEA). This body dates its founding to 1904. The National Catholic Education Association, "About the National Catholic Education Association," http://www.ncea.org/about/index.asp. Another such national body was the Conference of Catholic Charities, now known as Catholic Charities USA. It was established in the early twentieth century as a network of Catholic entities that provided social services for the poor. Catholic Charities USA, "Who We Are," http://www.catholiccharitiesusa.org/NetCommunity/Page.aspx?pid=290&srcid=193.

25. Ahlstrom, *A Religious History of the American People*, 569. "In proportion to its numbers," Sidney Ahlstrom has said, "the Jewish community in America was more profoundly revolutionized by nineteenth-century immigration than any other." Ibid. Although the American Jewish community was a "tiny group that numbered scarcely a half-dozen active congregations when the [nineteenth] century opened grew eight-fold in as many years, largely due to the immigration of German Jews." Ibid. Another wave of immigration during the years 1881–1914 brought about one third of all Eastern European Jews to the United States. Gregg Ivers, *To Build a Wall: American Jews and the Separation of Church and State* (Charlottesville, VA: University Press of Virginia, 1995), 35.

26. These entities were in addition to the various associations of synagogues and rabbis that served what ultimately became the three branches of Judaism, Reform, Conservative, and Orthodox. Beumler, "Church and State at the Turn of the Century," in *Church and State in America*, 157. The Union of American Hebrew Congregations, an umbrella organization for most synagogues in the Reform Jewish tradition, was established in 1873, and the organization of the reformed Jewish rabbinate, known as the Central Conference of American Rabbis, in 1889. Ibid. The Union of Orthodox Jewish Congregations in America was founded in 1898, and in 1902 the Union of Orthodox Rabbis was established. Ibid. Conservative Judaism planted a major flag for its movement when a reorganized Jewish Theological Seminary opened its doors in New York City in 1902. Ibid. In 1913, the United Synagogue of America, what James Beumler has called the "central Conservative body of Judaism" formed, and conservative rabbis established the Rabbinical

Assembly of America in 1919 to serve as their national membership group. Accordingly, as James Beumler has noted, "as in Protestantism, these can be seen as key years for denominational bureaucratic organization." Ibid.

27. Ivers, *To Build a Wall*, 36; J.J. Goldberg. *Jewish Power: Inside the American Jewish Establishment* (Reading: Addison-Wesley, 1996), 101.

28. Ivers, *To Build a Wall*, 36; Goldberg, *Jewish Power*, 101–102.

29. Goldberg, *Jewish Power*, 102.

30. Steve Windmueller, "'Defenders': National Jewish Community Relations Agencies," in *Jewish Polity and American Civil Society: Communal Agencies and Religious Movements in the American Public Square*, eds. Alan Mittleman, Jonathan D. Sarna, and Robert Licht (Lanham, MD: Rowman and Littlefield Publishers, Inc., 2002), 28.

31. Goldberg, *Jewish Power*, 93, 103–104.

32. Ibid., 104.

33. Ibid. In its early years, ADL focused on religious stereotyping in a range of venues, including the media, entertainment industries, and government. Steve Windmueller, "Defenders," in *Jewish Polity and American Civil Society*, 31.

34. Ivers, *To Build a Wall*, 60–61.

35. Ibid., 46–56.

36. Goldberg, *Jewish Power*, 103; Ivers, *To Build a Wall*, 46.

37. Ivers, *To Build a Wall*, 46.

38. Ibid., 50-56.

39. Askew and Pierard, *The American Church Experience*, 149.

40. Ahlstrom, *A Religious History of the American People*, 804.

41. Askew and Pierard, *The American Church Experience*, 138–140; Ahlstrom, *A Religious History of the American People*, 815–816.

42. Askew and Pierard, *The American Church Experience*, 138–140.

43. Ibid., 171.

44. Clyde Wilcox, *Onward Christian Soldiers? The Religious Right in American Politics*, 2nd ed. (Washington, DC: Georgetown University Press, 2000), 30–31.

45. Reichley, *Faith in Politics*, 206.

46. John C. Green, "Seeking a Place: Evangelical Protestants and Public Engagement in the Twentieth Century" in *Toward an Evangelical Public Policy: Political Strategies for the Health of the Nation*, eds. Ron J. Sider and Diane Knippers (Grand Rapids, MI: Baker Books, 2005), 18–19.

47. Reichley, *Faith in Politics*, 207; Green, "Seeking a Place" in *Toward an Evangelical Public Policy*, 18.

48. Reichley, *Faith in Politics*, 207.

49. Green, "Seeking a Place," in *Toward an Evangelical Public Policy*, 19.

50. Ibid.; Wilcox, *Onward Christian Soldiers?*, 30–34.

51. Wilcox, *Onward Christian Soldiers?*, 31. According to Wilcox, it was "[n]ot until the Soviet Union launched the Sputnik satellite into space in 1957 [that] evolution again bec[a]me a major component of high school biology classes, as Americans sought to catch up to the perceived Soviet lead in science and technology." Ibid.

52. Reichley, *Faith in Politics*, 207.

53. John C. Green, "Seeking a Place" in *Toward an Evangelical Public Policy*, 19. It is important to recognize that these Christians did not stop organizing and building institutions—they simply concentrated primarily on building institutions that, at least at the time, faced mostly inward, including Bible institutes, seminaries, religious publications and publishing houses, denominational structures, missionary societies and associations,

and radio ministries. Askew and Pierard, *The American Church Experience*, 171. As Thomas Askew and Richard Pierard note, "[f]rom this network developed an institutional base for evangelical advances later in the century," including advances in political activism. Ibid.

54. The ACCC was founded in 1941. Askew and Pierard, *The American Church Experience*, 185, 175–185; Wilcox, *Onward Christian Soldiers?*, 33–35; Reichley, *Faith in Politics*, 289–291.

55. Wilcox, *Onward Christian Soldiers?* 33–34.

56. Green, "Seeking a Place" in *Toward an Evangelical Public Policy*, 22.

57. Wilcox, *Onward Christian Soldiers?*, 30–34.

58. Allen D. Hertzke, *Representing God in Washington: The Role of Religious Lobbies in the American Polity* (Knoxville: University of Tennessee Press, 1988), 40.

59. Ibid.

60. Ibid. Ahlstrom, *A Religious History of the American People*, 958. The NAE "did not admit whole denominations that belonged to the Federal Council of Churches, but it would admit disaffected subdivisions thereof." Ibid., 958 n.11.

61. Green, "Seeking a Place," in *Toward an Evangelical Public Policy*, 24.

62. Luke Eugene Ebersole, *Church Lobbying in the Nation's Capital* (New York: The Macmillan Company, 1951), 25; Hertzke, *Representing God in Washington*, 29. Friends Committee on National Legislation, "About Us: Sixty Years of Quaker Action," http://www.fcnl.org/about/

63. Ebersole, *Church Lobbying in the Nation's Capital*, 24–27.

64. Ibid., 15.

65. Ibid., 15–17. Others opposed the bill because they believed that "every man must be left free to serve the state with his conscience," in the words of Reverend Eugene M. Austin, who spoke for an interfaith group. Ibid., 15. Some religious leaders did not oppose the bill but urged that ministers be explicitly exempted from the military draft. Ibid. The bill addressed this matter with the following provision: "Regular or duly ordained ministers of religion, and students who are preparing for the ministry in theological or divinity schools recognized as such for more than one year prior to the date of enactment of this Act, shall be exempt from training and service (but not from registration) under the Act." Ibid., 18–19, quoting Public Law 783, sec. 5(d), 76th Congress.

66. Ibid., 16–17. According to Luke Ebersole, the Selective Training and Service Act that went into effect in September 1940 provided in part: "Nothing contained in this Act shall be construed to require any person to be subject to combatant training and service in the land or naval forces of the United States who, by reason of religious training and belief, is conscientiously opposed to participation in war in any form." Ibid., 18.
In the 1965 case of *United States v. Seeger*, the U.S. Supreme Court reviewed some of the relevant history of these provisions:

> The Draft Act of 1917, 40 Stat. 76, 78, afforded exemptions to conscientious objectors who were affiliated with a "well-recognized religious sect or organization [then] organized and existing and whose existing creed or principles [forbade] its members to participate in war in any form. . . ." The Act required that all persons be inducted into the armed services, but allowed the conscientious objectors to perform noncombatant service in capacities designated by the President of the United States. Although the 1917 Act excused religious objectors only, in December 1917, the Secretary of War instructed that "personal scruples against war" be considered as constituting "conscientious objection." Selective Service System Monograph No. 11, Conscientious Objection 54-55 (1950). This Act, including its conscientious objector provisions, was upheld against constitutional attack in the *Selective Draft Law Cases*, 245 U.S. 366, 389–390 (1918).

In adopting the 1940 Selective Training and Service Act Congress broadened the exemption afforded in the 1917 Act by making it unnecessary to belong
to a pacifist religious sect if the claimant's own opposition to war was based on
"religious training and belief." 54 Stat. 889. Those found to be within the
exemption were not inducted into the armed services but were assigned to
noncombatant service under the supervision of the Selective Service System.
The Congress recognized that one might be religious without belonging to an
organized church just as surely as minority members of a faith not opposed to
war might through religious reading reach a conviction against participation in
war. Congress Looks at the Conscientious Objector (National Service Board for
Religious Objectors, 1943) 71, 79, 83, 87, 88, 89. Indeed, the consensus of the
witnesses appearing before the congressional committees was that individual
belief—rather than membership in a church or sect—determined the duties
that God imposed upon a person in his everyday conduct; and that "there is a
higher loyalty than loyalty to this country, loyalty to God." *Id.*, at 29–31. See
also the proposals that were made to the House Military Affairs Committee but
rejected. *Id.*, at 21–23, 82–83, 85. Thus, while shifting the test from membership
in such a church to one's individual belief the Congress nevertheless continued
its historic practice of excusing from armed service those who believed that
they owed an obligation, superior to that due the state, of not participating in
war in any form.

United States v. Seeger, 380 U.S. 163 (1965), 171–173. The National Service Board for
Religious Objectors referred to in this passage was an entity with religious representation
that was organized to handle the work assigned to conscientious objectors and related
matters. Ebersole, *Church Lobbying in the Nation's Capital*, 21.

67. John Lee Eighmy, *Churches in Cultural Captivity: A History of Social Attitudes of
Southern Baptists* (Knoxville, TN: The University of Tennessee Press, 1972), 142–143; Pam
Parry, *On Guard for Religious Liberty* (Macon: Smyth & Helwys, 1996), 8.

68. Ibid.

69. Parry, On Guard for Religious Liberty, 1–10.

70. Ibid., 9–10.

71. Ibid., 11–12.

72. Hertzke, *Representing God in Washington*, 40–41M; Ahlstrom, *A Religious History
of the American People*, 480–481; General Conference of Seventh-day Adventists, "Religious
Liberty" http://www.adventist.org/mission_and_service/religious_liberty.html.
en?&template=printer.html.

73. Hertzke, *Representing God in Washington*, 40–41; Ahlstrom. *A Religious History of
the American People*, 480–481; General Conference of Seventh-day Adventists, "Religious
Liberty" http://www.adventist.org/mission_and_service/religious_liberty.html.
en?&template=printer.html

74. *Everson v. Board of Education*, 330 U.S. 1 (1947).

75. Ibid.

76. Brief of General Conference of Seventh-day Adventists and the Joint Conference
Committee on Public Relations Representing the Southern Baptist Convention, the Northern
Baptist Convention, the National Baptist Convention, Inc. as Amici Curiae (filed with the
U.S. Supreme Court on October 7, 1946) in *Everson v. Board of Education*, 330 U.S. 1 (1947).

77. Ibid., 7.

78. Ibid., 11. Luke Ebersole reports that, at this time, federal aid for nonpublic schools
was broadly opposed by the Federal Council of Churches and the National Association of

Evangelicals, although they did not file any briefs in this case. Ebersole, *Church Lobbying in the Nation's Capital*, 174.

79. Brief Amicus Curiae of National Council of Catholic Men and National Council of Catholic Women as Amici Curiae (filed with the U.S. Supreme Court on November 18, 1946) in *Everson v. Board of Education*, 330 U.S. 1 (1947), i.

80. Ebersole, *Church Lobbying in the Nation's Capital*, 170–173.

81. Ibid., 172.

82. Ibid., 170–173.

83. *Everson v. Board of Education*, 330 U.S. 1 (1947).

84. Ibid. The Free Exercise Clause had been recognized to apply to states and localities in the 1940 case of *Cantwell v. Connecticut. Cantwell v. Connecticut*, 310 U.S. 296 (1940).

85. Goldberg, *Jewish Power: Inside the American Jewish Establishment*, 119–125.

86. Ibid., 122.

87. Ibid.

88. Ibid.

89. Ibid., 119–120.

90. Ibid., 121.

91. *McCollum v. Board of Education*, 333 U.S. 203 (1947).

92. Ibid.

93. Brief of the Synagogue Council of America and the National Community Relations Advisory Council as Amici Curiae (filed with the U.S. Supreme Court on November 24, 1947) in *McCollum v. Board of Education*, 333 U.S. 203 (1948).

94. Goldberg, *Jewish Power*, 105. The National Community Relations Advisory Council added the word "Jewish" to its name in 1971. Ibid. In 1997, it changed its name, but not its mission, to the Jewish Council for Public Affairs. Jewish Council on Public Affairs, "About the JCPA," http://www.jewishpublicaffairs.org/organizations.php3?action=printContentItem&orgid=54&typeID=1366&itemID=21761.

95. Brief of the Synagogue Council of America and the National Community Relations Advisory Council as Amici Curiae (filed with the U.S. Supreme Court on November 10, 1947) in *McCollum v. Board of Education*, 333 U.S. 203 (1948), xiii.

96. Ibid., 40–41.

97. Ibid., 33.

98. Brief of the General Conference of Seventh-day Adventists as Amicus Curiae (filed with the U.S. Supreme Court in December 1947) in *McCollum v. Board of Education*, 333 U.S. 203 (1948); Brief of the Joint Conference Committee on Public Relations Set Up by the Southern Baptist Convention, the Northern Baptist Convention, the National Baptist Convention, Inc., and the National Baptist Convention as Amici Curiae (filed with the U.S. Supreme Court on November 24, 1947) in *McCollum v. Board of Education*, 333 U.S. 203 (1948).

99. Brief of the Protestant Council of the City of New York as Amicus Curiae (filed with the U.S. Supreme Court on November 24, 1947) in *McCollum v. Board of Education*, 333 U.S. 203 (1948).

100. Ibid., at 21.

101. *McCollum v. Board of Education*, 333 U.S. 203 (1948).

102. *Zorach v. Clauson*, 343 U.S. 306 (1952).

103. Motion for Leave to File a Brief as Amicus Curiae by the National Council of the Churches of Christ in the USA (filed with the U.S. Supreme Court in January 5, 1952) in *Zorach v. Clauson*, 343 U.S. 306 (1952).

The Federal Council changed its name in 1950 when it united with several other religious bodies, including Eastern Orthodox churches. James D. Beumler, "America Emerges as a World Power: Religion, Politics, and Nationhood, 1940–1960," in *Church and State in America: A Bibliographical Guide: The Civil War to the Present Day*, ed. John F. Wilson (New York: Greenwood Press, 1987), 230. At the time, the NCC represented 29 denominations, had a membership of 33 million, and a string of offices in New York, Chicago, and Washington, DC. Pete J. Thuesen, "The Logic of Mainline Churchliness: Historical Background since the Reformation," in *The Quiet Hand of God: Faith-based Activism and the Public Role of Mainline Protestants*, eds. Robert Wuthnow and John Evans (Berkley, CA: University of California Press, 2002), 44. Indeed, one observer said that the NCC was "the most complex and intricate piece of ecclesiastical machinery this planet has ever witnessed." Ibid., quoted in Samuel McCrea Cavert, *The American Churches in the Ecumenical Movement, 1900–1968* (New York: Association Press, 1968), 210. James Reichley has noted that "[s]everal large Protestant denominations, including the Southern Baptists and the Missouri Synod of Lutherans, as well as the Catholic Church and the independent fundamentalists, have never joined the NCC." Reichley, *Faith in Politics*, 233.

At the founding meeting of the NCC, representatives of participating denominations and churches gathered under a large banner that said, "One Nation under God." Reichley, *Faith in Politics*, 233. The founding message sent by the NCC to the people of the United States included these words: "The nation may expect in the National Council a sturdy ally of the forces of liberty." Beumler, "America Emerges as a World Power" in *Church and State in America*, 230, quoting NCC, Christian Faith in Action, 150–151.

104. Motion for Leave to File a Brief as Amicus Curiae by the National Council of the Churches of Christ in the USA (filed with the U.S. Supreme Court in January 5, 1952) in *Zorach v. Clauson*, 343 U.S. 306 (1952), 4.

105. Ibid., 4–5.

106. Ibid., 4.

107. Brief for Appellants (filed with the U.S. Supreme Court in January 23, 1952) in *Zorach v. Clauson*, 343 U.S. 306 (1952).

108. *Zorach v. Clauson*, 343 U.S. 306 (1952).

109. Goldberg, *Jewish Power*, 125.

110. Ibid. J.J. Goldberg has noted that although the Commission "[ran] on a shoe-string from the New York offices of the Reform synagogue union, it could mobilize an army of congregants through the social-action committees of hundreds of Reform temples nationwide." Ibid.

111. Public Law 88-352; Religious Action Center of Reform Judaism, "About Us: History of the RAC," http://rac.org/aboutrac/rachistory/

112. Reichley, *Faith in Politics*, 160.

113. Public Law 88-352 (1964); Melissa Rogers, "Federal Funding and Religion-Based Employment Decisions," in *Sanctioning Religion? Politics, Law, and Faith-Based Social Services*, eds. David K. Ryden and Jeffrey Polet (Boulder, CO: Lynn Rienner Publishers, 2005), 105–124.

114. Rogers, "Federal Funding and Religion-Based Employment Decisions" in *Sanctioning Religion?*, 105–124.

115. *Trans World Airlines v. Hardison*, 432 U.S. 63 (1977).

116. Reichley, *Faith in Politics*, 269. Beumler, "America Emerges as a World Power," in *Church and State in America*, 235.

117. Dolan, *In Search of American Catholicism*, 158; Beumler, "America Emerges as a World Power" in *Church and State in America*, 235–236.

118. Reichley, *Faith in Politics*, 269; Vatican, *Declaration on Religious Freedom, Dignitatis Humanae, On the Right of the Person and of Communities to Social and Civil Freedom in Matters Religious, Promulgated by His Holiness, Pope Paul VI on December 7, 1965*, http://www.vatican.va/archive/hist_councils/ii_vatican_council/documents/vat-ii_decl_19651207_dignitatis-humanae_en.html; Dolan, *In Search of American Catholicism*, 157–161.

119. Dolan, *In Search of American Catholicism*, 161.

120. Ibid.

121. Reichley, *Faith in Politics*, 209–210; and United States Catholic Conference of Catholic Bishops, "About Us: Brief History," http://www.usccb.org/whoweare.shtml. The American bishops addressed public issues through the USCC. According to Allen Hertzke, the USCC "owe[d] its origins to Vatican II, which, among other things, granted greater authority to the bishops in each country, thus setting the stage for the American Bishops' [1980s] pastoral letters on nuclear arms, abortion, and the economy." Hertzke, *Representing God in Washington*, 36. In 2001, the National Conference of Catholic Bishops and the United States Catholic Conference were combined to create the United States Conference of Catholic Bishops (USCCB), an entity through which the bishops do all the work they did previously through these two preexisting bodies. Ibid.

122. *Engel v. Vitale*, 370 U.S. 421 (1962); *Abington Township v. Schempp*, 374 U.S. 203 (1963).

123. Brief of the Synagogue Council of America and the National Community Relations Advisory Council as Amici Curiae (filed with the U.S. Supreme Court on March 22, 1962) in *Engel v. Vitale*, 370 U.S. 421 (1962).

124. Ibid., 7.

125. Ibid., 14–24.

126. Ibid., 25–27.

127. Brief of the American Jewish Committee and Anti-Defamation League of B'nai B'rith as Amici Curiae (filed with the U.S. Supreme Court on December February 2, 1962) in *Engel v. Vitale*, 370 U.S. 421 (1962).

128. Brief of the American Jewish Committee and Anti-Defamation League of B'nai B'rith as Amici Curiae (filed with the U.S. Supreme Court on December 24, 1962) in *Abington Township v. Schempp*, 374 U.S. 203 (1963).

129. Brief of the Synagogue Council of America and the National Community Relations Advisory Council as Amicus Curiae (filed with the U.S. Supreme Court on February 18, 1963) in *Abington Township v. Schempp*, 374 U.S. 203 (1963).

130. *Epperson v. Arkansas*, 393 U.S. 97 (1968).

131. Brief of the American Civil Liberties Union and American Jewish Congress as Amici Curiae (filed with the U.S. Supreme Court on May 13, 1968) in *Epperson v. Arkansas*, 393 U.S. 97 (1968).

132. Ibid., 12–13.

133. Ibid., 13.

134. *Epperson v. Arkansas*, 393 U.S. 97 (1968).

135. Ivers, *To Build a Wall*, 151.

136. Ibid.

137. Ibid.

138. Ibid., 152–153.

139. Ibid., 151–152.

140. Lawrence Grossman, "Mainstream Orthodoxy and the American Public Square," in *Jewish Polity and American Civil Society*, eds. Alan Mittleman, Jonathan D. Sarna, and Robert Licht (Lanham, MD: Rowman and Littlefield Publishers, Inc., 2002), 297.

141. Ivers, *To Build a Wall*, 153.

142. Ibid., 152. Apparently there was some indecision within the Orthodox Jewish community about making this kind of statement before the consideration of ESEA. But the way President Johnson structured the aid in ESEA helped settle the debate: "A joke began making the rounds that 'Rabbi Johnson has *paskened* the *sha'alah*' (answered the *halakhic* question) of whether the Orthodox community should seek government aid for its day schools," according to Lawrence Grossman. Grossman, "Mainstream Orthodoxy and the American Public Square," in *Jewish Polity and American Civil Society*, 297.

143. Grossman, "Mainstream Orthodoxy and the American Public Square," in *Jewish Polity and American Civil Society*, 304, 283–306.

144. Ibid., 298.

145. See, e.g., Brief of the Synagogue Council of America and the National Community Relations Advisory Council as Amici Curiae (filed with the U.S. Supreme Court on November 10, 1947) in *McCollum v. Board of Education*, 333 U.S. 203 (1948); Brief of the Synagogue Council of America and the National Community Relations Advisory Council as Amici Curiae (filed with the U.S. Supreme Court on March 22, 1962) in *Engel v. Vitale*, 370 U.S. 421 (1962); Brief of the Synagogue Council of America and the National Community Relations Advisory Council as Amicus Curiae (filed with the U.S. Supreme Court on February 18, 1963) in *Abington Township v. Schempp*, 374 U.S. 203 (1963).

146. See, for example, Brief of the National Jewish Commission on Law and Public Affairs as Amicus Curiae (filed with the U.S. Supreme Court in 1970) in *Tilton v. Richardson*, 403 U.S. 672 (1971), 8–9.

147. Brief of National Jewish Commission on Law and Public Affairs as Amicus Curiae (filed with the U.S. Supreme Court on April 16, 1973) in *Committee for Public Education & Religious Liberty v. Nyquist*, 413 U.S. 756 (1973); Brief of National Jewish Commission on Law and Public Affairs as Amicus Curiae (filed with the U.S. Supreme Court in 1984) in *City of Grand Rapids v. Ball*, 473 U.S. 373 (1985); Brief of United States Catholic Conference as Amicus Curiae (filed with the U.S. Supreme Court on May 11, 1984) in *City of Grand Rapids v. Ball*, 473 U.S. 373 (1985); Brief of National Jewish Commission on Law and Public Affairs as Amicus Curiae (filed with the U.S. Supreme Court on October 15, 1984) in *Aguilar v. Felton*, 473 U.S. 402 (1985); Brief Amicus Curiae of United States Catholic Conference (filed with the U.S. Supreme Court on October 15, 1984) in *Aguilar v. Felton*, 473 U.S. 402 (1985); Brief of National Jewish Commission on Law and Public Affairs as Amicus Curiae (filed with the U.S. Supreme Court on January 7, 1988) in *Bowen v. Kendrick*, 487 U.S. 589 (1988); Brief of United States Catholic Conference as Amicus Curiae (filed with the U.S. Supreme Court on January 7, 1988) in *Bowen v. Kendrick*, 487 U.S. 589 (1988).

148. See, for example, Brief of Protestants and Other Americans United for Separation of Church and State as Amicus Curiae (filed with the U.S. Supreme Court on August 8, 1970) in *Tilton v. Richardson*, 403 U.S. 672 (1971); Brief of Baptist Joint Committee on Public Affairs as Amicus Curiae (filed with the U.S. Supreme Court on March 2, 1973) in *Committee for Public Education & Religious Liberty v. Nyquist*, 413 U.S. 756 (1973); Brief of Baptist Joint Committee on Public Affairs, the National Council of Churches of Christ in the U.S.A., and the American Jewish Committee as Amici Curiae (filed with the U.S. Supreme Court on June 8, 1984) in *City of Grand Rapids v. Ball*, 473 U.S. 373 (1985); Brief of Americans United for Separation of Church and State as Amicus Curiae (filed with the U.S. Supreme Court on June 11, 1984) in *City of Grand Rapids v. Ball*, 473 U.S. 373 (1985); Brief of American Jewish Congress on behalf of itself, the American Civil Liberties Union, Americans for Religious Liberty, the Anti-Defamation League of B'nai B'rith, the National

Committee on Public Education and Religious Liberty, and the National Education Association as Amici Curiae (filed with the U.S. Supreme Court on June 18, 1984) in *City of Grand Rapids v. Ball*, 473 U.S. 373 (1985); Brief of the Anti-Defamation League of B'nai B'rith (filed with the U.S. Supreme Court on November 15, 1984) as Amicus Curiae in *Aguilar v. Felton*, 473 U.S. 402 (1985); Brief of the American Civil Liberties Union, the American Jewish Congress, the National Education Association, and the National Coalition for Public Education and Religious Liberty as Amici Curiae (filed with the U.S. Supreme Court on November 15, 1984) in *Aguilar v. Felton*, 473 U.S. 402 (1985); Brief of the Anti-Defamation League of B'nai B'rith as Amicus Curiae (filed with the U.S. Supreme Court on November 15, 1984) in *Aguilar v. Felton*, 473 U.S. 402 (1985); Brief of Americans United for Separation of Church and State as Amicus Curiae (filed with the U.S. Supreme Court on November 15, 1984) in *Aguilar v. Felton*, 473 U.S. 402 (1985); Brief of Anti-Defamation League of B'nai B'rith on behalf of itself and Americans for Religious Liberty as Amici Curiae (filed with the U.S. Supreme Court on February 13, 1988) in *Bowen v. Kendrick*, 487 U.S. 589 (1988); Brief of the Baptist Joint Committee on Public Affairs, the American Jewish Committee, and Americans United for Separation of Church and State as Amici Curiae (filed with the U.S. Supreme Court on February 12, 1988) in *Bowen v. Kendrick*, 487 U.S. 589 (1988).

149. *Wisconsin v. Yoder*, 406 U.S. 205 (1972).

150. Brief of the National Council of the Churches of Christ in the United States of America as Amicus Curiae (filed with the U.S. Supreme Court on September 15, 1971) in *Wisconsin v. Yoder*, 406 U.S. 205 (1972), 3.

151. Brief of the National Jewish Commission on Law and Public Affairs as Amicus Curiae (filed with the U.S. Supreme Court on September 20, 1971) in *Wisconsin v. Yoder*, 406 U.S. 205 (1972), 2.

152. Brief of the Synagogue Council of America and the American Jewish Congress as Amicus Curiae (filed with the U.S. Supreme Court on September 20, 1971) in *Wisconsin v. Yoder*, 406 U.S. 205 (1972), 2.

153. *Wisconsin v. Yoder*, 406 U.S. 205 (1972).

154. *Trans World Airlines v. Hardison*, 432 U.S. 63 (1977).

155. Ibid.

156. Testimony of Richard T. Foltin, Legislative Director and Counsel, Office of Government and International Affairs of the American Jewish Committee with respect to the Workplace Religious Freedom Act (H.R. 1431) at a hearing of the House Education and Labor Subcommittee on Health, Employment, Labor and Pensions on "Protecting Americans from Workplace Discrimination," (February 12, 2008) at http://edworkforce. house.gov/testimony/2008-02-12-RichardFoltin.pdf.

Testimony of James D. Standish, Director of Legislative Affairs, Seventh-day Adventist Church World Headquarters, submitted pursuant to the request of the Subcommittee on Health, Employment, Labor and Pensions United States House of Representatives on the Workplace Religious Freedom Act (H.R. 1431) (February 12, 2008) at http://edworkforce. house.gov/testimony/2008-02-12-JamesStandish.pdf.

A later Title VII Supreme Court case, the 1987 *Corporation of Presiding Bishop v. Amos* case, also united many of these parties. *Corporation of the Presiding Bishop v. Amos*, 483 U.S. 327 (1987). This case considered the question of whether the exemption provided for religious organizations from Title VII's prohibition on religious discrimination in the workplace—an exemption that allowed them to discriminate on the basis of religion with respect to all job positions—violated the Establishment Clause. Those arguing in amicus briefs that the provision did not violate the Establishment Clause included the American

Jewish Congress, the Baptist Joint Committee, the Christian Legal Society, and COLPA. Brief of Concerned Women for America as Amicus Curiae (filed with the U.S. Supreme Court on December 19, 1986) in Corporation of *Presiding Bishop v. Amos*, 483 U.S. 327 (1987); Brief of the American Jewish Congress as Amicus Curiae (filed with the U.S. Supreme Court on January 5, 1987) in *Corporation of Presiding Bishop v. Amos*, 483 U.S. 327 (1987); Brief of the Baptist Joint Committee on Public Affairs as Amicus Curiae (filed with the U.S. Supreme Court on January 5, 1987) in *Corporation of Presiding Bishop v. Amos*, 483 U.S. 327 (1987); Brief of the Christian Legal Society, Lutheran Church-Missouri Synod, and National Association of Evangelicals as Amici Curiae (filed with the U.S. Supreme Court on January 5, 1987) in *Corporation of Presiding Bishop v. Amos*, 483 U.S. 327 (1987); Brief of the National Jewish Commission on Law and Public Affairs as Amicus Curiae (filed with the U.S. Supreme Court on January 5, 1987) in *Corporation of Presiding Bishop v. Amos*, 483 U.S. 327 (1987).

At least three religious groups, the ADL, the National Council of Jewish Women, and the Coalition of American Nuns, argued that at least aspects of the Title VII exemption violated the Establishment Clause. Brief of the Women's Legal Defense Fund, the National Council of Jewish Women, the National Coalition of American Nuns, and the Institute of Women Today as Amici Curiae (filed with the U.S. Supreme Court on February 23, 1987) in *Corporation of Presiding Bishop v. Amos*, 483 U.S. 327 (1987); Brief of the Anti-Defamation League of B'nai B'rith as Amicus Curiae (filed with the U.S. Supreme Court on February 29, 1987) in *Corporation of Presiding Bishop v. Amos*, 483 U.S. 327 (1987).

157. *Roe v. Wade*, 410 U.S. 113 (1973).

158. Reichley, *Faith in Politics*, 274–275.

159. Brief of American Ethical Union, American Friends Service Committee, American Humanist Association, the American Jewish Congress, Episcopal Diocese of New York, New York State Council of Churches, Union of American Hebrew Congregations, Unitarian Universalist Association, United Church of Christ and the Board of Christian Social Concerns of the United Methodist Church as Amici Curiae (filed with the U.S. Supreme Court) in *Roe v. Wade*, 410 U.S. 113 (1973), 13, i.

160. *Bob Jones University v. United States*, 461 U.S. 574, 578 (1983).

161. Ibid.

162. Ibid.

163. Brief of the American Civil Liberties Union and the American Jewish Committee as Amici Curiae (filed with the U.S. Supreme Court on January 5, 1982) in *Bob Jones University v. United States*, 461 U.S. 574 (1983), 5.

164. Brief of the National Association of Evangelicals as Amicus Curiae (filed with the U.S. Supreme Court on July 31, 1981) in *Bob Jones University v. United States*, 461 U.S. 574 (1983); Brief of the National Committee for Amish Religious Freedom as Amicus Curiae (filed with the U.S. Supreme Court on August 3, 1981) in *Bob Jones University v. United States*, 461 U.S. 574 (1983); Brief of the American Baptist Churches in the U.S.A. joined by the United Presbyterian Church in the U.S.A. as Amici Curiae (filed with the U.S. Supreme Court on November 25, 1981) in *Bob Jones University v. United States*, 461 U.S. 574 (1983); Brief of the Center for Law and Religious Freedom of the Christian Legal Society as Amicus Curiae (filed with the U.S. Supreme Court on November 25, 1981) in *Bob Jones University v. United States*, 461 U.S. 574 (1983).

165. Brief of the Center for Law and Religious Freedom of the Christian Legal Society as Amicus Curiae (filed with the U.S. Supreme Court on November 25, 1981) in *Bob Jones University v. United States*, 461 U.S. 574 (1983), 1–2. CLS established the Center for Law and Religious Freedom in 1975. Ibid.

166. Ibid., 3 n.2.

167. Ibid., 2.

168. Green, "Seeking a Place," in *Toward an Evangelical Public Policy*, 26–27.

169. Ibid.

170. Ibid., 27.

171. Ibid.

172. Ibid.

173. Kenneth D. Wald and Allison Calhoun-Brown, *Religion and Politics in the United States* (Lanham, MD: Rowman and Littlefield Publishers, 2007), 214–216.

174. *Wallace v. Jaffree*, 472 U.S. 38 (1985), 40.

175. Brief of the Moral Majority as Amicus Curiae (filed with the U.S. Supreme Court on July 8, 1984) in *Wallace v. Jaffree*, 472 U.S. 38 (1985), 60, 1.

176. Ibid.

177. Brief of the American Jewish Congress on Behalf of Itself and the National Jewish Community Relations Advisory Council as Amici Curiae (filed with the U.S. Supreme Court on September 4, 1984) in *Wallace v. Jaffree*, 472 U.S. 38, 60 (1985), xii.

178. Ibid., ix.

179. *Wallace v. Jaffree*, 472 U.S. 38, 60 (1985).

180. Green, "Seeking a Place," in *Toward an Evangelical Public Policy*, 28.

181. Hertzke, *Representing God in Washington*, 166–167. Clyde Wilcox has said that the Reagan administration "did not work to help pass" this amendment. Wilcox, *Onward Christian Soldiers?*, 89.

In 1998 Representative Ernest Istook (R-OK) proposed a related constitutional amendment. Bill Marshall, "The Constitution Under Clinton: A Critical Assessment: The Culture of Belief and the Politics of Religion," *Law & Contemp. Prob.* 63 (2000): 453.

Among other things, the proposed amendment said that "the people's right to pray and recognize their religious beliefs, heritage, or traditions on public property including schools, shall not be infringed." Ibid., 464. It also provided that the government shall not "deny equal access to a benefit on account of religion." Ibid. The amendment failed. Ibid.

182. Hertzke, *Representing God in Washington*, 166.

183. Ibid., 169. The Equal Access Act may be found at 20 U.S.C. Section 4071 (2008). The Equal Access Act applied the logic of the *Widmar v. Vincent* case to secondary public schools. *Widmar v. Vincent*, 454 U.S. 263 (1981). Allen Hertzke has said that the Christian Legal Society sponsored the *Widmar* litigation. Hertzke, *Representing God in Washington*, 163–164. *Widmar v. Vincent*, 454 U.S. 263 (1981). The Baptist Joint Committee on Public Affairs, COLPA, National Council of Churches, and the United States Catholic Conference, among others, filed amicus briefs on behalf of the prevailing side in the *Widmar* case. Motion for Leave to File Brief Amicus Curiae and Brief Amicus Curiae of Center for Constitutional Studies, National Council of Churches of Christ in the United States, National Institute for Campus Ministry, and United Ministries in Education as Amici Curiae (filed with the U.S. Supreme Court on June 1, 1981) in *Widmar v. Vincent*, 454 U.S. 263 (1981); Brief of the United States Catholic Conference as Amicus Curiae (filed with the U.S. Supreme Court on May 29, 1981) in *Widmar v. Vincent*, 454 U.S. 263 (1981); Brief of the Baptist Joint Committee on Public Affairs as Amicus Curiae (filed with the U.S. Supreme Court on November 30, 1981) in Widmar v. Vincent, 454 U.S. 263 (1981); Brief of the National Jewish Coalition on Law and Public Affairs as Amicus Curiae (filed with the U.S. Supreme Court on 1981) in *Widmar v. Vincent*, 454 U.S. 263 (1981).

Those filing on the other side in this case included the American Jewish Congress and the Anti-Defamation League of B'nai B'rith. Motion of the American Jewish Congress for

Leave to File Brief Amicus Curiae and Brief of the American Jewish Congress as Amicus Curiae (filed with the U.S. Supreme Court on April 13, 1981) in *Widmar v. Vincent*, 454 U.S. 263 (1981); Motion for Leave to File Brief Amicus Curiae and Brief Amicus Curiae of the Anti-Defamation League of B'nai B'rith (filed with the U.S. Supreme Court in 1981) in *Widmar v. Vincent*, 454 U.S. 263 (1981).

184. Hertzke, *Representing God in Washington*, 167–198.

185. Green,"Seeking a Place," in *Toward an Evangelical Public Policy*, 27. President Reagan's optimistic tone helped dampen the doom-and-gloom spirit that is so essential to the direct mail fundraising of these kinds of organizations, and the televangelist scandals of the 1980s, involving Oral Roberts and Jim and Tammy Faye Bakker, among others, also played a role in making Americans more cynical about the Christian Right. Wilcox, *Onward Christian Soldiers?*, 37–38.

186. Green, "Seeking a Place," in *Toward an Evangelical Public Policy*, 27.

187. Ibid.

188. Ibid., 28.

189. Green, "Seeking a Place," in *Toward an Evangelical Public Policy*, 28.

190. Alicia Caldwell, *Religious Liberty Group Takes Part in Case*, St. Petersburg Times, (December 4, 2000), A8.

191. Parry, *On Guard for Religious Liberty*, 45. The Joint Conference Committee changed its name to the Baptist Joint Committee on Public Affairs in 1950 and to the Baptist Joint Committee on Religious Liberty in 2005. Bill J. Leonard, *Baptist Ways: A History* (Valley Forge, PA: Judson Press, 2003), 409; Baptist Joint Committee for Religious Liberty, "Frequently Asked Questions," http://www.bjconline.org/about/faq.htm.

192. *Lee v. Weisman*, 505 U.S. 577 (1992).

193. Brief of the Southern Baptist Convention Christian Life Commission as Amicus Curiae (filed with the U.S. Supreme Court on May 14, 1991) in *Lee v. Weisman*, 505 U.S. 577 (1992), 5.

194. Brief of the American Jewish Congress, Baptist Joint Committee on Public Affairs, American Jewish Committee, National Council of Churches of Christ in the USA, Anti-defamation League of B'nai B'rith, General Conference of Seventh-day Adventists, People for the American Way, National Jewish Community Relations Advisory Council, New York Committee on Public Education and Religious Liberty, and James E. Andrews as Stated Clerk of the General Assembly of the Presbyterian Church (USA) as Amici Curiae (filed with the U.S. Supreme Court on July 10, 1991) in *Lee v. Weisman*, 505 U.S. 577 (1992), 48, 32–48.

195. *Lee v. Weisman*, 505 U.S. 577 (1992).

196. Brief of Christian Legal Society, National Association of Evangelicals, and the Fellowship of Legislative Chaplains, Inc., as Amici Curiae (filed with the U.S. Supreme Court on May 24, 1991) in *Lee v. Weisman*, 505 U.S. 577 (1992).

197. Green, "Seeking a Place," in *Toward an Evangelical Public Policy*, 28; Concerned Women for America, "About CWA," http://www.cwfa.org/history.asp; Brief of Concerned Women for America and Free Speech Advocates as Amicus Curiae (filed with the U.S. Supreme Court on May 24, 1991) in *Lee v. Weisman*, 505 U.S. 577 (1992).

198. Brief of Focus on the Family and Family Research Council as Amicus Curiae (filed with the U.S. Supreme Court on May 24, 1991) in *Lee v. Weisman*, 505 U.S. 577 (1992).

199. Brief of Liberty Counsel as Amicus Curiae (filed with the U.S. Supreme Court on May 2, 1991) in *Lee v. Weisman*, 505 U.S. 577 (1992).

200. Brief of The Rutherford Institute as Amicus Curiae (filed with the U.S. Supreme Court on May 8, 1991) in *Lee v. Weisman*, 505 U.S. 577 (1992);

The Rutherford Institute, "Our History," http://www.rutherford.org/About/ History.asp.

201. Brief of United States Catholic Conference as Amicus Curiae (filed with the U.S. Supreme Court on May 23, 1991) in *Lee v. Weisman*, 505 U.S. 577 (1992).

202. Brief of the American Jewish Congress, Baptist Joint Committee on Public Affairs, American Jewish Committee, National Council of Churches of Christ in the USA, Anti-defamation League of B'nai B'rith, General Conference of Seventh-day Adventists, People for the American Way, National Jewish Community Relations Advisory Council, New York Committee on Public Education and Religious Liberty, and James E. Andrews as stated clerk of the General Assembly of the Presbyterian Church (USA) as Amici Curiae (filed with the U.S. Supreme Court on July 10, 1991) in *Lee v. Weisman*, 505 U.S. 577 (1992).

203. Ivers, *To Build a Wall*, 190–191.

204. *See, e.g.*, Brief of the Rutherford Institute as Amicus Curiae (filed with the Supreme Court on November 12, 1992) in *Lamb's Chapel v. Center Moriches Union Free Sch. Dist.*, 508 U.S. 384 (1993); Brief of the National Jewish Commission on Law and Public Affairs as Amicus Curiae (filed with the Supreme Court on November 19, 1992) in *Lamb's Chapel v. Center Moriches Union Free Sch. Dist.*, 508 U.S. 384 (1993); Brief of the Concerned Women for America and Free Congress Foundation as Amicus Curiae (filed with the Supreme Court on November 26, 1992) in *Lamb's Chapel v. Center Moriches Union Free Sch. Dist.*, 508 U.S. 384 (1993).

Those filing amicus briefs on the other side of this case included Americans United for Separation of Church and State, the Union of American Hebrew Congregations, and the Anti-Defamation League. Brief of the American Civil Liberties Union, Americans United for Separation of Church and State, New York Civil Liberties Union, People for the American Way, and Union of American Hebrew Congregations as Amici Curiae (filed with the Supreme Court on November 19, 1992) in *Lamb's Chapel v. Center Moriches Union Free Sch. Dist.*, 508 U.S. 384 (1993). Brief of the New York State School Boards Association, the National School Boards Association, the Anti-Defamation League, and the Committee for Public Education and Religious Liberty as Amici Curiae (filed with the Supreme Court on December 18, 1992) in *Lamb's Chapel v. Center Moriches Union Free Sch. Dist.*, 508 U.S. 384 (1993).

205. *Widmar v. Vincent*, 454 U.S. 263 (1981).

206. *Agostini v. Felton*, 521 U.S. 203 (1997).

207. Brief of the American Jewish Committee and the Christian Legal Society as Amici Curiae (filed with the U.S. Supreme Court on September 3, 1985) in *Goldman v. Weinberger*, 475 U.S. 503 (1986).

208. *Goldman v. Weinberger*, 475 U.S. 503 (1986).

209. 10 U.S.C. Section 774 (1987).

210. *Employment Division v. Smith*, 494 U.S. 872 (1990). Parry, *On Guard for Religious Liberty*, 35.

211. 42 U.S.C. Section 2000bb *et seq.* (1993).

212. *City of Boerne v. Flores*, 521 U.S. 507 (1997).

213. Anthony Picarello, Jr. and Roman Storzer, "*The Religious Land Use and Institutionalized Persons Act of 2000: A Constitutional Response to Unconstitutional Zoning Practices,*" *George Mason Law Review*. (2001): 929.

214. 42 U.S.C. Section 2000cc *et seq.* (2000).

215. Ibid.

BIBLIOGRAPHY

Books

Ahlstrom, Sidney E. *A Religious History of the American People*. New Haven, CT: Yale University Press, 1972.

Askew, Thomas A. and Richard V. Pierard. *The American Church Experience*. Grand Rapids, MI: Baker Academic, 2004.

Dolan, Jay P. *In Search of American Catholicism: A History of Religion and Culture in Tension*. Oxford, UK: Oxford University Press, 2002.

Ebersole, Luke Eugene. *Church Lobbying in the Nation's Capital*. New York: The Macmillan Company, 1951.

Eighmy, John Lee. *Churches in Cultural Captivity: A History of Social Attitudes of Southern Baptists*. Knoxville: The University of Tennessee Press, 1972.

Goldberg, J.J. *Jewish Power: Inside the American Jewish Establishment*. Reading, PA: Addison-Wesley, 1996.

Hertzke, Allen D. *Representing God in Washington: The Role of Religious Lobbies in the American Polity*. Knoxville, TN: University of Tennessee Press, 1988.

Hutchison, John A. *We Are Not Divided: A Critical and Historical Study of the Federal Council of the Churches of Christ in America*. New York: Round Table Press, 1941.

Ivers, Gregg. *To Build a Wall: American Jews and the Separation of Church and State*. Charlottesville, VA: University Press of Virginia, 1995.

Leonard, Bill J. *Baptist Ways: A History*. Valley Forge, PA: Judson Press, 2003.

Mittleman, Alan, Jonathan D. Sarna, and Robert Licht, eds. *Jewish Polity and American Civil Society: Communal Agencies and Religious Movements in the American Public Square*. Lanham, MD: Rowman and Littlefield Publishers, Inc., 2002.

Parry, Pam. *On Guard for Religious Liberty*. Macon, GA: Smyth & Helwys, 1996.

Rauschenbusch, Paul, ed. *Christianity and the Social Crisis in the 21ˢᵗ Century*. New York City: HarperCollins Publishers, 2007.

Reichley, James A. *Faith in Politics*. Washington, DC: Brookings Institution Press, 2002.

Wald, Kenneth D. and Allison Calhoun-Brown. *Religion and Politics in the United States*. Lanham, MD: Rowman and Littlefield Publishers, 2007.

Wilcox, Clyde. *Onward Christian Soldiers? The Religious Right in American Politics*. 2nd ed. Washington, DC: Georgetown University Press, 2000.

Wilson, John F, ed. *Church and State in America: A Bibliographical Guide: The Civil War to the Present Day*. New York: Greenwood Press, 1987.

Wuthnow, Robert and John Evans, eds. "The Quiet Hand of God: Faith-based Activism and the Public Role of Mainline Protestantism." Berkeley, CA: University of California Press, 2002.

Articles/Chapters

Caldwell, Alicia. "Religious Liberty Group Takes Part in Case," *St Petersburg Times*, (December 4, 2000), A8.

Green, John. "Finding a Place; in *Toward an Evangelical Public Policy: Political Strategies for the Health of the Nation*, eds. Sider, Ron J. and Diane Knippers. Grand Rapids, MI: Baker Books, 2005.

Marshall, Bill. The Constitution Under Clinton: A Critical Assessment: The Culture of Belief and the Politics of Religion, *Law & Contemp. Prob.* 63(2000): 453.

Picarello, Anthony, Jr. and Roman Storzer. The Religious Land Use and Institutionalized
    Persons Act of 2000: A Constitutional Response to Unconstitutional Zoning Practices,
    George Mason Law Review 9 (2001): 929.
Rogers, Melissa. "Federal Funding and Religion-Based Employment Decisions" in
    Sanctioning Religion? Politics, Law, and Faith-Based Social Services, eds. Ryden, David
    K. and Jeffrey Polet. Boulder, CO: Lynn Rienner Publishers, 2005.

U.S. Supreme Court Cases

Abington Township v. Schempp, 374 U.S. 203 (1963).
Bob Jones University v. United States, 461 U.S. 574 (1983).
Bowen v. Kendrick, 487 U.S. 589 (1988).
Cantwell v. Connecticut, 310 U.S. 296 (1940).
City of Boerne v. Flores, 521 U.S. 507 (1997).
City of Grand Rapids v. Ball, 473 U.S. 373 (1985).
Committee for Public Education & Religious Liberty v. Nyquist, 413 U.S. 756 (1973).
Corporation of the Presiding Bishop v. Amos, 483 U.S. 327 (1987).
Employment Division v. Smith, 494 U.S. 872 (1990).
Engel v. Vitale, 370 U.S. 421 (1962).
Epperson v. Arkansas, 393 U.S. 97 (1968).
Everson v. Board of Education, 330 U.S.1 (1947).
Goldman v. Weinberger, 475 U.S. 503 (1986).
Lamb's Chapel v. Center Moriches Union Free Sch. Dist., 508 U.S. 384 (1993).
Lee v. Weisman, 505 U.S. 577 (1992).
McCollum v. Board of Education, 333 U.S. 203 (1948).
Roe v. Wade, 410 U.S. 113 (1973).
Tilton v. Richardson, 403 U.S. 672 (1971).
Trans World Airlines v. Hardison, 432 U.S. 63 (1977)
Zorach v. Clauson, 343 U.S. 306 (1952).
Wallace v. Jaffree, 472 U.S. 38 (1985).
Walz v. Tax Comm'n, 397 U.S. 664, 670 (1970).
Widmar v. Vincent, 454 U.S. 263 (1981).
Wisconsin v. Yoder, 406 U.S. 205 (1972).

Statutes

Public Law 88-352
10 U.S.C. Section 774 (1987).
20 U.S. C. Section 4071 (1984)
42 U.S.C. Section 2000bb *et seq.* (1996).
42 U.S.C. Section 2000cc *et seq.* (2000).

Amicus Curiae Briefs Filed with the U.S. Supreme Court
Amicus briefs filed in Everson v. Board of Education, 330 U.S.1 (1947)
Brief of the General Conference of Seventh-day Adventists and the Joint Conference
    Committee on Public Relations Representing the Southern Baptist Convention, the
    Northern Baptist Convention, and the National Baptist Convention, Inc. as Amici
    Curiae (filed with the U.S. Supreme Court on October 7, 1946) in *Everson v. Board of
    Education*, 330 U.S.1 (1947).

Brief of the National Council of Catholic Men and the National Council of Catholic Women as Amici Curiae (filed with the U.S. Supreme Court on November 18, 1946) in *Everson v. Board of Education*, 330 U.S.1 (1947).

Amicus briefs filed in *McCollum v. Board of Education*, 333 U.S. 203 (1948)

Brief of the Synagogue Council of America and the National Community Relations Advisory Council as Amici Curiae (filed with the U.S. Supreme Court on November 10, 1947) in *McCollum v. Board of Education*, 333 U.S. 203 (1948).

Brief of the Joint Conference Committee on Public Relations Set Up by the Southern Baptist Convention, the Northern Baptist Convention, the National Baptist Convention, Inc., and the National Baptist Convention as Amici Curiae (filed with the U.S. Supreme Court on November 24, 1947) in *McCollum v. Board of Education*, 333 U.S. 203 (1948).

Brief of the Protestant Council of the City of New York as Amicus Curiae (filed with the U.S. Supreme Court on November 24, 1947) in *McCollum v. Board of Education*, 333 U.S. 203 (1948).

Brief of the General Conference of Seventh-day Adventists as Amicus Curiae (filed with the U.S. Supreme Court in December 1947) in *McCollum v. Board of Education*, 333 U.S. 203 (1947).

Amicus brief filed in *Zorach v. Clauson*, 343 U.S. 306 (1952)

Motion for Leave to File a Brief as Amicus Curiae by the National Council of the Churches of Christ in the USA (filed with the U.S. Supreme Court in January 5, 1952) in *Zorach v. Clauson*, 343 U.S. 306 (1952).

Brief for Appellants (filed with the U.S. Supreme Court in January 23, 1952) in *Zorach v. Clauson*, 343 U.S. 306 (1952).

Amicus briefs filed in *Engel v. Vitale*, 370 U.S. 421 (1962)

Brief of the American Jewish Committee and Anti-Defamation League of B'nai B'rith as Amici Curiae (filed with the U.S. Supreme Court on December February 28, 1962) in *Engel v. Vitale*, 370 U.S. 421 (1962).

Brief of the Synagogue Council of America and the National Community Relations Advisory Council as Amici Curiae (filed with the U.S. Supreme Court on March 22, 1962) in *Engel v. Vitale*, 370 U.S. 421 (1962).

Amicus briefs filed in *Abingdon Township v. Schempp*, 374 U.S. 203 (1963)

Brief of the American Jewish Committee and Anti-Defamation League of B'nai B'rith as Amici Curiae (filed with the U.S. Supreme Court on December 24, 1962) in *Abingdon Township v. Schempp*, 374 U.S. 203 (1963).

Brief of the Synagogue Council of America and the National Community Relations Advisory Council as Amici Curiae (filed with the U.S. Supreme Court on February 18, 1963) in *Abingdon Township v. Schempp*, 374 U.S. 203 (1963).

Amicus brief filed in *Epperson v. Arkansas*, 393 U.S. 97 (1968).

Brief of American Civil Liberties Union and American Jewish Congress as Amici Curiae (filed with the U.S. Supreme Court on May 13, 1968) in *Epperson v. Arkansas*, 393 U.S. 97 (1968).

Amicus briefs filed in *Tilton v. Richardson*, 403 U.S. 672 (1971)

Brief of the National Jewish Commission on Law and Public Affairs as Amicus Curiae (filed with the U.S. Supreme Court in 1970) in *Tilton v. Richardson*, 403 U.S. 672(1971).

Brief of Protestants and Other Americans United for Separation of Church and State as Amicus Curiae (filed with the U.S. Supreme Court on August 8, 1970) in *Tilton v. Richardson*, 403 U.S. 672(1971).

Amicus briefs filed in *Wisconsin v. Yoder*, 406 U.S. 205 (1972)

Brief of the Mennonite Central Committee as Amicus Curiae (filed with the U.S. Supreme Court in 1971) in *Wisconsin v. Yoder*, 406 U.S. 205 (1972).

Brief of the General Conference of Seventh-day Adventists as Amicus Curiae (filed with the U.S. Supreme Court on August 30, 1971) in *Wisconsin v. Yoder*, 406 U.S. 205 (1972).

Brief of the National Council of the Churches of Christ in the United States of America as Amicus Curiae (filed with the U.S. Supreme Court on September 15, 1971) in *Wisconsin v. Yoder*, 406 U.S. 205 (1972).

Brief of the Synagogue Council of America and the American Jewish Congress as Amici Curiae (filed with the U.S. Supreme Court on September 20, 1971) in *Wisconsin v. Yoder*, 406 U.S. 205 (1972).

Brief of the National Jewish Commission on Law and Public Affairs as Amicus Curiae (filed with the U.S. Supreme Court on September 20, 1971) in *Wisconsin v. Yoder*, 406 U.S. 205 (1972).

Amicus brief filed in *Committee for Public Education & Religious Liberty v. Nyquist*, 413 U.S. 756 (1973)

Brief of Baptist Joint Committee on Public Affairs as Amicus Curiae (filed with the U.S. Supreme Court on March 2, 1973) in *Committee for Public Education & Religious Liberty v. Nyquist*, 413 U.S. 756 (1973).

Brief of National Jewish Commission on Law and Public Affairs as Amicus Curiae (filed with the U.S. Supreme Court on April 16, 1973) in *Committee for Public Education & Religious Liberty v. Nyquist*, 413 U.S. 756 (1973).

Brief of the National Jewish Commission on Law and Public Affairs as Amicus Curiae (filed with the U.S. Supreme Court on April 16, 1973) in *Committee for Public Education & Religious Liberty v. Nyquist*, 413 U.S. 756 (1973).

Amicus brief filed in *Roe v. Wade*, 410 U.S. 113 (1973)

Brief of American Ethical Union, American Friends Service Committee, American Humanist Association, the American Jewish Congress, Episcopal Diocese of New York, New York State Council of Churches, Union of American Hebrew Congregations, Unitarian Universalist Association, United Church of Christ and the Board of Christian Social Concerns of the United Methodist Church as Amici Curiae (filed with the U.S. Supreme Court) in *Roe v. Wade*, 410 U.S. 113 (1973).

Amicus briefs filed in *Widmar v. Vincent*, 454 U.S. 263 (1981)

Motion of the American Jewish Congress for Leave to File Brief Amicus Curiae and Brief of the American Jewish Congress as Amicus Curiae (filed with the U.S. Supreme Court on April 13, 1981) in *Widmar v. Vincent*, 454 U.S. 263 (1981).

Brief of the United States Catholic Conference as Amicus Curiae (filed with the U.S. Supreme Court on May 29, 1981) in *Widmar v. Vincent*, 454 U.S. 263 (1981).

Motion for Leave to File Brief Amicus Curiae and Brief Amicus Curiae of Center for Constitutional Studies, National Council of Churches of Christ in the United States, National Institute for Campus Ministry, and United Ministries in Education as Amici Curiae (filed with the U.S. Supreme Court on June 1, 1981) in *Widmar v. Vincent*, 454 U.S. 263 (1981).

Motion for Leave to File Brief Amicus Curiae and Brief Amicus Curiae of the Anti-Defamation League of B'nai B'rith (filed with the U.S. Supreme Court in 1981) in *Widmar v. Vincent*, 454 U.S. 263 (1981).

Brief of the Baptist Joint Committee on Public Affairs as Amicus Curiae (filed with the U.S. Supreme Court on November 30, 1981) in *Widmar v. Vincent*, 454 U.S. 263 (1981).

Brief of the National Jewish Coalition on Law and Public Affairs as Amicus Curiae (filed
with the U.S. Supreme Court in 1981) in *Widmar v. Vincent*, 454 U.S. 263 (1981).

Amicus briefs filed in *Bob Jones University v. United States*, 461 U.S. 574 (1983)

Brief of the National Association of Evangelicals as Amicus Curiae (filed with the U.S. Supreme
Court on July 31, 1981) in *Bob Jones University v. United States*, 461 U.S. 574 (1983).

Brief of the National Committee for Amish Religious Freedom as Amicus Curiae (filed
with the U.S. Supreme Court on August 3, 1981) in *Bob Jones University v. United
States*, 461 U.S. 574 (1983).

Brief of the American Baptist Churches in the U.S.A. joined by the United Presbyterian
Church in the U.S.A. as Amici Curiae (filed with the U.S. Supreme Court on November 25, 1981) in *Bob Jones University v. United States*, 461 U.S. 574 (1983).

Brief of the Center for Law and Religious Freedom of the Christian Legal Society as
Amicus Curiae (filed with the U.S. Supreme Court on November 25, 1981) in *Bob Jones
University v. United States*, 461 U.S. 574 (1983).

Brief of the American Civil Liberties Union and the American Jewish Committee as Amici
Curiae (filed with the U.S. Supreme Court on January 5, 1982) in *Bob Jones University
v. United States*, 461 U.S. 574 (1983).

Amicus briefs filed in *City of Grand Rapids v. Ball*, 473 U.S. 373 (1985).

Brief of the National Jewish Commission on Law and Public Affairs as Amicus Curiae
(filed with the U.S. Supreme Court in 1983) in *City of Grand Rapids v. Ball*, 473 U.S.
373 (1985).

Brief of United States Catholic Conference as Amicus Curiae (filed with the U.S. Supreme
Court on May 11, 1984) in *City of Grand Rapids v. Ball*, 473 U.S. 373 (1985);

Brief of Baptist Joint Committee on Public Affairs, the National Council of Churches of
Christ in the U.S.A., and the American Jewish Committee as Amici Curiae (filed with the
U.S. Supreme Court on June 8, 1984) in *City of Grand Rapids v. Ball*, 473 U.S. 373 (1985).

Brief of Protestants and Other Americans United for Separation of Church and State as
Amicus Curiae (filed with the U.S. Supreme Court on June 11, 1984) in *City of Grand
Rapids v. Ball*, 473 U.S. 373 (1985).

Brief of American Jewish Congress on behalf of itself, the American Civil Liberties Union,
Americans for Religious Liberty, the Anti-Defamation League of B'nai B'rith, the
National Committee on Public Education and Religious Liberty, and the National
Education Association as Amici Curiae (filed with the U.S. Supreme Court on June 18,
1984) in *City of Grand Rapids v. Ball*, 473 U.S. 373 (1985).

Amicus briefs filed in *Wallace v. Jaffree*, 472 U.S. 38, 40 (1985)

Brief of the Christian Legal Society and National Association of Evangelicals as Amici
Curiae Supporting Appellants (filed with the U.S. Supreme Court on July 3, 1984) in
Wallace v. Jaffree, 472 U.S. 38, 60 (1985).

Brief of the Moral Majority as Amicus Curiae (filed with the U.S. Supreme Court on July 8,
1984) in *Wallace v. Jaffree*, 472 U.S. 38, 60 (1985).

Brief of the American Jewish Congress on Behalf of Itself and the National Jewish Community Relations Advisory Council as Amici Curiae in Support of Appellees (filed
with the U.S. Supreme Court on September 4, 1984) in *Wallace v. Jaffree*, 472 U.S. 38,
60 (1985).

Amicus briefs filed in *Aguilar v. Felton*, 473 U.S. 402 (1985)

Brief of National Jewish Commission on Law and Public Affairs as Amicus Curiae (filed
with the U.S. Supreme Court on October 15, 1984) in *Aguilar v. Felton*, 473 U.S. 402
(1985).

Brief of the United States Catholic Conference as Amicus Curiae (filed with the U.S. Supreme Court on October 15, 1984) in *Aguilar v. Felton*, 473 U.S. 402 (1985).

Brief of the Anti-Defamation League of B'nai B'rith (filed with the U.S. Supreme Court on November 15, 1984) as Amicus Curiae in *Aguilar v. Felton*, 473 U.S. 402 (1985).

Brief of the American Civil Liberties Union, the American Jewish Congress, the National Education Association, and the National Coalition for Public Education and Religious Liberty as Amici Curiae (filed with the U.S. Supreme Court on November 15, 1984) in *Aguilar v. Felton*, 473 U.S. 402 (1985).

Brief of the Anti-Defamation League of B'nai B'rith as Amicus Curiae (filed with the U.S. Supreme Court on November 15, 1984) in *Aguilar v. Felton*, 473 U.S. 402 (1985).

Brief of Americans United for Separation of Church and State as Amicus Curiae (filed with the U.S. Supreme Court on November 15, 1984) in *Aguilar v. Felton*, 473 U.S. 402 (1985).

Amicus brief filed in *Goldman v. Weinberger*, 475 U.S. 503 (1986).

Brief of the American Jewish Committee and the Christian Legal Society as Amici Curiae (filed with the U.S. Supreme Court on September 3, 1985) in *Goldman v. Weinberger*, 475 U.S. 503 (1986).

Amicus briefs filed in *Corporation of Presiding Bishop v. Amos*, 483 U.S. 327 (1987)

Brief of Concerned Women for America as Amicus Curiae (filed with the U.S. Supreme Court on December 19, 1986) in *Corporation of Presiding Bishop v. Amos*, 483 U.S. 327 (1987);

Brief of the American Jewish Congress as Amicus Curiae (filed with the U.S. Supreme Court on January 5, 1987) in *Corporation of Presiding Bishop v. Amos*, 483 U.S. 327 (1987);

Brief of the Baptist Joint Committee on Public Affairs as Amicus Curiae (filed with the U.S. Supreme Court on January 5, 1987) in *Corporation of Presiding Bishop v. Amos*, 483 U.S. 327 (1987);

Brief of the Christian Legal Society, Lutheran Church-Missouri Synod, and National Association of Evangelicals as Amici Curiae (filed with the U.S. Supreme Court on January 5, 1987) in *Corporation of Presiding Bishop v. Amos*, 483 U.S. 327 (1987);

Brief of the National Jewish Commission on Law and Public Affairs as Amicus Curiae (filed with the U.S. Supreme Court on January 5, 1987) in *Corporation of Presiding Bishop v. Amos*, 483 U.S. 327 (1987).

Brief of the Women's Legal Defense Fund, the National Council of Jewish Women, the National Coalition of American Nuns and the Institute of Women Today as Amici Curiae (filed with the U.S. Supreme Court on February 23, 1987) in *Corporation of Presiding Bishop v. Amos*, 483 U.S. 327 (1987).

Brief of the Women's Legal Defense Fund, the National Council of Jewish Women, the National Coalition of American Nuns and the Institute of Women Today as Amici Curiae (filed with the U.S. Supreme Court on February 23, 1987) in *Corporation of Presiding Bishop v. Amos*, 483 U.S. 327 (1987).

Brief of the Anti-Defamation League of B'nai B'rith as Amicus Curiae (filed with the U.S. Supreme Court on February 29, 1987) in *Corporation of Presiding Bishop v. Amos*, 483 U.S. 327 (1987).

Amicus briefs filed in Bowen v. Kendrick, 487 U.S. 589 (1988)

Brief of the National Jewish Commission on Law and Public Affairs as Amicus Curiae (filed with the U.S. Supreme Court on January 7, 1988) in *Bowen v. Kendrick*, 487 U.S. 589 (1988).

Brief of United States Catholic Conference as Amicus Curiae (filed with the U.S. Supreme Court on January 7, 1988) in *Bowen v. Kendrick*, 487 U.S. 589 (1988).

Brief of the Baptist Joint Committee on Public Affairs, the American Jewish Committee, and Americans United for Separation of Church and State as Amici Curiae (filed with the U.S. Supreme Court on February 12, 1988) in *Bowen v. Kendrick*, 487 U.S. 589 (1988).

Brief of Anti-Defamation League of B'nai B'rith on behalf of itself and Americans for Religious Liberty as Amici Curiae (filed with the U.S. Supreme Court on February 13, 1988) in *Bowen v. Kendrick*, 487 U.S. 589 (1988).

Amicus briefs filed in *Lee v. Weisman*, 505 U.S. 577 (1992)
Brief of Liberty Counsel as Amicus Curiae (filed with the U.S. Supreme Court on May 2, 1991) in *Lee v. Weisman*, 505 U.S. 577 (1992).
Brief of The Rutherford Institute as Amicus Curiae (filed with the U.S. Supreme Court on May 8, 1991) in *Lee v. Weisman*, 505 U.S. 577 (1992);
Brief of the Southern Baptist Convention Christian Life Commission as Amicus Curiae (filed with the U.S. Supreme Court on May 14, 1991) in *Lee v. Weisman*, 505 U.S. 577 (1992).
Brief of United States Catholic Conference as Amicus Curiae (filed with the U.S. Supreme Court on May 23, 1991) in *Lee v. Weisman*, 505 U.S. 577 (1992).
Brief of Concerned Women for America and Free Speech Advocates as Amicus Curiae (filed with the U.S. Supreme Court on May 24, 1991) in *Lee v. Weisman*, 505 U.S. 577 (1992).
Brief of Christian Legal Society, National Association of Evangelicals, and the Fellowship of Legislative Chaplains, Inc., as Amici Curiae (filed with the U.S. Supreme Court on May 24, 1991) in *Lee v. Weisman*, 505 U.S. 577 (1992).
Brief of Focus on the Family and Family Research Council as Amicus Curiae (filed with the U.S. Supreme Court on May 24, 1991) in *Lee v. Weisman*, 505 U.S. 577 (1992).
Brief of the American Jewish Congress, Baptist Joint Committee on Public Affairs, American Jewish Committee, National Council of Churches of Christ in the USA, Anti-defamation League of B'nai B'rith, General Conference of Seventh-day Adventists, People for the American Way, National Jewish Community Relations Advisory Council, New York Committee on Public Education and Religious Liberty, and James E. Andrews as stated clerk of the General Assembly of the Presbyterian Church (USA) as Amici Curiae (filed with the U.S. Supreme Court on July 10, 1991) in *Lee v. Weisman*, 505 U.S. 577 (1992), 48.

Amicus briefs filed in *Lamb's Chapel v. Center Moriches Union Free Sch. Dist.*, 508 U.S. 384 (1993).
Brief of the Rutherford Institute as Amicus Curiae (filed with the Supreme Court on November 12, 1992) in *Lamb's Chapel v. Center Moriches Union Free Sch. Dist.*, 508 U.S. **384 (1993)**
Brief of the National Jewish Commission on Law and Public Affairs as Amicus Curiae (filed with the Supreme Court on November 19, 1992) in *Lamb's Chapel v. Center Moriches Union Free Sch. Dist.*, 508 U.S. 384 (1993).
Brief of the American Civil Liberties Union, Americans United for Separation of Church and State, New York Civil Liberties Union, People for the American Way, and Union of American Hebrew Congregations as Amici Curiae (filed with the Supreme Court on November 19, 1992) in *Lamb's Chapel v. Center Moriches Union Free Sch. Dist.*, 508 U.S. 384 (1993).
Brief of the Concerned Women for America as Amicus Curiae (filed with the Supreme Court on November 26, 1992) in *Lamb's Chapel v. Center Moriches Union Free Sch. Dist.*, 508 U.S. 384 (1993).
Brief of the New York State School Boards Association, the National School Boards Association, the Anti-Defamation League, and the Committee for Public Education and Religious Liberty as Amici Curiae (filed with the Supreme Court on December 18, 1992) in *Lamb's Chapel v. Center Moriches Union Free Sch. Dist.*, 508 U.S. 384 (1993).

Congressional Testimony

Testimony of Richard T. Foltin, Legislative Director and Counsel, Office of Government and International Affairs of the American Jewish Committee with respect to the Workplace Religious Freedom Act (H.R. 1431) at a hearing of the House Education and Labor Subcommittee on Health, Employment, Labor and Pensions on "Protecting Americans from Workplace Discrimination," (February 12, 2008) at http://edworkforce.house.gov/testimony/2008-02-12-RichardFoltin.pdf.

Testimony of James D. Standish, Director of Legislative Affairs, Seventh-day Adventist Church World Headquarters, submitted pursuant to the request of the Subcommittee on Health, Employment, Labor and Pensions United States House of Representatives on the Workplace Religious Freedom Act (H.R. 1431) (February 12, 2008) at http://edworkforce.house.gov/testimony/2008-02-12-JamesStandish.pdf.

Statements

Program of Social Reconstruction, National Catholic War Council (February 12, 1919) website of the Office of Social Justice of the Archdiocese of St. Paul and Minneapolis. http://www.osjspm.org/majordoc_us_bishops_statements_program_of_social_reconstruction.aspx.

Vatican, *Declaration on Religious Freedom, Dignitatis Humanae, On the Right of the Person and of Communities to Social and Civil Freedom in Matters Religious, Promulgated by His Holiness, Pope Paul VI on December 7, 1965*, http://www.vatican.va/archive/hist_councils/ii_vatican_council/documents/vat-ii_decl_19651207_dignitatis-humanae_en.html.

Websites

Baptist Joint Committee for Religious Liberty, "Frequently Asked Questions," http://www.bjconline.org/about/faq.htm

Catholic Charities USA, "Who We Are," http://www.catholiccharitiesusa.org/NetCommunity/Page.aspx?pid=290&srcid=193

Catholic University of American, "An Inventory of Record of the National Catholic War Council at the American Catholic History Research Center and University Archives" http://libraries.cua.edu/achrcua/NCWarCouncil.html

Concerned Women for America, "About CWA"http://www.cwfa.org/history.asp

Friends Committee on National Legislation, "About Us: Sixty Years of Quaker Action" http://www.fcnl.org/about/

The General Board of Church and Society of the United Methodist Church, "The United Methodist Building" http://www.umc-gbcs.org/site/c.frLJK2PKLqF/b.3791391/

General Conference of Seventh-day Adventists, "Religious Liberty" http://www.adventist.org/mission_and_service/religious_liberty.html.en?&template=printer.html

Jewish Council on Public Affairs, "About the JCPA" http://www.jewishpublicaffairs.org/organizations.php3?action=printContentItem&orgid=54&typeID=1366&itemID=21761

Leadership Conference on Civil Rights, "About LCCR" http://www.civilrights.org/about/lccr/

The National Catholic Education Association, "About the National Catholic Education Association"http://www.ncea.org/about/index.asp

Religious Action Center of Reform Judaism, "About Us: History of the RAC" http://rac.org/aboutrac/rachistory/

The Rutherford Institute, "Our History"http://www.rutherford.org/About/History.asp

United States Catholic Conference of Catholic Bishops, "About Us: Brief History" http://www.usccb.org/whoweare.shtml

PART II

CONSTITUTIONAL DIMENSIONS

CHAPTER 5

CONSTITUTIONAL LANGUAGE AND JUDICIAL INTERPRETATIONS OF THE FREE EXERCISE CLAUSE

BETTE NOVIT EVANS

THE opening words of the U.S. Bill of Rights symbolize a national commitment to religious liberty: "Congress shall make no law respecting an establishment of religion, or prohibiting the free exercise thereof." Almost every word or phrase of the religion clauses has been contested, interpreted, and reinterpreted by public officials at all levels, by constitutional litigants and their lawyers, scholars, historians, advocacy groups, and individuals who believe that their religious liberty has been burdened. When disputes about the meanings of these words are not resolved by the participants in a conflict, they often end up in court, and the most significant of these may find their way to the U.S. Supreme Court, whose interpretations are taken as authoritative.

Traditionally, we have understood these words to encompass two separate guarantees. The Establishment Clause protects us against state-sponsored or imposed religious obligations, and the Free Exercise Clause protects religious expressions from state penalties. Scholars and advocates debate whether these words should be understood as one guarantee or two, and whether the word "religion" in the Establishment Clause has the same meaning as the word "thereof" in the Free Exercise Clause. Many more constitutional controversies have arisen under the former than the latter, creating endless debate about the meaning of a religious establishment, and of course, what is meant by "respecting an establishment." Although the Supreme Court hears fewer Free Exercise Clause complaints, many constitutional scholars contend that the free exercise Clause is preeminent, giving meaning and purpose to the prohibition against religious establishment.

Some scholars and advocates insist that the best interpretation of these clauses is to seek the original understanding of the men who wrote, adopted, or ratified the First Amendment. This chapter does not proceed from that assumption, but on the premise that words mean what they have come to mean over time through precedents. In this view, meanings are not captured at the moment pen was put to paper, although the original meanings inform our understanding. Nor are they so fluid that only present usage counts. Meanings continually build upon each other through precedents, so that the entire history of a constitutional phrase becomes relevant to its understanding.

The meaning of the free exercise Clause cannot be identified by seeking literal definitions of the individual words. Although the first words of the First Amendment state that "Congress shall make no law . . . ," this prohibition, like the Bill of Rights generally, encompasses all governmental actors, federal, state, or local. Moreover, the guarantee does not protect every conceivable exercise of religion, and it provides no clue about how we are to understand the word "religion." Although the words specify that Congress shall make *no* law, legislators, administrators, and judges end up balancing religious rights against other important interests. Although the language forbids governments from "prohibiting" the free exercise of religion, the clause also offers protections against a wide range of "burdens" to religious freedom, whether intentional or inadvertent. Just as the range of religions and religious practices is almost unbounded, so are the ways in which people may perceive their religious exercise to be burdened by the actions of government. Every major controversy in religion clause jurisprudence is directly traceable to a dispute over some part of the constitutional language. This chapter analyzes contemporary free exercise jurisprudence by linking each major issue to the ambiguity of constitutional language. For example, the current debate over the status of neutral laws that incidentally burden religion is rooted in different interpretations of "prohibiting" a religious exercise. Debates over exemptions from such laws stem from different interpretations of the words "no law." My analysis of these issues will not follow the order in which the words appear in the free exercise Clause, but an order that highlights the logic of constitutional arguments.

CONGRESS

The First Amendment begins with the phrase, "Congress shall make no law. . . . " Some scholars have argued that the framers of the Constitution intended these words to prohibit only acts by the federal government, leaving the states free to make any religious policies they chose. Be that as it may, for contemporary purposes, the word "Congress" does not mean Congress. Since the incorporation of the

Bill of Rights into the Fourteenth Amendment, the word "Congress" has been understood to mean any governmental actor, whether local, state, or national.[1] These include not only legislators, but also administrators, public school teachers, military commanders, tax assessors, etc. This much has been settled law for more than a half century—or so it seemed until two Establishment Clause opinions brought that understanding into question. In the mid-1980s Federal District Court Judge Brevard Hand handed down some rather idiosyncratic opinions based on the notion that the Fourteenth Amendment never should have applied to the religion clauses, and the State of Alabama should be free to establish a religion if it chooses.[2] These quickly overruled opinions would have remained a constitutional oddity but for the fact that in 2005 Supreme Court Justice Clarence Thomas hinted at the same notion in his concurring opinion in *Van Orden v. Perry*.[3] Although these specula-tions applied only to the Establishment Clause, the logic would surely encompass the Free Exercise Clause as well, in effect nullifying its effect on state actors, and returning the meaning of "Congress" to the more literal designation of national decision makers. Justice Thomas' interpretation remains an "oddity," but reminds us that even settled constitutional meanings are open to reinterpretation.

Religion: What Is It?

Because the First Amendment singles out religion for special protection, the word "religion" serves as the threshold or gatekeeper to both constitutional guarantees, but the constitutional language gives no clue about what constitutes a religion. Most of the time, this threshold is passed without controversy, but occasionally courts are asked to decide whether the claim is a genuinely *religious* one. That ques-tion puts judges in the awkward role of deciding what counts as a religion for First Amendment purposes, and what criteria to use for making the judgment.

Defining religion for purposes of the First Amendment constitutes a paradox, because no definitions are neutral. Every effort to define a religion privileges some particular kind of belief or practice and discounts others. Steven Smith has made this argument persuasively in *Foreordained Failure*.[4] And more recently, Winnifred Fallers Sullivan has used an extensive case study of the trial in *City of Boca Raton v. Warner* to demonstrate the impossibility of capturing the diversity of religious experience in any workable legal definition.[5] History is singularly unhelpful. The authors of the Bill of Rights probably had a very limited understanding of what was a legitimate religion—often excluding the beliefs and practices of American Natives, and they had little experience thinking (in Madison's phrase) of "Jews, Turks, and infidels. . . ."[6] Although we remain guided by the broad goals the First Amend-ment's authors and ratifiers, our search for an understanding of religion will take us beyond their understanding and into the contemporary contexts in which religion is experienced.

Any comprehensive conception of religion must recognize the dual nature of religious experiences. Some of its manifestations concern individual spirituality, faith, or private conscience.[7] Other religious experiences are communal, and are experienced as senses of belonging and identity created and sustained by rituals, institutions, and communities. The First Amendment must protect both of these manifestations of religion.[8] The insights of religious sociologists and anthropologists are helpful in trying to identify common characteristics of religious experiences. Although their characterizations differ in detail, they agree that religions are characterized by beliefs (usually beliefs about some transcendent or "sacred" reality), rituals (including worship, holidays, etc.), and prescriptions for living.[9] These same themes show up in judicial attempts to identify the distinguishing characteristics of religion.

Beliefs

The earliest judicial attempts to define religion emphasized belief—particularly belief in a Supreme Being. A good example is the definition offered by the Supreme Court in the Mormon case of *Davis v. Beason:*

> the term "religion" has reference to one's own views of his relations with his Creator, and to the obligations they impose of reverence for his being and character and of obedience to His will. One cannot speak of religious liberty, without proper appreciation of its essential and historical significance, without assuming the existence of a belief in supreme allegiance to the will of God.[10]

A definition that limited "religion" only to belief in a single Supreme Being would encompass only the Abrahamic religions of Judaism, Islam, and Christianity, while omitting Hinduism, Buddhism, Taoism, as well as the beliefs of many Native Americans, animists, and polytheists at the very least. By the middle of the twentieth century, the United States was becoming too religiously pluralistic for such a definition to encompass the extent of religious experience. In 1961, in *Torcaso v. Watkins*,[11] the Supreme Court recognized non-theistic religions when it struck down a Maryland law requiring that public officials affirm a belief in God. In the Court's words, ". . . neither can [government] aid those religions based on a belief in the existence of God as against those religions founded on different beliefs."[12] By the time the conscientious objection statutes were interpreted during the Vietnam War era, the Court recognized that relying on a Supreme Being definition risked violating the Establishment Clause by preferring one kind of religious experience to others.

Still, defining religion in terms of belief alone resurfaces occasionally. In 2004, a Texas tax assessor briefly made headlines by ruling that the well-established Unitarian Universalist Church was not eligible for a tax exemption because it was not a religion. Her reasoning was that the church lacked a coherent doctrine and because: "For any organization to qualify as a religion, members must have "simply a belief in God, or gods, or a higher power."[13]

In spite of such occasional throwbacks, most thinkers understand the futility of defining religion by the *content* of a belief, and focus instead on the *comprehensiveness* of a belief system. Cross-culturally, religions offer comprehensive explanations of the universe and the human role in it. Theologian Franklin Gamwell captures this insight when he observes that all religions address both metaphysical questions about the nature of reality, and normative questions about how persons should lead their lives. Thus, he defines religion as "the primary form of culture in which the comprehensive question is explicitly asked and answered. . . . "[14]

The Church of Scientology's many legal tangles provided the courts numerous occasions to reflect on legal definitions of religion. In 1969, the D.C. Circuit decided that Scientology was a religion protected by the Free Exercise Clause, in part because of the comprehensiveness of the church's doctrines, especially the fact that its "fundamental writings contain a general account of man and his nature comparable in scope, if not in content, to those of some recognized religions."[15]

On the other hand, the absence of comprehensive doctrine may disqualify a religious claim. When prisoner Frank Africa attempted to declare his allegiance to the organization MOVE to be religious so as to receive dietary accommodations in the Pennsylvania prison, the Third Circuit held that however "deep" a sincerely held belief system might be, it did not qualify as a religion if it was not sufficiently "comprehensive."[16] And in *United States v. Meyers*, the lack of comprehensive doctrines addressing ultimate questions was among the indicators used by the District Court in denying demands for religious exemptions to criminal penalties on marijuana possession.[17]

The criterion of a comprehensive belief system raises some serious problems. First, a focus on comprehensiveness alone might not distinguish religion from any comprehensive philosophical system. Any attempt by judges to make this distinction would involve judges in the wholly inappropriate role of religious censors, deciding which beliefs are genuinely "comprehensive." Furthermore, the focus on comprehensive explanations reduces religion to a totally cognitive phenomenon, excluding from First Amendment protection persons and practices we conventionally consider religious—including the kinds of folk practices Sullivan described. Such a cognitive definition might well deny First Amendment protection to those who cannot articulate profound religious philosophy.

Rather than focusing on the nature of beliefs—whether on their content or comprehensiveness—one might look to the function of beliefs in the life of the believer. This functional approach takes its inspiration from the theology of Paul Tillich, whose characterization of religion as "ultimate concern" has been immensely influential in American legal thinking.[18] Tillich's insight directs attention not on a specific content, but on the kinds of issues addressed by a putative religion and its role in the life of the believer. Tillich defines religion, most simply, as that which concerns "the depth of your life, the source of your being, or your ultimate concern, or what you take most seriously, without reservation." Judges applying Tillich's approach in religious disputes look to the depth of a person's motivations as the defining characteristic of his putative religiosity. This was the approach the Supreme Court used in the Vietnam–era conscientious objector cases, which greatly broadened the concept of religion.

Congress has long granted conscientious objection exemptions from compulsory military service for persons with religious objections to war. To invoke this exemption, one must be able to show that his or her objection is a genuinely *religious* one. In *United States v. Kauten*, a 1943 conscientious objection case that foreshadowed those of a generation later, the Second Circuit used functional language in granting conscientious objector status to a religious dissenter.

> [Conscientious objection] may justly be regarded as a response of the individual to an inward mentor, call it conscience or God, that is for many persons at the present time the equivalent of what has always been thought of as an religious impulse.[19]

This decision provided a precedent for replacing theistic definitions of religion when the Court confronted the Vietnam–era conscientious objector cases. The opinions in these cases represent the most dramatic departure from traditional content-based definitions, and the clearest examples of functional ones. In the three cases that were combined in *U.S. v. Seeger*, the Court was asked to interpret a provision of the Selective Service Act that exempted from combat any person

> who, by reason of religious training and belief, is conscientiously opposed to participation in war in any form. Religious training and belief in this connection means an individual's belief in relation to a Supreme Being, involving duties superior to those arising from any human relation, but does not include essentially political sociological, or philosophical views or a merely personal moral code.[20]

Congress had explicitly used the term "Supreme Being" in defining religious belief, but the courts were aware, in the post-*Torcaso* era, that this kind of preference for one kind of religion risked violating the Establishment Clause. In one of the significant early Vietnam–era cases under this law, the trial judge constructed a very expansive reading of the statutory language. In *U.S. v. Jakobson*,[21] Judge Henry Jacob Friendly explicitly relied on Tillich's *Systematic Theology* to find that the applicants met the Supreme Being test, even though he referred to a belief in "Goodness" rather than God. This case was one of several that were combined in the landmark *Seeger* case. Seeger himself had given ambiguous answers to questions about his religion in his application for conscientious objector status, which left the Court in an awkward position. To deny his application would have limited "religion" to a belief in a Supreme Being—something difficult to do in light of *Torcaso*. Furthermore, to interpret the statute literally would have risked a violation of the Establishment Clause by granting a privilege for one kind of religious belief and denying it to others. Striking down the Selective Service Act as an Establishment Clause violation was a result no one wanted. The Court's solution was to "reinterpret" the statute, stretching the definition of religion so as to grant Seeger's application. The Court concluded that

> ... Congress, in using the expression "Supreme Being" rather than the designa-
> tion "God;" was merely clarifying the meaning of religious training and belief so
> as to embrace all religions. . . . [T]he test of belief 'in relation to a Supreme Being'
> is whether a given belief that is sincere and meaningful occupies a place in the life
> of its possessor parallel to that filled by the orthodox belief in God of one who
> clearly qualifies for the exemption.[22]

Justice Clark's opinion quoted Tillich's work, *The Shaking of the Foundation*, which defined religion as "the source of your being, of your ultimate concern, of what you take seriously without reservation."[23] Thus, the Court expanded religious exemptions from military service to persons whose moral and philosophical beliefs served for them the same *function* as the belief in God did for traditional religious believers. Seven years later, in *U.S. v. Welsh*, the Court continued this expansion, granting conscientious objector status to one who unambiguously rejected labeling his motivations as "religious":

> if an individual deeply and sincerely holds beliefs which are purely ethical or
> moral in source and content but that nevertheless impose upon him a duty of
> conscience to refrain from participation in any war at any time, those beliefs
> certainly occupy in the life of that individual a place parallel to that filled [by]
> God in traditionally religious persons.[24]

Although the *Seeger* and *Welsh* cases were important expansions of First Amendment protection, a definition of religion that included anyone's ultimate concern or anything that functions parallel to a belief in God, raises embarrassing problems for the judicial process. Ought judges to probe what is of "ultimate concern" to a complainant? Moreover, as Kent Greenawalt has observed, most individuals may simply not lexically order their motivations, and hence do not have "ultimate concerns."[25] Likely, "ultimate concerns" are not at the heart of religious experience for many people. Consider Jews who might "religiously" observe the laws of *kashrut* or Christians who might accept communion without ever pondering the profound teachings that these practices dramatize for theologians. Very likely, reflections on ultimate concerns, such as the nature of life and death or the grounding of morality, are simply less important to many conventionally religious persons than observing church teachings or participating in communal rituals. Hence, defining religion in terms of ultimate concerns could disadvantage religions or religious persons for whom *doing* or *being, as* opposed to *reflecting*, is at the heart of the religious experience.

Because a genuinely *religious* claim is the threshold to free exercise protection, judges are sometimes faced with the problem of judging the sincerity of a person's religious claims. Laws that provide exemptions from ordinary requirements to pro-tect religious behavior can tempt persons to make "strategic" religious claims; they might seek to shield nonreligious behavior under the umbrella of religious protection so as to gain advantages. Tax benefits and freedom from administrative regulation provide temptations for insincere religious claims, making investigation into the claimant's sincerity necessary. Conflicts over sincerity have occurred in a variety of other contexts, including attempts by draftees to obtain religious exemptions from military service, attempts by prisoners to seek recognition of novel religions in prisons, and cases brought by employees seeking religious accommodation in the workplace. Nontraditional ministries, especially those that actively seek financial contributions, raise continual problems about the distinction between religious fervor and fraud.[26]

The most important and sophisticated attempt by the Supreme Court to wrestle with religious sincerity came in the 1944 fraud conviction case of *United States v. Ballard*.[27] After experiencing a mystical revelation in 1930, Guy Ballard and his family founded a religious movement to propagate the supernatural messages he had received. After his death, his wife and son were indicted for mail fraud, specifically for making false claims (especially the power to heal) that "they well knew" were false. The trial judge was sensitive to the difficulty of judging religious beliefs, and separated the question of the truth of the Ballards' religious beliefs from their sincerity. When the case reached the Supreme Court, the Court was confronted for the first time with how to handle conflicts over veracity and sincerity of religious belief.

The Supreme Court split three ways: Three justices concluded that the veracity of religious claims could be considered by courts, and would have punished the Ballards for making false claims. Justice Douglas, writing for the majority, sustained the Ballards' mail fraud conviction, upholding both the trial judge's distinction between veracity and sincerity and his instruction that the jury consider only the sincerity of his claims, but not their veracity. Dissenting Justice Jackson argued that veracity and sincerity are inseparable, and both should be beyond the ken of the judiciary.

When a person's religious sincerity is in dispute, courts must confront evidence for ascertaining sincerity or its absence. Disregard for one's own teachings is evidence of insincerity. In addition, commercial or other self-serving motives, evidence of criminal behavior, and frivolity have provided evidence of insincerity. On the other hand, willingness to sacrifice for one's beliefs and longstanding commitment, especially to institutional groups who share one's faith, help to establish sincerity.

Conflicts involving the Church of Scientology exemplify the problem of distinguishing religious sincerity from commercial motives. Among Scientology's legal challenges were several civil suits brought against the church by former adherents for fraudulent misrepresentation of the benefits it offered. In *Van Schaick v. Church of Scientology*,[28] for example, plaintiffs in a fraud claim argued both that Scientology was not really a religion, and that its agents were not sincere in their profession of beliefs, but had commercial motives. These charges forced courts to consider not only the truth of that claim, but the more serious question of whether the religious sincerity and motivations of Scientology's founders was even relevant at all. Moreover, it raised an ancillary issue: How does one prove the sincerity or insincerity of an *institution*? Unlike *Ballard*, which turned on the sincerity of individuals, this case raised the problem of judging *institutional* motivations.

Conflicts between religious practices and narcotics laws are another source of disputes about religious sincerity.[29] In *U.S. v. Kuch*,[30] the evidence of insincerity was frivolity; here the District Court upheld the conviction for illegal marijuana possession and transportation against a primate of the New American Church who claimed that marijuana and LSD were sacraments of her church, and therefore protected by the First Amendment. Examining church documents, the Court found no belief in a Supreme Being, no religious discipline, ritual, or tenets to guide daily existence, and in general "goofy nonsense."

Although "goofy nonsense" may disqualify a claim to religious sincerity, a person making a religious claim need not be theologically sophisticated. Although faiths that are grounded in recognized religious groups have an easier time demonstrating their sincerity, neither individually held faiths,[31] nor disagreement with other members of one's faith,[32] are appropriate grounds for courts to reject the sincerity of one's religious motivations. Although obvious hypocrisy and cynicism may call one's sincerity into question, occasional lapses in consistency do not impugn one's sincerity. Courts may also inquire into the origins of beliefs (religious training, for example) to provide evidence of sincerity, but recently adopted faiths are fully protected.[33]

Codes, Conscience, and Religious Commands

Religions posit not just that an external reality exists, but that it imposes *duties* on human beings that are "higher" or more authoritative than the duties humans set for each other. It is not just belief in the existence of a transcendent reality that makes religion special; it is the belief that the other reality impinges on the human in a certain way. In short, religions impose obligations of conscience. James Madison's earliest drafts of the First Amendment religion clauses had proposed the words "freedom of conscience."[34] Further, Madison's *Memorial and Remonstrance against Religious Assessments* defined religion as "the duty we owe to our Creator."[35]

Madison's emphasis on duties or obligations of conscience has been one of the major conceptions for defining religion.[36] In fact, many contemporary constitutional thinkers understand burdens to religious conscience as the heart of both religion clauses.[37] This insight shifts our focus from the cognitive content of the belief to the fact that it is both prescriptive and authoritative. In sociologist Milton Yinger's words, "it is not the nature of *belief*, but the nature of *believing* that requires our study."[38]

Michael Sandel's powerful free exercise critique puts obligation, rather than freedom of choice, at the heart of the clause. Sandel argues that most people do not experience their religious practices as choices, but as *commands* or *obligations*.[39] Indeed, if religious practices were matters of choice, the reasons for protecting them would be far less powerful; it is their obligatory character that makes their protection so compelling.

The focus on conscience as the defining quality of religion raises what would have solved the problems of how to distinguish religious from nonreligious commands of conscience in the Vietnam–era conscientious objector cases. Perhaps, as Phillip Hammond has argued, there are none; in his view, the Free Exercise Clause ought to be understood as protecting individual conscience, whether based on institutionalized religions or not.[40] The protection of conscience is a very attractive way to understand the Free Exercise Clause, but it falls short of encompassing the full range of religious experiences because it would protect only those acts that are perceived as religious commands. Acts of government that do not require a person to violate her religious conscience would not be seen as free exercise violations, no matter how damaging they might be in other ways. In *Lyng v. Northwest Indian Cemetery Protective Association*, the destruction of Native American sacred lands did not literally require any individual to do something that his or her religion forbade.[41] Nor did paying a sales tax on religious items violate the religious obligation of Bible sellers; hence, the Court found no constitutional violation.[42]

To reduce religion to a body of commands leaves no protection for many of people's most meaningful ways of participating in the religious life of their communities—celebrating holidays, teaching Sunday School, and singing in the church choir, to name only a few common examples. Furthermore, a conscience-based definition could also have disastrous effects if applied to Establishment Clause controversies, although several judges have seen the coercion of conscience as the defining harm of establishment.[43] Public religious symbols, voluntary school prayers, and public support for religious schools do not require anyone to violate the commands of conscience, but infringe the Establishment Clause in other ways. Defining religion solely in terms of obligations of conscience would greatly constrict our understanding of both religion clauses.

Behavioral Indicators of Religion

Defining religion either in terms of beliefs or obligations entails major shortcomings. Both implicitly understand religion as an individual phenomenon—an internal state of mind for which courts lack empirical evidence. Not surprisingly, then, judges have attempted to identify religion by observable behaviors, including the collective practices of religious communities; for example, worship services and other rituals; institutionalized ways of propagating the faith to future generations; clergy, or some other form of teaching or leadership; and festivals and holidays or life-cycle events. These definitions approach religion as a collective phenomenon. Although theoretically a court could grant First Amendment protection to an individual who claims a personal religion not shared by others, I know of no decision that has done so. Indeed, the less institutionalized the collective practices of a group that claims to be religious, the less likely it is to receive First Amendment protection.

The foundational thinker of religious sociology, Emile Durkheim, captured this quality in his definition of religion: "A religion is a unified system of beliefs and practices relative to things sacred . . . beliefs and practices which unite into a single moral community called a Church all those who adhere to them."[44] For Durkheim, the sense of the sacred is essentially a communal and institutional one: "In all history, we do not find a single religion without a Church."[45] Like most contemporary sociologists, Milton Yinger defines religion by emphasizing its social nature:

> Religion, then, can be defined as a system of beliefs and practices by means of which *a group of people* struggles with these ultimate problems of human life.[46]

These insights have led some legal thinkers to focus on a family of characteristics, rather than a single essential element, in identifying a religion. Of course, not every religion or individual religious person partakes of every one of these characteristics. Some conventionally religious persons are almost totally ignorant of the doctrine of their faith, or unburdened by its moral commandments; others may partake in the spiritual life of their faith and ignore its communal manifestations. Still, taken in various combinations, these indicators help identify a wide range of religious phenomena.[47]

Judge Arlin Adams' use of this method in *Malnak v. Yogi* is considered a breakthrough in religion clause jurisprudence. In this Establishment Clause case, a public school program teaching the techniques of transcendental meditation was challenged as state inculcation of a religion. Proponents of the program denied that transcendental meditation was a religion; the Third Circuit concluded that it was. Judge Adams' concurring opinion defines religion with reference to three "indicia": the content of ideas that address "fundamental questions" of ultimate concerns, the claim to "an ultimate and comprehensive truth," and external manifestations such as formal services, ceremonial functions, clergy, efforts and propagation, etc.[48]

Several years after developing this test, Judge Adams had the opportunity to use it again, in considering a prisoner's petition for dietary accommodation of his religion. The threshold question was whether the movement on which he based his claims was a genuinely religious one. Judge Adams considered observable indicators and concluded that the organization was not a religion because its beliefs were not comprehensive and it lacked "formal services, ceremonial functions, the existence of clergy, structure and organization, efforts at propagation, observance of holidays, and other similar manifestations associated with traditional religions."[49] This approach places more weight on the social and institutional practices than on the conscience of believers, thus denying accommodation because the judges found the claimant's theology shallow and poorly articulated, and his "religion" lacked churches, holidays, and clergy.

The most elaborate attempt to identify a family of indicators was used by a U.S. District Court in *U.S. v. Meyers* (1995), in which a man convicted of marijuana possession and distribution claimed an exemption from drug laws because marijuana was at the heart of his religion.[50] Taking his claim seriously, the District Court used the following indicators to compare the "Church of Marijuana" to a general understanding of religion. His list of indicators includes:

1. Ultimate Ideas
2. Metaphysical Beliefs
3. Moral or Ethical System
4. Comprehensiveness of Beliefs
5. Accoutrements of Religion, including:
   a. Founder, Prophet, or Teacher
   b. Important Writings
   c. Gathering Places
   d. Keepers of Knowledge
   e. Ceremonies and Rituals
   f. Structure or Organization
   g. Holidays
   h. Diet or Fasting
   i. Appearance and Clothing
   j. Propagation

The District Court emphasized that "it cannot rely solely on established or recognized religions to guide it in determining whether a new and unique set of beliefs warrants inclusion" and that "no one of these factors is dispositive, and that the factors should be seen as criteria that, if minimally satisfied, counsel the inclusion of beliefs within the term 'religion.'"

The U.S. Internal Revenue Service often uses its own list of indicators for identifying religions:[51]

1. A Distinctive Legal Existence
2. A Recognized Creed and Form of Worship
3. A Definite and Distinct Ecclesiastical of Government
4. A Formal Code of Doctrine and Discipline
5. A Distinct Religious History
6. A Membership Not Associated with Any Other Church or Denomination
7. A Complete Organization of Ordained Ministers Ministering to Their Congregations and Selected After Completing Prescribed Courses of Study
8. A Literature of Its Own
9. Established Places of Worship
10. Regular Congregations
11. Regular Religious Services

12. Sunday Schools for the Religious Instruction of the Young
13. Schools for the Preparation of Its Ministers

Any application of these indicia that assumes all of them necessary for the existence of a religion would exclude religions lacking in formal structures. Still, this approach is promising because it recognizes both the individual and collective aspects of religion and provides a practical solution to the concrete problems judges most often confront. Most importantly, it avoids the necessity of a single, essentialist definition of religion, enabling a judge to focus specifically on the aspect of religion most relevant to the particular dispute. Thus, when a person claims that a law has violated his or her religious conscience, the nature of those beliefs is critical. When the dispute turns on whether an *organization* is religious, corporate activities become more relevant to the inquiry.

Free Exercise of

Constitutional observers often remind us that the First Amendment does not protect "religion" in the abstract, but the *exercise* of religion. But identifying a religious exercise proves to be even more difficult than attempting to define religion. The scope of religiously motivated behaviors is virtually incalculable. Religious codes dictate a variety of means by which people worship: kneeling, standing, eating, fasting, ingesting alcoholic beverages or hallucinogenic drugs, making symbolic sacrifices or sacrificing live animals, covering or uncovering their heads or feet in houses of worship, singing, meditating, chanting, preaching, and speaking in tongues, to name only a few. Religions frequently mandate certain kinds of personal care, including bathing, hygiene, dressing, health care, diet, and hair style. Religious mandates cover comportment in the world at large in such areas as social responsibility, education, child rearing, relations between the sexes, medical practices, appropriate employment, financial decisions, and countless other aspects of life. Religious practices include ceremonial activities performed in religious institutions and secular practices motivated by religious faith—both obligatory and optional practices, practices sanctioned by recognized churches and those based upon individual conscience, as well as the folk practices of religious communities. And to add further complications, free exercise protection also covers the actions of religions institutions—including financial management, employment practices, social services, zoning, and architecture.

Given the scope of both religious practices and the regulatory state, clashes between them are almost inevitable. One way to manage the problem of endless conflicts would be to limit the free exercise protection to practices that are central to the core doctrines or a faith. Such attempts proved unsuccessful, but raised extremely important issues.

Centrality: A False Start

Because of the intractability of reconciling an almost infinite variety of religious exercises with an equally extensive range of governmental regulations, some thinkers suggested simplifying the problem by extending First Amendment protection only to the central tenets and practices of a religion.[52] Judges have occasionally experimented with the concept of "centrality"; the more central the practice to the religion, the more constitutional protection it merited. There is a persuasive plausibility to this approach. Surely a core religious act—the sacrifice of the Eucharist—deserves more protection than an optional one that some members feel religiously encouraged to perform. Courts have sometimes asked for evidence about the centrality of the practice to the religious life of the person or group making a free exercise claim. But judging the centrality of a practice to religion is always tenuously close to evaluating religious doctrine. In Justice Scalia's words, "What principle of law or logic can be brought to bear to contradict a believer's assertion that a particular act is 'central' to his personal faith? Judging the centrality of different religious practices is akin to the unacceptable business of evaluating the relative merits of differing religious claims. . . . It is not within our judicial ken to question the centrality of particular beliefs or practices to a faith."[53]

Because few religions provide lexical lists of required or prohibited practices, it is not at all clear how crucial a challenged practice may be. How "central" is it for Jewish men or Muslim women to keep their heads covered? Was polygamy once central to Mormon belief? Was the objection to secular education for teenagers central to the Amish faith, or merely a strategy for protecting the religious subculture?

Moreover, the search for centrality comes perilously close to assuming that, at its core, religions consist of a body of required practices or rules, and hence fails to appreciate the social and communal aspects of religious life. Singing in a church choir may not be central to any religious belief system, but it may be precisely the activity that links an individual believer to a religious community.

Because of these difficulties, the courts have abandoned attempts to judge centrality in recent years. Justice O'Connor defended this refusal at some length in *Lyng v. Northwest Indian Cemetery Protective Association*, against the dissenters' arguments to retain it:

> [T]he dissent proposes a legal test under which it would decide which public lands are "central" or "dispensable" to which religions . . . and would then decide which government programs are "compelling" enough to justify infringement of those practices. . . . We would accordingly be required to weigh the value of every religious belief and practice that it said would be threatened by any government program. Unless a "showing of centrality" . . . is nothing but an assertion of centrality, . . . the dissent thus offers us the prospect of this court holding that some sincerely held religious beliefs and practices are not "central" to certain

religions, despite protestations to the contrary from the religious objectors who brought the lawsuit. In other words, the dissent's approach would require us to rule that some religious adherents misunderstood their own religious beliefs. We think such an approach cannot be squared with the Constitution.[54]

Although the centrality concept was problematic, abandoning it has permitted the Court to uphold laws that had devastating effects on practices that were indispensably central to a religion. Indeed, in *Lyng*, the devastating effect of the governmental road-building project was stipulated and beyond dispute. And in *Smith*, the majority upheld a prohibition on a core religious ritual without considering its centrality.

The Range of Religious Exercises

Abandoning the search for centrality has not relieved courts of the need to identify religious exercises and occasionally distinguish them from other activities. One way to think about the range of religious practices is to notice the contexts in which they occur: worship practices, religious mandates concerning personal care, religiously motivated practices diffused through the general culture, and institutional practices.

Worship practices include individual acts of spirituality, but more often, they occur in a communal setting in a specific location designated for that purpose. Likely these were the kinds of religious practices that most concerned the Constitution's founding generation. Because worship activities are mostly confined both in location and impact to willing participants, their impact on the wider community is circumscribed. Nevertheless, they have occasionally been the source of constitutional controversies. Examples include local prohibitions on the snake handling practices of Holiness Churches,[55] laws against the use[56] and importation[57] of hallucinogenic substances used in religious rituals, and laws against animal sacrifice.[58] In addition, controversies over freedom of worship have been raised within the special settings of prisons[59] and the U.S. military.

Another context for religious exercise encompasses religious mandates concerning the body and its care—dietary and cleanliness practices; religiously mandated health care; clothing, hair, and other appearance requirements or prohibitions; and the like. Many of these activities implicate constitutional privacy protections in addition to those of the Free Exercise Clause. Often these practices are crucial to people's religious identities: braids for Native Americans, head coverings and dietary restrictions for Jews and Muslims, and health practices of Christian Scientists have become the identifying symbols of religious identity. However, unlike worship practices, which are usually confined to specific settings, these activities are carried on in a variety of settings, in which opportunities for conflicts with state interests increase. Even on such a compelling public interest as vaccinations for communicable diseases, all but two states provide exemptions for persons with religious objections to them.

Conflicts regarding health practices still arise when Jehovah's Witnesses refuse blood transfusions for themselves and their children and when Christian Scientists refuse medical care. Other personal care conflicts concern orthodox Jews' and Muslims' insistence of head coverings, sweat baths for Native Americans, hair and beard requirements for Native Americans and Sikhs, and Orthodox Jews' refusal of autopsies. One example illustrates many: In 2006, a Florida appeals court upheld a ruling that a Muslim woman forego her *niquib* (face covering) on her driver's license identification photograph, holding that security of identification was sufficient to outweigh her religious objections, and therefore did not violate Florida's Religious Freedom Restoration Act.[60]

The most problematic kinds of religious activities are those that are conducted in society at large, and often in the idiom of the wider society. When religious individuals and institutions operate within the idiom of the broader culture, the opportunities for conflict grow and the interests of the state become more numerous. Here, the religious adherent is operating in multiple roles, including both citizen and religious observer.[61]

Religious practices in the workplace exemplify these kinds of role conflicts. Conflicts over the rights of religious employees often implicate not only the Free Exercise Clause, but also the 1964 Civil Rights Act with its mandates concerning religious accommodation by employers. Four of the most significant free exercise cases on unemployment compensation have protected the rights of members of religious minorities in the workplace.[62] In addition, religious employers and landlords also have asserted rights to conduct their businesses according to the demands of conscience.[63]

Finally, we must recall that many religious exercises are institutional and that religious institutions *as institutions* have First Amendment rights that protect them when their roles as employers, financial managers, providers of social services, etc. are manifestations of their religion.[64] Even before courts began to recognize religious institutional autonomy as a right in itself, judges were sensitive to the dangers of entanglement between church and state. The danger of entanglement was part of the Court's reasoning in 1970 in *Walz v. Tax Commission*, when the Supreme Court upheld tax exemptions for churches from an Establishment Clause challenge.[65] And when asked to intervene in internal church disputes, the Court developed "neutral principles" to avoid making judgments on doctrines, and deferring to internal decision-making procedures of religious institutions themselves. When the church itself provides an authority or a mechanism to resolve property disputes, courts must defer to that body—hence, insulating the autonomy of the church from judicial inquiry. The task of the courts is only to ascertain the appropriate decision-making structure of the church, and then withdraw itself from further consideration.[66]

The first strong statement of religious institutional autonomy was the 1973 decision in *National Labor Relations Board v. Catholic Bishop of Chicago*.[67] The diocese had refused to recognize and bargain in good faith with the teachers' union of the Chicago Catholic school system, which had been recognized by the NLRB. The diocese argued that submitting itself to NLRB jurisdiction would interfere with ecclesiastical control of a religious institution, and thus violate its First Amendment rights. The Supreme Court, expressing concern for church–state entanglement, agreed on statutory rather than constitutional grounds and held that the diocese was exempt from NLRB coverage. The justices accepted the church's argument that NLRB involvement in collective bargaining might impinge on church governance in matters of curriculum and religious doctrines.

Antidiscrimination laws are a frequent source of conflict between government and religious institutions. When churches profess racial separation as a matter of conscience, are they free to discriminate in ways that otherwise would violate federal law? The most celebrated of such cases arose when the Internal Revenue Service disallowed tax deductions for contributions to Bob Jones University because of its prohibitions against interracial dating. In a closely divided decision, the U.S. Supreme Court upheld the IRS policy on the grounds that the nation's commitment to racial equality is sufficiently important to override the school's religious claims, at least for the governmental *privilege* of a tax deduction.[68] However, statutory exemptions protect religious institutions from antidiscrimination laws for employees performing religious functions.[69]

Religious discrimination was at the heart of the dispute in *Corporation of the Presiding Bishop of the Church of Jesus Christ of Latter-Day Saints v. Amos* in 1987.[70] The church, acting as employer, and relying on the 1972 exemption for religious employers, had terminated as a custodian in a church-owned gymnasium, when he failed to remain a member in good standing of the church. Amos challenged his dismissal, as well as the exemption itself. This case raised important threshold questions, including whether a nonprofit gymnasium owned by a church is a religious institution and whether a custodian is performing a religious function.[71] In ruling in favor of the church, the Court suggested that fine distinctions between religious and nonreligious activities were inappropriate for government, and ought to be made only by the religious institution in question. The threshold question— whether an activity of a church is a religious activity—is a distinction reserved for the institution alone. Thus, it left determination of what was a religious function up to the church, reasoning that deference to the religion's own judgment is necessary to prevent courts from second-guessing religious doctrine.

An important conflict between religious institutions and secular law was decided by California's Supreme Court in 2004. California law requires all employers who offer prescription drug coverage benefits to employees to include coverage for contraceptives.[72] Because the Catholic Church holds contraception to be a "grave sin," Catholic Charities of Sacramento challenged the law on First Amendment grounds, arguing that the law presented it with the dilemma of either refusing to provide health insurance coverage for its employees or facilitating the sin of contraception, both of which violate its religious beliefs. The State Supreme Court found the state's interest in public health compelling, and ruled that the law was neither targeted nor discriminatory, that it did not compromise the church's autonomy, did not violate the Free Exercise Clause, and concluded that Catholic Charities was not entitled to an exemption.[73]

Conflicts between religious institutions and zoning ordinances are a final example of religious institutional conflict. In fact, zoning was at the heart of the case in which the Supreme Court struck down the 1993 federal Religious Freedom Restoration Act. The dispute began in 1993 when Saint Peter Church in Boerne, Texas applied for a building permit to enlarge its church building. Because the church was located in an area that had recently been designated as a historic district, the permit was denied. The church challenged the denial as a violation of the Religious Freedom Restoration Act, which forbids government from burdening religious exercise unless the burden is the least restrictive means of furthering a compelling governmental interest. When the case reached the Supreme Court, the justices not only denied the church's petition, but used the case to strike down the RFRA itself—a topic we will consider in the next section.[74]

Zoning conflicts involving churches seem to arise with increasing regularity, including disputes over parking and congestion, or aspects of church architecture such as steeples, or over the use of church property for "accessory" purposes such as homeless shelters.[75] The 1997 Religious Land Use and Institutionalized Persons Act tips the scales in favor of religious institutions in these cases by requiring that land use policies that restrict religious rights be justified by a compelling state interest.

No Law *PROHIBITING . . .*

The First Amendment provides that Congress shall pass no law "prohibiting" the free exercise of religion. To "prohibit" a religious exercise—making it a crime or subject to a civil penalty—is indeed a very serious infringement on religious liberty, but it is only one of the ways in which liberty may be trammeled. At least since *Sherbert v. Verner* (1963),[76] the Court has considered First Amendment issues invoked when religious exercise is *burdened*. In effect, the word "prohibiting" has come to mean "burdening;" thus the showing of a burden to religion is the threshold to free exercise protection. But what constitutes a burden and how serious must it be to present a constitutionally cognizable problem? How can we distinguish a major impediment to religion from a *de minimus* annoyance?

Harms to religious freedom are experienced in a variety of ways. Every understanding of burdens on religion implies its own view of what religion is and why it is important.[77] Some laws literally prohibit a religious exercise; some condition government benefits on behavior inconsistent with religion; others make a religious practice impossible. Some penalties or burdens on religious exercise are intentionally targeted at religious practices, but most are unintended burdens created when otherwise valid secular laws have the effect of burdening a religious practice. The difference may have great constitutional significance.

Penalties on Religious Acts

The most obvious burdens on religious freedom are those that literally prohibit a religious exercise. The very first free exercise case heard by the U.S. Supreme Court, *Reynolds v. United States*,[78] was of this nature. Congress had specifically outlawed polygamy, a tenet of the Church of Latter-day Saints, and the Court had no trouble upholding the law. Criminal penalties on religious practices—especially worship practices such as snake handling, peyote ingestion, and sacrifice—seem particularly egregious because they violate the most literal reading of the First Amendment. Laws authorizing civil damages have the same effect as criminal penalties. Civil penalties against "cults" for their recruiting practices in the 1980s illustrate this kind of burden.[79]

The 1990 *Smith* case illustrates some of the complexities of laws penalizing religious practices.[80] Because criminal penalties literally "prohibit" religious exercises, one might think such laws would be the most suspect. Oddly, however, Justice Scalia's majority opinion in *Smith* treats criminal laws as *least* likely to require accommodation. Even odder, the *Smith* majority treated what appeared to be an ordinary unemployment compensation dispute as a criminal case so as |to reach that conclusion. The very ambiguity of the legal issues provided the justices opportunities to reflect on the particular problems of criminal penalties against religious practices.

Recall briefly the situation: Smith and Black had been terminated from their jobs for using peyote during a ceremony of the Native American Church; their request for unemployment compensation was denied because they were fired for "job-related" wrongdoing. They appealed the denial, and both the appellate court and Oregon Supreme Court ruled that religious exercises could not be considered misconduct for purposes of denying state benefits. The criminal law was irrelevant at this point.

The U.S. Supreme Court vacated the state decisions, and remanded the case to the Oregon courts to determine whether state law prohibited sacramental peyote use. The Supreme Court reasoned that if a state could punish an act by criminal law, it could justify the lesser penalty of denying benefits. It is important to recall that *Smith* itself was not a criminal case. Neither Smith nor Black—nor anyone else—had been prosecuted in Oregon for peyote use in a religious ritual.

On remand, the Oregon Supreme Court concluded that (unlike 23 other states and the federal government) Oregon law "makes no exception for the sacramental use," but also noted that if the state should ever attempt to enforce the law against religious practice, that prosecution would violate the Free Exercise Clause. Hence, in the state court's view, the existence of the criminal law was irrelevant to the unemployment compensation issue. The U.S. Supreme Court again granted *certiorari*. In April 1990 it overturned Oregon's judgment that the application of the criminal statute to religious practices would be unconstitutional. The specific question before the Court in *Smith* was the denial of unemployment compensation for engaging in a religious ritual. The precedents requiring unemployment compensation when religious acts have led to job termination were too consistent to explain away. The only distinguishing factor in this case was the existence of a criminal law prohibiting peyote use. For the majority, the existence of the criminal statute distinguished *Smith* from the preceding cases. Consequently, the majority treated this as a criminal penalty case—although Oregon's highest court had twice ruled that the criminal penalty was irrelevant to Smith and Black's right to unemployment compensation, because a state criminal penalty on a religious observance would violate the Free Exercise Clause. Both Justice Blackmun's dissent and many critics have pointed out that the majority was thus ruling on a purely hypothetical issue— and resting a major constitutional ruling on an issue that had never arisen, and that the highest state court had ruled to be irrelevant. In short, the Court treated a case that was explicitly about the denial of benefits as though it were a penalty case.

A second penalty case quickly followed *Smith*, arising from a local ordinance specifically prohibiting animal sacrifices in religious rituals. The Afro-Caribbean religion known as Santeria worships its deities and celebrates life cycle events by offering sacrifices of chickens, goats, and other animals. When a congregation in Hialeah, Florida announced plans to open a church, the city council adopted a resolution that declared the city's commitment to prohibiting acts by religious groups "inconsistent with public morals, peace and safety." The council then adopted a number of resolutions prohibiting animal sacrifice, and the possession of animals intended for ritual sacrifice, but exempting virtually all other kinds of animal killing.

When the case reached the Supreme Court, the justices unanimously struck down the ordinances. Because there was no question that the ordinances prohibited a form of worship, the only question was whether the prohibition could be justified. Hialeah attempted to justify the ordinance as a public health measure, whereas the church characterized it as religious discrimination—the kind of laws that the *Smith* majority 3 years previously had declared to be prototypical free exercise violations. The decision in favor of the church was unanimous, largely because the ordinance so obviously targeted a specific religion and its practices.

Denial of Benefits

Far more common than outright prohibitions are denials of government benefits resulting from some aspect of religion. Typically in these instances, a government benefit is conditioned on foregoing some aspect of a religious practice. The landmark case on unconstitutional conditions of governmental benefits was a problem of this kind. Adelle Sherbert, a Seventh-day Adventist, was unable to continue her employment at a South Carolina textile mill when Saturday work became required.[81] She was terminated for refusing to work on Saturday, and denied unemployment compensation because her termination was viewed as voluntary. Typical regulations deny such benefits to persons who have quit their jobs voluntarily, have been terminated from their jobs for cause, or have refused to make themselves available for employment. However, when a person's religious practices are the source of the termination or unavailability, the denial of unemployment benefits implicates the state in obstructing religious freedom.

Thus, in *Sherbert v. Verner* (1963) the Court ruled that state denial of benefits to a person who refused to accept a job requiring her to work on her Sabbath violated the free exercise guarantee. The Court made it quite clear that the First Amendment forbids the denial of benefits as well as outright prohibitions.

> It is too late in the day to doubt that the liberties of religion and expression may be infringed by the denial or placing conditions upon a benefit or a privilege.
>
> . . . .
>
> [T]o condition the availability of benefits upon this appellant's willingness to violate a cardinal principle of her religious faith effectively penalizes the free exercise of her constitutional liberties.

Subsequent unemployment compensation cases have affirmed that unemployment compensation cannot be denied to persons who have lost their jobs for engaging in religious practices. In *Hobbie v. Unemployment Commission*, the Court applied this principle to a person who had adopted a new religion after accepting employment.[82] In *Thomas v. Review Board*, the Court ruled that the state could not deny compensation to a person who resigned his job because his religious conviction prohibited his working on armaments, even if other members of his faith felt no such moral restrictions. Chief Justice Burger made the reasoning regarding denial of benefits quite clear:

> Where the state conditions receipt of an important benefit upon conduct proscribed by a religious faith, or where it denies such benefits because of conduct mandated by religious belief, thereby putting substantial pressure on an adherent to violate his beliefs, a burden upon religion exists. Although the compulsion may be indirect, the infringement upon free exercise is nonetheless substantial.[83]

As was the case in the foregoing disputes, regulatory conditions that appear to be religiously neutral may conflict with religious commitments. These regulations may be as mundane as requiring social security numbers for administrative record keeping,[84] or as requiring drivers license photographs.[85] Before *Smith*, the general assumption was that the First Amendment required exemptions from these laws in the absence of a compelling state interest to the contrary. In spite of both state and federal efforts to restore that standard, the body of precedent remains ambiguous. We shall specifically consider the issues of exemptions from neutral laws in a later section.

Making Religious Acts Impossible

Some of the greatest burdens on religious practice are virtually invisible because the very possibility of these acts has been precluded by laws that simply make it impossible for a person to engage in a certain religious practice. For example, local courts may appoint a guardian *ad litem* to consent to blood transfusions on behalf of members of the Jehovah's Witness faith whose religion forbids it. When courts order blood transfusions, these people are often both physically and legally in no position to refuse.[86] Unlike laws penalizing religious actions, which a person may choose to violate, these laws simply remove the opportunity to engage in the act.

Governmental destruction of Native American sacred sites dramatically illustrates this kind of "burden." The analogy—although perhaps an exaggerated one—would be the "burden" on ancient Judaism by the destruction of the Temple; mandated rituals were simply no longer possible. Destruction of sacred sites simply precludes the religious associated with that site. The case of *Lyng v. Northwest Cemetery Association*[87] illustrates this kind of burden and the peril of ignoring it.

As part of the of the tragic history of U.S. acquisition of the North American continent from Native American peoples, many important native sites came to be owned by the U.S. government. As long as the lands were in remote places and "undeveloped," Native Americans continued to maintain the sacred sites and use the land for traditional worship practices. Pressure for land development often led to conflicts with traditional practices. Because the sites were considered sacred, once they were devoted to other uses, these religious rituals were no longer possible. The *Lyng* case grew out of a conflict between the continued ceremonial use of National Forest Service lands in Northern California, and the building of a logging road. A study by the National Forest Service had concluded that the road "would cause serious and irreparable damage to the sacred areas which are an integral and necessary part of the belief systems and lifeways of the Northwest California Indian peoples," and recommended abandoning the project. The Service nevertheless proceeded with the plan, prompting a free exercise challenge. Both the District Court and Court of Appeals enjoined the building of the road on free exercise grounds. The Supreme Court reversed and approved the road building project. First, by rejecting the centrality test, the Court refused to consider whether the ceremony in question was central to the religious life of the people in question. Second, the majority viewed the road project simply as internal governmental business. Justice O'Connor argued that no religious group could expect government to conduct *its own business* in conformity with that group's religious needs. Finally, and directly to the present point, the majority substantially diminished the notion of a harm to religious freedom. Justice O'Connor's decision rests on the word "prohibit" in the First Amendment; the government did not actually "prohibit" any religious practice by penalizing it or depriving its adherents of privileges enjoyed by others. Quoting *Sherbert v. Verner*, she wrote:

The crucial word in the constitutional text is "prohibit." For the Free Exercise Clause is written in terms of what the government cannot do to the individual, not in terms of what the individual can extract from the government.

According to this reasoning, the "incidental effects of the governmental program make it more difficult to practice certain religions, but . . . have no tendency to coerce individual into acting contrary to their religious beliefs. . . ."

Such burdens, the Court ruled, need not be justified by a compelling state interest. Because the Forest Service was merely redeploying one of its own resources, the government was not required to show a compelling state interest sufficient to override interests in maintaining the sacred site. By minimizing the notion of harm, the majority avoided the compelling state interest test, and relied instead on its finding that the challenged policy was religiously neutral and uniform in application.

The *Lyng* majority seemed to imply that rendering a religious practice impossible is somehow less burdensome on religious exercise than a penalty or the denial of a benefit. In fact, because it does not *compel* behavior, but only precludes it, it is no burden at all. Justice Brennan's dissent is devastating on this point:

> None of the religious adherents in *Hobbie, Thomas*, and *Sherbert*, for example, claimed or could have claimed that the denial of unemployment benefits rendered the practice of their religions impossible; at most, the challenged laws made those practices more expensive. Here, in sharp contrast, respondents have claimed—and proved that the desecration of the high country will prevent religious leaders from attaining the religious power or medicine indispensable to the success of virtually all their rituals and ceremonies. . . . Here the threat posed by the desecration of sacred lands that are indisputably essential to respondents' religious practices is both more direct and more substantial than that raised by a compulsory school law that simply exposed Amish children to an alien value system. And of course, respondents here do not even have the option, however unattractive it might be, of migrating to more hospitable locals; the site-specific nature of their belief system renders it nontransportable. . . . [R]eligious freedom is threatened no less by governmental action that makes the practice of one's chosen faith impossible than by governmental programs that pressure one to engage in conduct inconsistent with religious beliefs.[88]

Before ending this section, we make clear that this simple taxonomy does not encompass every alleged burden to religion. Nevertheless, the burdens summarized here exemplify a wide range of the harms alleged in free exercise complaints.

No Law

The wording of the First Amendment is stark: "Congress shall make *no* law. . . ." Not even judicial literalists have taken "no law" to mean "no law"; some laws may legitimately prohibit religious practices; the old standby example is a law that outlaws human sacrifice. The real question is, under what conditions may government prohibit or otherwise burden a religious exercise? Does "no law" mean no law that intentionally burdens a particular religion, or does it include secular laws that incidentally burden a religion or its practices? If so, does the First Amendment require that persons acting on sincere religious motives be granted exemptions from such laws? What kinds of justifications are sufficient to override religious burdens and refuse exemptions?

As long as the concept of a religion remained limited to traditional denominations, and the concept of religious exercises remained confined to their worship services, making these judgments was a reasonably constrained exercise. But once the courts recognized expanded conceptions of religion and its practices, as well as the concept of burdens to religious exercises, an almost infinite variety of regulations created an almost infinite variety of burdens on an almost infinite variety of religious exercises. Even apparently neutral laws can inadvertently burden someone's religious exercise. These problems are the heart of contemporary free exercise jurisprudence, and are the questions to which we now turn, beginning with the distinction between targeted and incidental religious burdens, then considering the problem of exemptions, and ending with the perpetually controversial compelling state interests debate.

Targeted and Incidental Burdens to Religion and the Problem of Neutrality

At least because *Sherbert v. Verner* in 1963, incidental burdens to religion had been treated much the same as intentional ones in free exercise jurisprudence. Among the many changes signaled by the controversial *Smith* decision was the sharp distinction made between laws that target a religious practice for unfavorable treatment and neutral laws that only incidentally burden religion. Justice Scalia's plurality opinion in *Smith* held that only laws that target religion for adverse treatment warrant compelling state interest analysis; neutral laws that burden religion only incidentally were to be presumed constitutional, and subject only to the rationality standard. Scalia correctly recognized that in a religiously plural society, virtually every ordinary policy, from labor to health policy, foreign policy to education could potentially burden the religious interests of some faith. Thus he concluded that to hold such laws presumptively invalid—at least as applied to religiously motivated persons, would be "to make an obligation to obey. . . a law contingent upon the law's coincidence with religious beliefs, except where the state's interest is compelling," permitting each person "to become a law unto himself." This danger is all the more troubling, he argued, because "we are a cosmopolitan nation made up of people of almost every conceivable religious preference." Hence, "we cannot afford the luxury of deeming *presumptively invalid*, as applied to the religious objector, every regulation of conduct that does not protect an interest of the highest order."[89] The only way to prevent that kind of anarchy, he argued, would be for courts to overlook the burdens created by otherwise-religiously neutral laws, leaving remedies to the normal political process. The full force of the Free Exercise Clause would be leveled only against laws that intentionally singled out religion or a particular religion for adverse treatment.

The four dissenters in *Smith* and Justice O'Connor, concurring, rejected this distinction. O'Connor stated the point powerfully:

> The First Amendment . . . does not distinguish between laws that are generally applicable and laws that target particular religious practices . . . .
> There is nothing talismanic about neutral laws of general applicability or general criminal prohibitions, for laws neutral toward religion can coerce a person to violate his religious conscience or intrude upon his religious duties just as effectively as laws aimed at religion.[90]

Fortunately, intentional or targeted burdens, such as the laws against polygamy aimed at Mormons in the Utah territory, are rare.[91] But in 1992, the justices confronted the City of Hialeah's law against animal sacrifice, specifically intended to prohibit a Santeria ritual, and unanimously struck the law down for that very reason.[92] The city adopted several ordinances prohibiting animal sacrifice and the possession of animals intended for ritual slaughter, but exempted other kinds of animal killing. When the church's free exercise petition ultimately reached the Supreme Court, the justices unanimously agreed, but they disagreed on the distinction between targeted and incidental burdens. Justice Kennedy, writing for himself and Justices Scalia, Rehnquist, White, and Thomas accepted that distinction, whereas Justices Souter, Blackmun, and O'Connor rejected it.

Justice Kennedy's majority opinion began from the premise that laws specifically targeting religions must meet compelling state interest scrutiny. The intentional targeting of Santeria was obvious, not only from the statute's use of words with religious significance, such as "ritual" and "sacrifice," but more significantly, from the "religious gerrymandering," that managed to prohibit the killing of animals in religious rituals, but to permit virtually every other kind of animal killing commonly practiced. Justice Kennedy concluded

> that each of Hialeah's ordinances pursues the city's interests only against conduct motivated by religious activity. The ordinances have every appearance of a prohibition that society is prepared to impose upon [Santeria worshipers] but not upon itself . . . . This precise evil is what the requirement of general applicability is designed to prevent.

What does the First Amendment require in such instances? For the majority, laws that target religious conduct for adverse treatment invoke the strictest scrutiny, which they will survive "only in rare cases." But Justice Blackmun, concurring for himself and Justice O'Connor, would simply hold that such laws could not meet the strict scrutiny test and therefore would be automatically unconstitutional. In either case, targeted laws are at the heart of the court's free exercise jurisprudence.

Because targeted laws such as the Hialeah one are rare, most free exercise jurisprudence concerns ordinary legislation that incidentally burdens religion. According
to the standard enunciated in *Smith*, these laws do not require religious exemptions,
nor need they be justified by the compelling state interest standard. In short, the Free
Exercise Clause requires only religious neutrality, reducing the variety of burdens to
religion to a single one—intentional discrimination. That standard reflects the interpretation proposed by one of the earliest religion clause scholars, Philip Kurland,
who understood the guarantees as preventing government from using religion as a
"standard for action or inaction," thus disabling government from using religion
"either to confer a benefit or to impose a burden."[93] Applied to the Establishment
Clause, this interpretation would only prevent government benefits that favor some
religions over others; it would not preclude symbolic or even financial support of all
religions as long as the benefits are not discriminatory. In this view, what the religion
clauses demand is *formal neutrality*.

The concept of neutrality is subject to the same ambiguities (perhaps even im-
possibilities) as the concept of formal neutrality under the Equal Protection Clause.
The past half century of American race relations have taught us that formal equality
can mask enormous substantive inequalities. Although it is difficult enough to
identify the characteristics of a racially neutral law, it is even more difficult (if not
impossible) to identify a religiously neutral law. Furthermore, the very distinction
between neutral and discriminatory laws is deeply flawed. The interests of religious
majorities are taken into account in ordinary governmental decision making without being noticed at all—i.e., schools and government offices are closed on Sundays,
Christmas, and Easter holidays. These accommodations to the Christian calendar
are so ordinary that they appear neutral to us. Only when religious outsiders seek
accommodation do we begin to notice the lack of neutrality and the requests for
"special treatment." Thus, laws that appear quite neutral to a majority may seriously burden a religious minority—even though that was never their intent. Certainly laws requiring basketball players to remain bareheaded was never intended to
discriminate against Jewish players, nor were the laws requiring full face photographs on drivers' licenses intended to discriminate against Muslim women. Sunday
closing laws were not intended to discriminate against Orthodox Jews who closed
their businesses on Saturdays. But the unfamiliarity of minority religious practices
may make legislators and administrators unaware, selectively indifferent, or insen-
sitive to the needs of persons out of the mainstream. Michael McConnell summarizes this problem succinctly:

> It should be apparent why a mere absence of attention to religious conse-
> quences on the part of the legislature cannot prove the legislation is neutral. In
> a world in which some beliefs are more prominent than others, the political
> branches will inevitably be selectively sensitive toward religious injuries. Laws
> that impinge upon the religious practices of larger or more prominent faiths
> will be noticed and remedied. When the laws impinge upon the practices of
> smaller groups, legislators will not even notice, and may not care even if they
> do notice. If believers of all creeds are to be protected in the "full and equal

rights of conscience," then selective sensitivity is not enough. The courts offer a forum in which the particular infringements of small religions can be brought to the attention of authorities (and assuming the judges perform their duties impartially) be given the same sort of hearing that more prominent religions already receive in the political process.[94]

Moreover, even if formal, genuinely equal treatment were possible, that is not what the Free Exercise Clause requires. That understanding of the Free Exercise Clause would render it "merely an adjunct to the Equal Protection Guarantee, requiring only that religion may not be treated more disfavorably than any other activity."[95] Reducing free exercise to mere equality would eliminate the substantive impact of the guarantee, as Laycock forcefully explains:

> [T]he Free Exercise Clause creates a substantive right, and the Court has reduced it to a mere equality right. The Free Exercise Clause does not say that Congress shall make no law discriminating against religion, or that no state shall deny to any religion within its jurisdiction the equal protection of the laws. Rather, it says that Congress shall make no laws prohibiting the free exercise of religion. . . . On its face, this is a substantive entitlement, not merely a pledge of non-discrimination.[96]

Substantively, the general goals of equality and religious freedom are normatively different. The goals of equality concern ignoring irrelevant differences, whereas the goals of the religion clauses foster differences in the interests of heterogeneity and pluralism. In McConnell's words:

> [T]he ideal of racial nondiscrimination is that individuals are fundamentally equal and must be treated as such; differences based on race are irrelevant and must be overcome. The ideal of free exercise of religion, by contrast, is that people of different religious convictions are different, and that those differences are precious and must not be disturbed. The ideal of racial justice is assimilationist and integrationist. The ideal of free exercise is counter-assimilationist; it serves to allow individuals of different religious faiths to maintain their differences in the face of powerful pressures to conform.[97]

For the critics, then, neutrality offers only a thin and inadequate approach to religious freedom. Moreover, its corollary that neutral laws do not require exemptions limits the role of courts in religious disputes, and returns them to the legislative or administrative context from which they developed.

Religious Exemptions

Persons who feel religiously burdened by secular laws usually do not ask that the law be withdrawn or overturned; they most often request exemptions. Religious exemptions to ordinary laws and policies are so common we often do not notice them at all. Most are made by administrators without controversy or even recognition. Legislation is full of religious exemptions, such as laws that exempt churches from zoning ordinances, exempt persons with religious objections from vaccination requirements, and state and federal exemptions for sacramental peyote use. Congress has engaged in legislative accommodation by providing for religious conscientious objection to military service, exempting persons with religious objections to receiving social security benefits from paying social security self-employment taxes, exempting those with religious objections to labor unions from paying union dues, and exempting religious institutions from some of the requirements of Title VII of the Civil Rights Act. Although these policies are criticized sometimes as violating the Establishment Clause by giving preferences to religion,[98] they do not raise free exercise problems. Free exercise disputes center not on whether legislators and administrators *may* grant exemptions, but on whether the constitution *requires* exemptions from otherwise valid, secular neutral laws so as to accommodate religious needs.

Beginning with *Sherbert v. Verner*, the general understanding was that such exemptions were required, unless there was a compelling state interest to the contrary. But as we have seen, the *Smith* decision reversed that understanding, holding that such exemptions were not constitutionally required. Although Justice Scalia denied any free exercise *right* to religious exemptions, he insisted that legislatures are free to grant them as part of the normal political process. Scalia recognizes that this approach moves religious protection from the courts back to the political process. "Values that are protected against government interferences through enshrinement in the Bill of Rights are not thereby banished from the political process." He readily admits that

> leaving accommodation to the political process will place at a relative disadvantage those religious practices that are not widely engaged in; but that unavoidable consequences of democratic government must be preferred to a system in which each conscience is a law unto itself . . . .

Hence, much of his argument turns on his preference for political solutions within the democratic process, rather than on an activist judiciary.

Frederick Gedicks situates Justice Scalia's argument in both constitutional history and changes in American religious patterns, particularly the decline of denominationalism and the growth of individualized religion. His point is powerful:

> Religious nondiscrimination is the only plausible understanding of what the Free Exercise Clause can require in a religiously plural postmodern United States marked by growing interest in spirituality and declining interest in traditional denominational religion. Denominational religion made the religious exemption doctrine plausible. Only when the definition of religion is strictly confined within clear boundaries can the state safely excuse citizens and others from obeying the law on the basis of religious beliefs or practices. Without a relatively narrow definition of religion, the effect of the exemption doctrine is to excuse unacceptably large numbers of people from complying with unacceptably large numbers of laws. As the Supreme Court observed in *Smith*, allowing religious belief to excuse the violation of law "would be to make the professed doctrines of religious belief superior to the law of the land, and in effect to permit every citizen to

become a law unto himself." The broader the definition of religion, the larger the potential number of people that might be excused from obeying the law . . . .

> The Draft Cases and the Amish Cases capture the dilemma of an exemption regime in a world of broad religious and moral difference, in which secular commitments have the same moral status as religious commitments, and in which it is common for individuals to manufacture their own idiosyncratic religions without the discipline of denominational boundaries: To avoid inequality and unfairness, exemptions must be extended beyond the traditional denominations to those with unusual religious beliefs, as well as to those whose beliefs are based upon secular morality. Yet, to extend the reach of exemptions so far would seriously undermine the observance, and thus the effectiveness, of law.[99]

Once again, we see a kind of circular problem: The more we expand the notion of religion and religious exercises, the more difficult it becomes to protect them.

Compelling State Interests: *Smith* and Its Aftermath

Because "no law" does not literally mean "no law," judges are asked to weigh the relative importance of an individual rights claim against the state's interest in its limitation. In ordinary balancing, the state must only show that the challenged law is reasonably related to legitimate interests, not necessarily that it is the best way to achieve them. This kind of balancing essentially replicates the legislative process; hence, dominant interests generally prevail. In fact, the very notion of balancing reduces *rights* to *interests*, and weighs them along with all other social interests.[100] Hence, balancing of interests often places the individual claimant at a disadvantage, because more widely shared interests can easily outweigh the interests of dissenting individuals or groups. Furthermore, this procedure allows for considerable judicial sleight of hand over exactly *what* is to be balanced. It makes an enormous difference whether the state weighs in with the entire policy, or simply its interest in not granting exemptions.[101]

To redress that imbalance (and put extra weight on the side of religious freedom), the courts developed the compelling state interest test. When a religious right is burdened, the burden of proof reverts to the state to show that the state's interest in burdening the religion is not only important, but *genuinely compelling*, and that no less burdensome strategies are available for achieving that interest. In striking that balance, courts are not to weigh the religious practice against the benefits of the law itself, but only against the costs of making a religious exception to that law. This method reflects the view that the whole point of having a Bill of Rights is to remove certain liberties from the ordinary balancing of the political process. Ordinarily, the person challenging the constitutionality of a law bears the burden of proof. Failing to overcome this burden leaves the law intact. In cases involving fundamental freedoms, the courts may reverse this burden of proof, and assume a law to be unconstitutional, leaving its defenders with the burden of establishing its constitutionality. Such laws are subjected to "strict scrutiny," requiring their defenders to show that (1) the challenged law served not just an important public purpose, but a genuinely *compelling* one, (2) the law was well tailored to achieve that purpose, and (3) the purpose could not be achieved by some less burdensome legislative method. In theory, the compelling state interest test poses a heavy burden on government to establish that burdens on fundamental rights are justified by extremely important state interests that could not be achieved in any less objectionable way.

The application of the compelling state interest standard to free exercise cases was made explicit in *Sherbert v. Verner*: "The compelling state interest standard requires that when religious practices are burdened by acts of government, the government must demonstrate that the burden is necessary to achieve a compelling state interest which can be achieved in no less burdensome way."[102] Perhaps the single clearest statement of this doctrine is in *Wisconsin v. Yoder*: "Only those interests of the highest order and those not otherwise served can overbalance legitimate claims to the free exercise of religion." *Yoder* offers a good example of how this method operates. In that case, the Court agreed with Wisconsin that the state had a compelling interest in fostering education, and agreed that the compulsory education laws in general were well tailored to achieve that purpose, but found that the state's educational goals would not be harmed by exempting Amish 14 to 16 year olds, because the Amish community's educational practices were capable of achieving many of the goals the state sought to accomplish.[103]

After *Yoder*, compelling state interest was widely understood to be the prevailing method of constitutional analysis in free exercise cases. Hence, when *Smith* reopened the question in 1990, litigants on both sides assumed the compelling state interest standard to be the appropriate standard of review, and neither party had challenged it. Thus, when the majority rejected this standard, they made a significant reversal in constitutional policy on an issue that was neither raised nor argued by the litigants. Because the majority, concurring, and dissenting opinions in *Smith* so pointedly capture the controversy surrounding the compelling state interest doctrine, we shall use those opinions as the focal point for discussing this doctrine.

As we have seen, the *Smith* majority held that the Free Exercise Clause is directly breached only by laws that specifically target religious practice for unfavorable treatment, not by generally applicable, religiously neutral laws. Consequently, laws inadvertently burdening religious exercise need not be justified by a compelling state interest. Hence, the *Smith* majority did not question either Oregon's interest in a drug policy, which included sacramental peyote use, or whether a religious exemption would have undermined the state's interests. Justice Scalia took great pains to suggest that the compelling state interest doctrine was itself an aberration, applicable only in unemployment compensation cases, but not in other circumstances, and most certainly not in cases involving criminal law.

The compelling state interest standard is vulnerable on another count as well. It is inconsistent with judicial restraint. The presumption of unconstitutionality is a presumption against the judgment of representative institutions. Scalia forcefully identified the counter-majoritarian implications of the compelling state interest approach, and the fact that it enabled a dissenting minority's interest to outweigh determinations made in the political process, thus disrupting the normal course of public policy. Furthermore, by removing the balancing from the legislative process and placing it in the hands of unelected judges, this process enhances the power of courts to substitute their judgment for those of elected officials. Justice Scalia's majoritarianism moved him not only to reject judicially mandated exemptions, but also to take a very permissive attitude toward legislative ones.

The majority's rejection of the compelling state interest test was opposed both in Justice O'Connor's concurring opinion and in the vigorous dissent authored by Justice Blackmun. To O'Connor, the test is not an anomaly, but "a fundamental part of our First Amendment doctrine." Without serious judicial scrutiny, the fate of minority religions would indeed be left up to the political process, which is precisely what the Bill of Rights is intended to prevent. "The very purpose of a Bill of Rights was to withdraw certain subjects from the vicissitudes of political controversy, to place them beyond the reach of majorities and officials and to establish them as legal principles to be applied by the courts." Further, she added:

> The compelling interest test effectuates the First Amendment's command that religious liberty is an independent liberty, that it occupies a preferred position, and that the Court will not permit encroachments upon this liberty, whether direct or indirect, unless required by clear and compelling governmental interests of the highest order. Only an especially important government interest pursued by narrowly tailored means can justify exacting a sacrifice of First Amendment freedoms as the price for an equal share of the rights, benefits, and privileges enjoyed by other citizens.[104]

Like the dissenters, she would maintain the compelling state interest test; unlike them, she believed that Oregon had shown a compelling state interest in maintaining the consistency of its antidrug policy.

Justices Harry Blackmun, William Brennan, and Thurgood Marshall joined Justice O'Connor in the two sections of her concurring opinion that challenged the majority's rejection of compelling state interest. They departed from her judgment that the state had shown a compelling interest in refusing to exempt sacramental peyote use. Their disagreement focuses on what is to be balanced, and how the balancing is to be done. Blackmun reminds the majority that individual interests are not to be balanced against the general purpose of the law; clearly, general public purposes would always prevail over individual interests. "It is not the state's broad interest in fighting the critical 'war on drugs' that must be weighed against respondents' claim, but the State's narrow interest in refusing to make an exception for the religious, ceremonial use of peyote." From this perspective, the dissenters conclude that virtually nothing is lost by granting the exemption.

Almost before the ink had dried on the *Smith* opinion, constitutional scholars and religious advocates assailed its devastating implications for the rights of religious minorities. An unusually broad coalition of religious interests groups formed the Coalition for the Free Exercise of Religion to petition Congress to reverse the effects of decision legislatively. In November 1993 Congress adopted and the president signed the Religious Freedom Restoration Act (RFRA), which legislatively restored the standard for constitutional review in cases in which federally supported programs were involved.[105] This statute, in force between 1993 and 1997, was a Congressional attempt to redress a perceived judicial imbalance in the understanding of the constitutional right to the free exercise of religion. The first stated purpose is the following:

> to restore the compelling interest test as set forth in *Sherbert v. Verner* and *Wisconsin v. Yoder*, and to guarantee its application in all cases where free exercise of religion is substantially burdened.

The key section of the bill states that government may restrict a person's free exercise of religion only if government can show that such a restriction "(1) is essential to further a compelling governmental interest; and (2) is the least restrictive means of furthering that compelling governmental interest" standard.

Under the traditional understanding of the separation of powers, Congress has no authority to reverse a Supreme Court decision by ordinary legislation. But Congress believed it was on safe grounds in adopting the RFRA under its Fourteenth Amendment authority to "enforce by appropriate legislation" constitutional guarantees. A constitutional challenge to this law reached the Supreme Court in 1997 in the case of *City of Boerne v. Flores*.[106] In that decision a divided Court struck down the Act as violating the separation of powers by infringing on the judicial power. The majority ruled that although the Fourteenth Amendment grants Congress the power to enforce a constitutional right, the RFRA went beyond enforcement and, in fact, altered the meaning of the right, thus usurping both judicial power and the prerogatives of states. As Justice Kennedy wrote, "Legislation which alters the Free Exercise Clause's meaning cannot be said to be enforcing the clause. Congress does not enforce a constitutional right by changing what the right is."

Since the demise of the RFRA—at least insofar as it applies to the states—a number of state legislatures have adopted their own versions of the statute, making many state courts friendlier to religious claims than are the federal courts. Thus, when litigants can choose between federal and state venues for hearing religious freedom cases, they may now choose state courts over federal ones, and state courts are often in the forefront of new developments in religion jurisprudence.

Meanwhile, in 2000 Congress adopted the much more limited Religious Land Use and Institutionalized Persons Act of 2000 (RLUIPA),[107] which forbids the federal government from implementing land uses regulations that impose a substantial burden on the religious exercise of a person, or impose a substantial burden on the religious exercise of a person confined to an institution, "unless that action is in furtherance of a compelling governmental interest and is the least restrictive means of furthering that compelling governmental interest." Rather than resting on Fourteenth Amendment grounds, as the RFRA had, this law was based on the commerce and spending clauses, and it therefore extends to all programs that receive federal money. In *Cutter V. Wilkinson*[108](2005) this law was upheld against an Establishment Clause challenge, ruling that it was permissible free exercise accommodation.

Conclusion

Some observers believe that the Free Exercise Clause has been in a period of eclipse since the *Smith* decision, and that religious petitioners can now make stronger statutory claims than constitutional ones. Whether this is a long- or short-term trend remains to be seen. We do know that constitutional arguments go in and out of fashion, and the understanding of constitutional language does not remain constant. This chapter has illustrated immense changes in interpretation of religion and its exercises, as well as of the standards for balancing religious claims against other interests. The origins of many of these changes lie beyond jurisprudence, with changes in the patterns of American religiosity itself. As American religion becomes more individual and diverse and less structured, free exercise jurisprudence changes with it. Given both the pervasive religious pluralism and the intense religiosity of the American people, religious conflicts will almost certainly continue to pervade American politics, and find their way into the courts. Eclipsed or re-emergent, the Free Exercise Clause will remain at the center of America's efforts to preserve both peace and religious freedom.

ENDNOTES

1. The Free Exercise Clause was incorporated into the Fourteenth Amendment, and hence held applicable to the states, in *Cantwell v. Connecticut*, 310 U.S. 296 (1940).
2. See his decisions in *Wallace v. Jaffree*, 472 US 38 (1985); and *Smith v. Board of Commissioners of Mobile County*, 655 F. Supp. 939 (S. Dist. Ala. 937) (1986).
3. *Van Orden v. Perry*, 545 U.S. 677 (2005).
4. Steven Smith, *Foreordained Failure* (New York: Oxford, 1995).
5. Winnifred Fallers Sullivan, *The Impossibility of Religious Freedom* (Princeton, NJ: Princeton University Press, 2005). Her book is an extended firsthand account of the case of *Warner v. City of Boca Raton*, 64 F. Supp. 2d 1272 (1999); 267 F.3d 122 (2001), 1227; 887 S.2d 1023 (Fla. 2004). This case arose when individuals erected memorial monuments at a municipal cemetery whose rules prohibited vertical displays. When the city demanded the removal of the monuments, the families claimed religious rights under Florida's Religious

Freedom Restoration Act. The city argued that these monuments were not "religious," and the trial focused on the meaning of a religious act. Sullivan concludes that "lived religion" is so infinitely diverse and personal that it simply cannot be captured by any of the attempts surveyed below, and advocates focusing on equality instead.

6. James Madison, Letter to Thomas Jefferson, 17 Oct. 1788. *Papers of James Madison*, Vol. 11, ed. by William T. Hutchinson, *et al.* (Charlottesville, VA: University Press of Virginia, 1977), 297–300.

7. On individualized religion, see Robert C. Fuller, *Spiritual, But Not Religious* (New York: Oxford University Press, 2001). See also Peter L. Berger, "Reflections on the Sociology of Religion Today," 62 *Sociology of Religion* 443 (2001), and Charles Trueheart, "Welcome to the Next Church," *The Atlantic Monthly*, August, 1996, 37.

8. See Bette Novit Evans, *Interpreting the Free Exercise of Religion* (Chapel Hill, NC: University of North Carolina Press, 1997), Chapter 2, for a more detailed discussion of this point.

9. Sociologist Catherine Albanese calls these creed, cult, and code. See Albanese, *America: Religions and Religion*, 4th ed. (Belmont, CA: Thomson Wadsworth, 2006).

10. *Davis v. Beason*, 133 U.S. 333 (1890), 342. The narrowest belief-type definitions insisted that religion meant the Christian religion, and mainstream Christianity at that. The 1922 Georgia Supreme Court case of *Wilkerson v. Rome*, quoted in Philip E. Hammond, "The Courts and Secular Humanism," in *Church State Relations: Tensions and Transitions*, eds. Thomas Robbins and Roland Robertson (New Brunswick, NJ: Transaction Books, 1987), 98–99.

11. 367 U.S. 488 (1961).

12. The footnote to this statement adds, "Among religions in this country which do not teach what would generally be considered a belief in the existence of God are Buddhism, Taoism, Ethical Culture, Secular Humanism, and others."

13. "Unitarian Group Denied Tax Status," by R.A. Dyer. Staff writer, *Fort Worth Star-Telegram*, via Knight Ridder Newspapers, USA, May 18, 2004.

14. Franklin Gamwell, *The Meaning of Religious Freedom* (Albany, NY: SUNY Press, 1995), 30. Gamwell's insight is echoed in the sociology of religion. Many sociologists recognize the *comprehensiveness of explanations* as one of the cross-cultural characteristics of religion. Milton Yinger, for example, writes that "Religion . . . can be defined as a system of beliefs and practices by means of which a group of people struggles with the ultimate problems of human life." Milton Yinger, *Religion, Society and the Individual* (New York: Macmillan, 1957), 9. And Clifford Geertz understands religion as a system of symbols which help one interpret the meaning of life itself by "formulating conceptions of a general order of existence." Geertz, "Religion as a Cultural System," in *Anthropological Approaches to the Study of Religion*, ed. Michael Banton, (London: Tavistock, 1966), 4.

15. *Founding Church of Scientology of Washington DC v. United States*, 409 F.2d 1146 (D.C. Cir.) *cert.* denied 296 US 963 (1969). On remand, however, the District Court required the church to cease making medical or scientific claims for its benefits, and to situate its claims in a religious context. But in 1977, in *Missouri Church of Scientology v. State Tax Commission*, 560 S.W.2d 837 (1977), a Missouri Court applied a belief in a Supreme Being test and disqualified Scientology from receiving state tax exemptions accorded to religions. See Marjorie Heins, "Other People's Faiths, The Scientology Litigation and the Justiciability of Religious Fraud," *Hastings Constitutional Law Quarterly* 9 (1981): 153. Scientology did not finally gain full recognition as a religion in the United States until 1993. For an excellent summary of Scientology's legal history, see Derek Davis, "The Church of Scientology: In Pursuit of Legal Recognition," Cesnur 2004 International

Conference on Religious Movements, Conflict, and Democracy: International Perspectives, June 17–20, 2004, Baylor University, Waco, Texas.

16. *Africa v. Pennsylvania*, 663 F.2d 1025 (3d Cir. 1981) *(cert. denied)* 456 U.S. 908 (1983). Judge Arlin Adams' opinion in this case also took account of several other indicators of religion, to be discussed below.

17. *United States v. Meyers*, 906 F. Sup 1494 (D. WY, 1995).

18. Tillich's works include *Systemic Theology* (Chicago: University of Chicago Press, 1951); *The Shaking of the Foundations* (New York: Charles Scribner's Sons, 1948); *The Courage to Be* (New Haven: Yale University Press, 1952); *Dynamics of Faith* (New York: Harper and Row, 1956), and *What Is Religion?* (New York: Harper and Row, 1969). See James McBride, "Paul Tillich and The Supreme Court: Tillich's 'Ultimate Concern' as a Standard in Judicial Interpretation," *Journal of Church and State* 30 (Spring, 1988): 245.

19. *U.S. v. Kauten*, 133 F. 2d 703 (2d Cir. 1943), 708.

20. 380 U.S. 163 (1965).

21. 325 F.2d 409 (1963).

22. *U.S. v. Seeger*, 380 U.S. 163 (1965).

23. Tillich, *Shaking of the Foundation* (New York: Charles Scribner's Sons, 1948), 26, 57.

24. 398 U.S. 333 (1972).

25. Kent Greenawalt, "Religion as a Concept in Constitutional Law," *California Law Review* 72 (1982): 753, 808–810.

26. The 1917 case of *New v. United States* illustrates one approach to making the distinction. Dr. New had claimed all kinds of supernatural powers, including the power to heal, which he professed to have received because of his rare virtue. In prosecuting him for mail fraud, the federal government denied both the truth of his claims and his sincerity in making them, thus attacking both veracity and sincerity. The Ninth Circuit made clear that Dr. New was entitled to believe anything he wanted, but not to *pretend* to hold beliefs "for false and fraudulent purposes of procuring money. . .." The evidence of Dr. New's "pretense" was hypocrisy: "he was also an habitual indulger in each and every of the sins and practices he pretended to condemn." *New v. United States* 245 F. 710 (9th Cir. 1917), *cert. denied* 246 U.S. 665 (1918). See Stephen Senn, "The Prosecution of Religious Fraud," 2 *Florida State University Law Review* 17 (1990): 325.

27. 322 U.S. 78 (1944). See John Noonan, "How Sincere Do You Have To Be To Be Religious?" 1988 *University of Illinois Law Review* 1988 (1988): 713.

28. *Van Schaick v. Church of Scientology*, 535 F. Supp. 1125 (D. Mass. 1982). Part of the conflict concerned the kinds of promises or enticements made by the church recruiters. If the benefits represented were spiritual ones, disgruntled former members could not be sued; if the promises were secular (better physical or mental health), they might be subject to fraud claims for failure to deliver the promised benefits. In claiming to be defrauded, the plaintiffs alleged that Scientology's founders and present leaders had purely commercial motives in creating the movement.

29. In *People v. Woody*, 61 Cal. 2d 716, 394 P.2d 813, 40 Cal. Rptr. 69 (1964) the California Supreme Court ruled that traditional ritual use of peyote by unquestionably sincere members of the Native American Church was protected by the Free Exercise Clause. In *State v. Bullard*, 267 N.C. 599, 48 S.D. 2d 565 (1966), this protection did not extend to drug use without evidence of religious sincerity, and in *Leary v. United States* 383 F.2d 851 (5th Cir. 1967), *rev'd on other grounds*, 395 U.S. 6 (1969), the Fifth Circuit ruled that Dr. Leary's religious faith was insufficient to outweigh the state interest in enforcement of its narcotics laws.

30. 288 Fed. Supp 439 (D.D.C. 1968). The ministers were called "Boo Hoos"; the symbol was a three-eyed toad; the bulletin was the "Divine Toad Sweat"; the church key was a bottle opener; the official songs were "Puff the Magic Dragon" and "Row, Row, Row Your Boat"; and the church motto was "Victory over Horseshit."

31. See *Frazee v. Illinois Department of Employment Security*, 489 U.S. 829 (1989).

32. See *Thomas v. Review Board of the Indiana Employment Security Division*, 450 U.S. 707 (1981).

33. See *Hobbie v. Unemployment Appeals Commission*, 480 U.S. 136 (1987).

34. Michael McConnell, discussing the origins of the Free Exercise Clause, makes much of the distinction between the "freedom of conscience" language proposed in James Madison's original draft, and the free exercise of "religion" that was ultimately adopted. The word "exercise," he notes, connotes activities—a far broader protection than the focus on mental states implied by the word "conscience." Furthermore, the word "religion" comprehends religion as a collective phenomenon. See his "The Origins and Historical Understanding of the Free Exercise of Religion," *Harvard Law Review* 103 (1990): 1409.

35. *The Papers of James Madison*, Vol. 8, ed. by W. Hutchinson and W. Rachal (Chicago: University of Chicago Press, 1986), 298–305.

36. An intriguing, but unsatisfying attempt to incorporate this insight has been offered by Jesse Choper, who understands the distinguishing characteristic of religion—for constitutional purposes—to be the belief that actions have "extratemporal consequences." Jesse Choper, *Securing Religious Liberty* (Chicago: University of Chicago Press, 1995). Choper reasons that the underlying insight of the Free Exercise Clause is to protect people from the agonizing choices between the commands of government and dangers to their immortal souls. Under these conditions—but *only* these conditions—people should be able to claim exemptions from ordinary legal obligations. This characterization excludes religions that do not rest on belief in an afterlife or in eternal reward and punishment as well as those practices which do not take the form of divine commands backed by threats. But the limited scope of this definition suits it well to a limited purpose Choper advocates. Thus, the First Amendment would only require exemptions from generally applicable laws that conflict with religious duties when that person can argue persuasively that he would suffer something akin to damnation.

37. The literature on a conscience-based understanding of the Free Exercise Clause is both enormous and impressive. Among the most influential works, see Christopher L. Eisgruber and Lawrence G. Sager, "The Vulnerability of Conscience: The Constitutional Basis for Protecting Religious Conduct," *University of Chicago Law Review* 61 (1994): 1245. See also Kent Greenawalt, "Objections in Conscience to Medical Procedures: Does Religion Make a Difference?" *Univ. of Illinois Law Review* (2006): 799; and Kent Greenawalt, "Law and Morality: Constitutional Law: Moral and Religious Convictions as Categories for Special Treatment: The Exemption Strategy," *William and Mary Law Review* 48 (April, 2007): 1605.

38. Milton Yinger, *The Scientific Study of Religion* (New York: Macmillan, 1970), 11.

39. Michael Sandel, "Religious Liberty: Freedom of Conscience or Freedom of Choice," *Utah Law Review* 1989 (1989): 597.

40. Phillip Hammond, *With Liberty for All: Freedom of Religion in the United States* (Westminster: John Knox Press, 1998).

41. *Lyng v. Northwest Indian Cemetery Protective Association*, 485 U.S. 439 (1988).

42. *Jimmy Swaggart Ministries v. Board of Equalization of California*, 493 US 378 (1990). See discussion of this point in Douglas Laycock, "The Remnants of Free Exercise," *Supreme Court Review* 1 (1990): 23–26. Also Frederick Mark Gedicks, "Toward a Constitutional Jurisprudence of Religious Group Rights," *Wisconsin Law Review* 1989 (1989): 99.

43. See, for example, Justice Kennedy's majority opinion in *Lee v. Weisman*, 505 U.S. 577 (1992).

44. Emile Durkheim, *The Elementary Forms of Religions Life*, trans. Joseph Swain (New York: Free Press, 1965), 62.

45. Ibid., 59.

46. Milton Yinger, *The Scientific Study of Religion* (New York: Macmillan, 1970), 9 (emphasis added).

47. In this spirit, Kent Greenawalt has suggested that judges seek analogies between the putative religion and that which is indisputably religious. See Greenawalt, "Defining Religions," 767–768. Greenawalt emphasizes that analogies to the external manifestations of religion, such as ceremonies, clergy, or institutional practices is dangerous; he prefers analogies to the kinds of concerns and motivations traditional religions include. See also George C. Freeman, "The Misguided Search for a Constitutional Definition of Religion," *Georgetown Law Journal* 71 (1983): 1519. Lawrence Tribe, arguing for a bifurcated definition, proposed that everything "arguably religious" should count as religious for free exercise purposes, but anything "arguably nonreligious" should be considered nonreligious for Establishment Clause purposes. Lawrence Tribe, *American Constitutional Law* (Foundation Press, 1978).

48. 592 F.2d 197 (3d Cir. 1979) (footnotes omitted). See also "Note: Transcendental Meditation and the Meaning of Religion Under the Establishment Clause," *Minnesota Law Review* 62 (1978): 887; Jesse Choper, "Defining Religion in the First Amendment," *University of Illinois Law Review* (1982): 579; "Note, Defining Religion," *University of Chicago Law Review* 32 (1965): 533; "Defining Religion in Operational and Institutional Terms," *University of Pennsylvania Law Review* 116 (1968): 479; "Note: The Sacred and the Profane: A First Amendment Definition of Religion," *University of Texas Law Review* (1982): 139; "Note: Toward a Constitutional Definition of Religion" 91 *Harvard Law Review* 91 (1978): 1056; and Derek Davis, "The Courts and the Constitutional Meaning of 'Religion': A History and Critique," in *The Role of Government in Monitoring and Regulating Religion in Public Life*, eds. James E. Wood, Jr. and Derek Davis (Waco, TX: J.M. Dawson Institute of Church-State Studies, 1993).

49. *Africa v. Pennsylvania*, 662 F.2d 1025, 1035 (3d Cir. 1981). See also *Church of the Chosen People v. United States*, 548 F. Supp. 1247 (D. Minn. 1982).

50. *United States v. Meyers*, 906 F. Supp. 1494 (D. Wyo. 1995), 1502–1503. The judge elaborates each of these indicators.

51. Reported by Derek Davis, "The Church of Scientology: In Pursuit of Legal Recognition," 2004. Davis provides an excellent critique of these criteria, both in general and as applied to Scientology.

52. See Bruce Bagni, "Discrimination in the Name of the Lord: A Critical Evaluation of Discrimination by Religious Organizations," *Columbia Law Review* 79 (1984): 1514. This proposal, which is specifically intended for evaluating the autonomy claims of religious institutions, is that the Free Exercise Clause protects "purely spiritual" matters at the epicenter of a church's functions, but as church activities emanate out from this core, they merit less constitutional protection.

53. *Employment Division v Smith*, 595 U.S. 872 (1990).

54. 485 U.S. 439 (1988). Justice Brennan, writing in dissent, would have retained the concept of centrality, but left claimants "the arbiters of which practice are central to their faith, subject only to the normal requirements that their claims be genuine and sincere."

55. *Lawson v. Commonwealth*, 291 Ky. 437, 164 S.W.2d 972 (1942). See also *Harden v. State* 188 Tenn. 17, 216 S.W. 2d 708 (1948), *State ex rel Swann v Pack*, Supreme Court of Tennessee, 1975, 527 S.W. 2d 99 (1975), *and State v. Massey*, 229 N.C. 734, 51 SE 2d (1979).

56. Employment Division v. Smith, 495 U.S. 872 (1990).

57. *Ashcroft v. O Centro Espirita Beneficento Uniao Do Vegetal*, 546 U.S. 418 (2006).

58. *Church of the Lukumi Babalu Aye, Inc. and Ernesto Pichado v. City of Hialeah*, 508 U.S. 520 (1993).

59. For numerous examples of requests for religious accommodation in prisons, see Marci A. Hamilton, *God vs. the Gavel: Religion and the Rule of Law* (New York: Cambridge University Press, 2005), 156–159.

60. *Sultaana Lakiana Myke Freeman v. State of Florida*, 924 So.2d 48 (Fla. App. 5 Dist. 2006),

61. Angela Carmella offers a theological explanation of these religious acts, grounded in the Catholic concept of "inculturation"—clothing the core faith in the cultural expressions of its particular adherents. Acculturated religious responses engage the prevailing secular world and are compatible with it, but are no less "religious" than those that are "pervasively sectarian"; they are equally legitimate ways in which religions encounter the world. But because they are such familiar "secular" activities, judges and juries fail to recognize them as religious, and to accord them First Amendment protection. Yet, failure to encompass these activities and the institutions that provide them misses some very important elements of contemporary religious exercise. See Angela Carmella, "A Theological Critique of Free Exercise Jurisprudence," *George Washington Law Review* 60 (1992): 782. The term "inculturation" comes from Reinhold Niebhur, *Christ and Culture* (New York: Harper and Row, 1951).

62. *Sherbert v. Verner*, 374 U.S. 398 (1963); *Hobbie v. Unemployment Commission*, 480 U.S. 136 (1987); *Thomas v. Review Board*, 450 U.S. 707 (1981); *Frazee v. Illinois Dept. of Employment Security*, 489 U.S. 829 (1989).

63. See EEOC v. Townley Engineering and Manufacturing Co., 859 F.2d 610 (9th Cir. 1988).

64. Carl Esbeck, "Church Autonomy and Establishments of Religion," *Brigham Young University Law Review* (2004): 1385.

65. *Walz v. Tax Commissioner*, 397 U.S. 664 (1970).

66. *Kedroff v. St. Nicholas Cathedral of the Russian Orthodox Church*, 344 U.S. 94 (1952), and *Serbian Eastern Orthodox Diocese v. Milivojevich*, 426 U.S. 696 (1975).

67. 440 U.S. 490 (1973). Douglas Laycock's work was extremely influential in laying the theoretical foundation for a right to church autonomy. See, for example, "Towards a General Theory of the Religion Clauses: The Case of Church Labor Relations and the Right to Church Autonomy," *Columbia Law Review* 81 (1981): 1378. For philosophical arguments for autonomy rights, see Frederick Mark Gedicks, "Toward a Constitutional Jurisprudence of Religious Group Rights," *Wisconsin Law Review* 1989 (1989): 99. See also Michael McConnell, "Accommodation of Religion," *Supreme Court Review* (1985): 1; Mary Ann Glendon and Raul F. Yanes, "Structural Free Exercise," *Michigan Law Review* 90 (1991): 477; and Howard Freedman, "Rethinking Free Exercise: Rediscovering Religious Community and Ritual," *Seton Hall Law Review* 24 (1994): 1800.

68. *Bob Jones University v. United States*, 461 U.S. 574 (1983).

69. 78 Stat. 255, as amended, 42 U.S.C. Sec. 2000e-1.

70. 438 U.S. 327 (1987).

71. If both were true, then the church would be protected by an exemption to the equal employment law for church employees performing religious functions.

72. The law does include a religious exemption, but its standards do not apply to Catholic Charities.

73. *Catholic Charities of Sacramento v Superior Court*, No. SO99822 (SC CA, 2004).

74. *City of Boerne v. Flores*, 521 U.S. 507 (1997).

75. For a theological analysis of the importance of church architecture, see Angella Carmella, "Houses of Worship and Religious Liberty: Constitutional Limits on Landmark Preservation and Architectural Review," *Villanova Law Review* 36 (1991): 401, 404–405; and "Land Use Regulation of Churches," *Religious Organizations in the United States: A Study of Identity, Liberty, and the Law* (Durham, NC: Carolina Academic Press, 2006). See also Douglas Laycock, "State RFRAs and Land Use Regulation," *University of California-Davis Law Review* 32 (1999): 755.

76. 374 U.S. 398 (1963).

77. Steven Smith, *Foreordained Failure*, offers a devastating critique of free exercise jurisprudence based on this point.

78. 98 U.S. 145 (1987).

79. See, for example, *Molko and Leal v. Holy Spirit Association*, 762 P.2d 46 (Cal. 1988); and *George v. ISKCON* 962 Cal. Rptr. 219 (Ct. App. 1989).

80. *Employment Division v. Smith*, 494 U.S. 872 (1990).

81. *Sherbert v. Verner*, 374 U.S. 398 (1963). See Kathleen Sullivan, "Unconstitutional Conditions," 102 *Harvard Law Review* (1989): 1413, 1435. Sullivan observed a seldom noticed peculiarity in this reasoning: "Ms. Sherbert could not have obtained unemployment compensation by violating her conscience; if she worked on Saturday, she would not have needed unemployment compensation."

82. 480 U.S. 136 (1987).

83. 450 U.S. 707 (1981).

84. *Bowen v. Roy*, 476 U.S. 693 (1986). The Court split five to four, and there were five separate opinions.

85. *Quaring v. Peterson*, 728 F.2d 1121 (8th Cir. 1984). *Jenson v. Quaring*, 572 U.S. 478 (1985) *(per curiam)* (affirmed by an equally divided Court). In *Sultaana Lakiana Myke Freeman v. State of Florida*, 924 So.2d 48 (Fla. App. 5 Dist. 2006),a Florida appeals court ruled that Florida's photograph requirement did not pose a substantial burden on a Muslim whose religion required her to keep her face covered, and thus did not violate the state's Religious Freedom Restoration Act.

86. See, for example, *Powell v. Columbian Presbyterian Medical Center*, 49 Misc. 2d 215, 267 N.Y.S. 2d 459 (Sup. Ct. 1965); *United States v. George*, 239 F. Supp. 752 (D. Conn. 1965); *Application of President and Directors of Georgetown College, Inc.*, 331 F. 2d 1000 (D.C. Cir. 1964).

87. 485 U.S. 439 (1988).

88. Justice Brennan also pointed out that the majority's decision relied on a distinction between government actions that "compel affirmative conduct inconsistent with religious beliefs," and those government actions that "prevent" conduct consistent with religious beliefs. He then noted that one of the dictionary definitions of "prohibit" is "to prevent from doing something." Ibid., 1334–1335, note 4.

89. 494 U.S. 872 (1990), quoting *Reynolds v. U.S.*, 98 U.S. 145 (1878).

90. 494 U.S. 872 (1990) (O'Connor, concurring).

91. *Reynolds v. United States*, 98 U.S. 145 (1878).

92. *Church of the Lukumi Babalu Aye v. City of Hialeah*, 508 U.S. 520 (1993).

93. Philip Kurland, *Religion and the Law* (Chicago: Aldine, 1961).

94. Michael McConnell, "Free Exercise Revisionism and the *Smith* Decision," *University of Chicago Law Review* 57 (1990): 1109, 1136. See Justice Souter's concurring opinion in *Church of Babalu Lukumi Aye* for further explication of this point.

95. Douglas Laycock, "The Remnants of Free Exercise," *Supreme Court Review* (1990):
1 See also Laycock, "Text, Intent, and the Religion Clauses," *Notre Dame Journal of Law
Ethics and Public Policy* 4 (1990): 683, and Laycock, "Formal, Substantive, and
Disaggregated Neutrality Toward Religion," *DePaul Law Review* 39 (1990): 993.

96. Laycock, "Remnants," 13.

97. McConnell, "Free Exercise Revisionism," 1139.

98. A classic example is *Estate of Thornton v. Caldor*, 472 U.S. 703 (1985). The State of
Connecticut repealed its Sunday closing laws, but created a statutory right for any
employee not to work on his or her Sabbath. In 1981, the U.S. Supreme Court ruled that
the law impermissibly advanced a particular religious practice by requiring employers and
fellow employers to adjust their behavior to the requirements of Sabbath observers. This
decision illustrates the very thin line between required and prohibited accommodation of
religion at the border between the two clauses.

99. Frederick Mark Gedicks, "Religious Exemptions, Formal Neutrality, and *Laicite*,"
Indiana Journal of Global Legislative Studies 13 (Summer 2006): 473. See also Philosophical
arguments on neutrality in L. Scott Smith, "Religion-Neutral Jurisprudence: An Examination
of Its Meanings and End," *William & Mary Bill of Rights Journal* 13 (February, 2005): 841.

100. Ronald Dworkin, *Taking Rights Seriously* (Cambridge, MA: Harvard University
Press, 1977).

101. Consider *Jensen v. Quaring*, 472 U.S. 478 (1985), in which a woman with religious
objections to personal images sought an exemption from the requirement of having her
picture on her driver's license. If her claim had been weighed against the general interest of
the state in photo identified drivers licenses, she would not have had much chance to prevail.
However, by weighing her claim not against the general policy, but against the anticipated
problems the exemption might create, her case was a far easier one. See also *Bowen v. Roy*,
476 U.S. 693 (1986). In both cases, the U.S. Solicitor General submitted briefs arguing that the
state need only support its general policy against the claimant's rights, rather than the state's
interests in not granting the exemption. This argument put Solicitor General Charles Fried in
an awkward position, because Fried's argument to the contrary had been a classic in
balancing of interests controversies. See Charles Fried, "Two Concepts of Interests," *Harvard
Law Review* 76 (1963): 755, and a critique in Stephen Pepper, "*Reynolds, Yoder*, and Beyond:
Alternatives for the Free Exercise Clause," *Utah Law Review* (1981): 309.

102. 347 U.S. 398 (1963).

103. 406 U.S. 205 (1972).

104. *Employment Division v. Smith*, 494 U.S. 872 (1990) (O'Connor concurring).

105. Pub. L. No. 103-144; 107 Stat. 1480.

106. 521 U.S. 507 (1997).

107. 42 U.S.C. sect. 2000cc et seq.

108. 544 U.S. 709 (2005).

BIBLIOGRAPHY

Books

Albanese, Catherine. *America: Religions and Religion*. 4th ed. Belmont, CA: Thomson
Wadsworth, 2006.

Durkheim, Emile. *The Elementary Forms of Religious Life*. Trans. Joseph Swain. New York: Free Press, 1965.

Eisgruber, Christopher and Lawrence Sager. *Religious Freedom and the Constitution*. Cambridge, MA: Harvard University Press, 2007.

Evans, Bette Novit. *Interpreting the Free Exercise of Religion*. Chapel Hill, NC: University of North Carolina Press, 1997.

Feldman, Noah. *Divided by God*. New York: Farrar, Straus and Giroux. 2005.

Fuller, Robert C. *Spiritual, But Not Religious*. New York: Oxford University Press, 2001.

Gamwell, Franklin. *The Meaning of Religious Freedom*. Albany: SUNY Press, 1995.

Greenawalt, Kent. *Religion and the Constitution*. Princeton, NJ: Princeton University Press, 2006.

Hamburger, Philip A. *Separation of Church and State*. Cambridge, MA: Harvard University Press, 2002.

Hammond, Phillip. *With Liberty for All: Freedom of Religion in the United States*. Westminster: John Knox Press, 1998.

McConnell, Michael, John Garvey and Thomas Berg, eds. *Religion and the Constitution*. 2nd ed. Aspen Publishers, 2006.

Smith, Steven. *Foreordained Failure*. New York: Oxford, 1995.

Sullivan, Winnifred Fallers. *The Impossibility of Religious Freedom*. Princeton, NJ: Princeton University Press, 2005.

Witte, John Jr. *Religion and the American Constitution*, 2nd ed. Boulder, CO: Westview Press, 2005.

Yinger, Milton. *Religion, Society and the Individual*. New York: Macmillan, 1957.

———— *The Scientific Study of Religion*. New York: Macmillan, 1970.

Articles/Chapters

Carmella, Angela. "Houses of Worship and Religious Liberty: Constitutional Limits on Landmark Preservation and Architectural Review." *Villanova Law Review* 36 (1991): 401.

Carmella, Angela. "A Theological Critique of Free Exercise Jurisprudence," *George Washington Law Review* 60 (1992): 782.

Eisgruber, Christopher L. and Lawrence G. Sager. "The Vulnerability of Conscience: The Constitutional Basis for Protecting Religious Conduct," *University of Chicago Law Review* 61 (1994): 1245.

Esbeck, Carl. "Church Autonomy and Establishments of Religion," *Brigham Young University Law Review* (2004): 1385.

Evans, Bette Novit. "The Constitutional Context of Religious Freedom in the United States." In *Piety, Politics, and Pluralism: Religion, the Courts, and the 2000 Election*, ed. Mary Segers. Lanham, MD: Rowman and Littlefield, 2002.

————. "A Proposed Best Account of Religious Liberty." *Forum on Public Policy* 4 (1: 2008): 25–35.

Freedman, Howard. "Rethinking Free Exercise: Rediscovering Religious Community and Ritual." *Seton Hall Law Review* 24 (1994): 1800.

Freeman, George C. "The Misguided Search for a Constitutional Definition of Religion." *Georgetown Law Journal* 71 (1983): 1519.

Gedicks, Frederick Mark. "Toward a Constitutional Jurisprudence of Religious Group Rights." *Wisconsin Law Review* 1989 (1989): 99.

————. "Religious Exemptions, Formal Neutrality, and *Laicite*." *Indiana Journal of Global Legislative Studies* 13 (Summer 2006): 473.

Glendon, Mary Ann and Raul F. Yanes. "Structural Free Exercise." *Michigan Law Review* 90 (1991): 477.

Greenawalt, Kent. "Religion as a Concept in Constitutional Law," *California Law Review* 72 (1982): 753.

———. "Objections in Conscience to Medical Procedures: Does Religion Make a Difference?" *University of Illinois Law Review* (2006): 799.

———. "Law and Morality: Constitutional Law: Moral and Religious Convictions as Categories for Special Treatment: The Exemption Strategy." *William and Mary Law Review* 48 (April 2007): 1605.

Laycock, Douglas. "The Remnants of Free Exercise." *Supreme Court Review* (1990): 23.

———. "Toward A General Theory of the Religion Clauses: The Case of Church Labor Relations and the Right to Church Autonomy," *Columbia Law Review* 81 (1981): 1378.

———. "Text, Intent, and the Religion Clauses." *Notre Dame Journal of Law Ethics and Public Policy* 4 (1990): 683.

———. "Formal, Substantive, and Disaggregated Neutrality Toward Religion." *DePaul Law Review* 39 (1990): 993.

McConnell, Michael. "The Origins and Historical Understanding of the Free Exercise of Religion," *Harvard Law Review* 103 (1990): 1409.

———. "Accommodation of Religion." *Supreme Court Review* (1985): 1.

Noonan, John. "How Sincere Do You Have To Be To Be Religious?" 1988 *Univ. of Illinois Law Review* (1988).

Sandel, Michael. "Religious Liberty: Freedom of Conscience or Freedom of Choice." *Utah Law Review* 1989 (1989): 597.

Court Cases

Africa v. Pennsylvania, 662 F.2d 1025 (3d Cir. 1981) *cert. denied* 456 U.S. 908 (1983).

Ashcroft v. O Centro Espirita Beneficento Uniao Do Vegetal, 546 U.S. 418 (2006).

Bob Jones University v. United States, 461 U.S. 574 (1983).

Cantwell v. Connecticut, 310 U.S. 296 (1940).

Catholic Charities of Sacramento v Superior Court, No. SO99822 (SC CA, 2004).

Church of the Lukumi Babalu Aye, Inc. and Ernesto Pichado v. City of Hialeah, 508 U.S. 520 (1993).

City of Boerne v. Flores, 521 U.S. 507 (1997).

Corporation of the Presiding Bishop of the Church of Jesus Christ of Latter-day Saints v. Amos, 438 U.S. 327 (1987).

Cutter v. Wilkinson, 544 U.S. 709 (2005).

Davis v. Beason, 133 U.S. 333, 342 (1890).

Employment Division, Department of Human Resources of Oregon v. Smith, 495 U.S. 872 (1990).

Estate of Thornton v. Caldor, 472 U.S. 703 (1985).

Founding Church of Scientology of Washington DC v. United States, 409 F.2d 1146 (D.C. Cir.) *cert. denied* 296 U.S. 963 (1969).

Frazee v. Illinois Department of Employment Security, 489 U.S. 829 (1989).

Goldman v Weinberger, 475 U.S. 503 (1986).

Hobbie v. Unemployment Appeals Commission, 480 U.S. 136 (1987).

Jimmy Swaggart Ministries v. Board of Equalization of California, 493 U.S. 378 (1990).

Kedroff v. St. Nicholas Cathedral of the Russian Orthodox Church, 344 U.S. 94 (1952).

Lee v. Weisman, 505 U.S. 577 (1992).

Lyng v. Northwest Indian Cemetery Protective Association, 485 U.S. 439 (1988

Malnak v Yogi, 592 F.2d 197 (3d Cir. 1979).

National Labor Relations Board v Catholic Bishop of Chicago, 440 U.S. 490 (1973).

Reynolds v. United States, 98 U.S. 145 (1878).

Serbian Eastern Orthodox Diocese v. Milivojevich, 426 U.S. 696 (1975).

Sherbert v. Verner, 374 U.S. 398 (1963).

Smith v. Board of Commissioners of Mobile County, 655 F. Supp. 939 (S. Dist. Ala 937) (1986).

Sultaana Lakiana Myke Freeman v. State of Florida, 924 So.2d 48 (Fla. App. 5 Dist. 2006).

Thomas v. Review Board of the Indiana Employment Security Division, 450 U.S. 707 (1981).

United States v. Ballard, 322 U.S. 78 (1944).

United States v. Kauten, 133 F. 2d 703, 708 (2d Cir. 1943).

United States v. Meyers, 906 F. Sup 1494 (D. Wyo., 1995).

United States v. Seeger, 380 U.S. 163 (1965).

United States v Welsh, 398 U.S. 333 (1972).

Van Orden v. Perry, 545 U.S. 677 (2005).

Wallace v. Jaffree, 472 U.S. 38 (1985)

Walz v. Tax Commissioner, 397 U.S. 664 (1970).

Warner v. City of Boca Raton, 64 F. Supp. 2d 1272 (1999), 267 F.3d 1223, 1227 (2001); 887 S.2d 1023 (Fla. 2004).

Wisconsin v. Yoder, 406 U.S. 205 (1972).

CHAPTER 6

....

THE U.S. SUPREME COURT AND NON-FIRST AMENDMENT RELIGION CASES

....

RONALD B. FLOWERS

THE United States Supreme Court decides most church–state cases on the basis of either the Establishment Clause or the Free Exercise Clause. However, because the religion clauses were not incorporated into the Due Process Clause of the Fourteenth Amendment and applied to the states until the 1940s,[1] the Court was required to decide some earlier religion cases through other means. Some were decided on the language of the Fourteenth Amendment itself.

Many cases, however, both before and after incorporation, have been decided on nonconstitutional grounds. The Court, from its earliest days, has said that cases should be decided at the lowest level possible, rather than raising them to the constitutional level. Chief Justice John Marshall wrote in 1804 "that an Act of Congress ought not be construed to violate the Constitution if any other possible construction remains available."[2] Some of the *Ashwander* rules," written in a concurrence by Justice Louis Brandeis,[3] make the point explicitly:

> 2. The Court will not "anticipate a question of constitutional law in advance
> of the necessity of deciding it." . . . "It is not the habit of the Court to
> decide questions of a constitutional nature unless absolutely necessary to a
> decision of the case." . . .[4]

4. The Court will not pass on a constitutional question, . . . if there is also present some other ground upon which the case may be disposed of. . . . Thus, if a case can be decided on either of two grounds, one involving a constitutional question, the other a question of statutory construction or general law, the Court will decide only the latter.[5] . . .

7. "When the validity of an act of the Congress is drawn in question, and even if a serious doubt of constitutionality is raised, it is a cardinal principle that this Court will first ascertain whether a construction of the statute is fairly possible by which the question may be avoided."[6]

The following statement from a 2004 case illustrates that this concept has been an abiding principle for the Court:

> The command to guard jealously and exercise rarely our power to make constitutional pronouncements requires strictest adherence when matters of great national significance are at stake. Even in cases concededly within our jurisdiction under Article III, we abide by "a series of rules under which [we have] avoided passing upon a large part of all the constitutional questions pressed upon [us] for decision."[7] . . . Always we must balance "the heavy obligation to exercise jurisdiction[8] . . . against the "deeply rooted" commitment "not to pass on questions of constitutionality" unless adjudication of the constitutional issue is necessary.[9]

Consequently, the Court frequently has decided cases by interpreting statutory language, i.e., reaching a decision by deciding whether the plaintiff acted consistently with the requirement of a law. This chapter examines a sample of church–state cases decided on grounds other than the Religion Clauses.

THE FOURTEENTH AMENDMENT

A famous Fourteenth Amendment church–state case was *Pierce v. Society of Sisters*,[10] about whether a state could compel children to attend public schools. The background of *Pierce* was massive immigration in the early twentieth century. Many Americans wanted immigrants to be assimilated into society quickly. Oregon, in 1922, passed legislation requiring all able children attend public schools. Oregon wanted immigrant children to learn English and American history and customs, thereby making them Americans.

However, a Catholic school and a secular military academy sued to nullify the law. They claimed a Fourteenth Amendment right to be able to make a living.[11] The Court decided for the private schools. "The inevitable practical result of enforcing the act under consideration would be destruction of appellees' primary schools, and perhaps all other private primary schools for normal children within the state of Oregon."[12] Because it allowed parochial schools to exist, *Pierce* has been called the "Magna Charta" of parochial schools.

Cochran v. Louisiana Board of Education[13] was another parochial school case decided on Fourteenth Amendment grounds. Louisiana law allocated money for books to be furnished to children in private and parochial schools. Taxpayers challenged the constitutionality of the law. They said the program violated the Fourteenth Amendment because it took private money and used it for a private purpose. Because taxation was to finance a public purpose, they argued, taxpayers were denied property, forbidden under the Fourteenth Amendment.

The Court disagreed. It ruled the money was used for a public purpose because education is a public good. Neither parochial schools nor the churches sponsoring the schools were the beneficiaries of the book program. The beneficiaries were the children and the state that needed an educated citizenry. This principle is the "child benefit theory," which has been used to circumvent Establishment Clause challenges to state expenditures.

In *Employment Division of Oregon v. Smith*[14] the Court decided a case that changed the rules for interpreting the Free Exercise Clause. Since 1963, government could not interfere with religious exercise without showing a compelling interest.[15] However, *Smith* said government could hinder religious exercise on the basis of generally applicable law. The new test made it more possible for government to inhibit religious behavior.

In response to *Smith*, Congress passed the Religious Freedom Restoration Act (RFRA),[16] which required courts to employ the "compelling state interest" test in deciding free exercise cases. However, questions arose about the constitutionality of RFRA. In Boerne, Texas, a Catholic church wanted to expand its sanctuary to accommodate crowds coming for worship. The city denied a building permit, however, because the church was in a historical preservation district. Claiming a right under RFRA to be able to enlarge its place of worship, the church sued, *Boerne v. Archbishop Flores*,[17] which became a landmark case. The Fourteenth Amendment guarantees civil rights to the citizens of the states. Section 5 of the amendment says: "The Congress shall have the power to enforce, by appropriate legislation, the provisions of this article." *Boerne* said this means Congress has the power to "remedy" and "prevent" unconstitutional conduct by state and local governments; but in passing RFRA Congress exceeded its power by requiring courts to use the "compelling state interest" test. In essence it made a substantive change in the Free Exercise Clause itself. Congress cannot do that. Stated differently, the separation of powers forbade Congress from going beyond its "remedial" and "preventive" powers to telling courts how to interpret the Constitution. RFRA was unconstitutional as it applied to state law, but not to federal law.[18]

The same principle was affirmed in *Gonzales v. O Centro Espirita Beneficente Uniao Do Vegetal* (UDV).[19] UDV is a church that uses *hoasca* ("wass-ca"), a hallucinogenic tea, as its sacrament. Because *hoasca* contains chemicals on the federal list of prohibited drugs, the government seized the church's tea and threatened prosecution for its further use. UDV sued for free exercise protection under the authority of RFRA. The Court ruled that RFRA was applicable because a *federal* drug law was in play. It found for UDV because the government could not show that it had a *compelling* interest (required by RFRA) in prohibiting the use of the tea. The Court rendered an important free exercise decision by strictly applying statutory language.

RELIGIOUS ORGANIZATIONS AND PERSONAL ASSETS

Some cases from the nineteenth and early twentieth centuries are about the ownership (or inheritance) of church property. Most of these cases involved the property of utopian groups. When people joined communistic forms of these groups, they gave all their wealth to the group to be used for the common good; but what happened if one wanted to leave the group? Could they get their property back? Or what if descendants of group members wanted to claim inheritance of the property their forebears had given to the group?

One of the groups involved in litigation was the "Harmony Society," founded in 1804 by George Rapp. Harmony was a communistic society. In 1819 Joshua Nachtrieb joined the group. He signed a statement transferring all his assets to the society. The document said that anyone who left the society had no claim on his former property. Nachtrieb quit his participation in Harmony in 1846 because he claimed that Rapp and other leaders were arbitrary, oppressive, dishonest, and impious. When he left, Rapp gave him $200, which Nachtrieb acknowledged by signing a paper. Later Nachtrieb sued to get property, equal to what he had contributed, from the society.

The Supreme Court, citing the papers Nachtrieb had signed when he joined the group and when he left, found against him. Given the communitarian nature of the group, he was not entitled to receive any property from it.[20]

There were also suits by descendants of former members who wanted to extract something of value from the religious groups as part of their inheritance. *Goesele v. Bimeler*[21] was lodged against the Society of Separatists of Zoar, Ohio. The Separatists also had members sign over their assets to the community with the understanding that the property would stay permanently with the community; neither members nor their heirs had any right to it. The case was about whether descendants of an original member could inherit the assets of their ancestor. The Court answered "no" on the basis of the nature of the community and the agreements signed by its members.

In *Order of St. Benedict v. Steinhauser*[22] the Court decided another inheritance case, except this time the organization was a Catholic monastic order, the deceased member was a priest, Father Augustin Wirth, and the one seeking assets was Albert Steinhauser, the administrator of his estate. Father Wirth had written some books. Steinhauser claimed that the proceeds of the books should be part of Wirth's estate and not go to the monastery. The Court ruled that the monastic order was a charitable organization, its constitution insisted that the assets of its members should go to the order, and the estate had no right to Father Wirth's assets. All the cases of this type were decided on contractual language, not constitutional principles.

A variation on these cases involved a dispute within a congregation about who owned and controlled church property, a common circumstance. During the Civil War, the Presbyterian Church divided into proslavery and antislavery factions. After the war, the church's general assembly insisted that formerly proslavery church members must renounce that belief before they could be considered Presbyterians again. Two groups in a Presbyterian congregation in Kentucky perpetuated the dispute; each claimed to be the rightful owners of their church's property. In *Watson v. Jones*[23] the Court not only addressed the question at hand, but also asserted principles by which courts should deal with church property disputes. It decided that civil courts must not intervene in disputes that required interpretation of theology, which was virtually always necessary in church property arguments.

In churches in which a bequest or donation required a certain theological belief, the party that believed the required theology was entitled to ownership of the property.

In churches with a congregational polity, i.e., a self-governing, autonomous church, majority rule would determine the property dispute.

Hierarchical churches, such as Presbyterian or Episcopalian, in which the local congregation was a part of a larger organization that had juridical control over the local churches, presented a harder problem. The Court said that because civil authority must not determine the truth or falsity of theology, in these disputes the courts must defer to the highest level in the church's judicatory that had rendered a decision in the case.

> The law knows no heresy, and is committed to the support of no dogma, the establishment of no sect. . . . It is not to be supposed that the judges of the civil courts can be as competent in the ecclesiastical law and religious faith of all these bodies as the ablest men in each are in reference to their own.[24]

The *Watson* principle was reaffirmed, with modification, in *Gonzales v. Archbishop*. There the Court opined that civil courts could review decisions of church authorities to determine if there had been "fraud, collusion, or arbitrariness" by the ecclesiastical body.[25]

THE UNITED STATES AS A CHRISTIAN NATION

Two nineteenth-century cases, decided on statutory grounds, are more famous for their *dicta* than for their decisions. The first is *Vidal v. Girard's Executors*.[26] Stephen Girard, a wealthy Frenchman, left a will that established an educational institution for "poor male white orphan children."[27] However, Girard left the money on the condition that no clergy person should ever administer or teach at the school.

Girard's heirs, including Francois Vidal, challenged his will. They claimed the prohibition of teaching by clergy was "derogatory and hostile to the Christian religion," and "against the common law and public policy of Pennsylvania."[28]

The Court acknowledged "that the Christian religion is a part of the common law of Pennsylvania." It quoted the religious freedom provisions of the state constitution and summarized them by saying, "Language more comprehensive for the complete protection of every variety of religious opinion could scarcely be used; . . . So that we are compelled to admit that although Christianity be a part of the common law of the state, yet it is so in this qualified sense; . . ."[29] Girard did not forbid teaching Christianity in the school, only that clergy could not teach. Girard only sought to protect the boys from the confusion of clashing sectarian doctrine. The principles of Christian morality could be taught by lay teachers and be within Girard's requirement. Girard's will was allowed to stand and the Court professed that Christianity was part of the law of Pennsylvania.

Immigration was a dominant social phenomenon in the nineteenth century. In its efforts to prevent foreigners coming into the country, in 1885 Congress forbade any individual or company from making a contract with any alien to come to this country to perform labor.[30] When a church hired an English clergyman to come to America to be its pastor, the United States prohibited his entry. The church sued. Did the law against contract laborers prohibit a church from hiring a foreign minister? The Court, in *Church of the Holy Trinity v. United States*,[31] answered "no."

The Court held that Congress intended to prohibit the importation of unskilled, uneducated manual laborers, those fit for menial labor. The Act did not intend to exclude professionals; certainly not clergy.

> Obviously the thought expressed in this reaches only to the work of the manual laborer, as distinguished from that of the professional man. No one . . . would suppose that Congress had in its mind any purpose of staying the coming into this country of ministers of the gospel, or, indeed, of any class whose toil is of the brain.[32]

This would have been enough to uphold the church's action; but apparently the Court felt strongly that the exclusion of clergy was wrong. So it argued further that such exclusion was wrong because the United States is a religious nation. "These, and many other matters that might be noticed, add a volume of unofficial declarations to the mass of organic utterances that this is a Christian nation. In the face of all these, shall it be believed that a Congress of the United States intended to make it a misdemeanor for a church of this country to contract for the services of a Christian minister residing in another nation?"[33]

Institutional Character

Occasionally the Court has avoided deciding a case on constitutional grounds by focusing on the nature of the institution at issue in the case. The classic example is *Bradfield v. Roberts*.[34] The lawsuit protested government money paid to operate a hospital run by Roman Catholics. The arrangement was alleged to violate the Establishment Clause. The Court, however, did not address that issue. It said that the religious nature of the proprietors of the hospital was immaterial; the real issue was whether the institution was being run for the purpose for which it was organized. "That the influence of any particular church may be powerful over the membership of a nonsectarian and secular corporation, incorporated for a certain defined purpose and with clearly stated powers, is surely not sufficient to convert such a corporation into a religious or sectarian body."[35] That the hospital admitted and cared for the sick, as it was supposed to do, justified government funding for its support. The religious nature of its management was irrelevant.

CONSCIENTIOUS OBJECTION

There are several nonconstitutional cases about conscientious objection to war decided by the Supreme Court. These are of two types—some about the admission of alien immigrants to citizenship, some about the interpretation of selective service laws. The first type came to the Court earlier than the second.

The earlier cases before the Court were of applicants for citizenship who were not willing to take up arms in defense of this country. The first case was that of Hungarian Rosika Schwimmer, a famous feminist and pacifist. She was a nonreligious, philosophical pacifist. When she applied for citizenship, she was 50 years old and obviously female. She was ineligible to serve in the military. She never dreamed she would be denied citizenship of because of her well-known resistance to war. But she was, because the government interpreted the "support and defend the Constitution and laws of the United States against all enemies, foreign and domestic" language of the naturalization law and the oath[36] to mean that applicants for citizenship must be willing to bear arms in defense of the country.

The Court decided against Schwimmer. It held "That it is the duty of citizens by force of arms to defend our government against all enemies whenever necessity arises is a fundamental principle of the Constitution." But she was an overage woman! Nevertheless, the Court held:

> The influence of conscientious objectors against the use of military force in defense of the principles of our government is apt to be more detrimental than their mere refusal to bear arms. The fact that, by reason of sex, age or other cause, they may be unfit to serve, does not lessen their purpose or power to influence others.[37]

Rosika Schwimmer lost her case because she was an outspoken pacifist.

Douglas Clyde Macintosh, a Canadian Baptist and an internationally known theologian who taught at Yale Divinity School, was also denied citizenship. He was not willing to promise that he would fight in any and all wars. He wanted to measure the rightness of any war against the will of God. The Court made short work of Macintosh's argument.

> It is not within the province of the courts to make bargains with those who seek
> naturalization. They must accept the grant and take the oath in accordance with
> the terms fixed by the law, or forego the privilege of citizenship. There is no
> middle choice. If one qualification of the oath be allowed, the door is opened for
> others, with utter confusion as the probable final result.[38]

There are important *dicta* in this case. In his brief to the Court, Macintosh's lawyer included the phrase "'[it is] a fixed principle of our Constitution, . . . that a citizen cannot be forced and need not bear arms in a war if he has conscientious scruples against doing so.'" The Court responded:

> This, if it means what it seems to say, is an astonishing statement. Of course,
> there is no such principle of the Constitution, fixed or otherwise. The conscien-
> tious objector is relieved from the obligation to bear arms in obedience to no
> constitutional provision, express or implied; but because, and only because, it has
> accorded with the policy of Congress to relieve him.[39]

The opportunity to be a conscientious objector is not a constitutionally given right, but only because Congress has legislated it.[40]

Another naturalization case followed *Macintosh* up the judicial ladder, *United States v. Bland*.[41] Marie Averil Bland, a Canadian Episcopalian, was opposed to war in any form. The Court also denied her citizenship and wrote no new or quotable language. It said, in essence, "We just decided this case in *Macintosh*."[42]

Before the quartet of naturalization conscientious objector cases was complete, the Court confronted the question of whether students in a state university that required military (ROTC) training could be exempted from that training. In the 1930s both the California and the General (national) Conferences of the Methodist Church passed pacifist resolutions. They asked universities requiring military training to exempt Methodist students who conscientiously objected to bearing arms. Some Methodist students at the University of California refused to take ROTC courses. They were expelled. They sued, claiming a denial of liberty guaran-teed by the Due Process Clause of the Fourteenth Amendment. They cited the res-olutions of their church, along with their own consciences, for their refusal to take the courses. The University cited its right to determine the conditions for attending. The Court, in *Hamilton v. Regents of the University of California*,[43] decided for the University. It cited *Schwimmer* and *Macintosh*, especially that conscientious objec-tion is not a constitutionally guaranteed right. Consequently, state universities could require military studies.

In the fourth naturalization conscientious objector case, James Louis Girouard, a Canadian Seventh-day Adventist, would serve in the military, but only in a non-combatant role.[44] The government opposed his application for citizenship. The Court, however, used this case to change its mind on the issue of conscientious objector applicants for citizenship. "We conclude that the *Schwimmer*, *Macintosh*,

and *Bland* cases do not state the correct rule of law."[45] Bearing arms was not the
only way a person could serve the nation in war.

> Refusal to bear arms is not necessarily a sign of disloyalty or a lack of attachment
> to our institutions. One may serve his country faithfully and devotedly, though
> his religious scruples make it impossible for him to shoulder a rifle. Devotion to
> one's country can be as real and as enduring among non-combatants as among
> combatants. . . .[46]

Because of *Girouard*, in 1952 Congress changed the immigration law and the
language of the oath.[47] Now, if an alien has conscientious objections based on "religious training and belief," he or she can become a citizen by taking an alternative
oath, to either do noncombatant service within the military, or do work of national
importance under civilian direction.[48]

Americans generally have been solicitous of domestic conscientious objectors.
In the colonial period and during the War of Independence and Civil War, colonies
and states exempted conscientious objectors from fighting. The exemption, however, typically excused only members of historic "peace churches," Anabaptists/
Mennonites, Church of the Brethren, Society of Friends/Quakers, and, more
recently, Jehovah's Witnesses. The first law of the modern period, the Draft Act of
1917, reflected that perspective:

> [N]othing in this Act contained shall be construed to require or compel any
> person to serve in any of the forces herein provided for who is found to be a
> member of a well-recognized religious sect . . . and whose existing creed or
> principles forbid its members to participate in war in any form. . . ."[49]

When Congress revisited the definition of conscientious objection in 1940, it
broadened the parameters of who qualified. "Nothing contained in this Act shall be
construed to require any person to be subject to combatant training and service in
the land or naval forces of the United States who, by reason of religious training and
belief, is conscientiously opposed to participation in war in any form."[50] When it
revised the law again, in 1948, Congress defined what it meant by "religious training
and belief." "Religious training and belief in this connection means an individual's
belief in relation to a Supreme Being involving duties superior to those arising from
any human relation, but does not include essentially political, sociological, or philosophical views or a merely personal moral code."[51]

What about persons claiming conscientious objector status who had unconventional religious beliefs? The Court confronted that issue in *United States v.
Seeger*.[52] During the unpopular Vietnam War, three persons who did not believe in
a "Supreme Being" had been denied conscientious objector status. They claimed
they fit the statutory requirement;[53] but did they? The linchpin of *Seeger* is this
language: "In spite of the elusive nature of the inquiry, we are not without certain
guidelines.

> In amending the 1940 Act, Congress adopted almost intact the language of Chief
> Justice Hughes in *United States v. Macintosh*: "The essence of religion is belief in a

relation to *God* involving duties superior to those arising from any human relation." (at 633–634; emphasis supplied)

By comparing the statutory definition with those words, however, it becomes readily apparent that the Congress deliberately broadened them by substituting the phrase "Supreme Being" for the appellation "God;" and in so doing it is also significant that Congress did not elaborate on the form or nature of this higher authority, which it chose to designate as a "Supreme Being."[54]

The Court, based on that rationale, broadened the statutory language to include nearly everyone. To determine who qualified, it formulated a "double sincerity test."[55] The test might be stated in these words: "A sincere and meaningful belief which occupies in the life of its possessor a place parallel to that filled by the God of those admittedly qualifying for the exemption comes within the statutory definition."[56] If the aversion to war is as sincerely held by the applicant with unconventional religious beliefs as the belief in God by one, either real or hypothetical, who clearly qualifies for conscientious objector status, then he or she qualifies.

On the basis of *Seeger*, Congress modified the law again by defining "religious training and belief" not in terms of what it is, but what it is not.[57] It removed the "Supreme Being" language altogether.

Later the Court considered *Welsh v. United States*,[58] in which it appeared that the applicant's "religious training and belief" was merely a personal moral code. However, given the elastic nature the Court had given "religious training and belief" in *Seeger*, the Court said that Welsh was more religious than he thought he was.

When a registrant states that his objections to war are "religious," that information is highly relevant to the question of the function his beliefs have in his life. But very few registrants are fully aware of the broad scope of the word "religious" as used in § 6(j), and accordingly a registrant's statement that his beliefs are nonreligious is a highly unreliable guide for those charged with administering the exemption.[59]

The Court held that Welsh was entitled to conscientious objector status; he met the statutory standard, despite the tenuous role of religion in his life.

Finally we come to the issue of selective conscientious objection. Every version of the draft laws state that for one to gain conscientious objector status, he or she must be opposed to participating "in war in any form." The Court confronted a version of this in *Gillette v. United States*.[60] Gillette would fight in wars of national defense or United Nations peacekeeping wars, but not Vietnam. A second plaintiff's objection to war was because he believed the Vietnam War was not just.

The Court made short work of these arguments. The statutory language, "conscientiously opposed to participation to war in any form" was straightforward and clear. It would bear no alternative reading.

Apart from the Government's need for manpower, perhaps the central interest involved in the administration of conscription laws is the interest in maintaining a fair system for determining "who serves when not all serve." When the Government exacts so much, the importance of fair, evenhanded, and uniform decision making is obviously intensified. The Government argues that the interest of fairness would be jeopardized by the expansion § 6(j) to include conscientious objection to a particular war. . . .[61]

STANDING

The issue of "standing" is the issue of whether or not one has the right to bring a lawsuit. Article III, section 2 of the Constitution, says that the courts shall adjudicate "cases" and "controversies." A case or controversy must be somebody against somebody, rather than answering an abstract philosophical question. Furthermore, it must be clear that the litigants will be affected by the outcome of the case. If one cannot show that he or she (or an organization) will be damaged or benefited by the decision, one may not bring suit.

The classic example of standing is taxpayer suits. The precedent-setting case was *Frothingham v. Mellon*.[62] The Federal Maternity Act of 1921 caused the federal government to give funds to the states "to reduce maternal and infant mortality and protect the health of mothers and infants."[63] Frothingham, suing as a taxpayer, claimed the law would "take her property, under the guise of taxation, without due process of law."[64] The Court ruled that she did not have standing because "The party who invokes the power must be able to show, . . . that he has sustained or is immediately in danger of sustaining some direct injury as the result of [the statute's] enforcement, and not merely that he suffers in some indefinite way in common with people generally."[65] Why does a taxpayer not meet that standard? Because the taxes from an individual taxpayer are such an infinitesimal part of the total federal budget that he or she is not directly affected by any federal spending program. "His interest in the moneys of the treasury . . . is shared with millions of others, is comparatively minute and indeterminable, and the effect on future taxation, of any payment out of the funds, so remote, fluctuating and uncertain, that no basis is afforded for an appeal to the preventive powers of a court of equity."[66] Consequently, taxpayers, as taxpayers, are not allowed to bring suits in federal court.[67]

However, the Court carved out an exception to *Frothingham* in *Flast v. Cohen*.[68] Some taxpayers attacked the Elementary and Secondary Education Act of 1965 because it permitted government money to finance instruction in church-related schools. The issue of their standing arose. The Court ruled that they had standing, but only by modifying the longstanding rule. Taxpayers have standing if they meet two conditions.

> First, the taxpayer must establish a logical link between that status and the type of legislative enactment attacked. Thus, a taxpayer will be a proper party to allege the unconstitutionality only of exercises of congressional power under the taxing and spending clause of Art. I, § 8 of the Constitution. It will not be sufficient to allege an incidental expenditure of tax funds in the administration of an

essentially regulatory statute. . . . Secondly, the taxpayer must establish a nexus between that status and the precise nature of the constitutional infringement alleged. . . . [T]he taxpayer must show that the challenged enactment exceeds specific constitutional limitations imposed on the exercise of the congressional taxing and spending power and not simply that the enactment is generally beyond the power delegated to Congress under Art. I, § 8. When both nexuses are established, the litigant will have shown a taxpayer's stake in the outcome of the controversy and will be a proper and appropriate party to invoke a federal court's jurisdiction.[69]

Flast made possible many Establishment Clause cases discussed elsewhere in this volume.

The Federal Property and Administrative Services Act of 1949 authorized the government to give properties no longer useful to the government to private or other public entities. In 1976 the Department of Health, Education, and Welfare gave a former Army hospital and 77 acres of property to an Assemblies of God school, Valley Forge Christian College, dedicated to teaching Christian doctrine and preparing people to serve the church. The gift was challenged as a violation of the Establishment Clause by a separationist organization, Americans United for Separation of Church and State.[70]

The case reached the Court on the question of whether the plaintiffs had standing. The Court ruled they did not because this case did not fit the *Flast* requirements.

Unlike the plaintiffs in *Flast*, respondents fail the first prong of the test for taxpayer standing. Their claim is deficient in two respects. First, the source of their complaint is not a congressional action, but a decision by HEW to transfer a parcel of federal property. . . .

Second, . . . the property transfer about which respondents complain was not an exercise of authority conferred by the taxing and spending clause of Art. I, § 8. The authorizing legislation, the Federal Property and Administrative Services Act of 1949, was an evident exercise of Congresses' power under the Property Clause, Art. IV, § 3, cl. 2. . . . [This] is decisive of any claim of taxpayer standing under the *Flast* precedent.[71]

Furthermore, Americans United could not demonstrate the giveaway that they protested would cause them any personal injury. Aside from being taxpayers and being committed to separation of church and state, they had no personal stake in the case. The *Frothingham* and *Flast* rules remain intact for taxpayer suits.

One of President George W. Bush's (2000–2008) favorite projects was to provide federal money to religious organizations to support their charitable work, a procedure authorized by the Welfare Reform Act of 1996.[72] To try to help religious welfare agencies "compete on a level playing field," he created the White House Office of Faith-Based and Community Initiatives within the Executive Office of the President.[73] White House personnel held conferences to encourage religious groups to apply for the available money. Those meetings stimulated the Freedom from

Religion Foundation to file suit, claiming that the faith-based initiative and the conferences promoting it violated the Establishment Clause. The government claimed the Foundation did not have standing, given that it sued as a group of tax-payers. The case, *Hein v. Freedom from Religion Foundation*,[74] reached the Court in that form.

The Freedom from Religion Foundation sued under *Flast*. It claimed a pres-idential order to spend funds ultimately came from the taxing and spending power of Congress, which allocated money to the executive branch. The Court disagreed. It said repeatedly that the challenged program was not the result of *direct* congressional action. That distinguished this case from the first *Flast* criterion.

> Because the expenditures that respondents challenge were not expressly autho-rized or mandated by any specific congressional enactment, respondents' lawsuit is not directed at an exercise of congressional power, . . . and thus lacks the requisite "logical nexus" between taxpayer status "and the type of legislative enactment attacked." *Flast*, 392 U.S., 102. . . .
>
> But *Flast* focused on congressional action, and we must decline the invitation to extend its holding to encompass discretionary Executive Branch expenditures. . . .[75]

Taxpayer suits are not allowed in federal courts, with certain narrowly defined exceptions delineated by *Flast v. Cohen*, to which the Court has given a very literal-istic interpretation.

Not all standing cases involve taxpayers. One of the most newsworthy church–state cases of 2004, *Elk Grove Unified School District v. Newdow*,[76] was resolved on standing, but without taxpayer facts. Under California law, children in the Elk Grove School District each day recited the pledge of allegiance to the flag. Michael Newdow, an atheist, argued that the school's practice was state-imposed religious indoctrination of his kindergarten-aged daughter, given that the pledge contained the phrase "under God." When the Ninth Circuit Court of Appeals agreed that the practice violated the First Amendment, it set off a firestorm of protest.[77] The Supreme Court defused the issue by ruling that Newdow lacked standing.

The Court recognized that, despite its constitutional dimension, the case was really about domestic relations, for the student's mother and father were not married. The father objected to his daughter saying the pledge, with its theological dimension. The mother, a Christian, wanted her daughter to say the pledge. The Court said that federal courts should not be involved in domestic relations cases, but should defer to the rulings of state courts. In this case a California court had ruled that when the mother and father disagreed over how to raise their daughter, the mother was to "exer-cise legal control," i.e., she had "a form of veto power" over the wishes of Newdow.[78] Given its deference to state courts in family law, and given the California ruling just described, the Court ruled that Newdow could not sue on behalf of his daughter.

> When hard questions of domestic relations are sure to affect the outcome, the prudent course is for the federal court to stay its hand rather than reach out to resolve a weighty question of federal constitutional law. . . . We conclude that,

having been deprived under California law of the right to sue as next friend, Newdow lacks prudential standing to bring this suit in federal court.[79]

Taxes

Because humans dislike paying taxes, it is not surprising that there are antitaxation church–state cases. In *Bob Jones University v. United States*[80] a Christian school lost its income tax exemption because its racial practices were contrary to public policy. Bob Jones University, a fundamentalist Christian school, believed the Bible forbade interracial marriage and dating. Before 1971, black students were forbidden admission. From 1971 to 1975, unmarried blacks were excluded, but blacks married within their race were admitted. After 1975, unmarried blacks were admitted, but strict campus rules prohibited interracial dating.

Was the university entitled to tax benefits under §§ 501 (c)(3) and 170 of the Internal Revenue Code?[81] The former exempts charitable organizations from paying income tax, the latter pertains to "deductibility," i.e., the ability of donors to exempt organizations to deduct donations from their individual taxes. The IRS removed both tax exemption and deductibility from Bob Jones. Because the university practiced various forms of racial discrimination, it was contrary to public policy established by the Civil Rights Act of 1964 and thus was not entitled to tax benefits.[82]

The university claimed Free Exercise Clause protection because its racial policy was based on religious beliefs. Although the Court took the argument seriously, it ultimately deflected it in favor of the view that the IRS was bound by law to deny tax benefits to institutions that violated public policy.

> [E]ntitlement to tax exemption depends on meeting certain common law standards of charity—namely, that an institution seeking tax-exempt status must serve a public purpose and not be contrary to established public policy. . . .
>   Whatever may be the rationale for such private schools' policies, and however sincere the rationale may be, racial discrimination in education is contrary to public policy. Racially discriminatory educational institutions cannot be viewed as conferring a public benefit within the "charitable" concept . . . or within the Congressional intent underlying § 170 and § 501(c)(3).[83]

Sometimes the issue was whether a taxpayer properly claimed tax deductions. Such a case was *Hernandez v. Commissioner of Internal Revenue*, about charitable contributions made to the Church of Scientology.[84] Two important practices of that church are "auditing" and "training." "Auditing" is a personal interview between a seasoned Scientologist and a novice for the purposed of identifying spiritual difficulties that cause behavioral and psychological problems. The goal is to eliminate the spiritual difficulties so that one might live a life clear of the problems. "Training" is instruction for Scientology members to learn the doctrines of the church and qualify to be auditors.

Scientology charges for both auditing and training. There are several layers of each procedure before one reaches a goal and, for each series of sessions, there is a fixed fee, i.e., the church has a fee schedule.

When various Scientologists deducted the expenses of auditing and training from their federal income taxes as § 170 charitable contributions, the IRS disallowed the deductions because they were not contributions. The Supreme Court agreed with the IRS. The government argued that "the term 'charitable contribution' in § 170 is synonymous with the word 'gift,' which case law has defined 'as a *voluntary transfer* of property by the owner to another *without consideration* therefore.'"[85] If one receives a benefit or service for which one pays, that money is not a gift or contribution and does not qualify as a tax deduction.

> [T]hese payments were part of a quintessential *quid pro quo* exchange: in return for their money, petitioners received an identifiable benefit, namely, auditing and training sessions. . ..
>
> [W]e conclude that petitioners' payments to the Church for auditing and training sessions are not "contribution[s] or gift[s]" within the meaning of that statutory expression.[86]

Donations to religious organizations must clearly be gifts, not *quid pro quo* payments for services or benefits.

PUBLIC PLACES

Virtually all religions desire to convince others of the veracity of their faith. Frequently they want to witness in public places. *Heffron v. International Society for Krishna Consciousness* (ISKCON)[87] considered whether such activity could take place at the Minnesota state fair. ISKCON (Hare Krishna) requires devotees to meet others in public places to evangelize and solicit funds. State fair rules required that it (and other similar groups, religious or secular) do its solicitation either outside the fair grounds or from a booth inside the grounds. ISKCON claimed the restriction violated its First Amendment rights. Neither Minnesota nor the Court denied that ISKCON had a constitutional right to express its viewpoint and solicit; but, because the confined area of the fairgrounds required crowd control, fair authorities argued the necessity for "time, place, and manner" restrictions.[88] The Court agreed. "It is also common ground, . . . that the First Amendment does not guarantee the right to communicate one's views at all times and places or in any manner that may be desired."[89]

A similar case couched the issue in terms of a public forum. A public forum is a government-owned area designated as a place suitable for the free expression of ideas. *International Society for Krishna Consciousness v. Lee*[90] considered whether ISKCON could solicit in airports. Although the case had freedom of religion and speech overtones, the Court decided it on nonconstitutional grounds, namely, that airports are not public forums and therefore not required to accommodate religious groups in their terminals.

The concept of a public forum has a long history, although airports do not. It is even more recent that groups have come to see them as fruitful places for solicitation or advocacy activity. "Thus, the tradition of airport activity does not demonstrate that airports have historically been made available for speech activity. Nor can we say that these particular terminals, or airport terminals generally, have been intentionally opened by their operators for such activity; . . ."[91]

ISKCON argued that because other "transportation nodes," e.g., train and bus stations, have been sites for expressive activity, airports should be as well. The Court noted that such places are typically privately owned and thus not subject to government public forum analysis. Also, airports are not typical "transportation nodes." They handle huge crowds of people on tight schedules in restricted space. Furthermore, if people stopped to respond to solicitors, it would impede foot traffic and snarl the terminals. "Thus, we think that neither by tradition nor purpose can the terminals be described as satisfying the standards we have set out for identifying a public forum."[92] Airports are not public forums.

WORKPLACE CASES

The issue of religion in the workplace is frequently a vexing issue. When the Court has adjudicated such disputes they frequently have been decided on nonconstitutional grounds.

Title VII of the Civil Rights Act of 1964[93] forbids an employer to discriminate against an employee because of religion. The nondiscrimination rule requires the employer to accommodate the religious practices of employees, so long as the accommodation does not cause the employer "undue hardship." In *Trans World Airlines v. Hardison*[94] the Court defined the nature of "undue hardship."

Hardison became a member of a sabbatarian group[95] and asked TWA for a work schedule to allow him to worship on Saturday. Because TWA's operation was huge and complex, which involved contractual relations, union structures, and seniority questions, it was not able to devise a work schedule to accommodate Hardison's religion. The question was whether TWA had done enough and whether further efforts by the company would have inflicted an "undue hardship" on it. What was an "undue hardship?"

The Court ruled that anything beyond a reasonable, and minimal, effort to accommodate an employee's religion was an "undue hardship" and not required by law. "To require TWA to bear more than a *de minimis* cost in order to give Hardison Saturdays off is an undue hardship."[96] Sabbatarians, such as Jews, Seventh-day Adventists, and Seventh-day Baptists, were dismayed at this decision.

Hardison was reinforced in a later decision about a public school teacher who needed days off to attend religious holidays, *Ansonia Board of Education v. Philbrook*.[97] Philbrook needed 6 days a year to attend holy days of his church, the Worldwide Church of God. His employer rejected an accommodation plan he suggested, so he sued. The Second Circuit Court of Appeals ruled that an— employer is obligated to accept an accommodation suggested by an employee unless it produced undue hardship.[98] The Supreme Court disagreed. Without rejecting *Hardison's de minimis* rule about undue hardship, the Court wrote: "[W]here the employer has already reasonably accommodated the employee's religious needs, the statutory inquiry is at an end. The employer need not further show that each of the employee's alternative accommodations would result in undue hardship."[99]

In *Hardison* and *Philbrook*, without reaching any constitutional question, the Court skewed Congress' Title VII protection of employees from religious discrimination in a way that favored employers.

Can lay teachers in religious schools unionize? The Court said "no" in *National Labor Relations Board v. Catholic Bishop of Chicago*.[100] Lay teachers in parochial schools were paid less than public school teachers. Teachers, in elections supervised by the NLRB, voted to unionize. The schools refused to recognize the elections and argued the NLRB had no jurisdiction over religious schools. For the NLRB to become involved in this parochial school salary dispute would involve it in both Establishment and Free Exercise Clause matters. The question before the Court was whether the National Labor Relations Act of 1935[101] and subsequent revisions authorized the NLRB to intervene in the affairs of church-related schools.

The Court examined the legislative history of the Act and its amendments. It noted that Congress was aware of the constitutionally sensitive nature of a federal regulatory agency being involved in the affairs of religious institutions. It concluded that in whatever efforts parochial school teachers made to unionize, the NLRB could not be involved.

That most of the cases reviewed in this chapter did not rise to the level of constitutionality does not mean they are less important than others. Abiding principles have emerged from some of them. Indeed, some of these cases have affected the lives of multitudes of people. One thinks of the conscientious objection cases, particularly those that made it possible for noncombatants to be naturalized. Some of them had huge impact on subsequent, constitutional, cases. This is particularly true of *Flast v. Cohen*, which opened the way for many Establishment Clause challenges of government funding of parochial schools.[102] Therefore, the Court's self-imposed restraint from using the heavy artillery of the Constitution does not mean that cases decided in that way are anemic or insignificant.

Conclusion

Virtually all religion cases addressed by the U.S. courts are adjudicated pursuant to the religion clauses of the First Amendment. However, there are exceptions. As this chapter has demonstrated, and for various legal reasons, the courts frequently decide religion cases on nonconstitutional grounds or pursuant to the U.S. Constitution's non-First Amendment provisions. That the courts are able to draw from a spectrum of constitutional and nonconstitutional sources in deciding cases is an asset rather than a liability to the American people.

ENDNOTES

1. A clause in section 1 of the Fourteenth Amendment provides: "[N]or shall any State deprive any person of life, liberty, or property, without due process of law." The Court ruled that one of the liberties guaranteed to the citizens of the states by this clause was the freedom of religion contained in the First Amendment. The Free Exercise Clause was applied to the states by *Cantwell v. Connecticut*, 310 U.S. 296 (1940) and the Establishment Clause in *Everson v. Board of Education*, 330 U.S. 1 (1947). Since this "incorporation," many more cases were decided on First Amendment grounds.

2. See *National Labor Relations Board v. Catholic Bishop*, 440 U.S. 490 (1979), 500. Chief Justice Marshall's words are: "It has also been observed that an act of congress ought never to be construed to violate the law of nations, if any other possible construction remains, and consequently can never be construed to violate neutral rights, or to affect neutral commerce, further than is warranted by the law of nations as understood in this country." *Murray v. The Charming Betsy*, 6 U.S. 64 (1804), 118.

3. *Ashwander v. TVA*, 297 U.S. 288 (1936), 346–348.

4. Quoting *Liverpool, N.Y. & P.S.S. Co. v. Emigration Commissioners*, 113 U.S. 33, 39, fn. 2/5 (1885) and *Burton v. United States* 196 U.S. 283 (1905), 295.

5. Citing *Siler v. Louisville & Nashville R. Co.*, 213 U.S. 175 (1909), 191; and *Light v United States*, 220 U.S. 523 (1911), 538.

6. Quoting *Crowell v. Benson*, 285 U.S. 22 (1932), 62, fn 2/8.

7. Quoting *Ashwander v. TVA*, 297 U.S. 288 (1936), 346.

8. Quoting *Colorado River Water Conservation Dist. v. United States*, 424 U.S. 800 (1976), 820.

9. *Elk Grove Unified School District v. Newdow*, 542 U.S. 1 (2005), 11, quoting *Spector Motor Service v. McLaughlin*, 323 U.S. 101 (1944), 105.

10. 268 U.S. 510 (1925).

11. The Due Process Clause of the Fourteenth Amendment (see note 1), protects property. The Court considered the opportunity for an institution to make a living to be personal property for purposes of this case.

12. 268 U.S. 510, 536, 534.

13. 281 U.S. 370 (1930).

14. 494 U.S. 872 (1990).

15. See *Sherbert v. Verner*, 374 U.S. 398 (1963).

16. 107 *Stat.* 1488 (1993).

17. 521 U.S. 507 (1997).

18. "As originally enacted, RFRA applied to States as well as the Federal Government. In *City of Boerne v. Flores*, 521 U.S. 507 (1997), we held the application to States to be beyond Congress' legislative authority under §5 of the 14th Amendment." *Gonzales v. O Centro Espirita Beneficente Uniao Do Vegetal*, 546 U.S. 418, 425 n. 1.

19. 546 U.S. 418 (2006).

20. *Baker v. Nachtrieb*, 19 Howard (60 U.S.) 126 (1856).

21. 55 U.S. 589 (1853).

22. 234 U.S. 640 (1914).

23. 13 Wallace (80 U.S.) 679 (1872).

24. 80 U.S. 679, 728–729.

25. 280 U.S. 1 (1929), 16.

26. 43 U.S. 127 (1844).

27. 43 U.S. 127, 129–130.

28. 43 U.S. 127, 197.

29. 43 U.S. 127, 198.

30. 23 *Stat.* 332, ch. 164 (1885).

31. 143 U.S. 457 (1893).

32. 143 U.S. 457, 463.

33. 143 U.S. 457, 471.

34. 175 U.S. 291 (1899).

35. 175 U.S. 291, 298–299.

36. 34 *Stat.* 596, ch. 3592; 54 *Stat.* 1157.

37. 279 U.S. 644 (1929), 650–651.

38. 283 U.S. 605 (1931), 626.

39. 283 U.S. 605, 623–624.

40. This is the reason that all the conscientious objector cases had to be decided on the basis of statutory language rather than either the Establishment or Free Exercise Clauses.

41. 283 U.S. 636 (1931).

42. However, Bland's story is interesting and dramatic. See Ronald B. Flowers, "In Praise of Conscience: Marie Averil Bland," *Anglican and Episcopal History* 62 (March 1993): 37–57.

43. 293 U.S. 245 (1934).

44. This is the traditional position of Adventists, who sometimes call themselves "conscientious cooperators" rather than conscientious objectors.

45. *Girouard v. United States*, 328 U.S. 61 (1946), 69.

46. 328 U.S. 61, 64.

47. 66 *Stat.* 163 (1952).

48. For a full explication of these conscientious objector naturalization cases, see Ronald B. Flowers, *To Defend the Constitution: Religion, Conscientious Objection, Naturalization, and the Supreme Court* (Lanham, MD: Scarecrow Press, 2003).

49. 40 *Stat.* 76, 78 § 4 (1917).

50. 54 *Stat.* 885, 889 § 5(g) (1940).

51. 62 *Stat.* 604, 613 § 6(j) (1948).

52. 380 U.S. 163 (1965).

53. Seeger, for example, said "that he was conscientiously opposed to participa-

tion in war in any form by reason of his 'religious' belief; that he preferred to leave the question as to his belief in a Supreme Being open, 'rather than answer 'yes' or 'no''; that his 'skepticism or disbelief in the existence of God' did 'not necessarily mean lack of faith in anything whatsoever'; that his was a 'belief in and devotion to goodness and virtue for their own sakes, and a religious faith in a purely ethical creed.'" 380 U.S. 163, 166.

54. 380 U.S. 163, 175.

55. This is my phrase.

56. 380 U.S. 163, 176, see also 184.

57. "As used in this subsection, the term 'religious training and belief' does not include essentially personal, sociological or philosophical views, or a merely personal moral code." 81 *Stat.* 100, 104 § (7) (1967).

58. 398 U.S. 333 (1970).

59. 398 U.S. 333, 340.

60. 401 U.S. 437 (1971). See also the earlier *Sicurella v. United States*, 348 U.S. 385 (1955).

61. 401 U.S. 437, 455.

62. 262 U.S. 447 (1923). Although *Frothingham* was not a church–state case, I review it because it is precedent for some church–state standing cases.

63. 262 U.S. 447, 479.

64. 262 U.S. 447, 480.

65. 262 U.S. 447, 488.

66. 262 U.S. 447, 487.

67. However, some states allow standing to taxpayers in their courts. One of the most important church–state cases, *Everson v. Board of Education*, 330 U.S. 1 (1947), was a taxpayer suit brought through the New Jersey state courts to which the U.S. Supreme Court granted certiorari.

68. 392 U.S. 83 (1968).

69. 392 U.S. 83, 102–103.

70. *Valley Forge Christian College v. Americans United for Separation of Church and State*, 454 U.S. 464 (1982).

71. 454 U.S. 464, 479–480.

72. 110 *Stat.* 2105 (1996).

73. Executive Order No. 13199, 3 CFR 752 (2001 Comp.), quoted in *Hein v. Freedom from Religion Foundation*, 551 U.S. 587 (2007), 593.

74. 127 S.Ct. 2553 (2007).

75. 551 U.S. 587, 608–609.

76. 542 U.S. 1 (2004).

77. See Ronald B. Flowers, *That Godless Court?: Supreme Court Decisions on Church-State Relations*, 2nd ed. (Louisville, KY: Westminster John Knox Press, 2005), 125–128.

78. 542 U.S. 1, 14, 17.

79. 542 U.S. 1, 17–18.

80. 461 U.S. 574 (1983).

81. 26 U.S.C., Section 501(c)(3), Section 170.

82. See Revenue Ruling 71-447, which asserted that exempt organizations must conform to public policy on race.

83. 461 U.S. 574, 586, 595–596.

84. 490 U.S. 680 (1989).

85. 490 U.S. 680, 687 (emphasis in original) quoting *DeJong v. Commissioner*, 36 T.C. 896, 899 (1961), aff'd 309 F.2d 373 (CA9 1962).

86. 490 U.S. 680, 691, 694.

87. 452 U.S. 640 (1981).

88. This was hardly a new idea. See, e.g., *Cox v. New Hampshire*, 312 U.S. 569 (1941).

89. 452 U.S. 640, 647.

90. 505 U.S. 672 (1992).

91. 505 U.S. 672, 680.

92. 505 US. 672, 683.

93. 78 *Stat.* 255 (1964).

94. 432 U.S. 63 (1977).

95. A group that worships on Saturday, the Sabbath. In *Hardison*, the group was the Worldwide Church of God.

96. 432 U.S. 63, 81, 84.

97. 479 U.S. 60 (1986).

98. 757 F.2d 476 (1985), 484.

99. 479 U.S. 60, 68.

100. 440 U.S. 490 (1979).

101. 49 *Stat.* 449 (1935).

102. Which, of course, had been given a "lease on life" by *Pierce v. Society of Sisters.*

BIBLIOGRAPHY

Books

Alley, Robert S., ed. *The Constitution and Religion: Leading Supreme Court Cases on Church and State*. Amherst, NY: Prometheus Books, 1999.

Flowers, Ronald B., Melissa Rogers, and Steven K. Green. *Religious Freedom and the Supreme Court*. Waco, TX: Baylor University Press, 2008.

Flowers, Ronald B. *That Godless Court?: Supreme Court Decisions on Church-State Relations*. 2nd ed. Louisville, KY: Westminster John Knox Press, 2005.

————. *To Defend the Constitution: Religion, Conscientious Objection, Naturalization, and the Supreme Court*. Lanham, MD: Scarecrow Press, 2003.

Hall, Kermit L., ed. *The Oxford Guide to United States Supreme Court Decisions*. New York: Oxford University Press, 1999.

Irons, Peter. *A People's History of the Supreme Court*. New York: Penguin Books, 1999.

————. *The Courage of Their Convictions: Sixteen Americans Who Fought Their Way to the Supreme Court*. New York: Penguin Books, 1990.

Lerner, Max. *Nine Scorpions in a Bottle: Great Judges and Cases of the Supreme Court*. New York: Arcade Publishing, 1994.

O'Brien, David. *Storm Center: The Supreme Court in American Politics*, 8th edition. New York: W.W. Norton, 2008.

O'Connor, Sandra Day. *The Majesty of the Law: Reflections of a Supreme Court Justice*. New York: Random House, 2003.

Schwartz, Bernard. *A History of the Supreme Court*. New York: Oxford University Press, 1993.

———. *Decision: How the Supreme Court Decides Cases*. New York: Oxford University Press, 1997.

Toobin, Jeffrey. *The Nine: Inside the Secret World of the Supreme Court*. New York: Doubleday, 2007.

Witte, John Jr. *Religion and the American Constitutional Experiment: Essential Rights and Liberties*. 2nd ed. Boulder, CO: Westview Press, 2004.

Wood, James E., Jr., ed. *Readings on Church and State*. Waco, TX: James M. Dawson Institute of Church State Studies, Baylor University, 1989.

Articles/Chapters

Flowers, Ronald B. "In Praise of Conscience: Marie Averil Bland," *Anglican and Episcopal History* 62 (March 1993): 37.

Court Cases

Ansonia Board of Education v. Philbrook, 479 U.S. 60 (1986).

Ashwander v. TVA, 297 U.S. 288 (1936).

Baker v. Nachtrieb 19 Howard, 60 U.S. 126 (1856).

Bob Jones University v. United States, 461 U.S. 574 (1983).

Boerne v. Archbishop Flores, 521 U.S. 507 (1997).

Bradfield v. Roberts, 175 U.S. 291 (1899).

Burton v. United States, 196 U.S. 283 (1905).

Cantwell v. Connecticut, 310 U.S. 296 (1940).

Church of the Holy Trinity v. United States, 143 U.S. 457 (1893).

Cochran v. Louisiana Board of Education, 281 U.S. 370 (1930).

Colorado River Water Conservation District v. United States, 424 U.S. 800 (1976).

Cox v. New Hampshire, 312 U.S. 569 (1941).

Crowell v. Benson, 285 U.S. 22 (1932).

DeJong v. Commissioner, 36 T.C. 896 (1961).

Elk Grove Unified School District v. Newdow, 542 U.S. 1 (2004).

Employment Division of Oregon v. Smith, 494 U.S. 872 (1990).

Everson v. Board of Education, 330 U.S. 1 (1947).

Flast v. Cohen, 392 U.S. 83 (1968).

Frothingham v. Mellon, 262 U.S. 447 (1923).

Gillette v. United States, 401 U.S. 437 (1971).

Girouard v. United States, 328 U.S. 61 (1946).

Goesele v. Bimeler, 55 U.S. 589 (1853).

Gonzales v. Archbishop, 280 U.S. 1 (1929).

Gonzales v. O Centro Espirita Beneficente Uniao Do Vegetal, 546 U.S. 418 (2006).

Hamilton v. Regents of the University of California, 293 U.S. 245 (1934).

Heffron v. International Society for Krishna Consciousness (ISKCON), 452 U.S. 640 (1981).

Hein v. Freedom from Religion Foundation, 551 U.S. 587 (2007).

Hernandez v. Commissioner of Internal Revenue, 490 U.S. 680 (1989).

International Society for Krishna Consciousness (ISKCON) v. Lee, 505 U.S. 672 (1992).

Light v. United States, 220 U.S. 523 (1911).

Liverpool, N.Y. & P.S.S. Co. v. Emigration Commissioners, 113 U.S. 33 (1885).

Murray v. The Charming Betsy, 6 U.S. 64 (1804).

National Labor Relations Board v. Catholic Bishop of Chicago, 440 U.S. 490 (1979).

Order of St. Benedict v. Steinhauser, 234 U.S. 640 (1914).

Pierce v. Society of Sisters, 268 U.S. 510 (1925).

Sherbert v. Verner, 374 U.S. 398 (1963).

Sicurella v. United States, 348 U.S. 385 (1955).

Siler v. Louisville & Nashville Railway Co., 213 U.S. 175 (1909).

Spector Motor Service v. McLaughlin, 323 U.S. 101 (1944).

Trans World Airlines v. Hardison, 432 U.S. 63 (1977).

United States v. Bland, 283 U.S. 636 (1931).

United States v. Macintosh, 283 U.S. 605 (1931).

United States v. Schwimmer, 279 U.S. 644 (1929).

United States v. Seeger, 380 U.S. 163 (1965).

Valley Forge Christian College v. Americans United for Separation of Church and State, 454 U.S. 464 (1982).

Vidal v. Girard's Executors, 43 U.S. 127 (1844).

Watson v. Jones 13 Wallace, 80 U.S. 679 (1872).

Welsh v. United States, 398 U.S. 333 (1970).

Statutes

Civil Rights Act of 1964, 78 *Statutes at Large* 255 (1964).

National Labor Relations Act of 1935, 49 *Statutes at Large* 449 (1935).

Religious Freedom Restoration Act (RFRA), 107 *Statutes at Large* 1488 (1993).

Welfare Reform Act of 1996, 110 *Statutes at Large* 2105 (1996).

CHAPTER 7

THE MEANING OF THE SEPARATION OF CHURCH AND STATE: COMPETING VIEWS

DANIEL L. DREISBACH

THEOCRATIC impulses and ecclesiastical establishments have long been features of Western political culture. This same culture has produced forceful advocates for a clear demarcation between the realms of the sacred and the secular—the church and the civil state. When asked whether or not it was lawful to pay taxes to Caesar, Jesus Christ answered, "Render unto Caesar the things which are Caesar's; and unto God the things that are God's."[1] This paralleled familiar biblical dualisms such as heaven and hell, spirit and flesh, life and death, light and dark, and faith and works.[2] Saint Augustine (354–430), the fourth-century Bishop of Hippo and one of the first great philosophers of the Christian era, similarly imagined two contrasting and separated realms, the city of God and the city of man. The "city of God," Augustine said, refers to those who love God, not the institutional church *per se,* and the "city of man" signifies those who love self.[3] As one scholar noted, "Even though Christianity became the one established religion of the Roman Empire, patronized and protected by the Roman state authorities, Augustine and other Church Fathers insisted that state power remain separate from church power."[4] Pope Gelasius I, in

Portions of this chapter were adapted from Daniel L. Dreisbach, *Thomas Jefferson and the Wall of Separation between Church and State* (New York: New York University Press, 2002).

an address chastening the Byzantine Emperor Anastasius I in 494 AD for interfering in church affairs, described "two powers by which this world is chiefly
ruled: the sacred authority of the Popes and the royal power. Of these," Gelasius
continued, "the priestly power is much more important, because it has to render
account for the kings of men themselves at the Divine tribunal [Last Judgment]."[5]
Drawing on the imagery of Luke 22:38, late-medieval Church authorities articulated a theory of two swords—a spiritual sword and a temporal sword. The church
and its clerics wielded the spiritual sword, generally expressed and enforced
through canon law. The church delegated the temporal sword to emperors, kings,
and lesser civil magistrates who promulgated civil laws, which were enforced "in
a manner consistent with canon law" and ultimately were subordinated to ecclesiastical authorities.[6]

The leaders of the Protestant Reformation distinguished between a spiritual
kingdom and a temporal kingdom. The reformers taught that God had ordained
these two kingdoms, but each had distinct functions in the divine order. They recognized that the kingdoms of this world were corrupted by sin and, by necessity,
governed by civil laws. The Christian is a citizen of both and has duties in each
realm. Early in his reformation ministry, Martin Luther (1483–1546) wrote of a
"paper wall" between the "spiritual estate" and the "temporal estate."[7] "In Luther's
view," John Witte writes, "the church was not a political or legal authority. The
church has no sword, no jurisdiction, no daily responsibility for law."[8] That was the
domain of the civil magistrate. The church and its leaders were called to preach and
attend to shepherding the faithful. In his *Institutes of the Christian Religion,* John
Calvin (1509–1564) asserted that the "spiritual kingdom" and "political kingdom"
"must always be considered separately" because there is a great "difference and
unlikeness . . . between ecclesiastical and civil power," and it would be unwise to
"mingle these two, which have a completely different nature."[9] The reformers
agreed that both church and state, although separate, were divinely ordained institutions under God's authority and that citizens were to be in submission to those
God had placed in positions of civil leadership (Romans 13).

Liberal theorists, such as John Locke (1632–1704), similarly distinguished
between the concerns of religion and the civil state. In *A Letter Concerning Toleration* (1689), Locke declared: "I esteem it above all things necessary to distinguish
exactly the business of civil government from that of religion, and to settle the just
bounds that lie between the one and the other."[10] "[T]he church itself," he continued, "is a thing absolutely separate and distinct from the commonwealth. The
boundaries on both sides are fixed and immovable. He jumbles heaven and earth
together, the things most remote and opposite, who mixes these societies, which
are, in their original, end, business, and in every thing, perfectly distinct, and infinitely different from each other."[11] Locke's writings were influential among intellectuals in the decades leading to the founding of the American constitutional
government.

Notwithstanding Augustine's imagery and the metaphors of two swords and
two kingdoms, ecclesiastical establishments have been persistent in the history of

Christendom. Distinguishing between the duties of the church and those of the civil state did not inevitably lead to disestablishment or religious liberty. Civil states for nearly two millennia have supported established churches, and established churches have not only accepted that support but also looked to the state to suppress religious dissent and rival institutions and dogmas. This was a legacy European settlers brought to the New World, even though many arrived seeking havens from the religious persecution experienced under establishmentarian regimes in the Old World. The New World, however, became the first great laboratory for church–state separation, disestablishment, and religious liberty.

THE AMERICAN EXPERIENCE

The first English colonies in the New World followed the European establishmentarian model. There were a few notable exceptions, however, such as Roger Williams' experiment in Rhode Island, which limited the town of Providence's jurisdiction to matters "only in civil things."[12] Around the mid-eighteenth century, religious dissenters and a few leading intellectuals began to challenge seriously the propriety of retaining exclusive ecclesiastical establishments. Critics of the old arrangement argued that ecclesiastical monopolies led to complacency, corruption, and intolerance within the religious community and that disestablishment facilitated a vibrant religious culture in which the best and purest religion would dominate in the public marketplace of ideas. This, they said, was good for the church, good for society, and good for the civil state. By the end of the century, a number of influential states had begun to terminate their formal establishments. Americans increasingly came to embrace a separation between the authority of the state and religious institutions and view this as an American principle.

"Separation of church and state" and "wall of separation between church and state" are two phrases that convey equivalent ideas and that, in modern times, have been ubiquitous in American church–state discourse. Indeed, few discussions—formal or informal—on church–state relationships fail to invoke this figurative language. In the American experience, Thomas Jefferson (1743–1826) is often credited with coining this metaphoric language. It has, however, been a part of Western theological and political discourse for at least half a millennium. The most celebrated use of this figurative language was a January 1802 missive to a Baptist Association in Danbury, Connecticut in which President Jefferson opined that the First Amendment to the U.S. Constitution had built "a wall of separation between church and state."

Few metaphors in American letters have had a greater influence on law and policy than Jefferson's "wall of separation." In the course of time, it has been accepted by many Americans as a pithy description of the constitutionally prescribed church–state arrangement. Most important, the judiciary has embraced

this figurative phrase as a virtual rule of constitutional law, even though the metaphor is not found in the U.S. Constitution or elsewhere in the organic laws of the
United States. In *Everson v. Board of Education* (1947), the U.S. Supreme Court was
asked to interpret the First Amendment's prohibition on laws "respecting an establishment of religion." "In the words of Jefferson," the justices famously declared,
the First Amendment has erected "'a wall of separation between church and State'. . . .
That wall must be kept high and impregnable. We could not approve the slightest
breach."[13] In *McCollum v. Board of Education*, the following term, Justice Hugo L.
Black asserted that the justices had "agreed that the First Amendment's language,
properly interpreted, had erected a wall of separation between Church and State."[14]
In the six decades since the landmark *Everson* ruling, the "wall of separation" has
become the *locus classicus* of the notion that the First Amendment separated religion and the civil state, thereby mandating a strictly secular polity.

After two centuries, Jefferson's trope remains influential, but enormously controversial, in American law and policy. The frequent use and pervasive influence of
this separationist rhetoric invite the question whether the figurative phrase "separation of church and state" and attendant formulation of a "wall of separation"
have illuminated or obfuscated our understanding of the prudential and constitutional relationships between church and state—and between religion and the civil
polity. This chapter considers briefly the promise of this separationist rhetoric and
then identifies and describes the perils posed by these figurative phrases.

Let me state clearly at the outset my own position. Despite my belief that, as a
matter of good ecclesiastical and public policy, church and state should operate in
distinct and *separate* institutional spheres, I have concluded that the phrases "separation of church and state" and "wall of separation" have done more to confound
than to inform prudential and constitutional principles. Accordingly, I counsel
caution in the use of this rhetoric.

The Promises and Perils of a (Wall of) Separation between Church and State

Much controversy surrounding the metaphoric language of "separation" and "wall
of separation" pertains to the purpose and propriety of a (wall of) separation
between church and state in a civil society. What is (or should be) the nature of the
wall of separation? Is it a wall of amity or enmity? Does it make for "good neigh-
bours," or does it "give offence?" "If nowhere else, in the relation between Church
and State," wrote Justice Felix Frankfurter, invoking the poet Robert Frost's
immortal line, "good fences make good neighbors."[15] "True enough!" J.M. O'Neill
retorted. "But only fences that allow for cooperation, friendly intercourse. Fences
so 'high and impregnable' as not to permit the slightest breach *never* make good

neighbors. They are called 'spite fences' and are *never* built by good neighbors. They are only the instruments of extreme unneighborliness."[16]

"Separation of church and state" and "wall of separation" express an alternative vision to the model of an exclusive ecclesiastical establishment. Proponents argue that a separation policy promotes private, voluntary religion, and freedom of conscience in a secular polity. A "wall of separation" prevents religious establishments and avoids sectarian conflict among denominations competing for the government's favor and aid. A restrictive barrier prohibits not only the formal recognition of, and legal preference for, one particular church (or sect), but also all other forms of government assistance or encouragement for religious objectives. A separation between religion and the civil state is a necessary precursor, they argue, to freedom of conscience and religious exercise. Adherents of the separation doctrine espouse a faith that a regime of strict separation is the best, if not the only, way to promote religious liberty, especially the rights of religious minorities. From the other side of the divide, separation frees the church from reliance on the civil state for sustaining aid and accompanying government oversight. Champions of the wall are fond of quoting the ancient proverb made famous by Robert Frost, "Good fences make good neighbors."[17]

Critics counter that this metaphoric language evades clear definition and predictable application in actual church–state conflicts. They also question whether this rhetoric accurately or adequately encapsulates American traditions and constitutional principles governing church–state relationships. Critics fear that a regime of separation restricts excessively the place for religion and the church in public life.

DEFINITION OF "CHURCH" AND "STATE"

Most major associations and denominations of Protestants, Catholics, and Jews, as well as atheists, secularists, and civil liberties associations, affirm support for "separation of church and state." And, yet, one finds very little consensus among these groups as to the precise meaning of "separation of church and state" in scope and application. This underscores the definitional problems with this terminology.

What is it about this language that lends itself to such ambiguity as to its meaning? First, and most fundamental, is the question what is meant by the words "church" and "state"? This question is more difficult to answer than it may seem at first blush. Indeed, uncertainty about the scope of these terms gives rise to much of the church–state conflict that spills over into courts and political fora. Is "church" limited to ecclesiastical institutions, or does it encompass, more broadly, any expression or manifestation of religion in public life? Does the "wall" disallow all governmental acknowledgments of God and all public roles for religion? Is "state" limited to official actions of civil government, or does it encompass both the public and private actions of public officials, and does it include all activities in the public square that are authorized or tolerated by civil government, including activities of private actors? Does "state" include civil government in all its forms at the local, state, and national levels? Ambiguity in the meaning of these key terms invites uncertainty and, eventually, disputes.

Purposes of the "Wall of Separation"

The concept of "separation" and the instrument of a "wall" can serve diverse objectives and interests. This metaphoric language—depending on one's perspective, ideology, and agenda—is susceptible to multiple interpretations. For at least 500 years, the wall of separation has been a prominent feature of church–state discourse. Some commentators have championed a wall of separation as a prudential, indeed an essential, fixture of church–state relationships. Others have denounced walls of separation as obstacles to healthy, cooperative relations between church and civil state.

A wall is a structure of unambiguous demarcation that, in this context, differentiates between the sacred and the temporal, between ecclesiastical and civil institutions. By marking this boundary with a wall and clearly identifying each side's respective jurisdictions, some writers have hoped that conflict between the two sides could be ameliorated. There are those who view a wall as a symbol of protection and freedom; for others it is a restrictive structure that imposes undue restraints on the legitimate roles of both church and state in a civil society. Some believe a "wall of separation" shields individual conscience from unwarranted intrusion by civil or clerical authorities. Religious dissenters, in particular, hope that placing a wall between church and state will provide a measure of autonomy from religious establishments in the exercise of religion. There are those who believe a wall safeguards the purity of religious truth and ecclesiastical institutions from the incursions and depredations of the world. Still others think a "wall of separation" protects the civil polity from ecclesiastical interference or domination. A high barrier between church and civil state also promises to avoid conflict among religious sects competing for government favor or assistance. All these functions are illustrated by various walls of separation proposed and described over the last half millennium.

The Anabaptists, who believed they were in the world but not of the world,[18] emphatically rejected the close identification of civil state and church that had been prevalent in Western Christendom since the reign of Constantine. Although they believed the civil state was instituted and ordained by God and is "necessary in the 'world,' that is, among those who do not heed or obey Christ's teachings, it is not necessary among the true disciples of Christ."[19] Anabaptists thus avoided participation in, and interaction with, the civil state. Menno Simons (1496–1561), a Dutch Anabaptist leader, spoke of a "Scheidingsmaurer"—a "separating wall" or "wall of separation"—between the realms of the true church and a fallen, outside world. In a December 1548 epistle, Menno Simons wrote: "You see, our people have always insisted that the church [Gemeende; religious community] must be entirely outside [buiten] the world. We must have a separating wall [Scheidings-maurer] between us."[20]

Richard Hooker (1554–1600), the sixteenth-century Anglican divine and apologist for the Elizabethan settlement, described "walles of separation between . . . the *Church* and the *Commonwealth*" in his *magnum opus Of the Laws of Ecclesiastical Polity*.[21] Both revelation and reason, he argued, supported the organic identity of church and state, as coextensive aspects of a unified Christian society. He believed, further, that "the episcopal form of government was best for the Church of England, and that Church and state were two aspects of the same commonwealth, a commonwealth in which both were rightly under the monarch."[22] Hooker viewed the English monarch as, in the words of Isaiah 49:23, a "nursing father" to the church. (This peculiar metaphor was a popular expression in Anglo-American literature of the duty of kings and civil magistrates to nurture and protect the true religion and Christ's church.)[23] He rejected the Puritan notion of church and commonwealth as two distinct and perpetually separated corporations, divided by "walls of separation" that denied the crown its divine prerogative to govern both the church and the commonwealth.

The seventeenth-century colonial advocate for religious liberty and founder of Rhode Island, Roger Williams (1603?–1683), championed a "hedge or wall of separation" so as to safeguard the religious purity of Christ's church from the corrupting wilderness of the world. Williams was a spiritual or theological separatist whose relentless quest was to separate the true church from theological impurity and the unclean world. He adamantly rejected the idea of a national church because he thought it improperly combined regenerate and unregenerate members of society. Where there was an established church, Williams instructed congregations to be separated from it so as to maintain spiritual purity. He further instructed individual believers to be fully separated from unbelievers. (Williams, his critics said, even refused fellowship with his own wife when he thought she was insufficiently pure in her spiritual life.)[24] Drawing on the imagery of Isaiah 5:5-6, Williams set forth in a 1644 tract the necessity for a "hedge or wall of separation":

> [T]he faithful labors of many witnesses of Jesus Christ, extant to the world, abundantly proving that . . . when they have opened a gap in the hedge or wall of separation between the garden of the church and the wilderness of the world, God hath ever broke down the wall itself, removed the candlestick, and made His garden a wilderness, as at this day. And that therefore if He will ever please to restore His garden and paradise again, it must of necessity be walled in peculiarly unto Himself from the world; and that all that shall be saved out of the world are to be transplanted out of the wilderness of the world, and added unto His church or garden.[25]

Williams proposed his wall, not to protect the outside world (including the civil polity or society at large) from religious influences, but to preserve the religious purity of the separated church from corrupting external influences.[26]

The eighteenth-century dissenting Scottish schoolmaster and radical Whig political reformer, James Burgh (1714–1775), advocated building "an impenetrable wall of *separation* between things *sacred* and *civil*."[27] He sought to prevent the church from "getting too much power into her hands, and turning religion into a mere state-engine."[28] Burgh was a man of faith as well as a man of reason.[29] He brought to his writings a dissenter's zeal for religious toleration and a profound distrust of established churches. Burgh thought religion was a matter between God and one's conscience; and he contended that two citizens with different religious views are "both equally fit for being employed, in the service of our country."[30] He alerted readers to the potential corrupting influences of established churches:

> I will fairly tell you what will be the consequences of your setting up such a
> mixed-mungrel-spiritual-temporal-secular-ecclesiastical establishment. You will
> make the dispensers of religion *despicable* and *odious* to all men of sense, and will
> destroy the *spirituality,* in which consists the whole *value,* of religion. . . .[31]

State support of religion corrupts church officers, whose comfortable reliance on, and favor with, the civil state encourages pride, indolence, and impiety, and ultimately profanes religion. For this reason, Burgh proposed building "an impenetrable wall of *separation* between things *sacred* and *civil*."[32]

In the early nineteenth century, one of Burgh's influential American admirers used the "wall" metaphor in an address to an obscure religious association. This use of the metaphor would have a profound impact on how subsequent generations of Americans would think about church–state relationships. On New Year's Day, 1802, President Thomas Jefferson penned a missive to the Danbury Baptist Association. The New England Baptists, who had supported Jefferson in the election of 1800, were a beleaguered religious and political minority in a region where a Congregationalist-Federalist axis dominated political life. Endorsing the persecuted Baptists' aspirations for religious liberty, Jefferson wrote:

> Believing with you that religion is a matter which lies solely between Man & his
> God, that he owes account to none other for his faith or his worship, that the
> legitimate powers of government reach actions only, & not opinions, I contemplate
> with sovereign reverence that act of the whole American people which declared
> that *their* legislature should "make no law respecting an establishment of religion,
> or prohibiting the free exercise thereof," thus building a wall of separation
> between Church & State.[33]

Jefferson allied himself with the New England Baptists in their struggle to enjoy the rights of conscience as an inalienable right and not merely as a favor granted, and subject to withdrawal, by the civil state.

According to his own account, Jefferson wanted to use his letter, with its metaphoric phrase, to explain why he, as president, had refrained from issuing executive proclamations setting aside days in the public calendar for prayer and thanksgiving. Because the national government could exercise only those powers expressly granted to it by the Constitution and because no power to issue religious proclamations had been granted to it, Jefferson maintained that the national government could not issue such proclamations. Insofar as Jefferson's wall was a metaphor for the First Amendment, it imposed restrictions on the national government only. As a matter of federalism, his wall had less to do with the separation between church and state than with the separation between state governments and the national government on matters pertaining to religion, such as religious proclamations.

Menno Simons, Richard Hooker, Roger Williams, James Burgh, and Thomas Jefferson described or proposed different walls of separation, each serving a function distinct from the others. (The modern Supreme Court, as I contend in the following, has described a still different wall of separation.) I regard these diverse and sometime incompatible functions as a *potential* peril of the wall metaphor. There is no consensus as to what this metaphor means or what function it serves. If we do not know what the phrase means, can we have confidence that it really will serve an intended or useful purpose?

The poet Robert Frost remarked, "Before I built a wall I'd ask to know / What I was walling in or walling out, / And to whom I was like to give offence."[34] We, too, I think, would do well to know what purpose or purposes are likely to be served by the walls we erect. What is the purpose for which one erects a "wall of separation between church and state"? And can one be sure that a wall built for one laudable objective will not be reassigned for some undesirable purpose? For example, should we fear that a wall built to protect religious liberties by limiting the power of civil government will be used to exclude religion from public life?

Does the Metaphor Represent Constitutional Principles?

In his treatise, *Separation of Church and State* (2002), Philip Hamburger argued that the rhetoric and attendant doctrine of church–state separation, in any sense resembling its modern usage, emerged in American political and legal thought much later than is often presumed. He traced the evolution of this rhetoric in America, starting as a political principle of separation between religion and politics, which began to gain currency in disestablishment debates of the late eighteenth century and in the presidential contest of 1800. Jeffersonian partisans adopted the rhetoric to silence the New England Congregationalist-Federalist clergymen who had criticized candidate Jefferson for being an infidel or atheist. In his 1802 letter to the Danbury Baptist Association, with its metaphoric "wall of separation," President Jefferson deftly transformed the political principle into a constitutional principle by equating the language of separation with the text of the First Amendment. Separation of church and state, despite this Jeffersonian endorsement, did not come to be widely viewed as a constitutional principle until well into the nineteenth century. The constitutional principle was eventually elevated to constitutional law by the U.S. Supreme Court in a series of influential mid–twentieth-century rulings, starting with *Everson v. Board of Education* (1947). Jefferson's wall, pursuant to the original construction of the First Amendment, separated church and national government only; whereas the wall described in *Everson* imposed restrictions on both national and state governments.

In the modern context, the phrases "separation of church and state" and "wall of separation" are typically used as figurative expressions for the First Amendment. An important legal and political consideration is whether these terms accurately represent the constitutional principles governing church–state relations. In *Everson,* the justices described a "high and impregnable" wall erected by the First Amendment. This First Amendment wall ensured that

> Neither a state nor the Federal Government can set up a church. Neither can pass laws which aid one religion, aid all religions, or prefer one religion over another. . . . No tax in any amount, large or small, can be levied to support any religious activities or institutions, whatever they may be called, or whatever form they may adopt to teach or practice religion.[35]

This construction of the First Amendment would have come as a surprise to the members of the first federal Congress who framed the amendment. This same Congress appropriated funds from the public treasury to pay for Congressional chaplains, enacted legislation pertaining to oaths, issued religious proclamations, and reauthorized the Northwest Ordinance with its affirmation that "Religion, Morality and knowledge [are] necessary to good government and the happiness of mankind." These actions are not easily reconciled with the *Everson* Court's construction of the First Amendment. The "high and impregnable" wall the Court erected in *Everson* has severely restricted the place and role of religion in the public square and, critics say, promoted the secularization of public life.

Although the language of "separation" may felicitously express some First Amendment principles, it seriously misrepresents or obscures others. "Separation of church and state" and the First Amendment concept of "nonestablishment" are often used interchangeably today; however, in the lexicon of the late eighteenth and early nineteenth centuries, the expansive notion of "separation" was distinct from the narrow institutional concepts of "nonestablishment" and "disestablishment."[36] Advocates of disestablishment or nonestablishment, such as evangelical dissenters, did not necessarily embrace the more expansive concept of "separation" because they feared it could sanction a divorce of religion's beneficent influences from public life and policy. Most citizens in the founding generation would have viewed such a divorce with alarm because they viewed religion, to paraphrase George Washington's Farewell Address, as an "indispensable" support for social order and political prosperity in a system of self-government.[37]

Furthermore, "separation of church and state" indicates an equivalent restriction on both the church and the civil state. Likewise, a wall is a bilateral barrier that inhibits the activities of both the civil government and religion. This is contrary to the explicit text and design of the First Amendment, which imposes restrictions solely on the civil government. The various First Amendment guarantees were entirely a check or restraint on civil government, specifically on Congress. The free press guarantee, for example, was not written to protect the civil state from the press; rather, it was designed to protect a free and independent press from control by the national government. Similarly, the religion provisions were added to the Constitution to protect religion and religious institutions from corrupting interference by the national government and not to protect the civil state from the influence of, or overreaching by, religion. As a bilateral barrier, however, the wall unavoidably restricts religion's ability to influence the conduct of civil government; thus, it necessarily exceeds the limitations imposed by the Constitution. A product of this separationist rhetoric, critics say, is that the First Amendment, which was written to limit civil government, has been reinterpreted to restrict religion in public life.

In application, this notion of separation has not only imposed an extraconstitutional restraint on religion, but also has dangerously granted the civil state *de facto* powers over religion. Having assumed the separation of church and state, the state has then exercised the prerogative to specify the legitimate jurisdictions of both the church and the state. The civil state, so as to determine that which is permissible or impermissible pursuant to the principle of separation, has presumed to define what is "religion" and what are the appropriate realm, duties, and functions of the "church" in a civil society. Yale University law professor Stephen L. Carter has denounced the state's construction of a "single-sided wall" that confines, indeed imprisons, the community of faith, but imposes few corresponding restraints on the civil state's ability to interfere with religion and religious institutions. The state, acting through its judges, "decides when religion has crossed the wall of separation. . . . Unsurprisingly, then, religion is often found to have breached the wall, whereas the state almost never is."[38] "[I]n its contemporary rendition," Carter continued in even more forceful language, separation of church and state "represents little more than an effort to subdue the power of religion, to twist it to the ends preferred by the state."[39] The separation principle is frequently invoked to restrict religion's place in public life, but all too infrequently is it used to insulate churches, clergy, and religious entities from the civil state's generally applicable criminal, employment, and zoning laws, as well as health and safety regulations. The result is that the First Amendment is transformed from being exclusively a restriction on the powers of civil government to being a grant of power to the state to define and, ultimately, restrict the place of the church in society.

Herein lies the danger of this metaphor and the reason why we should care about its use in law and policy. Today the wall is frequently used to separate religion from public life, thereby promoting a religion that is essentially private and a state that is strictly secular. The "high and impregnable" wall described in *Everson* and its progeny inhibits religion's ability to inform the public ethic and policy, deprives religious citizens of the civil liberty to participate in politics armed with ideas informed by their spiritual values, and infringes the right of religious communities and institutions to extend their prophetic ministries into the public square on the same terms as their secular counterparts. The "wall of separation" has become the sacred icon of a strict separationist dogma intolerant of religious influences in the public square.

Federal and state courts have used the "wall of separation" concept to justify censoring private religious expression (such as Christmas creches) in public fora, denying public benefits (such as education vouchers) for religious entities, and excluding religious citizens and organizations (such as faith-based social welfare agencies) from full participation in civic life on equal terms with their secular counterparts. The coerced removal of religion from public life not only is at war with our cultural traditions insofar as it evinces a callous indifference toward religion, but it also offends basic notions of freedom of religious exercise, expression, and association in a democratic and pluralistic society.

Walls are often structures of enmity, built to separate antagonists. The Court's construction of a "high and impregnable" barrier, critics argue, evinces hostility toward religion and the church. Jefferson's metaphor, sadly, has been used to silence the religious voice in the public marketplace of ideas and, in a form of religious apartheid, to segregate faith communities behind a restrictive barrier. The critics, too, quote the poet Robert Frost, who observed: "Something there is that doesn't love a wall / That wants it down."[40] This, rather than the more famous line, "Good fences make good neighbors," communicates Frost's true view of walls.[41]

Legacy of Intolerance

For much of American history, the phrase "separation of church and state" has often been an expression of exclusion, intolerance, and bigotry. It has been used to silence people and communities of faith and exclude them from full participation in civic life.

In the late eighteenth and early nineteenth centuries, establishmentarians sought to frighten pious Americans by deliberately mischaracterizing the religious dissenters' aspirations for disestablishment and liberty of conscience as advocacy for a separation of religion from public life that would inevitably lead to political atheism and rampant licentiousness. This was a political smear. Religious dissenters, indeed, agitated for disestablishment, but, like most Americans, they did not wish to separate religious values from public life and policy.

In the bitter presidential campaign of 1800, Jeffersonian Republicans cynically advocated the rhetoric and policy of separation, not to promote religious worship and expression, but to silence the New England clergy, who had vigorously denounced Jefferson as an infidel or atheist.

In *Separation of Church and State,* Philip Hamburger amply documented that the rhetoric of separation of church and state became fashionable in the 1830s, 1840s, and 1850s and, again, in the last quarter of the nineteenth century. Why? It accompanied two substantial waves of Catholic immigrants, with their peculiar liturgy and resistance to assimilation into the Protestant establishment: an initial wave of Irish in the first half of the century, and, then, more Irish along with other European immigrants later in the century. The rhetoric of separation was used by nativist elements, such as the Know Nothings and later the Ku Klux Klan, to marginalize Catholics and deny them entrance into the mainstream of public life, often through violence. By the end of the century, an allegiance to the so-called "American principle" of separation of church and state had been woven into the membership oaths of the Ku Klux Klan. Today we typically think of the Klan strictly in terms of their views on race, and we forget that their hatred of Catholics was equally odious.

Again, in the mid-twentieth century, the rhetoric of separation was revived and ultimately constitutionalized by anti-Catholic elites, such as Justice Hugo L. Black, and fellow-travelers in the American Civil Liberties Union and Protestants and Other Americans United for the Separation of Church and State (today known by the more politically correct appellation of "Americans United for Separation of Church and State"), who feared the influence and wealth of the Catholic Church and perceived parochial education as a threat to public schools and democratic values.

Justice Hugo L. Black, chief architect of the modern "wall," provides a fascinating case study of the role of anti-Catholicism in promoting a separationist agenda. Hamburger argued that Justice Black, a former Alabama Ku Klux Klansman, was the product of a remarkable "confluence of Protestant, nativist, and progressive anti-Catholic forces. . . . Black's association with the Klan has been much discussed in connection with his liberal views on race, but, in fact, his membership suggests more about [his] ideals of Americanism," especially his support for separation of church and state. "Black had long before sworn, under the light of flaming crosses, to preserve 'the sacred constitutional rights' of 'free public schools' and 'separation of church and state.'" Although he later distanced himself from the Klan on matters of race, "Black's distaste for Catholicism did not diminish." His admixture of progressive, Klan, and strict separationist views is best understood in terms of virulent anti-Catholicism and, more broadly, a deep hostility to assertions of ecclesiastical authority and hierarchy. Separation of church and state, Black believed, was an American ideal of freedom from oppressive ecclesiastical authority, especially that of the Roman Catholic Church. A regime of separation enabled Americans to assert their individual autonomy and practice democracy, which Black believed was Protestantism in its secular form. In *Everson*, Black "led the Court to declare itself in favor of the 'separation of church and state.'"[42]

Let me be clear. Diverse strains of political, religious, and intellectual thought have embraced notions of separation (I myself come from a faith tradition that believes church and state should operate in *separate* institutional spheres), but a particularly dominant strain in nineteenth-century America was this nativist strain. We must confront the uncomfortable fact that the terms "separation of church and state" and "wall of separation," although not necessarily expressions of intolerance, have, in the American experience, often been closely identified with the ugly impulses of nativism and bigotry.

CONCLUSION

"Separation of church and state" is a phrase fraught with ambiguity as to its definition, scope, and application. This alone is a compelling reason for employing alternative language more precise in its meaning. In any case, those who use this language
should clearly define what they mean by it.

The rhetoric of "separation of church and state" and "wall of separation" has been
instrumental in transforming judicial and popular constructions of the First Amendment from a provision protecting religion to one restricting religion's place and role in
public life. The rhetoric of separation, in other words, has reconceptualized the First
Amendment from a restriction on government only to a restriction on both government and religion. This has placed a new gloss on the First Amendment.

Moreover, this figurative language has provided little specific, practical guidance
for resolving difficult church–state controversies that require a delicate balancing of
competing constitutional values. This rhetoric has proved politically divisive. Because
a "wall," especially, is so concrete and unyielding, its very invocation forecloses
meaningful dialogue regarding the prudential and constitutional role of religion,
faith communities, and religious citizens in public life, and it inhibits the search for
common ground and compromise on vexing issues. In short, this metaphoric
language has not produced the practical solutions to real-world controversies that its
apparent clarity and directness led its proponents to expect.

"A phrase," Justice Felix Frankfurter observed, "begins life as a literary expression; its felicity leads to its lazy repetition; and repetition soon establishes it as a legal
formula, undiscriminatingly used to express different and sometimes contradictory
ideas."[43] Such has been the history of the phrase "separation of church and state."
Figures of speech designed to simplify and liberate thought often end by trivializing
or enslaving it. Therefore, as Judge Benjamin N. Cardozo counseled, "[m]etaphors in
law are to be narrowly watched."[44] This is advice we all would do well to heed.

ENDNOTES

    1. Matthew 22:21 (KJV); Mark 12:17; Luke 20:25; see also Romans 13:7.
    2. See John Witte, Jr., "That Serpentine Wall of Separation," *Michigan Law Review*
101 (2003): 1876.
    3. Augustine, *The City of God*, trans. Marcus Dods (New York: The Modern Library,
1950), bk. XIV, chap. 28.
    4. Witte, "Serpentine Wall," 1878.
    5. Pope Gelasius I to Emperor Anastasius I, 494 AD, reprinted in Sidney Z. Ehler and
John B. Morrall, trans. and eds., *Church and State Through the Centuries: A Collection of
Historic Documents with Commentaries* (New York: Biblo and Tannen, 1967), 11.
    6. Witte, "Serpentine Wall," 1880. For a classic expression of the two-swords theory,

see Bull "Unam sanctam" of Pope Boniface VIII, 18 November 1302, reprinted in *Church and State Through the Centuries*, 91–92. See generally Brian Tierney, *The Crisis of Church and State, 1050–1300* (Englewood Cliffs, NJ: Prentice-Hall, 1964).

7. Martin Luther, *To the Christian Nobility of the German Nation* (1520), in *Three Treatises* (Philadelphia: Fortress Press, 1970), 12, 16.

8. Witte, "Serpentine Wall," 1883.

9. John Calvin, *Institutes of the Christian Religion* (1559), ed. John T. McNeill, trans. Ford Lewis Battles, 2 vols., The Library of Christian Classics (Philadelphia: Westminster Press, 1960), bk. 3, chap. 19.15; bk. 4, chap. 11.3, bk. 4, chap. 20.1.

10. John Locke, *A Letter Concerning Toleration* (1689), in *The Works of John Locke*, 10 vols. (London, 1823), 6: 9.

11. Ibid., 6:21.

12. Providence Agreement (1637), in *Colonial Origins of the American Constitution: A Documentary History*, ed. Donald S. Lutz (Indianapolis, IN: Liberty Fund, 1998), 162.

13. *Everson v. Board of Education*, 330 U.S. 1 (1947), 16, 18.

14. *McCollum v. Board of Education*, 333 U.S. 203 (1948), 211.

15. *McCollum v. Board of Education*, 333 U.S. 203 (1948), 232 (Opinion of Frankfurter, J.); Robert Frost, "Mending Wall," in *Collected Poems of Robert Frost* (New York: Henry Holt and Co., 1930), 47–48.

16. J.M. O'Neill, *Religion and Education under the Constitution* (New York: Harper and Brothers, 1949), 243 (emphasis in the original).

17. Robert Frost, "Mending Wall," 48.

18. For biblical texts noting that Christians are in the world but not of the world, see John 15:19 and John 17:14-16. Anabaptists took to heart biblical admonitions that Christians should "be not conformed to this world" (Romans 12:2), but remain "separate" from the world and its temptations (1 Corinthians 6:14-17). For more on the biblical roots of Anabaptist separatism, see C. Arnold Snyder, ed., *Biblical Concordance of the Swiss Brethren, 1540*, trans. Gilbert Fast and Gaelen Peters (Scottdale, PA: Herald Press, 2001), 56–60.

19. Hans J. Hillerbrand, "An Early Anabaptist Treatise on the Christian and the State," *Mennonite Quarterly Review* 32 (1958): 30–31.

20. Letter from Menno Simons to "J.V." [perhaps Johannes Voetius, a Dutch jurist], December 1548. Menno enclosed a copy of the Schleitheim Confession (1527) in this correspondence with "J.V." This document in the Rijksarchief in the Hague, Netherlands, was brought to my attention by John Witte, Jr.

21. Richard Hooker, *Of the Laws of Ecclesiastical Polity: Books VI, VII, VIII*, ed. P.G. Stanwood, vol. 3, of *The Folger Library Edition of The Works of Richard Hooker*, ed. W. Speed Hill (Cambridge, MA: Belknap Press of Harvard University Press, 1981), 320. All other quotations in this section from *Ecclesiastical Polity*, with modernized spelling, are from Hooker, *Of the Laws of Ecclesiastical Polity: Preface, Book I, Book VIII*, ed. Arthur Stephen McGrade (Cambridge, UK: Cambridge University Press, 1989).

22. Kenneth Scott Latourette, *A History of Christianity* (New York: Harper and Brothers, 1953), 812.

23. James H. Hutson has observed that for centuries this metaphor "dominated the church-state dialogue in the Anglo-American world." A Calvinist interpretation of Isaiah 49:23 instructed kings and civil magistrates to "form a nurturing bond with religious institutions within [their] jurisdiction . . . [and,] in fact, become the 'nursing father[s]' of the church." The "nursing father" metaphor, according to Hutson, was transmitted to the American colonies, where it continued to inform church–state discourse until the

mid-nineteenth century. Although American constructions of the phrase evolved over time, at a minimum it stood for the proposition that civil magistrates had a duty to model and extol lives of Christian rectitude, protect and even encourage religion (and religious institutions), and promote laws and policies that facilitate and protect religious practices and resist laws that do not. In short, civil rulers must nurture religion as a good father cares for his children or as a shepherd attends to his flock. This was seen by some clergy as the first duty of civil rulers. James Hutson, *Forgotten Features of the Founding: The Recovery of Religious Themes in the Early American Republic* (Lanham, MD: Lexington Books, 2003), 45–46.

24. Timothy L. Hall, *Separating Church and State: Roger Williams and Religious Liberty* (Urbana, IL: University of Illinois Press, 1998), 27 and 42 n. 48; Philip Hamburger, *Separation of Church and State* (Cambridge, MA: Harvard University Press, 2002), 40.

25. Roger Williams, "Mr. Cotton's Letter Lately Printed, Examined and Answered," in *The Complete Writings of Roger Williams* (Providence, RI: Providence Press, 1866), 1: 392. The quotation is taken from Perry Miller's modernized version in Miller, *Roger Williams: His Contribution to the American Tradition* (Indianapolis, IN: Bobbs-Merrill, 1953; reprinted New York: Atheneum, 1962), 98.

26. See Mark DeWolfe Howe, *The Garden and the Wilderness: Religion and Government in American Constitutional History* (Chicago: University of Chicago Press, 1965).

27. [James Burgh], *Crito, or Essays on Various Subjects*, 2 vols. (London, 1766, 1767), 2: 119 (emphasis in the original).

28. *Crito*, 1: 7.

29. Carla H. Hay, *James Burgh, Spokesman for Reform in Hanoverian England* (Washington, DC: University Press of America, 1979), 49. Hay briefly traced the evolution of Burgh's religious beliefs from his early Calvinist training as the son of a Church of Scotland clergyman to a conversion "to some form of unitarianism." Hay, *James Burgh*, 49–55.

30. *Crito*, 2: 68.

31. Ibid., 2: 117 (emphasis in the original).

32. Ibid., 2: 119 (emphasis in the original). Of the four walls of separation mentioned thus far, Burgh's is the only wall that, based on history and intellectual content, one can plausibly argue informed Jefferson's figurative barrier. Although Jefferson probably encountered Hooker's wall in his reading, it is unlikely that he was familiar with Menno's or Williams' uses of the metaphor.

33. Letter from Jefferson to Messrs. Nehemiah Dodge, Ephraim Robbins, and Stephen S. Nelson, a committee of the Danbury Baptist association in the state of Connecticut, 1 January 1802, The Papers of Thomas Jefferson (Manuscript Division, Library of Congress), Series 1, Box 89, December 2, 1801–January 1, 1802.

34. Frost, "Mending Wall," 48.

35. *Everson*, 330 U.S. 1 (1947), 16.

36. If "separation of church and state" and nonestablishment or disestablishment were not synonymous terms in the lexicon of 1800, what did the members of the First Congress and their contemporaries mean by "establishment of religion?" The First Amendment was written at a time when the definition of "establishment" was in a state of flux. It meant different things to different groups in different regions of the country. Few late–eighteenth-century Americans dissented from the notion that, in a system of self-government, religion (and morality informed by religious values) provided a vital internal moral compass that would prompt citizens to behave in an orderly, disciplined manner without the prodding of an authoritarian ruler's whip. Thus, many Americans of the era regarded religion as indispensable to social order and political prosperity in a

regime of republican self-government. Few Americans of the era would have thought that the First Amendment prohibition on "law respecting an establishment of religion" proscribed all public acknowledgments of God and invocations of divine blessing for the civil polity. It also did not mean that religion could play no role in promoting civic virtue and social order. For most Americans, an "establishment of religion" meant an exclusive ecclesiastical establishment, such as existed in most European countries. Few Americans in the last quarter of the eighteenth century desired the establishment of a *national* church, and the First Amendment prohibitions endorsed this sentiment. For many Americans, especially in New England's old Puritan commonwealths, state support for churches and their ministers, as well as religious test oaths, did not necessarily constitute an establishment of religion and were not incompatible with the free exercise of religion. Most thought public leaders could and should promote religion through the example of their lives—by being models of moral rectitude, regularly attending church, and acknowledging God in their public pronouncements. A growing number of religious dissenters argued that legal preference for one religious sect over others was a form of religious establishment. A few, a very few, thought the civil state could take no action to promote religion and that religion must be encouraged through strictly private, nongovernmental means.

37. George Washington, Farewell Address, 19 September 1796, in *The Writings of George Washington,* ed. John C. Fitzpatrick, 37 vols. (Washington, DC: Government Printing Office, 1931–1940), 35: 229.

38. Stephen L. Carter, *God's Name in Vain: The Wrongs and Rights of Religion in Politics* (New York: Basic Books, 2000), 79–80.

39. Ibid., 78. This is a perversion of the historical and constitutional origins of the separation principle, Carter complained. The single-sided wall erected in the First Amendment was designed to protect religion from interference by the civil state, but not to protect the civil state from religious influences. Stephen L. Carter, *The Culture of Disbelief: How American Law and Politics Trivialize Religious Devotion* (New York: Basic Books, 1993), 105. See also Richard John Neuhaus, "Contending for the Future: Overcoming the Pfefferian Inversion," *Journal of Law and Religion* 8 (1990): 119.

40. Frost, "Mending Wall," 48.

41. Frost, "Mending Wall," 48. Frost clearly identified with the poem's narrator who questioned the need for a wall. See Jeffrey Meyers, ed., *Early Frost: The First Three Books* (Hopewell, NJ: The Ecco Press, 1996), xxiii (arguing that Frost "clearly stands with the narrator who questions the very need to have a wall and repeats his belief: 'Something there is that doesn't love a wall.' That 'something,' a natural force, which breaks down the wall and indicates the poet's point of view is—of course—frost."); Mordecai Marcus, *The Poems of Robert Frost: An Explication* (Boston: G.K. Hall and Co., 1991), 42 (noting that "Mending Wall," "often quoted out of context, is sometimes, mistakenly said to declare that 'Good fences make good neighbors,' which—as Frost sometimes had to point out—is the formula of the poem's antagonist"; noting the pun, in the poem's opening lines, that it is frost that does not love a wall and that "makes the stones in walls" tumble).

42. Hamburger, *Separation of Church and State,* 423, 434, 462, 463. These themes are also explored in John T. McGreevy, "Thinking on One's Own: Catholicism in the American Intellectual Imagination, 1928–1960," *Journal of American History* 84 (June 1997): 97–131.

43. *Tiller v. Atlantic Coast Line Railroad Co.,* 318 U.S. 54 (1943), 68 (Frankfurter, J., concurring).

44. *Berkey v. Third Ave. Ry. Co.,* 244 N.Y. 84, 94, 155 N.E. 58 (1926), 61.

BIBLIOGRAPHY

Books

Augustine. *The City of God*. Translated by Marcus Dods. New York: The Modern Library, 1950.

Burgh, James. *Crito, or Essays on Various Subjects*, 2 vols. London, 1766, 1767.

Calvin, John. *Institutes of the Christian Religion*. Edited by John T. McNeill, Translated by Ford Lewis Battles, 2 vols. The Library of Christian Classics. Philadelphia: Westminster Press, 1960.

Carter, Stephen L. *The Culture of Disbelief: How American Law and Politics Trivialize Religious Devotion*. New York: Basic Books, 1993.

———. *God's Name in Vain: The Wrongs and Rights of Religion in Politics*. New York: Basic Books, 2000.

Cord, Robert L. *Separation of Church and State: Historical Fact and Current Fiction*. New York: Lambeth Press, 1982.

Curry, Thomas J. *The First Freedoms: Church and State in America to the Passage of the First Amendment*. New York: Oxford University Press, 1986.

Dreisbach, Daniel L. *Thomas Jefferson and the Wall of Separation Between Church and State*. New York: New York University Press, 2002.

Dreisbach, Daniel L., and Mark David Hall, eds. *The Sacred Rights of Conscience: Selected Readings on Religious Liberty and Church-State Relations in the American Founding*. Indianapolis, IN: Liberty Fund, 2009.

Ehler, Sidney Z. and John B. Morrall, trans. and eds. *Church and State through the Centuries: A Collection of Historic Documents with Commentaries*. New York: Biblo and Tannen, 1967.

Frost, Robert. *Collected Poems of Robert Frost*. New York: Henry Holt and Co., 1930.

Hall, Timothy L. *Separating Church and State: Roger Williams and Religious Liberty*. Urbana, IL: University of Illinois Press, 1998.

Hamburger, Philip. *Separation of Church and State*. Cambridge, MA: Harvard University Press, 2002.

Hay, Carla H. *James Burgh, Spokesman for Reform in Hanoverian England*. Washington, DC: University Press of America, 1979.

Hooker, Richard. *Of the Laws of Ecclesiastical Polity: Books VI, VII, VIII*. Edited by P. G. Stanwood. Vol. 3 of The Folger Library Edition of The Works of Richard Hooker, edited by W. Speed Hill. Cambridge, MA.: Belknap Press of Harvard University Press, 1981.

———. *Of the Laws of Ecclesiastical Polity: Preface, Book I, Book VIII*. Edited by Arthur Stephen McGrade. Cambridge, UK: Cambridge University Press, 1989.

Howe, Mark DeWolfe. *The Garden and the Wilderness: Religion and Government in American Constitutional History*. Chicago: University of Chicago Press, 1965.

Hutson, James. *Church and State in America: The First Two Centuries*. New York: Cambridge University Press, 2008.

———. *Forgotten Features of the Founding: The Recovery of Religious Themes in the Early American Republic*. Lanham, MD: Lexington Books, 2003.

———. *Religion and the Founding of the American Republic*. Washington, DC: Library of Congress, 1998.

Latourette, Kenneth Scott. *A History of Christianity*. New York: Harper and Brothers, 1953.

Levy, Leonard W. *The Establishment Clause: Religion and the First Amendment*. 2d ed. Chapel Hill, NC: University of North Carolina Press, 1994.

Locke, John. *The Works of John Locke*, 10 vols. London, 1823.

Luther, Martin. *Three Treatises*. Philadelphia: Fortress Press, 1970.

Lutz, Donald S., ed. *Colonial Origins of the American Constitution: A Documentary History.* Indianapolis, IN: Liberty Fund, 1998.

Marcus, Mordecai. *The Poems of Robert Frost: An Explication.* Boston: G.K. Hall and Co., 1991.

Meyers, Jeffrey, ed. *Early Frost: The First Three Books.* Hopewell, NJ: The Ecco Press, 1996.

Miller, Perry. *Roger Williams: His Contribution to the American Tradition.* Indianapolis, IN: Bobbs-Merrill, 1953; reprinted New York: Atheneum, 1962.

O'Neill, J.M. *Religion and Education Under the Constitution.* New York: Harper and Brothers, 1949.

Snyder, C. Arnold, ed. *Biblical Concordance of the Swiss Brethren, 1540.* Translated by Gilbert Fast and Gaelen Peters. Scottdale, PA: Herald Press, 2001.

G. Stanwood. Vol. 3 of *The Folger Library Edition of The Works of Richard Hooker*, edited by W. Speed Hill. Cambridge, MA: Belknap Press of Harvard University Press, 1981.

Stokes, Anson Phelps. *Church and State in the United States.* 3 vols. New York: Harper and Brothers, 1950.

Tierney, Brian. *The Crisis of Church and State, 1050–1300.* Englewood Cliffs, NJ: Prentice-Hall, 1964.

Washington, George. *The Writings of George Washington.* Edited by John C. Fitzpatrick, 37 vols. Washington, DC: Government Printing Office, 1931–1940.

Williams, Roger. *The Complete Writings of Roger Williams.* 7 vols. New York: Russell and Russell, 1963.

Articles/Chapters

Dreisbach, Daniel L. "*Everson* and the Command of History: The Supreme Court, Lessons of History, and Church-State Debate in America." In *Everson Revisited: Religion, Education and Law at the Crossroads*, eds. Jo Renee Formicola and Hubert Morken. Lanham, MD: Rowman and Littlefield, 1997.

———. "Thomas Jefferson and the Danbury Baptists Revisited." *William and Mary Quarterly*, 3d series, 56, no. 4 (1999): 805.

Glenn, Gary D. "Forgotten Purposes of the First Amendment Religion Clauses." *Review of Politics* 49 (1987): 340.

Hillerbrand, Hans J. "An Early Anabaptist Treatise on the Christian and the State." *Mennonite Quarterly Review* 32 (1958): 28.

Hutson, James H. "Thomas Jefferson's Letter to the Danbury Baptists: A Controversy Rejoined." *William and Mary Quarterly*, 3d ser., 56, no. 4 (1999): 775.

McGreevy, John T. "Thinking on One's Own: Catholicism in the American Intellectual Imagination, 1928–1960." *Journal of American History* 84 (June 1997): 97.

Neuhaus, Richard John. "Contending for the Future: Overcoming the Pfefferian Inversion." *Journal of Law and Religion* 8 (1990): 115.

Witte, John, Jr., "That Serpentine Wall of Separation." Michigan Law Review 101 (2003): 1869.

CHAPTER 8

MANAGED PLURALISM: THE EMERGING CHURCH–STATE MODEL IN THE UNITED STATES?

NIKOLAS K. GVOSDEV

THE notion of America as a "nation of faith" is an important component of national self-identity. One of the founding myths that defines the United States is that the American experiment began as an ark of refuge for those seeking freedom of worship (beginning with the Pilgrim trek on the Mayflower) and became a "godly republic," but one that did not require the imposition of a state faith. In the words of John J. DiIulio, Jr., the United States is a republic whose "governmental institutions" "presuppose belief in the 'Supreme Being'" and that "respects, promotes and protects religious pluralism."[1] Former Massachusetts governor Mitt Romney sounded this theme during a 2007 address when he said, "[W]e do not insist on a single strain of religion—rather, we welcome our nation's symphony of faith."[2]

Indeed, as part of its efforts at public diplomacy, the U.S. State Department stresses the connection between American religiosity and freedom: "Religious freedom is one of the most prized liberties of the American people. . . . Religion is not absent from daily life in the United States; rather, the Constitution has created a system in which each individual and religious group can enjoy the full freedom to worship, free not only from the rein of government but from pressures by other sects as well."[3]

Religious diversity, in turn, is said to be the guarantee both of religious freedom and also the principal reason religion plays such a major role in American life, in contrast to other industrialized states.[4] In contrast to the 15 recognized religious communities of Romania, or the 22 religious and confessional communities authorized to function as public corporations in Austria, the United States has hundreds, if not thousands (depending on how one makes divisions and distinctions), of religious organizations.

Yet a symphony—to use Romney's characterization—requires a conductor to produce a pleasing melody. Absolute pluralism—in any society—is an impossibility. For the sake of civic peace and social cohesion, even at the cost of interfering with an individual's right to choose, a state will forbid (or require) certain beliefs and practices. International law, for instance, permits limitations "necessary to protect public safety, order, health or morals or the fundamental rights and freedoms of others" (Article 18.3, International Covenant on Civil and Political Rights)—but leaves the definitions of such matters such as "public safety" or "morals" in the hands of national governments. Peter Beyer concludes, "While most countries in the world today officially declare that their citizens enjoy freedom of religion, none of them actually allows the unfettered exercise of that freedom."[5] Thus, every country finds a way to "manage" pluralism—even the United States.

Most Americans take the 1876 ruling of the Ohio Supreme Court as the definitive statement on religious freedom in the United States: "It [the constitution] gives the state no power to declare which religion or religious sect is better or best. . . . This makes the state impartial and neutral between every creed, faith and sect existing among the people for the time being."[6] Yet the U.S. Supreme Court, in affirming pluralism in religious matters as the norm, nonetheless introduced the notion of limits. Only a few years earlier, in the landmark *Watson v. Jones* decision (1871), the Court had ruled: "The law knows no heresy, and is committed to the support of no dogma, the establishment of no sect." However, the justices also made clear: "In this country the full and free right to entertain any religious belief, to practice any religious principle and to teach any religious doctrine which does not violate the laws of morality and property, and which does not infringe personal rights, is conceded to all."[7] Thus the legal basis for managing America's religious pluralism was laid.

Defining Managed Pluralism

What is "managed pluralism?" As I have used the term, it is a system by which a state, while itself imposing no one ideology, nevertheless takes steps to regulate the number of options that are available by setting down the criteria that determine the extent to which divergence from prevailing norms is acceptable.[8] In turn, using its regulatory power, a government can then allow or exclude groups from being able to function openly in society as public associations.

Initially, I used this concept to evaluate developments in church–state relations across Central and Eastern Europe and Eurasia, where post-Communist governments, in freeing themselves from an *ancien regime* in which there had been a governing ideology (Marxism–Leninism) were coming to terms with the implications of a "free marketplace of ideas." "Managed pluralism" seemed a compromise approach; while accepting in principle the idea of state neutrality and free competition among different belief systems, governments could nonetheless engage in a process of vetting competing and diverse ideologies for overall compatibility with the "prevailing ethos" of society.[9]

In the Eastern European case, in the last decade two prevailing yardsticks have been used to limit the number of permitted options. The first has been for governments to use the concept of a "traditional faith"—usually defined in chronological terms. For instance, the "Law on Religious Communities and Associations," adopted by the Lithuanian legislature in 1995, defined nine groups as "traditional" (such as the Roman Catholics, the Russian Orthodox, and so on) on the grounds of having a documented presence in Lithuania of at least 300 years and as a result constituted a part of the country's historical, spiritual, and social heritage (Article 5). Other religious communities, defined as "non-traditional," could obtain state recognition "if they are backed by society and their instruction and rites are not contrary to laws and morality." After a challenge to the constitutionality of this act was mounted, on the grounds that religions deemed "non-traditional" faced discrimination, the Constitutional Court, in a June 2000 ruling, declared, "Tradition is neither created nor abolished by an act of the will of the legislator. Naming of churches and religious organizations as traditional is not an act of establishment as traditional organizations but an act stating both their tradition and the status of their relations in society."[10]

If the first method is to use history to arbitrarily create a dividing line between accepted and less-accepted options, the second takes a different tack. Here, the emphasis is on assessing the "compatibility" of any given faith or belief system with the prevailing values of the country, that permit the state to determine whether or not its right to interfere with a person's freedom of conscience can be justified by its prerogatives to take action in defense of "health" or "morals" or "public order." It should be stressed that the emphasis is not on ensuring any sort of theological conformity, but instead making sure that similar social norms are being promoted.

Take Russian President Vladimir Putin's 2000 Christmas message as an example. In it, he praised Russian Orthodoxy and its role in defining Russian culture and implied that Orthodox values (rather than specific dogmas of Orthodox theology) were normative for Russian society as a whole:

> [Orthodoxy] has been not only a moral touchstone for the believer but also an
> unbending spiritual core of the entire people and state. Based on the idea of love
> for one's neighbor and on the commandments of good, mercy and justice,
> Orthodoxy has largely determined the character of Russian civilization . . . its
> ideals will make it possible to strengthen mutual understanding and consensus in
> our society.[11]

Several months later, the patriarch of the Russian Orthodox Church, Aleksii II, renewed his calls for the government to restrict the rights of a number of religious groups, not on the grounds of dogma, but because they, in his opinion, threatened the good order of society. Prefacing his remarks with the statement that he respected "the right of every individual to confess a religion or to confess no religion," he nonetheless argued that there was an overriding state interest to "protect, in the interests of the people," against any religious organization that was a "negative influence" in society, such as groups that might cause their followers "to abandon their civic responsibilities and be anti-patriotic."[12] Throughout the region, the term "totalitarian sects" has often been introduced, usually in contradistinction to "traditional faiths," for religious movements deemed to be antisocial and thus subject to restrictive legislation—including denial of registration or the ability to function as a public corporation.[13]

Either method, in the end, produces the same result—identifying which religious groups, or often, more specifically, denominations—are permitted to operate in society.

American Managed Pluralism?
The Theories

At first glance, managed pluralism may not seem to hold much value as a concept for evaluating church–state relations in the United States. The First Amendment to the Constitution absolutely prohibits the management by the state—especially the executive branches of government—of the country's religious life in such a direct, blatant, and interventionist manner as is evident in eastern Europe. The U.S. government issues no lists of proscribed faiths, there is no legal definition of a protected class of religious groups that enjoy the designation "traditional" and thus special privileges (or denies to nontraditional groups the rights to register, own property, or spread their message through the media). Some of this may be a result of differences in political culture, from what Lev Kopelev and other Soviet-era intellectuals identified as a profound fear of disorder and anarchy that seems ingrained in the lands that lie between the Oder and the Urals—leading to the creation of legal cultures that limit the amount of individual freedom. However, even when contrasting this with the more liberal regimes of the West, especially Anglo-American constitutions, they noted that limits were still imposed on an individual's freedom of choice—but such limits were far less visible and more subtle.[14] Indeed, in the United States, groups that in Eastern Europe would be defined as "totalitarian sects" or as "threats" to public order and morals—the "Church of Satan" being a prime example—seem to enjoy the same full panoply of rights as those afforded to the predominant, mainline Christian denominations.

Yet, one can hear echoes of Putin in statements by leading American political figures, about a unifying set of common values that define American religions. Take Governor Romney:

> It is important to recognize that while differences in theology exist between the
> churches in America, we share a common creed of moral convictions . . . these
> American values: the equality of human kind, the obligation to serve one another,
> and a steadfast commitment to liberty. . . . They are not unique to any one
> denomination. They belong to the great moral inheritance we hold in common.
> They are the firm ground on which Americans of different faiths meet and stand
> as a nation, united.[15]

Left unsaid is what happens when a religious community does not share these
"American values;" so perhaps it would be more accurate to say that management of
pluralism in the United States is far more indirect than elsewhere in the world.

First and foremost, not even the United States can "institutionalize religion in
the abstract," as Veit Bader notes. Because a wide variety of benefits are made available to religious organizations, the United States, at both the federal and local
levels, must have definitions of what constitutes a religious group and religious
activity in place, since resorting to a system of self-definition would be to invite
wide-scale abuse.[16] As a result, a legal system "may explicitly or implicitly evaluate
(or rank) religions . . . between what is considered to be 'real' religion as opposed
to 'pseudo' religion."[17]

It is true that the United States has no "historical test" for religious groups, but
it would also be a mistake to assume that America's dominant religious tradition—
Protestant Christianity—has had no influence. Usually, the dominant religion or
tradition sets down defining criteria.[18] Yale law professor Guido Calabresi notes
that, in turn, many of these beliefs can pass into general standards:

> [M]ost of our secular beliefs are really part of older, accepted religions. They
> became part of our secular thinking because they were held by the first settlers—
> because they were widely held then.[19]

Over time, other religious traditions have undergone a process of "Americanization" whereby their own traditions have undergone a process of acclimatization
to prevailing American norms. This is why Alexis de Tocqueville could proclaim,
"The sects which exist in the United States are innumerable" but "they all agree in
respect to the duties which are due from man to man. Each sect adores the Deity in
its own peculiar manner, but all the sects preach the same moral law in the name of
God."[20] A century later, Will Herberg observed that America could sustain its religious pluralism because the multiplicity of religious organizations all taught values
that supported an "American way of life" defined by political liberty, free market
capitalism, limited government, and freedom of choice.[21]

In addition, the Protestant example—the de facto American standard—has
served "as an implicit model of what constitutes a legitimate religion," meaning, by
extension, that those who deviate too significantly from that form are perceived by
society as being less legitimate or not even constituting an actual religion.[22] As a
result, non-Christian faiths, in particular, have found it useful to adopt a number of
the outward features of a Protestant congregation and sometimes have even adopted
English-language terms drawn from the Protestant experience to describe their own

faith traditions and minimize differences.[23] One observer, contrasting the work and appearance of Hindu temples in India with Hindu communities in the United States, concluded: "In America, Hindu temples tend to become like other American voluntary associations and in time they will begin to resemble American synagogues and churches. . . ."[24] Similarly, the Buddhist Churches of America has sought to create "American forms of the dharma"—beginning with the adoption of the term "church," designating Sunday as the day for communal worship, and creating a leadership structure with bishops and ministers—giving its operations a "Protestant cast."[25] All of this, in turn, has enabled non-Protestant and even non-Christian faiths to assume the status Calabresi describes as "banquet religions"—those whose clergy and representatives are invited to give benedictions at civic gatherings as accepted representatives of the American community of faith.[26]

If one way of managing America's religious diversity is to encourage various faiths to take on the external features of the majority tradition, a related coping mechanism has been the notion of a "general" Christianity and the assigning of honorary Christian status to non-Christian religions. In the nineteenth century, Charles Franklin Thwing, president of the University of Michigan, was among those American intellectuals prepared to redefine the meaning of the generic term "Christian" to encompass any believer in the God of the Bible, laying the foundation for the concept of a "Judeo-Christian" tradition. Over time, many Americans came to understand religious pluralism as meaning a variety of denominations coexisting together but sharing some similar fundamental bedrock principles—such as the fatherhood of God and the brotherhood of man, with Jesus Christ respected as a moral figure and teacher.[27] In turn, a number of non-Christian religions in America—even those that historically had "no opinion" on the person and work of Jesus—were prepared to find a place for him in their own traditions—so that Jesus can be seen as a Bodhisattva, an incarnation of Vishnu or Krishna, or even a representation of the eternal Dao.[28] This trend began with Reform Judaism's endorsement, in the nineteenth century, of Jesus as a teacher and preacher in the Jewish tradition, breaking with more traditional Talmudic discussions of Christ as a sorcerer, a deceiver, and an illegitimate fraud—finding common ground with Unitarians and other Protestants who rejected the belief that Jesus Christ was God incarnate in favor of Christ as moral guide.

The "general Christian" approach can also coexist with another historic American model—an appeal to the Deism of the Founding Fathers. Whereas Thwing and others sought to expand the definition of "Christianity" by emphasizing belief in a common God revealed in the Bible, a number of America's founders, schooled in the Enlightenment emphasis on reason, not revealed scripture, as the guide to Truth, discussed religion in terms that, although perfectly acceptable to those who defined the Deity by referring to the Old and New Testaments, could also be acceptable to those who do not use the Bible as any point of reference for their own religious opinions. The existence of God and of a moral law (defined in terms of the Golden Rule) could be deduced from observing the universe and did not require proclamation by any specific prophetic figure.[29] Indeed, for some, different religions had taken these self-evident truths and added a mass of opinions and preferences—which a person should be free to follow but which were of no interest to the state or society. Jean-Jacques Rousseau had summarized them in Book 4, Chapter 8 of *The Social Contract*:

> There is therefore a purely civil profession of faith of which the Sovereign should fix the articles, not exactly as religious dogmas, but as social sentiments without which a man cannot be a good citizen or a faithful subject. . . . The dogmas of civil religion ought to be few, simple, and exactly worded, without explanation or commentary. The existence of a mighty, intelligent and beneficent Divinity, possessed of foresight and providence, the life to come, the happiness of the just, the punishment of the wicked, the sanctity of the social contract and the laws: these are its positive dogmas. Its negative dogmas I confine to one, intolerance, which is a part of the cults we have rejected.

These views found expression in many of the public statements of the Founders. For example, George Washington, the first president, never made reference to Jesus Christ and, although sometimes referring to "Almighty God," tended instead to use far more neutral terms such as "the Deity," "Superintending Power," "Providence," or the "Great Ruler of Events." Indeed, whether by design or accident, Washington's religious language strongly resembles that of the Roman Edict of Milan in its references to a generic Deity who can be identified with the specific Gods worshipped by different communities. Not surprisingly, Washington, during his two terms as president, found little difficulty in seeing Americans of diverse religious backgrounds as common citizens based on their allegiance to a common Deity—sentiments made perfectly clear in a series of addresses sent to various minority Protestant, Catholic, Quaker, Jewish, and Native American communities.[30]

A final approach to managing pluralism is to put limits on diversity that threatens the cohesiveness of the liberal-democratic state—based on a redefinition that the "American way of life" celebrated by Herberg is one predicated upon the supremacy of the individual. Bader argues that most modern Western states, even the United States, maintain that pluralism "must be compatible with the minimal requirements of a liberal-democratic constitution: in short, it must supplement, not replace representative democracy."[31] Building on this foundation, political theorist William Galston has put forward his concept of a "diversity state" in which all ideas and beliefs can be expressed—but with the following three limitations. First, he maintains, any group must, in its beliefs and rituals, protect human life. As he puts it, there is "no free exercise for Aztecs" who might want to engage in human sacrifice. The second requirement that the state can impose is to ensure the protection and promotion of the "normal development" of the "basic capacities" of all its citizens, including minors; the third is the overriding interest of the state in "social rationality"—that all citizens are capable of functioning in the larger society.[32]

All of the preceding methods for managing pluralism provide for a great deal of diversity—but even so, there are still limits. The "Protestant congregational" approach to defining religion either requires other religious traditions to adapt or risk losing benefits made available to religious organizations.[33] An appeal to Enlightenment Deism runs up against the challenge of nontheistic religions such as Buddhism, whereas "general Christianity" loses its appeal to groups unwilling or unable to find a common theological language that can encompass the God described in the Bible. The liberal standard has also, in recent years, faced challenges from Christian, Jewish, and Islamic traditionalists who fear the erosion of deeply held beliefs and traditions in public institutions, especially in education.

In turn, these various approaches to handling religious diversity are important, especially because they often find expression in legislation. After all, it was Congress that voted in 1954 to add the phrase "under God" to the Pledge of Allegiance; in more recent years, whether out of conviction or respect for the growing economic clout of Native American communities, members of Congress have proved themselves willing to expand the definitions of what constitutes a religion and religious activity. Across the United States, a whole host of state, city, and local governments pass measures that may either accommodate or hinder the work of religious groups. Some might use James Madison's standard, expressed in his "Memorial and Remonstrance Against Religious Assessments," that religion is the "duty we owe the Creator" and require that a group, to be considered a religion, must demonstrate a belief in a Supreme Being. This was the standard used by Congress when amending the Universal Military Training and Service Act in 1948, to define "religious training and belief" as "an individual's belief in a relation to a Supreme Being involving duties superior to those arising from any human relation"—and specifically differentiated religious sentiment from "essentially political, sociological or philosophical views or a merely personal moral code." Others might take as their starting point whether a group engages in recognizable religious activities—say a congregation assembling in a specific building to sing hymns and receive instruction, to solemnize momentous occasions such as births and marriages, or engage in charitable activity.[34]

Yet, under the American principle of judicial review, legislation dealing with religious pluralism is ultimately subject to the interpretation of the courts.

WHAT THE COURTS SAY

Suffice it to say, no United States court has ever used the term "managed pluralism" to discuss church–state relations; but the judicial branch, especially the Supreme Court, has been well aware of the need to provide definitions.

Over the last century, the Supreme Court has steadily expanded the legal definition of what constitutes a religion—and in so doing precluded the emergence of any sort of religious regulatory regime that one finds in Europe or other places around the world. Initially, in the 1892 decision *Holy Trinity Church v. United States,* the Court had seemed to set down the standard of "general Christianity," citing state court rulings that "general Christianity is, and always has been, a part of the common law . . . not Christianity with an established church and tithes and spiritual courts, but Christianity with liberty of conscience to all men" and "the people of this country profess the general doctrines of Christianity as the rule of their faith."[35]

However, the Supreme Court has been steadily backing away from that stance ever since, especially the implication in the *Holy Trinity* case that Christianity enjoyed a constitutionally more protected status than Islam or Buddhism.[36] Then Chief Justice Charles Evan Hughes noted in the 1931 case, *United States v. Macintosh*, "The essence of religion is belief in a relation to God involving duties superior to those arising from any human relation."[37]

This move, toward a more generic standard of Deism, continued in the 1952 *Zorach v. Clauson* decision (which upheld a New York program that allowed for public school students to be excused from attending religious education classes). The Court declared, "We are a religious people whose institutions presuppose a Supreme Being. We guarantee the freedom to worship as one chooses. We make room for as wide a variety of beliefs and creeds as the spiritual needs of man deem necessary."[38] Although the Court kept the phrasing found in the *Holy Trinity* decision—that Americans are a "religious people"—it also dispensed with any use of a standard of "general Christianity" to assess religion in favor of a reference to a generic "Supreme Being."

Here matters might have stayed, given that this statement could also be said to reflect what several of the Founding Fathers would have seen as a good definition.[39] Yet, little more than a decade later, the Supreme Court again expanded the scope of religion. This was due, in part, to concerns, raised by Buddhists, Ethical Humanists, and others, that the use of a "Supreme Being" as a reference point for defining religion was still too limiting.[40] Therefore, in deciding in favor of a conscientious objector who did not base his refusal—on religious grounds—to serve in the military on the basis of Hughes' earlier criteria that religion was based on duties owed to a Supreme Being or God, the Court decided on a standard that "a sincere and meaningful belief which occupies in the life of its possessor a place parallel to that" occupied by God in a theistic religion would qualify.[41] This is the standard that remains in effect to this day.

The *Seeger* decision also reiterated another constitutional principle that would inhibit one of the principal tools used by other societies in managing pluralism—subjecting beliefs to the scrutiny of the larger society—or government officials—to determine their reasonableness or suitability. *Seeger* built on the earlier precedent set down in *United States v. Ballard* (1944), when the majority decision held that freedom of religion embraces the right to maintain theories of life and death and the hereafter that are rank heresy to followers of the orthodox faiths. Heresy trials are foreign to our Constitution. Men may believe what they cannot prove. They may not be put to the proof of their religious doctrines or beliefs. . . .

The religious views espoused by respondents might seem incredible, if not preposterous, to most people; but if those doctrines are subject to trial before a jury charged with finding their truth or falsity, then the same can be done with the religious beliefs of any sect. When the triers of fact undertake that task, they enter a forbidden domain. The First Amendment does not select any one group or any one type of religion for preferred treatment. It puts them all in that position.[42]

The *Seeger* decision reiterated that, in determining whether or not a person is acting from religiously derived motives, "The validity of what he believes cannot be questioned." Moreover, "courts in this sense are not free to reject beliefs because they consider them 'incomprehensible.'"

Overt regulation of groups based on the contents of their beliefs, therefore, is very difficult to sustain under current Supreme Court guidelines. However, an interesting recent development was the Supreme Court's refusal to hear a case arising out of the decision of the U.S. Fourth Circuit Court of Appeals (*Simpson v. Chesterfield County*, 04-1141), arising out of the refusal of Chesterfield County, Virginia, to add a Wiccan leader to the list of local religious leaders who are asked to offer non-denominational prayers at the opening of county board sessions. The board had refused on the grounds that "non-sectarian invocations are traditionally made to a divinity that is consistent with the Judeo-Christian tradition." The appeals court, in finding for the board, found their system of clergy selection to, in essence, be diverse enough and that those who offered a prayer should follow the ecumenical guidelines laid out in the 1983 *Marsh v. Chambers* case: There should be "no indication that the prayer opportunity has been exploited to proselytize or advance any one, or to disparage any other, faith or belief" and that it should be broad based to encompass "beliefs widely held among the people of this country."[43] In turn, the Court, in the *Marsh* decision, went to its 1961 *McGowan* ruling, where it had noted: "the Founding Fathers looked at invocations as 'conduct whose . . . effect . . . harmonize[d] with the tenets of some or all religions.'"[44] The district court acknowledged that the clergy selection process of the county might not be as diverse as some might like—but at the same time also raised the issue as to whether some faiths represented in the community would be prepared to render invocations of a common nature without invoking specific deities (such as Kore or Pan). The amicus brief filed by the Hindu American Foundation to the Supreme Court, asking for a writ of certiorari, argued that the Chesterfield precedent created a two-tiered system of faiths and argued it would set a precedent across the country. Although the brief did not use the term "managed pluralism," it implied that the *Zorach v. Clauson* standard—that American institutions presuppose belief in a Supreme Being—could be used to suggest that, as a result, "They do not presuppose no Supreme Being and they do not presuppose many Supreme Beings. They presuppose monotheism." Thus a recognition of that fact "is not disparaging any other religion; it is simply operating within the very presuppositions of the society of which it is a part." At present, since it is not clear whether the Supreme Court will, at some point in the future, decide to hear a series of cases relating to invocations, whether the standard set by the appeals court will remain intact or not cannot be determined. Nevertheless, it does show that there remains significant interest in finding ways to mediate and manage America's religious pluralism around a set of common assumptions.

If belief remains largely off limits, regulation of activity is another matter. The Court made this quite clear in its 1940 *Cantwell v. Connecticut* decision: ". . . the [First] Amendment embraces two concepts—freedom to believe and freedom to act. The first is absolute, but, in the nature of things, the second cannot be. Conduct remains subject to regulation for the protection of society."[45]

The classic statement of this principle is the 1878 decision in *Reynolds v. United States,* in which the Court rejected the defense mounted by a member of the Church of Jesus Christ of Latter-day Saints that his right to free exercise of religion permitted him to engage in polygamy—which had been outlawed by act of Congress. The Court ruled, "Laws are made for the government of actions, and while they cannot interfere with mere religious belief and opinions, they may with practices."[46]

To make that conclusion, the Supreme Court fell back on the "original intent" of the Founding Fathers. In particular, Thomas Jefferson's famous 1802 letter to the Danbury Baptist Association was cited in which he wrote, "Believing with you that religion is a matter which lies solely between man and his God, that he owes account to none other for his faith or his worship, that the legislative powers of the government reach actions only, and not opinions . . . I shall see with sincere satisfaction the progress of those sentiments which tend to restore man to all his natural rights, convinced he has no natural right in opposition to his social duties." The Court therefore concluded, citing the "almost authoritative declaration" of Jefferson, that Congress and other legislatures were indeed free to proscribe actions "which were in violation of social duties or subversive of good order."

The *Reynolds* precedent has been continuously upheld by subsequent Court decisions. The Supreme Court has upheld regulations against different activities "if the religious practices themselves conflicted with the public interest"[47] and has maintained that government "may justify a limitation on religious liberty by showing that it is essential to accomplish an overriding governmental interest."[48]

However, this opens up the possibility of managing religious pluralism through the back door. Evaluating whether acts are prejudicial to public morals and good order can be a highly selective process. The Court, in the *Reynolds* decision, did list a number of practices that could be banned even though they might be backed by religious sanction—human sacrifice or the immolation of a widow on the funeral pyre of her dead husband—that few would find objectionable. However, in determining that Congress had an overriding interest in prohibiting polygamy outright (instead of simply limiting the state interest to whether or not additional wives entered into a polygamous union with informed consent), the Supreme Court relied on a number of different criteria. The Court made an appeal to cultural primacy of European Christian norms for American society (that "polygamy has been treated as an offence against society") as well as principles of family law that, although they had originated in Christian religious teachings, had become part of the secular legal inheritance of the United States (via transmission from Great Britain). Because they were no longer ecclesiastical in nature, prohibitions against polygamy therefore could not be seen as a type of establishment of a particular faith's canon law. Finally, anticipating the arguments made by Galston and others, the Court also invoked the right of the legislature to take steps that would preserve and enhance the liberal democratic system. Chief Justice Morrison Waite wrote that "according as monogamous or polygamous marriages are allowed, do we find the principles on which the government of the people, to a greater or less extent, rests" and that, over time, the existence of polygamy "fetters the people in stationary despotism."[49]

So the *Reynolds* precedent created a distinction between opinion that could not be regulated—one presumably is free to believe that human sacrifice is required by the gods—and actions that could. It also laid the basis for several of the standards previously discussed to be used to determine whether an activity is in fact religious and whether it might be prejudicial to good order or the interests of society—and for such activity to be limited or barred outright—without violating the First Amendment. Another option has been to draw distinctions between an act being "religious" versus it falling under the rubric of a "way of life"—and therefore lying outside the scope of First Amendment protections.[50] Finally, the landmark 1990 case *Employment Division, Oregon Department of Human Resources v. Smith*[51] reiterated the principle that "an individual's religious beliefs" cannot "excuse him from compliance with an otherwise valid law prohibiting conduct that the state is free to regulate."[52]

Usually, that regulation will be based on majoritarian views as to what constitutes religious activity—and what constitutes reasonable exceptions. For example, in the *Cantwell v. Connecticut* decision, the Court upheld the right of a state, "by general and nondiscriminatory legislation," to regulate how, where, and when meetings convened for religious purposes could take place.[53] The default assumption, however, is that religious activity should take place in a church or some other defined and consecrated structure—and that a site can and should be territorially limited. When confronted, however, with Native American religious groups that claim not only specific natural features, but also large tracts of land as sacred areas, the courts have been far more inconsistent in guaranteeing religious rights, especially if there are other countervailing interests. This was made clear in the Supreme Court's 1988 ruling on the request of several California Native American groups to prevent the construction of a road and commercial logging from occurring on what they considered to be sacred land.

The Government does not dispute, and we have no reason to doubt, that the logging and road-building projects at issue in this case could have devastating effects on traditional Indian religious practices. Those practices are intimately and inextricably bound up with the unique features of the Chimney Rock area, which is known to the Indians as the "high country." Individual practitioners use this area for personal spiritual development; some of their activities are believed to be critically important in advancing the welfare of the Tribe, and indeed, of mankind itself. The Indians use this area, as they have used it for a very long time, to conduct a wide variety of specific rituals that aim to accomplish their religious goals. According to their beliefs, the rituals would not be efficacious if conducted at other sites than the ones traditionally used, and too much disturbance of the area's natural state would clearly render any meaningful continuation of traditional practices impossible. . . . [But] government simply could not operate if it were required to satisfy every citizen's religious needs and desires. A broad range of government activities—from social welfare programs to foreign aid to conservation projects—will always be considered essential to the spiritual well-being of some citizens, often on the basis of sincerely held religious beliefs. Others will find the very same activities deeply offensive, and perhaps incompatible with their own search for spiritual fulfillment and with the tenets of their religion.[54]

The Court acknowledged that if there was an effort made to ban Native Americans from visiting the area altogether, "this would raise a different set of constitutional questions. Whatever rights the Indians may have to the use of the area, however, those rights do not divest the Government of its right to use what is, after all, its land."[55]

The *Lyng* case paved the way for a more controversial ruling, in the aforementioned *Smith* decision 2 years later, when in essence, the Court maintained that Oregon's ban on peyote encompassed even a ban on its use as a sacramental substance (in contrast, the Volstead Act, which paved the way for Prohibition, included a specific exception for sacramental wine). The court, in declining to find on behalf of the peyote users—both members of the Native American Church—instead opined that the best way forward would be for the Oregon legislature to enact a religious exemption rather than have the Court impose one. This is in keeping with what they had said 2 years earlier in *Lyng*, when the Supreme Court offered its opinion that "courts cannot, offer to reconcile the various competing demands on government, many of them rooted in sincere religious belief, that inevitably arise in so diverse a society as ours. That task, to the extent that it is feasible, is for the legislatures and other institutions." In the *Smith* decision, the Court acknowledged that local, state, and federal governments can make specific exemptions for religions in laws if they desire; that is not prohibited, but courts cannot compel this:

> But to say that a nondiscriminatory religious practice exemption is permitted, or even that it is desirable, is not to say that it is constitutionally required. . . . It may fairly be said that leaving accommodation to the political process will place at a relative disadvantage those religious practices that are not widely engaged in; but that unavoidable consequence of democratic governance must be preferred to a system in which each conscience is a law unto itself or in which judges weigh the social importance of all laws against the centrality of all religious beliefs.[56]

The Court seemed, therefore, to suggest that majority was free to determine what it considered to be a religious practice—and whether the practices of minority faiths—those which simply did not have the weight of numbers or public opinion behind them—should also receive exemptions or consideration.

Many observers assumed that the decision reached in the 1993 *Church of Lukumi Babalu Aye v. City of Hialeah,* in which the Supreme Court struck down a ban enacted by the city of Hialeah, Florida, against animal sacrifice—with the unstated but generally understood motive of curtailing the worship practices of Santeria, an

Afro-Caribbean religion, provides constitutional guarantees for religious groups whose practices fall outside the general mainstream and indeed may be targeted by the majority as repugnant. However, the Court's problem was with a city regulation that in essence, had been targeted to impact a specific religious community—the Santeria faith—while permitting the same activities to those engaged in "secular" purposes—rather than to uphold the right of a religious community to engage in animal sacrifice. Justice Anthony Kennedy's decision stressed this: "Under the Free Exercise Clause, a law that burdens religious practice need not be justified by a compelling governmental interest if it is neutral and of general applicability. . . . A law failing to satisfy these requirements must be justified by a compelling governmental interest, and must be narrowly tailored to advance that interest."[57] Indeed, had the city passed a general ordinance that would still have had the impact of making animal sacrifice illegal, it is not apparent that the Supreme Court would have overturned it; Justice Blackmun, in his concurring opinion, nonetheless felt it necessary to point out:

> A harder case would be presented if petitioners were requesting an exemption
> from a generally applicable anticruelty law. The result in the case before the
> Court today, and the fact that every Member of the Court concurs in that result,
> does not necessarily reflect this Court's views of the strength of a State's interest
> in prohibiting cruelty to animals. This case does not present, and I therefore
> decline to reach, the question whether the Free Exercise Clause would require a
> religious exemption from a law that sincerely pursued the goal of protecting
> animals from cruel treatment.[58]

In the aftermath of the Smith decision, Congress (and many state legislatures) passed legislation (most notably, the 1993 Federal Religious Freedom Restoration Act) that mandated that the government would have the burden of proof to demonstrate its "compelling interest" in overriding the free exercise clause of the First Amendment.[59] Yet I believe that the 2006 *Gonzales v. O Centro Espírita Beneficente União do Vegetal* decision, which many people see as a validation of that Act, should be read carefully. The Supreme Court agreed that the U.S. government had failed to demonstrate its compelling interest, at the preliminary injunction stage, in prohibiting this Brazilian-based religious group from using a tea brewed from a substance called *hoasca,* which is covered by the Controlled Substances Act—but does not rule out the possibility that the government, in the future, can in fact demonstrate it does has a compelling interest, in which case the ban can be upheld.[60]

In addition, legislation passed by Congress in the aftermath of the *Smith* decision (the "American Indian Religious Freedom Act Amendments of 1994") to protect the sacramental use of peyote specifically limited the application of that protection to members of recognized Native American communities. Therefore, the right to practice the rituals set down by groups such as the Native American Church are limited to those who fall under specified ethnic criteria; non-Indians who are not members of a "Federally Recognized Tribal entity" have no similar First Amendment protection—even if they have converted to an Indian-derived faith. To extend the analogy of the Volstead Act, this would be as if, in 1920, the exception for sacramental wine was not made for religious adherents (e.g., Roman Catholics) but specific ethnicities (e.g., Italians, Irish).

Accordingly, where we stand today is somewhat confusing: The overarching *Reynolds* precedent that allows the state to ban religious activities, modified by the government's need to show a compelling interest, with loopholes permitted by legislative action to exempt specific groups and practices—and one "protected class" of U.S. citizens so recognized by Congress—Native Americans—whose right to engage in activities deemed to be religious but that are not sanctioned by the mainstream (such as hunting of animals, a type of animal sacrifice)—is more often than not guaranteed—but such rights are enjoyed on the basis of ethnicity and are not transferable to converts or members of religious groups that have similar beliefs but are not recognized to be Native Americans.

This is why Calabresi, among others, has criticized the argument that the United States does not prohibit beliefs, only acts as a "distinction that makes no sense"[61]—that by prohibiting acts one can in fact affect religion. In his dissent in the *Lyng* opinion, Justice William J. Brennan, Jr. sounded a similar note, complaining, "Having thus stripped respondents and all other Native Americans of any constitutional protection against perhaps the most serious threat to their age-old religious practices, and indeed to their entire way of life, the Court assures us that nothing in its decision 'should be read to encourage governmental insensitivity to the religious needs of any citizen.'"[62] Two years later, in his dissent to the *Smith* decision, Justice Harry Blackmun raised the issue that the state of Oregon, by banning the sacramental use of a substance deemed to be essential for entering into communion with the Great Spirit, had essentially created a hostile environment for members of the Native American Church—which he viewed as inimical to the spirit of the First Amendment.[63]

Although the Native American cases affected very few people, they did lay out the outer bounds of what the Court was prepared to recognize as religion and over what actions it was prepared to give the protection of the Free Exercise clause. Even when beliefs may odd or strange, if the forms approximate those used by the mainstream faiths, they are more likely to be accepted.

Conclusion

In the eastern European case, managed pluralism has been about the outright banning of whole traditions or specific denominations, or otherwise restricting their abilities to function in the public square.

In the United States, managed pluralism is far more indirect. All faith traditions are welcomed; but the long-term impact of regulation on behavior and actions seems to be to create specifically American versions of different faiths. Stephen

Macedo notes that the political values of a liberal system cannot help but spill over into other spheres of life, including the religious; and this means that diversity needs to be shaped so that it does not interfere with the demands of a shared civic life.[64] (Examining Macedo's work, one reviewer noted that, in some cases, this may mean that "Oppression can and does occur when people take 'reasonable measures to secure the survival and health of our liberal civic order.'")[65]

Hence it might be said that, in the end, managed pluralism in the United States is designed to bring about de Tocqueville's outcome—a myriad number of different sects, preaching different theologies, upholding different scriptures, practicing different rituals—but promoting and sustaining the same values and sense of morality—the "American way of life."

ENDNOTES

1. John J. DiIulio, Jr., *Godly Republic: A Centrist Blueprint for America's Faith Based-Future* (Berkeley, CA: University of California Press, 2007), 29.

2. Governor Mitt Romney, "Faith in America," remarks delivered at the George Bush Presidential Library, College Station, Texas, on December 6, 2007, and archived at http://www.mittromney.com/News/Speeches/Faith_In_America.

3. Taken from the State Department's "Rights of the People" series, at http://usinfo.state.gov/products/pubs/rightsof/roots.htm.p.1.

4. "Among Wealthy Nations . . . The United States Stands Alone in its Embrace of Religion," report released by the Pew Global Attitudes Project, December 19, 2002, and available at http://pewglobal.org/reports/display.php?ReportID=167.

5. Peter Beyer, "Constitutional Privilege and Constituting Pluralism: Religious Freedom in National, Global and Legal Contexts," *Journal for the Scientific Study of Religion* 42:3 (September 2003): 333.

6. *Humphreys v. Little Sisters of the Poor,* 7 Ohio Dec. (1876), 194.

7. *Watson v. Jones,* 80 U.S. 679 (1871), 728.

8. Nikolas K. Gvosdev, "Tolerance versus Pluralism: The Eurasian Dilemma," *Analysis of Current Events* 12:7–8 (December 2000): 10.

9. See, for example, "'Managed Pluralism' and Civil Religion in Post-Soviet Russia," *Civil Society and the Search for Justice in Russia,* eds. Christopher Marsh and Nikolas K. Gvosdev (Lanham, MD: Lexington Books, 2002), esp. 79, and "Managing Pluralism: The Human Rights Challenge of the New Century," *World Policy Journal* (Winter 2001/02).

10. Ringolds Balodis, "State and Church in the Baltic States" (Riga: Latvian Association for Religious Freedom, 2001), 76–77.

11. *Interfax,* January 6, 2000.

12. Interview in *Rossiiskaia Gazeta,* January 6, 2001.

13. Balodis, 75.

14. See the discussion in Hedrick Smith, *The Russians* (New York: Quadrangle, 1976), 251–253.

15. Mitt Romney, "Faith in America," op cit.

16. Bader, 284.

17. T. Jeremy Gunn, "The Complexity of Religion and the Definition of 'Religion' in International Law," *Harvard Human Rights Journal* 16 (Spring 2003): 196.

18. For a discussion of religious hegemony and its role in influencing legal systems, see Lori G. Beaman, "The Myth of Pluralism, Diversity and Vigor: The Constitutional Privilege of Protestantism in the United States and Canada," *Journal for the Scientific Study of Religion* 42:3 (September 2003): 311–325.

19. Quoted in Chris Goodrich, *Anarchy and Elegance* (Boston: Little, Brown and Co., 1991), 174. An excellent example is the reasoning of the Supreme Court in upholding state laws requiring businesses to be closed on Sundays—that this was no longer predicated on religious requirements, but "with the establishment of a day of community tranquility, respite and recreation, a day when the atmosphere is one of calm and relaxation, rather than one of commercialism, as it is during the other six days of the week." *Braunfeld v. Brown,* 366 U. S. 599 (1961), 602.

20. This is something that Alexis de Tocqueville observed in chapter 17 of the first volume of *Democracy in America* in discussing Catholic immigrants to the United States, from which the above observation is also taken. How religious traditions can evolve to support new values—and how this can happen in the United States—is described in, among other sources, Lawrence Harrison, *The Central Liberal Truth* (Oxford, UK: Oxford University Press, 2006).

21. Will Herberg, *Protestant, Cathoic, Jew: An Essay in American Religious Sociology* (Garden City, NY: Doubleday, 1955).

22. Beyer, 333.

23. See, for instance, Prema Kurien, "Becoming American by becoming Hindu," and Rogaia Mustafa Abusharaf, "Structural Adaptations in an Immigrant Muslim Congregation in New York," both in *Gatherings in Diaspora: Religious Communities and the New Immigration,* eds. R. Stephen Warner and Judith G. Wittner (Philadelphia: Temple University Press, 1998), 37–70 and 235–264.

24. John Fenton, *Transplanting Religious Traditions: Asian Indians in America* (New York: Praeger, 1988), 179.

25. Richard Hughes Seager, *Buddhism in America* (New York: Columbia University Press, 1999), esp. 51–69.

26. Goodrich, 171.

27. See Richard E. Wentz, *The Culture of Religious Pluralism* (Boulder, CO: Westview Press, 1998), 13, 81.

28. See Stephen Prothero, "Hindus for Jesus," at http://www.beliefnet.com/story/97/story_9719_1.html.

29. See, for example, John Adams' assessment that one could rationally deduce the existence of a Higher Power and a moral law based on the Golden Rule, as quoted in Brooke Allen, *Moral Minority: Our Skeptical Founding Fathers* (Chicago: Ivan R. Dee, 2006), 68.

30. Washington's letters are available in the collection *George Washington: A Collection,* compiled and edited by W.B. Allen (Indianapolis, IN: Liberty Fund, 1988).

31. Bader, 284.

32. William A. Galston, "Two Concepts of Liberalism," *Ethics* 105 (April 1995): 524–525.

33. For instance, Muslim communities in the United States have moved in the direction of creating a professional class of full-time "clergy" who serve mosques that are legally incorporated as congregations, in contrast to the situation in many Muslim-majority countries, in order to be eligible for tax breaks, zoning considerations, access to hospitals

and prisons, and so on. See Abusharaf, esp. 250–258.

34. For example, a Rastafarian community in New York, the "Church of Haile Selassie I," is the only recognized, tax-exempt Rastafarian group in the United States, in part because although its beliefs in the divinity of the late Ethiopian emperor might seem at odds with the mainstream, the church nonetheless engages in behaviors that the larger community recognizes as being "religious." See Randal L. Hepner, "The House That Rasta Built: Church-Building and Fundamentalism among New York Rastafarians," in *Gatherings*, 197–234.

35. *Holy Trinity v. United States*, 143 U.S. 457 (1892), 470.

36. This comes when Justice Josiah Brewer continues to cite the opinion of New York Chancellor James Kent's opinion that—at least state governments—are not required to give the same degree of protection to "the religion of Mahomet or of the Grand Lama" because "we are a Christian people." Ibid., 471.

37. *United States v. Macintosh*, 238 U.S. 605 (1931), 626.

38. *Zorach v. Clauson*, 343 U.S. 306 (1952), 313.

39. Benjamin Franklin's "creed"—expressed in a letter to Yale's president Ezra Stiles—is belief in the Creator who governs the universe "by his providence" and that "the most acceptable service we render to him is doing good to his other children." Quoted in Allen, 24.

40. A standard argument made by the Buddhist Churches of America, for instance, is that Buddhists do "not believe in a Supreme Being or God" and that using that definition creates effective state sanction of belief in a Supreme Being and, by extension, a need for prayer. See Seager, *Buddhism in America*, 59–60.

41. *United States v. Seeger*, 380 U.S. 163 (1965).

42. *United States v. Ballard*, 322 U.S. 78 (1944), 87.

43. *Marsh v. Chambers*, 463 U. S. 783 (1983), 792.

44. *McGowan v. Maryland*, 366 U. S. 420 (1961), 442.

45. *Cantwell v. Connecticut*, 310 U. S. 296 (1940), 303.

46. *Reynolds v. United States*, 98 U.S. 145 (1878), 166.

47. *Braunfeld v. Brown*, 366 U. S. 599 (1961), 605.

48. *United States v. Lee*, 455 U.S. 252 (1982, 257). The so-called "Sherbert test," arising out of a 1963 case, set down criteria for determining if an individual's ability to practice his or her faith has been violated by state action. The individual would have to demonstrate a claim based on "sincere religious belief" and show that the state regulation posed a "substantial burden" on the person's ability to exercise his or her religion. The government, in turn, would have to show its compelling interest in the matter and that it had tried to ensure that it had acted in a manner that was least likely to affect a person's right to free exercise. *Sherbert v. Verner*, 374 U.S. 398 (1963).

49. *Reynolds v. United States*, 98 U.S. 145 (1878), 165–166.

50. See, for instance, Michael D. McNally's 2005 research report for Harvard University's Pluralism Project, "Native American Religious and Cultural Freedom: An Introductory Essay," at http://www.pluralism.org.

51. This case determined that a state—in this case, Oregon—could legally fire persons for violating a state prohibition on the use of controlled substances—in this particular case, peyote—even though the use of the drug was part of a religious ritual of the Native American Church and the drug was not made available or used outside of a religious context.

52. *Employment Division v. Smith*, 494 U.S. 872 (1990), 879.

53. *Cantwell v. Connecticut*, 310 U. S. 296 (1940), 304.

54. *Lyng v. Northwest Indian Cemetery*, 485 U.S 439 (1988), 451–452.

55. Ibid., 453.

56. *Employment Division v. Smith,* 494 U.S. 872 (1990), 890.

57. *Church of Lukumi Babalu Aye v. City of Hialeah,* 508 U.S. 520 (1993), 531.

58. Ibid, 580.

59. In 1997, the Supreme Court, in *City of Boerne v. Flores,* 521 U.S. 507 (1997), ruled that Congress could not define the substantive rights guaranteed by the Fourteenth Amendment, which can be imposed on the states. In response to this ruling, Congress passed the Religious Land Use and Institutionalized Persons Act in 2000—but the original 1993 act is still held to be applicable to federal actions.

60. 546 U.S. 418 (2006).

61. Quoted in Goodrich, 172.

62. *Lyng v. Northwest Indian Cemetery,* 485 U.S 439 (1988), 476-77.

63. *Employment Division v. Smith,* 494 U.S. 872 (1990), 920.

64. Stephen Macedo, "Liberal Civic Education and Religious Fundamentalism: The Case of. God v. John Rawls," *Ethics,* 45:3 (April 1995): 475. This theme is developed much further in his *Diversity and Distrust: Civic Education in a Multicultural Democracy* (Cambridge, MA: Harvard University Press, 2000).

65. See Michele S. Moses' review of *Diversity and Distrust,* archived at http://edrev.asu.edu/reviews/rev171.htm.

BIBLIOGRAPHY

Books

Allen, Brooke. *Moral Minority: Our Skeptical Founding Fathers.* Chicago: Ivan R. Dee, 2006.

Balodis, Ringolds. *State and Church in the Baltic States.* Riga: Latvian Association for Religious Freedom, 2001.

Casanova, Jose. *Public Religions in the Modern World.* Chicago: University of Chicago Press, 1994.

DiIulio, John J., Jr. *Godly Republic: A Centrist Blueprint for America's Faith Based-Future.* Berkeley, CA: University of California Press, 2007.

Fenton, John. *Transplanting Religious Traditions: Asian Indians in America.* New York: Praeger, 1988.

Harrison, Lawrence. *The Central Liberal Truth.* Oxford, UK: Oxford University Press, 2006.

Herberg, Will. *Protestant, Catholic, Jew: An Essay in American Religious Sociology.* Garden City, NY: Doubleday, 1955.

Kidwell, Clara Sue, Homer Nolan, and George E. "Tink" Tinker. *A Native American Theology.* Maryknoll, NY: Orbis Books, 2001.

Long, Carolyn. *Religious Freedom and Indian Rights: The Case of Oregon v. Smith.* Lawrence, KS: University of Kansas Press, 2001.

Martin, Joel W. *The Land Looks After Us: A History of Native American Religion.* New York: Oxford University Press, 1999-2000.

Meacham, Jon. *American Gospel: God, the Founding Fathers and the Making of a Nation.* New York: Random House Trade Paperbacks, 2007.

Norris, Pippa and Ronald Ingelhart. *The Sacred and the Secular.* Cambridge, UK: Cambridge University Press, 2004.

Pew Global Attitudes Project. *Among Wealthy Nations . . . The United States Stands Alone in its Embrace of Religion.* Washington, DC: Pew Research Center, 2002.

Seager, Richard Hughes. *Buddhism in America*. New York: Columbia University Press, 1999.

Wald, Kenneth and Allison Calhoun-Brown. *Religion and Politics in the United States*. 5th edition. Lanham, MD: Rowman and Littlefield, 2007.

Waldman, Steven. *Founding Faith: How Our Founding Fathers Forged a Radical New Approach to Religious Liberty*. New York: Random House, 2008.

Warner, R. Stephen and Judith G. Wittner, eds. *Gatherings in Diaspora: Religious Communities and the New Immigration*. Philadelphia: Temple University Press, 1998.

Wentz, Richard E. *The Culture of Religious Pluralism*. Boulder, CO: Westview Press, 1998.

Articles/Chapters

Beaman, Lori G. "The Myth of Pluralism, Diversity and Vigor: The Constitutional Privilege of Protestantism in the United States and Canada." *Journal for the Scientific Study of Religion* 42:3 (September 2003).

Bellah, Robert N. "Civil Religion in America." *Dædalus* 96 (Winter 1967): 1.

Beyer, Peter. "Constitutional Privilege and Constituting Pluralism: Religious Freedom in National, Global and Legal Contexts." *Journal for the Scientific Study of Religion* 42 (September 2003): 3.

Deloria, Vine, Jr. "Secularism, Civil Religion, and the Religious Freedom of American Indians." *American Indian Culture and Research Journal* 16 (1992): 9.

———. "Trouble in High Places: Erosion of American Indian Rights to Religious Freedom in the United States." in *The State of Native America: Genocide, Colonization, and Resistance*, ed. M. Annette Jaimes. Boston: South End Press, 1992.

Galston, William A. "Two Concepts of Liberalism." *Ethics* 105 (April 1995).

Gunn, T. Jeremy. "The Complexity of Religion and the Definition of 'Religion' in International Law." *Harvard Human Rights Journal* 16 (Spring 2003).

Gvosdev, Nikolas K. "'Managed Pluralism' and Civil Religion in Post-Soviet Russia." *Civil Society and the Search for Justice in Russia*, eds. Christopher Marsh and Nikolas K. Gvosdev. Lanham, MD: Lexington Books, 2002.

———. "Managing Pluralism: The Human Rights Challenge of the New Century," *World Policy Journal* (Winter 2001/02).

———. "Tolerance versus Pluralism: The Eurasian Dilemma." *Analysis of Current Events* 12 (December 2000): 7–8.

Leavitt, Peggy. "God Needs No Passport." *Harvard Divinity School* 34 (Autumn 2006): 3.

Machacek, David W. "The Problem of Pluralism." *Sociology of Religion* 64 (2003).

McNally, Michael D. "Native American Religious and Cultural Freedom: an Introductory Essay (2005),"published at *The Pluralism Project at Harvard University*, at http://www.pluralism.org/research/profiles/display.php?profile=73332.

Ray, S. Alan. "Native American Sacred Sites under Federal Law." *Church-State Issues in America*, eds. Ann W. Duncan and Steven L. Jones. Westport, CT: Greenwood Publishing Co., 2008.

Speeches and Presentations

Eck, Diana. "American Religious Pluralism: Civic and Theological Discourse." Draft paper presented at Georgetown University, April 21–22, 2005.

Romney, Mitt. "Faith in America." Remarks delivered at the George Bush Presidential Library, College Station, Texas, on December 6, 2007, and archived at http://www.mittromney.com/News/Speeches/Faith_In_America [accessed May 5, 2008].

PART III

THEOLOGICAL AND PHILOSOPHICAL DIMENSIONS

CHAPTER 9

....

RELIGIOUS LIBERTY AND RELIGIOUS MINORITIES IN THE UNITED STATES

....

ELIZABETH A. SEWELL[1]

THE United States has always been one of the most religiously diverse countries in the world. At its founding, it was formed by states with predominantly Episcopalian, Puritan, and other Protestant populations, as well as a few states such as Pennsylvania and Rhode Island that were already marked by broad religious pluralism.[2] The desire for unity among these religiously diverse states as they came together to form a nation was in sharp contrast to the European post-Westphalian model of *cuis regio, eius religio* (whose region, his religion). Religious pluralism in America has only continued to increase, with massive Catholic influxes of the nineteenth and twentieth centuries and contemporary immigrants bringing a tremendous variety of religions, not to mention the impact of home-grown new religious movements such as Jehovah's Witnesses, Seventh-day Adventists, and Mormons. By the 1890s, Catholicism had become the largest single denominational family, but the other dominant ones were still all mainline Protestant: (listed largest to smallest) Methodist, Baptist, Presbyterian, Lutheran, Disciples of Christ, Episcopalian, and Congregational.[3] As of 2008, however, all Protestant Christians together barely made up a majority of the population, claiming 51.3% of Americans.[4] The remaining 48.7% is a broad smattering of other Christian denominations, Jews, Buddhists, Muslims, Hindus, Native American religions, and individuals unaffiliated with any religion (16.1%).[5] Members of the Roman Catholic Church comprise 23.9% and mainline Protestant churches only comprise 18.1% of the population. Of traditional Protestants, the most populous tradition is the Methodists, with only

5.4% of the population. For a country that is often assumed to be dominated by traditional Protestants, it is clear that diversity is very much the order of the day. There are as many Mormons as there are Jews, and more of each of those individually than there are Episcopalians.[6]

This scenario, in which every denomination is a minority, paints a very different picture than that seen in most of the rest of the world. In Brazil, by comparison, 73.6% of the population belongs to the Roman Catholic Church.[7] Seventy percent of Russians consider themselves Russian Orthodox,[8] and 98% of Iran is Muslim.[9] Approximately 97% of Greeks consider themselves Greek Orthodox,[10] 81% of Philippinos are Roman Catholic,[11] and 80.5% of Indians are Hindu.[12] These results are not surprising when one considers that religion, along with language, was traditionally seen as a core element binding together a kingdom and, later, a nation.[13] As a result of modern nationalism and colonialism's attempts to blend formerly independent tribes or countries, some modern nations do have a pluralist mishmash of religious groups, such as many countries in Africa, or even Germany with its two dominant Christian denominations (Catholic and Lutheran).

What is particularly unique about religious pluralism in the United States, however, is the historical depth of its denominational breadth, and, quite strikingly in the international context, the sense in which religious pluralism has been largely embraced as a public good. Religious diversity is deeply intertwined with religious freedom in the minds of many Americans, which grants it a place in American self-conception and its national founding mythos. Associating religious diversity and protection of religious minorities with a strong and stable state has increasing empirical support as well. A recent study published in *Foreign Affairs* shows a very strong correlation between religious intolerance and "failed states" (measured using 12 social, economic, political, and military indicators, and ranked in order of their vulnerability to violent internal conflict and societal deterioration).[14] On the positive side, there is a growing body of empirical evidence that protection of religious freedom is strongly correlated with a variety of positive factors evidencing stability and productivity.[15]

In the broad scope of history, this understanding is quite unique. Historically, stability of the state was associated with religious unity,[16] not pluralism. The king or ruler was often seen as at least semidivine, and was an earthly representative of the gods or considered to have the mandate of heaven. Commonality in religion was seen as guaranteeing the binding power of oaths and contracts and thus maintaining order in the state.[17] Disunity in religion was considered to be disloyalty to the state. It has been speculated, for example, that this is the origin of some of the severe consequences for apostasy in Islam.[18] In a radical turn from such assumptions, Enlightenment thinkers, such as John Locke, recognized that protecting minorities can add to the stability of a state.[19] "It is not the diversity of opinions (which cannot be avoided)," wrote Locke, "but the refusal of toleration to those that are of different opinions (which might have been granted), that has produced all the bustles and wars that have been in the Christian world upon the account of religion."[20]

The United States was the first national experiment in extreme religious pluralism. Contemporary thinkers have recognized that, in many ways, religious diversity and the existence of religious minorities is a core precondition for religious
freedom, and, indeed, the development of modern political liberalism. To perhaps
belabor the obvious, being able to worship freely has little meaning unless there are
multiple choices available. Rawls has argued that without the fragmentation of religious belief in the West during the Protestant Reformation, modern toleration and
political liberalism would not be possible; i.e., "pluralism made religious liberty
possible."[21] He explains: "Political liberalism assumes the fact of reasonable pluralism as a pluralism of comprehensive doctrines, including both religious and
nonreligious doctrines. This pluralism is not seen as disaster but rather as the natural outcome of the activities of human reason under enduring free institutions. To
see reasonable pluralism as a disaster is to see the exercise of reason under the conditions of freedom itself as a disaster."[22]

In what is perhaps an interesting paradox, the religious pluralism underlying the
United States' commitment to religious freedom has become so much a staple of
American life that its value appears at times to have been forgotten. In *Employment
Division v. Smith*,[23] for example, Justice Scalia rejected claims that the First Amendment should protect religious exemptions from generally applicable laws, suggesting
that religious groups could obtain exemptions through the legislative process: "a society that believes in the negative protection accorded to religious belief can be
expected to be solicitous of that value in its legislation as well."[24] The absurdity of
expecting minorities to successfully lobby legislatures, which proceed by majority
vote, has been abundantly noted.[25] Justice Scalia himself recognized this, but saw it as
an unfortunate result of taking judges out of decision making on exemptions:

> . . . leaving accommodation to the political process will place at a relative
> disadvantage those religious practices that are not widely engaged in; but that
> unavoidable consequence of democratic government must be preferred to a
> system in which each conscience is a law unto itself or in which judges weigh the
> social importance of all laws against the centrality of all religious beliefs.[26]

In light of this result, some commentators have suggested a return to looking at the
law through a "religious minority perspective"[27] or understanding the underlying unity
of the Constitution's religion clauses as attempts to protect religious minorities.[28]

A SAMPLING OF RELIGIOUS MINORITIES

This chapter highlights the role religious minorities have played in establishing religious freedom in the United States. Without unduly instrumentalizing religious
minorities, it is worthwhile to underline the role they have played in the United
States in creating an often vibrant tradition of religious freedom. In many ways, it

has been the jostling of religious groups and their claims against the majority that have established what religious freedom protections the United States enjoys. This chapter examines the role of religious traditions individually in contrast to a more traditional historical narrative. Limitations of space preclude accounting for all groups that have played a role in establishing religious freedom, or even tracing in depth the contributions made by any one tradition. The focus is on the role religious groups have played in creating religion law, largely as shaped by U.S. Supreme Court cases.

Although it is true that there is a certain amount of chance in which parties were involved in cases, making major turning points in U.S. jurisprudence not necessarily deeply connected to the plaintiff, still, especially in recent years, other religious groups facing similar issues often weigh in as *amici,* and thus connect most of the logically related parties to the case. By tracking the contributions of various religious groups individually, a different angle is provided on the role that minority religions have played in establishing religious freedom in the United States, and the importance of minority religious players in creating the U.S. system is reemphasized. Not surprisingly, the resulting narrative does not necessarily yield a deep insight into the theology of different groups, but rather a practical story about how the United States legal system has been able to accommodate practical differences and has thereby enriched American law.

Amish

The Amish are one of the seven groups of Anabaptists in the Evangelical tradition with significant representation in the United States.[29] As of 2008, all these groups together constituted less than 0.3% of American adults.[30] There are two major U.S. Supreme Court cases in which the Amish raised challenges to limits on religious freedom: *Wisconsin v. Yoder*[31] and *United States v. Lee.*[32] The traditional agrarian lifestyle of the Amish, with minimal reliance on preindustrial technologies, led them to object to seemingly innocuous general laws: mandatory public education beyond the eighth grade and social security tax. The Amish's challenge to mandatory post-eighth grade public education was successful in *Yoder,* and serves as the high-water mark of Supreme Court protection of free exercise exemptions. *Yoder* also articulated the classical test for free exercise protection: A state action that burdens a religious interest may be permitted only when a compelling state interest is involved, which can be furthered in no less restrictive way. Although the Supreme Court abrogated this test in *Employment Division v. Smith,* it remains the basis of the test articulated by Congress in the Religious Freedom Restoration Act[33] and Religious Land Use and Incarcerated Persons Act.[34] This "compelling state interest" test also has been extensively used by state courts to interpret state constitutional protections of religious freedom.[35] The Amish's challenge to the social security tax in *Lee* was less successful, as the Court held that the state had an overriding interest in the uniformity of the social security tax.[36]

Atheists

Although strictly speaking, atheists would not consider themselves to be a religious minority, as a minority belief community they have played a significant role in extending the protections of the Establishment Clause against dominant religious traditions. Atheists are very much a minority in the United States: as of 2008, one poll indicated that only 1.56% of the adult population identified themselves as atheists, whereas another indicated that 15% of Americans are "nones"—atheists, agnostics, and secularists, up from 8.6% in 1990.[37] Whatever their actual number, atheists have brought a few extremely significant challenges to religious language in public schools and a challenge to religious tests for state offices. In *McCollum v. Board of Education*,[38] an atheist parent successfully challenged release-time religious instruction in public school buildings. Atheists also played a key role in school prayer and Bible reading cases.[39] In a similar vein, an atheist parent challenged the use of the phrase "under God" in the pledge of allegiance in *Elk Grove Unified School District v. Newdow*.[40] Although the Supreme Court decided this case on standing grounds, it seems likely that the Court will address a similar challenge on the merits before long. A classic case brought by an atheist was *Torcaso v. Watkins*.[41] *Torcaso* involved the challenge to a religious test for state office. The Court held that the incorporation of the First Amendment religion clauses prohibits religious tests by states. Although not specifically addressing whether atheism is a protected belief, the Court recognized that some religions, such as Buddhism, Taoism, and "secular humanism" are nontheistic and a requirement of a belief in God for state office would violate their religious freedom.

Baptists and Other Early Dissenters

Baptists, although now the largest single Protestant tradition in the United States,[42] were a beleaguered minority at the time of the founding. Unlike many other Protestants, Baptists were never the established religion of any state or colony; traditionally they retained a strong stance supporting disestablishment and separation of church and state.[43] Baptist thought was pragmatic and "grew up out of the experience of living as second-class citizens under the reigning orthodoxy—self-interest with a spark of righteous indignation at injustice."[44] Building on Roger Williams' claims for liberty of conscience, Isaac Backus, a prominent spokesman for the Baptists, argued that freedom of belief and practice is essential to truth itself and to a life lived in accordance with truth.[45] Baptists saw power as flowing from the people and sought recognition of minority rights but still promoted a generally Christian state. Baptists petitioned George Washington for a constitutional guarantee of separation of church and state[46] and concern over the persecution of Baptists in Virginia led James Madison to launch his public career, which included framing the Virginia Bill of Rights, drafting the classic opposition to religious establishment in The Memorial and Remonstrance Against Religious Assessments, securing passage of Jefferson's Statute for Religious Freedom, and playing crucial roles in drafting and adopting the U.S. Constitution and Bill of Rights.[47]

Buddhists

Buddhists, which comprise 0.7% of the population as of 2008,[48]brought a Supreme Court case that is notable for establishing some of the limits of protection for particularly small minorities. In *Cruz v. Beto*,[49] in response to a challenge by a Buddhist prisoner seeking a place of worship, the U.S. Supreme Court held that a special chapel or place of worship need not be provided for every faith regardless of size, nor must a chaplain, priest, or minister be provided without regard for the extent of the demand, but reasonable opportunities must be afforded to all prisoners to exercise the religious freedom guaranteed by the First and Fourteenth Amendments without fear of penalty. This basic principle continues to be respected under RLUIPA.[50]

Roman Catholics

Contributions by Roman Catholics to advancing religious freedom in the United States are too numerous to adequately detail here. As the largest single minority in what has traditionally been a largely Protestant country,[51] Catholics have often been on the front lines of religious discrimination and intolerance from the early days of the American colonies. For example, many of the colonies barred Catholics from holding public office.[52] Anti-Catholic animus abated some after the revolution, but flared again as numbers of Catholics in the United States dramatically increased in the mid-nineteenth century with massive Irish immigration[53] and in the early twentieth century. During the period from the beginning of the twentieth to the mid-twentieth century, the U.S. Catholic population increased from 8 million to more than 25 million.[54] In both the mid-nineteenth and early twentieth century, anti-Catholic activities dramatically increased in response to these massive influxes.[55] The Catholic population continued to grow quickly in the late twentieth century, largely as a result of an influx of Latino immigrants. As of 2008, the Catholic population was greater than 73 million (approximately 23.9% of the American public).[56]

The major nineteenth-century battle between "ascendant American Protestantism and an assertive, 'foreign' Catholic community" was fought over education and the rise of public schools.[57] Catholic private schools developed in response to this, and were bitterly opposed by Protestant majorities. The so-called "Blaine Amendment," proposed in 1875, would have revised the First Amendment to have made it specifically unconstitutional to provide public funds to sectarian schools.[58] This measure passed the House and barely missed passing the Senate.[59] Although this effort was not successful at the federal level, several states amended their constitutions to impose such strict separation requirements in the area of education.[60]

Catholics attending the public schools of nineteenth and early twentieth centuries were faced with a de facto Protestant establishment in which instruction had a Protestant cast and Bible instruction was from the Protestant King James version. Catholics made several attempts both to remove this Protestant influence from public schools and to gain access to public school funds for support of the sectarian schools they had created in response to what they perceived as education-based religious coercion. Each of these attempts met with vehement resistance by the Protestant majority. In one of the rounds of this struggle, anti-Catholic sentiment led to attempts to bar students from attending Catholic schools. In *Pierce v. Society of Sisters*,[61] however, Catholics successfully challenged a law requiring students to attend only public schools, and the right to establish religiously oriented private schools has been secure ever since.

The incorporation of the First Amendment accomplished to some degree what the Blaine Amendment attempted. In what must be acknowledged as an unfortunate example of prejudice in the application of the religion clauses themselves, anti-Catholic animus lies at the root of many of the "no-aid" cases in the American separationist tradition. In 1971, *Lemon v. Kurtzman*[62] barred most forms of state aid to Catholic schools. The notoriously vague *Lemon* test for establishment of religion has led to a series of cases trying to spell out what form of support to parochial schools is possible while retaining a secular purpose, not impermissibly advancing religion, and not creating excessive government entanglement with religion. Most of these cases have involved Catholic parochial schools, such as *Tilton v. Richardson*,[63] *Mueller v. Allen*,[64] *Aguilar v. Felton*,[65] *School Dist. of City of Grand Rapids v. Ball*,[66] *Zobrest v. Catalina School District*,[67] and *Agostini v. Felton*.[68] Over the course of these cases, however, the Supreme Court has softened limitations on aid to parochial schools.

Catholics have also been involved in other major Free Exercise and Establishment Clause cases. In *City of Boerne v. Flores*,[69] a Catholic parish church attempted to defend its exemption to zoning restrictions under the Religious Freedom Restoration Act (RFRA). Even though they had prevailed at the Court of Appeals, the Catholics did not contest the petition for certiorari in the Supreme Court. The Supreme Court, however, ruled against them, holding that RFRA was unconstitutional as applied to the states. The Catholic plaintiff (along with a Latter-day Saint plaintiff), was more successful in *Santa Fe Independent School Dist. v. Doe*.[70] In this case, the two students successfully challenged a broadcast of student-led prayer at high school football games.

Jehovah's Witnesses

Jehovah's Witnesses, formally known from approximately 1884 to 1931 as the Watchtower Bible and Tract Society,[71] are another denomination that has been heavily involved in the fight for religious freedom in the United States. The group now known as Jehovah's Witnesses was founded in Pennsylvania in 1868. As of 2008, 0.7% of American adults identified themselves as Jehovah's Witnesses. Jehovah's Witnesses have aroused the ire of others because of their strident attacks on Protestantism and Catholicism, active proselytizing, and their refusal to participate in blood transfusion, military service, or any form of religious or secular ceremony, such as saluting the flag.

Jehovah's Witnesses have won 48 cases before the United States Supreme Court.[72] Some of these were decided under freedoms of press and speech, and some under the Free Exercise Clause,[73] but they provide an important bulwark of religious freedom. Jehovah's Witnesses have not only filed federal court cases, but also sought to resolve religious liberty concerns through administrative law, state law, and use of governmental persuasion.[74]

Several significant cases in the middle decades of the twentieth century involved the Jehovah's Witnesses.[75] Cities throughout the country attempted to stop their "aggressive missionary"[76] activities with a variety of ordinances, including solicitation licensing schemes worded so as to allow city officials' virtually unbounded discretion to deny licenses to whomever they wished. The Witnesses routinely refused to comply with these ordinances, claiming the government had no right to regulate religion, and local authorities just as routinely arrested and jailed them for their noncompliance.[77]

The decision in *Cantwell v. Connecticut*[78] was particularly significant in that it was the first case to expressly hold that the Free Exercise Clause, which as originally drafted operated as a constraint only on Congress and the federal government, was applicable to state action as part of Fourteenth Amendment due process liberty. In the years since *Cantwell* was decided, this has been the primary basis for federal free exercise claims. The Court also expressly moved beyond the belief–action dichotomy of *Reynolds*, holding that free exercise of religion "embraces two concepts—freedom to believe and freedom to act."[79]

Other particularly significant court cases brought by or against Jehovah's Witnesses include ones that established the right for public school students not to salute the flag or say the pledge of allegiance,[80] cases detailing rights of conscientious objectors to military service,[81] and the right to retain unemployment benefits when leaving a job for conscientious objection reasons.[82] These cases illustrate clearly how distinctive behavioral beliefs of a minority group create problems, which in turn result in cases that further establish the boundaries of free exercise law.

Jews

A small number of Jewish groups were present in the United States at its founding, and Judaism is the longest-established non-Christian minority in the United States.[83] Jews experienced considerable discrimination, especially at first, with bans on voting, holding public office, and even an attempt to ban Jews from New York City.[84] Nineteenth-century immigration dramatically increased the number of Jews in America.[85] Between 1887 and 1927, the total population of American Jews increased from 229,000 to over 4,228,000.[86] As of 2008, 1.7% of American adults identified themselves as Jewish. Less than 1% (0.7%) of Americans were Reform; 0.5% were Conservative; less than 0.3% were Orthodox; less than 0.3% belonged to other Jewish groups; and less than 0.3% did not specify a particular group.[87]

Jews have been the most significant challengers to Sunday-closing laws, and brought two significant Supreme Court cases on this topic, *Braunfeld v. Brown*,[88] and *Gallagher v. Crown Kosher Super Market of Massachusetts.*[89] The Supreme Court, however, rejected their reasoning and upheld the Sunday-closing laws as advancing a legitimate state interest in a uniform day of rest.

Like Catholics, Jews have been concerned by the Protestant practices once typical in public schools, although unlike Catholics, Jews have typically not responded by establishing a large system of parochial schools. In the nineteenth century, along with Catholics, Jewish groups protested the reading of the Protestant Bible in Cincinnati schools, and successfully lobbied to have the practice outlawed. When a group of taxpayers sued to reinstate the practice, the Ohio Supreme Court upheld the ban on religious liberty grounds.[90]

In the early twentieth century, Jews actively lobbied against religious practices in schools, and were heavily involved in cases opposing prayer and Bible reading in public schools. Jewish organizations' litigation approach has generally been to bring claims under the Establishment Clause, but not to ask for any special treatment for themselves.[91] Jews were two of the five plaintiffs in *Engel v. Vitale,* which held that reciting a set prayer in public schools violated the Establishment Clause.[92] Jewish groups wrote amicus briefs in that case and were the only religious groups to do so in *School District of Abington Township v. Schempp,*[93] which struck down a law requiring Bible reading in public schools.[94] Divisions within the Jewish community have led to a split on cases involving aid to parochial schools, with some groups, such as the Jewish Committee on Law and Political Action, writing amicus briefs supporting aid and some, such as the American Jewish Congress, working with the American Civil Liberties Union to oppose aid.[95] A final and somewhat atypical school case in which Jews were key players was *Board of Education of Kiryas Joel Village School Dist. v. Grumet.*[96] In that case, the Supreme Court held that the creation of a school district to map a Hasidic Orthodox Jewish community in New York violated the Establishment Clause.

A final significant case brought by a Jew was *Goldman v. Weinberger.*[97] An Orthodox Jewish officer in the Air Force sought to wear his yarmulke as part of his uniform. The U.S. Supreme Court held that the compelling state interest test did not apply in the distinctive military setting, and that the Orthodox Jewish officer could be forbidden to wear his yarmulke. Although the officer's case was unsuccessful, later lobbying by Jewish groups led to a change in the military regulations to permit yarmulkes.

Krishna Consciousness

The Krishna Consciousness movement is a monotheistic branch of Hinduism, which requires its most dedicated followers to actively proselytize and solicit donations. The growth of this movement in the United States has been relatively recent; as of 1921, this group, called the Vedanta Society, only had 350 members.[98] Currently, American Hindus as a whole comprise 0.4% of the U.S. adult population, although this includes more than just followers of the Krishna Consciousness movement.[99]

The International Society for Krishna Consciousness (ISKCON) has been involved in two significant U.S. Supreme Court cases, *Heffron v. Int'l Soc. For Krishna Consciousness, Inc.*,[100] and *International Soc. For Krishna Consciousness, Inc. v. Lee*,[101] both involving the practice of Sankirtan, "a ritual with ancient roots which requires adherents to reach out and preach to, and to solicit aid from, potentially receptive members of the public."[102] In both cases, ISKCON challenged limits on where they could distribute material and solicit donations, and in both cases lost. *Heffron* held that the rule requiring members of ISKCON to limit performance of Sankirtan to fixed areas of fair grounds was not unconstitutional, as the rule applies evenhandedly to all speech, and *Lee* held that an airport terminal is a nonpublic forum for First Amendment purposes.

Latter-day Saints

The Church of Jesus Christ of Latter-day Saints was founded in New York in 1830. In the nearly two centuries since then, it has demonstrated consistent growth and has the largest population of the religions originating in the United States. As of 2008, 1.7% of American adults identified themselves as Latter-day Saints, also known as Mormons.

Latter-day Saints had the most significant early experiences litigating under the Free Exercise Clause in the U.S. Supreme Court. These arose from the practice of polygamy, since discontinued. Because of religious persecution, Latter-day Saints emigrated beyond the western borders of the United States. Because they were subsequently under federal territorial rule, their challenges to antipolygamy legislation under the First Amendment were heard in federal courts at an early date, before the incorporation of the First Amendment into the Fourteenth Amendment. Notable Supreme Court cases from this era include *Reynolds v. United States*,[103] and *Davis v. Beason*.[104]

In *Reynolds*, the Court rejected a free exercise objection to the criminalization of bigamy on the basis that "[l]aws are made for the government of actions, and while they cannot interfere with mere religious belief and opinions, they may with practices."[105] This was the first U.S. Supreme Court case interpreting the Free Exercise Clause, and established the action–belief dichotomy, which returned in *Employment Division v. Smith*.[106] In *Beason*, the Court held that an Idaho territorial law requiring prospective voters to give an oath not to practice or advocate polygamy did not violate the Establishment Clause.

More recently, Latter-day Saints have been involved in institutional litigation, both through *amicus* briefs and in the landmark case of *Corp. of Presiding Bishopric of the Church of Jesus Christ of Latter-day Saints v. Amos*.[107] This case involved a challenge to the religious exemption to Title VII's prohibition against religious discrimination in employment. The Court held that permitted religious discrimination in employment in secular nonprofit activities of religious organization did not violate the Establishment Clause. An individual Latter-day Saint, along with a

Catholic student, brought an Establishment Clause case in *Santa Fe Independent School Dist. v. Doe.*[108] In *Santa Fe,* the Court held that broadcasts of student-led prayer at football games violate the Establishment Clause.

Muslims

Islam has grown rapidly in the United States in a comparatively short time period. The growth of Islam in the United States is primarily a result of twentieth-century immigration and conversion of native U.S. citizens.[109] As of 2008, 0.6% of American adults identified themselves as Muslim.[110]

Muslims have been party to one significant Supreme Court case, as well as a significant case coming out of the Third Circuit. In *O'Lone v. Estate of Shabazz,*[111] a Muslim prisoner challenged prison regulations that he claimed prevented him from attending Jumu'ah, a weekly Muslim congregational service, but lost, as the Court held that prison regulations that prevent prisoners' free exercise of religion need only meet the less burdensome standard of being reasonably related to a legitimate state interest. In *Fraternal Order of Police Newark Lodge No. 12 v. City of Newark,*[112] a Muslim plaintiff brought a significant case broadening free exercise rights after *City of Boerne* limited the Religious Freedom Restoration Act to federal action.[113] In *Fraternal Order of Police,* a Muslim police officer challenged a denial of a religious exemption to a no-beard requirement. The Third Circuit held that the state's failure to make a religious exemption when it permitted other exemptions, such as health reasons, violated the Free Exercise Clause.

Native American Faiths

The fate of Native American faiths in the United States directly corresponds to the fate of Native Americans, including persecution, attempts to force religious and cultural assimilation, and limitations on sovereignty.[114] A number of particularly significant Native American cases were heard in the U.S. Supreme Court during the 1980s and 1990s, which also corresponds with a low point of free exercise protection. Some of these involved the "Native American Church," which was founded around the turn of the twentieth century as an attempt to blend elements of Christianity with a number of different traditional Native American religions.[115] Many elements of Native American faiths, such as sacred space or burial grounds and the ceremonial use of peyote, have proved difficult for U.S. courts to accommodate. As of 2008, less than 0.3% of American adults identified themselves being affiliated with a Native American faith.[116]

In three major cases, the U.S. Supreme Court ostensibly applied the compelling state interest/least restrictive means test from *Sherbert*[117] and *Yoder,*[118] but in all three cases the Native Americans lost on their religious claims. In *Bowen v. Roy,*[119] the Court held that the federal government did not unconstitutionally restrict freedom of religion by assigning a social security number to Native American girl. In *Northwest Indian Cemetery Protective Association v. Peterson*,[120] and *Lyng v. Northwest Indian Cemetery Protective Ass'n*,[121] the Court permitted state construction and timber harvesting on sacred lands despite free exercise claims.

The most notable case involving Native American faiths is *Employment Division v. Smith*,[122] which ended the use of the least restrictive means/compelling state interest test to judge religious exemptions under the Free Exercise Clause. The *Smith* court permitted laws that burden religion to override religious freedom claims, so long as they are general and neutral, and do not specifically target religious belief. In *Smith*, the Court held that members of the Native American Church could be denied unemployment benefits after their jobs were terminated for smoking peyote in accordance with their Native American religious practices. This case had a stormy wake. Religious and civil liberty groups across the spectrum unified behind a congressional attempt to restore the least restrictive means/compelling state interest test for religious exemptions to state action, which passed as the Religious Freedom Restoration Act (RFRA).[123] In turn, the U.S. Supreme Court struck down RFRA as applied to the states as exceeding congressional authority in *City of Boerne v. Flores,* mentioned earlier. In response, Congress passed a more narrowly tailored version of RFRA, the Religious Land Use and Institutionalized Persons Act.[124] In addition, Congress amended to American Indian Religious Freedom Act in 1994 to prohibit federal and state governments from banning the ceremonial use of peyote or discriminating against Indians based on such use.[125]

Orthodox

Although there has been a continuous Russian Orthodox presence in Alaska, most Orthodox Americans stem from twentieth-century immigration.[126] As of 2008, 0.3% of American adults identified themselves as Russian Orthodox.[127] Orthodoxy's hierarchical and predominantly country-based organizing system led to a significant U.S. Supreme Court case, *Kedroff v. St. Nicholas Cathedral of Russian Orthodox Church in North America*.[128]

After the Russian Revolution, in 1919, an "All-American Convention" declared that Russian Orthodoxy in America would be independent of the Russian Orthodox Church in Russia.[129] In the 1920s, the Russian Orthodox Church Moscow Patriarchy contested the American Orthodox Church's right to retain Saint Nicholas Cathedral in New York City. In *Kedroff v. St. Nicholas Cathedral of Russian Orthodox Church in North America*,[130] the Supreme Court held that a New York statute undertaking to transfer control of the New York churches of the Russian Orthodox religion from the central governing hierarchy of the Russian Orthodox Church to the governing authorities of the Russian Church in America was unconstitutional as prohibiting free exercise of religion.

Scientologists

The Church of Scientology is an esoteric Gnostic system founded in the 1960s by L. Ron Hubbard.[131] It has proved the source of much litigation, particularly over debates as to whether its practices can be classed as religious. Some of the controversial financial practices of Scientology include the rituals of "auditing," which is a one-on-one session with an "auditor" to attain higher spiritual enlightenment, and "training," in which parishioners study "the doctrine, tenets, codes, policies and practices of Scientology" and can perform audits on others.[132] In *Hernandez v. Comm'r of Internal Revenue*,[133] the U.S. Supreme Court held that payments to the Church of Scientology for auditing and training are not deductible as charitable donations. In 1993, however, the IRS restored the Church of Scientology's tax-exempt status.[134]

Seventh-day Adventists

Seventh-day Adventists are another home-grown American religion, established in the mid-nineteenth century.[135] Among other beliefs, Seventh-day Adventists observe the Sabbath on Saturday, and have had various clashes with the United States on this basis. As of 2008, 0.4% of American adults identified themselves as Seventh-day Adventists.[136]

The most significant case involving Seventh-day Adventists was *Sherbert v. Verner*,[137] in which a Seventh-day Adventist was denied unemployment compensation when she was fired for refusing to work on Saturdays. The U.S. Supreme Court held for the Seventh-day Adventist, using the compelling state interest/least restrictive means test, for which this case has become known. Like the Amish case of *Yoder, Sherbert* represents a high water mark in the protection of religious exemptions by the U.S. Supreme Court under the Free Exercise Clause.

Another Seventh-day Adventist case, *Girouard v. United States*,[138] established some limits to conscientious objection. The Court upheld denial of citizenship to a Seventh-day Adventist conscientious objector where the oath of allegiance prescribed by Congress for aliens seeking naturalization was that they would support and defend the Constitution and laws of the United States against all enemies.

CONCLUSION

This discussion of the role minority religious groups play in developing religion law in the United States is a useful reminder that religious liberty does not spring full-blown, but in a common-law system like that of the U.S., depends on independent actors to bring about religious liberty. "Groups and individuals decide—sometimes purposefully, sometimes willy-nilly—which issues will appear on the judicial dockets and which ones will not. They and their attorneys decide in what form questions will come to the courts, in what facts and argument they will be encased. . . . In some areas of constitutional law, however, the process is considerably less haphazard."[139]

In the religion field, religious groups are often repeat players on issues of importance to them. For example, Catholics repeatedly defend parochial education, Jehovah's Witnesses defend proselytizing, atheists attack evidences of religion in public schools, etc. One simply needs to think of the impact on Baptists on theory and practice of religious freedom during in the U.S. establishment, or the role of Catholics and Jews on the law governing religion in public and private schools to see the central role individual minorities can play. Justice Harlan Fisk Stone similarly commented in a letter on the role of Jehovah's Witnesses in litigating proselyting cases in 1940s: "I think the Jehovah's Witnesses ought to have an endowment in view of the aid they give in solving legal problems of civil liberty."[140] In this sense, the role of these groups is akin to the institutional litigants in separationist cases detailed by Frank Sorauf.[141] His comment on the dialogic role that institutional litigants and judges play applies as well to religious minorities: "Probing question precedes precise—perhaps even cagey—answer, which in turn suggests—even invites—the next artful query. *And in the dialogue, even when it is far more fragmented and discontinuous, one must understand the questions and the questioners if one is to understand the answers.*"[142]

Understanding religious minorities is vital to understanding why U.S. religion law has developed as it has. For example, the rights of institutional autonomy in selecting religious leaders,[143] or the right of religious organizations to have reasonable access to juridical status,[144] which have become an important part of the case law of the European Court of Human Rights simply have no similar prominence in U.S. law.[145] The relative paucity of cases dealing with Islam, Orthodoxy, or Hinduism necessarily means that their unique religious freedom concerns will not be reflected to a great degree in U.S. law. Perhaps as these and other new minorities grow, U.S. religion law will respond to more of these concerns.

This chapter concludes with two interesting paradoxes in the role of religious minorities and religious liberty. Although protections of religious liberty have predominantly been established by the efforts and suffering of religious minorities, it is a paradox that sometimes the majority will use ostensible protections of religious freedom against minorities, or invoke the protections but use them in name only. The most obvious example is the Blaine Amendment and the use of the Establishment Clause against Catholic schools coming out of anti-Catholic movements.[146] Even after the compelling state interest test was applied, it was repeatedly found insufficient to protect some of the newest or least Protestant-like religions such as Scientology or Native American religions. Perhaps the "foreignness" of some minorities has been at times too much a challenge; our founding commitment to religious liberty and the protection of religious minorities has waxed thin.

Another interesting paradox is the point that even minorities can be majorities somewhere and that even majorities can be minorities, when looking in history or defined locations. The case of *Kiriyas Joel*[147] is instructive. In that case, Hasidic Jews were a majority in their would-be New York school district, and lost on Establishment Clause grounds. Jewish groups often use the Establishment Clause to challenge pro-religious educational arrangements, which is obviously beneficial to them when they are in the minority, but worked against them in *Kiryas Joel*. Another similar case, seen over time, is American Baptists, now a majority in much of the South. Separationist ideas that they actively promoted as a minority during the founding era now work against them, such as in *Santa Fe Independent School Dist. v. Doe*,[148] in which the Court held that broadcasts of student-led prayer at football games violate the Establishment Clause. Either locational happenstance or temporal ascendancy of majorities challenge groups' ability to articulate a consistent position on church–state roles. This challenge is significant not only for groups within the United States, but also internationally, where even majority U.S. groups suddenly become small minorities. This realization of global minority status was one factor that led even majority U.S. religious groups to support the International Religious Freedom Act,[149] an attempt to increase the role of protecting religious freedom in U.S. foreign policy.[150]

ENDNOTES

1. The author would like to thank David Brown, Megan Grant, and especially Suzanne Disparte for research assistance, and W. Cole Durham, Jr. for his comments. Any mistakes are the author's.

2. See, e.g., John F. Wilson, ed., vol. 1, *Church and State in America: A Bibliographical Guide: The Colonial and Early National Periods* (New York: Greenwood Press, 1986).

3. Edwin S. Gaustad, *A Religious History of America* (New Haven, CT: Yale University Press, 1966), 242.

4. The Pew Forum on Religion and Public Life, *U.S. Religious Landscape Survey* (2008), 5. This is the source of all the statistics in this paragraph.

5. Ibid.

6. Ibid. (listing Mormons 1.7%, Jews 1.7%, Anglican/Episcopal 1.4%).

7. "Religious Demographic Profile, Brazil," *The Pew Forum on Religion and Public Life*, http://pewforum.org/world-affairs/countries/?CountryID=29 (citing 2000 Brazil Census at http://www.ibge.gov.br/english/).

8. U.S. Department of State, "International Religious Freedom Report 2007, Russia," http://www.state.gov/g/drl/rls/irf/2007/90196.htm.

9. U.S. Department of State, "International Religious Freedom Report 2007, Iran," http://www.state.gov/g/drl/rls/irf/2007/90210.htm.

10. U.S. Department of State, "International Religious Freedom Report 2007, Greece," http://www.state.gov/g/drl/rls/irf/2007/90178.htm.

11. "Religious Demographic Profile, Philippines," *The Pew Forum on Religion and Public Life*, http://pewforum.org/world-affairs/countries/?CountryID=163 (citing 2000 Philippine Census, archived at http://unstats.un.org/).

12. "Religious Demographic Profile, India," *The Pew Forum on Religion and Public Life*, http://pewforum.org/world-affairs/countries/?CountryID=94 (citing 2001 India Census, *archived at* http://unstats.un.org and http://www.censusindia.net).

13. See, e.g., Benedict Anderson, *Imagined Communities: Reflections on the Origin and Spread of Nationalism* (London: Verso, 1991), 12–16.

14. The Fund for Peace and Foreign Policy, "The Failed State Index 2007," in *Foreign Policy* (July/August 2007).

15. Brian J. Grim, "Religion: Good for What Ails Us?," *The Review of Faith and International Affairs* 6 (Summer 2008), 3–7 (available online at: http://www.cfia.org/ArticlesAndReports/ArticlesDetail.aspx?id=10368&hId=3672); Brian J. Grim, "God's Economy: Religious Freedom and Socioeconomic Well-Being" in Paul A. Marshall, ed., *Religious Freedom in the World* (Lanham, MD: Rowman and Littlefield, 2008), 42–47.

16. Malcolm D. Evans, *Religious Liberty and International Law in Europe* (Cambridge, UK: Cambridge University Press, 1997), 6–7.

17. Ibid., 1–2, 6–7.

18. See, e.g., Nazila Ghanea, "Apostasy and Freedom to Change Religion or Belief," in Tore Lindholm et al., eds. *Facilitating Freedom of Religion or Belief: A Deskbook* (Leiden: Martinus Nijhoff, 2004), 669, 683–684.

19. See Joshua Mitchell, "John Locke: A Theology of Religious Liberty," in *Religious Liberty in Western Thought*, eds. Noel B. Reynolds and W. Cole Durham, Jr. (Grand Rapids, MI: Scholars Press, 1996), 143.

20. John Locke, *A Letter Concerning Toleration* (Indianapolis, IN: Bobs-Merrill, 1955), 57.

21. John Rawls, *Political Liberalism* (New York: Columbia University Press, 1993), xxiv.

22. Ibid. xxiv–xxv.

23. *Employment Division, Department of Human Resources of Oregon v. Smith*, 494 U.S. 872 (1990).

24. Ibid., 890.

25. See, e.g., Michael McConnell, "Free Exercise Revisionism and the Smith Decision," *University of Chicago Law Review* 57 (Fall, 1990): 1129; Jesse H. Choper, "A Century of Religious Freedom," *California Law Review* 88 (2000): 1727; Michael McConnell, "Freedom from Persecution or Protection of the Rights of Conscience?: A Critique of Justice Scalia's Historical Arguments in *City of Boerne v. Flores*," *William & Mary Law Review* 39 (1998): 824.

26. *Employment Division, Department of Human Resources of Oregon v. Smith*, 494 U.S. 872 (1990), 90.

27. Samuel J. Levine, "Toward a Religious Minority Voice: A Look at Free Exercise Law through a Religious Minority Perspective," *William & Mary Bill of Rights Journal* 5 (1996): 153.

28. Thomas C. Berg, "Minority Religions and the Religion Clauses," *Washington University Law Quarterly* 82 (2004): 919; Stephen M. Feldman, *Please Don't Wish Me a Merry Christmas: A Critical History of Separation of Church and State* (1997); Stephen M. Feldman, "Religious Minorities and the First Amendment: The History, the Doctrine, and the Future," *University of Pennsylvania Journal of Constitutional Law* 6 (2003): 222; Rosalie Berger Levinson, "First Monday—The Dark Side of Federalism in the Nineties: Restricting Rights of Religious Minorities," *Valpariso University Law Review* 33 (1998): 47; Suzanna Sherry, "Religion and the Public Square: Making Democracy Safe for Religious Minorities," *DePaul Law Review* 47 (1998): 499; David E. Steinberg, "Religious Exemptions as Affirmative Action," *Emory Law Journal* 40 (1991): 77.

29. The Pew Forum on Religion and Public Life, *U.S. Religious Landscape Survey* (2008), 105.

30. The Pew Forum on Religion and Public Life, *U.S. Religious Landscape Survey* (2008), 128.

31. 406 U.S. 205 (1972).

32. 455 U.S. 252 (1982).

33. *Religious Freedom Restoration Act,* U.S. Code 42, §2000bb-1 (year).

34. *Religious Land Use and Incarcerated Persons Act,* U.S. Code 42, §2000cc-1 (year).

35. *Larson v. Cooper,* 90 P.3d 125, 131 & 131, n. 31 (Alaska. 2004); *City Chapel Evangelical Free Inc. v. City of South Bend,* 744 N.E.2d 443, 445-51 (Ind. 2001); *State v. Evans,* 796 P.2d 178 (Kan. App. 1990); *Fiscal Court v. Brady,* 885 S.W.2d 681, 690 (Ky. 1994); *Fortin v. Roman Catholic Bishop of Portland,* 2005 ME 57 (Me. 2005); *Att'y Gen. v. Desilets,* 636 N.E.2d 233 (Mass. 1994), 235-41; *McCready v. Hoffius,* 586 N.W.2d 723 (Mich. 1998), 729; *State v. Hershberger,* 462 N.W.2d 393 (Minn. 1990), 396-99; *St. John's Lutheran Church v. State Comp. Ins. Fund,* 830 P.2d 1271 (Mont. 1992); *Rourke v. N.Y. State Dep't of Corr. Servs.,* 603 N.Y.S.2d 647(N.Y. Sup. Ct. 1993), 649-50; *In re Browning,* 476 S.E.2d 465 (N.C. App. 1996); *State ex rel. Heitkamp v. Family Life Servs.,* 560 N.W.2d 526, 530 (N.D. 1997); *Humphrey v. Lane,* 728 N.E.2d 1039 (Ohio 2000), 1043-45; *Hunt v. Hunt,* 648 A.2d 843 (Vt. 1994), 852-53; *Horen v. Commonwealth,* 479 S.E.2d 553, 556-57 (Va. Ct. App. 1997); *Open Door Baptist Church v. Clark County,* 995 P.2d 33(Wash. 2000), 39; *State v. Miller,* 549 N.W.2d 23 (Wis. 1996), 238-42.

36. *United States v. Lee,* 455 U.S. 252 (1982).

37. The Pew Forum on Religion and Public Life, *U.S. Religious Landscape Survey* (2008), 12; American Religious Identification Survey (ARIS), 2008, sponsored by Trinity College, Hartford, Connecticut.

38. 333 U.S. 203 (1948).

39 See, e.g., *Engel v. Vitale,* 370 U.S. 421 (1962); *Wallace v. Jaffree,* 472 US 38 (1985).

40. 542 U.S. 1 (2004).

41. 367 U.S. 488 (1961).

42. The Pew Forum on Religion and Public Life, *U.S. Religious Landscape Survey* (2008), 12.

43. See., e.g., James T. Baker, "Baptists in Early America and the Separation of Church and State," in *Religion and American Law: An Encyclopedia,* ed. Paul Finkelman (New York: Garland Publishing, 2000), 20.

44. John F. Wilson, ed., vol. 1, *Church and State in America: A Bibliographical Guide, The Colonial and Early National Periods* (New York: Greenwood Press, 1986), 159.

45. Isaac Backus, *An Appeal to the Public for Religious Liberty* (Boston: John Boyle, 1773); see also Ellis Sandoz, "Religious Liberty and Religion in the American Founding Revisited," in *Religious Liberty in Western Thought,* eds. Noel B. Reynolds and W. Cole Durham, Jr. (Grand Rapids, Michigan: Scholars Press, 1996), 145, 267.

46. See, e.g., James T. Baker, "Baptists in Early America and the Separation of Church and State," in *Religion and American Law: An Encyclopedia,* 20, 23.

47. See, e.g., Ellis Sandoz, "Religious Liberty and Religion in the American Founding Revisited," in *Religious Liberty in Western Thought,* 145, 268–269.

48. The Pew Forum on Religion and Public Life, *U.S. Religious Landscape Survey* (2008), 12.

49. 405 U.S. 319 (1972).

50. *Religious Land Use and Incarcerated Persons Act,* U.S. Code 42, §2000cc-1 (year).

51. The Pew Forum on Religion and Public Life, *U.S. Religious Landscape Survey* (2008), 12 (As of 2008, 23.9% of American adults identified themselves as Catholic).

52. Arlin M. Adams and Charles J. Emmerich, *A Nation Dedicated to Religious Liberty: The Constitutional Heritage of the Religion Clauses* (Philadelphia: University of Pennsylvania Press, 1990), 14. (New Jersey and North Carolina limited officeholders to Protestants; Georgia, South Carolina, and New Hampshire permitted only Protestants to sit in legislatures.).

53. Sydney E. Ahlstrom, *A Religious History of the American People* (New Haven, CT: Yale University Press, 1972), 541–542 (Four and one-half million Irish came to the United States in the century after 1820, with most coming during and shortly after the Irish famines of 1847–1850).

54. Edwin Scott Gaustad, *A Religious History of America, New Revised Edition* (1966), 245–246.

55. Ahlstrom, *A Religious History of the American People*, 558–568, 900–901.

56. The Pew Forum on Religion and Public Life, *U.S Religious Landscape Survey* (2008), 12.

57. Richard E. Morgan, *The Supreme Court and Religion* (London: Collier-Macmillan, 1972), 15–16.

58. Richard Aynes, "Blaine Amendment," in *Religion and American Law: An Encyclopedia*, ed. Finkelman, 39.

59. Ibid., 40.

60. W. Cole Durham, "Treatment of Religious Minorities in the United States," in European Consortium for Church-State Research, *The Legal Status of Religious Minorities* (Thessaloniki: Sakkoulas Publications, 1994), 323, 333.

61. 268 U.S. 510 (1925).

62. *Lemon v. Kurtzman,* 403 U.S 602 (1971).

63. 403 U.S. 672 (1971).

64. 463 U.S. 388 (1983).

65. 473 U.S. 402 (1985). Eighty-four percent of the private schools receiving funds were Catholic; eight percent of the private schools receiving funds were Jewish.

66. 473 U.S. 373 (1985). Twenty-eight of the schools were Roman Catholic, seven were Christian Reformed, three were Lutheran, one was Seventh-day Adventist, and one was Baptist.

67. 509 U.S. 1 (1993).

68. 521 U.S. 203 (1997).

69. 521 U.S. 507 (1997).

70. 530 U.S. 290 (2000).

71. See Renee C. Redman, "Jehovah's Witnesses," in *Religion and American Law: An Encyclopedia*, ed. Finkelman, 245.

72. Eileen W. Lindner, ed., *Yearbook of American and Canadian Churches* (Nashville, TN: Abingdon Press 2007), 134.

73. Redman, "Jehovah's Witnesses," in *Religion and American Law: An Encyclopedia*, ed. Finkelman, 245.

74. Chuck Smith, "The Persecution of the West Virginia Jehovah's Witnesses and the Expansion of Legal Protection for Religious Liberty," in *New Religious Movements and Religious Liberty in America*, eds. Derek H. Davis and Barry Hankins, 2d ed. (Waco, TX: Baylor University Press, 2003), 155 (giving examples of these types of resolutions).

75. For example, *Coleman v. City of Griffin,* 302 U.S. 636 (1937); *Lovell v. City of Griffin,* 303 U.S 444 (1938); *Schneider v. New Jersey,* 308 U.S. 147 (1939); *Cox v. New Hampshire,* 312 U.S. 569 (1941); *Chaplinsky v. New Hampshire,* 315 U.S. 568 (1942); *Jones v. City of Opelika,* 316 U.S. 584 (1942); *Largent v. Texas,* 318 U.S. 418 (1943); *Jamison v. Texas,*

318 U.S. 413 (1943); *Douglas v. City of Jeanette,* 319 U.S. 157 (1943); *Follett v. Town of McCormick,* 321 U.S. 573 (1944); *Marsh v. Alabama,* 326 U.S. 501 (1946); *Tucker v. Texas,* 326 U.S. 517 (1946); *Saia v. New York,* 334 U.S. 558 (1948); *Niemotko v. Maryland,* 340 U.S. 268 (1951); *Fowler v. Rhode Island,* 345 U.S. 67 (1953); *Poulos v. New Hampshire,* 395 U.S. 95 (1953).

76. Richard E. Morgan, *Supreme Court and Religion* (London: Collier-Macmillan, 1972), 58.

77. Durham, "Treatment of Religious Minorities in the United States," in *European Consortium for Church-State Research,* 323, 335.

78. *Cantwell v. Connecticut,* 310 U.S. 296 (1940).

79. Ibid., 303.

80. *Minersville School Dist. v. Gobitis,* 310 U.S. 586 (1940), which the Jehovah's Witnesses lost, but which was subsequently overturned in their case *West Va. State Bd. of Ed. v. Barnette,* 319 U.S. 624 (1943).

81. The Supreme Court decided eleven Selective Service cases involving Jehovah's Witnesses, although the Witnesses only prevailed in *Falbo v. United States,* 320 U.S. 549 (1944), and *Estep v. United States,* 327 U.S. 114 (1946). See Redman, "Jehovah's Witnesses," in Finkelman, ed., *Religion and American Law: An Encyclopedia,* 245, 247–248.

82. *Thomas v. Review Bd. of Ind. Employment Sec. Div.,* 450 U.S. 707 (1981).

83. See Ahlstrom, *A Religious History of the American People,* 573.

84. William G. Ross, "Jews and American Religious Liberty," in *Religion and American Law: An Encyclopedia,* ed. Finkelman, 253.

85. Ahlstrom, *A Religious History of the American People,* 569.

86. Stephen M. Feldman, "Religious Minorities and the First Amendment: The History, the Doctrine, and the Future," *University of Pennsylvania Journal of Constitutional Law* 6 (2003): 222, 236.

87. The Pew Forum on Religion and Public Life, *U.S. Religious Landscape Survey* (2008), 12.

88. 366 U.S. 599 (1961).

89. 366 U.S. 617 (1961).

90. *Bd. of Ed. v. Minor,* 23 Granger (23 Ohio St.) 211 (1873). See also John F. Wilson, ed., vol. 2, *Church and State in America: A Bibliographic Guide, The Civil War to the Present Day* (New York: Greenwood Press, 1987), 341.

91. Feldman, "Religious Minorities and the First Amendment: The History, the Doctrine, and the Future," 222, 246.

92. *Engel v. Vitale,* 370 U.S. 421 (1962).

93. *Sch. Dist. of Abington Twp., Pa. v. Schempp,* 374 U.S. 203 (1963).

94. The groups writing amicus briefs in both cases were the National Jewish Community Relations Advisory Council, the Synagogue Council of America, the American Jewish Committee, and the Anti-Defamation League. See William G. Ross, "Jews and American Religious Liberty," in *Religion and American Law: An Encyclopedia,* ed. Finkelman, 253, 254–255.

95. Frank J. Sorauf, *The Wall of Separation: The Constitutional Politics of Church and State* (Princeton, NJ: Princeton University Press, 1976), 31–32; Ross, "Jews and American Religious Liberty," in *Religion and American Law: An Encyclopedia,* ed. Finkelman, 253, 255.

96. 512 U.S. 687 (1994).

97. 475 U.S. 503 (1986).

98. E.O. Watson, ed., *Yearbook of the Churches* (Washington, DC: Hayworth Publishing House, 1922), 361, http://books.google.com/books?hl=en&id=9sF07qbDVhcC&dq=yea

rbook+of+american+churches&printsec=frontcover&source=web&ots=n1Sm3fE2EF&
sig=sYPaNJPu7E388wIm7PAA9PwrTIs#PPA359,M1.

99. The Pew Forum on Religion and Public Life, *U.S. Religious Landscape Survey,*
2008), 5.

100. 452 U.S. 640 (1981).

101. 505 U.S. 672 (1992).

102. Brief of Respondents at 5, *Heffron v. Int'l Soc. For Krishna Consciousness, Inc.,* 452
U.S. 640 (1981) (No. 80-795).

103. 98 U.S. 145 (1878).

104. 133 U.S. 333 (1890).

105. 98 U.S. at 166.

106. 494 U.S. 872 (1990).

107. 483 U.S. 327 (1987).

108. 530 U.S. 290 (2000).

109. See Y. Haddad, *A Century of Islam in America* (American Institute for Islamic
Affairs, American University, Occasional Paper No. 4) (1986), 1.

110. The Pew Forum on Religion and Public Life, *U.S. Religious Landscape Survey*
(2008), 12.

111. 482 U.S. 342 (1987).

112. 170 F.3d 359 (3rd Cir. 1999).

113. *City of Boerne v. Flores,* 521 U.S. 507 (1997).

114. See generally, Bryan H. Wildenthal and Patrick M. O'Neil, "Native American
Religious Rights" in *Religion and American Law: An Encyclopedia,* ed. Finkelman, 330–338.

115. Frank S. Mead, *Handbook of Denominations in the United States,* ed. Samuel S.
Hill (New York: Abingdon-Cokesbury, 1951), 214.

116. The Pew Forum on Religion and Public Life, *U.S. Religious Landscape Survey*
(2008), 12.

117. 374 U.S. 398 (1963).

118. 406 U.S. 205 (1972).

119. 476 U.S. 693 (1986).

120. 485 U.S. 439 (1988).

121. 485 U.S. 439 (1988).

122. 494 U.S. 872 (1990).

123. U.S. Code 42, §2000bb-1 (2008).

124. U.S. Code 42, §2000cc-1(2008).

125. U.S. Code 42, §1996 (2008).

126. Gaustad, *Religious History of America,* 251.

127. The Pew Forum on Religion and Public Life, *U.S. Religious Landscape Survey* (2008), 12.

128. 344 U.S. 94 (1952).

129. Gaustad, *Religious History of America,* 252.

130. 344 U.S. 94 (1952).

131. See, e.g., J. Gordon Melton, "A Contemporary Ordered Religious Community:
The Sea Organization," in *New Religious Movements and Religious Liberty in America,* 2d
ed., eds. Davis and Hankins, 43, 45.

132. Brief for the Petitioners at 5, *Hernandez v. Comm'r of Internal Revenue,* 490 U.S.
680 (1989).

133. 490 U.S. 680 (1989).

134. Michal Belknap and Cathy Shipe, "Cults and the Law," in *Religion and American
Law: An Encyclopedia,* ed.Finkelman, 112, 114.

135. Ahlstrom, *A Religious History of the American People,* 478–481.

136. The Pew Forum on Religion and Public Life, *U.S. Religious Landscape Survey* (2008), 12.

137. 374 U.S. 398 (1963).

138. 401 U.S. 437 (1946).

139. Sorauf, *The Wall of Separation: The Constitutional Politics of Church and State,* 3–4.

140. Chuck Smith, "The Persecution of the West Virginia Jehovah's Witnesses and the Expansion of Legal Protection for Religious Liberty," in Davis and Hankins, eds., *New Religious Movements and Religious Liberty in America,* 2d ed., 155, 155–156 (quoting letter of Harland Fiske Stone to Charles Evans Hughes, 24 March 1941, quoted in Shawn Francis Peters, *Judging Jehovah's Witnesses: Religious Persecution and the Dawn of the Rights Revolution* (Lawrence, KS: University Press of Kansas, 2000), 186.

141. Sorauf, *The Wall of Separation: The Constitutional Politics of Church and State.*

142. Ibid., 4 (emphasis added).

143. *Hasan and Chaush v. Bulgaria,* App. No. 309985/96, Eur. Ct. H.R. Decision of 26 Oct. 2000; *Serif v. Greece,* App. No. 38178/97, Eur. Ct. H.R., Decision of 14 Dec. 1999.

144. *Metropolitan Church of Bessarabia v. Moldova,* App. No. 45701/99, Eur. Ct. H.R., , Decision of 13 Dec. 2001.

145. Although these cases also reflect the different governmental approaches to religion between the U.S. and countries such as Greece, Bulgaria, and Moldova, it is also relevant that the plaintiffs were Muslim and Orthodox. Some of the questions created when Muslim or Orthodox organizations split apart are different than with Protestants, where this issue has usually arisen in the U.S. Orthodoxy's hierarchy and geographical ties, for example, create new complications, as reflected in the case of *Kedroff v. St. Nicholas Cathedral of Russian Orthodox Church in North America,* 344 U.S. 94 (1952), as noted previously. Other issues that have not become prominent in U.S. law include regulation of Muslim veils, calls to prayer, and hajj, or the wearing of Sikh turbans or ceremonial knives.

146. See, e.g., Philip Hamburger, *Separation of Church and State* (Cambridge, MA: Harvard University Press, 2002), 15-16.

147. *Bd. of Ed. of Kiryas Joel Village Sch. Dist. v. Grumet,* 512 U.S. 687 (1994).

148. *Santa Fe Indep. Sch. Dist. v. Doe,* 530 U.S. 290 (2000).

149. U.S. Code 22, § 6401 (2008) (Public Law 105-292, *U.S. Statutes at Large* 112 (2008): 2787, as amended by Public Law 106-55, *U.S. Statutes at Large* 113 (1999): 401 and Public Law 107-228, *U.S. Statutes at Large* 116 (2002): 1350.

150. See generally T. Jeremy Gunn, "The United States and the Promotion of Freedom of Religion and Belief," in *Facilitating Freedom of Religion or Belief: A Deskbook,* eds. Tore Lindholm, et al., 721.

BIBLIOGRAPHY

....

Books

Adams, Arlin M. and Charles J. Emmerich. *A Nation Dedicated to Religious Liberty: The Constitutional Heritage of the Religion Clauses.* Philadelphia: University of Pennsylvania Press, 1990.

Ahlstrom, Sydney E. *A Religious History of the American People*. New Haven, CT: Yale University Press, 1972.

Anderson, Benedict. *Imagined Communities: Reflections on the Origin and Spread of Nationalism*. London: Verso, 1991.

Backus, Isaac. *An Appeal to the Public for Religious Liberty*. Boston: John Boyle, 1773.

Berg, Thomas C. *Minority Religions and the Religion Clauses*. St. Louis: School of Law, Washington University, 2004.

Davis, Derek H. and Barry Hankins, eds. *New Religious Movements and Religious Liberty in America,* 2nd ed. Waco: Baylor University Press, 2003.

Evans, Malcolm D. *Religious Liberty and International Law in Europe*. Cambridge, UK: Cambridge University Press, 1997.

Feldman, Stephen M. *Please Don't Wish Me a Merry Christmas: A Critical History of Separation of Church and State*. New York: New York University Press, 1997.

Gaustad, Edwin S. *A Religious History of America*. New Haven, CT: Yale University Press, 1966.

Hamburger, Philip. *Separation of Church and State*. Cambridge, MA: Harvard University Press, 2002.

Lindner, Eileen W., ed. *Yearbook of American and Canadian Churches*. Nashville, TN: Abingdon Press 2007.

Locke, John. *A Letter Concerning Toleration*. Indianapolis, IN: Bobs-Merrill, 1955.

Mazur, Eric Michael. *The Americanization of Religious Minorities: Confronting the Constitutional Order*. Baltimore: John Hopkins University Press, 1999.

Mead, Frank S. *Handbook of Denominations in the United States*. Ed. Samuel S. Hill. New York : Abingdon-Cokesbury, 1951.

Miller, Randall M. *Immigrants and Religion in Urban America*. Philadelphia: Temple University Press, 1977.

Morgan, Richard E. *The Supreme Court and Religion*. London : Collier-MacMillan, 1972.

Peters, Shawn Francis. *Judging Jehovah's Witnesses: Religious Persecution and the Dawn of the Rights Revolution*. Lawrence, KS: University Press of Kansas, 2000.

Ravitch, Frank S. *School Prayer and Discrimination: The Civil Rights of Religious Minorities and Dissenters*. Boston: Northeastern University Press, 1999.

Rawls, John. *Political Liberalism*. New York: Columbia University Press, 1993.

Sorauf, Frank J. *The Wall of Separation: The Constitutional Politics of Church and State*. Princeton, NJ: Princeton University Press, 1976.

Watson, E.O., ed. *Yearbook of the Churches*. Washington, DC: Hayworth Publishing House, 1922. http://books.google.com/books?hl=en&id=9sFo7qbDVhcC&dq=yearbook+of+american+churches&printsec=frontcover&source=web&ots=n1Sm3fE2EF&sig=sYPaNJPu7E388wIm7PAA9PwrTIs#PPA359,M1.

Wilson, John F., ed. *Church and State in America: A Bibliographical Guide: The Colonial and Early National Periods*. 2 volumes. New York: Greenwood Press, 1986–1987.

Articles/Chapters

Aynes, Richard. "Blaine Amendment." In *Religion and American Law: An Encyclopedia,* ed. Paul Finkelman. New York: Garland Publishing, 2000.

Baker, James T. "Baptists in Early America and the Separation of Church and State." In *Religion and American Law: An Encyclopedia,* ed. Paul Finkelman. New York: Garland Publishing, 2000.

Belknap, Michal, and Cathy Shipe. "Cults and the Law." In *Religion and American Law: An Encyclopedia,* edited by Paul Finkelman. New York: Garland Publishing, 2000.

Berg, Thomas C. "Minority Religions and the Religion Clauses." *Washington University Law Quarterly* 82 (Fall 2004): 919.

Carlson, John D. "God, War, and the Secular: Varieties of Religious and Ethical Traditions." *Barry Law Review* 7 (Fall 2006): 1.

Choper, Jesse H. "A Century of Religious Freedom." *California Law Review* 88 (December 2000): 1709–1741.

Dargo, George. "Religious Toleration and its Limits in Early America." *Northern Illinois University Law Review* 16 (Spring 1996): 341.

DeForrest, Mark Edward. "An Overview and Evaluation of State Blaine Amendments: Origins, Scope, and First Amendment Concerns." *Harvard Journal of Law & Public Policy* 26 (Spring 2003): 551.

Durham, Cole W. "Treatment of Religious Minorities in the United States." In *The Legal Status of Religious Minorities in the Countries of the European Union*, ed. European Consortium for Church-State Research. Thessaloniki: Sakkoulas Publications, 1994.

Feldman, Stephen M. "Religious Minorities and the First Amendment: The History, the Doctrine, and the Future." *University of Pennsylvania Journal of Constitutional Law* 6 (November 2003): 222.

Garry, Patrick M. "The Democratic Aspect of the Establishment Clause: A Refutation of the Argument that the Clause Serves to Protect Religious or Nonreligious Minorities." *Mercer Law Review* 59 (Winter 2008): 595.

Gedicks, Frederick Mark. "Religions, Fragmentations, and Doctrinal Limits." *The William and Mary Bill of Rights Journal* 15 (Oct 2006): 25.

Ghanea, Nazila. "Apostasy and Freedom to Change Religion or Belief." In *Facilitating Freedom of Religion or Belief: A Deskbook*, eds. Tore Lindholm, W. Cole Durham, Jr., Bahia G. Tahzib-Lie, Elizabeth A. Sewell, and Lena Larson. Leiden: Martinus Nijhoff, 2004.

Grim, Brian J. "God's Economy: Religious Freedom and Socioeconomic Well-Being." In *Religious Freedom in the World*, ed. Paul A. Marshall. Lanham, MD: Rowman and Littlefield, 2008.

Grim, Brian J. "Religion: Good for What Ails Us?" *The Review of Faith and International Affairs* 6 (Summer 2008): 3. http://www.cfia.org/ArticlesAndReports/ArticlesDetail.aspx?id=10368&hId=3672.

Gunn, T. Jeremy. "The United State and the Promotion of Freedom of Religion and Belief." In *Facilitating Freedom of Religion or Belief: A Deskbook*, eds. Tore Lindholm, W. Cole Durham, Jr., Bahia G. Tahzib-Lie, Elizabeth A. Sewell, and Lena Larson. Leiden: Martinus Nijhoff, 2004.

Haddad, Y. "A Century of Islam in America." Occasional Paper No. 4, American Institute for Islamic Affairs, American University, 1986.

Laycock, Douglas. "Church and State in the United States: Competing Conceptions and Historic Changes." *Indiana Journal of Global Legal Studies* 13 (Summer 2006): 503.

Levine, Samuel J. "Toward a Religious Minority Voice: A Look at Free Exercise Law Through a Religious Minority Perspective." *William & Mary Bill of Rights Journal* 5 (Winter 1996): 153.

Levinson, Rosalie Berger. "First Monday—The Dark Side of Federalism in the Nineties: Restricting Rights of Religious Minorities." *Valparaiso University Law Review* 33 (Fall 1998): 47.

Luna, Guadalupe T. "Cultural, Ethnic, and Religious Fragmentation." *St. Thomas Law Review* 20.3 (Spring 2008): 622.

McConnell, Michael. "Free Exercise Revisionism and the *Smith* Decision." *University of Chicago Law Review* 57 (Fall 1990): 1109.

———. "Freedom From Persecution or Protection of the Rights of Conscience?: A Critique of Justice Scalia's Historical Arguments in *City of Boerne v. Flores*." *William & Mary Law Review* 39 (February 1998): 819–847.

Milne, Elijah L. "Blaine Amendments and Polygamy Laws: The Constitutionality of Anti-Polygamy Laws Targeting Religion." *Western New England Law Review* 28 (Winter 2006): 257.

Melton, J. Gordon "A Contemporary Ordered Religious Community: The Sea Organization." In *New Religious Movements and Religious Liberty in America*, 2d ed., eds. Derek H. Davis and Barry Hankins. Waco, TX: Baylor University Press, 2003.

Mitchell, Joshua. "John Locke: A Theology of Religious Liberty." In *Religious Liberty in Western Thought*, eds. Noel B. Reynolds and W. Cole Durham, Jr. Grand Rapids Mich.: Scholars Press, 1996.

Piar, Daniel F. "Majority Rights, Minority Freedoms: Protestant Culture, Personal Autonomy, and Civil Liberties in Nineteenth-Century America." *The William and Mary Bill of Rights Journal* 14 (February 2006): 987.

Redman, Renee C. "Jehovah's Witnesses." In *Religion and American Law: An Encyclopedia*, ed. Paul Finkelman. New York: Garland Publishing, 2000.

Ross, William G. "Jews and American Religious Liberty." In *Religion and American Law: An Encyclopedia*, edited by Paul Finkelman. New York: Garland Publishing, 2000.

Sandoz, Ellis. "Religious Liberty and Religion in the American Founding Revisited." In *Religious Liberty in Western Thought*, eds. Noel B. Reynolds and W. Cole Durham, Jr. Grand Rapids, MI: Scholars Press, 1996.

Sherry, Suzanna. "Religion and the Public Square: Making Democracy Safe for Religious Minorities." *DePaul Law Review* 47 (Spring 1998): 499–517.

Smith, Chuck. "The Persecution of the West Virginia Jehovah's Witnesses and the Expansion of Legal Protection for Religious Liberty." In *New Religious Movements and Religious Liberty in America*, 2nd ed., eds. Derek H. Davis and Barry Hankins. Waco, TX: Baylor University Press, 2003.

Steinberg, David E. "Religious Exemptions as Affirmative Action." *Emory Law Journal* 40 (Winter 1991): 77–139.

The Fund for Peace and Foreign Policy. "The Failed State Index 2007." *Foreign Policy*, July/ August 2007, 54–63.

Wildenthal, Bryan H., and Patrick M. O'Neil. "Native American Religious Rights." In *Religion and American Law: An Encyclopedia*, ed. Paul Finkelman. New York: Garland Publishing, 2000.

Williams, Cynthia Norman. "America's Opposition to New Religious Movements: Limiting the Freedom of Religion." *Law and Psychology Review* 27 (Spring 2003): 171–182.

Court Cases

Agostini v. Felton, 521 U.S. 203 (1997).

Aguilar v. Felton, 473 U.S. 402 (1985).

Att'y Gen. v. Desilets, 636 N.E.2d 233 (Mass. 1994).

Bd. of Educ. of Kiryas Joel Village Sch. Dist. v. Grumet, 512 U.S. 687 (1994).

Bd. of Educ. v. Minor, 23 Ohio St. 211 (1873).

Bowen v. Roy, 476 U.S. 693 (1986).

Braunfeld v. Brown, 366 U.S. 599 (1961).

Cantwell v. Connecticut, 310 U.S. 296 (1940).

Chaplinsky v. New Hampshire, 315 U.S. 568 (1942).

City Chapel Evangelical Free Inc. v. City of South Bend, 744 N.E.2d 443 (Ind. 2001).

City of Boerne v. Flores, 521 U.S. 507 (1997).

Coleman v. City of Griffin, 302 U.S. 636 (1937).

Corp. of Presiding Bishop of Church of Jesus Christ of Latter-day Saints v. Amos, 483 U.S. 327 (1987).

Cox v. New Hampshire, 312 U.S. 569 (1941).

Cruz v. Beto, 405 U.S. 319 (1972).

Davis v. Beason, 133 U.S. 333 (1890).

Douglas v. City of Jeanette, 319 U.S. 157 (1943).

Elk Grove Unified Sch. Dist. v. Newdow, 542 U.S. 1 (2004).

Employment Div., Dep't of Human Resources of Or. v. Smith, 494 U.S. 872 (1990).

Engel v. Vitale, 370 U.S. 421 (1962).

Estep v. United States, 327 U.S. 114 (1946).

Falbo v. United States, 320 U.S. 549 (1944).

Fiscal Court v. Brady, 885 S.W.2d 681 (Ky. 1994).

Follett v. Town of McCormick, 321 U.S. 573 (1944).

Fortin v. Roman Catholic Bishop of Portland, 871 A.2d 1208 (Me. 2005).

Fowler v. Rhode Island, 345 U.S. 67 (1953).

Fraternal Order of Police Newark Lodge No. 12 v. City of Newark, 170 F.3d 359 (3rd Cir. 1999).

Gallagher v. Crown Kosher Super Market of Mass., Inc., 366 U.S. 617 (1961).

Gillette v. United States, 401 U.S. 437 (1946).

Goldman v. Weinberger, 475 U.S. 503 (1986).

Hasan and Chaush v. Bulgaria, App. No. 309985/96, Eur. Ct. H.R. Decision of 26 Oct. 2000.

Heffron v. Int'l Soc'y for Krishna Consciousness, Inc., 452 U.S. 640 (1981).

Brief of Respondents, *Heffron v. Int'l Soc. For Krishna Consciousness, Inc.*, 452 U.S. 640 (1981) (No. 80-795).

Hernandez v. Comm'r, 490 U.S. 680 (1989).

Brief for the Petitioners at 5, *Hernandez v. Comm'r of Internal Revenue*, 490 U.S. 680 (1989). (Nos. 87-963, 87-1616).

Horen v. Commonwealth, 479 S.E.2d 553 (Va. Ct. App. 1997).

Humphrey v. Lane, 728 N.E.2d 1039 (Ohio 2000).

Hunt v. Hunt, 648 A.2d 843 (Vt. 1994).

Illinois ex rel. McCollum v. Bd. of Educ. of Sch. Dist. No. 71, 333 U.S. 203 (1948).

In re Browning, 476 S.E.2d 465 (N.C. Ct. App. 1996).

Int'l Soc'y for Krishna Consciousness, Inc., v. Lee, 505 U.S. 672 (1992).

Jamison v. Texas, 318 U.S. 413 (1943).

Jones v. City of Opelika, 316 U.S. 584 (1942).

Kedroff v. St. Nicholas Cathedral of Russian Orthodox Church in North America, 344 U.S. 94 (1952).

Largent v. Texas, 318 U.S. 418 (1943).

Larson v. Cooper, 90 P.3d 125 (Alaska 2004).

Lemon v. Kurtzman, 403 U.S. 602 (1971).

Lovell v. City of Griffin, 303 U.S. 444 (1938).

Lying v. Northwest Indian Cemetery Protective Ass'n, 485 U.S. 439 (1988).

Marsh v. Alabama, 326 U.S. 501 (1946).

McCready v. Hoffius, 586 N.W.2d 723 (Mich. 1998).

Metropolitan Church of Bessarabia v. Moldova, App. No. 45701/99, Eur. Ct. H.R., Decision
        of 13 Dec. 2001.
Minersville Sch. Dist. v. Gobitis, 310 U.S. 586 (1940), *overruled by W. Va. State Bd. of Educ. v.
        Barnette,* 319 U.S. 624 (1943).
Mueller v. Allen, 463 U.S. 388 (1983).
Niemotko v. Maryland, 340 U.S. 268 (1951).
O'Lone v. Estate of Shabazz, 482 U.S. 342 (1987).
Open Door Baptist Church v. Clark County, 995 P.2d 33 (Wash. 2000).
Pierce v. Soc'y of the Sisters of the Holy Names of Jesus and Mary, 268 U.S. 510 (1925).
Poulos v. New Hampshire, 345 U.S. 395 (1953).
Rourke v. N.Y. State Dep't of Corr. Servs., 603 N.Y.S. 2d 647 (N.Y. Sup. Ct. 1993).
Reynolds v. United States, 98 U.S. 145 (1878).
Saia v. New York, 334 U.S. 558 (1948).
St. John's Lutheran Church v. State Comp. Ins. Fund, 830 P.2d 1271 (Mont. 1992).
Santa Fe Indep. Sch. Dist. v. Doe, 530 U.S. 290 (2000).
Sch. Dist. of Abington Twp., Pa. v. Schempp, 374 U.S. 203 (1963).
Sch. Dist. of City of Grand Rapids v. Ball, 473 U.S. 373 (1985).
Schneider v. New Jersey, 308 U.S. 147 (1939).
Serif v. Greece, App. No. 38178/97, Eur. Ct. H.R., Decision of 14 Dec. 1999.
Sherbert v. Verner, 374 U.S. 398 (1963).
State ex rel. Heitkamp v. Family Life Servs., 560 N.W.2d 526 (N.D. 1997).
State v. Evans, 796 P.2d 178 (Kan. App. 1990).
State v. Hershberger, 462 N.W.2d 393 (Minn. 1990).
State v. Miller, 549 N.W.2d 235, 238-42 (Wis. 1996).
Thomas v. Review Bd. of Ind. Employment Sec. Div. , 450 U.S. 707 (1981).
Tilton v. Richardson, 403 U.S. 672 (1971).
Torcaso v. Watkins, 367 U.S. 488 (1961).
Tucker v. Texas, 326 U.S. 517 (1946).
United States v. Lee, 455 U.S. 252 (1982).
Wallace v. Jaffree, 472 U.S. 38 (1985).
Wisconsin v. Yoder, 406 U.S. 205 (1972).
Zobrest v. Catalina Foothills Sch. Dist., 509 U.S. 1 (1993).

Government Material

International Religious Freedom Act, U.S. Code 22, § 6401 (2008) (Public Law 105-292,
        U.S. Statutes at Large 112 (2008): 2787, as amended by Public Law 106-55, *U.S.
        Statutes at Large* 113 (1999): 401 and Public Law 107-228, *U.S. Statutes at Large* 116
        (2002): 1350).
Protection and Preservation of Traditional Religions of Native Americans, U.S. Code 42,
        §1996 (2008).
Religious Freedom Restoration Act, U.S. Code 42, §2000bb-1 (2008).
Religious Land Use and Incarcerated Persons Act, U.S. Code 42, §2000cc-1 (2008).U.S.
        Department of State. "International Religious Freedom Report 2007, Russia," http://
        www.state.gov/g/drl/rls/irf/2007/90196.htm.
U.S. Department of State. "International Religious Freedom Report 2007, Iran," http://
        www.state.gov/g/drl/rls/irf/2007/90210.htm.
U.S. Department of State. "International Religious Freedom Report 2007, Greece," http://
        www.state.gov/g/drl/rls/irf/2007/90178.htm.

Miscellaneous

The Pew Forum on Religion and Public Life. "U.S. Religious Landscape Survey (2008)." http://religions.pewforum.org/.

The Pew Forum on Religion and Public Life. "Religious Demographic Profile, Brazil," http://pewforum.org/world-affairs/countries/?CountryID=29 (citing 2000 Brazil Census at http://www.ibge.gov.br/english/).

The Pew Forum on Religion and Public Life. "Religious Demographic Profile, India," http://pewforum.org/world-affairs/countries/?CountryID=94 (citing 2001 India Census, *archived at* http://unstats.un.org and http://www.censusindia.net).

The Pew Forum on Religion and Public Life. "Religious Demographic Profile, Philippines," http://pewforum.org/world-affairs/countries/?CountryID=163 (citing 2000 Philippine Census, archived at http://unstats.un.org/).

CHAPTER 10

RELIGIOUS SYMBOLS AND RELIGIOUS EXPRESSION IN THE PUBLIC SQUARE

T. JEREMY GUNN

RELIGIOUS symbols and religious discourse pervade the public square in the United States. In the twenty-first century, radio and television airwaves, not to mention the Internet and cable television, are filled with preachers delivering religious messages. Concert halls and sports arenas have been rented out for religious revivals for decades. Scores of radio stations broadcast Christian music. Pedestrians on sidewalks in any city in the United States can see, from Main Street to Wall Street, churches, crosses, temples, menorahs, mosques, and other religious institutions and symbols. People are free to worship one God, no god, or many gods—and they do so. Church attendance is higher in the United States than in any other developed country in the world. Religious books are widely published, sold, and handed out, and the U.S. Postal Service delivers them in the mail without government censorship or restraint. Street preachers preach. Missionaries walk up and down sidewalks and knock on doors to convey their message to any who will listen. School children at public schools freely wear religious attire (whether a *hijab,* cross, turban, or yarmulke). Religious parades and manifestations take place on streets and in parks. Candidates for public office deliver speeches about their religious beliefs, whether for the purpose of enlightening the public or pandering to it.

Not only do all of these religious activities appear in a vibrant way in the public square in America, but they are also protected by the First Amendment of the Constitution. Organizations ranging from the secular American Civil Liberties Union to the faith-based Becket Fund for Religious Liberty have filed numerous lawsuits in support of such rights when they are perceived as being infringed by government officials (federal, state, or local). Dozens of organizations—from the ideological left, right, and center—vigorously work to ensure that American citizens are free to practice, manifest, broadcast, and otherwise express their religious beliefs in public. For most practical purposes, the basic laws governing religious activities by individuals in the public square are now well established and generally (although certainly not always) respected.

Although religion has long played an active role in American public life, and continues to play a greater role in politics in the United States than it does in any other industrialized country in the world, warnings that religion is under assault and at imminent risk of being stripped from the public square have been issued repeatedly since the early 1980s. Perhaps the most famous and influential discussion of this perceived threat came from Father Richard John Neuhaus, whose 1984 book *The Naked Public Square* has played a major role in framing the debate.[1] Following Neuhaus, conservatives repeatedly warn Americans in ominous terms about dangerous elites who are seeking to "purge religion from the public square."[2] The fear of the naked public square has now crossed political lines to the point that those perceived to be on the left now echo the same warnings. United States Supreme Court Justice Stephen Breyer assures us that he too rejects those who wish to "compel the government to purge from the public sphere all that in any way partakes of the religious."[3] He finds that such "absolutism is . . . inconsistent with our national traditions. . . ."[4] Justice Breyer does not identify who these "absolutists" are. Similarly, President Barack Obama has been careful to distinguish himself from "some" (unnamed) persons "who bristle at the notion that faith has a place in the public square."[5] Journalist Eboo Patel insists that that it would be "fundamentally illiberal to exclude religious voices from the public square," without identifying who these illiberal excluders might be.[6] He further explains that "to close the civic door to some—or all—religious voices is contrary to our nation's ideal of fairness."[7] Both conservatives and liberals thus speak as if the future survival of religion in the public sphere were somehow in doubt. Although discussions about the role that religion should play in public life, politics, society, and government has been an enduring issue in North America since the seventeenth century, the suggestion that religion and religious symbols are actually at risk of being removed from the religiously vibrant public square is a relatively recent phenomenon and requires some attention and conceptual clarification.

Although there are of course "some" people who are hostile to religion and who believe that religious discourse of any kind should be excluded from public debates, the number is so small and their voices are so fully drowned out in the political and legal sphere that it is difficult to find any public official at any level of government who openly espouses such beliefs.[8] Therefore, why are there so many calls to defend religion's right to be present in the public square when the possibility of its disappearance is so slight? The answer lies, in part, in some ambiguity in the meaning of the words "public" and "private" and how they are used (and abused) in political and popular discourse.

Of the many meanings of the word "public," two should be placed in particular focus. First, "public" may invoke "openness" and "visibility." A "public concert" is one that is open to anyone who might wish to attend. Something that is on public display is readily visible, whether indoors or out. A meeting that is open to the public means that anyone may come.

A second, and quite different, meaning of the word "public" is something that is owned or operated by the government. A "public school" is one that is operated by, for example, a local school board and is paid for by taxpayers rather than private tuition. If a person holds a "public office," it likely means that she is an elected government official or has been appointed by a political body. "Public services" typically (although not necessarily) are social programs that are operated by government agencies. If something is "public property" (such as a "public library"), it presumably means that it is owned by a government entity or the population as a whole.

Among the various meanings of the word "private," there are two that are of particular importance here. The first bears almost the opposite meaning of "openness," and suggests something that is conducted out of view of the population generally. It may include actions that are conducted in secret, behind closed doors, or out of public view. Thus a "private club" is one in which members decide who may be admitted. A "private matter" is one that should be left alone by others, and something that is done "in private" should not be seen. Things that should be left "private" are often embarrassing or shameful.

The second meaning of "private," unlike the first, has nothing to do with visibility, but simply means "nongovernmental" (and thus is the opposite of the second meaning of "public" described in the preceding). CBS and McDonalds are "private" businesses with very visible public faces. Disney World is situated on "private property" and is owned by "private shareholders," but is one of the most publicly visited and frequently photographed sites in the world. One might become confused if the rather different meanings of the words "public" and "private" were not kept straight, and there may be ambiguity even if one is paying close attention.[9]

It is in these different, ambiguous, and sometimes deliberately manipulated uses of the words "public" and "private" that much of the confusion originates when people allege that "some" are trying to "purge religion from the public square."[10] The real debate in the United States, contrary to what the polemicists portray, is not about whether religion should be seen or practiced in *public* (i.e., in the open), but rather the role that the *government* (the other meaning of "public") should play in financing, supporting, sponsoring, favoring, and endorsing religious symbols and religious speech. Those individuals and organizations who are often accused of attempting to remove religious symbols from the public square typically defend the public expression of religion and religious symbols when made by individuals, families, and religious communities.[11] In other words, when the statements of those who fear the "purging" of religion are examined closely, they typically use the word "public" when the actual meaning is "government." Rather than arguing explicitly that *they favor government promotion of religion* (which is of questionable constitutional and popular merit), they use the vague and misleading allegation that "others" are trying to "purge religion from the public square."

The remainder of this chapter is divided into three parts. First, it offers a brief historical overview of some of the major forms of religious expression and religious symbolism that have been promoted by government entities since the founding of the United States. Next, it provides a synopsis of current constitutional law regarding government-sponsored religious expression. The concluding section provides an overview of the law regarding religious expression by "private" individuals in the "public square." In short, the widespread concern that traditional religious symbols and discourses face imminent extinction is misplaced. The public sphere has always been populated by robust expressions of religious faith, and will continue to be so. However, many if not most of the government-sponsored religious displays that citizens now believe to be long-cherished aspects of American public life are actually quite recent innovations, introduced during the 1950s in response to Cold War tensions. Contrary to those who raise the alarming specter of the "naked public square," the true danger is not that these religious symbols will be eliminated, but that government-sponsored religious displays will receive the imprimatur of constitutionality on the faulty assumption that such displays have "always" been a part of American public life. Ultimately, *governmental* promotion of religious messages is constitutionally deeply problematic, whereas *citizen expression* of religion is generally not. The conflating of these two very different concepts ("government promotion" and "citizen expression") into the single term—"public square"—falsely suggests that opposition to governmental promotion of religion is equivalent to stripping religion from the public square.

HISTORICAL OVERVIEW OF GOVERNMENT-SPONSORED RELIGIOUS EXPRESSIONS

Although one might at first imagine that governmental support of religious monuments and symbols has long been a recognized part of American tradition and that it became a subject of controversy only recently, this is not entirely the case. Although some governmental involvement in religious expression has long been part of American history, particularly in the authorization of chaplains and presidential proclamations of thanksgiving and prayer, many forms of government support for religion are of much more recent origin and emerged specifically in response to Cold War tensions in the 1940s and 1950s.[12]

Before the 1950s, when there was a burst of official sponsorship of religious symbols and expression, governmental activities related to religion had been much more circumscribed. Although there are many important exceptions to this general rule—many of which will be identified below—it was not until after World War II that the U.S. governments became actively involved in promoting religious and quasireligious symbols and declarations. The erection of Ten Commandments monuments and the disputes about their constitutionality are largely phenomena that emerged in the 1950s, as shall be discussed below.

The clearest and most persistent form of federal government involvement in promoting religious messages since the eighteenth century has been through prayer proclamations issued by the president. The American tradition of issuing such proclamations began with the Puritans in the seventeenth century and was long associated with them.[13]The Continental Congress issued several such proclamations, and they often encouraged the population to commit themselves to prayer, fasting, and humiliation (typically in the spring) and thanksgiving (typically in the fall).[14] The more demanding calls for fasting and humiliation have long since fallen from favor. Presidents George Washington and John Adams issued prayer proclamations, but Thomas Jefferson believed them to be unconstitutional and refused to do so. After writing a draft letter explaining his constitutional objections (which was originally part of his famous letter to the Baptists of Danbury, Connecticut), Jefferson was advised that it would be politically unwise to detail his constitutional objections inasmuch as it would alienate the New Englanders, who in many ways continued to imbibe the spirit of their Puritan ancestors. He made the politically expedient decision and passed up the opportunity to explain his objections.[15] Although Jefferson did not issue prayer proclamations, according to at least one historian, he started attending religious services in the Capitol building so as to deflect accusations that his piety was suspect.[16] President James Madison also believed the proclamations to be unconstitutional, although he lapsed and issued them during the War of 1812, something that he later regretted according to private notes that were not published until long after his death. Although presidents Jefferson, Madison, and Andrew Jackson had constitutional objections to the proclamations, their successors in office continued to issue them during the nineteenth century. These periodic exhortations to prayer reached a crescendo with President William McKinley, who delivered an extraordinarily boastful "prayer proclamation" in 1898 following several successful battles in the Spanish-American War. President Woodrow Wilson also issued pointed proclamations in support of his political positions, both during World War I and immediately after, as he sought ratification of the Treaty of Paris. President Harry S. Truman issued three modest proclamations in 1945 that urged Americans to reflect prayerfully following the death of President Franklin Roosevelt, the surrender of Germany, and the surrender of Japan. As described in the following, the number and frequency of presidential prayer proclamations jumped sharply during 1947 and has stayed at a high rate ever since.

The tradition of legislative prayer has been connected with the United States since the Continental Congress convened in 1774 and retained a chaplain, Jacob Duché, to offer prayers.[17] Duché's piety was warmly praised until he objected to the issuance of the Declaration of Independence, whereupon he was denounced as a "traitor." Although the Continental Congress continued to have chaplains and prayers, the practice was not followed during the Constitutional Convention in Philadelphia in 1789. There is a frequently recounted story that the constitution-writing body had become enmeshed in conflict until Benjamin Franklin suggested that they hold a prayer, after which harmony returned to the body. Like the story of General Washington having been seen praying at Valley Forge, this anecdote is false. General Washington did, however, employ military chaplains during the Revolutionary War—and the practice continued in the U.S. military thereafter, over the objections of prominent constitutionalists such as Madison, who insisted that they were unconstitutional despite their popularity with politicians.[18] Beginning with the First Congress, the federal legislature has had chaplains who provide spiritual advice to members of Congress and who frequently offer prayers at the beginning of the legislative day. The Supreme Court held the practice of conducting nonsectarian legislative prayers to be constitutional in 1983, largely on the grounds of longstanding practice, and because the practice was followed by the same First Congress that drafted the First Amendment.[19]

Although members of the Continental Congress originally had considered adopting national mottos and seals with explicitly religious messages, the proposals as they finally emerged eliminated almost all religious references. Six years after beginning its work, and after having rejected numerous alternatives the Continental Congress adopted in 1782 what became the two-sided "Great Seal of the United States."[20] (It has been revised at least five times since.) The original obverse side displays an eagle protected by a shield bearing 13 alternating red and white stripes, just as there are 13 stars above the eagle's head. The left talon clutches the arrows of war and the right an olive branch. The motto on the seal includes the Latin "*E Pluribus Unum*" (out of many, one). The reverse side of the Great Seal is noted for having more of a religious message than the obverse, but this should not be overly emphasized.[21] The reverse side contains an unfinished pyramid of 13 layers, with an eye inside a triangle appearing in rays of glory at the summit of the pyramid. Across the bottom is a draped motto bearing the words "*Novus Ordo Seclorum*" (a new order of the ages) and across the top are the two words "*Annuit Coeptis,*" often translated as "God has favored our undertakings."[22] Although this translation is not wrong, there are two problems with it. First, if the Congress had wanted to say this in Latin the obvious and correct choice would have been to say "*Deo Favente,*" which was in fact proposed on draft designs but was never approved. *Annuit Coeptis* does not include the Latin word for "God" and would more accurately be translated as "our undertakings have been favored," leaving the reader to infer *who* or *what* was responsible for such undertakings. The eye in glory is generally described as being either the "all-seeing eye" or the "eye of Providence," both of which have religious connotations but neither of which emerged from orthodox Christianity or Judaism. The descriptive language used by the Continental Congress includes only the term "Eye" and does not explicitly attribute any religious significance to it.[23] Although there is no question that the eye and the phrase *Annuit Coeptis* evoke religious themes, they are indirect and vague when compared to the explicit religious themes and language that were considered and rejected. Moreover (and somewhat curiously), the reverse side of the original Great Seal that contained this imagery was never cut and no dye was ever cast. It was only after later revisions of the seal were adopted that the reverse side appeared.

The art and architecture of the Federalist period, for most practical purposes, did not evoke Christian or biblical themes. Rather, the style and imagery was derived from the classical period. The statues and paintings of Washington and other leaders portrayed them in the style of Greek or Roman warriors or statesman rather than as biblical prophets or priests. The Capitol Building was constructed in a Greco-Roman style, rather than in a Gothic or Puritan vein. To the extent that there were other historical influences in the art and architecture of the first half of the nineteenth century, they typically came from the Renaissance. The monuments constructed in the nineteenth and twentieth centuries that were designed to honor some of America's great presidents also were designed following classical and not religious motifs: the Washington Monument, the Jefferson Memorial, and the Lincoln Memorial.[24]

In 1863, in the midst of the Civil War, the phrase "In God We Trust" was first adopted as an expression to be placed on a two-cent coin by the (North's) Secretary of the Treasury Salmon P. Chase. A variation of this phrase appeared in the fourth and last stanza of the Star-Spangled Banner, written in 1812: "And this be our motto: In God is our trust." Although President Theodore Roosevelt opposed engraving the phrase onto the ten-dollar gold piece, believing it trivialized God, his objection was overruled by Congress.

With these exceptions, the remainder of the religious symbols and language that are at the heart of the American "culture wars" had their origins in the 1950s.[25]

TRUSTING IN ONE NATION UNDER GOD

A significant number of the now famous governmental and political declarations about religion and God emerged during the 1950s, and were explicitly promoted as constituting America's "first line of defense" against Soviet communism.[26] Although President Truman had issued only three prayer proclamations during the first years of his presidency, Congress began to enact laws that either urged or required him to do so, and more than a dozen soon followed. The first Presidential Prayer Breakfast was launched by President Eisenhower in 1953, and the tradition has continued without interruption every year since.[27] The famous statement by Justice William O. Douglas that Americans are "a religious people" was made in 1952, further evidence of the emerging religious *Zeitgeist* that was quickly permeating American public life.[28] Congress enacted several laws and adopted several resolutions announcing days of prayer and calling for the president to issue proclamations in support of them.

The words "under God" were inserted by law into the Pledge of Allegiance in 1954 and were explicitly justified as a way of showing how different Americans were from their communist enemies. In 1955, a law was enacted requiring placing the words "In God We Trust" on all United States currency.[29] In 1955, Congress voted funds to construct an interdenominational "prayer room" inside the U.S. Capitol Building.[30] In 1956, Congress officially adopted "In God We Trust" as the national motto, thereby displacing the trinity of *"E Pluribus Unum," "Novo Ordo Seclorum,"* and *"Annuit Coeptis,"* all of which had appeared in various combinations on seals, documents, coins, and currency since the eighteenth century. In the 1950s, stamps and postmarks also began to bear the logos "In God We Trust" and "Pray for Peace."

TEN COMMANDMENT MONUMENTS

Ten Commandments monuments illustrate what is perhaps the archetypal and most salient dispute over government sponsorship of religious symbols. Supporters of such monuments typically argue that they simply recognize the Judeo-Christian heritage and values upon which the United States was founded, and highlight the influence that the Mosaic law had on Western law.[31] Whether or not this is true, the heightened public interest in displaying the Ten Commandments is relatively recent. It dates not to the seventeenth-century Puritans or eighteenth-century Founders, but almost entirely to the 1950s, when they were erected in response to the perceived ideological threat of Soviet communism.[32]

Emerging contemporaneously with these other declarations about God and religion, some civic and religious leaders in the 1950s began to draw attention to the particular importance of the Ten Commandments. In January 1951, a New York rabbi proposed that copies of the Ten Commandments be placed on the walls of every schoolroom in the country. Another rabbi preached that closer attention to the Ten Commandments would enhance the American democratic character.[33] Some enterprising people converted a formerly nondescript hill in North Carolina into "Ten Commandments Mountain," which visitors could climb while reading the sacred words that were "written in concrete, with letters five feet high and four feet wide."[34] However, the most enduring effort to promote the Ten Commandments was launched by the Fraternal Order of Eagles, which convinced the State of Minnesota in 1951 to support its effort to distribute paper copies of the Ten Commandments to churches, schools groups, courts, and government offices throughout the country. The idea was proposed to the Eagles by a state court judge in Minnesota named E.J. Ruegemer. Judge Ruegemer decided to promote the Ten Commandments after learning just how little a particular juvenile convict knew about them; the young delinquent's ignorance inspired the judge to launch a nationwide crusade to distribute the Decalogue. The printed version of the Eagles

Ten Commandments was a quasiecumenical, quasisanitized version of scripture that had been abridged and approved by Protestant, Catholic, and Jewish clergy. The printed version distributed by the Eagles included decorative drawings of an eagle, an American flag, the Star of David, the Chi-Rho cross, and a pyramid with an all-seeing eye. According to the Eagles, thousands of framed versions were distributed throughout the country during the next few years.[35]

In 1952, the famous Hollywood director Cecil B. DeMille "officially confirmed a long-standing rumor" that his next film undertaking would be *The Ten Commandments*. Three years later, while filming on location at Mt. Sinai, DeMille was inspired to distribute brass versions of Ten Commandment monuments throughout the country. DeMille no doubt had both pious and pecuniary motives.[36] After some inquiries, DeMille learned about Judge Ruegemer's campaign in Minnesota and called him to ask his opinion on the brass monument idea. The judge made a counterproposal to have the commandments carved on stone tablets, just as God Himself had done on Mt. Sinai. DeMille readily accepted the suggestion and began to make arrangements with the Eagles to help pay for the stone monuments. The campaign to erect monuments would help him advertise the pending release of his blockbuster film while simultaneously promoting public awareness of the Decalogue. With DeMille's encouragement, and against the backdrop of his film's pending release, Ten Commandments monuments began to spring up in 1955 and continued to proliferate for several years thereafter.[37]

CHRISTMAS AND OTHER HOLIDAY DISPLAYS

Every December since the 1990s, the media has been overrun with warnings about an insidious "war against Christmas" that is allegedly being waged by people who wish to remove all trappings of Christmas from public view. One best-selling book, for example, advises that secularists are trying to undermine "normal and traditional Christmas representations such as Christmas trees, Santa Claus, treetop stars, wreaths, the singing of and listening to Christmas carols or Christmas instrumental music, attending a performance of Dickens' *A Christmas Carol*. . . ."[38] The elements of Christmas that author John Gibson identifies—Santa Claus, decorated trees and wreaths, Christmas music, and Charles Dickens' *A Christmas Carol*—are actually less "normal and traditional" than might popularly be believed. They emerged from a variety of conflicting sources and traditions that finally coalesced in America only in the 1950s.

The origins of the celebration of Christmas are somewhat obscure. There is no documented evidence of any type of Christmas observance during the first 300 years of the Christian era. The New Testament does not identify the date of Jesus' birth, and during the early years of Christianity there was no traditional date ascribed to the nativity. The only two gospels that mention the birth of Jesus, Matthew and

Luke, offer little factual information, and the New Testament does not suggest that it is a date that should be commemorated. During the first centuries of Christianity there were no Christmas celebrations and the principal liturgical focus of the early Christian calendar was Easter.[39] The first documented reference to the observance of Jesus' birth was in 354, almost two decades after the death of the first Christian emperor, Constantine. Because no specific date was associated with the birth of Jesus, the Christians of the fourth century had some latitude when they finally selected a date to celebrate the nativity.

> With the choice of December 25, the Western church settled on a date that was precisely in the middle of three wildly popular Roman midwinter festivals. The First was Saturnalia . . . with a legendary reputation of excessive partying. A few days later came the New Year's festival. . . . Between these two celebrations fell December 25, the winter solstice by calendars of the time. Romans celebrated December 25 as the birthday of Sol Invictus, the Unconquered Sun. . . .[40]

After having selected the conventional date of the Winter Solstice to recognize the birth of their Lord, the early followers of Jesus "gave an overlay of Christian meaning to some preexisting winter festivities."[41] Having selected December 25 as a date that corresponded with pagan celebrations, they also burnished it with pagan ornamentation.

> In pre-Christian times, Romans used evergreens, symbols of fertility and rege- neration, to trim their houses at the [first] of January. Eventually, Christians appropriated the use of evergreens for their Christmas celebration. To remove the taint of paganism, they associated it with new beginnings and man's second chance with God.[42]

The later folk traditions of the pagan German and Scandinavian peoples provided a second and separate overlay of evergreen trees and wreaths to celebrate the Winter Solstice and the birth of Jesus. In the sixteenth century, German Chris- tians began bringing trees into their homes, and in the seventeenth century they began to decorate them.[43]

In the same fourth century that the Western Church selected December 25 as the feast day for the nativity (and the Eastern Church selected January 6), a pious bishop named Nicholas of Myra (in present-day Turkey) gained the reputation of being particularly generous to children. Over time, as hagiography mixed with history, St. Nicholas (Sinterklaas in Dutch) became recognized as the patron saint of children, and his feast day was commemorated on December 6.[44] Unbeknownst to the original St. Nicholas or those who contemporaneously selected December 25 as the feast day for the Nativity, the two celebrations and the two holy figures would be merged into a massive consumer extravaganza by the late twentieth century.

Christmas, or "Christ's Mass," became a part of the liturgical calendar in the West, and was increasingly recognized as a particularly holy day during the Middle Ages. Legend credits St. Francis of Assisi with the introduction of the crèche as a symbolic representative of the manger in which the infant Jesus was laid and which became surrounded by additional carvings of a kneeling Mary and Joseph, shepherds, animals, and wise men. With the coming of the Reformation, some Protestants began to question not only the perceived idolatry in what they thought was Catholic worship of the carved nativity figures, but also the entire celebration of Christmas with its legacy of pagan decorations. During the Reformation many Protestant churches saw Christmas as an intrinsically Catholic holiday and deemphasized its importance. English Puritans and Scottish Presbyterians in particular voiced their disapproval of the Christmas holiday. The most vociferous opponents of Christmas were the English and American Puritans, but Calvinists and Presbyterians also were offended by the Catholic-tainted pageantry of the Christmas holiday.[45] In 1644, the English Parliament, seeing too much frivolity and irreligion associated with Christmas festivities, declared by law that it should be a day of penance rather than a feast day. By 1652, Christmas observance in England was banned both in and out of church.[46]

On the other side of the Atlantic, the New Englanders who gave America the traditions of thanksgiving day, thanksgiving-day proclamations, the Mayflower Compact, John Winthrop's "City on a Hill," and election-day sermons criminalized the celebration of Christmas.

> In 1659, in an atmosphere of tension over Anglicanism, other heresies, new trade, and general disarray, the Massachusetts Bay General Court banned the keeping of Christmas by 'forebearing of labour, feasting, or any other way.' The law aimed to prevent the recurrence of further, unspecified 'disorders' which had apparently arisen in 'seurerall places. . .by reason of some still observing such Festiualls,' and provided that 'whosoeuer shall be found observing any such day as Xmas or the like. . .' would be fined.[47]

Thus, devout English-speaking conservative Christian Protestants were the first and most vociferous warriors against Christmas and banned its celebration because it had so far departed from their version of the true Christian message.

The Massachusetts and English Puritans ultimately retracted their total ban on Christmas celebrations.[48] A hundred years later, by the last quarter of the eighteenth century, some Protestant denominations, including Baptists, slowly began to incorporate Christmas into their religious services. Although it was not an official holiday, and government institutions continued to take no note of it, it became an increasingly popular annual event, albeit for a minority of Americans.[49] Many prominent figures, including the man who was perhaps the nineteenth century's most famous preacher, Henry Ward Beecher, continued to keep the holiday at arm's length.[50] Thus, in the 100 years after the War for Independence, Americans had still not integrated Christmas celebrations into their lives. Elizabeth Cady Stanton and Samuel Goodrich, both New Englanders, recalled the Fourth of July, Thanksgiving, and "training day" as the only "great festivals" of their childhood in the early nineteenth century. "An 80-year-old New Yorker wrote that in 1818 his boarding school allowed only two week-long vacations, plus the Fourth of July and Thanksgiving, during the entire year. Christmas and New Year's were ignored."[51]

"The *Youth's Friend*, an American Sunday School Union magazine for children, did not mention Christmas as anything more than a date until 1846."[52]

By the 1830s Christmas trees had been introduced to Scandinavia, and by the 1840s to France, England, and America.[53] Apparently the first royal Christmas tree was introduced in England when Prince Albert gave one to Victoria in 1840. The innovation was so new, however, that the most famous English language Christmas story ever published, *A Christmas Carol* by Charles Dickens in 1843, makes no reference to Christmas trees, Santa Claus, or Christmas stockings.[54] Many religious aspects of Christmas also are absent in Dickens. There are no crèches, shepherds, or kings bearing gifts. Indeed the words "Jesus" and "Christ" and "Mary" and "Joseph" appear nowhere in the famous story, although there are references to church attendance and to one Christmas carol: "God Rest Ye Merry, Gentleman," a traditional Christmas song that was first published only in 1833—just 10 years before the Dickens story.

The absence of traditional religious themes in *A Christmas Carol* becomes even more striking when the pagan aspects of it are examined more closely.[55] The original title of the story, now rarely mentioned, was *A Christmas Carol in Prose, Being a Ghost Story of Christmas*. And indeed the other-worldly characters are not religious figures (there is no visitation from Christ or the Virgin Mary), but the "ghosts" and "spirits" of Jacob Marley and the decidedly unchristian ghosts of Christmas past, present, and future. The deceased Jacob Marley and the three spirits do not describe a recognizable Christian, theological afterlife; and although Tiny Tim and Bob Cratchit are praised for their goodness, the person who emerges in the end as the most generous giver of gifts is none other than the very unreligious but newly transformed Ebenezer Scrooge, who was brought to a love of Christmas not by Christ, but by specters from the netherworld who seem uninformed by Christian theology.

One of the most important American literary contributions toward the modern de-sacralization of Christmas was the famous children's poem "Twas the Night Before Christmas," which was published anonymously in 1823 as *A Visit from St. Nicholas*.[56] Although the poem, like Dickens' famous story, makes explicit references to "Christmas," it is otherwise fully pagan and is completely divorced from orthodox Christian tradition and theology.[57] The relationship between the protagonist and the fourth-century saint is purely nominal. St. Nick has been transformed from a kindly bishop to a magical "right jolly old elf" who is transported by a "miniature sleigh, and eight tiny reindeer." (Modern readers of the original poem have been so influenced by subsequent depictions of a robust and larger-than-life Santa Claus that they generally fail to note that the original in the poem was a tiny, elfin figure who was able to travel so easily through the chimney because his size was so small.) His reindeer bear the thoroughly pagan names of "Comet," "Cupid," and, in translation, "Thunder," and "Lightning." Although, like his successors, the 1823 St. Nick is rotund (albeit an elf), comes down through the chimney, and fills stockings with gifts, he is not yet dressed in red (but in fur), nor does he live at the North Pole. The birth of Jesus is not mentioned in the poem. Although not yet

named "Santa Claus," this magical, well-nourished St. Nick would soon be promoted by merchants in lieu of Jesus Christ, whose birthday they were ostensibly
honoring. The phrase "Merry Christmas" has no biblical roots, but was shouted
aloud by the fictional gift-giving elf named "St. Nick" in the children's poem, and
by Ebenezer Scrooge after being transformed by his encounter with spirits from
beyond. The greeting "Merry Christmas," then, comes not from the Bible, but from
popular culture.

Despite the increasing public awareness of Christmas in the United States
during the nineteenth century, it remained without legal status as a holiday and
employers, like Ebenezer Scrooge, had the authority to decide whether or not to
allow workers time off to attend church. Federal employees were required to show
up for work. "Congress met on Christmas Day every year from 1789 to 1855, with
only three exceptions" and "public schools met on Christmas day in parts of New
England at least until 1870."[58] It was not until June 1870—3 weeks after the death of
the author of A Christmas Carol—that the U.S. Congress made Christmas into an
official national holiday.

Meanwhile, however, the religious dimension of Christmas had begun to give
way to its commercial aspects. As early as the 1820s

> New York's stores in the city stayed open until midnight during the Christmas
> season. Bright gas lights illuminated "[w]hole rows of confectionery stores and
> toy shops, fancifully, and often splendidly, decorated with festoons of bright silk
> drapery, interspersed with flowers and evergreens." In the evenings and into the
> late night, "visitors of both sexes and all ages" filled the streets, "some selecting
> toys and fruit for holiday presents; others merely lounging from shop to shop to
> enjoy the varied scene."[59]

Denunciations of the commercialization of Christmas immediately followed.
Some newspapers began to call for a "more marked observance of Christmas day."[60]
However, such warnings were not heeded. Amidst the backdrop of the second
industrial revolution and the rise of consumerism

> Christmas trees were sold on the streets of New York as early as 1840, light bulbs
> for Christmas trees first appeared in the 1880s, and glass ornaments appeared in
> the 1890s. Wrapping paper appeared at the end of the nineteenth century and
> became more colorful in the twentieth. . . . Gifts certainly have become central to
> the modern American Christmas.[61]

The popular, contemporary image of Santa Claus, which began with the miniature
St. Nick of "Twas the Night before Christmas," expanded into the full-sized modern
character with the help of Coca-Cola advertisements illustrated by Haddon Sundblom after 1931. Unlike the gaunt St. Nicholas of the fourth century, Sundblom's
Santa Claus "lost his religious authority and became a kindly, even jolly, grandfather
figure who delivered presents. . . ."[62] It was the gift-giving Santa Claus rather than the
pious Saint Nicholas that captured the merchants' idea of the true meaning of Christmas. A new and vastly more commercialized era of Christmas began "when businesses recognized the marketing possibilities associated with holidays."[63]

Over time, St. Nicholas was separated from his original feast day (December 6), christened with a mispronunciation of his Dutch name (Sinterklass), secularized and stripped of his clerical garb, fattened up, equipped with a magical sleigh pulled by flying Scandinavian reindeer, taught how to descend through chimneys with a magical touch to his nose, given a house decorated with pagan evergreens, married to a jolly Mrs. Claus, provided with a nonunion workshop at the North Pole operated by sexually ambiguous elves, and turned into a theologically incorrect but commercially triumphant competitor to Jesus Christ on the very day that had originally been set aside to celebrate the latter's birth.[64]

Even into the 1940s the nativity crèche was still associated with specifically Catholic religious traditions; but it too was about to be transferred from the sanctuary to a display in department store windows. "Display of crèches came with Catholic immigrants and has represented and continues to represent, for many Americans, a distinctively Catholic piety."[65] Yet it too, after having been desacralized and thoroughly commercialized by department stores and other business establishments, worked its way into broader popular culture.[66] The final incorporation of the distinctly Catholic into the fully American might be symbolized by the Christmas display at New York's Metropolitan Museum of Art beginning in 1957 (three years before the first Catholic was elected president):

> The annual Christmas display is the result of the generosity, enthusiasm, and dedication of the late Loretta Hines Howard, who began collecting crèche figures in 1925 and soon after conceived the idea of combining the Roman Catholic custom of elaborate Nativity scenes with the tradition of decorated Christmas trees that had developed among the largely Protestant people of northern Europe. This unusual combination first was presented to the public in 1957. . . .[67]

At the high point of the Eisenhower era, when so many quasi-religious images were being linked with religio-political symbols, the competing northern European Christmas tree and the Catholic nativity scene were finally brought together by one of the iconic secular institutions of art in America. The courts would soon be asked to sort out the sacred from the secular in this entangled history.

THE COURTS AND GOVERNMENT-SPONSORED RELIGIOUS EXPRESSION

Immediately after the 1950s, a decade characterized by its aggressive infusion of religious and quasi-religious symbolism into governmental actions, the courts were called upon to decide whether official promotion of religious activities had crossed a constitutional line.

THE COURTS AND CEREMONIAL DEISM

In 1962, Eugene V. Rostow, Dean of the Yale Law School, coined the term "ceremonial deism" as a way of describing the numerous official and quasi-official governmental invocations of God and religion that he believed fell short of government endorsement of sectarian beliefs or violations of the Establishment Clause.[68] Although the Supreme Court itself has never adopted Dean Rostow's term, the concept has been endorsed by individual justices. In a concurring opinion, Justice O'Connor wrote:

> I would suggest that such practices as the designation of 'In God We Trust' as our national motto, or the references to God contained in the Pledge of Allegiance can best be understood, in Dean Rostow's apt phrase, as a form a 'ceremonial deism,' protected from Establishment Clause scrutiny chiefly because they have lost through rote repetition any significant religious content.[69]

Justices Brennan and Stevens joined Justice O'Connor when she later wrote that:

> Practices such as legislative prayers or opening Court sessions with 'God save the United States and this honorable Court' serve the secular purposes of 'solemnizing public occasions' and 'expressing confidence in the future.' These examples of ceremonial deism do not survive Establishment Clause scrutiny simply by virtue of their historical longevity alone.[70]

Although the term "ceremonial deism" itself is not a term of art and has no legal standing, it does capture the sense of many court decisions that recognize the religious dimensions of the action at issue, but that nevertheless find that they fall short of violating the Constitution. In 1970, the federal Ninth Circuit Court of Appeals heard a case challenging the use of "In God We Trust" as the national motto and its appearance on coins, currency, and government documents. In a very short opinion that did not explore any of the factual evidence surrounding the circumstances in which the motto came into existence, the Ninth Circuit summarily held that:

> It is quite obvious that the national motto and the slogan on coinage and currency . . . has nothing whatsoever to do with the establishment of religion. Its use is of a patriotic or ceremonial character and bears no true resemblance to a governmental sponsorship of a religious exercise.[71]

The court could not find "any religious significance" or "theological or ritualistic impact" in the phrase "In God We Trust."[72] The concept has subsequently been employed to permit the use of the term "under God" in the Pledge of Allegiance,[73] the state motto "With God, All Things are Possible,"[74] the engraving of "In God We Trust" on U.S. coinage,[75] and to explain the permissibility of a wide range of similar actions.[76]

Although judges may decide cases by suggesting that they raise only questions of ceremonial deism, the strongest supporters of the symbols advocate their use precisely *because* they believe the symbols are religious. An examination of the organizations that most zealously promote "under God" in the Pledge, "In God We Trust," the Ten Commandments monuments, and prayer proclamations reveals them to be religiously inspired advocates who want to bring God, religion, and often even Christ into government; the promotion of a vague "ceremonial deism" appears nowhere on their agenda.

And yet when the constitutionality of these expressions is questioned, their defenders often argue to the courts that they are not really religious at all. One of the most extraordinary examples illustrating this denial of a religious message pertains to constitutional challenge to a painting that hung in a high school auditorium. The court described the painting at issue as follows:

> The central figure in the painting portrays a man nailed to a wooden cross. This figure is bleeding from the left side of his chest. Across his forehead are two intertwined white lines containing red highlighting which appears to be a crown of thorns. . . . Other figures in the painting include two other men nailed to crosses, a man tossing a net into the water, a woman mourning. . . .[77]

Although the ordinary observer would have no difficulty understanding that the painting depicts the crucifixion of Jesus Christ, the painting's defenders denied it. The supporters of the painting asserted, under oath, that the painting merely represented "various examples of 'man's inhumanity to man' rather than having any religious significance" and that "the painting in no way provokes religious thoughts."[78] In another case in which a public school hung reproductions of the famous Warner Sallman painting entitled "Head of Christ" outside the principal's office and the school gymnasium, its defenders argued, in the words of the court, "that the picture has meaning to all religions and that it is not inherently a symbol of Christianity."[79] Although these cases are slightly unusual in the blatancy of the defenders' denials of the obvious religious messages in the images, it is fully typical of the effort to downplay the religious message so as to keep it from being removed. Thus we frequently have the odd circumstance that there is a popular clamor for these government-sponsored expressions because they *are religious,* whereas the courts agree to permit them because they are *not religious.*

THE TEN COMMANDMENTS CASES

The first Supreme Court case regarding the display of the Ten Commandments on public property was *Stone v. Graham*.[80] In a 5-4 decision, the Court held that a Kentucky law requiring the posting of the Ten Commandments in each public school classroom in the state violated the Establishment Clause. Although the posters of the Ten Commandments were provided by private donors and state funds were not used, the Court nevertheless said that the law had an unconstitutional purpose:

The preeminent purpose for posting the Ten Commandments on schoolroom walls is plainly religious in nature. The Ten Commandments are undeniably a sacred text in the Jewish and Christian faiths, and no legislative recitation of a supposed secular purpose can blind us to that fact. The Commandments do not confine themselves to arguably secular matters, such as honoring one's parents, killing or murder, adultery, stealing, false witness, and covetousness. Rather, the first part of the Commandments concerns the religious duties of believers: worshipping the Lord God alone, avoiding idolatry, not using the Lord's name in vain, and observing the Sabbath Day.[81]

In declaring that the Ten Commandments are "plainly religious in nature" and are "undeniably a sacred text in the Jewish and Christian faiths," the Court signaled a difference from the "ceremonial deism" that had made other government actions permissible.

The Court's most detailed consideration of Ten Commandments displays came in two separate decisions that were handed down on the same day in 2005: *McCreary County v. ACLU of Kentucky* and *Van Orden v. Perry*.[82] In *McCreary*, five justices struck down a display that included the Ten Commandments in two Kentucky courthouses, whereas in *Van Orden* five justices agreed to allow a stone Ten Commandments monument, erected by a private group in 1961, to remain on the Texas State House grounds. Although there was a majority opinion of five justices in *McCreary*, the *Van Orden* case had a plurality of four justices with a separate concurring opinion written by Justice Breyer.[83] Four justices would have permitted both displays and four justices would have struck both displays. For practical purposes, only Justice Breyer saw a constitutionally significant difference between the two.

Also, unlike the "ceremonial deism" cases, in which courts have suggested that prayers and official statements about God are more civic and patriotic than religious, the justices basically agreed that the Ten Commandments are religious, although they disagreed about the significance of that fact. For four justices, the fact that the displays were religious was a basis for finding them unconstitutional (O'Connor, Stevens, Souter, Ginsburg), whereas four justices found that the monotheism and "Judeo-Christian" aspect of the displays reflected American history and traditions and was not inconsistent with the Constitution.

In *McCreary*, two Kentucky counties posted highly visible gold-framed copies of an abridgement of the Ten Commandments in their courthouses. After being challenged by the ACLU, the counties twice revised their displays by adding other documents and furnishing supposedly "secular" explanations as justifications for posting them. The Court held that when "the government acts with the ostensible and predominant purpose of advancing religion, it violates that central Establishment Clause value of official religious neutrality, there being no neutrality when the government's ostensible object is to take sides."[84] The *McCreary* Court found that the subsequent revisions of the display were a "sham" and that the two counties in fact had a "predominantly religious purpose" in promoting the displays.[85]

Dissenting in *McCreary*, Justice Scalia (joined in part by Justices Rehnquist, Thomas, and Kennedy), offered a litany of examples from the past in which political leaders and government bodies promulgated expressions favoring religion and then referred to an earlier opinion in which he "catalogued . . . the variety of circumstances in which this Court . . . has approved government action 'undertaken with the specific intention of improving the position of religion.'"[86] Although recognizing some value to the "neutrality principle" that the majority had adopted as a rationale for striking the Ten Commandments displays in Kentucky, he rejected its applicability in certain types of case. "With respect to public acknowledgment of religious belief, it is entirely clear from our Nation's historical practices that the Establishment Clause permits this disregard of polytheists and believers in unconcerned deities, just as it permits the disregard of devout atheists."[87]Thus, for Justice Scalia, although the literal text of the U.S. Constitution itself does not differentiate between believers and unbelievers or theists and polytheists, the longstanding historical practice of government actions favoring monotheism means that they have become constitutional. It is a "demonstrably false principle [to argue] that the government cannot favor religion over irreligion."[88]However, notably, it was historical practices that made this principle false, not the text of the Constitution.

In *Van Orden,* five justices, in two separate opinions, decided that a stone marker on the Texas State Capitol grounds bearing an abridged version of the Ten Commandments did not violate the Establishment Clause. According to the plurality opinion of four justices:

> The monolith challenged here stands 6-feet high and 3-feet wide. It is located to the north of the Capitol building, between the Capitol and the Supreme Court building. Its primary content is the text of the Ten Commandments. An eagle grasping the American flag, an eye inside of a pyramid, and two small tablets with what appears to be an ancient script are carved above the text of the Ten Commandments. Below the text are two Stars of David and the superimposed Greek letters Chi and Rho, which represent Christ. The bottom of the monument bears the inscription "PRESENTED TO THE PEOPLE AND YOUTH OF TEXAS BY THE FRATERNAL ORDER OF EAGLES OF TEXAS 1961."[89]

The 22 acres of the Texas State Capitol grounds contained 17 monuments and 21 historical markers commemorating events from Texas and American history. Like the majority in *McCreary,* the *Van Orden* plurality recognized that "of course" the monument pertained to religion.

> Of course, the Ten Commandments are religious—they were so viewed at their inception and so remain. The monument, therefore, has religious significance. According to Judeo-Christian belief, the Ten Commandments were given to Moses by God on Mt. Sinai.[90]

However, unlike the majority in *McCreary,* a case that was decided that same day, the *Van Orden* plurality (who were also the *McCreary* dissenters) noted that

> Moses was a lawgiver as well as a religious leader. And the Ten Commandments have an undeniable historical meaning, as the foregoing examples demonstrate. Simply having religious content or promoting a message consistent with a religious doctrine does not run afoul of the Establishment Clause.[91]

The plurality appears to be suggesting that the impetus to erect these monuments was to honor history and a famous lawgiver, as if it were coincidental that they contain a message that is "consistent with a religious doctrine. . . ." Visitors to the websites of many of the strongest proponents of the Ten Commandments monuments will quickly recognize that the monuments are being promoted *because* they are sacred religious messages—God's law—and not because they are historical reminders that happen to be "consistent" with religion, as the plurality suggests.[92]

Justice Breyer's controlling decision, which was joined by no other justice, discussed both the religious and the secular aspects of the monument, and found that the organization that was largely responsible for erecting it, the Fraternal Order of Eagles, had principally "ethics-based motives."[93] After considering this background, Justice Breyer seized upon what he called the "determinative" factor:[94]

> As far as I can tell, 40 years passed in which the presence of this monument, legally speaking, went unchallenged (until the single legal objection raised by petitioner). And I am not aware of any evidence suggesting that this was due to a climate of intimidation. Hence, those 40 years suggest more strongly than can any set of formulaic tests that few individuals, whatever their system of beliefs, are likely to have understood the monument as amounting, in any significantly detrimental way, to a government effort to favor a particular religious sect, primarily to promote religion over nonreligion, to "engage in" any "religious practic[e]," to "compel" any "religious practic[e]," or to "work deterrence" of any "religious belief." Those 40 years suggest that the public visiting the capitol grounds has considered the religious aspect of the tablets' message as part of what is a broader moral and historical message reflective of a cultural heritage.[95]

Thus it appears that for Justice Breyer, in a case in which there may be mixed religious and nonreligious elements underlying the case, the "determinative" factor is that because the monument had gone unchallenged for 40 years, "few individuals" would have understood the monument to be favoring any religious sect or religion over nonreligion. This analysis, which persuaded no other justice, became the law of the land in June 2005.

The Law of Holiday Displays

The U.S. Supreme Court has twice directly addressed the constitutionality of Christmas displays. The first case, *Lynch v. Donnelly,* was decided in 1984, and arose in Pawtucket, Rhode Island, 3 miles north of Providence. The Court's opening description of the display beautifully, if unintentionally, illustrates the mixture of religious, American, and commercialized Christmas themes described in the preceding. Just as John Gibson lumped together the sacred, pagan, secular, and popular, so too the Court sees a menagerie of figures.

> Each year, in cooperation with the downtown retail merchants' association, the city of Pawtucket, R.I., erects a Christmas display as part of its observance of the Christmas holiday season. . . . The Pawtucket display comprises many of the figures and decorations traditionally associated with Christmas, including, among other things, a Santa Claus house, reindeer pulling Santa's sleigh, candy-striped poles, a Christmas tree, carolers, cutout figures representing such characters as a clown, an elephant, and a teddy bear, hundreds of colored lights, a large banner that reads 'SEASONS GREETINGS,' and the crèche at issue here.[96]

The Pawtucket Christmas display was jointly sponsored by the local government and the local merchants, rather than local churches or religious leaders. Although the display was on private property—which otherwise would have immunized it against an Establishment Clause challenge—the various figures in the display were purchased with taxpayer dollars and thus raised the question whether the display was promoting government-sponsored religion.

Chief Justice Burger, writing for a five-justice majority, does not begin by subjecting the facts of the case to a serious doctrinal analysis of whether the display is the equivalent of a law establishing a religion in violation of the First Amendment, but instead offers a litany of examples from American history in which government officials and government institutions have promoted or acknowledged religion. He begins with legislative prayers, and follows with Justice Douglas' assertion that "We are a religious people whose institutions presuppose a Supreme Being." He mentions in turn Thanksgiving celebrations, and thanksgiving proclamations, the motto "In God We Trust," and the National Gallery of Art's display of religious paintings. Thus, Chief Justice Burger pursues the strategy seen in Scalia's *McCreary* dissent of judging an act's constitutionality by an accretion of practices.

The Court then turns to the tripartite *Lemon* purpose-effect-entanglement test, beginning with the question of whether Pawtucket had a secular purpose in creating the display. The lower court is first criticized for having "plainly erred" in "focusing almost exclusively on the crèche."[97] Although such an error might have been understandable in that it was the crèche and not the candy cane figures that were under challenge, the Court held instead that the crèche must be "viewed in the proper context of the Christmas Holiday season . . . "[capitalization in original].[98] The Court did not find that the inclusion of the crèche expressed "some kind of subtle governmental advocacy of a particular religious message."[99] Rather, the City of Pawtucket had "principally taken note of a significant historical religious event long celebrated in the Western World. The crèche in the display depicts the historical origins of this traditional event long recognized as a National Holiday."[100] (Without offering any evidence, the Court later decided that the display "engenders a friendly community spirit of goodwill in keeping with the season.")[101] The Court thereupon concluded that the recognition of this historical event was a sufficiently "secular purpose" to pass constitutional muster.[102]

This observation by the *Lynch* Court about the "significant historical religious event" commemorated by the crèche must surely be one of the Court's most curious statements in its entire corpus of religion cases. The role of the crèche, which had remained contested and controversial within Christendom from the time of the Reformation until the 1950s in America, as shown in the preceding, was suddenly transformed by the court into a self-evident historical fact. Whether Jesus was in fact laid in a manger following his miraculous birth and whether wise men were led by a star to visit this sacred nativity scene is most decidedly not a verifiable "historical religious event," but a profoundly contested matter of religious faith.

In turning to the question of whether the Pawtucket display had the unconstitutional "primary effect" of advancing religion, the Court again failed to pose the question of how much aid might be permissible, and instead sought out examples in which aid had previously been provided to religion while asking whether the Pawtucket case provided "more" aid than had previously been found permissible. After surveying other instances, the Court concluded that it was "unable to discern a greater aid to religion deriving from inclusion of the crèche than from the benefits and endorsements previously held not violative of the Establishment Clause."[103] For the final prong of the *Lemon* test, the Court accepted the finding of the lower court that there was an absence of impermissible entanglements.

In previous Establishment Clause cases, most famously in the preceding year's *Marsh v. Chambers*,[104] the Court had looked to historical examples of the practice being used as a guide to help determine whether the practice before it could be justified. In *Marsh*, for example, it had found a tradition of legislative prayer going back to the First Congress in 1789 to be an important indication that the practice in question was both widely accepted and historically uncontroversial. Had the Court looked to the historical use of the crèche in *Lynch*, as described in the preceding section, it would have found that the crèche had in fact been controversial in American history and that it had only recently been incorporated into a sentimentalized and commercialized popular culture. Rather than seriously looking at "history," which it purported to undertake in finding the birth of Jesus to be a recognized historical event, the Court accepted Pawtucket's "goodwill" display of Christmas trees, commercialism, Santa Claus, carolers, candy canes, and crèches. Although the Court's decision might be heartening to proponents of a sentimentalized postwar American culture, it should be deeply disturbing to anyone who takes either their Christianity or their history very seriously.

In its second Christmas holiday display case, *County of Allegheny v. ACLU of Pittsburgh*,[105] the Court's analysis was both more sophisticated and more fractured than in *Lynch v. Donnelly*. The justices published six separate opinions regarding the permissibility of the two religious displays at issue. The first of the two symbols was a crèche that was prominently placed on the Grand Staircase inside the Allegheny County Courthouse, and that bore a sign identifying the crèche as having been donated by the Catholic Holy Name Society along with a crest bearing the legend "Gloria in Exelsis Deo" (Glory to God in the Highest). Aside from the sign, flowers, and a small fence surrounding the crèche, there were no competing or commercial symbols as had been the case in *Lynch*. The setting in the Courthouse was used for an annual Christmas carol program in which local high school choirs were invited to attend and perform. Near the grand staircase was the "gallery forum," which was used for artistic and other cultural exhibits.

The second contested display, an 18-foot high Jewish Chanukah menorah, was erected a block away at the City-County Building and was placed next to a 45-foot Christmas tree and alongside a sign advertising the city's "salute to liberty." The menorah was owned by Chabad, a Jewish group, but was stored and maintained by the city. Unlike *Lynch,* the religious symbols were displayed on government and not private property; also contrasting with *Lynch,* the religious symbols were not purchased by the government (although the government maintained them).

In December 1986, 2 years after the Supreme Court handed down the *Lynch v. Donnelly* decision, several citizens, in conjunction with the local ACLU, filed suit. In brief, and with conflicting rationales, a divided majority of the Supreme Court ultimately found that the prominent display of the crèche violated the Establishment Clause, whereas the menorah, in a less prominent position and in the company of a Christmas tree, was found not to be unconstitutional. With competing rationales, three justices (Brennan, Marshall, and Stevens) would have found both displays to be unconstitutional, four justices (Chief Justice Rehnquist, White, Scalia, and Kennedy) would have found both displays to be constitutional, and two justices (Blackmun and O'Connor) found the crèche display to be unconstitutional and the menorah to be constitutional.

The reasons for the outcome can be summarized as follows, although it should be remembered that the justices disagreed among themselves. The crèche was singled out for display in a particularly prominent place and was not surrounded by other seasonal messages. It also conveyed a particularly religious message, being inextricably associated with the birth of the founder of the Christian religion. The menorah, however, communicated less of a particularized religious message and was associated less with the doctrines of the Jewish religion and more with a cultural holiday associated with Jews. In addition, the menorah was part of a larger seasonal and religious display that did not promote a single religion to the exclusion of others.

There have been several important lower court decisions that are not entirely consistent with each other.[106] It can be said, however, that as a general rule of thumb the following two doctrines pertaining to holiday displays are likely to prevail, although the constitutional merits of the arguments are in sharp dispute and will likely continue to be contested.

First, the government may not finance, erect, display, or endorse stand-alone religious displays that suggest that the government is promoting particular religious doctrines and beliefs.

Second, religious displays on government property are most likely to be found constitutional when they are financed by private groups, are part of larger displays that include a variety of religious and cultural beliefs, and when observers are unlikely to mistake the display for government approval of a particular religious belief.

THE LAW OF "PRIVATE" RELIGIOUS EXPRESSION IN PUBLIC

From the perspective of public conflicts over religion in the public square, perhaps the least polemical area pertains to religious expression and religious symbols by private individuals and associations; but saying "the least polemical" does not mean that the subject is without controversy or that the law is completely clear. The topic of "private" religious expression can be divided into two general areas. First, there is religious expression that is temporary in nature, such as a speech, a parade, or posters that might be carried during a march. The second involves the erection of a religious display that, although not permanent, may be visible for several days or weeks. The first area, and the more typical, will be treated in this section; the second further on.

The Free Exercise and Free Speech Clauses of the Constitution provide broad protections for religious expression. There are, however, different standards that apply, depending on the particular forum in which the expression is made.

First, with regard to private (i.e., nongovernmental) property, such as the grounds of a church or a store that is owned by those wishing to manifest their religion, the First Amendment provides the greatest extent of free expression that the owners of the land and the Constitution otherwise allow. The First Amendment provides a full range of protections for private religious and commercial speech. Stores may freely display holiday decorations and churches may advertise their religious services. For practical purposes, the only limitations on religious speech or the erection of displays or monuments come from zoning laws and tax laws.[107] A church is free to erect a cross on a steeple and synagogues may place a menorah on an exterior wall so long as they comply with general, content-neutral land use and zoning restrictions. Under the Religious Land Use and Institutionalized Persons Act (RLUIPA), government bodies may not impose land-use restrictions on individuals or entities if those restrictions impose a "substantial burden" on the free-exercise of religion, unless the government is able to prove that the restriction was in furtherance of a "compelling government interest" and that it was the "least restrictive means" of furthering that compelling interest.[108] Finally, the Internal Revenue Code requires that all nonprofit organizations, including churches, that wish to qualify for tax-exempt status comply with tax laws prohibiting partisan political activity or a substantial amount of lobbying.[109]

Second, with regard to government property such as public sidewalks, public streets, and government-owned parks—land that has historically been open to the free exchange of ideas and is described as "a traditional public forum"—free expression is broadly protected. Government officials may exclude speakers from such locations based on the content of their speech "only when the exclusion is necessary to serve a compelling state interest and the exclusion is narrowly drawn to achieve that interest."[110] "The state may also enforce regulations of the time, place, and manner of expression which are content-neutral, are narrowly tailored to serve a significant government interest, and leave open ample alternative channels of communication."[111] Thus, government officials may decide, for example, that speech must take place only during daylight hours and that audio amplification is not allowed. These restrictions, however, must be uniformly applied and cannot single out disfavored messages for restriction. Further, in 1995, the Supreme Court expressly clarified that the First Amendment does not permit, and the Establishment Clause does not require, private religious speech to be excluded from such traditional public forum because it is religious.[112]

Third, in some contexts, the government invites private entities to speak on government property for limited purposes. A public school, for example, may decide to open its classrooms during after-school hours to private groups that offer educational opportunities for children; or a public library may allow groups to use certain spaces for community meetings. As is not the case in a traditional public forum, the government may broadly exclude private speech from these spaces, which are sometimes referred to as a "limited public forum"; and it may constitutionally open such spaces only for speech with particular "content" or "subject-matter."[113] The government may not, however, restrict the "viewpoint" of private speech on this type of government property.[114] For example, the school may restrict use of its classrooms to "educational" programs for children, but it may not then exclude educational programs because they are led by religious groups or educate from a religious perspective.[115] Similarly, if the government opens an auditorium to political debate, it may not permit Democrats but deny Republicans access.

Conclusion

As explained in the Introduction, two of the important and distinct meanings of the word *public* in the phrase "religion in the public square" are first, "open" and "visible" and second, "governmental" and "official." Whereas the First Amendment broadly protects the rights of individuals and groups to express and manifest religion in the open and in public, it nevertheless contains limitations on the power of the government to promote religion (or irreligion) or to favor, subsidize, or endorse some religious doctrines or religion in general. To avoid confusion and unnecessary polemics, it is important to keep these different aspects of "public" with their different constitutional implications clear and distinct. The protections for religious expression by individuals and the general public are broad and generally respected. The question of the role of the government in promoting religion, however, is highly contested.

Although religious and quasireligious symbolism and language have been part of American history from its beginnings, they also have been controversial since the founding of the United States of America in 1789. In keeping with the principle of religious freedom enshrined in the First Amendment, the drafters of the Constitution and those who immediately followed them largely eschewed governmental use of religious symbolism and language in favor of a more universal and inclusive public language. As shown, a closer examination of the historical origins of these developments, as well as of Christmas and other holiday displays, reveals that their origins are at once much more recent and far less pious than their supporters often imagine.

Since the 1950s, American courts generally have been protective of religious expression in public, although they have allowed restrictions on religiously motivated behavior. However, the record of courts with regard to government-promoted religious and quasireligious expression has been far less clear. Although advocates of government-supported religious expression promote it *because* they favor such religious expressions, courts have more typically either disapproved of it on constitutional grounds or have suggested that it is permissible because it is not really religious and is something akin to "ceremonial deism." Even more distressingly, the Supreme Court has at times adopted an ahistorical view of government-sponsored religious displays that assumes their roots are both much wider and much deeper than they actually are. A better understanding of the history of these displays might guide the Court toward a more coherent Establishment Clause jurisprudence.

ENDNOTES

1. Richard John Neuhaus, *The Naked Public Square* (Grand Rapids, MI: William B. Eerdmans Publishing Company, 1984). Neuhaus was a Lutheran priest who subsequently converted to Roman Catholicism. He argued that religious discourse was increasingly being excluded from the "public square" by secular elitists and intellectuals.
2. There are many examples of such language being used:

"Since 1947 and *Everson* v. *Board of Education*, the Supreme Court has—with a few recent exceptions—sought to purge religion from the public square." Lee J. Strang, "The *Lemon* Cliffs of *Dover*," *National Review Online*, Dec. 21, 2005, http://www.nationalreview.com/comment/strang200512211205.asp.

The "modern-day civil libertarians have, in many ways, gained the momentum in the effort to purge religion from the public square." Jerry Falwell, "Diversity in Education . . . For All But Those in Religious Studies," newxmax.com, Mar. 05, 2004, http://archive.newsmax.com/archives/articles/2004/3/5/151230.shtml.

"Americans are tired of special-interest groups like the ACLU profiting from their efforts to purge religion from the public square." Senator Sam Brownback, as quoted in The American Legion, *In the Footsteps of the Founders: A Guide to Defending American Values* (Indianapolis, IN [2007]), 4.

"For more than 50 years, the ACLU and other radical activist groups have attempted to eliminate public expression of our nation's faith and heritage."

Alliance Defense Fund, http://www.alliancedefensefund.org/issues/ReligiousFree-dom/Default.aspx.

"[C]ourts and bureaucrats often rule that religion belongs entirely in private and so should be purged from public life." http://www.becketfund.org/index. php/topic/2.html?PHPSESSID=e81144f5966a274fae0208e32a10d2f9.

3. *Van Orden v. Perry,* 545 U.S. 677 (2005), 699 (Breyer, J., concurring).

4. Ibid.

5. Barack Obama, speech at Eastside Community Church in Zanesville, Ohio, July 1, 2008.

6. Eboo Patel, "Religious Pluralism in the Public Square," in *Debating the Divine: Religion in 21st Century American Democracy,* ed. Sally Steenland (Washington, DC: Center for American Democracy, 2008), 18.

7. Ibid.

8. Among the three best known denouncers of religion (two of whom are British) are Christopher Hitchens, *God is Not Great: How Religion Poisons Everything* (New York: Twelve/Warner Books, 2007), Richard Dawkins, *The God Delusion* (New York: Bantam Press, 2006), and Sam Harris, *The End of Faith: Religion, Terror, and the Future of Reason* (New York: W.W. Norton & Company, 2005). To the extent that leading politicians cite these books and authors it is for the purpose of denouncing them and warning of their supposed influence.

9. "Public transportation" might mean that anyone is free to ride who is willing to pay the fare, but it could also refer to a bus system that is owned by a municipality. Both Greyhound Lines, Inc. and the Washington Metropolitan Transport Authority provide "public transportation," but one is a private corporation and the other is publicly owned. These distinct and potentially confusing meanings can be seen when the terms are juxtaposed. For example, Exxon-Mobil is a *public* (visible) corporation that is *privately* owned by shareholders at the same time that it is a *"public* corporation" whose shares can be purchased by the general *public,* each of whom is a *private* person. The shares of Exxon-Mobil are listed on the *privately* owned New York Stock Exchange that is the *public* face of the American *private*-enterprise system.

10. See examples listed in note 2.

11. For example, the document "ACLU Defense of Freedom of Religious Practice and Expression" identifies dozens of its cases brought on behalf of people seeking to manifest their religion in public.

12. In 1876, the Reverend Dr. Samuel T. Spear, a Presbyterian clergyman and legal scholar, published a 400-page book entitled *Religion and the State.* Many of the subjects covered in Spear's book, which examined the legal aspects of church–state controversies of the day, are familiar to Americans in the twenty-first century: the role of public schools, the meaning of "secular" education, the role of state constitutions, chaplains in the military, and presidential proclamations of thanksgiving and prayer. Subjects that are conspicuously absent from the nineteenth-century treatise, however, concern the extent to which the government should be able to promote religious symbols and monuments (such as Ten Commandments displays and crèches) and whether the government should be involved in promoting religious expressions such as "In God We Trust" on currency or "one nation under God" in the Pledge of Allegiance.

13. Derek H. Davis, *Religion and the Continental Congress 1774–1789: Contributions to Original Intent* (Oxford, UK: Oxford University Press, 2000), 83–84; W. De Loss Love, Jr., *The Fast and Thanksgiving Days of New England* (Boston: Houghton, Mifflin & Co., 1895).

14. Davis, *Religion and the Continental Congress*, 84–89.

15. James H. Hutson, *Religion and the Founding of the American Republic* (Washington, DC: Library of Congress, 1998), 85, 93.

16. Ibid. James Madison's "Memorial and Remonstrance" (1785) suggests that when politics and religion mix, it tends to encourage politicians to engage in activities that imply their piety.

17. Davis, *Religion and the Continental Congress*, 73–76.

18. Ibid., 80–83.

19. *Marsh v. Chambers*, 463 U.S. 783 (1983). The Supreme Court has not explicitly decided the questions whether "sectarian" prayers are permissible or whether non-legislative bodies (such as school boards and county commissions) may conduct prayers. Although these questions have resulted in conflicting decisions in lower courts, the majority of cases have found both practices to be unconstitutional.

20. Davis, *Religion and the Continental Congress*, 137–143.

21. Ibid., 144.

22. Ibid.

23. The all-seeing eye (though not in a pyramid) was a symbol from Freemasonry, where it referred to the Great Architect rather than the God of Abraham, and the image itself dates to ancient Egypt.

24. The odd duck on the Washington Mall, the neo-Gothic "Smithsonian Castle," was completed in 1855 and was designed by the same architect, James Renwick, Jr., who built St. Patrick's Cathedral in New York City.

25. The term "culture wars" was given life immediately after the collapse of the Soviet Union in 1991 by Professor James Davison Hunter in his book *Culture Wars: The Struggle to Define America* (New York: Basic Books, 1991) and the famous speech of erstwhile presidential candidate Pat Buchanan in 1992 when he declared on August 17, 1992, at the Republican National Convention: "There is a religious war going on in our country for the soul of America. It is a cultural war, as critical to the kind of nation we will one day be as was the Cold War itself."

26. See T. Jeremy Gunn, *Spiritual Weapons: The Cold War and the Forging of an American National Religion* (New York: Praeger, 2009).

27. They are now called National Prayer Breakfasts. For background information on the sponsoring organization, see Jeff Sharlet, *The Family: The Secret Fundamentalism at the Heart of American Power* (New York: Harpers, 2008).

28. *Zorach v. Clauson*, 343 U.S. 306 (1952), 313. There are two other frequently cited cases in which the U.S. Supreme Court made statements about the religious character of the American people. During the nineteenth century, the Court once referred to the United States as a "Christian country," *Vidal v. Girard's Executors*, 43 U.S. 127 (1844), 198, and once as a "Christian nation." *Holy Trinity Church v. United States*, 143 U.S. 457 (1892), 471. In the case *United States v. Macintosh*, 283 U.S. 605 (1931), 625, the Supreme Court cited *Holy Trinity* in support of the proposition that Americans are a "Christian people" in a case denying citizenship to an otherwise qualified immigrant who had religious scruples against taking up arms in the military.

These and similar quotations are sometimes cited as if they are scriptures that are themselves *proof* that the United States was founded on religious (or even explicitly Christian) principles. For those who use these quotations in such a way, the fact that "Washington said it" or the "Supreme Court said it" means that "it must be true." Those who use such quotations as "proof texts" do not, of course, accept counter-examples. The lists of quotations and governmental actions favoring religion typically are offered without placing the evidence in its rich historical context and without providing the telling counter-examples that show the American story to be far more complicated and nuanced than is wished. One semiofficial example of using quotations as "proof" of the underlying proposition is the 2007 proposed congressional resolution entitled: *Affirming the rich spiritual and religious history of our Nation's founding and subsequent history and expressing support for designation of the first week in May as 'American Religious History Week' for the appreciation of and education on America's history of religious faith,* 110th Cong., 1st sess., H.R. 888, which provides the now-typical litany of official and quasiofficial declarations about God and religion in American history. A leading writer, though unreliable from a scholarly perspective, is David Barton, *The Myth of Separation: What Is the Correct Relationship Between Church and State* (Aledo, TX: WallBuilder Press, 1989).

29. As discussed, the phrase was first placed on a two-cent coin during the Civil War. It was gradually added to many coins thereafter, albeit not without controversy. It first appeared on paper money in 1957, following the enactment of the law 2 years earlier. The Star-Spangled Banner, written in 1812, is sometimes credited with originating a variation of the phrase in the lyric: "and this be our motto, in God is our trust."

30. The room includes a depiction of General George Washington praying at Valley Forge, thereby incorporating into official iconography the spurious story that Parson Weems added to his biography of Washington.

31. Although the term "Judeo-Christian" had been in existence for several years, it was not until the 1950s that it began to be used as a generic term to identify the perceived religio-political foundations of the United States. Mark Silk, "Notes on the Judeo-Christian Tradition in America," *American Quarterly* 36 (Spring, 1984): 65–85.

32. Among the rare cases of a Ten Commandments monument from before the 1950s involved the posting of a brass Ten Commandments plaque on the exterior wall of the Chester County Courthouse (Pennsylvania) in the 1920s. The text quoted was from the entire King James version of the Bible (from Exodus and Deuteronomy) and also included a "summary" that was drawn from Matthew 22:37, 39. Although the District Court struck down the plaque as a violation of the Establishment Clause, the Third Circuit reversed and allowed the brass plaque to remain. *Freethought Society of Greater Philadelphia v. Chester County,* 334 F.3d 247 (3d. Cir. 2003). Another case, *Modrovich v. Allegheny County,* 385 F.3d 397 (3d Cir. 2004), similarly involved a Ten Commandments plaque that had been attached to a courthouse wall since 1918. For a discussion of the Ten Commandments cases, see the following.

33. *The New York Times,* Jan. 28, 1951. In addition, in May 1950, Rabbi Alexander Burnstein proposed at an interfaith breakfast in New York City that nations, and not just individuals, should obey the Ten Commandments. *The New York Times,* May 1, 1950. A few months later, yet another rabbi "described the Decalogue as the foundation of modern civilization." *The New York Times,* June 11, 1951.

34. *The New York Times,* May 18, 1952.

35. For a discussion of the text of the Eagles version in comparison with other versions of the Ten Commandments, see Paul Finkelman, "The Ten Commandments on the Courthouse Lawn and Elsewhere," *Fordham Law Review* 73 (2005): 1477.

36. *The New York Times* bureau chief in Los Angeles described DeMille as "a cultivated and ultra-conservative combination of dramatic impresario and business man, with an array of outside financial interests. . . ." *The New York Times,* Aug. 12, 1956.

37. Although the exact number of Eagles monuments is not known, it is probably in excess of 200—although some have asserted that as many as 2,000 were erected.

38. John Gibson, *The War on Christmas* (New York: Sentinel, 2005), xviii.

39. Forbes, "Christmas Was Not Always Like This," 400, 401.

40. Ibid., 401.

41. Ibid., 402. See also Forbes, *Christmas: A Candid History*, 29–30 and Sullivan, *Paying the Words Extra*, 141–143.

42. Restad, *Christmas in America*, 57.

43. Ibid., 58.

44. Forbes, "Christmas Was Not Always Like This," 404. In modern-day Netherlands and Belgium, the popular Sinterklaas—who is dressed in clerical red robes and who wears a bishop's miter—rides on a white horse on the eve of his feast day and delivers presents to good children.

45. Ibid., 402.

46. Ibid., 403.

47. Restad, *Christmas in America*, 14. See also Winnifred Fallers Sullivan, *Paying the Words Extra: Religious Discourse in the Supreme Court of the United States* (Cambridge, MA: Harvard University Press, 1994), 93.

48. "Finally in 1681, Massachusetts issued a repeal. . . . Still, in 1686, Puritan militants barred newly appointed English Governor Andros from holding his Christmas services in their meeting house and forced him to move to the Boston Town Hall." Restad, *Christmas in America*, 14.

49. Restad, 29 ff.

50. Ibid., 31–32. Justice William Brennan quoted Beecher in his dissent in *Lynch v. Donnelly*.

51. Ibid., 17.

52. Ibid., 62.

53. Ibid., 58. "At least some Christians had been bringing trees into their homes since the Reformation. However, not until the seventeenth century is there any record of trimming the Christmas evergreens. A diarist in Strasbourg wrote about Christmas in 1605: 'they set up fir-trees in the parlours. . .and hang thereon roses cut out of many-coloured paper, apples, wafers, gold foil, sweets, &c.' By the first decades of the nineteenth century, German Protestants had taken the tree as an emblem of their faith. German Catholics, inspired by Francis of Assisi, had already adopted the *Krippe,* or holy manger, as an icon distinctly theirs." Ibid. The Christmas tree was introduced to America in the early nineteenth century by German immigrants to Pennsylvania (wrongly called "Dutch" rather than "Deutsch"). Ibid. However, during these early years non-German Americans associated the tree with the German ethnic group more than with the holiday itself. Ibid., 59. The tree began to spread throughout the country after the 1830s and 40s. Ibid., 59–60. But it was not universally accepted as a neutral symbol. Calvinists, for example, objected to them. Ibid., 61. One of the earliest tree-selling ventures was in 1840 when a farmer's wife from Monmouth County, New Jersey packed a bundle of pine greens along hogs and chickens to sell in New York City. The *New York Tribune* carried advertisements for Christmas trees and decorations as early as 1843. Ibid., 63.

54. *A Christmas Carol* "became popular in American soon after its publication and has remained popular to the present, making it the most widely read literary statement on Christian charity." William B. Waits, *The Modern Christmas in America: A Cultural History of Gift Giving* (New York: New York University Press, 1993), 164, 249 n. 2.

55. Although "Jesus" and "Christ" do not appear in *A Christmas Carol*, the word "God" appears frequently, although typically in exclamations such as "God knows," "Oh God," "God love it," and "God forbid," with the principal positive invocation being Tiny Tim's wish that "God bless us, every one."

56. There is a controversy about authorship, though Clement Clarke Moore is generally credited. See Forbes, *Christmas: A Candid History,* 84.

57. The same could be said for the most popular ballet associated with Christmas, *The Nutcracker* (1892), which is set on a Christmas eve and is replete with dancing fairies, dolls that come to life, and animals that are able to communicate with humans.

58. Forbes, "Christmas Was Not Always Like This," 403.

59. Restad, *Christmas in America,* 33–34, 180 n. 10 quoting "Stranger's Account," in Horatio Smith, *Festivals, Games and Amusements* (New York, 1831).

60. Ibid., 34.

61. Forbes, "Christmas Was Not Always Like This," 405.

62. Forbes, *Christmas: A Candid History,* 93.

63. Forbes, "Christmas Was Not Always Like This," 405. For a critique of the commercial aspects of Christmas, see *Christmas Unwrapped: Consumerism, Christ, and Culture,* ed. Richard Horsley and James Tracy (Harrisburg, PA: Trinity Press International, 2001) and Waits, *The Modern Christmas in America.* The popular holiday film "The Miracle on 34th Street" appeared in 1947, which included a scene in which the U.S. Postal Service officially recognized Kris Kringle as the "one and only true Santa Claus" who, conveniently enough, was an employee of Macy's Department Store.

64. Before the Surgeon General warned of the health risks of tobacco, the grandfatherly Santa Claus smoked a pipe.

65. Sullivan, *Paying the Words Extra,* 144–145.

66. Ibid., 149.

67. http://www.metmuseum.org/press_room/full_release.asp?prid={A345B35B-88DF-11D6-942D-00902786BF44} (June 3, 2002).

68. See Steven B. Epstein, "Rethinking the Constitutionality of Ceremonial Deism," *Columbia Law Review* 96 (1996): 2083–2174.

69. *Lynch v. Donnelly,* 465 U.S. 668 (1984), 716 (O'Connor, J., concurring) (citations omitted).

70. *County of Allegheny v. ACLU of Greater Pittsburgh,* 492 U.S. 573 (1989), 630 (O'Connor, J., concurring).

71. *Aronow v. United States,* 432 F.2d 242 (9th Cir. 1970), 243. Although the lower court held that the pro se plaintiff did not have standing as a taxpayer to bring the suit, the Ninth Circuit decided to set aside the question of standing so as to reach the merits.

72. Ibid.

73. *Sherman v. Community Consolidated School District,* 980 F.2d 437(7th Cir. 1992), 445 ("ceremonial references" and "ceremonial invocations"), cert. denied, 508 U.S. 950 (1993).

74. "The motto is merely a broadly worded expression of a religious/philosophical sentiment that happens to be widely shared by the citizens of Ohio. As such, we believe, the motto fits comfortably within this country's long and deeply entrenched tradition of civic piety, or 'ceremonial deism,' as Yale Law School's Eugene Rostow called it." *ACLU of Ohio v. Capitol Square Review and Advisory Board,* 243 F.3d 289 (6th Cir. 2001), 299–300.

75. *Gaylor v. United States,* 74 F.3d 214 (10th Cir. 1996).

76. Without using the term "ceremonial deism" per se, Justice Brennan developed the concept in his concurring opinion in *Schempp.*

[T]he use of the motto 'In God We Trust' on currency, on documents and public buildings and the like may not offend the clause. It is not that the use of those four words can be dismissed as 'de minimis'—for I suspect there would be intense opposition to the abandonment of that motto. The truth is that we have simply interwoven the motto so deeply into the fabric of our civil polity that its present use may well not present that type of involvement which the First Amendment prohibits.

This general principle might also serve to insulate the various patriotic exercises and activities used in the public schools and elsewhere which, whatever may have been their origins, no longer have a religious purpose or meaning. The reference to divinity in the revised pledge of allegiance, for example, may merely recognize the historical fact that our Nation was believed to have been founded 'under God.' Thus reciting the pledge may be no more of a religious exercise than the reading aloud of Lincoln's Gettysburg Address, which contains an allusion to the same historical fact.

Abington Township v. Schempp, 374 U.S. 203 (1963), 303–304 (Brennan, J., concurring).

77. *Joki v. Board of Educ. of Schuylerville Cent. School Dist.*, 745 F. Supp 823(N.D.N.Y.,1990), 824–825 (citations omitted).

78. *Joki*, 745 F.Supp. at 825. The District Court found otherwise.

79. *Washegesic v. Bloomingdale Public Schools*, 33 F.3d 679 (6th Cir. 1994), 684. The Court of Appeals rejected the assertion that the painting did not promote Christianity.

80. *Stone v. Graham*, 449 U.S. 39 (1980). The Supreme Court took the somewhat unusual step of issuing a *per curiam* opinion on the petition for a writ of certiorari rather than granting certiorari and receiving a full briefing and oral argument. Some of the dissenters believed that certiorari should have been granted and there should have been a full consideration of the matter.

81. 449 U.S. at 41–42 (citations omitted).

82. *McCreary County v. ACLU of Kentucky*, 545 U.S. 844 (2005) and *Van Orden v. Perry*, 545 U.S. 677 (2005).

83. Under Supreme Court law and practice, the opinion of Justice Breyer, because it provides the narrowest basis for the judgment, is controlling.

84. *McCreary*, 545 U.S. at 890.

85. *McCreary*, 545 U.S. at 859.

86. *McCreary*, 545 U.S. at 891 (Scalia, J., dissenting).

87. *McCreary*, 545 U.S. at 893 (Scalia, J., dissenting).

88. Ibid.

89. *Van Orden*, 545 U.S. at 681–682.

90. *Van Orden*, 545 U.S. at 690.

91. Ibid.

92. In a separate concurring opinion, Justice Scalia stated: "I would prefer to reach the same result by adopting an Establishment Clause jurisprudence that is in accord with our Nation's past and present practices, and that can be consistently applied—the central relevant feature of which is that there is nothing unconstitutional in a State's favoring religion generally, honoring God through public prayer and acknowledgment, or, in a non-proselytizing manner, venerating the Ten Commandments." *Van Orden*, 545 U.S. at 692 (Scalia, J., concurring).

93. *Van Orden*, 545 U.S. at 701 (Breyer, J., concurring).

94. *Van Orden*, 545 U.S. at 702 (Breyer, J., concurring).

95. *Van Orden*, 545 U.S. at 678–679 (Breyer, J., concurring) (citing concurrence of Justice Goldberg in *Schemmp*, 374 U.S. at 305).

96. *Lynch v. Donnelly,* 465 U.S. 668 (1984), 671. The Court found that the crèche had been included in the display for 40 or more years, which suggests that it was added only in the mid-1940s. Ibid.

97. *Lynch,* 465 U.S. 680.

98. Ibid.

99. Ibid.

100. Ibid.

101. *Lynch,* 465 U.S. at 668.

102. *Lynch,* 465 U.S. at 681.

103. *Lynch,* 465 U.S. at 682.

104. 463 U.S. 783 (1983).

105. 492 U.S. 573 (1989).

106. *Skoros v. New York,* 437 F.3d 1 (2d Cir. 2006) (permitting New York's Department of Education to display secular and cultural holiday symbols such as stars, menorahs, and Christmas trees but not crèches or nativity scenes); *Knights of Columbus v. Lexington,* 272 F.3d 25 (1st Cir. 2001) (upholding a town regulation that prevented a Catholic fraternal organization from erecting a crèche on an historic battleground site during the holiday season); *Wells v. Denver,* 257 F.3d 1132 (10th Cir. 2001) (refusing to allow plaintiff to include a so-called "Winter Solstice" sign, stating that Jesus was a myth and the government should not endorse Christianity, in a city holiday display erected on the steps of its City and County Building that included a crèche, a Happy Holidays sign, and Christmas decorations); *ACLU v. Schundler,* 168 F.3d 92 (3d Cir. 1999) (permitting the city to maintain, on the city hall's plaza, a holiday display containing a crèche, menorah, Christmas tree, and Kwanzaa symbols, as well as a banner announcing celebration of the city residents' diverse cultural and ethnic heritages); *Warren v. Fairfax County,* 196 F.3d 186 (4th Cir. 1999) (overturning the County's refusal to allow nonresident to erect a Christmas display on an outdoor mall in front of the county government center); *Koenick v. Felton,* 190 F.3d 259 (4th Cir. 1999) (upholding a statute providing for public school holidays on Good Friday and Monday after Easter); *Metzl v. Leininger,* 57 F.3d 618 (7th Cir. 1995) (striking down a state law requiring school closures on Good Friday); *ACLU v. Florissant,* 186 F.3d 1095 (8th Cir. 1999), 1096 (authorizing a city display containing holiday decorations, including a crèche, candy canes, Santa Clause, and a "Seasons Greetings" banner, in front of entrance to civic center); *American Jewish Congress v. City of Beverly Hills,* 90 F.3d 379 (9th Cir. 1996) (striking down the city's decision to allow a Jewish group to erect large menorah display during Chanukah); *Elewski v. Syracuse,* 123 F.3d 51 (2d Cir. 1997) (permitting the city to display a crèche in a downtown public park during holiday season); *Grossbau v. Indianapolis,* 100 F.3d 1287 (7th Cir. 1996) (authorizing a county government to prohibit public groups from displaying exhibits in the lobby of the City County building); *Congregation Lubavitch v. City of Cincinnati,* 997 F.2d 1160 (6th Cir. 1993) (striking down a city ordinance, intended to avoid controversy over a Ku Klux Klan Latin Cross and a menorah during Chanukah, that banned displays sponsored by private entities in the public square between the hours of 10:00 P.M. and 6:00 A.M.); *Kreisner v. San Diego,* 1 F.3d 775 (9th Cir. 1993) (allowing a private, overtly religious display of eight scenes depicting the Biblical story of the birth of Jesus, accompanied by Bible verses, to be erected in a public park); *Florey v. Sioux Falls,* 619 F.2d 1311 (8th Cir. 1980) (upholding a school district policy that permitted religious holiday activities but prohibited religious exercises or celebration of "solely religious" holidays).

107. There are other obvious but atypical restraints, such as offering speech that immediately incites people to riot.

108. Religious Land Use and Institutionalized Persons Act, Pub.L. 106-274, 42 U.S.C. §2000cc-1 et seq. Although the Supreme Court has upheld the constitutionality of other parts of RLUIPA, *Cutter v. Wilkinson,* 544 U.S. 709 (2005), it has not specifically ruled on the constitutionality of the land-use provisions cited.

109. Internal Revenue Code, 26 U.S.C. § 501(c).

110. *Cornelius v. NAACP Legal Defense & Educational Fund, Inc.,* 473 U.S. 788 (1985), 800.

111. *Perry Educ. Ass'n v. Perry Local Educators' Ass'n,* 460 U.S. 37, 45 (1983).

112. In *Capitol Square Review & Advisory Bd. v. Pinette,* 515 U.S. 753 (1995), the Court held that a government entity violated the First Amendment by denying the Ku Klux Klan a permit to display an unattended cross in a plaza, otherwise open to free expression as a traditional public forum, near the Ohio state capitol building. Although concerns on the part of the State about violating the Establishment Clause could constitute a compelling state interest for First Amendment purposes, the private cross in this case—displayed in a forum that had been generally open for private speech, erected pursuant to a neutral permit process, and posted with a disclaimer highlighting its private rather than governmental ownership—did not violate the Establishment Clause by signaling government endorsement or promotion of religion.

113. *Rosenberger v. Rector & Visitors of Univ. of Va.,* 515 U.S. 819 (1995), 829.

114. Ibid.

115. *Good News Club v. Milford Central School,* 533 U.S. 98 (2001); *Lamb's Chapel v. Center Moriches Union Free School District,* 508 U.S. 384 (1993).

BIBLIOGRAPHY

Books

Barton, David. *The Myth of Separation: What Is the Correct Relationship between Church and State.* Aledo, TX: WallBuilder Press, 1989.

Davis, Derek H. *Religion and the Continental Congress 1774–1789: Contributions to Original Intent.* Oxford, UK: Oxford University Press, 2000.

Dawkins, Richard. *The God Delusion.* New York: Bantam Press, 2006.

Gibson, John. *The War on Christmas.* New York: Sentinel, 2005.

Gunn, T. Jeremy. *Spiritual Weapons: The Cold War and the Forging of an American National Religion.* New York: Praeger, 2009.

Harris, Sam. *The End of Faith: Religion, Terror, and the Future of Reason.* New York: W.W. Norton & Company, 2005.

Hitchens, Christopher. *God Is Not Great: How Religion Poisons Everything.* New York: Twelve/Warner Books, 2007.

Horsley, Richard and James Tracy, eds. *Christmas Unwrapped: Consumerism, Christ, and Culture.* Harrisburg, PA: Trinity Press International, 2001.

Hunter, James Davison. *Culture Wars: The Struggle to Define America.* New York: Basic Books, 1991.

Hutson, James H. *Religion and the Founding of the American Republic.* Washington, DC: Library of Congress, 1998.

Love, W. DeLoss, Jr. *The Fast and Thanksgiving Days of New England.* Boston: Houghton, Mifflin & Co., 1895.

Neuhaus, Richard John. *The Naked Public Square.* Grand Rapids, MI: William B. Eerdmans Publishing Company, 1984.

Sharlet, Jeff. *The Family: The Secret Fundamentalism at the Heart of American Power.* New York: Harpers, 2008.

Sullivan, Winnifred Fallers. *Paying the Words Extra: Religious Discourse in the Supreme Court of the United States.* Cambridge, MA: Harvard University Press, 1994.

The American Legion. *In the Footsteps of the Founders: A Guide to Defending American Values.* Indianapolis, IN, 2007.

Waits, William B. *The Modern Christmas in America: A Cultural History of Gift Giving.* New York: New York University Press, 1993.

Articles/Chapters

Alliance Defense Fund: http://www.alliancedefensefund.org/issues/ReligiousFreedom/Default.aspx.

Becket Fund: http://www.becketfund.org/index.php/topic/2.html?PHPSESSID=e81144f596 6a274fae0208e32a10d2f9.Epstein, Steven B. "Rethinking the Constitutionality of Ceremonial Deism." *Columbia Law Review* 96 (1996): 2083.

Falwell, Jerry. "Diversity in Education . . . For All But Those in Religious Studies," newxmax.com, March 5, 2004: Met Museum: http://archive.newsmax.com/archives/articles/2004/3/5/151230.shtml.

Finkelman, Paul. "The Ten Commandments on the Courthouse Lawn and Elsewhere." *Fordham Law Review* 73 (2005): 1477.

Met Museum: http://www.metmuseum.org/press_room/full_release.asp?prid={A345B35B-88DF-11D6-942D-00902786BF44} (June 3, 2002)Patel, Eboo. "Religious Pluralism in the Public Square." In *Debating the Divine: Religion in 21st Century American Democracy,* ed. Sally Steenland. Washington, DC: Center for American Democracy, 2008.

Silk, Mark. "Notes on the Judeo-Christian Tradition in America." *American Quarterly* 36 (Spring, 1984): 65.

Strang, Lee J. "The *Lemon* Cliffs of *Dover.*" *National Review Online,* Dec. 21, 2005, http://www.nationalreview.com/comment/strang200512211205.asp.

Court Cases

Abington Township v. Schempp, 374 U.S. 203 (1963).

ACLU v. Florissant, 186 F.3d 1095 (8th Cir. 1999).

ACLU of Ohio v. Capitol Square Review and Advisory Board, 243 F.3d 289 (6th Cir. 2001).

ACLU v. Schundler, 168 F.3d 92 (3d Cir. 1999).

American Jewish Congress v. City of Beverly Hills, 90 F.3d 379 (9th Cir. 1996).

Aronov v. United States, 432 F.2d 242 (9th Cir. 1970).

Capitol Square Review & Advisory Bd. v. Pinette, 515 U.S. 753 (1995),

Congregation Lubavitch v. City of Cincinnati, 997 F.2d 1160 (6th Cir. 1993).

Cornelius v. NAACP Legal Defense & Educational Fund, Inc., 473 U.S. 788 (1985).

County of Allegheny v. ACLU of Greater Pittsburgh, 492 U.S. 573 (1989).

Cutter v. Wilkinson, 544 U.S. 709 (2005).

Elewski v. Syracuse, 123 F.3d 51 (2d Cir. 1997).

Florey v. Sioux Falls, 619 F.2d 1311 (8th Cir. 1980).

Freethought Society of Greater Philadelphia v. Chester County, 334 F.3d 247 (3d. Cir. 2003).

Gaylor v. United States, 74 F.3d 214 (10th Cir. 1996).

Good News Club v. Milford Central School, 533 U.S. 98 (2001).

Grossbau v. Indianapolis, 100 F.3d 1287 (7th Cir. 1996).

Holy Trinity Church v. United States, 143 U.S. 457 (1892).

Joki v. Board of Educ. of Schuylerville Cent. School Dist., 745 F. Supp 823 (N.D.N.Y., 1990).

Knights of Columbus v. Lexington, 272 F.3d 25 (1st Cir. 2001).

Koenick v. Felton, 190 F.3d 259 (4th Cir. 1999).

Kreisner v. San Diego, 1 F.3d 775 (9th Cir. 1993).

Lamb's Chapel v. Center Moriches Union Free School District, 508 U.S. 384 (1993).

Lynch v. Donnelly, 465 U.S. 668 (1984).

Marsh v. Chambers, 463 U.S. 783 (1983).

McCreary County v. ACLU of Kentucky, 545 U.S. 844 (2005).

Metzl v. Leininger, 57 F.3d 618 (7th Cir. 1995).

Modrovich v. Allegheny County, 385 F.3d 397 (3d Cir. 2004).

Perry Educ. Ass'n v. Perry Local Educators' Ass'n, 460 U.S. 37 (1983).

Rosenberger v. Rector & Visitors of Univ. of Va., 515 U.S. 819 (1995).

Sherman v. Community Consolidated School District, 980 F.2d 437(7th Cir. 1992), 445 cert. denied, 508 U.S. 950 (1993).

Skoros v. New York, 437 F.3d 1 (2d Cir. 2006).

Stone v. Graham, 449 U.S. 39 (1980).

United States v. Macintosh, 283 U.S. 605 (1931).

Van Orden v. Perry, 545 U.S. 677 (2005).

Vidal v. Girard's Executors, 43 U.S. 127 (1844).

Warren v. Fairfax County, 196 F.3d 186 (4th Cir. 1999).

Washegesic v. Bloomingdale Public Schools, 33 F.3d 679 (6th Cir. 1994).

Wells v. Denver, 257 F.3d 1132 (10th Cir. 2001).

Zorach v. Clauson, 343 U.S. 306 (1952).

Statutes

Religious Land Use and Institutionalized Persons Act, Pub.L. 106-274, 42 U.S.C. §2000cc-1 et seq.

Internal Revenue Code, 26 U.S.C. § 501(c).

CHAPTER 11

RELIGIOUS LIBERTY AS A DEMOCRATIC INSTITUTION

TED G. JELEN

In the early twenty-first century, the political role of religion is a central question in the United States and the world. The rise of a resurgent, politically assertive Islam is perhaps the dominant fact of international relations in the first decade of the new century. The permissible limitation on religious liberty is a central question in societies as diverse as Tibet, Turkey, France, Myanmar, and the People's Republic of China. In the United States, the appropriate relationship between religion and politics, and church and state, remains at center stage in national political discourse. Religion informs and animates public debate on issues such as abortion, same-sex marriage, and has begun to enter the public dialogue on issues such as health care and environmental protection.

In late 2007, former governor and Republican presidential candidate Mitt Romney gave a nationally televised speech in which he defended the right of a Mormon to run for president. Despite the provision in Article VI of the United States Constitution that prohibits religious tests for public office, the fact that a leading contender for the presidency felt it necessary to defend his faith suggests that questions of religious liberty remain important in American politics.

Does religious liberty contribute to democracy? This chapter answers this question with a qualified affirmative. Religious liberty does, in the United States and elsewhere, facilitate the self-governance of citizens living in ostensibly democratic systems. However, the contributions of religion and religious liberty to democratic governance are not unlimited, and they carry certain substantial risks.

As I attempt to address this important and complex question, it is necessary to delimit the scope of this chapter. In the first place, I do not intend to address directly theological claims. I regard the truth value of claims about religious reality, and indeed, assertions concerning the moral or policy implications of religious belief, as beyond my competence as a political scientist. Second, to as great an extent as possible, I plan to eschew direct discussion of constitutional interpretation. Again, questions of the "correct" meaning of the Establishment or Free Exercise Clauses, or the "original intent" of the authors of the religion clauses of the First Amendment, have been considered at great length elsewhere, and are ably addressed by other contributors to this volume.

Third, I do not intend to rely on discussions of constitutional or human rights in my analysis of the role of religious liberty in democracy. "Rights talk" tends to obscure as much as it illuminates, and has been described as a source of the "impoverishment" of public discourse.[1] Rather, it is my intention to attempt to assess the consequences of religious liberty for the practice of democratic governance. My main focus will be the United States, although I regard my observations as having general applicability.

Even with these self-imposed limitations, the task of assessing the role of religious liberty in democratic governance is quite daunting. Democracy is a complex, multifaceted phenomenon, and it is necessary to isolate certain essential (I hope) aspects of democracy for consideration.

This chapter focuses on democracy as "self-governance." The notion of self-governance has both individual and collective aspects. The "self" to be governed includes the individual citizen's mastery over her or his own self, as well as the collective and reciprocal responsibility to govern one another. Religion poses both risks and opportunities for the task of individual and collective self-governance.

Religious Liberty and Individual Self-Governance

Obviously, any conception of democracy must entail a strong procedural component. Citizens must be able to make choices among meaningful and genuinely competitive alternatives, and to have those choices aggregated in a fair and impartial manner. Indeed, analysts such as John Rawls have suggested that consensus on such fundamental practices may be essential to democratic governance.[2]

These considerations were most conspicuously discussed during the presidential election of 2000. Third-party candidate Ralph Nader brushed aside criticisms of his candidacy as providing assistance to George W. Bush by asserting that both major party candidates were beholden to "corporate America," and that the choice between Bush and Al Gore presented no meaningful alternatives to the American people. Similarly, the controversy over the vote counting in Florida during the 2000 presidential election was extremely bitter, and remains controversial years after the fact.

Nevertheless, although procedural fairness may be a necessary condition for democratic governance, few would suggest that such fairness is sufficient for an election, or a political system, to be characterized as authentically "democratic." One would also require that the preferences expressed through democratic institutions (such as elections) be uncoerced, and, to some extent, unmanipulated.

Obviously, the requirement that preferences be unmanipulated is unrealistic, and perhaps unreasonable. All of us are subject to a variety of influences, including religion, education, family and peers, government, and mass media. However, it is perhaps important that individual citizens be free to choose among the available communications that might influence their preferences and values. This is essential if citizens are to govern themselves, and participate in the formation of their own characters. This notion of "self-determination" makes possible self-governance at the individual level.[3]

For example, as a political liberal who identifies with the Democratic Party in the United States, I am much more likely to read *The New Republic* or the *Nation* than I am to peruse *The National Review* or *The American Spectator*. As a former Roman Catholic, I am much more familiar with the writings of St. Thomas Aquinas and St. Augustine than I am with those of Martin Luther, John Calvin, or Mohammed. These choices of reading material are likely to have clear implications for my political and religious preferences. Although I would not claim to be completely autonomous in my own thinking (nor would I desire to be so), the ability to choose my reading material allows me to participate in the formulation of my own character. This sort to self-determination or "authenticity" is, to some extent, what distinguishes "genuine" democratic politics from those settings that observe the form, but not the substance, of popular sovereignty.[4] It is difficult for citizens to govern one another collectively if they lack the capacity to govern themselves individually.

Indeed, it might be argued that the diverse liberties listed in the First Amendment to the United States Constitution (freedom of religion, speech, press, and assembly) have in common the characteristic of facilitating the self-determination and self-governance of individual citizens. Such freedoms provide for a range of choices of messages and influences from which citizens can choose, and legitimize the interactions that make possible the reflective governance of the self.

This point can be approached from another angle. A common topic of debate in university classrooms (and dormitories) is the question of "free will versus determinism." Stated as polar opposites, neither alternative is plausible. Relatively few social scientists would subscribe to a hard view of behavioral determinism, and no one would claim that anyone is free from influences (often unconscious) on their own beliefs and behaviors. A more reasonable take on this issue might be to regard the extent to which any individual actively participates in the development of her or his own character as a *variable,* which differs across persons, and indeed, within any given person at different periods of her or his life, or in different areas of endeavor.[5]

For example, in his *Autobiography,* John Stuart Mill reports receiving a somewhat painful message; namely, that many of his acquaintances regard him as a "made man," capable of reproducing the opinions of others, but not able to think for himself. Mill describes this event as a "crisis in [his] mental history," and he sets upon an ambitious project of self-improvement.[6] Mill's individual project (which he extends to politics in *On Liberty* and *Considerations on Representative Government*) corresponds nicely to my conception of individual self-governance.[7]

Arguably, religion and religious freedom may enhance the potential for such self-governance at the individual (psychological) level. Nearly two centuries ago, Alexis de Tocqueville noted the conformist tendencies of democratic societies. Tocqueville's conception of the "tyranny of the majority" makes clear that individual self-determination or authenticity may be difficult even in ostensibly "free" societies, and in the absence of overt coercion.[8] Public opinion, communicated to citizens through the mass media in contemporary society, is a formidable force, which may make dissent difficult socially (if not legally). Empirical support for the power of popular opinion to suppress minority opinion has been provided by Elisabeth Noelle-Neuman.[9]

In *Democracy in America,* Tocqueville asserts that religion is an important check on the tyranny of the majority. Religion, for Tocqueville, provides a moral and psychological mooring that enables citizens to resist the power of public opinion. Indeed, popular sentiment is thought by Tocqueville to derive its power from the egalitarian nature of democratic societies, and the corresponding lack of respect accorded authorities (whether political, intellectual, or moral). Religion is a source of authoritative, transcendent values that may enable citizens to resist the persuasive power of mass opinions.

Supporters of an active public role for religion have argued that religiously motivated citizens have been at the forefront of a number of mass movements, including those associated with abolition, civil rights, opposition to the Vietnam War, and the contemporary Christian Right. Although the value of these movements (especially the most recent) certainly can be debated, my point here is more limited: Religious activists have traditionally been willing to make public witness to unpopular positions based on their religious convictions.[10]

Of course, there are many historical instances in which religious activists have resisted authority in the face of active suppression.[11] However, it seems likely that religious beliefs and values will provide counterweights to prevailing public opinion in settings in which religious liberty is legally protected and socially respected. This assertion seems especially plausible if one grants the legitimacy of two empirical claims: First, that religious liberty promotes religious pluralism; and second, that religious pluralism occasions higher levels of religious participation.

It seems obvious that, absent legal repression or restriction on the formation of religious bodies, a variety of religious perspectives and organizations may emerge. Indeed, it is arguably the case that the religious diversity that characterizes the

United States can be attributed to the fact that, in the United States, religion is neither supported nor regulated by government. Not only are minority religions tolerated, and their liberties protected, but religious organizations are largely freed from administrative burdens and governmentally imposed costs, which are common in other democratic systems.[12] Second, the notion that religious pluralism results in higher levels of religious activity has received a good deal of theoretical and empirical support from adherents of the "supply-side" school of religious activity.[13] Using an economic analogy, religious entrepreneurs are required to provide religious "goods" (experiences, fellowship, plausible promises of salvation, etc.) attractive to members and potential members. Such competition is thought to make religious good more generally responsive to the needs and desires of the laity. To the extent that religious leaders have incentives to provide such attractive "products" (as opposed to situations in which one church has a monopoly or near monopoly), the aggregate level of religious participation can be expected to increase. Although the market approach to religious participation is controversial,[14] religious liberty may enhance the countermajoritarian effects of religion by increasing the number of actively religious citizens.

Nor is this all. To the extent that the market model of religion seems plausible, it follows that religious entrepreneurs might be required to engage in "product differentiation." That is, in a more standard economic setting, McDonald's spends a great deal of money to convince consumers that a Big Mac really tastes better that a Burger King Whopper. Similarly, if religious bodies must compete for adherents, it might be that different religious denominations may need to distinguish themselves from one another. Southern Baptists might explain why their brand of baptism is preferable to that offered by the American Baptist Church, or the General Association of Regular Baptist Churches.[15] If this is the case, it might also follow that members of the laity may come to exhibit "brand loyalty" in the sense of valuing the distinctive nature of their denomination or tradition.

If the foregoing considerations seem reasonable, it might follow that religiously active citizens inhabit congregational environments in which they are encouraged to regard themselves as distinct from the rest of the population. Many churches provide explicitly countermajoritarian messages, in which lay members may be encouraged (for example) to be "in the world, but not of it." Such "particularistic" religious bodies might further enhance the ability of their members to resist the powerful influence of the popular culture.[16]

Thus, following Tocqueville and others, my argument to this point is that authentic democratic citizenship requires that individual citizens be able to participate in self-determination. Religion provides an essential check on the power of public opinion to limit the ability of members of democratic societies to participate actively in the formation of their own characters and preferences. Religious freedom enhances this role of religion by encouraging diversity in belief and practice, and diversity may well increase the frequency and intensity of religious behavior.

To illustrate this point, it is noteworthy that public opinion in the United States is increasingly accepting of the rights of gays and lesbians, and this trend applies even to the divisive question of same-sex marriage.[17] Although there is no consensus on the rights of gays and lesbians, the trends in the popular culture are quite clear. Nor is this difficult to understand: A dominant theme in the political culture of the United States is individual autonomy. The "master narrative" of American culture is autonomous individuals making uncoerced choices,[18] and the treatment of gays and lesbians in the popular media in the United States has begun to apply this principle to gays and lesbians over the past two decades or so. Acting on one's sexual orientation is seen by growing numbers of Americans as a personal, autonomous choice, to which anyone is entitled.

Much of the opposition to increased acceptance of homosexuality in the United States has a religious basis.[19] Although the denial of full citizenship to people of unconventional sexual orientation poses problems for individual self-determination (which I will address in the following), the point here is that, for many citizens of the United States, religious conviction provides the intellectual and psychological resources to resist a powerful trend in public opinion.

There is another sense in which religion may enhance democratic citizenship. Numerous analysts have shown that religious participation is an important source of "social capital," or political and social skills.[20] Participation in religious organizations, such as congregations, appears to enhance the development of such traits as political efficacy, the ability to negotiate with people with alternative viewpoints, and the ability to communicate one's own viewpoints to other people. Although religion is not the only source of social capital, Verba and colleagues have suggested that religion is a particularly important source of social capital for citizens who are otherwise disadvantaged.[21] That is, most of the other sources of social capital, such as high levels of education and income, an occupation in which one's communication skills are developed, or social contact with influential people, tend to accrue to people already well-equipped with such skills. By contrast, participation in religious organizations tends to provide opportunities for people of lower education, income, and occupation prestige to develop the skills necessary for active, efficacious participation in democratic politics.

Again, if it is the case that religious liberty occasions religious diversity, and that religious diversity in turn increases aggregate religious participation, it seems clear that religious freedom is an important component to the development of authentic democratic citizenship. By encouraging an active and diverse religious environment, then, the protection of religious freedom may enhance the development of democratic citizenship in several ways. Religious participation may provide the moral, intellectual, and psychological resources for individual believers to resist the power of mass culture. Religious activity and belief may facilitate the development of authentic, or at least uncoerced, political preferences. Engagement in religious activities may also impart the skills necessary to act upon those preferences in complex political and social environments.

Of course these benefits do not come without costs. In some instances, the exercise of religious liberty may retard the potential for self-determination and individual development for others. Indeed, it seems clear that the public assertion of religious values may (indeed, has) limited the opportunities for self-development and efficacious participation for those lying outside an apparent religious or moral consensus.

The basis of this possible paradox is that religious belief and activity may be an important source of individual self-determination, but is not the only source. Indeed, citizens make many choices that have serious implications for the development of their preferences and their values. Two examples may suffice here: Among the most profound choices available to citizens are the choices of whether (and whom) to marry and whether to conceive or bear children. Citizens who are married (or have decided not to marry), or who are parents will surely attest to the fact that attaining the statuses of spouse or parent are among the most far-reaching perceptual shifts that can occur to an individual person. Marriage and parenthood are profoundly self-defining acts, which affect virtually every subsequent decision (and preference) a person can make.

From the foregoing, it follows that restrictions on same-sex marriage, or on abortion, represent the potential denial of self-determination of gays and lesbians, or sexually active heterosexuals who do not wish to become parents.[22] This is not a libertarian argument about the autonomy of individual marital or reproductive choices. I do not wish to invoke a right to "privacy" to support marital or reproductive freedom.[23] Rather, I mean to suggest that if religiously motivated citizens are successful in enacting their preferences about marriage and abortion into public policy, citizens who would seek to marry a member of their own sex, or who would seek reproductive freedom, are being denied the opportunity to develop the capacity to participate fully in the social and political life of the nation.

This tendency of religion to limit the possibilities for self-development is perhaps especially apparent when applied to the education of the young. Indeed, an enormous proportion of court decisions in the church–state arena in the United States deal with issues surrounding public education. These would include the teaching of evolution (or creationism), school prayer, the public display of religious symbols (e.g., the Ten Commandments) on school property, or compulsory attendance laws. It would be a strange conception of religious freedom that did not include the right to raise one's children in the faith. Nevertheless, it may be that the exercise of religious freedom to the education of children could restrict the opportunities for self-development for the younger generation.

To take one example, in the 1972 case of *Wisconsin v. Yoder,* the Supreme Court ruled that Amish families could be allowed to remove their children from public schools at the age of 14 (as their religion required), even though the state of Wisconsin had mandated compulsory school attendance until the age of 16. The basis for the Court's decision was the Free Exercise Clause of the First Amendment. In his dissenting opinion, Justice William O. Douglas argued that the premature removal of children from school would limit their social and economic opportunities, and indeed, would make it more difficult for them to leave the Amish communities themselves.[24] To the extent that a lack of formal education would limit the economic opportunities of children brought up in Amish communities, the exercise of religious liberty of the parents might well limit the subsequent religious liberty (in this case, the liberty to leave the faith and the community) of their children.

Similarly, religiously motivated legal restrictions on the teaching of evolution (which are extraordinarily common in the United States) might well inhibit the scientific education of high school students, and might engender skepticism about the methods of science. So far, courts have limited the ability of state governments to proscribe the teaching of evolution, require "equal treatment" between evolution and creationism, or mandate the teaching of "intelligent design." However, opponents of evolution have continued to press for accommodation of their views, which are, to a large extent, religiously based,[25] and many biology teachers have responded to the public pressure by omitting the topic of evolution from the curriculum altogether. If indeed evolution is a central explanatory framework for the study of biology, this limitation on scientific training might, in turn, limit the opportunities of students so educated to pursue careers in science or medicine.[26]

Thus, the protection and enhancement of religious freedom carries with it an apparent paradox. If religion is, to any extent, a public matter, then religiously motivated citizens exercising their religious liberty may well limit the opportunities for self-development and self-determination for people outside a religious tradition, or for their own children. This limitation may well extend to the exercise of religious freedom itself.

The foregoing assumes that an authentic religious liberty cannot be limited to a private sphere of activity. If one is allowed to form and hold individual religious beliefs, it is clearly inappropriate to deny religious citizens the opportunity to promote the affirmation of these beliefs in public life. Although it seems clear, both morally and legally, that religious conduct cannot be accorded the same degree of protection as religious belief, it is not reasonable to suppose that authentic religious liberty can be limited to beliefs.[27]

Certainly the assertions in the preceding paragraph are controversial. Several analysts have suggested that religious values should only be put forth in public discourse if such values are either publicly accessible to those outside the religious tradition, or if no publicly accessible arguments are available with respect to the topic in question.[28] The concept of "public accessibility" is essentially a requirement that assertions made in public discourse be justified by premises that are shared among those making arguments and those whose support is sought. To take an extreme example, an assertion that one might have believed that Barack Obama should be elected president because "God told me so" in a private revelation would not meet the criterion of public accessibility, because the revelation on which the assertion is based was not available to all, but rather confined to the person who made the claim supporting Obama.

Whether or not a justification or a warrant is publicly accessible is clearly dependent on the social and ideological context in which a discourse is taking place. If the United States were indeed a "Christian nation," the assertion of Jesus' divinity would likely be publicly accessible in the sense of being widely shared. In a society in which Jews, Muslims, and atheists make up a substantial proportion of the population, the same assertion would not be considered publicly accessible. Similarly, justifying opposition to gay rights by invoking passages from the Hebrew scriptures might be publicly accessible to an audience of evangelical Protestants, but would not meet the criterion in a more religiously pluralistic setting.

The requirement of public accessibility requires a distinction between the source of a theological or political position and its public justification. One might (given the importance placed in this chapter on individual self-determination) derive one's values and preferences from any of a number of sources, including scripture, private revelation, or the extension of natural law. However, the position must be justified on grounds acceptable to people who might not share one's premises. Thus, although opponents of same-sex marriage might base their lack of support for such unions on their reading of scripture, the requirement of public accessibility requires that the policy preference not be justified on biblical grounds to an audience that does not share a belief in the authority of the Bible.

Ultimately, the requirement of public accessibility is a normative one, based in large part on the respect democratic citizens owe one another.[29] As an ethical principle to guide the public discourse of democratic citizens, the assertion of the desirability of public accessibility may well be appropriate. However, insistence on such a requirement might well violate the values of free expression, as well as religious free exercise. Clearly, a person engaged in public political discourse (a political candidate, journalist, or academic, for example) cannot be prevented from invoking religious beliefs and values that might not be widely shared among the members of one's audience. Moreover, the demand of public accessibility may privilege some religious traditions over others. For example, a highly rationalistic religious discourse, such as Roman Catholic natural law theology, might come closer to meeting the requirement of public accessibility than a more experiential tradition, such as Pentecostalism. To this extent, a dialogue in which public accessibility is valued might render some religious traditions "more equal than others."

However, as an empirical question, and as a practical consideration, the admonition that religiously motivated arguments be framed in a publicly accessible manner has a great deal of merit. Again, in a religiously pluralistic society in which religious freedom is valued, political positions that are not based on widely shared assumptions are unlikely to be persuasive. For example, I have argued elsewhere that in the United States, religiously based arguments are more persuasive to the extent that they are framed in the language of individual rights and personal autonomy.[30] Thus, it may be that the aforementioned increase in the acceptance of homosexuality, and the growing support for legal equality for gays and lesbians, and same-sex marriage, can be attributed in part to the failure of opponents of gay rights to produce a plausible (e.g., rights-based) counterframe to the autonomy-based arguments in favor of legal and political equality for homosexuals. Although religious opposition to gay rights remains substantial, religious conservatives are clearly not dominating the public debate over this issue. By contrast, public opinion on issues such as abortion and aspects of the evolution/creation controversy has been much more stable.[31] In part, the distinctive dynamics (or, perhaps more accurately, statics) of opinion on abortion and evolution may be attributed, in part, to the availability of a conservative, rights-based frame for each issue. With respect to abortion, the "right to choose" held by the woman may be offset by a fetal "right to life," or the right of parents to supervise their children (when issues of parental consent are raised). Similarly, opponents of evolution, even if their positions are motivated by religious conviction, have used the language of "equal time," allowing students to "make up their own minds" or "be open to opposing viewpoints." Because considerations of equality and autonomy are widely shared and therefore publicly accessible in the United States, religious conservatives have been able to hold their own in public discourse on these issues, but are clearly losing the battle for public opinion with respect to issues surrounding the question of gay rights.

Thus, perhaps a possible solution to the problem of religiously based restrictions on individual self-determination may lie in the religious pluralism that religious liberty encourages. Given the religious and moral diversity that characterizes the contemporary United States (a point to which I shall return in the following section), explicitly religious arguments are unlikely to prevail in public discourse. Even if the values in question are derived from religious belief, secular public justifications are likely to be required to translate religiously based moral judgments into public policy.

Religious liberty may thus enhance the ability of individual citizens to engage in self-determination, and participate in the formation of their own characters and preferences. Conversely, the exercise of religion may enable believers to restrict the opportunities for individual self-development for others. It can be hoped that the diversity that seems likely to result from the exercise of religious freedom may mitigate the latter risk.

Religious Liberty and Public Religion

Thus far, the discussion has been limited to the role of religion and religious liberty on the development of self-governance as governance of the self. This section examines the role of religious liberty in a more public sense, as a source of developing the capacity for collective self-governance, or the governance of democratic citizens over one another.

It is appropriate to begin with a discussion of an intellectual tradition of religion and democracy that places a high value on the shared values of religious citizens. Analysts as diverse as Alexis de Tocqueville, Peter Berger, A. James Reichley, and Richard Neuhaus have suggested that religion makes its primary contribution to democratic discourse though its consensual character.[32] To oversimplify for the sake of brevity, these analysts share a sense that democratic deliberation is only possible if shared ethical and moral principles exist among citizens. Berger's metaphor of a "sacred canopy" suggests that religiously shared values provide a common intellectual framework within which democratic deliberation and disagreement may take place. Similarly, Neuhaus' notion of a "naked public square" is intended to suggest that the secularism that characterizes contemporary political life in the United States has deprived our public life of the sacred canopy, to the detriment of democratic discourse and civility. In a similar vein, Reichley suggests that the religious values of theism–humanism uniquely provide a basis for political authority and respect for the individual, and that these values are the consequence of a generally shared Judeo-Christian tradition in the United States. Although there are important differences among these analysts,[33] the general argument is that democratic dialogue is dependent on the existence of shared premises (which, as discussed in the preceding section, should be publicly accessible). In the United States, the claim is often advanced that these shared moral and ethical premises have a religious basis.[34]

To the extent that the position outlined in the preceding paragraph has merit, it follows that religious liberty might legitimately be limited to those religious beliefs and practices that contribute to the prevailing moral consensus. If religion derives its political value from its ability to impart a common ethical framework and moral vocabulary, it is not clear that religious liberty should be extended to religious traditions that do not share in the social consensus without substantial qualifications. Thus, the desire of many democratic citizens in the United States and elsewhere to restrict the activities of cults becomes understandable, even if those activities would be legal if conducted by representatives of more "mainstream" traditions. Given the intellectual tradition of the sacred canopy, religious liberty is a qualified and instrumental value.[35]

However, the canopy model is ultimately based on a false premise; namely, that a religious or moral consensus might exist in the United States or elsewhere. First, in a religiously pluralistic nation such as the United States, any consensus on religion or morality is likely to be quite thin. Apart from likely societal agreement condemning murder or theft, it is difficult to discern large areas of agreement on questions of morality, let alone religious doctrine. In a nation in which the morality of such practices as abortion, homosexuality, or capital punishment (to name a few) is contested, the assertion of anything approaching a moral consensus is quite implausible. Moreover, such issues of morality are not simply contested on the basis of a "culture war" between "orthodox" and "progressive" citizens,[36] but are also the subject of controversy within Christian religious traditions. The question of the morality of homosexuality has been debated in a number of religious denominations,[37] and the question of gay ordination threatens to tear apart the fabric of the Episcopalian Church in the United States.

Religious pluralism (the likely result of the exercise of religious liberty) may render the notion of a widely shared "sacred canopy" of religious or moral convictions unlikely. If this is the case, it may follow that there is no compelling reason to restrict the religious freedom of practitioners of faith traditions outside a cultural mainstream.[38] The benefits of religious liberty, described in the previous section and in the material that follows, seem likely to result from the exercise of religious freedom among conventional and unorthodox faith traditions alike. Moreover, the presumed social cohesion that might result from a religious or moral consensus seems illusory, and is often challenged by adherents of denominations widely characterized as "mainline."

Further, the sacred canopy model does not seem to fare much better in societies that are characterized by much lower levels of religious diversity. Moral questions such as divorce and abortion are contested in nations in which the overwhelming majority is Roman Catholic, such as Poland and Ireland,[39] and in predominantly Islamic societies such as Iran.[40] In each of these nations, an apparent consensus on religion does not appear to result in agreement on political or moral issues.

There are two general reasons why the sacred canopy is not effective in religiously homogeneous cultures. First, some analysts have suggested that a lack of religious competition leads to a "lazy monopoly" in which the dominant religious tradition can survive with relatively low levels of lay religious participation.[41] Whether the religious monopoly is *de jure* (as in Iran and some Scandinavian countries) or *de facto* (as in Poland or France), religious leaders are thought to lack incentives to engage the desires and needs of laity without the spur of competition. A generally shared adherence to a single religious tradition allows many citizens to be nominally affiliated with that tradition.

Second, the effects of modernity and globalization ensure that religious values will necessarily compete with aspects of secularization. Jose Casanova has argued that, although the inhabitants of most nations are not becoming more secular in the sense of declining religious belief or membership, religion is becoming compartmentalized and privatized, and religious beliefs are applied to an increasingly narrow range of phenomena.[42] For many modern citizens, the world is becoming "disenchanted" as science, technology, and cosmopolitan exposure to different cultures render the tenets of a locally dominant theological tradition less certain, and perhaps less plausible.

Thus, even in cultures that do not exhibit the religious diversity of the United States, a dominant, widely shared religious tradition may not offer the social cohesion on issues of politics or morality. Ethically, then, there is no compelling reason for governments in religiously monopolistic settings to restrict the freedom of religious minorities, because the social fabric that such groups seem to threaten has already been torn by indifference and modernity.

If religion is no longer a plausible source of social agreement (if it ever was), what political role can religion play in democratic politics? One important political function is that of social critic. The countermajoritarian tendencies of religion, described in the preceding section at the level of the individual citizen, may also apply to macro-level politics in the arena of policy making. Religion can provide the resources for public assertion of unpopular positions based on transcendent values.

To illustrate, much public discourse in the United States during the early years of the Reagan administration was characterized by a new assertiveness in foreign affairs (including incautious statements about the possibility of "winning" a nuclear exchange with the USSR), and a belief that economic programs designed to assist the poor were unjust and counterproductive. Arguably, the early 1980s was a period in which it was difficult for secular politicians to assert arguments from the political left. I would suggest that the Catholic Church (specifically, the National Council of Catholic Bishops)[43] stepped into the rhetorical void by publishing pastoral letters on the morality of nuclear war and economic justice (National Council of Catholic Bishops, 1983, 1986). These documents were addressed both to adherents of Catholic doctrine ("people of faith") and to sympathetic non-Catholics ("people of goodwill"). Most importantly for present purposes, the pastoral letters on war and economics were presented as "prophetic" documents, flowing against the prevailing tide of public opinion (or, at least, public discourse).

There is, of course, nothing unusual about religious bodies engaging in "prophetic" politics in the United States. Social and political movements such as abolitionism, Prohibition, civil rights, and opposition to the Vietnam War all had the support of religious leaders, even when such causes were initially unpopular. Religion can serve and has served as a social critic, reminding citizens of the transcendent values underlying political rhetoric and policy choices available to democratic citizens. If politics is "the art of the possible," religious politics may involve the art of the (perhaps temporarily) impossible.

Clearly, a prophetic role for religion in democratic politics requires that religious citizens and organizations maintain a respectful distance from political authority.[44] Close involvement between religious leaders and political authorities may compromise the integrity and independence of the former. Indeed, it has been argued that the separation of church and state serves to protect religion from politics as much as separation protects political activity from religion.[45] Wilcox and Larson have argued that the prophetic voice of the Christian Right in the United States may have been compromised by what is now a longstanding relationship between the movement and the Republican Party.[46] During the contests for the Republican presidential nomination in 2008, evangelical leaders such as James Dobson of Focus on the Family and others suggested that evangelicals should seek to form and support a third-party candidacy if the Republican nominee did not hold acceptable positions on such issues as abortion and same-sex marriage.[47]

Thus, there is reason to suppose that religion can and does serve an important role as social critic. Although this public role of religion has been conducted effectively even in the face of official repression—as in Communist Poland[48]—the important consideration here is an independence of religion from the state, or from close involvement with political groups such as parties. Close identification between church and state may affect the independence of prophetic religious voices. Authentic religious liberty may thus involve eschewing even apparently benevolent contact between the sacred and the secular. Thus, although critics of a separationist reading of the Establishment Clause of the US Constitution may regard strong church–state separationism as antireligious, it may be that the political influence of religious values are enhanced by vigilant maintenance of the boundary between the sacred and the secular.

CONCLUSION

This chapter has suggested that religious liberty has a positive effect on the practice of democratic politics in two general ways. First, religious liberty may enhance individual autonomy and authenticity. Democratic self-governance may, in the first instance, require the ability to engage in governance of the self. Religion appears to provide the means to resist the power of mass culture (what Tocqueville has termed the "tyranny of the majority"), apply transcendent values to the often profane world of politics, and develop the political and social skills necessary to participate effectively in democratic politics.

At the system or societal level, religion may serve as a means by which transcendent values enter the public debate, and provide counterweights to the often short-term and pragmatic imperatives of democratic politics. Religious voices in the public dialogue may serve as potent reminders that some policy issues involve higher stakes than success or failure in the next election.

The benefits of religious participation in public affairs, which are likely enhanced by the protection of religious liberty, are not obtained without costs or risks. The enactment of religious values in public policy may inhibit the very freedom and autonomy that religious liberty is intended to protect, and close identification between church and state may limit the ability of the former to engage in its prophetic role as social critic. The role of religion in democratic politics is complex and multifaceted, and religious liberty is thus a double-edged sword in the quest for individual and popular sovereignty.

ENDNOTES

1. Mary Ann Glendon, *Rights Talk* (New York: Free Press, 1991).

2. John Rawls, *Political Liberalism* (New York: Columbia University Press, 1993).

3. L. Kent Sezer, "The Constitutional Underpinnings of the Abortion Debate," in *Perspectives on the Politics of Abortion,* ed. Ted G. Jelen (Westport, CT: Praeger, 1995), 123–153.

4. Marshall Berman, *The Politics of Authenticity* (New York: Antheneum, 1970).

5. For example, I like to think that my attachment to the Democratic Party is the result of careful and continuous deliberation and assimilation of new information (some of my friends might disagree). However, I freely admit that my psychological attachment to the Chicago White Sox (which is held much more intensely than my identification as a Democrat) is the result of childhood socialization, which I have neither the energy nor desire to reconsider.

6. John Stuart Mill, *Autobiography* (Boston: Houghton-Mifflin, 1969).

7. John Stuart Mill, *On Liberty* (New York: Oxford University Press, 1975); and John Stuart Mill, *Considerations on Representative Government* (New York: Oxford University Press, 1975).

8. Alexis de Tocqueville, *Democracy in America,* 2 vols., ed. Bradley Phillips (New York: Vintage, 1945).

9. Elisabeth Noelle-Neuman, *The Spiral of Silence: Public Opinion—Our Social Skin* (Chicago: University of Chicago Press, 1993).

10. One important difference between Tocqueville's argument and the position I am describing is that Tocqueville attributes the importance of religion to the mitigation of the tyranny of the majority to the consensual nature of Christianity in the United States. By contrast, I would suggest that the countermajoritarian tendencies of religion do not depend directly on the nature of the religious market, and further, that the indirect effects are more pronounced in religiously pluralistic settings.

11. Timothy Byrnes, "The Challenge of Pluralism: The Catholic Church in Democratic Poland," in *Religion and Politics in Comparative Perspective: The One, the Few, and the Many,* eds. Ted Gerard Jelen and Clyde Wilcox (New York: Cambridge University Press, 2002), 27–44.

12. See Frank Way and Barbara Burt, "Religious Marginality and the Free Exercise Clause," *American Political Science Review* 77 (1983): 654–665; and Stephen V. Monsma and J. Christopher Soper, *The Challenge of Pluralism: Church and State in Five Democracies* (Lanham, MD: Rowman and Littlefield, 1997).

13. See Laurence Iannaccone, "The Consequences of Religious Market Structure," *Rationality and Society* 3 (1991): 156–177; Roger Finke and Rodney Stark, *The Churching of America, 1776–1990* (New Brunswick, NJ: Rutgers University Press, 1992); and Rodney Stark and Roger Finke, *Acts of Faith: Explaining the Human Side of Religion* (Berkeley: University of California Press, 2000).

14. See Steve Bruce, "The Poverty of Economism, or the Social Limits on Maximizing," in *Sacred Markets, Sacred Canopies: Essays on Religious Markets and Religious Pluralism,* ed. Ted G. Jelen (Lanham, MD: Rowman and Littlefield, 2002), 167–186; and Ted G. Jelen, "Relections on the 'New Paradigm:' Unfinished Business and an Agenda for Research," in *Sacred Markets, Sacred Canopies: Essays on Religious Markets and Religious Pluralism,* ed. Ted G. Jelen, 187–204.

15. See Ted G. Jelen, *The Political World of the Clergy* (Westport, CT: Praeger, 1993).

16. Ted G. Jelen, *The Political Mobilization of Religious Beliefs* (Westport, CT: Praeger, 1991); and Clyde Wilcox, *God's Warriors: The Christian Right in the 20th Century* (Baltimore: Johns Hopkins University Press, 1992).

17. Clyde Wilcox and Barbara Norrander, "Of Moods and Morals: The Dynamics of Opinion on Abortion and Gay Rights," in *Understanding Public Opinion,* eds. Barbara Norrander and Clyde Wilcox, 2nd ed. (Washington, DC: CQ Press, 2002), 121–148; and Clyde Wilcox, Paul R. Brewer, Shauna Shames, and Celinda Lake, "'If I Bend This Far, I Will Break?' Public Opinion and Same Sex Marriage," in *The Politics of Same-Sex Marriage,* eds. Craig A. Rimmerman and Clyde Wilcox (Chicago: University of Chicago Press, 2007), 215–242.

18. Ted G. Jelen, "Political Esperanto: Rhetorical Resources and Limitations of the Christian Right," *Sociology of Religion* 66 (2005): 303–321.

19. This is not to suggest that all, or even most, religious people are opposed to gay and lesbian rights; indeed, some denominations (e.g., Episcopalians) are sharply divided over this issue. Rather, my more limited point is that much of the extant opposition to gay rights is motivated by religious beliefs, and public arguments against the social and legal acceptance of homosexuality are often made by religious leaders such as Marion "Pat" Robertson.

20. See Sidney Verba, Kay Lehman Scholzman, and Henry E. Brady, *Voice and*

Equality: Civic Voluntarism in American Politics (Cambridge, MA: Harvard University Press, 1995); and Robert Putnam, *Bowling Alone: The Collapse and Revival of American Community* (New York: Simon and Schuster, 2000). For an overview of this literature, see Corwin E. Smidt, Kevin denDulk, Douglas L. Koopman, Stephen V. Monsma, and James M. Penning, *Pews, Prayers, and Participation: The Role of Religion in Fostering Civic Responsibility* (Washington, DC: Georgetown University Press, 2008).

21. Verba et al., *Civic Voluntarism in American Politics.*

22. Ted G. Jelen, "In Defense of Religious Minimalism," in *A Wall of Separation? Debating the Public Role of Religion,* eds. Mary C. Segers and Ted G. Jelen (Lanham, MD: Rowman and Littlefield, 1998), 3–51.

23. Constitutionally, marital and reproductive choices have been legally protected on the basis of a right to privacy, as asserted in *Griswold v. Connecticut* (1965); *Loving v. Virginia* (1967); and *Roe v. Wade* (1973).

24. Shawn Frances Peters, *The Yoder Case: Religious Freedom, Education, and Parental Rights* (Lawrence, KS: University Press of Kansas, 2002).

25. Donald P. Haider-Markell and Maryk R. Joslyn, "Pulpits Versus Ivory Towers: Socializing Agents and Evolution Attitudes," *Social Science Quarterly* 89 (September 2008) 665.

26. In the film version of *Inherit the Wind,* one character argues against the prosecution of Bert Cates (the fictional name of the character representing Scopes) by saying "I may want my son to go to Yale."

27. See Jesse Choper, *Securing Religious Liberty* (Chicago: University of Chicago Press, 1995).

28. See Kent Greenawalt, *Religious Convictions and Political Choice* (New York: Oxford University Press, 1988); Michael J. Perry, *Love and Power: The Role of Religion and Morality in American Politics* (New York: Oxford University Press, 1991); and Ronald Thiemann, *Religion in Public Life: A Dilemma for Democracy* (Washington, DC: Georgetown University Press, 1996).

29. See especially Perry, *Love and Power.*

30. Ted G. Jelen, "Religion and American Public Opinion: Social Issues," in *Oxford Handbook on Religion and American Politics,* eds. Corwin E. Smidt, Lyman A. Kellstedt, and James Guth (New York: Oxford University Press, forthcoming 2009).

31. George F. Bishop, "Evolution, Religion, and the 'Culture War' in American Politics," paper presented at the annual meeting of the American Political Science Association, Chicago, September, 2007.

32. Tocqueville, *Democracy in America;* Peter Berger, *The Sacred Canopy: Elements of a Sociological Theory of Religion* (New York: Doubleday, 1967); A. James Reichley, *Religion in American Public Life* (Washington, DC: Brookings, 1985); Richard John Neuhaus, *The Naked Public Square* (Grand Rapids, MI: Eerdmans, 1984).

33. In particular, Reichley's argument seems more directly theological than those of Neuhaus or Berger.

34. For a more detailed analysis of these considerations, see Jelen, "In Defense of Religious Minimalism."

35. See Ted G. Jelen and Clyde Wilcox, "The Political Roles of Religion," in *Religion and Politics in Comparative Perspective: The One, the Few and the Many,* eds. Ted G. Jelen and Clyde Wilcox (New York: Cambridge University Press, 2002), 314–324.

36. James Davison Hunter, *Culture Wars* (New York: Basic Books, 1991); Rhys Williams, ed., *Culture Wars in American Politics* (New York: Aldine Transaction, 1997).

37. See Richard N. Ostling, "What Does God Really Think About Sex?" *Time* (June 24, 1991), 48–50.

38. This would suggest that from a political standpoint (as opposed to a legal one) the Supreme Court's relatively libertarian positions in *Sherbert v. Verner* (1963) and *Wisconsin v. Yoder* (1972) may represent more authentically the nature of the Free Exercise Clause than the Court's more recent (and restrictive) decisions in *Employment Division v. Smith* (1990) and *City of Boerne v. Flores* (1997).

39. See Byrnes, "The Challenge of Pluralism," and Michele Dillon, "Catholicism, Politics and Culture in the Republic or Ireland," in *Religion and Politics in Comparative Perspective: The One, the Few and the Many,* eds. Ted G. Jelen and Clyde Wilcox (New York: Cambridge University Press, 2002), 47–70.

40. Mehran Tamadonfar and Ted G. Jelen, "Religion and Regime Change in Iran and Poland," paper presented at the annual meeting of the Southern Political Science Association, New Orleans, Louisiana, January 2006.

41. See Stark and Finke, *Acts of Faith.*

42. Jose Casanova, *Public Religions in the Modern World* (Chicago: University of Chicago Press, 1994).

43. Now the United States Council of Catholic Bishops.

44. See especially Clarke Cochran, *Religion in Public and Private Life* (New York: Routledge, 1991).

45. For an elaboration of these arguments, see Jelen, "In Defense of Religious Minimalism."

46. Clyde Wilcox and Carin Larson, *Onward Christian Soldiers: The Religious Right in American Politics* (Boulder, CO: Westview Press, 2002).

47. David D. Kirkpatrick, "Guiliani Inspires Threat of a Third-Party Run," *New York Times* (October 1, 2007).

48. Tamadonfar and Jelen, "Religion and Regime Change."

BIBLIOGRAPHY

Books

Berger, Peter. *The Sacred Canopy: Elements of a Sociological Theory of Religion.* New York: Doubleday, 1967.

Berman, Marshall. *The Politics of Authenticity.* New York: Atheneum, 1970.

Casanova, Jose. *Public Religions in the Modern World.* Chicago: University of Chicago Press, 1994.

Choper, Jesse. *Securing Religious Liberty.* Chicago: University of Chicago Press, 1994.

Cochran, Clarke. *Religion in Public and Private Life.* New York: Routledge, 1991.

Finke, Roger, and Rodney Stark. *The Churching of America, 1776–1990.* New Brusnwick, NJ: Rutgers University Press, 1992.

Glendon, Mary Ann. *Rights Talk.* New York: Free Press, 1991.

Greenawalt, Kent. *Religious Convictions and Political Choice.* New York: Oxford University Press, 1991.

Hunter, James Davison. *Culture Wars.* New York: Basic Books, 1991.

Jelen, Ted G. *The Political Mobilization of Religious Beliefs.* Westport, CT: Praeger, 1991.

———. *The Political World of the Clergy.* Westport, CT: Praeger, 1993.

Mill, John Stuart. *Autobiography.* Boston: Houghton-Mifflin, 1969.

———. *On Liberty.* New York: Oxford University Press, 1975.

Mill, John Stuart. *Considerations on Representative Government.* New York: Oxford University Press, 1975.

Monsma, Stephen V. and J. Christoper Soper. *The Challenge of Pluralism: Church and State in Five Democracies.* Lanham, MD: Rowman and Littlefield, 1997.

National Council of Catholic Bishops. *The Challenge of Peace: God's Promise and Our Response.* Washington, DC: United States Catholic Conference, 1983.

National Council of Catholic Bishops. *Economic Justice for All.* Washington, DC: United States Catholic Conference, 1986.

Neuhaus, Richard John. *The Naked Public Square.* Grand Rapids, MI: Eerdmans, 1984.

Noelle-Neuman, Elisabeth. *The Spiral of Silence: Public Opinion—Our Social Skin.* Chicago: University of Chicago Press, 1993.

Perry, Michael J. *Love and Power: The Role of Religion and Morality in American Politics.* New York: Oxford University Press, 1991.

Peters, Shawn Frances. *The Yoder Case: Religious Freedom, Education, and Parental Rights.* Lawrence, KS: University Press of Kansas, 2003.

Putnam, Robert. *Bowling Alone: The Collapse and Revival of American Community.* New York: Simon and Schuster, 2000.

Rawls, John. *Political Liberalism.* New York: Columbia University Press, 1993.

Reichely, A. James. *Religion in American Public Life.* Washington, DC: Brookings Institution, 1985.

Smidt,. Corwin E., Kevin denDulk, Douglas L. Kopman, Stephen V. Monsma, and James M. Penning. *Pews, Prayers, and Participation: The Role of Religion in Fostering Civic Responsibility* Washington, DC: Georgetown University Press (2008).

Stark, Rodney and Roger Finke. *Acts of Faith: Explaining the Human Side of Religion.* Berkeley, CA: University of California Press, 2000.

Thiemann, Ronald. *Religion in Public Life: A Dilemma for Democracy.* Washington, DC: Georgetown University Press, 1996.

Tocqueville, Alexis de. *Democracy in America.* 2 vols. Ed. Bradley Phillips. New York: Vintage Books, 1945.

Verba, Sidney, Kay Lehman Schlozman, and Henry E. Brady. *Voice and Equality: Civic Voluntarism in American Politics.* Cambridge, MA: Harvard University Press, 1995.

Wilcox, Clyde. *God's Warriors: The Christian Right in the 20th Century.* Baltimore: Johns Hopkins University Press, 1992.

Wilcox, Clyde and Carin Larson. *Onward Christian Soldiers: The Religious Right in American Politics.* Boulder, CO: Westview Press, 2002.

Williams, Rhys, ed. *Culture Wars in American Politics.* New York: Aldine Transaction, 1997.

Articles/Chapters

Bishop, George F. "Evolution, Religion, and the 'Culture War' in American Politics," paper presented at the annual meeting of the American Political Science Association, Chicago, September, 2007.

Bruce, Steve. "The Poverty of Economism or the Social Limits on Maximizing." In *Sacred Markets, Sacred Canopies: Essays on Religious Markets and Religious Pluralism,* ed. Ted G. Jelen. Lanham, MD: Rowman and Littlefield, 2002.

Byrnes, Timothy. "The Challenge of Pluralism: The Catholic Church in Democratic Poland," in *Religion and Politics in Comparative Perspective: The One, the Few, and the*

Many, eds. Ted G. Jelen and Clyde Wilcox. New York: Cambridge University Press, 2002.

Dillon, Michele. "Catholicism, Politics, and Culture in the Republic of Ireland," in *Religion and Politics in Comparative Perspective: The One, the Few, and the Many*, eds. Ted G. Jelen and Clyde Wilcox. New York: Cambridge University Press, 2002.

Haider-Markell, Donald P., and Mark R. Joslyn. "Pulpits versus Ivory Towers: Socializing Agents and Evolution Attitudes," *Social Science Quarterly* 89 (September 2008) 665.

Iannaccone, Laurence. "The Consequences of Religious Market Structure." *Rationality and Society* 3 (1991): 156.

Jelen, Ted G. "In Defense of Religious Minimalism," in *A Wall of Separation? Debating the Public Role of Religion, eds.* Mary Segers and Ted G. Jelen. Lanham, MD: Rowman and Littlefield, 1998.

Jelen, Ted G. "Reflections on the 'New Paradigm:' Unfinished Business, and an Agenda for Research." in *Sacred Markets, Sacred Canopies: Essays on Religious Markets and Religious Pluralism,* ed. Ted G. Jelen. Lanham, MD: Rowman and Littlefield, 2002.

Jelen, Ted G. "Political Esperanto: Rhetorical Resources and Limitations of the Christian Right in the United States." *Sociology of Religion* 66 (2005): 303.

Jelen, Ted G. "Religion and American Public Opinion: Social Issues." in *Handbook on Religion and American Politics, eds.* Corwin E. Smidt, et al. Oxford, UK: Oxford University Press 89 (September 2008) 665.

Jelen, Ted G. and Clyde Wilcox. "The Political Roles of Religion." in *Religion and Politics in Comparative Perspective: The One, the Few, and the Many,* eds. Ted G. Jelen and Clyde Wilcox. New York: Cambridge University Press, 2002.

Kirkpatrick, David D. "Guliani Inspires Threat of a Third-Party Run." *The New York Times*, October 1, 2007.

Ostling, Richard N. "What Does God Really Think About Sex?" *Time* (June 24, 1991), 48.

Sezer, L. Kent. "The Constitutional Underpinnings of the Abortion Debate," in *Perspectives on the Politics of Abortion,* ed. Ted G. Jelen. Westport, CT: Praeger, 1995.

Tamadonfar, Mehran, and Ted G. Jelen. "Religion and Regime Change in Iran and Poland," paper presented at the annual meeting of the Southern Political Science Association, New Orleans, January 2006.

Way, Frank and Barbara Burt. "Religious Marginality and the Free Exercise Clause." *American Political Science Review* 77 (1983): 654.

Wilcox, Clyde, Paul R. Brewer, Shauna Shames, and Celinda Lake. "'If I Bend This Far, I Will Break?' Public Opinion and Same-Sex Marriage," in *The Politics of Same-Sex Marriage,* eds. Craig A. Rimmerman and Clyde Wilcox. Chicago: University of Chicago Press, 2007.

CHAPTER 12

....

PURSUIT OF THE MORAL GOOD AND THE CHURCH–STATE CONUNDRUM IN THE UNITED STATES: THE POLITICS OF SEXUAL ORIENTATION

....

ANDREW R. MURPHY

AND CAITLIN KERR

FORMER United States Solicitor General and Justice of Massachusetts' Supreme Judicial Court Charles Fried recently wrote that "[t]he greatest enemy of liberty has always been some vision of the good."[1] Fried's claim provides a provocative point of entry into the complex relationship among morality, ethics, religion, and American law in the early twenty-first century. How does the American constitutional system promote or impede talking about, or acting upon, moral visions? How does it seek to balance the aspirations of democratic majorities with the protection of minority perspectives on the good? This chapter focuses on one specific area of the law that has been deeply enmeshed in conflicting ideas about human morality in recent years: the intersection between individual liberty, autonomy, and evolving notions of human sexuality and appropriate sexual behavior.

How could a vision of the good be the enemy of liberty? All individuals hold some sense of the good, often derived from what John Rawls has called "comprehensive doctrines;" that is, "conceptions of what is of value in human life, as well as ideals of personal virtue and character, that . . . inform much of our nonpolitical conduct."[2] Visions of the good dictate how adherents ought to structure their pursuits, which faculties to develop and which to suppress, and suggest the sort of life plan most conducive to the realization of fundamental values. In a constitutional democracy, liberties of speech, assembly, and the press can promote a diverse moral landscape by ensuring that adherents of various visions of the moral good can gather and promote their views in the public sphere. At the same time, however, visions of the good that command the allegiance of majorities often find their way into legal codes and criminal statutes, when democratic majorities, in the course of the political process, enact particularistic moral views into law. Even lacking explicit political or legal sanction, conceptions of the good often work through the more subtle mechanisms of custom, culture, and tradition, privileging some values while discouraging or stigmatizing others. In Fried's view, granting political or social power to a substantive moral vision—about the values that people should hold, and the significance of those values for individual and communal life—threatens to run roughshod over the rights of individuals or the moral visions of minority communities.

This chapter begins with a brief look at the historical and theoretical foundations of the American approach to moral pluralism among its citizenry, which focused largely on religious matters but laid constitutional foundations that illuminate broader issues of diversity on a host of moral issues.[3] It then turns more specifically to questions of privacy and sexuality and examines a series of cases culminating in *Bowers v. Hardwick* (1986) and *Lawrence v. Texas* (2003).[4] The differing outcomes of these two cases illustrate clearly the way that the Court has reflected public uncertainty about moral diversity over the course of the past two decades. In both *Bowers* and *Lawrence,* the Court faced criminal statutes embodying moral views regarding proper sexual behavior. Insofar as the issues at stake in *Bowers* and *Lawrence* involve sexual behavior, and particularly the kind of sexual behavior at the heart of moral debate in America,[5] a closer look at these two cases will illuminate broader questions of liberty, privacy, and the good that have become central to American politics and culture in the twenty-first century. It concludes with some reflections on possible future trajectories involving same-sex marriage and the implications of *Lawrence.*

Historical Foundations: American Colonization and the Founding

American colonization grew out of, yet departed sharply from, its English roots.[6] The Church of England served important functions in maintaining and reinforcing social cohesion, and English rulers had long expected church leaders to use their positions to inculcate morality, piety, allegiance, and obedience. (Even after the Toleration Act of 1689—in which most Protestant sects achieved permission to exist alongside the Anglican Church—a number of social, political, and legal privileges continued to attach to membership in the Church of England.)

Visions of the good—many of them rooted in religion—have flourished throughout American history. The interplay of moral visions and American public life predates the nation's founding as well, reaching back into the colonial period. Indeed, the pursuit of a moral vision, grounded in Puritanism, spurred the Great Migration to America during the 1620s and 1630s. Puritan elites imagined themselves erecting godly settlements in this New World, settlements that would allow them to live out their understandings of true Protestantism in ways unavailable to them under England's established church. The restrictions on personal liberty so common in early New England, then, must be viewed against the backdrop of this search for a godly community, a community that regulated individual behavior in the service of a moral vision. Puritan elites did not object to the idea that government ought to enforce moral and religious orthodoxy; rather, they insisted that the English Church was fatally flawed and that its coercive presence in their lives made godliness nearly impossible. After risking a dangerous ocean crossing in the pursuit of their moral vision, Puritan elites were decidedly unsympathetic to those whose conceptions diverged sharply from their own. As a result, the first several decades of New England settlement saw a number of deeply divisive conflicts over the rights of religious dissenters, and a relatively successful defense of orthodoxy by New England elites.

Much of the early history of American settlement is the story of the gradual, protracted, contested, and always precarious growth of religious liberty in the colonies.[7] However, such liberty could and did coexist with governmental regulation of public morality. Fifty years after the settlement of the Massachusetts Bay colony, William Penn journeyed to Pennsylvania to initiate his "holy experiment" in which colonists of various faiths would live together under a regime of religious toleration. Penn denied that civil government possessed the right to dictate the consciences of its subjects, and he sought to allow religious minorities a wider degree of participation in public life than existed in England at the time. Penn denied the Puritan contention that government should enforce religious orthodoxy, but he insisted that government must enforce general tenets of public morality.[8] Penn retained a substantive moral vision—grounded, in his view, in natural law and the nature of conscience—about what ought to be allowed in public life more generally. As he put it in his *Laws Agreed Upon in England,* "there shall be no taverns, nor alehouses, endured in the [province], nor any playhouses, nor morris dances, nor games as dice, cards, board tables, lotteries, bowling greens, horse races, bear baitings, bull baitings, and such like sports, which tend only to idleness and looseness."[9] The raucous, at times chaotic, nature of early Pennsylvania politics mirrored and reinforced the colony's religiously pluralistic public life: The benevolent Quaker hegemony envisioned by Penn quickly turned into a contentious public sphere in which Quakers and non-Quakers vied for influence. In many ways, then, despite its English background, the Pennsylvania experience resembled the Dutch tradition of toleration so important in the history of the middle colonies, especially New York, as much as it did the English.[10]

At the time of the nation's founding, the American constitutional system took a rather different approach than the English, eschewing a national establishment by announcing in the First Amendment to the Constitution that "Congress shall make no law respecting an establishment of religion, or prohibiting the free exercise thereof." The product of an alliance between evangelicals who sought to protect the church's purity from state corruption and Deist skeptics who sought to safeguard the political realm from power-hungry priests, American disestablishment recognized religious diversity (a diversity, we might say, of views of the good) as a fundamental fact of the American landscape. It was a fact in which Americans took a great deal of pride.[11] The Constitution's prohibition on religious tests for office-holding, furthermore, represented a rejection of English practice and sought to ensure that a wide variety of religious perspectives would be represented in the halls of government. Of course individual states could and did retain establishments, but by the 1830s the final one, in Massachusetts, had fallen, a further concession (if a grudging one) to moral and religious pluralism in American society.

Throughout the early national period, American society witnessed waves of religious revival and reformism, and religious energy continued to contribute to a vibrant, often conflictual, social and political landscape. Religious energy was instrumental in the Second Great Awakening of the early nineteenth century, the steady acceptance of marginalized religions (Mormons, Millerites) into a Protestant-dominated religious culture, and the heavy involvement of evangelical Protestants in movements for moral reform (e.g., temperance, women's rights, antipoverty, abolition). Americans, Tocqueville commented, are constantly joining with their fellow citizens to express their views on a host of public issues, including controversies over the moral good.

> Americans are taught from birth that they must overcome life's woes and impediments on their own . . . . In the United States, people associate for purposes pertaining to public security, commerce and industry, morality and religion. There is nothing the human will despairs of achieving through the free action of the collective power of individuals . . . . Although religion in the United States never intervenes directly in government, it must be regarded as the first of America's political institutions, for even if religion does not give Americans their taste for liberty, it does notably facilitate their use of that liberty.[12]

Such a phenomenon is not without dangers, of course, and Tocqueville also noted that "freedom of association has become a necessary guarantee against the tyranny of the majority . . . . [n]owhere are associations more necessary to prevent either the despotism of the parties or the arbitrariness of the prince than in countries whose social state is democratic."[13]

Much of this energy of early American society, mentioned in the preceding, was fed by religious diversity. Religious diversity, in turn, was fostered by basic social and geographical facts: the availability of land to the west, which beckoned to groups who dissented from predominant notions of community; the localism so central to early

American identity; concrete aspects of the constitutional system (its division of authority between local, state, federal governments, its reservation of unenumerated rights to the states; its protection of concurrent rights such as speech and assembly along with religion). These elements combined to form a powerful impediment to any group wishing to impose, through law or custom, a sectarian identity on the nation. Even within the broad contours of Protestant hegemony and its associated anti-Catholicism, the varieties of American Protestantism often fought bitterly among themselves.[14]

Moral Diversity, American Constitutionalism, and Liberal Theory

The American constitutional system recognizes moral pluralism and diversity as an ineradicable element of modern social life. Such an understanding was fundamental to arguments in favor of the Constitution's ratification, and remains crucial to the protections afforded to a wide range of individuals and groups in the twenty-first century.

Madison famously acknowledged in *Federalist 10* that "[a]s long as the reason of man continues fallible, and he is at liberty to exercise it, different opinions will be formed." As he elaborated,

> The latent causes of faction are thus sown in the nature of man; and we see them everywhere brought into different degrees of activity, according to the different circumstances of civil society. A zeal for different opinions concerning religion, concerning government, and many other points, as well of speculation as of practice; an attachment to different leaders ambitiously contending for pre-eminence and power; or to persons of other descriptions whose fortunes have been interesting to the human passions, have, in turn, divided mankind into parties, inflamed them with mutual animosity, and rendered them much more disposed to vex and oppress each other than to co-operate for their common good.

Madison expressed his hope that enlightened leaders would be chosen by the people, and that an active and engaged citizenry would vigilantly guard their own liberties. However, he did not rest his hope there, invoking the large scale of the American territories and its ability to frustrate the ambitions of factious leaders:

> Extend the sphere, and you take in a greater variety of parties and interests; you make it less probable that a majority of the whole will have a common motive to invade the rights of other citizens; or if such a common motive exists, it will be more difficult for all who feel it to discover their own strength, and to act in unison with each other.

Thus, he concluded, we find "a republican remedy for the diseases most incident to republican government."

Such efforts to neutralize the potential for majorities to impose their visions of the good on society, of course, did not end with Madison. The Civil War amendments represented an attempt to protect minorities from a hostile surrounding culture (although in this case one based not on belief or religious views, but rather on ideologies of racial supremacy). Madison's insights—that it is not possible to "give every citizen the same opinions, the same passions, and the same interests"—and their early modern context of religious conflict continue to inform much contemporary liberal thinking about the relationship between religion and politics, which has been heavily influenced by John Stuart Mill's *On Liberty*. Mill argued stridently in favor of marginalized or minority viewpoints, concerning himself far more with social tyranny (the influence of custom and tradition, in which "society is itself the tyrant") than with explicit political tyranny.

In our own time, John Rawls' "political liberalism" builds its system of basic liberties on the recognition of reasonable pluralism:

> [P]olitical liberalism takes for granted not simply pluralism but reasonable pluralism . . . . [R]easonable pluralism is not a mere historical condition that may soon pass away . . . but the long-run outcome of the work of human reason under enduring free institutions.[15]

Consequently, Rawls argues, because a diversity of views of the good is a fundamental fact of modern life, societies should give up the ideal of political community understood as "united on one (partial or fully) comprehensive religious, philosophical, or moral doctrine."[16] Rather, modern liberal societies should insist on the priority of the right over the good, ensuring citizens the autonomy to choose and pursue their own plans of life.

In a similar vein, David A.J. Richards sees toleration and the protection of conscience—the refusal to sanction a particular moral view into law—as the "central constitutional ideal" that underwrites liberationist movements around issues of religion, gender, and sexual orientation. Richards compares the movement for gay and lesbian rights in American law to struggles for religious, gender, and racial equality, concluding his most recent book with the argument that same-sex marriage represents the logical fulfillment of the Constitution's tolerationist ideals. Echoing Justice Kennedy's opinion in *Romer v. Evans,* Richards argues that anti-gay initiatives "express constitutionally forbidden sectarian religious intolerance through public law . . ."[17]

Privacy, Liberty, and Sexuality in Politics and the Law: Fundamental Rights, Strict Scrutiny, and the Conflict of Moralities

Issues of religious belief and practice—the classic "church and state" cases—have long represented, institutionally speaking, the most obvious ways in which visions of the good and American politics have intersected throughout American history.

In *Reynolds v. United States* (1878), the Supreme Court upheld criminal laws against polygamy over the free exercise objections of Mormon defendants: In the noted words of that decision, "Laws are made for the government of actions, and while they cannot interfere with mere religious belief and opinions, they may with practices."[18] The flag-salute cases of the 1940s dealt squarely with the circumstances under which one community's notion of the good may legitimately be imposed upon a subcommunity that finds such expressions odious. Reversing a decision that the Court had made just three years earlier, Justice Jackson wrote in *Barnette* that "[i]f there is any fixed star in our constitutional constellation, it is that no official, high or petty, can prescribe what shall be orthodox in politics, nationalism, religion, or other matters of opinion, or force citizens to confess by word or act their faith therein."[19]

The Court's decision in *Schempp*, striking down organized prayer in public schools, represented another significant step in the removal of religious practices from the nation's public life.[20] During that same decade, the Court's conscientious objection cases noted "the richness and variety of spiritual life in our country," and the challenges that such diversity posed for lawmakers.

> Over 250 sects inhabit our land. Some believe in a purely personal God, some in a supernatural deity; others think of religion as a way of life envisioning as its ultimate goal the day when all men can live together in perfect understanding and peace. There are those who think of God as the depth of our being; others, such as the Buddhists, strive for a state of lasting rest through self-denial and inner purification; in Hindu philosophy, the Supreme Being is the transcendental reality which is truth, knowledge and bliss. Even those religious groups which have traditionally opposed war in every form have splintered into various denominations. . .[21]

The Court went on to redefine the acceptable definition of "religious" exemptions from military service, part of a broader process often referred to as "the secularization of conscience."[22]

The preceding cases deal with situations in which the tensions between religious and moral views on the one hand and the claims of governmental decision makers on the other are relatively overt and explicit. However, there are other ways in which conflicting notions of the moral good—both individual and communal—intersect with legal and political affairs. The remainder of this chapter explores a slightly different set of issues that shed light on the pursuit of these moral goods. The relevant background for our inquiry lies in a series of cases from the 1960s and 1970s, cases that highlight the evolving nature of visions of the good as they pertain to human sexuality and the role of sexual behavior in the construction of individual identity.

Given the intimate nature of sexual behavior, and the way that notions of proper sexual conduct grow out of larger moral systems and views of human nature, these cases articulated and developed a line of interpretation around the concept of privacy and its connection with individual liberty and autonomy. In *Griswold v. Connecticut* (1965), the Court invalidated a Connecticut drug that prohibited the use of "any drug, medicinal article or instrument for the purpose of preventing conception" by referring to a "right to marital privacy."[23] Seven years later, in *Eisenstadt v. Baird* (1972), the Court extended the ruling in *Griswold* to unmarried citizens, again referring to privacy rights: "If the right of privacy means anything, it is the right of the individual, married or single, to be free from unwarranted governmental intrusion into matters so fundamentally affecting a person as the decision whether to bear or beget a child."[24] Finally, and perhaps most controversially, we find in Justice Blackmun's majority opinion in *Roe*, that "[t]his right of privacy . . . is broad enough to encompass a woman's decision whether or not to terminate her pregnancy."[25] Against the backdrop of this increasingly robust defense of the right of privacy as related to issues surrounding (hetero)sexual ideas and practices, the *Bowers* case in 1986 presented the Court with an opportunity to extend such privacy rights to homosexual conduct. The Court declined this opportunity.

HOMOSEXUAL RIGHTS AND *BOWERS V. HARDWICK*

In *Bowers*, the Court upheld a Georgia statute criminalizing sodomy. In doing so, the Court ruled against a respondent who claimed that laws criminalizing private, consensual homosexual behavior violated his fundamental rights, and that the government should thus be required to demonstrate a compelling interest, and show that the legislation represented the most narrowly drawn means of achieving that interest.[26] Relying on such cases as *Griswold, Eisenstadt, Stanley,* and *Roe,* the Georgia Court of Appeals for the Eleventh Circuit had agreed, holding that homosexual activity was a "private and intimate association" beyond the realm of state regulation under the Ninth Amendment and the Due Process Clause of the Fourteenth Amendment.[27]

Despite Hardwick's attempts to have the case viewed broadly as one involving fundamental rights, the U.S. Supreme Court insisted on the narrowest drawing of the rights at stake. In Justice White's opinion for the Court, "the issue presented is whether the Federal Constitution confers a fundamental right upon homosexuals to engage in sodomy and hence invalidates the laws of the many states that still make such conduct illegal and have done so for a very long time."[28] The important expansions of the right to privacy notwithstanding—the succession of cases including *Griswold* through *Roe*—in *Bowers* the Court steadfastly denied that such a privacy right extended to homosexual activity. To be considered a "fundamental right" and thus qualify for the heightened protection sought by Hardwick, homosexual activity would have to have been "deeply rooted in this nation's history and tradition" or "implicit in the concept of ordered liberty."[29] Returning to the focus on homosexual behavior, White concluded that "It is obvious to us that neither of these formulations would extend a fundamental right to homosexuals to engage in acts of consensual sodomy."[30]

The denial that laws criminalizing sodomy infringed on fundamental rights changed, of course, the Court's analysis of the legislation in question; and the fact that moral disapproval of homosexual behavior likely lay behind antisodomy legislation did not automatically threaten those laws' legitimacy. In denying Hardwick's claim that the fundamental right to privacy pertains to homosexual activity, it affirmed that a "rational basis" for Georgia's antisodomy legislation did, in fact, exist:

> Even if the conduct at issue here is not a fundamental right, respondent asserts that there must be a rational basis for the law and that there is none in this case other than the presumed belief of a majority of the electorate in Georgia that homosexual sodomy is immoral and unacceptable. This is said to be an inade-quate rationale to support the law. The law, however, is constantly based on notions of morality, and if all laws representing essentially moral choices are to be invalidated under the Due Process Clause, the courts will be very busy indeed.[31]

White shifted the focus from the case at hand to a consideration of the nature of law more generally. The law, said White, is consistently reflective of notions of morality, and the Court risks its own legitimacy if it appears to be inventing new fundamental rights "having little or no cognizable roots in the language or design of the Constitution."[32] At the very least, the Court held, the fact that a particular piece of legislation is based upon a majority's moral opinions unpersuasive as a reason to invalidate such legislation.

If White laid out, in dispassionate and rather general ways, the reasons for hes-itating to declare homosexual conduct a fundamental right, Chief Justice Burger's brief concurrence in *Bowers* provides a more detailed discussion of the specific moral visions at work. Burger's concurrence invokes language indicative not only of moral but also of religious considerations, and shows, even more clearly than the majority opinion, the ways in which liberty and visions of the good (to return to Fried's formulation) may come into direct conflict. He supplemented the Court's evidence with the additional fact that "condemnation of those practices is firmly rooted in Judeo-Christian moral and ethical standards. . .under Roman law. . .and during the English Reformation."[33] The English common law prohibition of sod-omy entered the American legal tradition during colonial times, and a declaration of sodomy as a fundamental right would cast aside "millennia of moral teaching."[34]

Justice Blackmun's dissent, joined by Justices Brennan, Marshall, and Stevens, argued that the Court erred in focusing on homosexual sodomy as opposed to the right to privacy: "[T]his case is about the most comprehensive of rights and rights most valued by civilized men, namely, the right to be let alone."[35] The fact that the State of Georgia had decided that this "right to be let alone" did not apply to sexual conduct of one particular kind reflected longstanding moral disapproval of homo-sexuality, a justification that Blackmun refused to endorse. He echoed the words of Justice Holmes in *Lochner v. New York*:

> [I]t is revolting to have no better reason for a rule of law than that so it was laid down in the time of Henry IV. It is still more revolting if the grounds upon which

it was laid down have vanished long since, and the rule simply persists from blind imitation of the past . . . [in which sodomy was] 'an abominable crime not fit to be named among Christians.'[36]

In approaching the issues raised by *Bowers*, Blackmun cited *Lochner*'s holding that the majority's moral opinion "ought not to conclude our judgment upon the question whether statutes embodying them conflict with the Constitution of the United States."[37] Instead, Blackmun returned the focus to privacy rights, the "right to be let alone."

The privacy right, according to Blackmun, involves both "decisional" and "spatial" aspects. With regard to the spatial aspects, Blackmun made special note of the fact that the behavior in question took place in the privacy of his own home, "a place to which the Fourth Amendment attaches special significance."[38] Within the right of privacy, considered in its spatial dimensions, lies a presumption against the restriction of one's decisions that occur and play out primarily in the home: "Indeed, the right of an individual to conduct intimate relationships in the intimacy of his or her own home seems to me to be at the heart of the Constitution's protection of privacy." The right to privacy, in Blackmun's opinion, is thus not just about "the breaking of a person's doors, and the rummaging of his drawers, but rather is the invasion of his indefensible right of personal security, personal liberty, and private property."[39]

The decisional aspect of the privacy right deals with issues related to individual identity: Blackmun described marriage and procreation as protected rights "not because they contribute in some direct and material way, to the general public welfare, but because they form so central a part of an individual's life . . . [including] the happiness of individuals."[40] This right to personal happiness is further connected with the nation's diversity, because "in a Nation as diverse as ours, that there may be many "right" ways of conducting those relationships, and . . . much of the richness of a relationship will come from the *freedom an individual has to choose* the form and nature of these intensely personal bonds."[41] The "form and nature" of such personal bonds epitomize the diverse visions of the moral good in a diverse society.

Blackmun identified a concern for public decency as the core justification offered by the State of Georgia for its antisodomy legislation. Yet any such notions of decency ultimately involve moral, perhaps even religious, notions based on longstanding animus toward homosexuality; Blackmun noted that the state's invocation of Leviticus, Romans, Aquinas, and medieval sources fails to establish a legitimate justification for such legislation:

> That certain, but by no means all, religious groups condemn the behavior at issue gives the State no license to impose their judgments on the entire citizenry. The legitimacy of sexual legislation depends instead on whether the State can advance some justification for its law beyond its conformity to religious doctrine. . . . A State can no more punish private behavior because of religious intolerance than it can punish such behavior because of racial animus. . . . Private biases may be outside the reach of the law, but the law cannot, directly or indirectly, give them effect.[42]

Although the Court should remain mindful of the majority will, the religious majority's approval of a certain behavior is not a singularly legitimate support for the Court's judgment in this and other cases. To do so, in Blackmun's view, is to allow the moral good as understood by the majority to deprive minorities of their liberty in this most private of human behaviors.

We have dwelt at some length on Blackmun's dissent in this brief account of the Court's decision in *Bowers,* in large part because it raised many of the issues that would later appear in Justice Kennedy's majority opinion in *Lawrence.* We now turn to *Lawrence.*

HOMOSEXUAL RIGHTS AND *LAWRENCE V. TEXAS*

Seventeen years after its decision in *Bowers,* the Court revisited the issue of antisodomy legislation in *Lawrence v. Texas.* The facts of the case, although not identical, were broadly similar: Two defendants were arrested in the bedroom of a private residence while engaging in conduct forbidden by state statute. (Although the Texas statute forbade only sodomy between same-sex couples—and thus an equal protection claim formed part of Lawrence's objection to the legislation—this element did not figure into the majority or dissenting opinions in the case, and will be set aside here.)[43] The fact that the Texas Court of Appeals held *Bowers* to be controlling in its decision against Lawrence required the Court to revisit *Bowers* in its consideration of Lawrence's challenge.

After setting the broad context of its consideration of *Lawrence* in the privacy cases mentioned in the preceding (*Griswold, Eisenstadt, Roe, Carey*), Justice Kennedy, writing for the *Lawrence* majority, signaled the Court's departure from *Bowers* almost immediately, criticizing the earlier Court's exclusive focus on a so-called fundamental right to sodomy as "disclos[ing] the Court's failure to appreciate the extent of the liberty at stake."[44] In the majority opinion's first sentence, Kennedy placed issues of liberty and privacy front and center: "Liberty protects the person from unwarranted government intrusions into a dwelling or other private places." Such liberty was closely associated with the right of privacy laid out from *Griswold* to *Carey:*

> The laws involved in *Bowers* and here are . . . statutes that purport to do no more
> than prohibit a particular sexual act. Their penalties and purposes, though, have
> more far-reaching consequences, touching upon the most private human
> conduct, sexual behavior, and in the most private of places, the home. The
> statutes do seek to control a personal relationship that, whether or not entitled to
> formal recognition in the law, is within the liberty of persons to choose without
> being punished as criminals.[45]

However, Kennedy's opinion went farther than simply connecting liberty and privacy: It also highlighted the role played by sexuality with respect to deeper notions of human personality and identity: "When sexuality finds overt expression in intimate conduct with another person, the conduct can be but one element in a personal bond that is more enduring."[46] The Court did not address whether there is a fundamental right to engage in sodomy laid out in so many words in the Constitution, but did hold that one's sexual decisions fall under the fundamental right to privacy so key to *Griswold, Eisenstadt,* and *Roe.*

Thus the fact that antisodomy legislation represents the expression of a majority's will through the political process can not be the final word on its constitutional legitimacy.

> It must be acknowledged, of course, that the Court in *Bowers* was making the broader point that for centuries there have been powerful voices to condemn homosexual behavior as immoral. The condemnation has been shaped by religious beliefs, conceptions of right and acceptable behavior, and respect for the traditional family. For many persons these are not trivial concerns but profound and deep convictions accepted as ethical and moral principles to which they aspire and which thus determine the course of their lives. These considerations do not answer that question before us, however. The issue is whether the majority may use the power of the State to enforce these views on the whole society through operation of the criminal law.[47]

Although, as mentioned, in *Lawrence* the Court never clarified the status of "fundamental rights"—nor did it proclaim whether sexual activity is one of those rights—it clearly views the outlawing of a specific form of sexual intimacy, especially when that sanction is founded on historically religious or moral grounds, as constitutionally questionable. *Lawrence* seeks to carve out a space in which personal liberty is protected from majoritarian democratic processes and the majority's sectarian vision of the good (in this sense, the good of normative heterosexuality). In other words, the Court views its objective as separating the state from visions of the moral and religious good that attempt to infringe on liberty. In doing so, the Court must determine whether the will of the majority finds a basis outside of moral teaching by which to legitimize its intrusion into the citizens' private sphere. Although the *Bowers* Court suggested that it would risk its own legitimacy if it invented a new fundamental right (not to mention a right to homosexual sodomy), the *Lawrence* Court views the denial of privacy as risking its legitimacy: quoting its opinion in *Casey,* Kennedy argued that "the Court's obligation is to define the liberty of all, not to mandate its own moral code."[48]

Given the contemporary view of the importance of sexuality to one's identity, the Court found even less of a foundation on which to continue to endorse *Bowers. Griswold,* as we have seen, established that the right to privacy has consistently protected personal decisions, ruling that "If the right to privacy means anything, it is the right of the *individual,* married or single, to be free from unwarranted governmental intrusion into matters . . . fundamentally affecting a person." Decisions fundamental to a person's identity are included within the right to privacy, echoing Blackmun's language of the right to determine one's identity as fundamental to personal happiness and fulfillment in the *Bowers* dissent. Just as Blackmun recognized that certain relationships enhance one's personal happiness, *Lawrence* recognizes that decisions about entering into these relationships and engaging in behaviors appropriate to them are integral to one's identity. Whereas the *Bowers* majority viewed the case as simply involving one's right to engage in a sexual act, *Lawrence* considers the greater implications of the *decisions* to engage in this act and the meaning that such a decision carries for issues of identity and character. *Griswold* and other cases are evidence of the "emerging awareness that liberty gives substantial protection to adult persons in deciding how to conduct their private lives in matters pertaining to sex."[49]

Justice Scalia's dissent restated the language of fundamental rights so central to *Bowers,* and took issue with the *Lawrence* majority's unwillingness to say whether or not homosexual sodomy is such a right. Absent such a clarification, Scalia suggested, it is unclear on what grounds a court can invalidate properly enacted laws meant to discourage it.[50] In elaborating the societal reliance on *Bowers* that would argue against reversal, Scalia relied on the large number of legislative and judicial decisions that are based on moral perspectives: "Countless judicial decisions and legislative enactments have relied on ancient propositions that a governing majority's belief that certain sexual behavior is immoral and unacceptable constitutes a rational basis for regulation."[51] Visions of the moral good that govern the extent of one's liberty are not only legitimate, but expected catalysts in democratic systems. Furthermore, the invalidation of morality as a means of establishing legislation causes the proverbial slippery slope. The overruling of *Bowers* is dangerous because "state laws against bigamy, same-sex marriage, adult incest, prostitution, masturbation, adultery, fornication, bestiality, and obscenity are likewise sustainable only in light of *Bowers'* validation of laws based on moral choices."[52] The invalidation of *Bowers* illegitimizes moral disapproval as a means of legislation, and simultaneously invalidates all other state laws regarding these activities.

Scalia viewed the parameters of liberty in a democratic society as subject to the will of the majority. The extent of liberty may change as society's moral visions change. He suggested that "social perception of sexual and other morality can change over time, and every group has the right to persuade its fellow citizens that its view of such matters is best. . ."

> But persuading one's fellow citizens is one thing, and imposing one's views in absence of democratic majority will is something else. I would no more require a State to criminalize homosexual acts—or, for that matter, display any moral disapprobation of them—than I would forbid it to do so. . . . It is indeed true that "later generations can see that laws once thought necessary and proper in fact serve only to oppress," ante, at 18; and when that happens, later generations can repeal those laws. But it is the premise of our system that those judgments are to be made by the people, and not imposed by a governing caste that knows best.[53]

The determination of concepts such as liberty should rest with the will of the majority, expressed through the political process, and not with unelected judges. Of course, such definitions of liberty are likely to be shaped by moral visions held by majorities as well as minorities, but such is the nature of democratic politics. The solution to the shortcomings of democratic politics, suggests Scalia, is not activist judges legislating from the bench, but active legislators engaging in a vigorous political process.

MORALITY, POLITICS, AND LAW
BEYOND *LAWRENCE*

This chapter has looked at the way in which competing notions of the moral good are implicated in one of the more contentious issues of early–twenty-first century American law and politics. Since *Lawrence,* questions surrounding gay and lesbian rights have been engaged in at virtually every level of government. It remains to be seen, however, how any of these developments bear on the longstanding American debates over morality, autonomy, or liberty; or what the future might hold, either for the legal status of sexual behavior more generally, or for issues such as same-sex marriage.

Certainly *Lawrence* has animated critics from a variety of perspectives in American politics. For Robert P. George, the lesson of *Lawrence* is clear: "A majority of justices have made clear that they share the view, common in elite circles, that traditional standards of sexual morality are outmoded, and distinctions of any kind between heterosexual and homosexual conduct are rooted in animus and amount to bigotry." Andrew Sullivan sees *Lawrence* as opening the question of gay marriage and maintaining it insistently before both sympathizers and critics alike: "One of the key benefits of marriage, after all, is that it also upholds a common ideal of mutual support and caring; it not only enables such acts of responsibility but rewards and celebrates them. In the past you could argue that such measures were inappropriate for a criminal or would-be criminal subgroup. But after *Lawrence,* that is no longer the case."[54]

We have maintained throughout this chapter that legal and political debates over competing views of the good often occur outside of the narrow and traditional formulations of "church" and "state." We touched earlier on David A.J. Richards' argument that sexual identity involves issues analogous to religious conscience; indeed, Richards goes beyond analogy, and claims that sexual orientation involves a notion of moral conscience that operates at "exactly the same level" as religious faith.[55] More recently, he has argued that "claims of gay and lesbian identity— whether irreligiously, non-religiously, or religiously grounded—are decidedly among the dissident forms of conscience that should fully enjoy protection under the American tradition of religious liberty."[56] It is hardly coincidental, Richards adds, that the organized movements most active in seeking to deny civil and marriage rights to gay and lesbian Americans are themselves explicitly religious in nature. Thus, for Richards, fully comprehending the many dimensions of the struggle for gay and lesbian rights involves fundamentally rethinking terms such as conscience, religion, and identity; and noting their broad parallels with issues of sexuality and sexual orientation.

However, is this expansive notion of conscience the best way to understand the importance of *Lawrence* and what it might portend for the future? Perhaps a more stepwise analysis will enable us to track the progression of legal and political protection for sexual behavior. Yuval Merin's comparative work on the politics of gay and lesbian rights in European countries may be instructive here; Merin suggest a three-stage progression in which decriminalization of gay and lesbian sex acts sets a basic, minimal standard of toleration on which gay rights activists build a movement seeking antidiscrimination legislation on par with race and gender. From there, the campaign moves on to argue for legal recognition of same-sex partnerships on terms of equality with opposite-sex partnerships, including same-sex marriage.[57] Following this template, we might say that the United States achieved the first stage with *Lawrence v. Texas;* whereas the Court's 1997 ruling in *Romer v. Evans* indicates that aspects of the second may not be far off—although such claims must be tempered, given the many different levels and jurisdictions in which discrimination can persist.[58]

But when moving from such "negative" goals—decriminalization, for example, and nondiscrimination—to more "positive" agendas involving government recognition of same-sex relationships, the situation seems much more complicated. After all, marriage rights would raise intricate and intertwined legal issues including (although certainly not limited to) tax law, inheritance, and probate; authority over healthcare and end-of-life decisions, child-related issues such as adoption and custody, and the disposition of retirement, pension, and other insurance benefits. (Some of these aspects of the relationship, legally speaking, would no doubt mirror analogous issues in heterosexual marriages, but others would certainly require rethinking in the context of same-sex partnerships.) Richards' confident assertion that "the lack of any legal recognition for same-sex partnerships unconstitutionally burdens a right to intimate life [protected by *Lawrence*]" depends heavily on his empirical prediction that "once American culture comes reasonably to understand what gay/lesbian relationships really are, that understanding will require such [legal] recognition."[59] Richards' claims that same-sex marriage follows logically in the wake of *Lawrence* blurs the distinction between Merin's first and third stages, and runs the risk of misconstruing the historical development of conscience-based politics, which always sought "negative" rights of nonpersecution and shied away from more expansive claims about public recognition for same-sex marriage. Basic toleration, *a la Lawrence,* is a significant achievement, but should not be confused with the more ambitious, and more contested, agendas that might seek to build on it.

Indeed, broader social acceptance of same-sex marriage remained a distant hope for gay and lesbian activists. On November 2, 2004, 11 states voted on same-sex marriage bans as part of statewide ballots. All 11 passed. Six of these states (Arkansas, Georgia, Kentucky, Mississippi, North Dakota, and Oklahoma) passed the measures by comfortable margins. According to the National Conference of Legislatures, these same-sex marriage bans define marriage as between one man and one woman (Mississippi, Missouri, Montana, Oregon). Many others go further and state that a legal status which is substantially similar to marriage, such as a civil union, may not be recognized in the state (Arkansas, Georgia, Kentucky, Louisiana, Michigan, North Dakota, Ohio, Oklahoma, Utah). Nine ban civil unions too (including Louisiana's primary measure).[60]

Forty-one states currently have Defense of Marriage Acts of some sort, defining marriage as the union of one man and one woman.

Although the relatively short 17-year span between *Bowers* and its reversal in *Lawrence* suggests, for some, rapid progress in the Court's shifting approach to such moral conflicts, the road to positive rights appears much longer and certainly more controversial. Conflicting signals from various state courts promise to keep issues of sexuality, morality, and liberty in the news for years to come. In 2004, the Massachusetts Supreme Judicial Court, in *Goodridge v. Department of Public Health*, ruled that denying same-sex couples the right to marry violated the constitution. *Goodridge* was a major victory for advocates of same-sex marriage, and sources estimate that about 8,500 same-sex marriages have taken place since that time.[61] Opponents began a petition against the ruling in December 2005, arguing in favor of a Constitutional ban against same sex marriage. The petition was presented to both state houses, and was defeated on June 14, 2007. Later that same year, however, in *Deane and Polyak v. Conaway,* the Maryland Court of Appeals denied an equal-protection claim seeking same-sex marriage, denying that the denial of same-sex marriage did not violate fundamental rights.[62]

The *Deane* ruling suggests that the legal and political maneuvering around issues of marriage present more complex issues than the removal of sanctions for consensual behavior engaged in the privacy of one's home. The volatile nature of these decisions demonstrates that issues of sexuality and morality, and the public status of each, will continue to occupy the nation's attention—as well as that of its courts—for years to come. Although we do not intend this chapter to stake out a position on the issue of same-sex marriage, it seems clear that the privacy and liberty arguments so central to Kennedy's opinion in *Lawrence,* although powerful in their ability to articulate the right to intimate sexual conduct free from state interference, do not in and of themselves make the case for same-sex marriage.[63] To make such a case, scholars and activists will need to attend more explicitly to the connection between removing punitive sanctions for *private* behavior, and conferring benefits and *public* recognition on committed same-sex relationships.

ENDNOTES

1. Charles Fried, *Modern Liberty and the Limits of Government* (New York: Norton, 2007), 17.

2. John Rawls, *Political Liberalism* (New York: Columbia University Press, 1993), 175.

3. This is not to say that issues such as gay rights represent a mere "generalization" or "expansion" of the arguments for religious toleration. We are claiming that the two sets of issues—religious toleration and gay rights—possess some broad parallels, but do not push the argument further than that. In fact, one of us has argued against attempts (by both Rawls and David A.J. Richards) to generalize from early modern religious toleration debates to contemporary issues of sexuality. See Andrew R. Murphy, *Conscience and Community: Revisiting Toleration and Religious Dissent in Early Modern England and America* (University Park, PA: Penn State University Press, 2001), ch. 8.

4. *Bowers v. Hardwick,* 478 U.S. 186 (1986); *Lawrence v. Texas,* 539 U.S. 558 (2003).

5. Robert George, *The Clash of Orthodoxies: Law, Religion, and Morality in Crisis* (ISI, 2001).

6. For the purposes of this chapter, we set aside Dutch, French, and Spanish influences, not because they are unimportant, but because of the predominance of English legal and political heritage on the eventual shape of the United States' constitutional system.

7. See, e.g., Chris Beneke, *Beyond Toleration: The Religious Roots of American Pluralism* (New York: Oxford University Press, 2006).

8. Sally A. Schwartz, *"A Mixed Multitude": The Struggle for Toleration in Colonial Pennsylvania* (New York: New York University Press, 1988); Andrew R. Murphy, Introduction to *The Political Writings of William Penn* (Indianapolis, IN: Liberty Fund, 2002).

9. Fundamental Constitutions of Pennsylvania," in *The Papers of William Penn,* ed. Mary Maples Dunn, et al. (Philadelphia: University of Pennsylvania Press, 1981–1986), II: 151. In Penn's draft of the *Laws Agreed Upon in England* (ca. April 1682), he restates his opposition to "all prizes, plays, may games, gamesters, masques, revels, bullbaitings, cockfightings, bear baitings, and the like, which excite the people to rudeness, looseness, and irreligion," accounting them petty treason (*Papers,* II: 209).

10. See Russell Shorto, *The Island at the Center of the World: The Epic Story of Dutch Manhattan and the Forgotten Colony that Shaped America* (New York: Doubleday, 2004).

11. Beneke, *Beyond Toleration.*

12. Alexis de Tocqueville, *Democracy in America,* trans. Arthur Goldhammer (New York: Library of America, 2004), Vol. I, Pt. II, ch. 4, 215–216; Vol, I, Pt. II, ch. 9, 338.

13. Tocqueville, *Democracy in America,* trans. Goldhammer, Vol. I, Pt. II, ch. 4, 218, 219.

14. See, e.g. John McGreevy, *Catholicism and American Freedom: A History* (New York: Norton, 2004); Philip Hamburger, *Separation of Church and State* (Cambridge, MA: Harvard University Press, 2002).

15. John Rawls, *Political Liberalism* (New York: Columbia University Press, 1993), xviii, 36, 129.

16. Ibid., 201.

17. David A. J. Richards, *The Case for Gay Rights: From* Bowers *to* Lawrence *and Beyond* (Lawrence, KS: University Press of Kansas, 2007), 117. For toleration as the "central constitutional ideal," see David A. J. Richards, *Toleration and the Constitution* (New York: Oxford University Press, 1986), xx; also *Identity and the Case for Gay Rights: Religion, Race, Gender as Analogies* (Chicago: University of Chicago Press, 1998).

18. *Reynolds v. United States,* 98 U. S. 145 (1878), 166.

19. *West Virginia State Board of Education v. Barnette,* 319 U.S. 624 (1943), 642; overruling *Minersville School District* v. *Gobitis,* 310 U.S. 586 (1940).

20. *Abington School District v. Schempp,* 374 U.S. 203 (1963).

21. *United States v. Seeger,* 380 U.S. 163 (1965), 175.

22. See Charles Moskos and John W. Chambers, *The New Conscientious Objection: From Sacred to Secular Resistance* (New York: Oxford University Press, 1993), 6; also Murphy, *Conscience and Community,* 276–279.

23. *Griswold v. Connecticut,* 381 U.S. 479 (1965).

24. *Eisenstadt v. Baird,* 405 U.S. 438 (1972), 453.

25. *Roe v. Wade,* 410 U.S. 113 (1973), 153.

26. *Bowers,* 189. Some clarification on the term "fundamental rights" and the commonly accepted "three-tiered" model of judicial review relating to fundamental rights is in order. The highest level of judicial review, known as *strict scrutiny,* is applied to legislation that infringes upon personal rights or interests deemed fundamental. (A fundamental right is one deemed "of the very essence of a scheme of ordered liberty," such that to abolish it would violate a "principle of justice so rooted in the traditions and conscience of our people as to be ranked as fundamental"; see *Palko v. Connecticut,* 302 U. S. 319 (1937), 325). *Strict scrutiny* requires that the state demonstrate that its action is necessary to further a compelling government interest and that this action be drawn sufficiently narrowly that it is the least restrictive means for accomplishing that end. A less demanding level of judicial review, *rational basis,* allows laws to pass muster if they are rationally related to a legitimate governmental interest. (The rational basis test is currently applied in cases involving sexual orientation.)

In practical terms, as we shall see in *Bowers,* the government is much more likely to prevail in cases in which rational basis is required; strict scrutiny is a much more demanding level of scrutiny, often with decidedly different results.

27. *Bowers,* 189.

28. Ibid., 190.

29. Ibid., 191–192.

30. Ibid., 192.

31. Ibid., 195.

32. Ibid., 194.

33. Ibid., 196.

34. Ibid., 197. Interestingly, 14 years before the ruling in *Bowers,* Burger had been the lone dissenter in *Eisenstadt.*

35. Ibid., 199.

36. Ibid.

37. Ibid.

38. Ibid., 206.

39. Ibid., 206–207.

40. Ibid., 204–205.

41. Ibid., 205 (emphasis added).

42. Ibid., 212.

43. O'Connor's concurrence did emphasize the equal-protection aspects of the case, but we focus on the privacy–liberty nexus outlined by Kennedy's opinion for the Court, and Scalia's dissent.

44. *Lawrence,* 567.

45. Ibid.

46. Ibid., 567.

47. Ibid., 571.

48. Ibid.

49. Ibid., 572.

50. In fact, much of Scalia's dissent consists of an extended argument that, if *Bowers* was wrongly decided and thus liable to reversal, the same must be said about *Roe* at least, and the cases leading to *Roe*—*Griswold*, *Eisenstadt*, *Carey*—and the Court should certainly be willing to reconsider *Roe*.

51. *Lawrence*, 589.

52. Ibid., 590.

53. Ibid., 603.

54. Robert P. George, "One Man, One Woman: The Case for Preserving the Definition of Marriage." *Wall Street Journal Online*. (http://www.opinionjournal.com/editorial/feature.html?id=110004356), accessed 1 March 2008; Andrew Sullivan, "If It's Not a Crime to be Gay, Why Can't We Get Married?" online at http://www.indegayforum.org/news/show/26930.html, accessed 1 March 2008.

55. Richards, *Identity and the Case for Gay Rights*, 180.

56. Ibid., 106.

57. Yuval Merin, *Equality for Same-Sex Couples: The Legal Recognition of Gay Partnerships in Europe and the United States* (Chicago: University of Chicago Press, 2002); see also Richards, *The Case for Gay Rights*, 101. Without equating previous movements with those for gay and lesbian rights, one of us has argued that the sort of progression that Merin lays out does bear a general resemblance to the movement for religious liberty, which began with the achievement of basic toleration and further agitated for more "positive" forms of recognition. See Murphy, *Conscience and Community*, esp. ch. 8.

58. *Romer v. Evans*, 517 U.S. 620 (1996), invalidating an amendment to the Colorado state constitution that would have prevented any locality from protecting homosexual citizens from discrimination on the basis of sexual orientation.

59. Richards, *The Case for Gay Rights*, 131, 134.

60. http://www.ncsl.org/programs/cyf/samesex.htm; and http://www.ncsl.org/programs/legismgt/statevote/marriage-mea.htm.

61. Pam Belluck, "Massachusetts Gay Marriage to Remain Legal," *The New York Times*, 15 June 2007; http://www.nytimes.com/2007/06/15/us/15gay.html?ref=us (accessed 18 February 2008).

62. Maryland Court of Appeals, case #24-C-04-005390 (2007).

63. Again, we refer the reader to Chapter 8 of Murphy's *Conscience and Community* for a more extensive discussion of the parallels and divergences of the conscience–toleration argument on the one hand, and the equality–respect argument on the other.

BIBLIOGRAPHY

Books

Ahlstrom, Sydney. *A Religious History of the American People*. New Haven, CT: Yale University Press, 1972.

Beneke, Chris. *Beyond Toleration: The Religious Roots of American Pluralism*. New York: Oxford University Press, 2006.

Eskridge, William N. *Gay Marriage: For Better or For Worse? What We've Learned from the Evidence*. New York: Oxford University Press, 2006.

Eskridge, William N., Jr. *The Case for Same-Sex Marriage: from Sexual Liberty to Civilized Commitment*. New York: Free Press, 1996.

Fried, Charles. *Modern Liberty and the Limits of Government*. New York: Norton, 2007.

George, Robert P. *The Clash of Orthodoxies: Law, Religion, and Morality in Crisis*. Wilmington, DE: ISI, 2001.

Gerstmann, Evan. *Same-Sex Marriage and the Constitution*. Cambridge, UK: Cambridge University Press, 2008 [2004].

Hamburger, Philip. *Separation of Church and State*. Cambridge, MA: Harvard University Press, 2002.

McGreevy, John. *Catholicism and American Freedom: A History*. New York: Norton, 2004.

Merin, Yuval. *Equality for Same-Sex Couples: The Legal Recognition of Gay Partnerships in Europe and the United States*. Chicago: University of Chicago Press, 2002.

Moskos, Charles, and John W. Chambers. *The New Conscientious Objection: From Sacred to Secular Resistance*. New York: Oxford University Press, 1993.

Murphy, Andrew R. *Conscience and Community: Revisiting Toleration and Religious Dissent in Early Modern England and America*. University Park, PA: Penn State University Press, 2001.

The Papers of William Penn. Ed. Mary Maples Dunn et al. 5 vols. Philadelphia: University of Pennsylvania Press, 1981–1986.

Rawls, John. *Political Liberalism*. New York: Columbia University Press, 1993.

Richards, David A. J. *The Case for Gay Rights: From* Bowers *to* Lawrence *and Beyond*. Lawrence, KS: University Press of Kansas, 2007.

————. *Identity and the Case for Gay Rights: Religion, Race, Gender as Analogies*. Chicago: University of Chicago Press, 1998.

Richards, David A. J. *Toleration and the Constitution*. New York: Oxford University Press, 1986.

Baird, Robert M. and Stuart E. Rosenbaum, eds. *Same-Sex Marriage: The Moral and Legal Debate*. New York: Prometheus Books, 1997.

Schwartz, Sally A. *"A Mixed Multitude": The Struggle for Toleration in Colonial Pennsylvania*. New York: New York University Press, 1988.

Shorto, Russell. *The Island at the Center of the World: The Epic Story of Dutch Manhattan and the Forgotten Colony that Shaped America*. New York: Doubleday, 2004.

Sullivan, Andrew, ed. *Same-Sex Marriage: Pro and Con: A Reader*. New York: Vintage Books, 1997.

de Tocqueville, Alexis. *Democracy in America*. Transl. Arthur Goldhammer. New York: Library of America, 2004.

Articles/Chapters

Ball, Carlos A. "The Positive in the Fundamental Right to Marry: Same-Sex Marriage in the Aftermath of *Lawrence v. Texas*." *Minnesota Law Review* 88 (2004):1184.

Belluck, Pam. "Massachusetts Gay Marriage to Remain Legal." *The New York Times*, 15 June 2007; http://www.nytimes.com/2007/06/15/us/15gay.html?ref=us, accessed 18 February 2008.

Dent, George W. Jr. "The Defense of Traditional Marriage." *The Journal of Law and Politics* 15 (Fall 1999): 581.

Finnis, John. "The Good of Marriage and the Morality of Sexual Relations: Some Philosophical and Historical Observations." *American Journal of Jurisprudence* 42 (1997): 97.

George, Robert P. "One Man, One Woman: The Case for Preserving the Definition of Marriage." *Wall Street Journal Online* (http://www.opinionjournal.com/editorial/feature.html?id=110004356), accessed 1 March 2008.

Katz, Pamela S. "The Case for Legal Recognition of Same-Sex Marriage." *Journal of Law & Policy* 8 (1999): 61.

Murphy, Andrew R. "William Penn: His Life, His Times, and His Work." In *The Political Writings of William Penn*. Indianapolis, IN: Liberty Fund, 2002.

Reid, Eric. "Assessing and Responding to Same-Sex 'Marriage' in Light of Natural Law." *Georgetown Journal of Law & Public Policy* 3 (2005): 523.

Spaht, Katherine Shaw. "Revolution and Counter-Revolution: The Future of Marriage in the Law." *Loyola Law Review* 49 (2003): 1.

Strasser, Mark. "Loving in the New Millennium: On Equal Protection and the Right to Marry." *University of Chicago Law School Roundtable* 7 (2000): 61.

Strasser, Mark. "Same-Sex Marriage Referenda and the Constitution: On Hunter, Romer, and Electoral Process Guarantees." *Albany Law Review* 64 (Spring 2001): 949.

Strasser, Mark. "Same-Sex Marriages and Civil Unions: On Meaning, Free Exercise, and Constitutional Guarantees." *Loyola University of Chicago Law Journal* 33 (2002): 597.

Strasser, Mark. "Toleration, Approval, and the Right to Marry: On Constitutional Limitations and Preferential Treatment." *Loyola of Los Angeles Law Revie* 35 (Nov.2001): 65.

Sullivan, Andrew. "If It's Not a Crime to be Gay, Why Can't We Get Married?" http://www.indegayforum.org/news/show/26930.html, accessed 1 March 2008.

Wardle, Lynn D. &Lincoln C. Oliphant. "In Praise of *Loving*: Reflections on the '*Loving* Analogy' for Same-Sex Marriage." *Howard Law Journal* 51 (2007): 117.

Wardle, Lynn D. "'Multiply and Replenish': Considering Same-Sex Marriage in Light of State Interests in Marital Procreation." *Harvard Journal of Law & Public Policy* 24 (Summer 2001): 771.

Wedgwood, Ralph. "The Fundamental Argument for Same-Sex Marriage." *Journal of Political Philosophy* 7 (Sept.1999): 225.

Court Cases

Abington School District v. Schempp, 374 U.S. 203 (1963).

Bowers v. Hardwick, 478 U.S. 186 (1986)

Eisenstadt v. Baird, 405 U.S. 438 (1972).

Griswold v. Connecticut, 381 U.S. 479 (1965).

Lawrence v. Texas, 539 U.S. 558 (2003).

Maryland Court of Appeals, 24-C-04-005390 (2007).

Minersville School District v. Gobitis, 310 U.S. 586 (1940).

Palko v. Connecticut, 302 U. S. (1937).

Reynolds v. United States, 98 U. S. 145 (1878).

Roe v. Wade, 410 U.S. 113 (1973).

Romer v. Evans, 517 U.S. 620 (1996).

United States v. Seeger, 380 U.S. 163 (1965).

West Virginia State Board of Education v. Barnette, 319 U.S. 624 (1943).

PART IV

POLITICAL DIMENSIONS

CHAPTER 13

....

MONITORING AND SURVEILLANCE OF RELIGIOUS GROUPS IN THE UNITED STATES

....

JAMES T. RICHARDSON AND THOMAS ROBBINS

THIS chapter briefly examines the many ways that government at various levels in the United States monitors and engages in surveillance of religious groups. What we discuss may surprise some readers, but confirm with others the growing pervasiveness of government into the religious life of American citizens. It may also come as a surprise that some of the monitoring and surveillance that takes place is a direct result of religious groups getting more involved in society. As religions expand the public space they occupy in American society, political leaders and governmental bureaucrats may assume that they have a right and even a responsibility to know what the religious entities are doing, especially if they are involved in receiving public funds, or performing functions usually performed by the government. Our analysis begins with some results of a major survey concerning the willingness of citizens and opinion leaders to engage in surveillance of unpopular religious groups. Following that discussion we will attempt to establish an international context, with a few comments about the prevalence of surveillance and monitoring by governments in other countries, including other Western democracies.

PUBLIC SUPPORT FOR SURVEILLANCE OF
MINORITY RELIGIOUS GROUPS

David Bromley and Edward Breschel presented some relevant data gathered in 1987 on the issue of public support for surveillance of religious "cults."[1] The issue was presented, among many others, to a large randomly drawn sample of 1,708 members of the general public in the United States, as well as to a sample of 863 members of "institutional elites," which included business, political, academic, and religious leaders. The exact wording of the question, to which participants were instructed to indicate "agree" or "disagree," was: "The FBI should keep a close watch on religious cults." Note that the severely negatively connoted word but popular term "cult" was used in the question, something that may have affected the results obtained.[2]

In the general public sample an overall agreement of 63% was obtained, whereas 26% of the elite sample agreed. When the data were broken down by typical demographic categories, some interesting patterns were found in the general public sample. For instance, older respondents were more prone to agree, as were women, less educated, and lower income respondents. Protestants, both mainline and "reborn," were also more prone to agree than were Catholics and others, including "nones." More frequent church attendees were more prone to favor surveillance than were those who never attended or did so infrequently. In the elite sample the pattern was similar except with lower percentages, with two interesting differences. Frequent attendees were much more prone to favor surveillance than other attendance categories, and mainline Protestants were considerably less favorable than other categories.

For context, it should be noted that these data were gathered 10 years after the Jonestown tragedy, but before the more recent events in Waco with the Branch Davidians and the Solar Temple suicide deaths in Europe and Canada, as well as the Heaven's Gate suicides of 39 people in San Diego. Also, because the term "cult" was used in the question, one might wonder what the results would have been if a term such as "minority religion" had been used instead. Notwithstanding these caveats, the fact that two thirds of the general public sample and greater than one fourth of the elite sample agreed with the statement serves as an interesting backdrop to the following discussion of official governmental surveillance and monitoring of religious groups in the United States and other countries.

SURVEILLANCE AND MONITORING AROUND
THE GLOBE

It is not unusual for governments, including those in Western democracies, to engage in official action designed to maintain close observation of religious groups, especially minority faiths that differ in beliefs and practices from the dominant religion of the society. Many governments around the world have official agencies whose task is to regulate religion, a charge that implies, if not directly requires, considerable knowledge about religion and religious groups operating within the society. Such knowledge can be gained by onerous requirements for registration and other self-reporting that demand considerable self-disclosure. However, government agencies can and do engage in surveillance and monitoring as well, with a sometimes quite clear mandate to do so to fulfill their function as entities whose job it is to regulate religion. There are many examples of both overt self-disclosure requirements and more covert monitoring activities that can serve as examples. This type of action by governmental agencies has sometimes been focused on what may seem to many observers to be rather ordinary religious groups. However, controversial New Religious Movements (NRMs) and other minority faiths have been targeted, as have Muslim groups operating within various countries. A number of examples of this type of activity can be cited.

In Germany, courts have ruled that surveillance of the Church of Scientology and its members is properly within the purview of the Federal Office for the Protection of the Constitution, which is Germany's domestic intelligence agency.[3] In Germany there are additional reports of government surveillance of German converts to Islam;[4] a high-level governmental commission reviewed this entire area a few years ago, gathering considerable information on minority faiths operating within the country.[5] France has apparently placed one religious group headed by an Australian New Age guru, "Jasmuheen," under "high surveillance,"[6] and has engaged in surveillance and monitoring of a number of other minority faiths.[7] Belgium has followed the lead of France, establishing an official governmental agency to monitor "sects."[8] In Belgium, federal intelligence services are surveilling mosques in a claimed effort to combat racism and violence.[9] Similarly in Australia the former Prime Minister, John Howard, stated that he favored infiltration of mosques to discover if they were promoting violence.[10] In Australia accusations have been made by Falun Gong practitioners that Chinese government operatives have infiltrated the sect and are spying on meetings and attempting to disrupt activities of the group.[11] In Poland a controversy erupted in 2003 over plans issued by a Gdansk police official to collect information about minority religious groups, including Baptists, Adventists, Pentecostals, and others.[12] The plans included surreptitious visits by various police officials to gather information on various minority religions. The European Union has also considered a plan, supported by security officials from its largest and oldest members, to monitor mosques for indications that they were promoting radicalism and violent actions.

The government of Brazil was engaged for some years in a battle with the Unification Church[13] over efforts of the UC to acquire large land holdings and build major facilities there. The government investigated the UC for possible money laundering, tax evasion, and abetting illegal immigration. Some governmental actions in the investigation apparently involved covert surveillance as well as overt raids on UC facilities to obtain information. Japan has continued its focus on Aum Shinrikyo and some remaining splinter groups since the tragic sarin gas attacks of 1995.[14]

In Russia many complaints have been lodged concerning monitoring of religious groups by government agencies,[15] and new laws have increased this sort of activity considerably.[16] In Uzbekistan, there are reports that police officers monitor activities of all religious groups; moreover, they are very overt about it in an apparent effort to frighten participants.[17] China also has implemented a policy toward all unofficial churches that justifies monitoring and surveillance, and this has often led to actions against such groups and their leadership.[18]

MONITORING WITHIN THE UNITED STATES

In the United States, efforts to exert control over religious groups are usually much more diffuse than is the case with many other nations. The Establishment and Free Exercise Clauses of the First Amendment are generally understood to mean that governments at all levels are to avoid direct efforts to monitor religion. Early in the "cult wars" that broke out in the 1970s in the United States an effort was made to have the federal Justice Department take action to control certain controversial New Religious Movements (NRMs).[19] However, the effort was rebuffed by Attorney General Benjamin Civiletti, who cited First Amendment concerns as precluding such official actions.[20]

Because the First Amendment guarantees the free exercise of religion, there is no "ministry of religion" in the United States at the federal, state, or local level. This does not mean, however, that no governmental agencies are involved with direct efforts to regulate religion. Diverse agencies that include federal entities such as the Internal Revenue Service, the Immigration and Naturalization Service, and the Food and Drug Administration all have reason to gather information about religious groups engaged in activities within the purview of that agency, and these agencies have implemented policies affecting those groups. Local government zoning boards, local and state social services and welfare organizations, state, and local jail and prison administrations, and many more entities also deal with religion within their particular sphere of activity. This means that various agencies need and seek information about religion, and sometimes such information might be gained via surveillance and monitoring.

One particular area involving surveillance and monitoring of religious groups by government officials at several levels involves the concern for children. The "child saver" movement[21] has raised concern about the welfare of children in American society in recent decades, and has contributed to the passage of laws in many states that require reporting of possible abuse to officials. Those same laws either explicitly or implicitly sanction observation of religious groups that might be accused of harming children. Indeed, such accusations have become a major method of exerting control over religious groups.[22] Many such investigations involve monitoring and surveillance of various kinds by government officials who believe they have no choice about whether to engage in such activities, if claims of child abuse are made.

Our review of the situation in the United States will examine other instances of direct monitoring and secret surveillance of religious groups, such as what happened with the Sanctuary Movement in the 1980s as well as with the surveillance of some Islamic religious groups being done currently. The latter can all be seen as part of the aftermath of the tragedy of the destruction of the World Trade Center in 2001. Additionally we will focus on examples of what we call "forced self-monitoring" in which religious organizations are required by law and court precedents and processes to furnish information on many of their activities to governmental entities, thus permitting those entities considerable power to intrude, monitor, and regulate religious groups. Also covered will be the monitoring and regulatory activities stimulated by former members of religious organizations who often become, in the perception of governmental officials and the media, credible witnesses to actions allegedly taking place in the religious groups. This includes claims made against some well-known religious organizations such as Christian Science, Jehovah's Witnesses, the Church of Latter-day Saints, and even the Catholic Church. We will also cover claims made by former members of controversial New Religious Movements (NRMs), popularly known as "cults." We begin with a discussion of some important historical coverage of surveillance and monitoring activities within the United States.

HISTORICAL ANALYSES IN THE UNITED STATES

William Thompson, in his "Opening Statement"[23] to *Government Intervention in Religious Affairs,* edited by Dean Kelley, lists several ways that government surveillance and monitoring has taken place, including some patterns that might not be expected. Examples of "forced self-surveillance" include such things as requiring reports on: (1) lobbying activities by religious groups;[24] (2) business activities undertaken by religious groups, including taxes paid to workers as well as income generated, and from what activities; (3) certification levels of teachers in religious schools; and (4) demographic make-up of staffs and faculties in church-related schools, seminaries, and universities. Closely related are more overt interventions involving grand jury investigations of alleged wrongdoing by religious organizations, their leaders, and third parties with whom they might be involved;[25] use of clergy as informants in investigations by various law enforcement agencies, both internally and abroad; and subpoenas for church records in civil and criminal actions involving religious groups and persons.

Kelley's volume contains several important chapters dealing with various facets of monitoring and surveillance of religious groups. For example, Braiterman and Kelley discuss efforts of individual state attorneys general to monitor fundraising through the promotion of a model statute that would force religious groups to report such activities.[26] The logic used asserts that religious groups are public charities that should be willing to report contributions received to insure the government and the public that funds are being raised for proper purposes. Similarly, they discuss required reporting on lobbying efforts by religious bodies, and object to such governmental requirements. However, they do note significantly that when religious organizations accept governmental funding it opens the organization to governmental reporting requirements and other monitoring procedures.

Another useful chapter in the Kelley volume is that by Sharon Worthing, who writes about the growing tendency of governmental surveillance of religious groups using forced self-reports by religious organizations.[27] She discusses the area of fundraising, as well as local and state governments' efforts to control such activities with various requirements for reporting and long waiting periods for approvals. Her analysis raises serious questions about any simplistic view that the early (mid-twentieth century) Jehovah's Witness decisions by the United States Supreme Court fully protected fundraising by religious groups in contemporary society.

Another very useful volume that concerns monitoring and surveillance of religious groups is that of James E. Wood, Jr. and Derek Davis, *The Role of Government in Monitoring and Regulating Religion in Public Life.*[28] In the introduction Wood discusses the growing trend toward monitoring and surveillance as a product of the growth of government activities in many spheres of life.[29] However, he also points out that institutional religion has expanded into many areas of life as well. This expansion includes a dramatic growth of lobbying activities as religious groups attempt to affect public policy development, as well as access public funding. This situation has led to conflict between the two spheres of activity and to enhanced interest on the part of local, state, and federal governments in what religious groups are doing.

Wood laments the intrusion of governments into the realm of religion, and asserts that governments have overreached what should be the proper relationship between religion and the state. He discusses implications of the watershed 1990 *Smith* case,[30] noting that the legal and philosophical underpinnings of this decision imply a greater authority for governments to regulate and monitor religious activities of all kinds. He maintains that this major Supreme Court decision exemplifies a pattern of cases that expand governmental rights of regulation and monitoring of many religious activities in the name of the public interest.

The Wood and Davis volume contains several papers of interest to our present concerns. Some discuss the growing efforts to force religious organizations to self-report information that might be used to regulate their activities. Included is the chapter by David Gregory concerning regulation by the federal government of the employment relations of religious organizations,[31] and the chapter by Stanley Weithorn and Douglas Allen on tax policies as they impact advocacy of churches on public policy issues,[32] as well as Jeffrey Hadden's chapter dealing with regulation of religious broadcasting.[33] Sharon Vaino expands on her earlier discussion of governmental monitoring mentioned above, focusing on required reporting by the

IRS, by state governments, and by the courts.[34] She notes that the tremendous growth of data collecting by governmental agencies lends itself to more regulation and monitoring by governments of activities that traditionally have been outside their purview.

Of special note is the chapter by Robin Johansen and Kathleen Purcell dealing with the Sanctuary Movement.[35] They describe in some detail the secret monitoring and surveillance activities by law enforcement of this movement in the 1980s, and the impacts and implications of such actions. "Operation Sojourner" was the name given surveillance efforts developed in the 1980s to deal with the Sanctuary Movement, a religiously motivated effort among middle class churchgoers in the Southwest U.S. to assist refugees from political violence in some Central American countries. The operation, directed by an Immigration and Naturalization Administrator and a U.S. Attorney assigned to the Phoenix area, involved infiltrating the movement by two undercover agents, one of whom was a convicted felon. They passed as devoted Christians interested in the movement, and attended Bible study classes and worship services in two Tucson churches, wearing tape recording devices and taking down license numbers of cars in church parking lots.

These actions, apparently taken as a result of the negative publicity generated by the Sanctuary Movement toward governmental policies concerning political refugees, resulted in indictments of 16 church leaders and members on several different felony charges, including smuggling, transporting, and harboring undocumented refuges. The case resulted in convictions of some of those indicted, with the courts stating that what the government did was justified, and that there was no infringement of religious beliefs or moral duties that outweighed the strong interest of the government.[36]

MONITORING NRMs AND OTHER MINORITY FAITHS IN THE UNITED STATES

There have been accusations of monitoring and surveillance of NRMs in the United States during their controversial history over the past few decades, although few credible claims for direct secret surveillance can be documented. There are, however, numerous instances of monitoring of various kinds, given that NRMs are, like their counterparts in the realm of traditional religious groups, subject to a growing array of reporting requirements and legal precedents that make them vulnerable to regulation in various areas of group life and activity. Some of that monitoring has been provoked by claims made by former members about various aspects of life in the groups. Such claims are subject to the criticism of their being self-interested,[37] but such claims are sometimes taken quite seriously by authorities, who may then take action based upon the claims.

Richardson discusses a number of such instances involving apostates from NRMs as well as more traditional religious groups who attempt to define themselves as whistleblowers, thereby gaining the positive resonance of that term in modern American society.[38] Such efforts can be categorized as a form of "self-help" in exerting control over religious groups.[39] These self-help efforts have been undertaken by some parents concerned about their children being involved in strange and unfamiliar religious groups, and sometimes such claims have been promoted by some former members or apostates from the groups. Self-help efforts often include attempts to make governmental authorities, including law enforcement officials and the courts, take action of one kind or another against the religious group. Thus in the 1960s and 1970s, when NRMs first burst onto the American scene, claims that some of the groups were "brainwashing" participants, and exploiting them economically, were quite prevalent.[40] However, the First Amendment has usually precluded direct efforts at surveillance and monitoring by governmental authorities, although there are occasional claims of such activities having taken place. Groups such as the Unification Church became embroiled in continual battles with tax and immigration officials largely because of their desire to bring people into the country from Korea and to raise money through various forms of street solicitation. Claims by detractors made the group subject to review by governmental officials, and sometimes decisions were made that were detrimental to the group by officials acting on such information.

One major tragic incident in the annals of minority faiths in America that involved surveillance and monitoring concerns the Branch Davidians, whose compound outside of Waco, Texas was raided by government forces in 1993. More than 80 people, including a number of children, eventually lost their lives in that episode, which resulted in a 50-day siege culminating in an attack by FBI forces. As is well known, the group was under surveillance before the raid, and they had even been infiltrated to some extent by one member of the surveillance team stationed in a nearby house. The Davidians knew they were under surveillance, and they were aware that ATF authorities were asking questions about them with gun dealers and others. That knowledge, however, did not help when the elaborate attack came from 200 well-armed ATF officers.

Of special note according to Richardson is the use of claims of child abuse, including sex abuse, to force authorities to exert social control over religious groups.[41] Such claims have not only been made against some NRMs, but have also against some well-known older religious groups such as the Catholic Church.[42] This type of claim played a major role in the tragedy at Waco, as we learned later,[43] and apparently helped justify for authorities the initial decision to place the group under surveillance and attempt to serve a warrant that prominently mentioned child abuse concerns, even though such issues do not fall within federal purview.[44] The welfare of children is a very high value in modern American society, and someone willing to make a claim of child abuse, especially sex abuse, can almost guarantee that authorities will take some action, as noted.

There are a number of examples of this process of claims-making concerning children's welfare, and action being taken by authorities that might involve surveillance or monitoring of some sort. Gretchen Seigler, in her research during the 1980s on In Search of Truth, a northern California communal group, tells of how during her research she interacted with a person who was in fact a paid employee of the State of California who had feigned an interest in the group so as to infiltrate it.[45] The agent sought to gain evidence concerning activities within a group home for troubled youth the ISOT group was operating. The state then used the information gathered to shut down the group home they had been operating. This example demonstrates how easy it is for a religious group seeking converts to be infiltrated if the state is willing to use such tactics. However, it also shows how vulnerable groups can become if they seek and accept state largess such as payment for operating a group home for nonmember youth. Operation of the group home had led to tension with neighbors who complained to state authorities. Those authorities then took action that involved infiltration of the group.

Susan Palmer writes about actions of authorities toward the Island Pond Messianic Community group in Vermont in the 1980s and 1990s.[46] An array of people and groups associated with the anticult movement in America assisted state authorities and encouraged them to take action, using child abuse claims as their leverage. A series of custody battles had developed between member couples who had divorced, and claims of child abuse were made in these battles. The state then sent a team to interview people in seven states about activities in the Island Pond group, and used information gathered to justify a raid that resulted in 112 children being taken away on June 22, 1984. The children were returned quickly after a judge ruled the action illegal, however. The custody battles involving the Messianic Community also included self-help efforts by at least one former member who hired a group of investigators to monitor the group for a time.

Richardson writes of similar developments concerning The Family, formerly known as the Children of God. Custody battles between couples who had been members of the group and then divorced led to orchestrated accusations of child abuse, which in turn triggered state action in several different countries, including Spain, Argentina, France, and Australia.[47] The orchestration involved former members plus other apostates and members of the Anti-Cult Movement who were intent on bringing attention and even harm to the group. In the United States, one Family group in southern California attempted successfully to pre-empt state action by inviting authorities into the community to see for themselves what was happening, and that no children were being abused. This tactic worked, and a raid similar to what had happened in other countries was averted. Note, however, that the tactic chosen by the group involved an overt recognition that the state had extensive authority, and that those in authority in the child care arena of the state had a right or even obligation to observe activities within the group whenever accusations of child abuse were made.

Better known religious groups such as the Christian Scientists also are not immune to claims of child abuse, and the attendant state action that follows such accusations. Richardson and John DeWitt describe the many legal battles around the country resulting from use of Spiritual Healing practices with ill children in the group.[48] In some instances children died, and although there might have been exemptions in the state law protecting those using spiritual healing with their children, some state authorities brought charges of child endangerment and even manslaughter against a few parents whose children had died. When a prosecuting attorney brings such charges, that action by the state typically opens the group to all sorts of monitoring and investigation, and this was the case in this spate of such actions in the 1980s.

Raids in 2008 by Texas authorities against the Fundamentalist Latter-day Saints group resulted in over 400 children being taken into custody for a time. This clearly demonstrates that claims of child abuse are very powerful indeed. Although the Texas courts have since ordered the children returned to their parents, the setting of rigorous conditions for that return shows that state authorities, including the courts, think the state does have the right and responsibility to protect children, even if actual claims being made are questionable as to the vast majority of children who are involved.

The Texas FLDS case demonstrates the kind of monitoring that can take place if a group is unpopular, especially if claims of child abuse are involved. Stuart Wright discusses the strong connections between an apostate from the FLDS group and Texas authorities, and how that apostate's credibility led state authorities to accept the false claims made by a 33-year-old woman from Colorado who feigned being an abused young girl living in the Eldorado compound. The "career apostate" who passed on information received from phone calls from the Colorado woman was continually monitoring the group, and had been for years, passing on any damaging information obtained to authorities, even if not credible, whenever possible.[49]

This case shows the willingness of authorities to accept without verification information received from private monitors of unpopular groups, and it also demonstrates the interaction and collusion that can take place between private individuals with an agenda and state authorities. The possibility of manipulation of state social control mechanisms by private individuals willing to make claims of child abuse is shown in the FLDS situation, as it has been in other cases described, including those of The Family and Christian Science. A similar situation also developed with the Waco tragedy, in which it eventually became evident that federal authorities had depended heavily on information furnished by apostates and well-known members of the Anti-Cult Movement as they planned the raid, and then tried to handle the aftermath of the botched and tragic attempt to gain entry into the Davidian compound.[50]

The Texas FLDS case also reveals yet another new facet of social control of minority faiths that involved more open and permanent monitoring. It is a fact that the Texas appeal courts, including the State Supreme Court, overruled the State District Court and ordered the return of the children to their parents.[51] However, the appellate courts allowed the District Court to impose unprecedented conditions on the group in exchange for the children's return. Those conditions included having the children finger-printed and their picture taken; DNA testing of parents and children; medical, psychological, and psychiatric testing of the children; unannounced home visits; parenting classes for parents; supplying current addresses and phone numbers for all children and parents; providing the names of all adults who were living in the home; notification of any change of residence with 7 days' notice, and requiring that the children not be taken from the state of Texas. These unprecedented conditions forced on the FLDS group by the court means that there can be a permanent monitoring of all persons in the group, with the group being responsible for furnishing the key information needed by the state for the monitoring. The effect of these conditions is to make the children, and even their parents, virtual wards of the state, a situation with possible quite significant long-term consequences for the group.

Conclusion

We have attempted to set the issue of monitoring and surveillance of religious groups in both a comparative and historical context. It is important to note that the frequency of such actions by state authorities in the United States is usually less than can occur in a number of other societies, including Western democracies. In many societies the state takes a somewhat (and in some cases, an extremely) paternalistic approach to monitoring religious activities, justified by authorities as a way of protecting citizens within the society. However, having made this important point, it should be acknowledged by all observers in the United States that the interest state authorities take in religious groups, especially unpopular newer ones, is on the rise. Whereas early efforts at exerting social control by state authorities over newer religions were usually not very effective because of First Amendment protections afforded groups claiming to be religious, later efforts have been more successful for at least two reasons.

One major reason is the growth of the liberal state that envelops more and more areas of life in America.[52] This spread of governmental interest and intervention in the religious realm suggests that the United States is moving closer to the more paternalistic model of church–state relations found in other parts of the world. This tendency has been exacerbated significantly by the willingness of many religious groups to accept the largess of the state, thereby opening them to more intrusive monitoring by the state. What is happening with a number of religious groups in America, including some well-known and venerable ones, seems to be a good demonstration of the old adage "be careful what you wish for, because you might get it" (with all its implications for social control).

A second reason why more recent monitoring actions toward religious groups by the state have been accepted concerns the use of claims about children in efforts at social control. Whereas earlier "brainwashing" based claims against new religions eventually were rejected by the courts as violative of First Amendment protections, concern about children has trumped such considerations in more recent times.[53] These legal developments have especially affected second-generation NRMs and other minority religions, some of which have many children. Reporting laws govern a number of professions involving people with regular contact with children, and other laws require governmental officials to take action when credible claims of child abuse are made. That action may, as demonstrated in the cases described herein, include monitoring, covert surveillance, and sometimes considerable intrusion into the lives of those living in religious communities. The conditions required for the FLDS group members to regain access to their children is an extreme example of how far governments may be allowed to go in oversight of religious groups in contemporary American society.

Given these considerations, it seems safe to say that more actions of state authorities that involve monitoring of religious groups will occur in the future, and that these state actions may become more and more intrusive. There have been few developments that suggest otherwise.

ENDNOTES

1. David Bromley and Edward Breschel, 1992, "General Population and Institutional Elite Support for Social Control of New Religious Movements: Evidence from National Survey Data," *Behavioral Sciences & the Law* 10 (1992): 39–52.

2. See James T. Richardson, "Definitions of Cult: From Sociological-Technical to Popular-Negative," *Review of Religious Research* 34 (1993): 348–356.

3. *Deutche Welle,* "Court Rules Surveillance of Scientology Legal," Feb. 12, 2008.

4. Mathew Schofield, "Germany Considers Increased Spying on Muslims," *McClatchy Newspapers,* Sept. 6, 2007.

5. Hubert Seiwert, "The German Enquete Commission on Sects: Political Conflicts and Compromises," in *Regulating Religion: Case Studies from Around the Globe,* ed. J.T. Richardson (New York: Kluwer, 2004), 85–102.

6. *The Australian,* "Breath Guru Under Surveillance," Nov. 21, 2005.

7. Rodolphe Landais, "French Police Fear Collective Suicide by Sect Members," *Reuters,* Sept. 10, 2002; James Beckford, "'Laicite,' 'Dystopia,' and the Reaction to New Religious Movements in France," in *Regulating Religion: Case Studies from around the Globe,* ed. J.T. Richardson (New York: Kluwer, 2004), 27–40; Cyrille Duvert, "Anticultism in the French Parliament," in *Regulating Religion: Case Studies from around the Globe,* ed. J.T. Richardson (New York: Kluwer, 2004), 41–52; Nathalie Luca, "Is There a Unique French Policy of Cults? A European Perspective," in *Regulating Religion: Case Studies from around the Globe,* ed. J.T. Richardson (New York: Kluwer, 2004), 53–72; Massimo Introvigne, "Holy Mountains and Anti-Cult Ecology: The Campaign Against the Aumist Religion in France," in *Regulating Religion: Case Studies from around the Globe,* ed. J.T. Richardson (New York: Kluwer, 2004), 73–84.

8. Willy Fautre, "Belgium's Antisect Policy," in *Regulating Religion: Case Studies from around the Globe,* ed. J.T. Richardson (New York: Kluwer, 2004), 113–126.

9. *Expatica,* "Belgium Steps Up Mosque Surveillance," July 15, 2004.

10. *Reuters,* "Australian Prime Minister Backs Surveillance in Mosques," August 24, 2005.

11. Andra Jackson, "Spies Watch, Bug Falun Gong: Claim," *The Age,* June 8, 2005.

12. Felix Corley, "Poland: Secret Instructions Order Religious Surveillance, *Forum 18 News Service,* May 16, 2003.

13. *WND.com,* "Unification Church Under Siege in Brazil," May 14, 2002.

14. Mari Yamaguchi, "Officers of Cult Splinter Group Raided." *Associated Press,* May 10, 2007.

15. Geraldine Fagan, "Russia: Will NGO Regulations Restrict Religious Communities?" *Forum 18 News Service,* Nov. 14, 2006.

16. James T. Richardson, Galina Krylova, and Marat Shterin, "Legal Regulation of Religions in Russia: New Developments," in *Regulating Religion: Case Studies from around the Globe,* ed. J.T. Richardson (New York: Kluwer, 2004), 247–258.

17. Reuel Hanks, "Religion and Law in Uzbekistan: Renaissance and Repression in an Authoritarian Context," in *Regulating Religion: Case Studies from around the Globe,* ed. J.T. Richardson (New York: Kluwer, 2004), 319–330.

18. Bryan Edleman and James T. Richardson, "Imposed Limitations on Freedom of Religion in China and the Margin of Appreciation Doctrine," *Journal of Church and State* 47 (2005): 243–268.

19. Thomas Robbins and Dick Anthony, "Deprogramming, Brainwashing and the Medicalization of Deviant Religion," *Social Problems* 29 (1982): 283–297.

20. This official posture of the government led, of course, to many "self-help" actions by citizens and groups in America to exert control over unpopular religions. Many of those self-help remedies such as deprogramming NRM members skirted the law in various ways, and sometimes involved government officials turning a blind eye to what was happening. However, governments at all levels in the United States were usually precluded from direct involvement in exerting social control over religious groups unless such groups were accused of breaking specific laws of one kind or another.

21. Joel Best, *Threatened Children* (Chicago: University of Chicago Press, 1990).

22. James T. Richardson, "Social Control of New Religions: From 'Brainwashing' Claims to Child Sex Abuse Allegations," in *Children in New Religions,* eds. Susan Palmer and Charlotte Hardman (New Brunswick, NJ: Rutgers University Press, 1999), 172–186; Mike Homer, 'The Precarious Balance Between Freedom of Religion and Best Interests of the Child," in *Children in New Religions,* eds. Susan Palmer and Charlotte Hardman (New Brunswick, NJ: Rutgers University Press, 1999), 187–209; Susan Palmer, "Frontiers and Families: The Children of Island Pond," in Palmer and Hardman, eds., *Children in New Religions,* eds. Susan Palmer and Charlotte Hardman (New Brunswick, NJ: Rutgers University Press, 1999), 153–171.

23. William Thompson, "Opening Statement of the Chairperson," in *Government Intervention in Religious Affairs*, ed. Dean Kelley (New York: Pilgrim Press, 1982), 16–19.

24. Dean Kelley, *Government Intervention in Religious Affairs* (New York: Pilgrim Press, 1982).

25. Eugene Scheiman, "Obtaining Information from Religious Bodies by Compulsory Process," in *Government Intervention in Religious Affairs* (New York: Pilgrim Press, 1982), 141–150.

26. Marvin Braiterman and Dean Kelley, "When Is Governmental Intervention Legitimate?" in Kelley, ed., *Government Intervention in Religious Affairs* (New York: Pilgrim Press, 1982), 170–193.

27. Sharon Worthing Vaino, "The Potential in Recent Statues for Government Surveillance of Religious Organizations," in *Government Intervention in Religious Affairs*(New York: Pilgrim Press, 1982), 11–128.

28. James E. Wood, Jr. and Derek Davis, *The Role of Government in Monitoring and Regulating Religion in Public Life* (Waco, TX: JM Dawson Institute of Church-State Studies, 1993).

29. James Wood, "Government Intervention in Religious Affairs: An Introduction," in *The Role of Government in Monitoring and Regulating Religion in Public Life* (Waco, TX: JM Dawson Institute of Church-State Studies, 1993), 1–20.

30. *Employment Division of Oregon v. Smith,* 494 U.S. 872 (1990).

31. David Gregory, "Government Regulation of Religion Through Labor and Employment Discrimination Laws," in *The Role of Government in Monitoring and Regulating Religion in Public Life* (Waco, TX: JM Dawson Institute of Church-State Studies, 1993) 121–160.

32. Stanley Weithorn and Douglas Allen, "Taxation and the Advocacy Role of Churches in Public Affairs," in *The Role of Government in Monitoring and Regulating Religion in Public Life* (Waco, TX: JM Dawson Institute of Church-State Studies, 1993), 51–64.

33. Jeffrey Hadden, "Regulating Religious Broadcasting: Some Old Patterns and New Trends," in *The Role of Government in Monitoring and Regulating Religion in Public Life* (Waco, TX: JM Dawson Institute of Church-State Studies, 1993), 179–204.

34. Sharon Worthing Vaino, "Government Monitoring of Religious Organizations," in *The Role of Government in Monitoring and Regulating Religion in Public Life* (Waco, TX: JM Dawson Institute of Church-State Studies, 1993), 65–88.

35. Robin Johansen and Kathleen Purcell, "Government Regulation of Sanctuary Activities, in *The Role of Government in Monitoring and Regulating Religion in Public Life* (Waco, TX: JM Dawson Institute of Church-State Studies, 1993), 161–178.

36. *United States v. Aguilar,* 883 F.2d 662 (1989).

37. David Bromley, *The Politics of Religious Apostasy* (Westport, CT: Praeger, 1998).

38. James T. Richardson, "Apostates, Whistleblowers, Law, and Social Control," in *The Politics of Religious Apostasy,* ed. David Bromley (Westport, CT: Praeger, 1998), 171–189.

39. James T. Richardson, "Regulating Religion: A Sociological and Historical Perspective," in Richardson, ed., *Regulating Religion: Case Studies from Around the Globe* (New York: Springer, 2003), 1–22.

40. David Bromley and James T. Richardson. *The Brainwashing/Deprogramming Controversy* (New York: Edwin Mellen, 1983); James T. Richardson, *Money and Power in the New Religions* (New York: Edwin Mellen, 1988); Thomas Robbins and Dick Anthony, "Deprogramming, Brainwashing and the Medicalization of Deviant Religion," *Social Problems* 29 (1982): 283–297.

41. James T. Richardson, "Social Control of New Religions: From 'Brainwashing' Claims to Child Sex Abuse Allegations," in *Children in New Religions,* eds. Susan Palmer and Charlotte Hardman (New Brunswick, NJ: Rutgers University Press, 1999), 172–186.

42. Anson Shupe, *Spoils of the Kingdom: Clergy Misconduct and Religious Community* (Urbana, IL: University of Illinois Press, 2007).

43. Christopher Ellison and John Bartkowski, "'Babies were Being Beaten': Exploring Child Abuse Allegations at Ranch Apocalypse," in *Armageddon in Waco,* ed. Stuart Wright (Chicago: University of Chicago Press, 1995), 111–152.

44. Stuart Wright, "A Critical Analysis of Evidentiary and Procedural Rulings in Branch Davidian Civil Case," in *New Religious Movements & Religious Liberty in America,* eds. Derek Davis and Barry Hankins (Waco, TX: Dawson Institute of Church-State

Studies, 2002), 101–114; James T. Richardson, "'Showtime' in Texas: Social Production of the Branch Davidian Trials," *Nova Religio* 5 (2001): 152–170.

45. Gretchen Seigler, "The Children of ISOT," in *Children in the New Religions*, eds. Susan Palmer and Charlotte Hardman (New Brunswick, NJ: Rutgers University Press, 1999), 124–137.

46. Susan Palmer, "Frontiers and Families: The Children of Island Pond," in Palmer and Hardman, eds., *Children in the New Religions*, eds. Susan Palmer and Charlotte Hardman (New Brunswick, NJ: Rutgers University Press, 1999), 153–171. Also see Jean Swantko, "The Twelve Tribes Messianic Communities, the Anti-Cult Movement, and Governmental Response," in *Regulating Religion: Case Studies from around the Globe,* ed. J.T. Richardson (New York: Kluwer, 2004), 179–202.

47. James T. Richardson, "'Social Control of New Religions: From 'Brainwashing' Claims to Child Sex Abuse Accusations," in *Children in the New Religions*, eds. Palmer and Hardman, 172–186.

48. James T. Richardson and John DeWitt, "Christian Science Spiritual Healing, the Law, and Public Opinion," *Journal of Church and State* 34 (1992): 549–562.

49. Stuart Wright, "Deconstructing Official Rationales for the State Raid on the FLDS." Presented at annual meeting of the Society for the Scientific Study of Religion, Louisville, KY (Oct., 2008).

50. Stuart Wright, *Armageddon in Waco* (Chicago: University of Chicago Press, 1995).

51. Tamatha Schreinert and James T. Richardson, "Appeal Courts Speak in Texas: An Analysis of Appeal Court Opinions Concerning the FLDS Children." Presented at annual meeting of the Society for the Scientific Study of Religion, Louisville, KY (Oct., 2008).

52. Thomas Robbins, "Government Regulatory Powers over Religious Movements: Deviant Religions as test Cases," *Journal for the Scientific Study of Religion* 24 (1985): 237–251.

53. James T. Richardson, "Social Control of New Religions," in *Children in New Religions* eds. Susan Palmer and Charlotte Hardman (New Brunswick, NJ: Rutgers University Press, 1999), 172–186.

BIBLIOGRAPHY

Books

Best, Joel. *Threatened Children.* Chicago: University of Chicago Press, 1990.
Bromley, David and James T. Richardson. *The Brainwashing/Deprogramming Debate.* New York: Edwin Mellen, 1983.
Bromley, David. *The Politics of Religious Apostasy.* Westport, CT: Praeger, 1998.
Kelley, Dean. *Government Intervention in Religious Affairs.* New York: Pilgrim Press, 1982.
Richardson, James T. *Money and Power in the New Religions.* New York: Edwin Mellen, 1998.
Shupe, Anson. *Spoils of the Kingdom: Clergy Misconduct and Religious Community.* Urbana, IL: University of Illinois Press, 2007.
Wood, James E. Jr. and Derek Davis, eds. *The Role of Government in Monitoring and Regulating Religion in Public Life.* Waco, TX: Dawson Institute of Church-State Studies, 1993.

Articles/Chapters

"Australian Prime Minister backs surveillance in mosques." *Reuters*, August 24, 2005.

Beckford, James. "'Laicite,' 'Dystopia,' and the Reaction to New Religious Movements in France." In *Regulating Religion: Case Studies from around the Globe*, ed. J.T. Richardson. New York: Kluwer, 2004.

"Breath guru under surveillance." *The Australian*, Nov. 21, 2005.

Corley, Felix. "Uzbekistan: Government issues orders to religious communities." *Forum 18 News Service*, May 21, 2007.

———. "Uzbekistan: Spies and videotape." *Forum 18 News Service*, Sept. 5, 2007.

———. "Poland: Secret instructions order religious surveillance." *Forum 18 News Service*, May 16, 2003.

"Court rules surveillance of Scientology legal." *Deutche Welle*, Feb. 12, 2008.

Duvert, Cyrille. "Anticultism in the French Parliament." *In Regulating Religion: Case Studies from around the Globe*, ed. J.T. Richardson. New York: Kluwer, 2004.

Ellison, Christopher and John Bartkowski. "'Babies were being beaten': Exploring child abuse allegations at Ranch Apocalypse." In *Armageddon in Waco*, ed. S. Wright. Chicago: University of Chicago Press, 1995.

"Belgium steps up mosque surveillance." *Expatica*, July 15, 2004.

Fagan, Geraldine, "Russia: Will NGO regulations restrict religious communities?" *Forum 18 News Service*, Nov. 14, 2006.

Fautre, Willy. "Belgium's Anti-sect Policy." In *Regulating Religion: Case Studies from around the Globe*, ed. J.T. Richardson. New York: Kluwer, 2004.

Gregory, David. "Government Regulation of Religion through Labor and Employment Discrimination Laws." In *The Role of Government in Monitoring and Regulating Religion in Public Life*, eds. James E. Wood, Jr. and Derek Davis. Waco, TX: Dawson Institute of Church-State Studies, 1993.

Hadden, Jeffrey. "Regulating Religious Broadcasting: Some old Patterns and New Trends." In *The Role of Government in Monitoring and Regulating Religion in Public Life*, eds. James E. Wood, Jr. and Derek Davis. Waco, TX: Dawson Institute of Church-State Studies, 1993.

Hanks, Reuel. "Religion and Law in Uzbekistan: Renaissance and Repression in an Authoritarian Context." In *Regulating Religion: Case Studies from around the Globe*, ed. James T. Richardson. New York: Kluwer, 2004.

Homer, Mike. "The Precarious Balance between Freedom of Religion and Best Interests of the Child." In *Children in New Religions*, eds. Susan Palmer and C. Hardman. New Brunswick: NJ: Rutgers University Press, 1999.

Introvigne, Massimo. "Holy Mountains and Anti-cult Ecology: The Campaign against the Aumist Religion in France." In *Regulating Religion: Case Studies from around the Globe*, ed. James T. Richardson. New York: Kluwer, 2004.

Jackson, Andra. "Spies Watch, Bug Falun Gong Claim." *The Age*, June 8, 2005.

Johansen, Robin and Kathleen Purcell. "Government Response to the Sanctuary Movement." In *The Role of Government in Monitoring and Regulating Religion in Public Life*, eds. James E. Wood, Jr. and Derek Davis. Waco, TX: Dawson Institute of Church-State Studies, 1993.

Luca, Nathalie. "Is there a Unique French Policy of Cults? A European Perspective." In *Regulating Religion: Case Studies from around the Globe*, ed. James T. Richardson. New York: Kluwer, 2004.

Landais, Rodolphe. "French police fear collective suicide by sect members." *Reuters*, Sept. 10, 2002.

Palmer, Susan. "Frontiers and Families: The Children of Island Pond." In *Children in New Religions*, eds. Susan Palmer and C. Hardman. New Brunswick, NJ: Rutgers University Press, 1999.

Richardson, James T. "Apostates, Whistleblowers, Law, and Social Control." In *The Politics of Religious Apostasy*, ed. David Bromley. Westport, CT: Praeger, 1998.

———. "From 'Brainwashing' Claims to Child Abuse Allegations." In *Children in New Religions*, eds. Susan Palmer and C. Hardman. New Brunswick, NJ: Rutgers University Press, 1999.

Richardson, James T. and John DeWitt. "Christian Science Spiritual Healing, Public Opinion, and the Law." *Journal of Church and State* 34 (1992): 549.

Richardson, James T. and Massimo Introvigne. "'Brainwashing' Theories in European Parliamentary and Administrative Reports on 'Cults and Sects.'" In *Regulating Religion: Case Studies from around the Globe*, ed. J.T. Richardson. New York: Kluwer, 2004.

Richardson, James T., Galina Krylova, and Marat Shterin. "Legal Regulation of Religions in Russia: New developments." in *Regulating Religion: Case Studies from around the Globe*, ed. J.T. Richardson. New York: Kluwer, 2004.

Robbins, Thomas and Dick Anthony. "Deprogramming, Brainwashing and the Medicalization of Religion." *Social Problems* 29 (1982, No. 3).

Scheiman, Eugene. "Obtaining Information from Religious bodies by Compulsory Process." In *Government Intervention in Religious Affairs*, ed. Dean Kelley. New York: Pilgrim Press, 1982.

Schofield, Matthew. "German considers increased spying on Muslims." *McClatchy Newspapers*, Sept. 6, 2007.

Schreinert, Tamatha and James T. Richardson. "Appeal Courts Speak in Texas: An Analysis of Appeal Court Opinions Concerning the FLDS Children." Presented at the annual meeting of the Society for the Scientific Study of Religion, Louisville, KY, Oct. 2, 2008.

Seiwert, Hubert. "The German Enquete Commission on Sects: Political Conflicts and Compromises." In *Regulating Religion: Case Studies from around the Globe*, ed. J.T. Richardson. New York: Kluwer, 2004.

Seigler, Gretchen. *The Children of ISOT*. In *Children in New Religions*, eds. Susan Palmer and C. Hardman. New Brunswick, NJ: Rutgers University Press, 1999.

Thompson, William. "Opening Statement of the Chairperson." In *Government Intervention in Religious Affairs*, ed. Dean Kelley. New York: Pilgrim Press, 1982.

"Unification Church under siege in Brazil." WND.com, May 14, 2002.

Vaino, Sharon W. "Government Monitoring of Religious Organizations." In *The Role of Government in Monitoring and Regulating Religion in Public Life*, eds. James E. Wood, Jr. and Derek Davis. Waco, TX: Dawson Institute of Church-State Studies, 1993.

Weithorn, Stanley & Douglas Allen (1993). "Taxation and the Advocacy Role of the Churches in Public Affairs." In *The Role of Government in Monitoring and Regulating Religion in Public Life*, eds. James E. Wood, Jr. and Derek Davis. Waco, TX: Dawson Institute of Church-State Studies, 1993.

Worthing, Sharon. "The Potential in Recent Statutes for Government Surveillance of Religious Organizations." In *Government Intervention in Religious Affairs*, ed. Dean Kelley. New York: Pilgrim Press, 1982.

Wright, Stuart. "Deconstructing Official Rationales for the State Raid on the FLDS." Presented at annual meeting of the Society for the Scientific Study of Religion, Louisville, KY, Oct. 2, 2008.

Yamaguchi, Mari. "Officers of cult splinter group raided." AP, May 10, 2007.

CHAPTER 14

THE U.S. CONGRESS: PROTECTING AND ACCOMMODATING RELIGION

ALLEN D. HERTZKE

ACCORDING to the conventional view, U.S. Supreme Court precedents define church–state relations in America. However, Congress has played a pivotal role in both protecting the free exercise of religion and demarcating the boundaries between church and state. Indeed, as we will see, Congress often has been a more consistent defender of religious freedom than the courts,[1] while simultaneously taking a more accommodating posture toward the constitutional prohibition against state establishment. This blend seems to reflect a view that the Establishment and Free Exercise Clauses of the First Amendment work in tandem to ensure an expansive practice of religion in the nation. On both fronts, however, we see limits beyond which Congress is unwilling to go. It denied free exercise claims of Mormons in the nineteenth century, for example, in prohibiting polygamy and aggressively prosecuting the group's members; and it has consistently resisted efforts to proclaim the United States a Christian nation and generally rebuffed attempts to sanction overt sectarian favoritism by the government.

Understanding the Congressional role begins, of course, with the First Congress of 1789, which drafted the fateful language of the First Amendment: "Congress shall make no law respecting an establishment of religion, or prohibiting the free exercise thereof." This bears stressing: it was an act of Congress, not the courts, which established the parameters of church–state law in America. And Congress did not abandon its constitutional role once the First Amendment took effect.

The debate over the First Amendment religion clauses provides clues to how members of Congress thought about protecting religious practice. Records of the Congressional debate indicate that bargaining and compromise contributed to the consensus language that became constitutional law. Introduced by James Madison in June 1789, the legislation went through several versions in both chambers before a conference committee bill passed by the necessary two thirds of the House on September 24 and the Senate on September 25.

One thing that emerges in deliberations is that Madison's sweeping approach had to be amended to accommodate critics. His original bill included what he called "rights of conscience," which was dropped as redundant, although it also could have been interpreted to cover nonreligious expression. A second concern was that the federal government might interfere with state practices and constitutions, some of which privileged Christianity or included officially establishment churches. Madison, in fact, wanted to prohibit both the national and state governments from infringing on religious liberty or establishing state churches, but the final version, acknowledging states' rights, applied only to the federal government.[2] Still, the grand national experiment, which departed from centuries of Western practice, set the stage for states to end their establishments and remove religious restrictions on citizenship.

What did the framers of the amendment have in mind when they passed it? On religious exercise they clearly envisioned a broad protection for religious freedom for both diverse Christian denominations and minorities such as Jews and even Muslims. An indication of the founders' thinking is contained in the oft-forgotten clause in Section VI of the unamended Constitution that barred any "religious test" for public office, and by implication for citizenship. With respect to the Establishment Clause there were greater differences of opinion. Madison, as president, interpreted it in strict separationist terms as prohibiting any government acknowledgment or support for religion, however general. The majority of Congress, however, operated on the assumption that the amendment did not prohibit nonsectarian support for religion. The same year it passed the First Amendment, for example, Congress re-enacted the Northwest Ordinance to govern territories and included the following language: "Religion, morality, and the knowledge being necessary to good government and the happiness of mankind, schools and the means of learning shall forever be encouraged."[3] Although its philosophy has evolved over time, Congress continues to play a role in defining the contours of the First Amendment.

Congressional Action on Establishment Boundaries

Throughout its history Congress has been heavily involved in issues demarcating the boundaries between church and state. Most of the time Congress has attempted to accommodate religion but stopped short of amending the Constitution to do so.

The one exception to this pattern involved early state aid to parochial schools, in which Congress moved to restrict, rather than accommodate, generalized support for religion. Although state governments followed the national government in disestablishing state churches, Protestant hegemony in the nineteenth century produced a form of cultural "establishment," complete with wide use of the King James Bible in public schools. In self-defense, Roman Catholics developed what would become the nation's most extensive parochial school system. As Catholics became more numerous they gained political clout in a number of northern states, aided by Democratic party machines that had assimilated successive waves of immigrants. With this new influence they pressed for various forms of state funding of church-run schools, which produced a backlash among the Protestant majority.

The issue came to a head during the administration of Ulysses S. Grant when Republicans sought to exploit Protestant fears of "papist" influence. The mechanism was a proposed amendment to the Constitution in 1875 baring state support for parochial schools. Introduced by Representative James G. Blaine of Maine, soon to be senator and presidential aspirant, the legislation would revise the religion clauses of the First Amendment with the following language:

> No state shall make any law respecting an establishment of religion or prohibiting the free exercise thereof; and no money raised by taxation in any State for the support of public schools, or derived from any public fund therefore, nor any public lands devoted thereto, shall ever be under the control of any religious sect, nor shall any money so raised or lands so devoted be divided between religious sects or denominations.[4]

The amendment became a symbol of anti-Catholic prejudice because of Blaine's association with the Republican charge that the Democrats were the party of "rum, Romanism, and rebellion." The proposal also revealed a number of things about the Congressional view of church–state law. First, it explicitly sought to extend the religion clauses to the states, indicating a federalist understanding of the existing First Amendment. Second, it suggested that Protestants did not see the courts at the time as a venue for their challenge to parochial aid, either at the federal or state level. Although twentieth-century courts would later interpret the First Amendment to bar direct public funds to parochial schools, this was apparently not the understanding at the time.

The amendment passed the house but fell short of the two thirds needed in the Senate. Strong Catholic opposition, coupled with a desire by some to leave the issue to the states, convinced enough senators to vote against the provision or abstain. Although Republican platforms from 1876 to 1892 called for an end to government aid to sectarian schools, the issue was not brought before Congress again. At the state level, however, Protestants were more successful, and a number of states passed their own amendments—so-called "Baby Blaines" that have been invoked in recent voucher cases.

Ironically, at the same time Congress deliberated the Blaine Amendment it was taking a different approach to federal Indian policy. Because the federal government did not operate schools, Congress had found it convenient from time to time to grant churches the privilege of providing schools on reservations. After the Civil War church leaders (notably Quakers) demanded reform of corrupt Indian agencies. President Grant responded by agreeing to appoint Indian agents from lists the churchmen provided, a practice that expanded from 1869 onward, to the point that different denominations were formally assigned to particular tribes and given responsibility for education and relief of specific Indian groups.[5]

Thus the same House of Representatives that passed the Blaine Amendment appropriated enormous sums to diverse sectarian religious schools on reservations. Indeed, in the last quarter of the nineteenth century Roman Catholics alone received $4.5 million from the federal government for their Indian schools in the West. Although the policy thrived from the 1870s to the end of the century, some Protestant groups became skittish about receiving government support and withdrew from the program. Catholics, in contrast, expanded their federally funded efforts with private money, sparking renewed anti-Catholic agitation. In 1894 Congress began debating the wisdom of the policy, and thereafter appropriations were cut, until in 1899 legislation declared an end to this notable experiment in federal support for religious schools.[6]

Although Congress has accommodated generalized acknowledgment and support for religion, it has resisted overt endorsement of a particular faith. Periodically in American history groups have petitioned Congress to amend the Constitution to declare the United States a Christian nation. During the Civil War a group of ministers formed the National Reform Association, declaring their purpose "to secure such an amendment to the Constitution of the United States as will declare the nation's allegiance to Jesus Christ and its acceptance of the moral laws of the Christian religion, and so indicate that this is a Christian nation."[7] An amendment was subsequently introduced in Congress in 1864 to amend the preamble of the Constitution. Proposed language acknowledged "Almighty God as the source of all authority and power in civil government, the Lord Jesus Christ, as the Ruler among the nations, and His revealed will as of supreme authority. . ." The amendment languished in the House Judiciary Committee, whose chairman termed it "unnecessary and injudicious." A decade later the committee officially voted against its adoption.[8]

Nearly a century later, in 1947 and again in 1954, the National Association of Evangelicals similarly proposed amending the Constitution to declare that "This nation divinely recognizes the authority and law of Jesus Christ, Savior and Ruler of Nations, through whom are bestowed the blessings of Almighty God." It too got nowhere in a Congress that nonetheless felt comfortable with a less sectarian acknowledgment of the nation's religious character by inserting "under God" into the pledge of Allegiance.[9]

A similar fate has fallen on attempts to amend the Constitution to allow organized school prayer. A common practice for more than a century, state-sponsored school prayer and Bible reading were banned as unconstitutional in the early 1960s by the Warren Court. In *Engel v. Vitale* (1962) the court struck down a New York practice of teachers reading a designated prayer at the beginning of each day. *Abington Township School District v. Schempp* (1963) declared unconstitutional a Pennsylvania law that required the reading of Bible verses before class. These and subsequent cases caused a firestorm of protest, leading to "hundreds of proposals" for Congressional action, "some favoring a constitutional amendment to overturn the Supreme Court's rulings, others favoring measures to remove the issue from the jurisdiction of Federal courts."[10]

From the beginning of the controversy Christian evangelicals and fundamentalists have spearheaded efforts to reverse these Supreme Court rulings. It took two decades of mobilization and the election of a sympathetic president, however, to bring the issue to a head. With public opinion polls showing wide support for school prayer, President Reagan proposed in 1982 that Congress pass a constitutional amendment explicitly allowing organized recited prayer in public schools. Introduced as S.J. Res. 73, the measure proposed this language:

> Nothing in this Constitution shall be construed to prohibit individual or group prayer in public schools or other public institutions. No person shall be required by the United States or any state to participate in prayer. Neither the United States nor any state shall compose the words of any prayer to be said in public schools.[11]

Note that the proposed amendment accepted a key premise in the *Engel* decision: that state authorities should not be in the business of composing prayers for students to recite. Moreover, advocates averred that the language pertained to voluntary prayer only. Critics, however, charged that organized group prayer in a public school setting stretched beyond credulity the voluntary nature of such practice.

Fundamentalist groups, such as the Moral Majority, Christian Voice, and Concerned Women for America initiated a massive mobilization effort for the amendment, whereas the network of TV and radio evangelists called the faithful to political action. This resulted in an unprecedented outpouring of support, as Congress was flooded with millions of calls and letters. New phone lines had to be installed and members had to pass by vigils held on the Capitol steps.[12]

As in the case of the Blaine Amendment, however, advocates faced the daunting obstacle of achieving a two thirds vote of both houses of Congress before the amendment could be sent to the states. Moreover, extensive opposition by Jewish, mainline Protestant, and even some evangelical leaders provided cover for Congressional members chary about amending the Constitution or breaching the boundary separating church and state. Thus when the Senate vote was taken on March 20, 1984, 44 senators voted against the measure, leaving it 11 votes short of two thirds.

The failure of the school prayer amendment, in the face of such intense public support, made Congressional members especially receptive to a compromise law that would address some of the concerns of school prayer advocates. One of those concerns was that school authorities went far beyond the limited scope of Supreme Court edicts and infringed on students' free exercise of religion, creating a chilling environment for religious freedom. Congressional testimony and press reports were replete with "horror stories" of overzealous administrators taking such actions as ordering a blind girl to stop praying the rosary on a school bus and confiscating religiously oriented valentines from a pupil.[13] The problem, therefore, was not so much Supreme Court decisions as it was the ignorance of school authorities, acting out of fear that any religious activity, however voluntary or student-initiated, could be challenged in the courts, necessitating costly legal fees.

Simultaneously, so-called "equal access" legislation addressing this kind of concern was working its way through Congress. Backed by such groups as the Christian Legal Society, a moderate evangelical organization, the proposed legislation focused on how student-run religious clubs were routinely banned from using school property, even though other clubs were free to do so. Contradictory lower court rulings, moreover, fostered legal confusion about such action.

After much legislative maneuvering and careful re-working of bill language, the act gained the strong support of a broad coalition of religious organizations and leaders. As passed, the Equal Access Act (PL 98-377) mandated that if a secondary school allowed noncurricular student clubs to meet on school property, before or after school, it could not deny the same privilege to religious clubs. To ensure minimal confusion about the new law, a coalition of religious and civil liberties associations sent guidelines to all school districts in the country.[14]

Equal Access, which was upheld as constitutional by the Supreme Court (*Westside Board of Education v. Mergens* [1990]), came to symbolize a broader effort to address the secularization of schools that the 1960s rulings did not require. Thus, even though it focused solely on student clubs, the spirit of the law equipped students with ammunition to challenge limitations on their voluntary religious activity. Equal Access also epitomized how some Congressional initiatives "accommodating" religion hinged on how such accommodation would expand genuine free exercise of religion.

Passage of Equal Access, however, did not end agitation for school prayer because subsequent Supreme Court decisions went beyond the 1960s rulings that dealt with teacher-led religious observances. In *Wallace v. Jaffree* (1985) the Court struck down Alabama's statute for a moment of silent meditation and in *Lee v. Weisman* (1992) found unconstitutional minister-led prayers at graduation ceremonies. The last straw was Court opposition to student-led prayer at sporting events (*Santa Fe Independent School District v. Doe* [2000]). Adding fuel to the fire were overreactions by some school authorities, such as denying students the prerogative of invoking their faith in valedictorian speeches.

However, it was also a series of related Court decisions that reignited agitation for constitutional amendments. In highly controversial cases the Court struck down religious displays on public grounds, such as Christmas creche scenes at civic centers or the Ten Commandments at courthouses. This led school prayer advocates to broaden the scope of their initiatives.

Leading this most recent charge was Oklahoma representative Ernest Istook, who introduced a series of proposed amendments that emphasized religious freedom as their theme. His first attempt was titled the Religious Freedom Amendment of 1998, which achieved majority support but not the two thirds needed for passage. Istook persisted and introduced a bill in December 2001, in the wake of patriotic fervor after the September 11 attacks. Similar to the one defeated, it read as follows:

> To secure the people's right to acknowledge God according to the dictates of conscience:
>
> - Neither the United States nor any State shall establish any official religion, but the people's right to pray and to recognize their religious beliefs, heritage, and traditions on public property, including schools, shall not be infringed.
> - The United States and the States shall not compose school prayers, nor require any person to join in prayer or other religious activities.

The proposal was vigorously attacked by civil liberties and strict separation advocates as opening up schools to a variety of intrusive practices, such as allowing students to read sectarian prayers over PA systems or invite clergy to pray at compulsory school events. In addition, opponents argued that the "right to voluntary prayer already exists and requires no special action by Congress."[15] This amendment did not come up for a vote before the 107th Congress adjourned, but a new version, H. J. Res 46, was introduced in April of 2003.

Responding to legal challenges to the phrase "under God" in the pledge of allegiance, the preamble of this resolution stated the amendment's intention to protect "the Pledge of Allegiance to the Flag, the display of the Ten Commandments, and voluntary school prayer." The amendment language was briefer than previous proposals:

> To secure the people's right to acknowledge God according to the dictates of conscience:
>
> - The people retain the right to pray and to recognize their religious beliefs, heritage, and traditions on public property, including schools.
> - The United States and the States shall not establish any official religion nor require any person to join in prayer or religious activity.[16]

The proposal was referred to committee but no action was taken. It may be that in the midst of the global war on terror the attentions of members were focused elsewhere and they had no stomach or sense of urgency in tackling another bruising church–state battle.

The point of this extended discussion of the school prayer controversy is that Congress, despite public agitation, continues to rebuff attempts to amend the Constitution, because enough members see such a radical move as a minefield fraught with potential unintended legal and political consequences.

One area that Congress discerned a means of accommodating religion—and arguably expanding its free exercise—involved various "choice" options in the implementation of education and welfare programs. The paradigm example was the GI Bill, which allowed World War II veterans to use their federal college grants for tuition at private sectarian institutions. Widely popular, the program created a precedent that choice advocates often cite in their efforts to promote a similar approach in other initiatives.

An example involves federal subsidies for child day care. Although the federal government had periodically provided such support, the major enduring program—the Child Care and Development Block Grant (CCDBG)—was created by Congress in 1990. Originally introduced as the Act for Better Child Care (or ABC bill), the legislation was championed by the Children's Defense Fund, a liberal advocacy group, which sought to expand quality child care services for poor families. Although originally introduced by Democratic members in 1987, the concept enjoyed some bipartisan support because it was seen by conservatives as a means of helping move welfare recipients, especially single mothers, into work.

What caught proponents off guard was a thorny church–state issue: What do you do when at least a third of the potential venders of child care to be subsidized by the federal government are churches or organizations housed in churches? The original bill allowed subsidies for such church-based care, but because of constitutional concerns mandated its secularization, even to the point of covering religious objects and pictures. Moreover, vendors were prohibited from exercising any preference in hiring employees who shared the faith of the organization. This was unacceptable to many religious organizations and led to a groping for compromise language.[17]

That language, proposed by the U.S. Catholic Conference, entailed an expansive "parental choice" provision. As amended the bill mandated that states receiving the child care block grant provide parents the option of receiving "certificates" that they could use at overtly sectarian providers (as long as they were properly licensed). In addition, although it prohibited discrimination in hiring, it allowed such sectarian organizations to require that employees adhere to their religious tenets and teachings.[18]

This language was opposed by strict separationist organizations, such as the Baptist Joint Committee (BJC) and Americans United for Separation of Church and State. James Dunn of BJC argued that to keep churches pure the law should forbid any government aid to sectarian programs, either directly or indirectly. On the other hand, Sam Ericsson of the Christian Legal Society countered that without the amendment the bill would "condition a benefit on the foregoing of a constitutional right." A certificate program, on the other hand, entails "a transaction between government and families," with the provider only an indirect recipient of federal assistance, receiving benefits "only after the family has made a private, individual choice."[19] This rationale ultimately won the day and the amended law[20] continues to be funded to this day.

One of the most vociferous critics of the parental choice provision of CCDGB was the National Education Association. Because it viewed day care programs as entailing education, it feared that the choice provision would set a precedent for educational vouchers. Such fears were probably warranted as subsequent Congresses debated various proposals for expanding parental choice in secondary education. The concept generally involved providing parents in failing schools with vouchers that enable them to send their children to either public or private schools of their choice (including religious ones). Voucher proposals flow from the combination of discontent with the widespread failure of inner-city schools coupled with a philosophical position that the poor should enjoy the same choice the wealthy do to send their children to good schools that embody their moral or religious values.

Although the states have taken the lead in experimenting with voucher schemes, Congress took initiative with its governance over the District of Columbia. In 2004 it passed H.R. 2556, The D.C. Choice Initiative Act, which created the first federally funded voucher program. As one account noted, by 2007 some "1,800 students, with an average family income of $21,100, are using opportunity scholarships to attend 66 participating private schools in Washington."[21] Although popular in the District, the law was vehemently opposed by teachers unions, which successfully lobbied the new Democratic Congress in 2009 to delete future funding for the program, putting it on the road to likely extinction.

The final Congressional foray into the church–state thicket began with welfare reform legislation of 1996, which replaced open-ended government support to the poor (AFDC) with temporary assistance and strong incentives to move into the work force (TANF). A key amendment sponsored by Senator John Ashcroft mandated that religious nonprofit social service agencies be given equal opportunity to apply for federal grants that support "welfare to work" initiatives and the like. This so-called "charitable choice" provision established a precedent upon which President George W. Bush based his signature "faith-based initiative."

As advanced by the president, the charitable choice concept would be applied to a host of other federal grant programs and possibly expanded to more "pervasively sectarian" providers. The president's proposed legislation thus moved beyond the certificate option of day care and the circumscribed arena of welfare reform. This raised an acute issue: Under what conditions could "pervasively sectarian" providers be eligible for federal grants, and what strings would be attached? Some religious organizations, including evangelical churches, feared that the program would involve federal intrusion into their financial books or lead faith-based charities to downplay their religious message. Liberal groups, particularly the Congressional Black Caucus, opposed the legislation because it would allow sectarian organizations to hire only employees of their own faith and thus be discriminatory. Strict separationists saw direct government support for religious organizations as fraught with constitutional and practical problems.

The sweeping nature of the Bush proposal moved into the arena of direct government subsidies of faith-based organizations that tie their success in addressing such problems as drug and alcohol addiction, teen pregnancies, or recidivism to religiously based methods of treatment. Congress could not come up with a consensus formula to provide grants to such providers without overtly promoting religious practices. This was a boundary it was loath to cross. The president ultimately had to settle for executive orders as a means of implementing part of his vision for marshaling "armies of compassion" through partnerships with the faith-based sector. The debate over this practice, however, is far from over.

Throughout Congressional history, as we have seen, religious groups have lobbied to define the boundaries between church and state. The general pattern of such effort is summarized well by Congressional scholar Louis Fisher: When religious lobbies "operate in concert for broad national goals, they have exercised a positive and constructive influence. When they pursue narrow, sectarian objectives, they are checked by other interest groups."[22] The Congressional system, with its numerous veto points and consensus-building norms, is largely responsible for producing this outcome.

CONGRESS AND FREE EXERCISE

In a sense it is not surprising that Congress, as the Constitution's "majoritarian" branch, would reflect popular sentiment and accommodate widespread religious practice. What is more surprising, perhaps, is its role in protecting minority rights to free exercise of religion. However, as Louis Fisher has exhaustively documented, Congress has played a pivotal role in defending religious freedom, often more aggressively and consistently than the courts.[23] As we will see, this stems from several related factors. At least some religious minorities enjoy the sympathy of the broader public, and they can form effective alliances with other minority faiths. Moreover, the enormous pluralism of American religious life ensures that virtually all religious communities can see themselves as minorities under certain circumstances and thus ban together to protect expansive applications of religious freedom. Congress, in a way, ratifies this outcome.

Before cataloguing the ways Congress has protected religious minorities, we must address the singular exception: Mormons and polygamy. Mormons trace their origins to the vision of Joseph Smith, of Palmyra, New York. In 1827 he claimed to have found sacred tablets describing the migration of a lost tribe of Israel to the new world and the subsequent visitation by Christ. The new religious movement Smith fashioned (The Church of Jesus Christ of Latter-day Saints) was fervent, disciplined, and clearly situated outside the mainstream, which aroused the enmity of neighbors. After being chased successively out of New York, Ohio, Missouri, and Illinois (where Smith was killed by a mob) the Latter-day Saints settled in Utah and established in essence a theocratic state under the leadership of Brigham Young. The safe haven was short-lived because the territory of Utah came under United States control in 1848 after the Mexican-American War.

Although Brigham Young was initially appointed territorial governor, that ended when a general church conference openly acknowledged the practice of polygamy, which was deeply repugnant to the majority of Americans. Thus ensued an extended and at times bloody effort by the federal government to tame Mormon theocracy and enforce prohibition against polygamy. In 1862 Congress passed a law establishing punishments for polygamy in the territory. Because local courts failed to enforce the law, Congress followed up in 1874 by giving federal judges authority over Utah courts. This was still not enough to stem noncompliance of the law, so Congress passed draconian legislation in 1887 that confiscated church property. Mormons went to court, claiming that these laws violated their free exercise of religion. Citing a distinction between belief and practice, the Court disagreed and upheld the laws. After these defeats the head of the Mormon Church announced the abandonment of polygamy and the acceptance of federal laws, thus paving the way for statehood in 1894.[24] Thus did the majority enforce its will on an unorthodox religious group.

In contrast to the Mormon case, Congress generally has been generous to religious minorities. One of the most vivid examples of Congress extending protection for such religious groups concerns exemption from military service. Legislative protection of conscientious objectors extends far back in American history. Many colonial legislatures exempted members from pacifist sects from serving in combat. The Continental Congress followed suit during the War for Independence by allowing those who "from religious principles cannot bear arms" to perform noncombat service to the cause.[25] Although the First Congress chose not to include an explicit exemption in the First Amendment for those "scrupulous of bearing arms," it generally provided such protection by laws.

Neither the War of 1812 nor the Mexican-American War involved conscription, but the magnitude of the Civil War required a draft, both in the South and the North. In the North, Quakers and other pacifists initially had to rely on the provision of the conscription law that allowed payment of $300 in lieu of military service. This, of course, did not satisfy them, and they petitioned the Congress for redress. This lobbying by Quakers, a tiny minority at the time, gained Congressional passage of a law in 1864 that allowed "those conscientiously opposed to the bearing of arms" to be assigned "to duty in the hospitals, or to the care of freedman" or to pay into a fund for wounded soldiers. Subsequent legislation and executive interpretation even relaxed the requirement for alternative service.[26]

With this as a well-established precedent, Congress extended exemptions for conscientious objectors during World War I. What is striking is that Congress debated extending such status not only to members of a "well-recognized religious sect," but also to those who oppose war on religious grounds but do not belong to pacifist denominations.[27] Although this provision did not pass, it anticipated the more generous contours of conscientious objection to come.

The 1940 conscription act that Congress deliberated on the eve of World War II initially lifted language from the World War I law exempting from the draft those individuals belonging to a "well-recognized religious sect whose creed or principles forbid its members to participate in way in any form;" but lobbying by a diverse array of churches led Congress to broaden exemptions to anyone who, "by reason of religious training and belief, is conscientiously opposed to participation in war in any form." To take into account religious belief that does not affirm a Supreme

Being, such as Buddhism, Congress (during the Vietnam War) removed the necessity of belief in a "Supreme Being" for an individual to qualify for exemption.[28] As we see clearly in this discussion, it was primarily Congress, not the courts, that defined and expanded religious exemption from military service.

Congress has also weighed in to provide other exemptions. When the Supreme Court upheld an Air Force regulation prohibiting an observant Jew from wearing a yarmulke while on duty, Congress passed a law permitting members of the military to wear any "neat, conservative, and unobtrusive" religious apparel. Again, Congress secured a more expansive free exercise than provided by the courts.[29]

This example is by no means isolated. As summarized by Louis Fisher:

> On hundreds of occasions, Congress has decided to protect religious interests by exempting them from general laws on taxation, social security, military service, peyote use, labor laws, discrimination in housing and employment, census questions, rehabilitative services, medical examinations, and public health measures.[30]

Two areas from the preceding list deserve elaboration. A longstanding Congressional practice is exempting churches and religious nonprofits from taxation. Not only is this a fiscal boon to religious communities and institutions, but it also prevents the government from engaging in intrusive investigations into the internal life of religious entities.[31] With respect to civil rights laws, Congress has pursued a dual track. On the one hand its statutes prohibit employers from discriminating against employees on the basis of religion; on the other hand houses of worship are exempt from such provisions so that they can exercise a hiring preference for members of the same faith.

One of the more notable instances of Congressional engagement in free exercise explicitly for religious minorities involves Indian tribes. Beginning in the 1960s Congress passed a series of measures protecting the religious practice of Native Americans. In legislation to preserve the Bald Eagle, for example, Congress provided certain exemptions for "the religious purposes of Indian tribes" (mostly to allow use of eagle feathers). Similarly, Congress acted to provide an exemption from federal drug laws for the religious use of peyote by members of the Native American Church.[32]

This was only the beginning of a succession of Congressional acts. In 1968 Congress enacted the Indian Civil Rights Act, which mandated that tribal governments protect the free exercise of religion. In 1978 it passed the American Indian Religious Freedom Act, in part to protect access to sacred sites. In 1990 it passed the Native American Graves Protection and Repatriation Act, designed to prevent removal of sacred objects from plunder and return human remains or funerary objects to tribes of origin.[33]

The lesson from this discussion is that religious minorities have gained legislative relief from Congress. In part this is because American civic culture cultivates a respect for religious practice, thus generating public sympathy for religious minorities. Small sects can also form alliances.

Nowhere is this more vividly displayed than in the Congressional response to a narrowing of free exercise relief by the Supreme Court. Up until 1990 the Supreme Court had generally adhered to the doctrine of "strict scrutiny" in adjudicating religious free exercise claims. This meant that when an otherwise valid secular law incidentally burdened someone's religious freedom the government had to show that it had used the "least restrictive means" to achieve some "compelling state interest." Otherwise the Court mandated a religious exception. This gave leverage to religious litigants when they bumped up against the plethora of laws and regulations of the administrative state.

The apparently settled nature of free exercise law was shattered when the Supreme Court departed from prior decisions in *Employment Division of Oregon v. Smith* (1990). The case involved two Native Americans who sought unemployment benefits from the State of Oregon after being fired from state jobs for using peyote as part of religious ritual. Writing for the majority, Justice Antonin Scalia argued that religious practices are not exempt from generally applicable state laws unless legislators explicitly write those exemptions into law.

This overturning of the "compelling state interest" test caused a firestorm in the religious community and united religious groups across the ideological and theological spectrum. In part this stemmed from their philosophical commitment to generous contours of free exercise; but it also reflected the fact that just about any religious group or church could imagine situations in which some law or regulation might burden its religious practice.

In response to *Oregon v. Smith* a broad coalition of religious groups—from liberal Jews to conservative evangelicals, Catholics to Muslims—lobbied Congress to restore the compelling state interest test by statute. In testimony before Congressional committees they provided extensive documentation of the deleterious impact of the ruling on the rights of religious litigants. Congress responded by passing the Religious Freedom Restoration Act (RFRA) of 1993 (PL 103-141), which relied on the clause of the Fourteenth Amendment giving Congress the power to enforce the rest of the amendment's provisions. RFRA stipulated that laws or regulations that burden religious freedom must be "least restrictive means" of furthering a "compelling governmental interest."[34]

The Supreme Court, however, viewed the law as an intrusion upon its turf. In *Boerne v. Flores* (1997) the Court found that Congress lacked the authority to interpret the Fourteenth Amendment and struck down as unconstitutional the application of RFRA to state and local governments (although the law still applies to actions of the federal government).[35]

Religious freedom advocates did not abandon the struggle. Again they sought a mechanism to reinstate the RFRA's intent, but this time relied on Congress' authority to regulate interstate commerce. New legislation, titled the Religious Liberty Protection Act, passed the House but stalled in the Senate when fears emerged that it might grant exemptions from antidiscrimination ordinances. A broad consensus remained, however, on the need to address mounting cases of local zoning restrictions that increasingly limit the freedom of worship and assembly for churches (the issue in the *Boerne* case), as well as restrictions on the religious exercise of prisoners. Therefore, in 2000 Congress passed more narrowly targeted legislation, the Religious Land Use and Institutionalized Persons Act, which prohibits regulations that impose a substantial burden on religious exercise unless the government can show a compelling interest in doing so. The Supreme Court has yet to test the constitutionality of this law, so the battle continues.

Intriguingly, the unlikely alliances forged in this struggle facilitated a remarkable foray by Congress into the international arena. Mounting concern about religious persecution around the world led to agitation by a broad coalition of domestic and international religious groups demanding a vigorous American response. After a tortuous legislative battle, Congress unanimously passed the International Religious Freedom Act of 1998 (PL 105-292), which mandated that promotion of religious freedom be a basic aim of American foreign policy. The law created a new State Department office tasked with producing an annual report on the status of religious freedom in every country on earth. It also stipulated that the State Department designate "countries of concern," egregious deniers of religious freedom subject to American sanctions. Finally, the law created a U.S. Commission on International Religious Freedom, a high-level independent body to investigate instances of religious persecution around the world and make recommendations for U.S. policy responses. The Commission acts as a watchdog, often critiquing aspects of the State Department report that it feels soft pedals religious violations by strategic nations. Congressional backers continue to hold hearings about the implementation of the law and generally demand stronger enforcement by the U.S. government.[36] Clearly, the interest of Congress in religious freedom now transcends national boundaries.

Conclusion

A pattern emerges in the discussion of the role of Congress in defining the contours of First Amendment religious provisions. On establishment issues Congress has taken a generally accommodationist position, although not an unlimited one, as there have been boundaries beyond which it will not go. Generally it acted to accommodate religion when it saw such accommodation as furthering the cause of free exercise of religion. On free exercise Congress has often taken a more expansive position than the Supreme Court, particularly in providing religious exemptions from otherwise valid secular law or practice. These two positions, I would suggest, are philosophically compatible, and they demonstrate that the elected branch of government, not just the courts, has played a pivotal role in securing the "first freedom" of the American system.

ENDNOTES

1. Louis Fisher, *Religious Liberty in America: Political Safeguards* (Lawrence, KS: University Press of Kansas, 2002).

2. Michael Malbin, *Religion and Politics: The Intentions of the Authors of the First Amendment* (Washington, DC: American Enterprise Institute, 1978).

3. 1 Stat. 50,52 (1789), Section 3.

4. Jon Meacham, *American Gospel: God, the Founding Fathers, and the Making of a Nation* (New York: Random House, 2006), 143.

5. Anson Phelps Stokes and Leo Pfeffer, *Church and State in the United States,* vol. 2 (New York: Harper & Row, 1964), 285–292.

6. Ibid., 2: 285–292.

7. James E. Wood, Jr., "Public Religion vis a vis the Prophetic Role of Religion," *Journal of Church and State* 41 (Winter 1999): 62.

8. Jon Meacham, *American Gospel*: 129–130; "Is America a 'Christian Nation"? Americans United for Separation of Church and State (www.au.org), accessed September 14, 2007.

9. Meacham, *American Gospel,* 175.

10. Charles Whittier, "The School Prayer Controversy: Pro-Con Arguments," Congressional Research Service, August 26, 1985: 1.

11. Ibid., 2.

12. An extended discussion of the Congressional Equal Access battle is provided by Allen D. Hertzke, *Representing God in Washington: The Role of Religious Lobbies in the American Polity* (Knoxville, TN: University of Tennessee Press 1988), Chapter 6.

13. Ibid., 164.

14. Ibid., 172–173.

15. Whittier, "The School Prayer Controversy," 4.

16. H. J. Res. 46, introduced in the House of Representatives on April 9, 2003.

17. Allen D. Hertzke and Mary Scribner, "The Politics of Federal Day Care: The Nexus of Family, Church, and the Positive State," presented at the 1990 annual meeting of the American Political Science Association.

18. Alice Butler and Melinda Gish, "The Child Care and Development Block Grant: Background and Funding," Report to Congress, Congressional Research Service, April 7, 2003.

19. Congressional Record, 1989, 101st Cong., 1st sess. Vol. 135, S7161–7169.

20. Child Care and Development Block Grant Act of 1990, included in the Omnibus Budget and Reconciliation Act of 1990, PL 101-508, Title V, Chapter 6, Subsection C.

21. Evan Feinberg, "How Members of Congress Practice Private School Choice," *Backgrounder,* The Heritage Foundation, September 4, 2007.

22. Louis Fisher, *Religious Liberty in America: Political Safeguards* (Lawrence, KS: University of Kansas Press, 2002), 2.

23. Ibid.

24. Ibid., 20–26.

25. Ibid., 82–83.

26. Ibid., 90

27. Ibid., 92.

28. Ibid., 96–103.

29. Ibid., 114–122.

30. Ibid., 231.

31. Dean M. Kelley, *Why Churches Should Not be Taxed* (New York: Harper & Row, 1977).

32. Fisher, 164, 181–182.

33. Ibid., 165–174.

34. Jay Wexler, "Protecting Religion Through Stature: The Mixed Case of the United States," *The Review of Faith & International Affairs* 5 (Fall 2007): 17–25.

35. Allen D. Hertzke and Kevin R. den Dulk, "The 'First Freedom' and Church-State Policy in the U.S.A., in *Jahrbuch Fur Europanische Verwaltungsgeschichte (JEV)*, ed. Jos Raadschelders (Nomos Verlagsgesellschaft: Baden-Baden, 2002).

36. Allen D. Hertzke, *Freeing God's Children: The Unlikely Alliance for Global Human Rights* (Lanham, MD: Rowman & Littlefield, 2004), Chapter 6.

BIBLIOGRAPHY

Books

Fisher, Louis. *Religious Liberty in America: Political Safeguards.* Lawrence, KS: University Press of Kansas, 2002.

Hertzke, Allen D. *Freeing God's Children: The Unlikely Alliance for Global Human Rights.* Lanham, MD: Rowman & Littlefield, 2004.

Hertzke, Allen D. *Representing God in Washington: The Role of Religious Lobbies in the American Polity.* Knoxville, TN: University of Tennessee Press, 1988.

Kelley, Dean M. *Why Churches Should Not be Taxed.* New York: Harper & Row, 1977.

Malbin, Michael. *Religion and Politics: The Intentions of the Authors of the First Amendment.* Washington, DC: American Enterprise Institute, 1978.

Meacham, Jon. *American Gospel: God, the Founding Fathers, and the Making of a Nation.* New York: Random House, 2006.

Stokes, Anson Phelps and Leo Pfeffer. *Church and State in the United States,* vol. 2. New York: Harper & Row, 1964.

Articles/Chapters

Butler, Alice, and Melinda Gish. "The Child Care and Development Block Grant: Background and Funding." Report to Congress, Congressional Research Service, April 7, 2003.

Child Care and Development Block Grant Act of 1990, included in the Omnibus Budget and Reconciliation Act of 1990, PL 101-508, Title V, Chapter 6, Subsection C.

Congressional Record, 1989, 101st Congress, 1st session, Vol. 135, S7161-7169.Feinberg, Evan. "How Members of Congress Practice Private School Choice." *Backgrounder,* The Heritage Foundation: September 4, 2007.

Hertzke, Allen D. and Kevin R. den Dulk, "The 'First Freedom' and Church-State Policy in the U.S.A." in *Jahrbuch Fur Europanische Verwaltungsgeschichte (JEV).* Nomos Verlagsgesellschaft: Baden-Baden, 2002.

Hertzke, Allen D., and Mary Scribner. "The Politics of Federal Day Care: The Nexus of Family, Church, and the Positive State." Presented at the 1990 annual meeting of the American Political Science Association.

Wexler, Jay. "Protecting Religion Through Stature: The Mixed Case of the United States."
    The Review of Faith & International Affairs 5 (Fall 2007): 17.
Wittier, Charles. "The School Prayer Controversy: Pro-Con Arguments." Congressional
    Research Service, August 26, 1985: 1.
Wood, James E. Jr. "Public Religion vis a vis the Prophetic Role of Religion." *Journal of
    Church and State* 41 (Winter 1999): 62.

CHAPTER 15

THE CHRISTIAN RIGHT AND CHURCH–STATE ISSUES

CLYDE WILCOX AND SAM POTOLICCHIO

In late September, 2008, Pastor Wiley Drake of the First Southern Baptist Church in Los Angeles announced from the pulpit that "There is no way in the world a Christian could vote for Barack Hussein Obama." Pastor Jody Hice of the Bethlehem First Baptist Church outside Atlanta, Georgia told his congregation "When you go into that voting booth, I urge you not to vote for Obama."[1] These pastors, along with more than 30 others across the country, mailed videos or transcripts of their sermons to the Internal Revenue Service as part of a coordinated effort to challenge tax law that bars Internal Revenue Code Section 501(c)(3) charities from endorsing candidates. Their efforts were orchestrated by the Alliance Defense Fund, an Arizona-based Christian Right legal foundation that promised to defend pastors who joined the action all the way to the Supreme Court. The Alliance Defense Fund is itself a 501(c)(3) organization.

This coordinated challenge to established tax laws barring endorsements by tax-exempt churches is a mixture of old and new movement tactics. After the formation of the Moral Majority and other Christian Right groups in the late 1970s, the movement focused primarily on electing Republican candidates and lobbying GOP policymakers to accomplish its policy goals.[2] During the 1990s, however, a parallel effort to modify the law through the courts achieved some success.[3] During this period the Christian Right changed its rhetorical focus from a challenge to church–state separation to a call for greater free exercise and free speech rights for conservative Christians.

Over the last 30 years or so, the Christian Right has been active in nearly every political and legal dispute in the national church–state domain. Movement leaders and activists have proclaimed that the United States is a Christian nation, and that failure to recognize this in public displays, public schools, and public policy will lead to God's punishment. They have worked to mobilize conservative Christians, lobby government, influence elections, and change the underlying constitutional interpretation of church–state issues. Their actions have sparked the creation of new groups such as People for the American Way and the rejuvenation of opposition groups such as Americans United for Separation of Church and State.

Like all social movements, the Christian Right has leaders and organizations that cooperate, but also compete, to define the movement's ideology and agenda; and like all movements, there is great diversity in what leaders and activists seek. Some movement leaders have proclaimed America to be a Christian nation, with little room for those of other faiths, whereas others have defended in court the right of religious minorities. Some argue that they merely wish to protect religious freedoms for conservative Christians, but others movement activists argue that America's Constitution and laws should be consistent with the Bible. Some have proclaimed that they seek only "a seat at the table" where policy is made; others have suggested the need for Christian conservatives to have dominion over society and government.[4]

Christian Right activists frequently argue that theirs is a defensive movement seeking to reestablish a balance on church–state issues, and to represent conservative Christians in the policy process.[5] They argue that conservative Christians face a hostile media and academy that has ignored their views, and that they must mobilize to win a place at the table of policy negotiations. Many charge that liberals seek to limit the religious rights of conservative Christians, and urge their followers to help them "take back" America for Christ.

Opponents describe a radical fundamentalist movement that resembles Islamist parties abroad in its desire to limit the rights of women and cultural liberals, and to write its religious views into the Constitution and law.[6] They suggest that Christian Right leaders seek to break down the separation of church and state and establish evangelical Christianity as the dominant American religion. More moderate proclamations by Christian Right leaders are discounted as public relations efforts that conceal more radical plans.

The rhetoric on each side has been heated. Consider the following:

Modern U.S. Supreme Courts have raped the Constitution and raped the churches by misinterpreting what the founders had in mind in the First Amendment of the Constitution . . . We must fight against those radical minorities who are trying to remove God from our textbooks, Christ from our nation. We must never allow our children to forget that this is a Christian nation. (Jerry Falwell, March 1993 sermon)[7]

We often hear of the constitutionally mandated 'separation of church and state.' Of course, as you know, this phrase appears nowhere in the Constitution or the Bill of Rights. . . We do find this phrase in the constitution . . . of the Union of Soviet Socialist Republics—an atheistic nation sworn to the destruction of the United States. (Pat Robertson, testimony to Senate Judiciary Committee, August 18, 1982)[8]

And also:

The Religious Right seeks to reorder society by insisting that the country embrace a rigid set of rules based on a narrow definition of Christianity. The movement's leaders would use the power of government to force all of us to follow its dictates. This is the Religious Right's greatest mistake—and its biggest threat. (Barry Lynn, director of Americans United for Separation of Church and State)

Talk about a Christian theocracy in this country, many evangelical Christians believe . . . that's what we should have, that government should favor people who have the right and understand what God wants us to do. (Sam Donaldson, December 9, 2007)[9]

What Does the Christian Right Want?

The Christian Right is a social movement that seeks to mobilize primarily white evangelical Protestants into political action. The movement has attracted the support of a smaller number of white conservative Catholics, a few African American evangelicals, and a scattering of other religious groups, including Orthodox Jews. The movement has included large membership organizations such as the Moral Majority, Concerned Women for America, and the Christian Coalition, ministries with political muscle such as Focus on the Family, organizations that focus on a narrower range of policies, such as Citizens for Excellence in Education, and legal organization such as the Alliance Defense Fund. It has also included state organizations such as the Virginia Family Foundation, and countless local organizations.

Christian Right leaders and groups stake different public positions on church–state issues, but it is difficult to assess how much this reflects differences in real agendas or differences in political tactics. Movement leaders in the 1990s began to train activists to use more moderate and inclusive rhetoric; scholars have disagreed to what extent this reflects genuine moderation and to what extent it reflects instrumental politics.[10] There is diversity in the Christian Right, however, both in policy preferences, and in views of how church and state should interact.

At the radical fringe of the Christian Right are those who espouse Christian Reconstructionism, dominion theology, and/or theonomy. The leaders of this movement disagree on some matters, but agree that Christians have a biblical mandate to reconstruct all aspects of society, beginning with the United States government. They proclaim a broad agenda from eliminating public schools, replacing government authority in many areas with religious authority, and enforcing Old Testament death penalty sanctions against homosexuality, adultery, blasphemy, and other sins. Reconstructionists do not generally support religious tolerance or pluralism, and make it clear that non-Christians should not be involved in government. Indeed, some argue that only members of "biblically correct" churches should be allowed to vote. These views represent a small minority of the Christian

Right, although the writings of authors in this tradition have been cited by Pat Robertson, Jerry Falwell, and other leaders.[11]

A majority of Christian Right leaders agree that U.S. laws should reflect biblical teachings, although they support broader democratic processes and at least some pluralism. Many have endorsed an electoral strategy that would lead to a Christian conservative dominated government that could change laws and eventually change constitutional understandings of establishment and free exercise issues. At an early meeting of the Christian Coalition, Pat Robertson proclaimed the goal of Christian conservative majorities in state legislatures, in Congress, and "the White House in pro-family, Christian hands by 2000, if the Lord permits."[12]

A smaller number Christian Right activists claim to seek only a seat at the bargaining table. They argue that conservative Christians have been traditionally underrepresented in government, and that their voices have been excluded from the pluralist choir. Generally these activists assert that their policy preferences either have majority support, or that they would be majority positions if fully understood.

Movement activists believe that presidents should proclaim their faith and serve as a moral example to the nation. And like Israel, America will be punished if it strays from God's will—a view embodied by statements by Pat Robertson that God would punish Florida for allowing Disney World to host a gay pride day, and by Jerry Falwell that the September 11, 2001 terrorist attacks were in part God's judgment against "pagans, abortionists, feminists, gays and lesbians and the ACLU, People For the American Way, all of them who have tried to secularize America."[13]

Movement activists proclaim the importance of the role of elected officials (especially presidents) proclaiming their faith and serving as moral example to the nation. Christian Right leaders were very critical of Bill Clinton's various moral transgressions, and were drawn to George W. Bush's public proclamations of faith, as well as his appropriation of evangelical language as in his call for the "wonder working power of private charity."[14] Some movement activists welcomed the increased religious rhetoric of Democratic presidential candidates Hillary Clinton and Barack Obama, but Dr. James Dobson accused Obama, who became president in 2009, of "dragging biblical understanding through the gutter."[15]

ESTABLISHMENT CLAUSE ISSUES

Christian Right leaders almost universally argue that a constitutional separation of church and state is a myth. Dr. James Kennedy argued that "If we are committed and involved in taking back the nation for Christian moral values, and if we are willing to risk the scorn of the secular media and the bureaucracy that stand against us, there is no doubt we can witness the dismantling of not just the Berlin Wall but the even more diabolical 'wall of separation' that has led to increasing secularization, godlessness, immorality, and corruption in our country."[16] Christian Right activists argue that the establishment clause merely prohibits national endorsement of a single Christian denomination, but allows endorsement of faith in general, and (for most) Christianity.

Christian Right leaders seek public statements of faith by elected and appointed leaders, and to allow public prayer in some public meetings and events. They support public displays of the Ten Commandments on schoolhouse walls or outside of public courtrooms, and to have public displays of Christian symbols on public land at Easter and Christmas. Most also support limited displays of Jewish symbols, especially the Menorah at Hanukkah, but there is more opposition to displays of other faiths.

Christian Right activists place special emphasis on education, and they believe that cultural liberals have systematically removed religion from public schools and replaced it with active advocacy of secularism. The most moderate seek primarily to allow voluntary prayer before and after school, at graduation and at football games, and to include some discussion of religion in the public school curriculum.[17] Others seek to alter public school curricula, and have worked to mandate abstinence-only sex education and the teaching of "Intelligent Design" as an alternative to evolution among other changes.[18] These activists seek to fill school boards with sympathetic Christians. The Christian Coalition has held several training seminars for Christian Right candidates, and Citizens for Excellence in Education claims to have helped at least 25,000 Christians in a 10-year period.[19] In 1994, Ralph Reed declared that he "would exchange the Presidency for 2,000 school seats."[20] Still others have declared the public schools unsalvageable, and have urged parents to either home-school their children or send them to private religious schools.[21] In 2004 The National Center for Education (NCES) reported that conservative Christian schools comprised 18.9% of all private schools.[22] These proponents of private religious schools seek to provide tax credits to parents who send their children there, or establish vouchers to help pay for religious schools.

Christian Right activists see the family as the central social unit, and believe that it is under siege by a secular culture that glamorizes sexuality, disrupts the natural relationships between men and women, and undermines parental authority. Family and sexuality issues include sex education, abortion, policy toward gays and lesbians, and policies that make it easier for mothers of small children to work outside the home. Most activists would like to ban abortions, although a majority of rank-and-file members would allow abortion to protect the health of the mother and in case of rape.[23] A few activists would like to jail doctors and (less often) women if illegal abortions occur. Recognizing the long odds of banning abortions, Christian Right activists work actively in states to pass a variety of limits on abortion, including waiting periods, parental consent, "informed" consent, among many others.[24]

Christian Right groups proclaim that homosexuality is a serious sin, and much Christian Right fundraising centers on anti-gay themes. Many of these materials argue that gays and lesbians are a danger to children—one Moral Majority fundraising letter spoke of "known, practicing and soliciting homosexual teachers," and a Focus on the Family document argued that the gay rights agenda was really "promoting pedophiles as prophets of the new world order."[25] In Oregon, a state level Christian Right group sought to amend the state constitution to declare that no level of government would promote, facilitate, or encourage homosexuality, pedophilia, sadism, or masochism, and that government (and especially the public schools) should set the standard that homosexuality is "abnormal, wrong, unnatural and perverse."[26]

Although Christian Right groups universally denounced the Supreme Court's decision overturning state sodomy laws, the reaction to state court decisions allowing same-sex marriage was far more vigorous and organized. In the late 2000s, Christian Right groups worked with others to amend state constitutions to ban same-sex marriage.

Many but not all Christian Right activists proclaim that the ideal family includes a father working for wages, and a woman who is primarily a homemaker. Some have worked to alter tax and other policies to create financial incentives for mothers to remain at home to care for small children, although some groups supported welfare reform measures that forced women who received government-supplied AFDC or TANF payments to seek employment. Others seek to put active barriers in the path of mothers who seek to work outside the home.

In many of these issues the Christian Right opposes organized social movements that promote gender equality, abortion rights, and equality for gays and lesbians. The public debate has been cast as between Christian moral values on the one hand, and equality and human rights on the other. Where court rulings establish constitutional rights for abortion or gay rights, leaders advocate constitutional amendments. Former Arkansas governor Mike Huckabee summarized this position after he dropped out of the GOP presidential race: "I have opponents in this race who do not want to change the Constitution. But I believe it's a lot easier to change the Constitution than it would be to change the word of the living God. And that's what we need to do—is to amend the Constitution so it's in God's standards rather than try to change God's standards so it lines up with some contemporary view of how we treat each other and how we treat the family."[27]

FREE EXERCISE CLAUSE ISSUES

Although Christian Right groups in the early 1980s framed many issues around the Establishment Clause, in more recent times they have frequently focused on free exercise and even free speech issues. There are several reasons for this shift. First, some Christian Right leaders came to believe that they could never reshape the culture. In 1999, Paul Weyrich, who helped form the Moral Majority, announced that he no longer believed that there was a moral majority. In a letter to supporters he proclaimed: "We probably have lost the culture war. We need to drop out of this culture, and find places where we can live godly, righteous and sober lives."[28]

Second, by the 1990s it was obvious that Establishment Clause arguments would not prevail in the Supreme Court, at least with its then-current membership. But free exercise claims resonate more strongly within the broader pluralist culture, in which liberal groups have frequently supported religious minorities who sought exceptions from secular law. Strategically, it was easier to argue for the rights of a high school valedictorian to pray or thank Jesus than it was to argue for a constitutional amendment to allow spoken prayer in classrooms. Finally, the free exercise claims allowed the Christian Right to broaden their coalition, at least on some issues. Many conservative Baptists and Catholics were uncomfortable with a teacher-led, spoken prayer in public school, but they would agree that if the school allowed the scuba club to meet after school it should also allow the Bible club to meet.

Christian Right groups nevertheless have differed on how far to extend free exercise protections to faiths outside the Judeo-Christian tradition. Consider two statements by leaders of the Christian Coalition. In *After the Revolution*, Ralph Reed wrote, "If religious conservatives took their proper, proportionate place as leaders in the political and cultural life of the country, we would work to create the kind of society in which presumably all of us would want to live: safe neighborhoods, strong families, schools that work, a smaller government, and lower taxes. Civil rights protections would be afforded to all Americans without regard to gender, race, religious beliefs, ethnicity, age, or physical handicap."[29] Reed's reassuring rhetoric suggests an America that is open to non-Christians, and he includes Muslims in a few passages of the book as elements of the "people of faith."

Yet Pat Robertson has sounded far less welcoming of non-Christians. He has suggested that "America was founded as a Christian nation. Our institutions presuppose the existence of a Supreme Being, a Being after the Bible. And we as Americans believe in the god of the Bible. And the fact that somebody comes with what amounts to an alien religion to these shores doesn't mean that we're going to give up all of our cherished religious beliefs to accommodate a few people who happen to believe in something else."[30] He argued in 2008 that Muslims should not be appointed to the U.S. cabinet or as judges.

In general, Christian Right mass organizations (which depend on membership for contributions) have been less supportive of free exercise rights for religious minorities than Christian Right legal firms. Although most cases brought by Christian Right firms have focused on free exercise or free speech of Christians, some groups have filed amicus briefs on behalf of religious minorities. For example, the Christian Legal Society has filed briefs on behalf of Islamic prisoners, Native Americans objecting to timbering on sacred land, and a Santeria church that had been banned by local governments from animal sacrifice.[31]

CHRISTIAN RIGHT STRATEGIES

The Christian Right has employed a variety of strategies to accomplish its agenda, each with implications for church and state in America. Like all movements and interest groups, they have sought to lobby government to change policies. Second, they have been active in nominations and elections. Finally, they have sought to change constitutions and to influence the interpretation of constitutions and laws.

LOBBYING GOVERNMENT

The Christian Right has lobbied national, state, and local governments in an effort to influence laws and policies. These efforts have included crude, unsophisticated efforts and professional, polished presentations. The movement has used a mixture of inside lobbying featuring professional lobbyists making arguments, and outside campaigns of letter writing, phone calls, and other grassroots pressure.

In the 1980s, groups like the Moral Majority mounted grassroots pressure on friend and foe alike, irritating both sets of policymakers. Although the movement won symbolic statements from President Reagan (and to a lesser extent Bush) on issues such as abortion, they were unable to persuade these presidents to push their agenda, including a constitutional amendment to allow school prayer.[32] In state legislatures and local governments, Christian Right lobbyists pushed for extreme proposals using explicitly religious language. This continues today in some states and especially in local governments.

During the 1990s, the lobbying strategies of some Christian Right groups became more professional. The Christian Coalition for a time employed an experienced and ecumenical lobby team, and Ralph Reed worked closely with GOP leaders after the party won control in the 1994 elections. Focus on the Family built effective state chapters that frequently lobbied state governments, and the Family Research Council prepared research reports that were shared with other groups. Concerned Women for America (CWA) built a network of women who met lawmakers in their district and pressed them to adopt the movement's agenda.[33] Christian Right lobbying has been more successful when Republicans are in office. Yet they have also been constrained by their links to the GOP. When the Republican Congress passed welfare reform that required poor mothers to enter the labor force, CWA did not lobby to change the proposal. When the Republican state legislature in Virginia accidentally guaranteed all citizens of the state a day off for family life and worship, the Family Foundation stood mutely by as the legislature quickly reversed this provision.

However, many activists have been disappointed in their victories with Republican lawmakers. They have nonetheless worked with Republicans in elections, because GOP policymakers are more likely to share their views than Democrats. Chuck Cunningham, who handled voter guides for the Christian Coalition, explained that "to change the kinds of policies we care about, you have to change politicians."[34]

WORKING WITH PARTIES AND IN ELECTIONS

The Christian Right in the 1980s to 2000s has been heavily involved in electoral mobilization. The Moral Majority and other Christian Right groups were formed in the late 1970s with the express intent of helping Ronald Reagan win the White House, and Republicans to gain in the Senate and House, and Pat Robertson proclaimed in 1989 that the goal of the Christian Coalition was to elect pro-family Republicans to the White House and Congress.

Electoral activity by the Christian Right has consisted of three elements. First, movement leaders seek to register and turn out voters. The Moral Majority in 1980 focused its efforts on voter registration in several southern states that were strategically vital to Reagan's contest against Jimmy Carter. The Christian Coalition a decade later designed voter guides that they distributed in churches on the Sunday before the election, seeking to mobilize conservative Christians and perhaps help influence their votes. The Christian Coalition also sought to build a database of conservative Christian Republican voters, and to call them before the election to urge them to vote. There is some evidence that these efforts did increase evangelical turnout, although not so much as movement leaders had hoped.[35]

Second, the Christian Right sought to recruit candidates to run for office, train them to run effectively, and help create a corps of activists to help them win office. In the 1980s, Christian Right groups frequently recruited pastors and other religious activists who staked extreme positions on issues and used religious reasons in public debates.[36] Although these candidates succeeded in mobilizing activists and evangelical voters, they frequently sparked a backlash among moderate voters that ensured their defeat.[37]

In 1988 Pat Robertson ran for president, and surprised the Republican establishment with both his fundraising prowess and his support in the caucuses.[38] Robertson laid out a populist platform that included debt relief as well as a ban on abortions, and promised to hire only Christians and Jews in his administration. Since 1990, Christian Right leaders have helped to recruit candidates who have at least some other support within the GOP, and who have some experience in winning elections. These "bilingual" candidates can use religious and secular arguments depending on the audience, and have proved far more successful than movement ideologues. In 2000, movement leaders endorsed George W. Bush in the primary, even though he ran against movement activists Gary Bauer, Patrick Buchanan, and Alan Keyes, in part because they believed him to be more electable.

Finally, the Christian Right has sought to work within the Republican Party to gain control of state and local party committees and influence party platforms. In many states, GOP platforms show strong Christian Right influence. The Republican platform in Texas, for example, proclaims that "America is a Christian nation, founded on Judeo-Christian principles," and that "we affirm that the public acknowledgement of God is undeniable in our history and is vital to our freedom, prosperity and strength as a nation." By working within the GOP, the Christian Right has gradually increased support for their platform among Republican policymakers.[39]

However, electoral efforts by the Christian Right did not succeed in altering policy in the way activists had hoped. First, when activists campaigned openly on a Christian Right platform they frequently were defeated, even in conservative states. Many moderate Republicans—including some with strong religious credentials—resisted efforts to redefine their party.[40] Moderate voters mobilized against Christian Right candidates, and Democrats frequently were successful in "morphing" pictures of Christian Right candidates into those of Jerry Falwell and Pat Robertson, who were very unpopular figures in most states.

In addition, candidates who won with Christian Right support frequently did not prioritize movement policies. Ronald Reagan did little to push a school prayer movement in Congress in the 1980s, and George W. Bush did little to promote a movement barring same-sex marriage 25 years later. When the Republicans gained control of Congress in 1994, their "Contract with America" did not include abortion or school prayer, and the "Christian Coalition Contract with America" was not taken up by GOP leaders. GOP leaders believed that actively promoting the movement's agenda would risk a backlash that might sweep them from office.

The electoral strategy failed for a second reason—many policies that the movement sought to implement were constitutionally impossible under national or state court rulings. The Supreme Court legalized abortion with *Roe v. Wade* in 1973, and although later court rulings allowed for state restrictions, outright bans on abortion would clearly not pass constitutional muster. The movement's agenda on schools, families, and public endorsements of Christianity also faced insurmountable barriers with current constitutional interpretations.

To overcome this barrier, the Christian Right sought to change the meaning of the U.S. and state constitutions by amendment, changing the composition of courts, and reframing arguments considered by courts.

THE COURTS AND CONSTITUTION

Christian Right activists have denounced U.S. Supreme Court decisions and those of state courts, using phrases such as "judicial tyranny." The movement has been frustrated repeatedly when victories in local and state governments are later overturned by courts. They have responded to this in three different ways.

First, the Christian Right has sought to amend the national and state constitutions to take interpretative power away from justices. In the early 1980s the Moral Majority pushed for national amendments to allow prayer in school and ban abortion. In the 2000s groups also pushed for a national amendment to bar same-sex marriage. Although the Christian Right was not the primary sponsor of an amendment barring flag burning in the late 1980s, most leaders supported it.

Efforts to change state constitutions have varied widely, based in part on the ideology of dominant state and local groups. In the 1980s and early 1990s several states considered constitutional changes to bar antidiscrimination laws against gays and lesbians. Many were worded more moderately than the Oregon initiative discussed previously, but nevertheless had broad implications. In 1992, Colorado voters approved an amendment sponsored by Colorado for Family Values that barred any level of government from protecting sexual minorities. In 1996, the U.S. Supreme Court ruled that the amendment violated the Equal Protection Clause of the U.S. Constitution.

Second, Christian Right groups have worked to replace justices with those more friendly to their positions. In states with elected courts, the Christian Right has been active in elections. At the national level, the movement has worked assiduously to try to change the ideological balance of all levels of courts. In 2005 and 2006, Family Research Council and Focus on the Family sponsored "Justice Sundays" to build support for a number of individuals nominated by George W. Bush for the federal bench. Speakers at these events included prominent GOP policymakers, who claimed that Democrats were filibustering their nominations because of their religious views. In 2005, Pat Robertson in a televised prayer asked God for additional vacancies on the Supreme Court. Activists believe that courts have asserted a liberal agenda in place of sound jurisprudence.

George Bush consulted carefully with Christian Right leaders before nominating Supreme Court justices. Focus on the Family president James Dobson initially supported Harriet Miers, but her nomination was withdrawn after pressure from religious and secular conservatives, and especially after Concerned Women for America called for her withdrawal. This strategy has been somewhat successful, and there is no doubt that the federal bench is more supportive of religious accommodation today in part because of Christian Right efforts.

Finally, the Christian Right has formed a number of law firms that litigate on behalf of clients, file amicus briefs, and negotiate settlements with local governments.[41] These groups, such as The Center for Law and Policy, The Rutherford Institute, The Alliance Defense Fund, American Center for Law and Justice, and the Liberty Council, have different goals and strategies. For instance, Jay Sekulow's ACLJ is renowned for its pragmatism and savvy navigation of the appellate process, whereas the CLP is more uncompromising, rooting its legal strategy to its theological beliefs. However, overall these firms have moved from framing arguments on the establishment clause to framing them in terms of free exercise. In the early part of the twenty-first century, some but not all groups went further, framing religious claims around the free speech clause, because of its stronger protective language. In particular, the Rutherford Institute framed its religious free expression arguments as part of a broad national conversation; as Lienesch relates, they were not arguing "to have a Christian nation, but to enable religious people to survive."[42] This strategy proved controversial, because proponents acknowledged that any victories they won will apply to religious minorities and atheists as well.

The ultimate impact of this activity will become apparent as the (Chief Justice) Roberts court builds an opus of rulings. Where the activity has been unquestionably effective is in dealing with local governments—where a high school principal denies a student the right to read Bible in study hall, or where there are other obvious infringements on religious freedom. With a successful litigation record (The Alliance Defense Fund claims a 75% success rate) and impressive resources, Christian Right attorneys frequently have merely to show up and discuss legal precedent to solve these problems, and if this not enough the threat of a lawsuit may be successful.

ONE NATION UNDER GOD(S)?

After nearly 30 years of activity, the Christian Right has been a very successful electoral movement, but has been less successful in implementing its agenda. Yet it is important to understand that the agenda itself is disputed within the movement. A few seek to restructure society and institutions to fit their understanding of Christian principles, a majority would use democratic processes to enact laws that they believe conform to biblical principles, and a few merely seek to enter the public debate. Some want to proclaim a Christian nation with little room for other faiths in politics and perhaps in the culture, others are more focused on protecting the freedom exercise of religion for conservative Christians and others.

A survey of Christian Right activists in the Republican Party in 2000 is revealing about the distribution of these positions in the movement. More than 94% of Christian Right activists believed that the greatest problem facing America is moral decay, and 94% also agreed that the United States is a Christian nation and that its laws should be consistent with Christian teachings. On some issues, activists were more moderate than generally perceived; only half would ban abortion under all circumstances (although most would limit exceptions to health, rape, and fetal defect), and a clear majority favored equal roles for women in politics and society.

However, other questions revealed a more radical movement. Nearly half agreed that sodomy is a crime and that known homosexuals should be arrested, and although a majority would allow all kinds of groups to demonstrate, majorities opposed allowing gays and lesbians, atheists, and even feminists to teach in public schools. More than a third would bar environmentalists from teaching.[43] A majority believed that attacks on Christian schools come from Satan, and that God works through elections and parties—an apocalyptic world view that makes political compromise difficult.

Ultimately the Christian Right is best conceived somewhere between its apologists' claims and its opponents' fears. Most activists want more than a seat at the table; they want to make U.S. law and constitutional understandings consistent with their religious views. Yet only a radical fringe wants a theocracy, and most are content to contest politics through democratic means.

CONCLUSION

As the first decade of the twenty-first century ended, the Christian Right was in disarray. The leaders of the organizations of the 1980s were aging or dead, the Moral Majority had disbanded, and the Christian Coalition was bankrupt. Movement nemesis John McCain won the GOP nomination, and Democrat Barack Obama won the presidency with the support of substantial numbers of younger white evangelicals. More generally, younger evangelicals are conservative, but more tolerant and inclusive than the Christian Right, and less focused on restoring visions of past constitutional orders.

However, over the twentieth century, Christian Right movements surged and declined, and scholars have reported the death of the Christian Right before, only to discover these rumors to be exaggerated.[44] As the United States becomes more religiously diverse, two strands of Christian Right activism may come into conflict. Those who want a bolder proclamation that the United States is a Christian nation may find free exercise and free speech arguments by other movement leaders unpalatable, because they will be useful to Sikhs, Buddhists, Muslims, and others. But those who seek to build a broader conception of religious freedom may increasingly find the religious particularism of some Christian Right groups a hindrance.

ENDNOTES

1. Taken from CNN Video.

2. See generally, Clyde Wilcox, *God's Warriors: The Christian Right in Twentieth Century America* (Baltimore: Johns Hopkins University Press, 1992).

3. See generally, Steven P. Brown, *Trumping Religion: The New Christian Right, the Free Speech Clause, and the Courts* (Tuscaloosa, AL: University of Alabama Press, 2004).

4. Ralph Reed, *After the Revolution* (Dallas: Word Publishers, 1994); Ralph Reed, *Politically Incorrect: The Emerging Faith Factor in American Politics* (Dallas: Word Publishers, 1994); and Francis A. Schaeffer, *A Christian Manifesto*, rev. ed. (Westchester, IL: Crossway Books, published in association with Nims Communications, 1992).

5. Reed, *Politically Incorrect.*

6. Robert Boston, *Close Encounters with the Religious Right: Journeys into the Twilight Zone of Religion and Politics* (Amherst, NY: Prometheus, 2000).

7. Reported in *Church & State,* May 1993, 14.

8. Reported in *Church & State,* April, 1996, 10.

9. Appearing on "This Week."

10. Mark J. Rozell and Clyde Wilcox, *Second Coming: The New Christian Right in Virginia Politics* (Baltimore: Johns Hopkins University Press, 1996); Matthew C. Moen, "The Evolving Politics of the Christian Right," *Political Science and Politics* 29 (3; 1996): 461–464; and Jon A.Shields, "Between Passion and Deliberation: The Christian Right and Democratic Ideals," *Political Science Quarterly* 12 (1; 2007): 89–113.

11. William Martin, *With God on Our Side: The Rise of the Religious Right in America* (New York: Broadway Books, 1996).

12. From Pat Robertson speech, "How to Turn America Back to God," November, 1991.

13. Transcript, "The 700 Club" with Rev. Pat Robertson on September 13, 2001.

14. Rozell and Wilcox, *Second Coming;* David Aikman, *A Man of Faith: The Spiritual Journey of George W. Bush* (Nashville, TN: W. Publishing Group, 2004); Clyde Wilcox and Carin Robinson, "The Faith of George W. Bush: The Personal, Practical, and Political," in *Religion and American Presidents*, eds. M.J. Rozell and G. Whitney (New York: Palmgrave/McMillan, 2004).

15. Dobson, J. "Focus on the Family Radio Program," July 24, 2008, accessed at http://abcnews.go.com/Politics/wireStory?id=5231473p.1.

16. James D. Kennedy (with J.N. Black), *Character and Destiny: A Nation on Search of Its Soul* (Grand Rapids, MI: Zondervan, 1994), 126–127.

17. Joseph P. Viteritti, *The Last Freedom: Religion From the Public School to the Public Square* (Princeton, NJ: Princeton University Press, 2007).

18. Stephen Bates, *Battleground: One Mother's Crusade, the Religious Right, and the Struggle for Control of Our Classrooms* (New York: Poseidon Press, 1993).

19. Melisa M. Deckman, *School Board Battles: The Christian Right in Local Politics* (Washington, DC: Georgetown University Press, 2004).

20. K. Vail, "Conservatively Speaking," *American School Board Journal* 182 (12; 1995): 30–32.

21. Rozell and Wilcox, *Second Coming.*

22. S. P. Broughman and K.W. Pugh, "Characteristics of Private Schools in The United States: Results From The 2001–2002 Private School Universe Survey (NCES 2005-305)," U.S. Department of Education. National Center for Educational Statistics, Washington, DC.

23. Clyde Wilcox, and Carin Larson, *Onward Christian Soldiers: The Christian Right in American Politics,* 3rd ed. (Boulder, CO: Westview Press, 2006).

24. Carin Larson, David Madland, and Clyde Wilcox, "Religious Lobbying in Virginia: How Institutions Can Quiet Prophetic Voices," in *Representing God in the Statehouse: Religion and Politics in the American States*, eds. E. Cleary and A. Hertzke (Lanham, MD: Rowman & Littlefield, 2005).

25. Clyde Wilcox, "The Christian Right and Civic Virtues," paper for the American Political Science Association Task Force on Religion and American Politics, 2008.

26. Luncheon conversation, 1995.

27. Mike Huckabee, Campaign Speech, Warren, Michigan, January 14, 2008, accessed at http://firstread.msnbc.msn.com/archive/2008/01/15/579265.aspx.

28. Paul Weyrich, "Letter to Supporters," February 16, 1999, accessed at http://www.rfcnet.org/archives/weyrich.htm.

29. Ralph Reed, *After the Revolution,* 10.

30. Pat Robertson, "The 700 Club," October 5, 2000, accessed at http://www.rightwingwatch.org/content/christian-coalition.

31. Brown, *Trumping Religion.* The Christian Legal Society does not neatly fit into the Christian Right category, for they also devote significant resources to providing legal help for the poor. But their central mission statements focus on protecting religious citizens from equality claims by sexual minorities, and protecting pro-life activists.

32. Moen, "The Evolving Politics of the Christian Right."

33. Wilcox and Larson, *Onward Christian Soldiers.*

34. Private communication, 2003.

35. James L. Guth, Lyman A. Kellstedt, John C. Green, and Corwin E. Smidt, "Getting the Spirit? Religious and Partisan Mobilization in the 2004 Elections," in *Interest Group Politics,* eds. A. J. Cigler and B. A. Loomis, 7th ed. (Washington, DC: CQ Press, 2007); Clyde Wilcox and Lee Sigelman, "Political Mobilization in the Pews: Religious Contacting and Electoral Turnout," *Social Science Quarterly* 83 (2; 2001): 524–535.

36. Andrew M. Appleton and Daniel Francis, "Washington: Mobilizing for Victory," in *God at the Grassroots 1996: The Christian Right in the 1996 Elections,* eds. by M.J. Rozell and Clyde Wilcox (Lanham, MD: Rowman & Littlefield, 1997); Christopher P. Gilbert and David A. Peterson, "Minnesota: Christians and Quistians in the GOP," in *God at the Grassroots;* John Clifford Green, Mark J. Rozell, and Clyde Wilcox, *The Christian Right in American Politics: Marching to the Millennium* (Washington, DC: Georgetown University Press, 2003).

37. Green, Rozell, and Wilcox, *The Christian Right in American Politics.*

38. Allen D. Hertzke, *Echoes of Discontent: Jesse Jackson, Pat Robertson, and the Resurgence of Populism* (Washington, DC: CQ Press, 1993).

39. Greg D. Adams, "Abortion: Evidence of an Issue Evolution," *American Journal of Political Science* 41 (3; 1997): 718–737.

40. John C. Danforth, "In the Name of Politics," *The New York Times,* March 30, 2005; Hans J. Hacker, *The Culture of Conservative Christian Litigation* (Lanham, MD: Rowman & Littlefield, 2005).

41. Brown, *Trumping Religion;* Hacker, *The Culture of Conservative Christian Litigation.*

42. M. Lienesch, "Redeeming America: Piety and Politics," in *The New Christian Right* (Chapel Hill, NC: University of North Carolina Press, 1993).

43. Clyde Wilcox, "The Christian Right and Civic Virtues," paper for the American Political Science Association Task Force on Religion and American Politics, 2008.

44. Steve Bruce, *The Rise and Fall of the New Christian Right* (Oxford, UK: Clarendon Press, 1988).

BIBLIOGRAPHY

Books

Aikman, D. *A Man of Faith: The Spiritual Journey of George W. Bush.* Nashville, TN: W Publishing Group, 2004.

Bates, S. *Battleground: One Mother's Crusade, the Religious Right, and the Struggle for Control of Our Classrooms.* New York: Poseidon Press, 1993.

Boston, R. *Close Encounters with the Religious Right: Journeys into the Twilight Zone of Religion and Politics.* Amherst, NY: Prometheus Books, 2000.

Brown, S. P. *Trumping Religion: The New Christian Right, the Free Speech Clause, and the Courts.* Tuscaloosa, AL: University of Alabama Press, 2004.

Bruce, S. *The Rise and Fall of the New Christian Right.* Oxford, UK: Clarendon Press, 1988.

Deckman, M.M. *School Board Battles: The Christian Right in Local Politics.* Washington, DC: Georgetown University Press, 2004.

Green, J.C., J.L. Guth, C.E. Smidt, and L.A. Kellstedt. *Religion and the Culture Wars: Dispatches from the Front.* Lanham, MD: Rowman & Littlefield, 1996.

Green, J.C., M.J. Rozell, and C. Wilcox. *Prayers in the Precincts: The Christian Right in the 1998 Elections.* Washington, DC: Georgetown University Press, 2000.

Green, J.C., M.J. Rozell, and C. Wilcox. *The Christian Right in American Politics: Marching to the Millennium.* Washington, DC: Georgetown University Press, 2003.

Hacker, H.J. *The Culture of Conservative Christian Litigation.* Lanham, MD: Rowman & Littlefield, 2003.

Hertzke, A.D. *Representing God in Washington.* Knoxville, TN: University of Tennessee Press, 1988.

Hertzke, A.D. *Echoes of Discontent: Jesse Jackson, Pat Robertson, and the Resurgence of Populism.* Washington, DC: CQ Press, 1993.

Jelen, T.G. *The Political Mobilization of Religious Belief.* Westport, CT: Praeger, 1991.

Martin, W. *With God on Our Side: The Rise of the Religious Right in America.* New York: Broadway Books, 1996.

Moen, M.C. *The Christian Right and Congress.* Tuscaloosa, AL: University of Alabama Press, 1989.

Reed, Ralph. *After the Revolution.* Dallas, TX: Word Publishers, 1994a.

———. *Politically Incorrect: the Emerging Faith Factor in American Politics.* (Dallas, TX: Word Publishing, 1994b.

Rozell, M.J., and C. Wilcox. *Second Coming: The New Christian Right in Virginia Politics.* Baltimore: Johns Hopkins University Press, 1996.

Schaeffer, F.A. *A Christian Manifesto.* Rev. ed. Westchester, IL: Crossway Books, published in association with Nims Communications, 1982.

Smidt, C.E. and J.M. Penning. *Sojourners in the Wilderness: The Christian Right in Comparative Perpsective.* Lanham, MD.: Rowman & Littlefield, 1999.

Viteritti, J.P. *The Last Freedom: Religion from the Public School to the Public Square.* Princeton, NJ: Princeton University Press, 2007.

Wilcox, C. *God's Warriors: The Christian Right in Twentieth Century America.* Baltimore: Johns Hopkins University Press, 1992.

Wilcox, C. and C. Larson. *Onward Christian Soldiers: The Christian Right in American Politics.* 3rd ed. Boulder, CO: Westview Press, 2006.

Articles/Chapters

Adams, G.D. "Abortion: Evidence of an Issue Evolution." *American Journal of Political Science* 41 (1997): 718.

Appleton, A.M. and Francis, D. "Washington: Mobilizing for Victory." In *God at the Grassroots 1996: The Christian Right in the 1996 Elections,* eds. M.J. Rozell and C. Wilcox. Lanham, MD.: Rowman & Littlefield, 1997.

Gilbert, C.P. and Peterson, D.A. "Minnesota: Christians and Quistians in the GOP." In *God at the Grassroots: The Christian Right in the 1994 Elections,* eds. M.J. Rozell and C. Wilcox. Lanham, MD: Rowman & Littlefield, 1997.

Green, J.C., Rozell, M. J., and Wilcox, C. "The Christian Right's Long March." In *The Christian Right in American Elections: Marching to the Millennium,* eds. J.C. Green, M.J. Rozell and C. Wilcox. Washington, DC: Georgetown University Press, 2003.

Guth, J.L., Kellstedt, L.A., Green, J.C., and Smidt, C.E. "Getting the Spirit? Religious and Partisan Mobilization in the 2004 Elections." In *Interest Group Politics*, eds. A.J. Cigler and B.A. Loomis. 7th ed. Washington, DC: CQ Press, 2007.

Larson, C., Madland, D., and Wilcox, C. "Religious Lobbying in Virginia: How Institutions Can Quiet Prophetic Voices." In *Representing God in the Statehouse: Religion and Politics in the American States*, eds. E. Cleary and A. Hertzke. Lanham, MD: Rowman & Littlefield, 2005.

Lunch, W.M. "Oregon: Identity Politics in the Northeast." *In God at the Grassroots: The Christian Right in the 1994 Election*, eds. M.J. Rozell and C. Wilcox. Lanham, MD: Rowman & Littlefield, 1995.

Moen, M.C. "The Evolving Politics of the Christian Right." *Political Science and Politics* 29 (1996): 461.

Rozell, M.J., and Wilcox, C. "Second Coming: The Strategies of the New Christian Right." *Political Science Quarterly* 111 (1996): 271.

Rozell, M.J., Wilcox, C., and Green, J.C. "Religious Constituencies and Support for the Christian Right in the 1990's." *Social Science Quarterly* 79 (1998): 815.

Shields, J. A. "Between Passion and Deliberation: The Christian Right and Democratic Ideals." *Political Science Quarterly* 12 (2007): 89.

Wilcox, C. "Premillenialists at the Millenium: Some Reflections on the Christian Right in the Twenty-first Century." *Sociology of Religion* 55 (1994): 243.

Wilcox, C., and Robinson, C. "The Faith of George W. Bush: The Personal, Practical, and Political." In *Religion and American Presidents*, eds. M. J. Rozell and G. Whitney. New York: Palmgrave/McMillan, 2007.

Wilcox, C., and Sigelman, L. "Political Mobilization in the Pews: Religious Contacting and Electoral Turnout." *Social Science Quarterly* 83 (2001): 524.

CHAPTER 16

....

AMERICAN RELIGIOUS LIBERTY IN INTERNATIONAL PERSPECTIVE

....

JOHN WITTE, JR.

WRITING in 1787, American founder and future president John Adams offered a robust appraisal of the place of the new American constitution in the history of the world:

> The United States have exhibited, perhaps, the first example of governments erected on the simple principles of nature; and if men are now sufficiently enlightened to disabuse themselves of artifice, imposture, hypocrisy, and superstition, they will consider this event as a [new] era in history. Although the detail of the formation of the American governments is at present little known or regarded either in Europe or in America, it may hereafter become an object of curiosity [for it is] destined to spread over the northern part of . . . the globe. The institutions now made in America will not wholly die out for thousands of years. It is of the last importance, then, that they should begin right. If they set out wrong, they will never be able to return, unless it be by accident to the right path.[1]

More than two centuries later, Adams' sentiments still prove remarkably prescient. Particularly on issues of religious liberty, Adams and other eighteenth-century American founders did, indeed, begin on the right constitutional path, and today most Americans enjoy ample freedom of religion as a consequence. American understandings of religious liberty have had a profound influence around the globe in the past century, and they now figure prominently in a number of national constitutions[2] and international human rights instruments.[3]

To be sure, as Adams predicated, there has always been "a glorious uncertainty in the law" of American religious liberty and a notable diversity of understandings of its details.[4] This was as true in Adams' day as in our own. In Adams' day, there were competing models of religious liberty more overtly theological than his—whether Anglican, Reformed, or Evangelical in inspiration. There were also competing models more overtly philosophical than his—whether classical, republican, or libertarian in inclination. However, despite their deep differences, most eighteenth-century American founders settled on six main principles of religious liberty: (1) liberty of conscience; (2) freedom of exercise; (3) religious pluralism; (4) religious equality; (5) separation of church and state; and (6) no federal establishment of religion. They designed the First Amendment religion clauses to balance these principles. The First Amendment Free Exercise Clause outlaws government proscriptions of religion—actions that unduly burden the conscience, restrict forms of religious exercise and expression, discriminate against religion, or invade the autonomy of churches and other religious bodies. The First Amendment Establishment Clause, in turn, outlaws government prescriptions of religion—actions that unduly coerce the conscience, mandate forms of religious exercise and expression, discriminate in favor of religion, or improperly ally the government with churches or other religious bodies. Both the Free Exercise and Establishment Clauses thereby provide complementary protections to the first principles of religious liberty that the eighteenth-century American founders championed.

Today, these founding models and principles of religious liberty have borne ample progeny, and the great rivalries among them are fought out in federal and state courts, legislatures, and agencies throughout the land. As several chapters in this volume have demonstrated, however, modern American constitutional laws on religious liberty are very much in transition today.[5] Strong and settled free exercise and establishment laws of the 1960s to 1980s have now fractured into a series of shifting lines of federal cases on discrete topics, most with weaker standards of review and none providing an integrated framework for resolving religious liberty questions. This weakening and fracturing of the First Amendment has, in turn, triggered a small explosion of new federal and state legislation on religion, yielding an intricate mosaic of special religious preferences and exemptions. It has also triggered a brisk new industry of religious liberty litigation in state courts. A neofederalist understanding of religious liberty, with separate state and federal tracks of religious liberty law, is becoming a growing reality in America today—to the delight of some and the dismay of others.

This chapter compares this modern American religious liberty law with prevailing international norms on point. Comparative legal analysis is always edifying—if for no other reason than to have confirmation, from a fresh perspective, of the validity and utility of one's own legal norms and practices and to gain an idea or two about reforming them. Especially at this time of transition in First Amendment law, such comparative legal analysis is particularly salutary. Moreover, a good deal of what appears in modern international human rights instruments captures the best of American constitutional learning on religious liberty. The Universal Declaration of Human Rights of 1948 and the great 1966 Covenants encapsulate and elaborate American President Franklin Roosevelt's famous "four freedoms"—including notably religious freedom.[6] More recent international provisions on religious liberty were forged, in no small measure, by the efforts of American politicians, scholars, and activists. To compare First Amendment law with international norms is, in a real sense, to judge American law by a standard of religious liberty that it has helped to shape.[7] It is also to judge America by the same international standard that the U.S. Department of State and the U.S. Office and Commission of International Religious Freedom now use each year to judge the laws and policies on religion of all other nations.[8]

Several common international legal principles help to confirm, refine, and integrate prevailing American First Amendment principles and cases. The prioritizing of the principles of liberty of conscience, free exercise, and religious equality in international human rights instruments suggests a prototype for the integration of American free exercise and establishment values. The insistence of international human rights instruments that state abridgments of religious rights and liberties be both "necessary" and "proportionate" confirms the strict scrutiny test of American free exercise jurisprudence and its statutory analogues. The heavy emphasis on the religious rights of groups in recent international instruments both confirms the American protection of corporate free exercise rights and one core understanding of the doctrine of separation of church and state. The international doctrine of granting "a margin of appreciation" for local religious and political practices could be put to particularly effective use in our federalist system of government.

What follows in this chapter is a brief review of the main teachings on religious liberty in the international human rights documents, and then a comparison of those teachings with prevailing First Amendment and related American laws on religious liberty.

The International Framework of
Religious Liberty[10]

International religious rights and liberties have deep roots in classical Roman law, medieval canon law, and early modern Protestant and Catholic legal traditions.[11] Their definitive modern formulation, however, came only after World War II, with the promulgation of the Universal Declaration of Human Rights (1948). Four international instruments, elaborating the Declaration, contain the most critical protections of religious rights and liberties: (1) the International Covenant on Civil and Political Rights (1966) ("the 1966 Covenant");[12] (2) the United Nations Declaration on the Elimination of All Forms of Intolerance and of Discrimination Based on

Religion or Belief (1981) ("the 1981 Declaration");[13] (3) the Concluding Document of the Vienna Follow-up Meeting of Representatives of the Participating States of the Conference on Security and Co-operation in Europe, which was promulgated in 1989 ("the 1989 Vienna Concluding Document");[14] and (4) the 1992 Declaration on the Rights of the Persons Belonging to National or Ethnic, Religious, and Linguistic Minorities ("the 1992 Minorities Declaration").[15]

The 1966 International Covenant on Civil and Political Rights largely repeats the capacious guarantee of religious rights and liberties first announced in the 1948 Universal Declaration of Human Rights. Article 18 reads:

1. Everyone shall have the right to freedom of thought, conscience and religion. This right shall include freedom to have or to adopt a religion or belief of his choice, and freedom, either individually or in community with others and in public or private, to manifest his religion or belief in worship, observance, practice and teaching.
2. No one shall be subject to coercion which would impair his freedom to have or to adopt a religion or belief of his choice.
3. Freedom to manifest one's religion or beliefs may be subject only to such limitations as are prescribed by law and are necessary to protect public safety, order, health, or morals or the fundamental rights and freedoms of others.
4. The States Parties to the present Covenant undertake to have respect for the liberty of parents and, when applicable, legal guardians to ensure the religious and moral education of their children in conformity with their own convictions.[16]

Article 18 distinguishes between the right to freedom of religion and the freedom to manifest one's religion—the rough equivalent to what American law labels as liberty of conscience and free exercise of religion, respectively. The right to freedom of religion—the freedom to have, alter, or adopt a religion of one's choice—is an absolute right from which no derogation may be made and that may not be restricted or impaired in any manner. Freedom to manifest or exercise one's religion—individually or collectively, publicly or privately—may be subject only to such limitations as are prescribed by law and are necessary to protect public safety, order, health, or morals or the fundamental rights and freedoms of others. The latter provision is an exhaustive list of the grounds allowed to limit the manifestation of religion. The requirement of necessity implies that any such limitation on the manifestation of religion must be proportionate to its aim to protect any of the listed state interests. Such limitations must not be applied in a manner that would vitiate the rights guaranteed in Article 18—an ideal that is often honored in the breach, even in many advanced Western countries.[17]

Article 20.2 of the 1966 Covenant calls for States Parties to prohibit "any advocacy of national, racial, or religious hatred that constitutes incitement to discrimination, hostility, or violence." Articles 2 and 26 require equal treatment of all persons before the law and prohibit discrimination based, among other grounds, on religion.

Article 27 further guarantees to religious and cultural minorities "the right to enjoy their own culture" and "to profess and practise their own religion."

The 1981 Declaration elaborates the religious liberty provisions that the 1966 Covenant adumbrated. Like the 1966 Covenant, the 1981 Declaration on its face applies to "everyone," whether "individually or in community," "in public or in private."[18] Articles 1 and 6 of the 1981 Declaration set forth a lengthy illustrative catalogue of rights to "freedom of thought, conscience, and religion"—repeating but also illustrating more concretely the 1966 Covenant's guarantees of liberty of conscience and free exercise of religion. Article 6 enumerates these rights as follows:

(a) To worship or assemble in connection with a religion or belief and to establish and maintain places for these purposes;

(b) To establish and maintain appropriate charitable or humanitarian institutions;

(c) To make, to acquire and use to an adequate extent the necessary articles and materials related to the rites or customs of a religion or belief;

(d) To write, issue, and disseminate relevant publications in these areas;

(e) To teach a religion or belief in places suitable for these purposes;

(f) To solicit and receive voluntary financial and other contributions from individuals and institutions;

(g) To train, to appoint, to elect, or to designate by succession appropriate leaders called for by the requirements and standards of any religion or belief;

(h) To observe days of rest and to celebrate holy days and ceremonies in accordance with the precepts of one's religion or belief; and

(i) To establish and maintain communications with individuals and communities in matters of religion and belief at the national and international levels.[19]

The 1981 Declaration also dwells specifically and at some length on the religious rights of children and their parents. It guarantees the rights of parents (or guardians) to organize life within their household and educate their children "in accordance with their religion or beliefs."[20] Such parental responsibility within and beyond the household, however, must be discharged in accordance with the "best interests of the child."[21] At minimum, the parents' religious upbringing or education of their child "must not be injurious to his physical or mental health or to his full development."[22] Moreover, the Declaration provides more generically, "the child shall be protected from any form of discrimination on the ground of religion or belief. He shall be brought up in a spirit of understanding, tolerance, friendship among peoples, peace and universal brotherhood, respect for freedom of religion or belief of others, and in full conscience that his energy and talents should be devoted to the service of his fellow men."[23] The Declaration leaves juxtaposed the parents' right to rear and educate their children in accordance with their own religion and beliefs and the state's power to protect the best interests of the child, including the lofty aspirations for the child's upbringing. Despite ample debate on point, the Declaration drafters offered no specific principles to resolve the disputes that would inevitably arise between the rights of parents and the powers of the state operating in loco parentis. Some further guidance on this subject is provided by the 1989 UN Convention on the Rights of the Child—although the issue of parental rights over their child's religious upbringing and welfare remains highly contested at international and domestic law.[24]

As these children's rights provisions illustrate, the 1981 Declaration, like the 1966 Covenant, allows the "manifestation of religion" to be subjected to "appropriate" state regulation and adjudication. The 1981 Declaration permits states to enforce against religious individuals and institutions general regulations designed to protect public safety, order, health, or morals, or the fundamental rights and freedoms of others. It is assumed, however, that in all such instances, the grounds for such regulations are enumerated and explicit and that such regulations abide by the international legal principles of necessity and proportionality.[25]

The 1981 Declaration includes more elaborate prohibitions than the 1966 Covenant on religious discrimination and intolerance. It bars religious "discrimination by any State, institution, group of persons, or person."[26] And it defines such discrimination as "any distinction, exclusion, restriction or preference based on religion or belief, and having as its purpose or as its effect nullification or impairment of the recognition, enjoyment or exercise of human rights or fundamental freedoms on an equal basis."[27] All such discrimination based on religion or belief, the Declaration insists, is "an affront to human dignity" and a "disavowal" of the "fundamental freedoms" that form the cornerstone of national and international peace and cooperation.[28] Accordingly, the Declaration calls on all States Parties "to take effective measures to prevent and eliminate" such discrimination "in all fields of civil, economic, political, social, and cultural life," including rescinding laws that foster discrimination and enacting laws that forbid it.[29]

The 1989 Vienna Concluding Document extends the religious liberty norms of the 1981 Declaration, particularly for religious groups. Principle 16 rounds out the list of enumerated rights guarantees quoted above from the 1981 Declaration:

16. In order to ensure the freedom of the individual to profess and practice religion or belief the participating States will, inter alia,
    A. take effective measures to prevent and eliminate discrimination against individuals or communities, on the grounds of religion or belief in the recognition, exercise and enjoyment of human rights and fundamental freedoms in all fields of civil, political, economic, social and cultural life, and ensure the effective equality between believers and non-believers;
    B. foster a climate of mutual tolerance and respect between believers of different communities as well as between believers and non-believers;
    C. grant upon their request to communities of believers, practicing or prepared to practice their faith within the constitutional

framework of their states, recognition of the status provided for them in
their respective countries;

D. respect the right of religious communities to establish and maintain
freely accessible places of worship or assembly; organize themselves
according to their own hierarchical and institutional structure; select,
appoint and replace their personnel in accordance with their respective
requirements and standards as well as with any freely accepted
arrangement between them and their State; solicit and receive voluntary
financial and other contributions;

E. engage in consultations with religious faiths, institutions and
organizations in order to achieve a better understanding of the
requirements of religious freedom;

F. respect the right of everyone to give and receive religious education
in the language of his choice, individually or in association with
others;

G. in this context respect, inter alia, the liberty of parents to ensure the
religious and moral education of their children in conformity with their
own convictions;

H. allow the training of religious personnel in appropriate institutions;

I. respect the right of individual believers and communities of believers to
acquire, possess, and use sacred books, religious publications in the
language of their choice and other articles and materials related to the
practice of religion or belief;

J. allow religious faiths, institutions and organizations to produce and
import and disseminate religious publications and materials;

K. favorably consider the interest of religious communities in participating
in public dialogue, inter alia, through mass media.

A number of these religious group rights provisions in the Vienna Concluding
Document reflect the international right to self-determination of peoples. This right
has long been recognized as a basic norm of international law, and is included, among
other places, in the 1966 Covenant.[30] The right to self-determination has its fullest
expression in the 1992 Minorities Declaration. This right belongs to "peoples" within
pluralistic societies. It guarantees a religious community the right to practice its religion, an ethnic community the right to promote its culture, and a linguistic community the right to speak its language without undue state interference or unnecessary
legal restrictions. The 1992 Minorities Declaration recognizes that "the promotion and
protection of the rights" of religious, cultural, and linguistic minorities is "an integral
part of the development of a society as a whole and within a democratic framework based on the rule of law." Accordingly, it calls upon states to respect and to
pass implementing legislation that protects and promotes the rights of cultural, religious, and linguistic minorities "to enjoy their own culture, to profess and practice
their own religion, and to use their own language, in private and in public, freely and
without interference or any form of discrimination."[31] It further provides that "States

shall take measures to create favorable conditions to enable persons belonging to minorities to express their characteristics and to develop their culture, language, religion, traditions and customs, except where specific practices are in violation of national law and contrary to international standards."[32] So conceived, the right to religious self-determination provides religious groups some of the same strong protections that are afforded to religious individuals under the freedom of conscience guarantee.

These are the basic international provisions on religious rights on the books. Various regional instruments, notably the European Charter on Human Rights (1950), the American Convention on Human Rights (1969), and the African Charter on Human and People's Rights (1981), elaborate some of these guarantees. Various religious declarations and treaties involving religious bodies, notably the recent concordats between the Vatican and Italy, Spain, and Israel as well as the Universal Islamic Declaration of Human Rights (1981) and the Cairo Declaration on Human Rights in Islam (1990), give particular accent to the religious concerns and constructions of their cosigners.[33] However, the foregoing four instruments capture the common lore of current international human rights norms on religious rights and liberties.

These instruments highlight a number of the most critical legal issues that have confronted national and international tribunals over the past half century: How to protect religious minorities within a majoritarian religious culture—particularly controversial groups such as Muslims, Mormons, Bahais, Jehovah's Witnesses, Scientologists, Unification Church members, and indigenous or first peoples who often bring charges of religious and cultural discrimination. How to place limits on religious and antireligious exercises and expressions that cause offense or harm to others. How to adjudicate challenges that a state's proscriptions or prescriptions run directly counter to a party's core claims of conscience or cardinal commandments of the faith. How to balance private and public exercises of religion, including the liberty of conscience of one party to be left alone and the free exercise right of another to proselytize. How to negotiate the complex needs and norms of religious groups without according them too much sovereignty over their members or too little relief from secular courts in the event of fundamental rights violations by religious tribunals. How to adjudicate intrareligious or interreligious disputes that come before secular courts for resolution. How to determine the proper levels of state cooperation with and support of religious officials and institutions in the delivery of vital social services—child care, education, charity, medical services, and disaster relief, among others.

INTERNATIONAL NORMS AND AMERICAN LAWS COMPARED

The United States has ratified the 1966 Covenant. None of the 14 reservations, understandings, or declarations that the United States put to the instrument seeks to avoid or evade the religious liberty standards set out in the document. The 1966 Covenant, however, is not self-executing. It "does not, by itself, create private rights enforceable in U.S. courts."[34] It requires implementing legislation to become effective, and no such law to date has been issued.[35] Yet, the 1966 Covenant holds out a high standard of religious liberty, which the United States has pledged to support.

The 1981 Declaration, 1989 Vienna Concluding Document, and 1992 Minorities Declaration are not binding legal instruments on the United States. Nonetheless, as collective expressions of common international opinion, if not common international law, on the meaning and measure of religious liberty, these instruments, too, carry ample moral, intellectual, and diplomatic suasion.

These international human rights instruments both confirm and prioritize several of the founding principles of religious liberty in America—liberty of conscience, freedom of exercise, religious equality, religious pluralism, separation of church and state, and disestablishment of religion. The principles of liberty of conscience, individual and corporate free exercise of religion, and equality of a plurality of religions before the law form the backbone of the international norms on religious liberty. Liberty of conscience rights, with their inherent protections of religious voluntarism and prohibitions against religious coercion, are absolute rights from which no derogation can be made. The exercise of religion may be regulated only to protect either the fundamental rights of others or public health, safety, welfare, and morals, and the burden caused by the regulation must be "proportionate" to achieving that stated interest. Equality of religions before the law must not only be protected, but affirmatively fostered by the state, particularly to ensure the equal protection and treatment of religious and cultural minorities. A vast pluralism of forms and forums of religion and belief deserve protection—whether ancient or new, individual or communal, internal or external, private or public, permanent or transient.

International human rights instruments further confirm the American principles of corporate free exercise rights and the basic separation of the state from churches and other religious groups. Religious groups organized for purposes of religious worship, education, charity, and other causes have the fundamental right to function in expression of their founding religious beliefs and values and must enjoy a level of autonomy of their own internal affairs. The state may regulate these religious groups only on stated grounds that are necessary and proportionate. Conspicuously absent from international human rights instruments, however, are the more radical demands for separationism, rooted in the popular American metaphor of a "wall of separation between church and state." *Everson v. Board of Education* (1948),[36] *McCollum v. Board of Education* (1948),[37] and other early establishment clause cases maintained that religious liberty requires the absolute separation of church and state and the cessation of state support for religion, particularly religious schools. Only the secular state can guarantee religious liberty, it was argued, and only separation can guarantee the state's neutrality on religious matters. Such views, which still pervade popular opinion in America, are not reflected in international human rights instruments nor, indeed, widely shared by other nation-states around the world.[38]

If they were hypothetically applied in the United States, the international instruments would commend several lines of Supreme Court cases protecting liberty of conscience rights. These include a series of cases, from *Arver v. United States* (1918)[39] to *United States v. Welsh* (1970),[40] in which the Court upheld federal statutes that granted conscientious objection status to religious pacifists. These also include several early free exercise cases, from *West Virginia Board of Education v. Barnette* (1943)[41] to *Torcaso v. Watkins* (1961),[42] that protected parties from coerced participation in swearing pledges and oaths as well as the later establishment cases of *Lee v. Weisman* (1992)[43] and *Santa Fe Independent School District v. Doe* (2000),[44] which protected parties from coerced participation in public prayers and ceremonies. These liberty of conscience cases include a series of sabbatarian cases, from *Sherbert v. Verner* (1963)[45] onward, that relieved parties from having to choose between adherence to a core commandment of conscience and a set of government benefits to which they were otherwise entitled. The international instruments norms make it unequivocally clear that private parties have the right to choose, change, or reject religion without compulsion, control, or conditions imposed by the state.

Particularly younger children, the 1981 Declaration and 1989 UN Convention on the Rights of the Child underscore, cannot be compelled to participate in religious or secular activities to which their parents object. Several American cases have confirmed this, based on the landmark case of *Wisconsin v. Yoder* (1972).[46] To be sure, parental rights to control their child's religious upbringing must be balanced against the state's duty to protect the best interest of that child. The international instruments would likely confirm the Supreme Court case of *Prince v. Massachusetts* (1944),[47] which insisted that a minor child could not proselytize on the street corner at night in violation of child labor laws, even if the child's guardian regarded that activity as essential to the child's religious upbringing. These instruments would also uphold *Jehovah's Witnesses v. King County Hospital* (1968),[48] which insisted that a minor child be given a necessary blood transfusion and other medical care, even though the parents wanted to treat the child by prayer alone as a test and testimony of faith. Endangering a child's life and limb is an automatic trigger for state intervention—notwithstanding parental religious interests to the contrary.

The international instruments would strongly commend the "strict scrutiny" test for free exercise claims. This was the test developed by the Supreme Court in *Sherbert v. Verner* (1963) and *Wisconsin v. Yoder* (1972) and recaptured by Congress in the Religious Freedom Restoration Act (RFRA) (1993)[49] and the Religious Land Use and Institutionalized Persons Act (RLUIPA)(2000).[50] The test provides that when the state imposes a substantial burden on the free exercise of a claimant's religion, the state must show that it is pursuing a compelling or overriding purpose, has used the least restrictive alternative for achieving that purpose, and has engaged in no religious discrimination in drafting or applying the law in question. Absent such showing, that state must either rescind the law or provide the burdened party with an exemption from full compliance. This American strict scrutiny test is the rough equivalent to the "necessity" and "proportionality" standard of the international human rights instruments, particularly as set forth in the 1966 Covenant.

Just as in international law, so in First Amendment law, this strict scrutiny regime of free exercise is not "strict in theory, but fatal in fact."[51] Even in the *Sherbert* and *Yoder* heyday of 1963 to 1989, when the Supreme Court had strict scrutiny as its stated free exercise standard, government won nearly half the time, especially in cases in which parties claimed free exercise exemption from taxation and social security laws. These holdings are consistent with prevaling international and comparative law standards that all parties, including religious parties, must comply with a fairly administered tax scheme.[52]

Although they would applaud a strict scrutiny regime, the international instruments would find little to commend in the much narrower reading of the Free Exercise Clause introduced by the Supreme Court in *Bowen v. Roy* (1986),[53] *Lyng v. Northwestern Indian Cemetery Protective Association* (1988),[54] and *Employment Division v. Smith* (1990).[55] These latter cases, which now control application of the First Amendment Free Exercise Clause by the federal courts, effectively reduce the free exercise guarantee to a type of heightened rational basis review.[56] In particular, the *Smith* Court has held that laws that are judged to be "neutral and generally applicable" will pass constitutional muster regardless of the burden cast on religion or the nature of the power exercised by government. Even a discretionary law or policy that crushes a central belief or practice of a free exercise claimant will survive constitutional challenge if it is neutrally drafted and generally applicable to all. Only if the law is not neutrally drafted or generally applicable will government be required to demonstrate a compelling government interest that overrides the burdened free exercise right. Such a harsh, religion-blind neutrality leaves religious minorities too vulnerable to the machinations of state legislators and state judges, who tend to keep their eyes on majoritarian sentiment and the next election. This runs directly counter to the strong solicitude for religious minorities mandated especially by the 1966 Covenant and the 1992 Minorities Declaration.

It is especially troublesome that the *Bowen, Lyng,* and *Smith* cases involved claims by Native American Indians to special protection for their religious sites and rites. The right to self-determination of indigenous peoples, particularly their religious self-determination, is an important international human rights principle, and it requires unusual solicitude by nation-states. Congress, in fact, had recognized this responsibility in passing the American Indian Religious Freedom Act (1978), which called officials "to protect and preserve for American Indians their inherent right of freedom to believe, express, and exercise the[ir] traditional religions . . . including but not limited to access to sites, use and possession of sacred objects, and the freedom to worship through ceremonials and traditional rites."[57] The Supreme Court's cavalier treatment of the Native Americans' religious liberty claims is a substantial blight on its First Amendment record. The Court's special accommodations of Adventist sabbatarianism in *Sherbert* and Amish communitarianism in *Yoder* come much closer to the solicitude mandated by international human rights instruments.

The international norms on equality and nondiscrimination would applaud the free speech "equal access" and "equal treatment" cases from *Widmar v. Vincent*

(1981)[58] to *Good News Club v. Milford Central School* (2001)[59] that give religious parties equal access to forums, facilities, and even funds made available to like-positioned nonreligious parties. They would likewise commend recent establishment clause cases such as *Agostini v. Felton* (1997),[60] *Mitchell v. Helms* (2000),[61] and *Zelman v. Simmons-Harris* (2002),[62] which treated religious and nonreligious schools alike in the distribution of general government-funded educational services and materials. Nothing in international law, nor in First Amendment law requires the state to make public forums or state funds available to private parties. However, when the state does offer these forums or funds, it may not discriminate against otherwise eligible religious claimants in granting access or distributing them.[63]

The international instruments would also commend cases such as *McDaniel v. Paty* (1978),[64] which removed special state prohibitions on religious ministers participating in political office. It would also uphold the recent case of *Watchtower Bible and Tract and Tract Society v. Village of Stratton* (2002)[65] and several earlier free exercise and free speech cases that prohibited discriminatory licensing requirements against religious solicitors in public places. Nondiscriminatory and neutrally applied "time, place, and manner" regulations on all public speech, including religious and political speech and activities, is as permissible under the international instruments as it is under First Amendment law.[66] However, again, singling out religious solicitors for special restrictions or requirements violates the essential religious liberty principle of equality and nondiscrimination.

The principles of structural pluralism (or group rights) set out in the international instruments would endorse the many lines of cases and statutes protecting the forms and functions of religious associations, whether worship centers, religious schools and charities, or other such groups.[67] Various Supreme Court cases upholding general regulation of these bodies in furtherance of health, safety, and welfare, and in exercise of regulatory, taxation, and police power, would likewise pass muster.[68] The principle of structural pluralism, especially as elaborated in the Vienna Concluding Document, would look askance, however, at a case such as *Jones v. Wolf* (1979),[69] which permitted government resolution of intrachurch disputes involving "neutral principles" of law. The "deference test," maintained by the Supreme Cout from *Watson v. Jones* (1871)[70] to *Serbian Orthodox Diocese v. Milivojevich* (1976),[71] would find greater favor under international human rights instruments as a proper form of intrareligious dispute resolution. Also favorably received at international law would be the cases of *NLRB v. Catholic Bishop of Chicago* (1979)[72] and *Presiding Bishop v. Amos* (1987),[73] which protected the employment decisions of religious employers, including their right to engage in religious discrimination in their core employment decisions. Neither international law nor American law would require a Catholic Church to hire a rabbi to say a mass, or require a synagogue to employ a Methodist minister to read the Torah on the Sabbath.

The absence of a disestablishment of religion principle in international human rights instruments would not call into question the entire line of disestablishment clause cases that have emerged since 1947, principally on issues of religion and education.[74] Many of these cases serve to protect the principles of liberty of conscience, free exercise, religious equality, and religious pluralism in a manner consistent with prevailing international instruments. But when there is a clash between such principles and the principle of nonreligious establishment, international norms would give preference to the former—as do American cases upholding the principle of accommodation.

The international instruments do not have an equivalent to the *Lemon* test that the Court developed in 1971 to apply the First Amendment Establishment Clause. This test requires that a law or policy will pass constitutional muster under the Establishment Clause only if it (1) has a secular purpose; (2) has a primary effect that neither inhibits or prohibits religion; and (3) fosters no excessive entanglement between religious and political officials.[75] This test, although ignored or reformulated by several later Supreme Court cases, still finds favor among lower federal courts in the absence of a consistently applied alternative. This *Lemon* test is consistent with international instruments in so far as it protects nonreligious or religious minorities from coerced support for or participation in majoritarian religions, and protects various religious communities from undue intrusion or regulation by the state. The *Lemon* test goes further than international instruments, however, in requiring a necessary "secular" purpose for a state law or policy. The key to international religious liberty is not the secular nature of the law, but the freedom of each individual to accept or reject the religions that are available.

Moreover, the realm of education—in which parental religious rights and preferences receive especially strong protection—is not the ideal place for undue zealotry in application of disestablishment values. To be sure, the international instruments would not countenance any more than the First Amendment coerced religious exercises in school classrooms—such as mandatory participation in prayers, pledges, confessions of faith, Bible reading, and the like—however strong the countervailing parental preferences. Nevertheless, the constitutional purging of tax-supported public schools of virtually all religious symbols, texts, and traditions, in favor of purportedly neutral and secular tropes, stands in considerable tension with international principles of religious equality and parental religious rights. It also fails to recognize what the international instruments have long recognized—that peaceable religious, nonreligious, and antireligious "thought, conscience, and beliefs" are all "religious" and are all deserving of religious liberty protection.

Conclusion

The ample vacillations in the Supreme Court's First Amendment cases can be explained, in part, on factual grounds. The application of a 16-word guarantee to dozens of diverse and complex issues over the course of a century and more has inevitably led to conflicting decisions. "The life of the law has not been logic: it has been experience," Oliver Wendell Holmes reminds us.[76] The American law of religious rights and liberties is no exception.

These vacillations, however, also betray the failure of the Court to develop a coherent framework for interpreting and applying the First Amendment. The Court has tended to rely too heavily on its mechanical tests of free exercise and establishment and to use these tests as substitutes, rather than as guides to legal analysis. The Court has tended to pit the First Amendment Establishment and Free Exercise Clauses against each other, rather than treating them as twin guarantees of religious rights and liberties. The Court has been too eager to reduce the religion clauses to one or two principles, thereby often ignoring the range of interlocking first principles of the American experiment in religious liberty. The accumulation of these interpretive shortcomings, particularly in the past two decades, has brought the American experiment to a state of acute crisis—both of law and faith in the law.

The Court needs to develop a more integrated approach to First Amendment questions that incorporates the first principles of religious rights and liberties on which the American experiment was founded and integrates them into the resolution of specific cases. Such a framework is easy enough to draw up on the blackboard or in the pages of a treatise—and a number of important integrative methodologies and frameworks have been offered of late.

Resort to international legal and human rights norms of religious liberty might seem a rather unpromising path to developing a more integrated American constitutional law of religious liberty. Not only have Americans been better at exporting their constitutional ideas and institutions than importing those of other peoples, but also the budding international norms on religious liberty seem, by conventional wisdom, to have rather little that is worth importing. The canon of applicable international human rights norms has developed only slowly and sporadically since World War II. Very few international cases are at hand, and those that have been reported do not follow the conventional form and format of American constitutional law. International human rights norms would thus seem to be better left outside the ambit of First Amendment inquiry.

To keep this parochial veil drawn shut, however, is to deprive the American experiment of religious liberty of a rich source of instruction and inspiration. There are more golden rules of religious liberty in the mountains of international human rights documents than was traditionally thought. A number of national and international tribunals, especially in Europe,[77] are now mining these documents with new alacrity in discerning the meanings and measures of religious liberty for the twenty-first century. Both the United States Congress and the United States Supreme Court have begun to consider international and comparative legal sources in defining and adjudicating other fundamental rights claims.[78] It is time to cast American laws of religious liberty in international perspective as well.

ENDNOTES

1. *The Works of John Adams,* ed. J.F. Adams, 10 vols. (Boston: Little, Brown & Company, 1850–1856), 4: 290, 292–293, 298.

2. John T. Noonan, Jr., *The Lustre of our Country: The American Experience of Religious Freedom* (Berkeley, CA: University of California Press, 1998), 263–356. For a good example of its influence on selected common law countries, see Symposium, "The Foundations and Frontiers of Religious Liberty: A 25th Anniversary Celebration of the 1981 UN Declaration on Religious Tolerance," *Emory International Law Review* 21 (2007): 1–276.

3. See detailed analysis in John Witte, Jr. and Johan D. van der Vyver, eds., *Religious Human Rights in Global Perspective,* 2 vols. (Hague: Martinus Nijhoff, 1996); Tore Lindholm, W. Cole Durham, Jr., and Bahia G. Tahzib-Lie, eds. *Facilitating Freedom of Religion or Belief: A Deskbook* (Leiden: Martinus Nijhoff, 2004); Natan Lerner, *Religion, Secular Beliefs, and Human Rights: 25 Years After the 1981 Declaration* (Leiden: Martinus Nijhoff, 2006).

4. Adams, *Works,* 9:629–632, 630.

5. See other chapters above.

6. See "Roosevelt's Eighth Annual Message to Congress (January 6, 1941)," in *State of the Union Messages of the Presidents, 1790–1966,* ed. F. Israel (New York: Chelsea House, 1966), 3: 1.

7. Louis Henkin, "Rights, American and Human," *Columbia Law Review* 79 (1979): 405.

8. International Religious Freedom Act of 1998, 112 Stat. 2787, 22 U.S.C.A. 6401. The act affirms the importance of religious freedom, as reflected in American history and law, and in various international human rights instruments. The act further decries the fresh rise of religious repression and persecution around the world and applies religious freedom standards in its assessment of diplomatic relations with foreign nations. An Office of International Religious Freedom, with an Ambassador-at-Large for International Religious Freedom publishes annual reports on the state of religious freedom in each of the 195 countries of the world, as well as in-depth studies of selected countries. The office also makes recommendations to Congress and the Executive branch on responses, including the imposition of economic sanctions, on countries that fall short of international standards.

9. Clovis C. Morrisson Jr., "Margin of Appreciation in European Human Rights Law," *Revue des droits de l'homme* 6 (1973): 263.

10. This section is adapted in part from John Witte, Jr., *Religion and the American Constitutional Experiment,* 2d ed. (Boulder, CO: Westview Press, 2005), 223–249; and John Witte, Jr., *God's Joust, God's Justice: Law and Religion in the Western Tradition* (Grand Rapids, MI: Eerdmans, 2006), 63–142.

11. John Witte, Jr., *The Reformation of Rights: Law, Religion, and Human Rights in Early Modern Calvinism* (Cambridge, UK: Cambridge University Press, 2008).

12. UN Doc. A/6316 (1968).

13. U.N. Doc. A/RES/36/55 (1982).

14. 28 I.L.M. 527.

15. Posted at http://www.ohchr.org/english/law/minorities.htm. (last visited December 20, 2007).

16. 1966 Covenant, art. 18.1–18.4.

17. Symposium, "The Permissible Scope of Legal Limitations on the Freedom of Religion and Belief," *Emory International Law Review* 19 (2005): 465–1320.

18. 1981 Declaration, supra note 2, art. 1.1.

19. Ibid., art. 6.

20. Ibid., art. 5.1.

21. Ibid., art. 5.2, 5.4.

22. Ibid., art. 5.5.

23. Ibid., art. 5.3.

24. U.N. Doc. A/44/25; see further Symposium, "What's Wrong with Rights for Children?" *Emory International Law Review* (2006): 1–239.

25. 1981 Declaration, art. 1.3.

26. Ibid., art. 2.1

27. Ibid., art. 2.2.

28. Ibid., art. 3.

29. Ibid., art. 4.1–2.

30. 1966 Covenant, art. 1.1.

31. 1992 Minorities Declaration, Preamble and arts. 1–2. See further Johan D. van der Vyver, *Leuven Lectures on Religious Institutions, Religious Communities, and Rights* (Leuven, 2004), 67–90.

32. 1992 Minorities Declaration, art. 4.2.

33. See the collection of documents in Tad Stanke and J. Paul Martin, *Religion and Human Rights: Basic Documents* (New York: Columbia University Press, 1988).

34. David P. Stewart, "United States Ratification of the Covenant on Civil and Political Rights: The Significance of the Reservations, Understandings, and Declarations," *DePaul Law Review* 42 (1993): 1183, 1202ff.

35. Louis Henkin, "U.S. Ratification of Human Rights Conventions: The Ghost of Senator Bricker," *American Journal of International Law* 89 (1995): 341; Gerald Neumann, "The Global Dimension of RFRA," *Constitutional Commentary* 14 (1997): 33.

36. 330 U.S. 1 (1947).

37. 333 U.S. 203 (1948).

38. See John Witte, Jr., "Facts and Fictions about the History of Separation of Church and State," *Journal of Church and State* 48 (2006): 15–45.

39. 245 U.S. 366 (1918).

40. 398 U.S. 333 (1970).

41. 319 U.S. 624 (1943).

42. 367 U.S. 488 (1961).

43. 505 U.S. 577 (1992).

44. 530 U.S. 290 (2000).

45. 374 U.S. 398 (1963), extended in *Thomas v. Review Board of Indiana Employment Security Division,* 450 U.S. 707 (1981); *Hobbie v. Unemployment Appeals Commission of Florida,* 480 U.S. 136 (1987); *Frazee v. Illinois Department of Employment Security,* 489 U.S. 829 (1989). The Court, however, has not always been consistent in its treatment of sabbatarian concerns. See, e.g., *Estate of Thornton v. Caldor,* 472 U.S. 703 (1985) (struck down state law that allowed private sector employees to pick their Sabbath, which employers must accommodate); *Braunfeld v. Brown,* 366 U.S. 599 (1961) (statute disallowing sales on Sunday does not violate free exercise rights of Jewish Saturday sabbatarian); and *Gallagher v. Crown Kosher Supermarket,* 366 U.S. 617 (1961) (Sunday closing law does not violate free exercise rights of owner of kosher super market, Orthodox Jewish customers, or rabbis with a duty to inspect kosher markets per Jewish dietary laws).

46. 406 U.S. 205 (1972) (exempted Amish from full compliance with compulsory school attendance law).

47. 321 U.S. 158 (1944).

48. 390 U.S. 598 (1968).

49. 42 U.S.C. secs. 2000bb to 2000b–4

50. 42 U.S.C.A. secs. 2000cc–2000cc5.

51. See Kent Greenawalt, *Religion and the Constitution: Free Exercise and Fairness* (Princeton, 2006), 215 (quoting Gerald Gunther).

52. See esp. *U.S. v. Lee*, 455 U.S. 252 (1982) (denied free exercise exemption from social security taxes for Amish employer); *Jimmy Swaggart Ministries v. Board of Equalization of California*, 493 U.S. 378 (1990) (levy of state sales and use taxes on religious articles is not a violation of religious crusader's free exercise rights).

53. 476 U.S. 693 (1986) (agency's use of social security number does not violate free exercise rights of native American, who believes such use would impair his child's spirit).

54. 485 U.S. 439 (1988) (construction of road through section of national forest regarded as sacred ground by three tribes does not violate free exercise clause; American Indian Religious Freedom Act provides no cause of action).

55. 494 U.S. 872 (1990) (denial of unemployment compensation benefits to Native American who was discharged for sacramental use of peyote, a proscribed narcotic, does not violate free exercise clause).

56. Save in cases involving blatant religious discrimination by the state. See, e.g., *Church of the Lukumi Babalu Aye, Inc. v. City of Hialeah*, 508 U.S. 520 (1993) (local ordinance transparently discriminating against Santerian ritual sacrifice of animals violates the free exercise clause). But cf. *Locke v. Davey*, 540 U.S. 712 (2004) (state scholarship program established to assist payment of academically gifted students' post-secondary education expenses for all students, except those pursuing a theology degree, does not violate the free exercise clause).

57. 42 U.S.C. sec. 1996 (1978).

58. 454 U.S. 263 (1981) (when a state university creates a limited public forum open to voluntary student groups, religious groups must be given "equal access" to that forum).

59. 533 U.S. 98 (2001) (public middle school's exclusion of Christian children's club from meeting on school property after hours was unconstitutional viewpoint discrimination, and was not required to avoid establishment of religion).

60. 521 U.S. 203 (1997).

61. 530 U.S. 793 (2000).

62. 536 U.S. 639 (2002).

63. Nor may the state discriminate in favor of religion for a nonessential accommodation. See, e.g. *Texas Monthly v. Bullock*, 489 U.S. 1 (1989) (state sales tax exemption exclusively for religious periodicals violates Establishment Clause).

64. 435 U.S. 618 (1978).

65. 536 U.S. 150 (2002).

66. See the early summary free exercise case, *Poulos v. New Hampshire*, 345 U.S. 395 (1953) and the summary free speech case in *Heffron v. International Society for Krishna Consciousness*, 452 U.S. 640 (1981).

67. See especially the classic early case, *Pierce v. Society of Sisters*, 268 U.S. 510 (1925) (invalidated state law mandating attendance at public schools as violation of rights of private schools and of parents).

68. See, e.g, a good summary case in *Tony and Susan Alamo Foundation v. Secretary of Labor*, 471 U.S. 290 (1985) (Application of Fair Labor Standards Act Does not obstruct core religious functions of a foundation). See generally William Bassett, *Relgious Organizations and the Law*, 2 vols. (St. Paul, MN: Clark, Boardman, Callahan, 1997-2007).

69. 443 U.S. 595 (1979).

70. 80 U.S. (13 Wall.) 679 (1871).

71. 426 U.S. 696 (1976).

72. 440 U.S. 490 (1979).

73. 483 U.S. 327 (1987).

74. See a detailed summary of these cases in my *Religion and the American Constitutional Experiment,* ch. 8.

75. *Lemon v. Kurtzman,* 403 U.S. 602 (1971). This test was used most recently by the plurality opinion of Justice Souter in *McCreary County v. ACLU, 545* U.S. 844 (2005), striking down a courthouse display of a Decalogue and other texts with prominent religious language.

76. Oliver Wendell Holmes Jr., *The Common Law* (Boston, 1881), 1.

77. See, e.g., Paul Taylor, *Freedom of Religion: UN and European Human Rights Law and Practice* (Cambridge, UK: Cambridge University Press, 2005); Carolyn Evans, *Freedom of Religion under the European Convention on Human Rights* (New York: Oxford University Press, 2001); Malcolm D. Evans, *Religious Liberty and International Law in Europe* (Cambridge, UK: Cambridge University Press, 1997).

78. See *Roper v. Simmons,* 543 U.S. 551 (2005); *Lawrence v. Texas,* 539 U.S. 558 (2003) and analysis in Thomas Alexander Aleinikoff, "Thinking outside the Sovereignty Box: Transnational Law and the U.S. Constitution, *Texas Law Review* 82 (2004): 1990.

BIBLIOGRAPHY

....

Books

Adams, John. *The Works of John Adams,* ed. J. F. Adams, 10 vols. Boston: Little Brown, 1850–1856.

Bassett, William, *Religious Organizations and the Law,* 2 vols. St. Paul, MN: West Publishing Co., 1997–2007.

Evans, Carolyn M. *Freedom of Religion under the European Convention on Human Rights.* New York: Oxford University Press, 2001.

Evans, Malcolm D. *Religious Liberty and International Law in Europe.* Cambridge, UK: Cambridge University Press, 1997.

Greenawalt, Kent. *Religion and the Constitution,* 2 vols. Princeton, NJ: Princeton University Press, 2006–2008.

Gunn, T. Jeremy. *Spiritual Weapons: The Cold War and the Forging of an American National Religion.* Westport, CT: Praeger, 2009.

———. "U.S. Ratification of Human Rights Conventions: The Ghost of Senator Bricker." *American Journal of International Law* 89 (1995): 341.

Holmes, Oliver Wendell, Jr. *The Common Law.* Boston: Little Brown, 1881.

Israel, Fred L., ed. *State of the Union Messages of the Presidents, 1790–1966,* 3 vols. New York: Chelsea House, 1966.

Lerner, Natan. *Religion, Secular Beliefs, and Human Rights: 25 Years After the 1981 Declaration.* Leiden: Martinus Nijhoff Publishers, 2006.

Lindholm, Tore, W. Cole Durham, Jr. and Bahia G. Tahzib-Lie, eds. *Facilitating Freedom of Religion or Belief: A Deskbook.* Leiden: Martinus Nijhoff Publishers, 2004.

Noonan, John T., Jr. *The Lustre of our Country: The American Experience of Religious Freedom.* Berkeley, CA: University of California Press, 1998.

Stahnke, Tad and J. Paul Martin. *Religion and Human Rights: Basic Documents.* New York: Columbia University Press, 1988.

Taylor, Paul. *Freedom of Religion: UN and European Human Rights Law and Practice.* New York/Cambridge, 2005.

Van der Vyver, Johan D. *Leuven Lectures on Religious Institutions, Religious Communities, and Rights.* Leuven: Peeters, 2004.

John Witte, Jr. *God's Joust, God's Justice: Law and Religion in the Western Tradition.* Grand Rapids, MI: Wm. B. Eerdmans Publishing Co., 2006.

——. *The Reformation of Rights: Law, Religion, and Human Rights in Early Modern Calvinism.* Cambridge, UK: Cambridge University Press, 2007.

——. *Religion and the American Constitutional Experiment,* 2d ed. Boulder, CO: Westview Press, 2005.

——. "Facts and Fictions About the History of Separation of Church and State." *Journal of Church and State* 48 (2006): 15.

Witte, John, Jr. and Johan D. van der Vyver, eds. *Religious Human Rights in Global Perspective,* 2 vols. The Hague: Martinus Nijhoff Publishers, 1996.

Articles/Chapters

Aleinikoff, Thomas Alexander. "Thinking Outside the Sovereignty Box: Transnational Law and the U.S. Constitution," *Texas Law Review* 82 (2004): 1990.

Henkin, Louis. "Rights, American and Human." *Columbia Law Review* 79 (1979): 405.

Morrisson, Clovis C. Jr. "Margin of Appreciation in European Human Rights Law." *Revue des droits de l'homme* 6 (1973): 263.

Neumann, Gerald. "The Global Dimension of RFRA." *Constitutional Commentary* 14 (1997): 33.

Stewart, David P. "United States Ratification of the Covenant on Civil and Political Rights: The Significance of the Reservations, Understandings, and Declarations." *DePaul Law Review* 42 (1993): 1183.

Symposium, "The Permissible Scope of Legal Limitations on the Freedom of Religion and Belief," *Emory International Law Review* 19 (2005): 465–1320.

Symposium, "What's Wrong with Rights for Children?" *Emory International Law Review* (2006): 1–239

Symposium, "The Foundations and Frontiers of Religious Liberty: A 25th Anniversary Celebration of the 1981 UN Declaration on Religious Tolerance." *Emory International Law Review* 21 (2007): 1–276.

PART V

SOCIOLOGICAL DIMENSIONS

CHAPTER 17

....

SUPPLY-SIDE CHANGES IN AMERICAN RELIGION: EXPLORING THE IMPLICATIONS OF CHURCH–STATE RELATIONS

....

ROGER FINKE

TRADITIONAL scholarship often approaches religious change from the "demand-side," attributing religious developments to the shifting desires, perceptions, and circumstances of the population. American religious historians describe the increased revivalism in the eighteenth and nineteenth centuries as "Great Awakenings" in which Americans demanded new world views more consistent with the existing political and economic environment.[1] Social scientists traced the 1960s surge in Asian-style cults to the birth of a "new religious consciousness" among America's youth.[2] And, more recently, scholars and journalists explain the rise of "independent" and "emergent" churches as a postmodernity preference for less religious authority.

This attention to shifting demands has masked the powerful influence of supply-side changes. Rather than emphasizing shifting preferences and demand, a growing body of research is now placing emphasis on the changing opportunities and restrictions on religious supply.[3]How are religious leaders and organizations restrained from supplying religion? Or, under what conditions are they unleashed to do so? I will argue that many of the most significant changes in religious history have resulted from changes in supply. This does not suggest that religious preferences fail to shape choices or that religious demands lack variation from one location to the next.[4] However, it does suggest that all religious choices are constrained by the availability and price of religious options. For this argument, understanding church–state relations, especially the state's restriction of religious freedoms, is essential for explaining religious change over time.

This chapter offers several examples of how and why these supply-side changes take place and the implications they hold for religion in the United States and beyond. My first example shows that early-American religion flourished in response to religious *deregulation*. I contend that the so-called Great Awakenings were nothing more (or less) than successful marketing campaigns of new religious suppliers. These campaigns arose when restrictions on new sects and itinerant preaching diminished. The second example will draw from more recent events in American history. Reviewing court decisions and legislative actions of the 1990s, I show how seemingly minor changes to religious freedoms can have powerful consequences. The final example moves beyond the United States to illustrate that the consequences of restrictions on religious freedoms are not confined to America. Before reviewing the examples, however, I begin with a brief overview of the argument.

Supply-side Religious Change

Throughout the discussion that follows I refer to all of the religious activity within a society as a religious economy. Within this economy I talk about a religious market of current and potential adherents and the religious organizations seeking to attract and retain these adherents. This vocabulary, however, does not imply that religious changes are merely a product of economic forces or slick marketing. To the contrary, previous work on supply-side religious changes has highlighted the importance of doctrines and beliefs in explaining religious changes.[5]

Yet the awareness that religious economies (like commercial economies) are sensitive to changes in market structure, calls attention to the important relationship between church and state and the powerful consequences of the state regulating religion. This regulation lies at the heart of a core supply-side thesis: *The state's regulation of religion restricts competition by changing the incentives and opportunities for religious producers (churches, preachers, revivalists, etc.) and the viable options for religious consumers (church members).*[6] This chapter tests this thesis and explores the implication that higher levels of state regulation result in less religious activity.[7]

When discussing regulation, attention will center on two forms: subsidy and suppression.[8] Suppression, the most obvious form of regulation, frequently targets the new and powerless religions.[9] The consequences of these regulations seem slight, at first, since the groups suppressed are initially small and attract members from the "fringes." Yet, these groups are a source of innovation and growth for any religious economy. Not only do they appeal to a segment of the population not reached by the more "refined" religions authorized by the state, they also serve as a testing ground for religious innovation. Although most will fail, a few succeed.[10] Suppression also changes the incentives for dominant religions. When state-supported religions can restrict competition through suppression, they find it far easier to suppress the activities of new religions and their itinerants than to compete with them. Incentives for institutional change or popular appeal soon fade, when the option of suppressing alternative religions is available.

Some might suggest that suppressing marginal sects in a religious economy has few significant or long-term consequences. Yet even a cursory glance at American religious history reveals that the religious outsiders of one era often join the mainstream in the next.[11] The revivalistic Methodists, often exuding untamed religious experiences in the early nineteenth century and reporting fewer than 5,000 members in the colonial America of 1776,[12] were the largest religious group in America by 1850. The once persecuted and struggling colonial Baptists now dominate the South, and the American Catholic Church, accused of supporting a papal conspiracy in the nineteenth century, is now the largest religious group in the nation.[13] A few of the religious outsiders of the early twentieth century, Mormons and Assemblies of God, now have burgeoning memberships and an increasing acceptance in the culture. Likewise, the once suspect immigrant religions, Lutherans and Jews, are now treated as America's own. Yet, the organizational success of each of these movements, especially the once-sectarian groups (i.e., Methodists, Baptists, Mormons, and Assemblies of God), relied on religious freedoms.

Regulations not only curb the growing minority religious movements, they curb another innovative segment of American religion. Religious groups targeting a specific mission or organizational objective, and often referred to as parachurch groups, rely on the courts for protection. They make no attempt to start new churches or create a new sect, yet they have shaped American religion for at least two centuries. The American Sunday School Union and American Tract Society serve as two of the most visible interdenominational groups in nineteenth-century America, with Campus Crusade for Christ, Prison Fellowship Ministries, and Promise Keepers serving as only a few of the approximately 2,000 contemporary examples.[14] These groups have introduced new forms of worship, evangelism, education, and small group fellowships that have been quickly incorporated into the mainstream of American religion.[15] Yet, they have little formal authority and lack a membership to initiate legislative actions.

Although suppression is the most obvious form of regulation, and the one most fully addressed in this chapter, subsidy is equally powerful and far more deceptive. Initially, subsidy appears to stimulate activity by supporting religious institutions and reducing the cost of involvement for the individual. However, on closer inspection we find that subsidy reduces the incentives of churches to gain popular support, and serves to limit competition by restricting the subsidy to a few select religions.

Whereas suppression penalizes unauthorized groups, subsidy rewards only selected religious groups.

Church subsidies make a striking change in the incentives of the clergy. When the state pays clergy salaries, the clergy have little incentive to mobilize popular support.[16] In 1837 Francis Grund of Austria offered this pithy assessment of American clergy: "In America, every clergyman may be said to do business on his own account, and under his own firm. . . . He always acts as principal, and is therefore more anxious, and will make greater efforts to obtain popularity, than one who serves for wages."

He contrasted these clergy with the "indolent and lazy" clergy of Europe's established churches, and explained that "a person provided for cannot, by the rules of common sense, be supposed to work as hard as one who has to exert himself for a living." When the market is unregulated, religious groups must garner popular support to survive.[17]

Finally, suppression and subsidy also change the incentives of the people. Suppression can burden dissenters with persecution, loss of privileges, fewer religious options, and the cost of concealing their membership. Subsidy inflates the cost of joining alternative religions. Just as parents choosing a private school must pay the full cost of the private education, forego the option of a "free" public education, and still make tax "contributions" to support the public schools, individuals selecting an alternative religion must forego the "free" or partially subsidized religion provided by the state. Thus, the state's preference for one religion reduces the individual's incentives for joining another.

Returning to the core supply-side thesis, the state's regulation of religion reduces religious competition and involvement by changing religious market structure. Whether the regulations involve subsidy or suppression, regulations change the incentives and opportunities for churches, preachers, revivalists, and the people. These changes in religious incentives and opportunities can be illustrated in early America.

CONSEQUENCES OF COLONIAL DEREGULATION

Histories of American religion devote much attention to the "Great Awakenings" that ran from 1730 to 1760 and 1800 to 1830. As the term "awakening" suggests, scholars view these years as periods of surging demand. But supply-side scholars contend that the so-called Great Awakenings arose when restrictions on new sects and itinerant preaching diminished. That is, early-American religion flourished in response to *religious deregulation*.

To appreciate the impact of deregulation, recall that the American colonies did not begin as bastions of religious freedom. Contrary to nostalgic stories of early American settlements, it was neither the intent nor the desire of most colonial leaders to grant religious freedoms for all or to deny select religious establishments. Historians have long acknowledged that religious liberties were born of necessity, not desire.[18] Although it is true that some immigrants came to the colonies for religious freedom, few desired religious freedom for all. Politicians and preachers alike considered the idea of religious freedom, or even religious toleration, a dangerous and heathen notion that was sure to undermine the authority of the state and the very survival of the church.

The religious liberties that gradually followed were offered as a solution to the immediate needs of a new nation, rather than an ideal for its future.[19] Most colonies initially had state-supported churches, and only by virtue of necessity were these establishments dismantled. Toleration grew in large part from the need for political compromise and economic development within the colonies. When combined with the difficulty of maintaining religious uniformity across a diverse immigrant population sparsely settled over vast areas, toleration soon emerged. The gradual transition to a free and competitive religious market, one in which minority religions were not only tolerated but were given equal rights, began in the late-colonial era and accelerated thereafter.[20] The new principles of religious freedom attained their clearest expression in the Constitution and Bill of Rights.[21]

Support for establishment ran deepest and lasted longest in New England. For nearly two centuries, New England's Congregational churches enjoyed the state's direct and indirect support. They received tax revenue and exercised local authority, whereas members of other religions paid taxes to subsidize the establishment and risked persecution, including imprisonment, for their support of a dissenting faith. All this changed in late eighteenth and early nineteenth centuries.[22] Deprived of its privileged position and financial support, Congregationalism lost market share at a remarkable rate. In 1776 it dominated the New England market, with more than two thirds of all religious adherents; by 1850 its share plummeted to only 28%. In contrast, the dissident upstarts—Baptists and Methodists now freed from regulatory constraint—rocketed from 12% of all adherents in 1776 to 41% in 1850. (See Table 17-1 for details.)[23] As the upstart sects successfully fought for followers, they also managed to enlarge the market. Total rates of religious adherence doubled, from a mere 17% of the population in 1776 to 34% in 1850.[24] One is hard-pressed to attribute these gains to crises or shifts within the American psyche. Increased competition, aggressive marketing, and religious entrepreneurship provide a much more credible explanation. The activities of George Whitefield in the 1740s offer an early glimpse of the new religious marketing.

By all accounts, the Grand Itinerant, George Whitefield, stood at the center of America's "First Great Awakening." Yet only a few scholars have appreciated Whitefield's marketing skills and religious entrepreneurship. Whitefield was a master of advance publicity who sent a constant stream of press releases, extolling the success of his previous revivals, to cities he intended to visit.[25] His success dramatically illustrates the producer's role in the promotion of faith. Conversely, the New England establishment's response to Whitefield illustrates how regulatory constraints can, and often do, stifle such faith-promoting entrepreneurship.

Table 17-1. Decline of the New England Establishment, 1776–1850

	1776	1850
NEW ENGLAND*		
Congregational Establishment	67%	28%
Baptist and Methodist	12%	41%
Roman Catholic	0%	11%
MAINE		
Congregational Establishment	61%	19%
Baptist and Methodist	8%	58%
Roman Catholics	0%	6%
NEW HAMPSHIRE		
Congregational Establishment	63%	30%
Baptist and Methodist	9%	46%
Roman Catholics	0%	3%
VERMONT		
Congregational Establishment	65%	29%
Baptist and Methodist	10%	44%
Roman Catholics	0%	6%
MASSACHUSETTS		
Congregational Establishment	72%	29%
Baptist and Methodist	15%	33%
Roman Catholics	0%	17%
CONNECTICUT		
Congregational Establishment	64%	37%
Baptist and Methodist	9%	39%
Roman Catholics	0%	11%

*New England totals exclude Rhode Island, which never supported an established church.
Sources: Rodney Stark and Roger Finke, "American Religion in 1776: A Statistical Portrait," *Sociological Analysis* 49 (1988): 39; and Roger Finke and Rodney Stark, "Turning Pews into People: Estimating Nineteenth Century Church Membership," *Journal for the Scientific Study of Religion* 25 (1986): 180.

Whitefield was a minister with credentials, being a graduate of Oxford University, and he made no attempt to found his own denomination. Yet his presence provoked heated resistance. The president and faculty of Harvard condemned Whitefield for "going about, in an Itinerant Way."[26] An association of Congregational ministers in Marlborough County bore "publick and faithfull *Testimony* . . . against Mr. *Whitefield's* appearing as an *Itinerant* Preacher, or *Evangelist*, and travelling from Town to Town." And the Congregational ministers of Bristol County complained that "for a Minister to invade another's Province and preach in his Charge without his leave, is disorderly and tends to Confusion, and hurteth the Work of God."[27]

To appreciate these attacks, one need only see that itinerants were *unregulated competitors* in the religious marketplace, "foreign" competition that threatened the privileges and profits of a "domestic" cartel. In Colonial America the established clergy maintained a system of territorial monopolies, dividing the land into geographical units (often called "parishes"), and granting each minister exclusive

authority over the religious activity in "his" area. Itinerants like Whitefield threatened to undermine this cartel, thereby reducing its power and profits.

New England's clergy moved quickly to defend their interests and squelch the
revival. In 1742, following a recommendation of the General Consocation of
ministers, the Connecticut legislature prohibited itinerants "from preaching in any
parish without the approval of the minister of that parish." Yale students and faculty
were required to take an "oath affirming their orthodoxy" and any clergy who protested the law were "called before the legislature, publicly rebuked, and deprived of
their offices."[28] Restrictions like these spelled the end of the First Great Awakening.

However, by the early nineteenth century, the erstwhile establishment no longer
enjoyed the official support needed to suppress competition. With the power of the
parish system in decline, a new generation of religious entrepreneurs sprang up.
Histories usually label this surge of itinerant evangelism and the concomitant
growth of Methodist and Baptist sects as the "Second Great Awakening." In fact, it
was the direct result of new religious freedoms.

This time around, the evangelists did not limit themselves to preaching, but
instead sought to found new churches wherever they went. The famous Methodist
itinerant, Peter Cartwright, emphasized this point when a Presbyterian minister
asked him not to start a church "in the bounds of his congregation."

> I told him that was not our way of doing business; that we seldom ever preached
> long at any place without trying to raise a society. He said I must not do it. I told
> him the people were a free people and lived in a free country, and must be
> allowed to do as they pleased. . . .[29]

Freed from restrictions, the upstart sects soon overtook the old-line faiths in
New England and throughout the nation.

Nevertheless, the story would read quite differently had the religious establishments remained strong and their regulatory power endured. To glimpse history as
it might have been, we need only compare the paths of American and English
Methodism. Whereas the American Methodists embraced itinerancy and camp
meetings, the Methodist hierarchy in England viewed both activities as a threat to
the "fragile nature of religious toleration."[30] According to British historian David
Hempton, "how far Methodism should be allowed to shelter under the umbrella of
the Church of England . . . became one of the most controversial legal problems of
the period between 1740 and 1820." Initially the Church of England had tolerated
the Methodists' rigorous behavioral standards, exclusive membership, and lay and
female itinerancy because Methodists had organized as a society within the Church
of England and because John Wesley could guarantee their allegiance to the English
church and state. However, by the 1790s, Wesley's death and the growth and independence of Methodist societies pushed Methodists beyond the protective shelter
of Anglicanism. The Methodists could no longer call themselves the "Church of
England at prayer"; they had become dissenters.[31] As a result, Hempton explains,
the English "Methodists realized that their preaching privileges depended upon
continued loyalty and good order."[32]

Thus Methodism in Great Britain faltered, while American Methodism soared. As the Methodists in Great Britain struggled to keep pace with population growth, the percent of Methodists in America continued to climb. From 1776 to 1850, Methodist membership in America rose from less than 3% of all church adherents to 34%, and Methodist congregations skyrocketed from 65 to more than 13,000.[33] Such meteoric growth could never have occurred under a hierarchy that restrained its itinerants and opposed camp meetings.

I would be remiss, however, to end the story of deregulation in 1850. Indeed, the forces of religious deregulation have shaped all of American religious history. Just as religious freedom allowed the upstart sects of the late eighteenth century to compete openly with the colonial establishment, the same freedoms allowed new sects to arise in the centuries that would follow. Multiple Adventist groups, the Mormons, Disciples of Christ, and a seemingly endless number of holiness groups would all arise in the nineteenth century, with a handful going on to become sizeable groups in the twentieth. Likewise a few of the Pentecostal groups that sprang up in the early twentieth century, such as the Assemblies of God and the Church of God in Christ, have shown remarkable growth and staying power. Needless to say, the vast majority of the new sects show little potential for growth, with most remaining small and obscure.[34] Yet, the successful sectarian movements have been a powerful force in shaping American religious history and continue to arise today.

However, the new sects are not the only groups to rely on religious freedoms. The freedoms of an unregulated market also allow new immigrants to worship without restraints and build religious and ethnic enclaves despite resistance. The most obvious example is the late nineteenth- and early twentieth-century Catholics, who were frequently charged with papal conspiracies, viewed with contempt, and targeted for political action.[35] Despite this public opposition, however, they worshiped freely and built institutions that paralleled the larger culture, such as schools, hospitals, and numerous civic, financial, and professional organizations. Concurrently, freed slaves, Jews, and Lutherans all relied on religious deregulation. Like the Catholics, each of these groups depended on religious freedoms to protect them from powerful nativist groups. More recently, with immigration from the east surging following 1965 amendments to the Immigration and Nationality Act, Buddhists, Hindus, Muslims, and many other immigrants now rely on these same freedoms for protection.[36]

Although the most obvious consequences of religious deregulation are the religious freedoms granted to the new and powerless religions, deregulation has consequences for established religions as well. No longer armed with the support of the state, the former colonial establishments had to rely on the support of the people for their very survival. Not only did the Methodists and Baptists of the nineteenth century offer alternative religions, they forced the existing establishments to revise how they did religion. Likewise, when the religious establishments of Europe were transplanted onto American soil, they faced immediate competition. When the Lutheran pastor Friedrich Wyneken wrote a Distress Call (*Notruf*) to German religious leaders in 1843, he described the Baptists and Methodists as "dangerous enemies" and "swarming pests" who would soon "wipe out the name of the Lutheran church in the [W]est" unless assistance was sent immediately.[37] Catholics also feared this new competition and quickly responded by holding their own version of the Protestant revival (i.e., parish mission).[38] Today Buddhists, Hindus, and Muslims are forming into congregations and providing services that are foreign to their countries of origin.[39] Moreover, all of the groups, whether they are former establishments, recent immigrants, or newly minted sects, must effectively appeal to a segment of the population for survival. Religious deregulation forces all religions to rely on the resources and loyalties of the people.

The end result of this increased religious supply and competition is what Rodney Stark and I call the "churching of America."[40] As shown in Figure 17-1, on the eve of the American Revolution only 17% of Americans were churched. This rate increased sharply in the nineteenth century until the dawn of the Civil War, when the immense dislocations of the War caused a serious decline in the South. However, the climb resumes following the War and slightly more than half of all Americans were religious adherents by 1906. Since then the rate has been stable, although inching up. This two-century trend has been fueled by the freedoms of religious deregulation. Not only were new sects and immigrant groups allowed equal freedoms, but all religious groups were forced to compete for adherents.

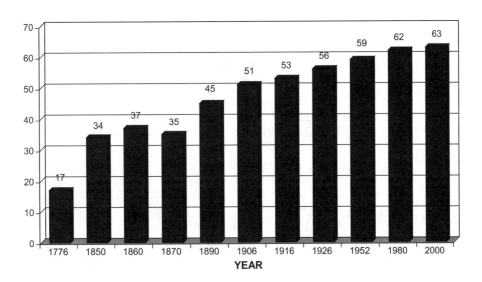

FIGURE 17-1. Rates of Adherence, 1776 to 2000.
Note: Adherents include all members of a congregation and their children.
Sources: Rodney Stark and Roger Finke, "American Religion in 1776: A Statistical Portrait," *Sociological Analysis* 49 (1988): 39; Roger Finke and Rodney Stark, "Turning Pews into People: Estimating Nineteenth Century Church Membership," *Journal for the Scientific Study of Religion* 25 (1986): 180; Roger Finke and Christopher P. Scheitle, "Accounting for the Uncounted: Computing Correctives for the 2000 RCMS Data," *Review of Religious Research* 47 (2005): 5–22. See also Roger Finke and Rodney Stark, *The Churching of America, 1776–2005* (New Brunswick, NJ: Rutgers University Press, 2005).

DEFENDING AMERICAN LIBERTIES

Religious liberties, like other civil liberties, are often inconvenient. They are inconvenient for those in power, who must acknowledge the rights of those opposing their authority, and inconvenient for sizeable majorities who see little merit in the minority's position. In his glowing assessment of the young American democracy, Alexis de Tocqueville cautioned that the "main evil" he found in this new system was not the "excessive liberty" that most Europeans feared, but the "inadequate securities . . . against tyranny." The tyranny of which he spoke was the "tyranny of the majority."[41] His concern was the ability of the majority to impose its will without regard to the sovereignty of all people. De Tocqueville recognized that because liberties are inconvenient, they are often conveniently overlooked.

When explaining America's long-held commitment to religious liberties, it is tempting to attribute this to the larger American culture or the American way of doing things, suggesting a secure stability and certainty. After all, it has been more than two centuries since the First Amendment was ratified, with clauses assuring both the free exercise of religion and the freedom from religious establishments. However, the territorial reach of each clause, as well as the boundary between them, continues to be negotiated. The civil rights of religious minorities must still be protected. In the words of de Tocqueville, the sovereignty of all people must be protected from the tyranny of the majority.

This section documents the impact of a single court decision. Returning to the 1990s and relying on data compiled by John Wybraniec, I show how even subtle judicial and legislative shifts can have powerful consequences.[42] Although documenting far more limited change, and largely confined to the Free Exercise Clause, this example illustrates that the supply-side implications of changing church–state relations is not confined to eighteenth- or nineteenth-century America.

RELIGIOUS FREEDOM AND THE *SMITH* DECISION

From 1963 to 1990, the courts frequently relied on the *Sherbert*[43] test (compelling interest) to offer guidelines on how courts accommodated the interest of public welfare without unduly burdening religious freedom. This test required courts to ask if undue burden was being placed on the plaintiff's religious freedom.[44] If the government did not cause an undue burden, the court ruled against the plaintiff. When the court discerned that a burden was present, it asked if there was a compelling interest to carry forth an action that might burden the plaintiff's free exercise of religion.[45] And, if the court felt that it must rule in the public's interest, it attempted to find an alternative way to satisfy the complaint without infringing upon religious freedom.[46]

In 1990, in *Employment Division of Oregon, Department of Human Resources of Oregon v. Smith,* the Supreme Court severely challenged the *Sherbert* test.[47]In this case the Employment Division of Oregon denied unemployment benefits to Alfred Smith and Galen Black, two rehabilitation counselors who had been fired for ingesting peyote during a Native American Church ceremony. The Court did not dispute the use of peyote as an ancient and genuine sacramental practice, but nevertheless concluded that: ". . . the nation cannot afford the luxury of deeming presumptively invalid, as applied to the religious objector, every regulation of conduct that does not protect an interest of the highest order."[48] Thus, the Court withdrew the compelling interest test that had been used for the previous three decades.

Many, including Justice Sandra Day O'Connor and Professor Michael W. McConnell, addressed the meaning of the controversial ruling. McConnell stated that the theoretical argument of the *Smith* case left "the court open to the charge of abandoning its traditional role as protector of minority rights against majoritarian oppression."[49] At the 1991 Bicentennial Conference on the Religion Clauses Justice O'Connor summed up the concerns of many when she explained, "The Free Exercise Clause does not mean very much if all a state has to do is make a law generally applicable in order to severely burden a very central aspect of our citizens' lives."[50] After *Smith,* Congress passed the Religious Freedom Restoration Act (RFRA), which was a legislative attempt to restore the *Sherbert* test. However, in the *City of Boerne v. Flores* case in June of 1997 the Supreme Court struck it down as unconstitutional, at least insofar as it applied to the states.[51]

What are the consequences of the *Smith* decision and RFRA? Did this decision reduce the court's role as a protectorate of minority faiths? Many bold claims have been made, but evidence is often anecdotal. In recent research, John Wybraniec, Amy Adamczyk, and I have attempted to eliminate the speculation by systematically analyzing and comparing the court cases from 1981 to 1997 (all levels of the judiciary).[52] Reading, coding, and analyzing over 2,000 religion cases making First Amendment claims, we divided the cases into three distinct legal time periods: before *Smith,* after *Smith* (but before RFRA), and during the RFRA period. This allowed us to more fully address the key question: What were the consequences of *Smith* and RFRA?

THE CONSEQUENCES OF *SMITH* AND RFRA

When reviewing the results of all 17 years, many of our findings support previous expectations. For example, when it comes to guarding their own religious freedoms, religious groups seek protection from the courts. Religious groups or individuals initiated the legal action for 76% of the cases on religious freedom. Conversely, when the separation of church and state was the issue (the Establishment Clause), 68% of the cases were brought by secular litigants. Also, as expected, religious minorities are the most likely religious groups to seek protection from the courts. Whereas 21% of all church members are in mainline Protestant denominations, they are involved in only 4% of the religion cases. In sharp contrast, "cults" represent only 1% of religious congregational membership, yet they are involved in over 16% of the free exercise court cases. When all minority religious groups are combined, we find that although they only make up about 18% of the church membership in the United States, they account for nearly 62% of the free exercise cases coming to the courts, and nearly one half of all court cases on religion. Finally, despite frequently initiating court cases, minority religions are more likely to receive unfavorable rulings. From 1981 to 1997 they received favorable rulings in 37% of their cases, compared with 70% for mainline Protestants. Thus, as expected, religious minorities more frequently turn to the courts for protection, despite receiving less favorable rulings.

What was the impact of *Smith* and RFRA? Contrary to the claims of Justice Anthony M. Kennedy and others, our results reveal that the consequences of the *Smith* decision were swift and immediate.[53] The courts' use of the compelling interest test plummeted after *Smith* and quickly rebounded following the passage of RFRA. At all court levels, the percentage of free exercise cases citing the compelling interest test was 23.6% before *Smith*, 11.9% after *Smith*, and before RFRA, and 25.4% following RFRA (Figure 17-2). The percentage of favorable decisions followed a similar pattern. For free exercise cases the percentage dropped from 39.5% before *Smith* to 28.4% following *Smith*, and rebounded to more than 45% after RFRA was passed (Table 17-2). Thus, the consequences of the *Smith* decision resulted in an immediate reduction in the use of the compelling interest test and a far lower rate of favorable free exercise decisions.

However, even this drop in favorable rulings underestimates the impact of *Smith*. Following *Smith* and before RFRA, we also found that religious groups were less likely to initiate free exercise claims. Whereas religious groups initiated 7.1 free

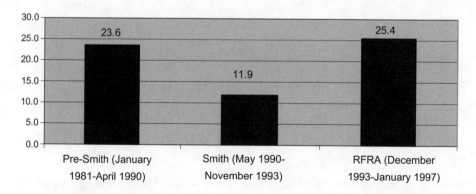

FIGURE 17-2. Percentage of cases citing a compelling interest test by legal period (*N* = 1,171 cases).
Source: John Wybraniec and Roger Finke "Religious Regulation and the Courts: The Judiciary's Changing Role in Protecting Minority Religions from Majoritarian Rule." *Journal for the Scientific Study of Religion* 40 (2001): 427.

Table 17-2. Percentage of Successful Decisions by Legal Period

	Legal Period		
Decision	Pre-Smith (January 1981–April 1990)	Smith (May 1990–1993)	RFRA (December 1993–January 1997)
Favorable	39.5% (310)	28.4% (38)	45.2% (114)

exercise cases per month before *Smith* (1981–1990), they only initiated 3.2 cases per month following the *Smith* case and before RFRA. Following RFRA the number of cases increased to 5.9 per month. When religious groups did not have recourse to the courts for free exercise exemptions, they very quickly limited its use.

This last result suggests that if religions were burdened by laws of general applicability, the courts would not know about it because so few religious groups would come requesting an exemption.[54] This concern echoes those raised by colonial Baptists in the late seventeenth and early eighteenth centuries. Historians tell us that Baptists chose not to appeal their cases to the courts because they had no representation "on the bench, none at the bar, and seldom any on the juries."[55] The religious minorities of the late 1990s had far more protections than the colonial Baptists, but the principle remains the same: When religious minorities receive fewer favorable rulings and appear to receive less protection from the courts, they initiate fewer court actions.

Following the *Smith* decision, the reduction in free exercise claims, the increase in unfavorable rulings, and the reduced use of the compelling interest test all weighed most heavily on religious minorities relying on the courts for protection. Justice O'Connor explains:

> . . . the First Amendment was enacted precisely to protect the rights of those whose religious practices are not shared by the majority and may be viewed with hostility. The history of our free exercise doctrine amply demonstrates the harsh impact majoritarian rule has had on unpopular or emerging religious groups such as the Jehovah's Witnesses and the Amish.[56]

Using multivariate models with this same data we found that Justice O'Connor is right: Minority religions are especially burdened by the removal of free exercise claims.[57] When controlling for region, level of court, legal period, citing the compelling interest test, and whether an individual or group brought the case forward, we found that minority religious groups were significantly less likely to receive favorable decisions when compared with mainline Protestant churches.[58] With the exception of Native American religions, the odds that sects, cults, and Muslims will receive a favorable ruling are about one third of the odds for mainline Protestants. General Christians, members of the Jewish faith, and Catholics were also *less* likely to receive a favorable decision when compared with mainline Protestant groups.[59]

The probability of a favorable decision in using the compelling interest test at the federal level for mainstream Protestants, 53% in the pre-*Smith* period, dropped to 40% during the *Smith* era (but before RFRA) and increased to 58% for the RFRA period. If a religious sect brought the case forward, the probability of success was much lower. If this group used the compelling interest test and brought their case to federal court, they had a success rate of 27% in the pre-*Smith* period, 18% during the *Smith* era (but before RFRA), and 31% during the RFRA period.

These results do not suggest that the *Smith* decision abolished the religious freedoms promised in the First Amendment. To the contrary, we are arguing that the changes were subtle and modest; but evidence taken from this brief window of time does illustrate how seemingly modest changes can have significant impact on implementing religious freedoms. This evidence has stressed the influence of the *Smith* decision on the courts' actions, but evidence could also be produced on how the *Smith* decision influenced the legislative actions of local governments (e.g., zoning and other building codes). Legislative actions might support the will of the majority, but can impose heavy burdens on the new and novel religions. The burden was described by de Tocqueville as the tyranny of the majority.

BEYOND AMERICA

When supply-side arguments were first introduced, many suggested that the arguments were uniquely American.[60] Whereas American religion responded to changing church–state relations, religions in other locations (or times) were less sensitive to changes in the structure of religious markets. Only in America, it was argued, could the market forces be applied to religion. However, a growing body of research is concluding that supply-side restrictions and regulations can curtail religious activity in any setting. Conversely, when regulations are removed, religions have room to flourish. Although the focus of this chapter is on the United States, I want to briefly document that the effects of church–state relations are not narrowly confined by time and space.

CONSEQUENCES OF DEREGULATION

When moving beyond the United States, supply-side changes have been documented most extensively in Latin America. Anthony Gill,[61] Andrew Chestnut,[62] and many others have charted the surge in religious competition and growth in Latin America after four centuries of monopoly religion were lifted. Evangelical Christians burst onto the scene as regulations were removed in the latter half of the twentieth century, with the percentage of evangelicals in the population doubling and tripling over the last 30 years.[63] When the state was no longer weeding out religious competitors, not only did the supply of new religions increase, the new competition forced the Roman Catholic Church to activate ministries, outreach, and services to the people. At first, the new religions limited their appeal to the areas most fully neglected by the Catholic Church (e.g., the poorest barrios);[64] but their presence has grown throughout the cities and countryside. A recent survey found that Brazil still has more Catholics than any other country, but it also has more Pentecostals than the United States.[65] The Pentecostals and other religious minorities initially arose in the market niches being ignored by the state churches, but as their freedoms grow and their numbers increase they compete on equal footing without restraints.

However, the changes are not restricted to the Americas or Christianity. Post-World War II Japan serves as one of many other examples. Before the end of World War II, the government strictly controlled religious activity in Japan. The state-subsidized Shinto shrines and participation in Shinto ceremonies was a matter of civic duty. Alternative religions required government recognition to legally exist, and once recognized, they faced interference, suppression, and persecution from the state.[66] However, the Japanese defeat and Allied Occupation in 1945 led to the immediate repeal of all laws controlling religion, disestablished the Shinto religion, and granted unprecedented religious freedom.[67]

The response was overwhelming. The period immediately following 1945 is called *kamigami no rasshu awa*, the "rush hour of the gods." It was said that "New Religions rose like mushrooms after a rainfall."[68] By 1949, 403 new religious groups were founded, and 1,546 other groups established independence through secession from the shrines, temples, or churches to which they had previously belonged. In contrast, only 43 religious groups had received official recognition in the decades before 1945—13 Shinto sects, 28 Buddhist denominations, and two Christian groups.[69] Some have argued that it was the *demand* for religion, not supply, that shifted most dramatically in the wake of World War II. I reject this argument for several reasons. First, Japanese defeat did not trigger widespread spiritual escapism; the traditional religions did not experience an increase in membership or devotion. Second, the growth of new religions continued long after the Japanese economy recovered and continues even today. Third, Germany shared Japan's defeat, but its religious economy remained highly regulated and did not experience a postwar boom in new religions. On the other hand, when South Korea was liberated from Japanese rule and Japanese religious restrictions, it displayed a similar flowering of new religions, with a sharp increase in the level of active membership.[70]

More recent examples can also be offered. Yungfeng Lu reports that when the 1989 Taiwanese Law on Civic Organizations allowed all religions to exist and removed multiple prohibitions, there was a 12-fold increase in the number of different religious groups in Taiwan (from 83 in 1990 to 1,062 in 2004) and the total number of temples and churches more than doubled.[71] Likewise, Paul Froese reports similar trends following the breakup of the Soviet Union and the initial religious freedoms provided. He found religious revivalism increased and atheism declined when regulations were initially lifted.[72] Also, in agreement with the theory, the trend has since slowed or even reversed as regulations have returned. Like the previous examples offered, shifts in religious regulation are associated with major religious change.

RESTRICTING LIBERTIES

Despite being described as the "orphan of human rights,"[73] the importance of religious freedom is widely acknowledged and consistently promised in international documents and an increasing number of nations promise religious freedoms in their constitutions.[74] However, just as the consequences of religious deregulation are not confined to America, so also the struggle to secure and retain promised liberties is not confined to a single nation. Recent data suggest that when it comes to religious freedom, there is a gaping chasm between promise and practice. This chasm has important implications for supply-side changes in religion.

A recent coding of all 196 nations in the U.S. State Department's *International Religious Freedom Reports* documents the gap between promise and practice of religious freedom around the globe.[75] The findings are striking. Eighty-three percent of all countries offer assurances of religious freedom in their constitutions

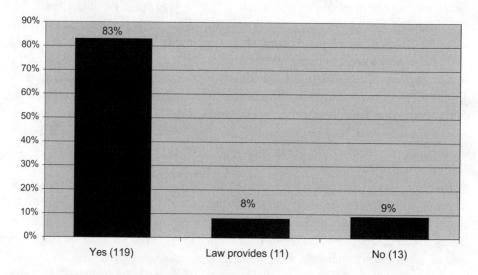

FIGURE 17-3. Does the Constitution provide for freedom of religion?
Source: The Association of Religion Data Archives "Cross-National Data" (http://www.thearda.com/Archive/Files/Descriptions/INTL2003.asp), Roger Finke and Brian J. Grim Principal Investigators. For more information on the data collection, see Brian J. Grim and Roger Finke. "International Religion Indexes: Government Regulation, Government Favoritism, and Social Regulation of Religion." *Interdisciplinary Journal of Research on Religion.* 2 (2006) Article 1: www.religjournal.com (2006).

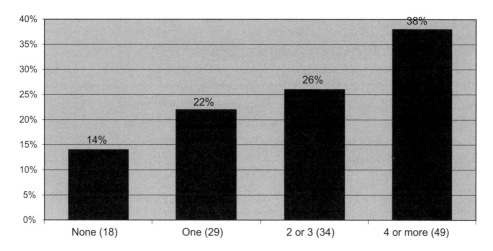

FIGURE 17-4. Laws restricting religious practice for 130 countries promising religious freedom in 2005.

Source: The Association of Religion Data Archives "Cross-National Data" (http://www.thearda.com/Archive/Files/Descriptions/INTL2003.asp), Roger Finke and Brian J. Grim Principal Investigators. For more information on the data collection, see Brian J. Grim and Roger Finke. "International Religion Indexes: Government Regulation, Government Favoritism, and Social Regulation of Religion." *Interdisciplinary Journal of Research on Religion.* 2 (2006) Article 1: www.religjournal.com (2006).

(Figure 17-3).[76] Another 8%, some without constitutions, hold laws providing such promises. Only 9%, or 13 nations, fail to offer promises of religious freedom. Thus, more than 90% of all nations offer legal assurances of religious freedom.

How do these promises translate into practice? Based on the evidence, the simple and obvious answer is: They don't! Despite constitutional promises, most nations openly denied the religious freedoms of individuals and restrained the activities of religious groups (Figure 17-4). Of the 130 countries promising religious freedom, 86% (112 countries) have at least one law denying a religious freedom and 38% have four or more such restrictions.[77] Of the 13 countries not promising religious freedom, all have four or more.

Our conclusions on the gap between promise and practice are confirmed by multiple other sources as well. Not only do a host of human rights and religious advocacy groups confirm these findings, the UN's Special Rapporteur on freedom of religion or belief offers very similar conclusions.[78] At the close of her 2007 report, Asma Jahangir writes that the implementation of the 1981 Declaration "is far from being a reality" and explained that "there still is a huge gap between rhetoric and practice in many instances."[79] She went on to express concern over the number of "urgent appeals" and "allegation letters" that receive no response. In her 2006 report she complained that the number of countries refusing to offer her an invitation to visit is increasing. She noted with special concern that after "numerous requests and reminders," Indonesia and the Russian Federation refused to grant her an invitation.[80] Thus, despite the many assurances of religious freedoms in country constitutions, as well as in the declarations, covenants, and resolutions of the UN, the wide chasm between promise and practice remains.

This cross-national research is still underway, but already it offers several insights for supply-side arguments.[81] First, the level of restrictions placed on religion varies widely from one nation to the next. Although we sometimes talk about regulated and unregulated religious economies, most fall somewhere between the two extremes. Second, the type of restrictions enacted varies dramatically from one country to the next and holds different implications for future religious change. Some are designed to protect the state, and others are protecting a dominant religion. Third, religious liberties, like many other civil liberties, are fragile. Even constitutional assurances offer no guarantee that religious liberties will be protected. Fourth, changes in religious liberty are closely associated with multiple other social and religious changes.

CONCLUSION

When attempting to understand the "why" of religious change, scholars frequently turn to demand-side explanations. Emphasizing the population's preferences and tastes (demands), they often overlook the supply-side factors that shape the incentives and opportunities of religious firms and religious entrepreneurs. Whereas demand-side explanations emphasize how cultural changes lead to sudden shifts in demand, this chapter emphasizes how government actions can constrain the actions of local congregations and the viable religious options of the people.

The supply-side emphasis draws attention to church–state relations and how the state restricts the religious activities of individuals and organizations. This chapter documents how major shifts in church–state relations of early America resulted in dramatic religious change. Unleashed by new religious liberties, a host of new sects arose and the so-called "Great Awakenings" soon followed. Within a 75-year span the upstart Methodists went from a small sect with few freedoms to the largest religious group in the nation. The examples of Latin America, Japan, and others confirmed that the impact of altering church–state relations is not constrained by time, location, or a specific culture. When regulations were lifted, new religions flourished. But the data reviewed on U.S. court cases in the 1980s and 1990s also demonstrates how even modest shifts in religious liberties can result in significant changes. After the *Smith* case in 1990 and before the Religious Freedom Restoration Act in 1993, free exercise cases received fewer favorable rulings and fewer religious groups turned to the courts for protection.

Supply-side arguments also draw attention to minority and marginal religions. Because these groups have faced the brunt of state regulations throughout American history, they are the first to notice increased restrictions. Even when changes seem negligible for majority groups, such as the *Smith* decision in the United States, the consequences are immediate for those on the fringes. Following *Smith*, favorable free exercise decisions fell for all, but they fell most abruptly for minority religions. This trend of minority religions being the first to face state restrictions has been documented as a global trend by researchers and human rights organizations.[82] Like canaries in the coal mine, they are the first to fall victim.

The temptation, of course, is to dismiss the minority groups as insignificant and not worthy of the burden they place on the majority. However, a growing body of historical research has documented the importance of religious outsiders in shaping American culture and the importance of religious liberties in allowing them to do so.[83] For new religious immigrants as well as racial, ethnic, and social minorities, religious liberties have provided an institutional free space for these outsiders. Whether it is the early immigrations of the Amish, Jews, Lutherans, and Catholics, or the more recent waves of Buddhists, Muslims, Pentecostals, and Catholics, this free space has given the new immigrants a haven for garnering social support and acclimating to a new culture.[84] Likewise, racial minorities, such as African Americans, have relied on this institutional free space for practicing their faith as well as mobilizing social and political support.[85] Religious liberties are even more essential for the religious minorities not limiting their appeal to a select ethnic or racial minority. Methodists, Mormons, and various forms of fundamentalism have all been religious outsiders at different points in American history. As noted earlier, however, the religious outsiders of one century often join the mainstream in the next.[86]

Finally, this chapter points to the fragility of the religious liberties that serve to lift regulations. Secular states (especially Communist regimes) and powerful state supported religions are the most obvious sources for freedoms denied. However, as de Tocqueville has warned, the "tyranny of the majority" also threatens liberties lacking adequate protections. Because religious liberties can be inconvenient, costly, and even threatening for the general population, liberties always run the risk of losing popular support—a risk that increases as the issues become more local.[87] This might all seem far removed for Americans, but consider the following recent change in public opinion. When the state of the First Amendment survey was conducted in 2000, 72% of the American population responded that "freedom to worship as one chooses . . . applies to all religious groups regardless of how extreme their beliefs are." Seven years later only 56% agreed with this statement.[88] Everyone wants liberties, but not everyone wants liberties for all.

ENDNOTES

1. William G. McLoughlin, *Revivals, Awakenings, and Reform* (Chicago: The University of Chicago Press, 1978).

2. See Roger Finke and Rodney Stark, *1776–1990* (New Brunswick, NJ: Rutgers University Press, 1992), 239–245.

3. Roger Finke and Rodney Stark, *The Churching of America, 1776–2005* (New Brunswick, NJ: Rutgers University Press, 2005); Roger Finke and Laurence R. Iannaccone, "Supply-Side Explanations for Religious Change," *The Annals of the American Academy of Political and Social Science* 527 (1993): 27; R. Stephen Warner, "Work in Progress Toward a New Paradigm for the Sociological Study of Religion in the United States," *American Journal of Sociology* 98 (1993): 1044; Rodney Stark and Laurence Iannaccone, "A Supply-Side Reinterpretation of the 'Secularization' of Europe," *Journal for the Scientific Study of Religion* 33 (1994): 230; Roger Finke, "Supply-side Explanations for Religious Change," in *Rational Choice Theory and Religion: Summary and Assessment,* ed. Lawrence A. Young (New York: Routledge, 1997); Laurence Iannaccone, Roger Finke and Rodney Stark, "Deregulating Religion," *Economic Inquiry* 35 (1997): 350.

4. For a discussion and illustration of the variation in religious preferences, see Rodney Stark and Roger Finke, *Acts of Faith: Explaining the Human Side of Religion* (Berkeley, CA: University of California Press, 2000), 196–203.

5. For an example, see Roger Finke and Rodney Stark, *The Churching of America, 1776–2005* (New Brunswick, NJ: Rutgers University Press, 2005).

6. Roger Finke, "Religious Deregulation: Origins and Consequences," *Journal of Church and State* 32 (1990): 609.

7. Although my attention will focus on the work of social scientists and historians, legal scholars have also recognized the implications of church–state relations on market structure. Richard A. Posner and University of Chicago law Professor Michael McConnell have argued that "the First Amendment can be understood as positing that the 'market'—realm of private choice—will reach the 'best' religious results; or, more accurately, that the government has no authority to alter such results." Michael W. McConnell and Richard A. Posner, "An Economic Approach to Issues of Religious Freedom," *Chicago Law Review* 56 (1989): 14.

8. See Roger Finke, "Supply-side Explanations for Religious Change," in Young, *Rational Choice Theory and Religion: Summary and Assessment.*

9. Sidney E. Mead, *The Lively Experiment: The Shaping of Christianity in America* (New York: Harper and Row, 1976 [1963]); William G. McLoughlin, *New England Dissent, 1630–1833, 2 Vols.* (Cambridge, MA: Harvard University Press, 1971); James A. Beckford, *Cult Controversies: The Societal Response to New Religious Movements* (London: Tavistock Publications, 1985); Thomas Robbins and James A. Beckford, "Religious Movements and Church-State Issues," in *Handbook of Cults and Sects,* eds. David Bromley and Jeffrey Hadden (Greenwich, CT: JAI Press, 1993), 199–218.

10. See Rodney Stark and William Sims Bainbridge, *The Future of Religion: Secularization, Revival, and Cult Formation* (Berkeley, CA: University of California Press, 1985); Roger Finke, "Innovative Returns to Tradition: Using Core Beliefs as the Foundation for Innovative Accommodation," *Journal for the Scientific Study of Religion* 43 (2004): 19.

11. R. Laurence Moore, *Religious Outsiders and the Making of Americans* (New York: Oxford University Press, 1986).

12. *Minutes of the Annual Conferences of the Methodist Episcopal Church, 1773–1828* (New York: T. Mason and G. Lane, 1840).

13. See Roger Finke and Rodney Stark, *The Churching of America, 1776–2005* (New Brunswick: Rutgers University Press, 2005).

14. Restricting his search to religious nonprofits with a national scope and an annual budget of over $200,000, Christopher P. Scheitle located 1,941 groups. Their annual budgets totaled to over $10 billion. See Christopher P. Scheitle, "Beyond the Congregation: Christian Nonprofits in the United States." (Ph.D. dissertation, Department of Sociology, Pennsylvania State University, University Park, PA, 2008).

15. For a more extensive discussion see Roger Finke, "Innovative Returns to Tradition: Using Core Beliefs as the Foundation for Innovative Accommodation." *Journal for the Scientific Study of Religion* 43 (2004): 19.

16. A religious dissenter from Connecticut offered this biting assessment in 1791: "Preachers that will not preach without a salary found for them by law are hirelings who seek the fleece and not the flock. As quoted in William G. McLoughlin, *New England Dissent, 1630–1833, Vol. II* (CambrIbidge: Harvard University Press, 1971), 927.

17. Francis Grund, *The Americans in Their Moral, Social, and Political Relations* (1837) as excerpted in Milton B. Powell, ed., *The Voluntary Church: Religious Life, 1740–1860, Seen Through the Eyes of European Visitors* (New York: Macmillan, 1967).

18. Robert Baird, *Religion in America; or, An Account of the Origin, Progress, Relation to the State, and Present Condition of the Evangelical Churches in the United States. With Notices of the Unevangelical Denominations* (Glasgow: Blackie and Co., 1844); Perry G. Miller, "The Contribution of the Protestant Churches to Religious Liberty in Colonial America," *Church History* 4 (1935): 57; Sidney E. Mead, *The Lively Experiment: The Shaping of Christianity in America* (New York: Harper and Row, 1976 [1963]). Frank Lambert, *The Founding Fathers and the Place of Religion in America* (Princeton, NJ: Princeton University Press, 2003).

19. Pennsylvania and Rhode Island were the only two colonies to consistently offer some form of religious freedom that was based on principle as well as necessity.

20. Sidney E. Mead, "From Coercion to Persuasion: Another Look at the Rise of Religious Liberty and the Emergence of Denominationalism," *Church History* 25 (1956): 317. Roger Finke, "Religious Deregulation: Origins and Consequences" *Journal of Church and State*, 32 (1990): 609. Frank Lambert, *The Founding Fathers and the Place of Religion in America* (Princeton, NJ: Princeton University Press, 2003).

21. Article IV of the constitution states that "no religious test shall ever be required as qualification to any office or public trust under the United States," and the First Amendment states that "Congress shall make no law respecting an establishment of religion, or prohibiting the free exercise thereof."

22. The profit from Vermont's Glebe rights or "ministry lands" were redistributed among *all* clergy (1794); New Hampshire passed toleration acts for Episcopalians (1792), Baptists (1804) and eventually all Christians (1819); Connecticut eased the standards of exemption from religious taxes (1784–1791); and Massachusetts' Religious Freedom Act of 1811 eased the constraints on dissenting religions. Religious taxation, the final remnant of the establishment, ceased in 1807 in Vermont, 1818 in Connecticut, 1819 in New Hampshire, and 1833 in Massachusetts. William G. McLoughlin, *New England Dissent, 1630–1833*, 2 vols. (Cambridge, UK: Cambridge University Press, 1971).

23. Although Catholics eventually became the largest denomination in New England, Catholic immigration had little to do with the Congregationalists' early decline. By 1850 Roman Catholics constituted only 11% of all religious adherents.

24. Adherence refers to all adult members and their children. For more detail on how the membership totals were computed go to: Rodney Stark and Roger Finke, "American Religion in 1776: A Statistical Portrait," *Sociological Analysis* 49 (1988): 39; and Roger Finke and Rodney Stark, "Turning Pews into People: Estimating Nineteenth Century Church Membership," *Journal for the Scientific Study of Religion* 25 (1986): 180.

25. See Frank Lambert's *"Pedlar in Divinity: George Whitefield and the Transatlantic Revivals, 1737–1770* (Princeton, NJ: Princeton University Press, 1994); and "Pedlar in Divinity: George Whitefield and the Great Awakening, 1737–1745," *Journal of American History* 77 (1990): 812.

26. *The Testimony of the President, Professors, Tutors and Hebrew Instructor of Harvard College in Cambridge, against the Reverend Mr. George Whitefield and His Conduct* (Boston, N.E.: T. Fleet, 1744), 3.

27. *The Testimony of an Association of Ministers Convened at Marlborough, January 22, 1744, against the Reverend George Whitefield and His Conduct* (Boston, N.E.: T. Fleet, 1745), 3. *The Testimony of a Number of Ministers in the County of Bristol against Mr. Whitefield* (Boston, N.E.: T. Fleet, 1745), 8.

28. William G. McLoughlin, *New England Dissent, 1630–1833, Volume 1* (Cambridge, UK: Cambridge University Press, 1971), 363.

29. Peter Cartwright, *Autobiography of Peter Cartwright, The Backwoods Preacher*, ed. W.P. Strickland (Cincinnati, OH: Cranston and Curts, 1856), 123.

30. Nathan O. Hatch, *The Democratization of American Christianity* (New Haven, CT: Yale University Press, 1989), 50.

31. David Hempton, "Methodism and the Law, 1740–1820," in *Sects and New Religious Movements*, eds. A. Dyson and E. Barker; *Bulletin of the John Rylands Library* 70 (1988): 94. Also, David Hempton, *Methodism and Politics in British Society, 1750–1850* (Palo Alto, CA: Stanford University Press, 1984).

32. David Hempton, *Methodism and Politics in British Society, 1750–1850* (Palo Alto, CA: Stanford University Press, 1984), 104.

33. For data on Methodist membership in Great Britain see Robert Currie, Alan Gilbert, and Lee Horsley, *Churches and Churchgoers: Patterns of Church Growth in the British Isles Since 1700* (Oxford, UK: Clarendon Press, 1977), 161–165. For data on Methodist membership in the U.S. see Roger Finke and Rodney Stark, *The Churching of America, 1776–2005: Winners and Losers in our Religious Economy* (New Brunswick, NJ: Rutgers University Press, 2005). Also see John H. Wigger, *Taking Heaven by Storm: Methodism and the Rise of Popular Christianity in America* (Urbana, IL: University of Illinois Press, 1998).

34. After collecting data on 417 American-born sects, Rodney Stark and William Sims Bainbridge report that "nearly a third of all sects (32 percent) reached their high-water mark on the day they began." See Rodney Stark and William Sims Bainbridge, *The Future of Religion: Secularization, Revival, and Cult Formation* (Berkeley, CA: University of California Press, 1985), 134.

35. Jay P. Dolan, *The American Catholic Experience: A History From Colonial Times to the Present* (Garden City, NY: Image Books, 1985).

36. The new amendments replaced country-of-origin quotas with a single quota for the Eastern and Western Hemisphere and resulted in an immediate surge in immigration from non-European nations. Immigration from India, for example, rose from 467 in 1965 to 2,293 the next year, and now runs around 30,000 a year. For Asia as a whole, immigration went from a modest 20,040 in 1965 to an average of nearly 150,000 per year in the 1970s and more than 250,000 in the 1980s. Immigration from Latin America, especially Mexico, was sizable before 1965, rose sharply throughout the 1970s, and remained the largest current of immigration in the 1980s and 1990s. In 1960 about 75% of all foreign-born residents were born in Europe. Forty years later (2000), 15% of the foreign-born were from Europe, 26% were from Asia, and 51% were from Latin America.

37. Friedrich Conrad Dietrich Wyneken, *The Distress of the German Lutherans in North America*, translated by S. Edgar Schmidt and edited by R.F. Rehmer (Fort Wayne, IN: Concordia Theological Seminary Press, [1843] 1982).

38. Jay P. Dolan, *Catholic Revivalism: The American Experience, 1830–1900* (Notre Dame: University of Notre Dame Press, 1978).

39. R. Stephen Warner, "The Place of the Congregation in the Contemporary American Religious Configuration," in *American Congregations,* eds. James P. Wind and James W. Lewis, vol. 2 (Chicago: University of Chicago Press, 1994); Helen Rose Ebaugh and Janet Saltzman Chafetz, *Religion and the New Immigrants: Continuities and Adaptations in Immigrant Congregations* (Walnut Creek, CA: AltaMira Press, 2000).

40. Roger Finke and Rodney Stark, *The Churching of America, 1776–2005* (New Brunswick, NJ: Rutgers University Press, 2005).

41. Alexis de Tocqueville, *Democracy in America* (New York: Vintage Books, 1945[1835]), 270–271.

42. John Wybraniec and Roger Finke, "Religious Regulation and the Courts: The Judiciary's Changing Role in Protecting Minority Religions from Majoritarian Rule," *Journal for the Scientific Study of Religion* 40 (2001): 427.

43. In *Sherbert v. Verner,* 374 U.S. 398 (1963), the defendant, a Seventh-day Adventist, refused on religious grounds to work Saturdays after her employer shifted her schedule to include this day. Seventh-day Adventists observe Saturday as the Sabbath and proper day of rest. When Sherbert could not find alternative work and applied for benefits, the state denied them. Claiming a breach of religious freedom, Sherbert sued and the Supreme Court found in her favor. When the Supreme Court overturned a lower court's denial of Sherbert's claim it established the tripartite *(Sherbert)* test that was used in free exercise cases until 1990.

44. Ibid. at 403.

45. Ibid. at 406.

46. Ibid. at 407.

47. 494 U.S. 872 (1990).

48. *Smith,* 494 U.S. 872 (1990).

49. Michael W. McConnell, "*Free* Exercise Revisionism and the Smith Decision," *Chicago Law Review* 57 (1990): 1109, 1129.

50. Ibid. at 677.

51. *Boerne v. Flores,* 521 U.S. 507 (1997).

52. John Wybraniec and Roger Finke, "Religious Regulation and the Courts: The Judiciary's Changing Role in Protecting Minority Religions from Majoritarian Rule," *Journal for the Scientific Study of Religion* 40 (2001): 427; and Amy Adamczyk, John Wybraniec, and Roger Finke, "Religious Regulation and the Courts: Documenting the Effects of *Smith* and RFRA," *Journal of Church and State* 46 (2004): 237.

53. While speaking for the majority in *City of Boerne v Flores,* Justice Kennedy asserted that laws of general applicability very rarely burden the free exercise of religion in America. *City of Boerne v. Flores,* 117 S. Ct. 2157 (1997). Also see Ira C. Lupu, "The Failure of RFRA," *University of Arkansas Little Rock Law Journal* 20 (1998): 589; and James E. Ryan, "Smith and the Religious Freedom Restoration Act: An Iconoclastic Assessment," *Virginia Law Review* 78 (1992): 1417.

54. Professor Drinan makes the similar point that we will not know what happens to religious individuals and persons if RFRA is not reinstated in some form. As he explains, "at the local level, zoning commissions will quietly deny access to Jewish temples, controversial denominations or Catholic schools. Appeals will not be taken nor will there be any public outcry. The number of individuals who will seek to vindicate their rights under the *Smith* decision will be small." See Robert F. Drinan, "Reflections on the Demise of the Religious Freedom Restoration Act," *Georgetown Law Journal* 89 (1997): 101, 115–116.

55. *See* William G. McLoughlin, *New England Dissent, 1630–1833,* 2 Vols. (Cambridge, MA: Harvard University Press, 1971).

56. Ibid., 902.

57. *See* John Wybraniec and Roger Finke, "Religious Regulation and the Courts: The Judiciary's Changing Role in Protecting Minority Religions from Majoritarian Rule," *Journal for the Scientific Study of Religion* 40 (2001): 427.

58. Aside from religious affiliation, legal period, and citing of the compelling interest test, the only other significant variable was level of court.

59. *See* note 35, at 437, table 4, model 2 in John Wybraniec and Roger Finke, "Religious Regulation and the Courts: The Judiciary's Changing Role in Protecting Minority Religions from Majoritarian Rule," *Journal for the Scientific Study of Religion* 40 (2001): 427.

60. Even some of the theory's proponents suggested the explanation was limited to America: See R. Stephen Warner, "Work in Progress Towards a New Paradigm for the Sociological Study of Religion in the United States," *American Journal of Sociology* 98 (1993): 1044.

61. Anthony Gill, *Rendering Unto Caesar: The Catholic Church and the State in Latin America* (Chicago: University of Chicago Press, 1994).

62. R. Andrew Chesnut, *Competitive Spirits: Latin America's New Religious Economy* (Oxford, UK: Oxford University Press, 2003).

63. Although sources vary on the number of evangelicals in Latin American countries, all show a rapid increase. For a more detailed report on the religious demography of Guatemala, Chile, and Brazil, download the Pew Forum's report "Spirit and Power: A 10 Country Survey of Pentecostals." http://pewforum.org/surveys/pentecostal/.

64. Anthony Gill, *Rendering Unto Caesar: The Catholic Church and the State in Latin America* (Chicago: University of Chicago Press, 1994).

65. For a detailed report on the religious demography of Brazil and 9 other countries, download the Pew Forum's report "Spirit and Power: A 10 Country Survey of Pentecostals." http://pewforum.org/surveys/pentecostal/.

66. H. Neill McFarland, *The Rush Hour of the Gods: A Study of New Religious Movements in Japan* (New York: Macmillan, 1967); Helen Hardacre, *Shinto and the State, 1868–1988* (Princeton, NJ: Princeton University Press, 1989).

67. Tsuyoshi Nakano, "The American Occupation and Reform of Japan's Religious System: A Few Notes on the Secularization Process in Postwar Japan," *The Journal of Oriental Studies* 26 (1987): 124.

68. H. Neill McFarland, *The Rush Hour of the Gods: A Study of New Religious Movements in Japan* (New York: Macmillan, 1967), 4.

69. Tsuyoshi Nakano, "The American Occupation and Reform of Japan's Religious System: A Few Notes on the Secularization Process in Postwar Japan," *The Journal of Oriental Studies* 26 (1987): 124.

70. The Government-General of Korea reported 67 new religions in 1945; by 1982 the Cultural Research Centre reported 303. A portion of this growth resulted from the missionary efforts of western nations, but the most substantial growth came from indigenous Protestant groups and the sects splitting off from the missionary churches. See Syn-Duk Choi, "A Comparative Study of Two New Religious Movements in the Republic of Korea." in *New Religious Movements and Rapid Social Change*, ed. James A. Beckford (Beverly Hills, CA: Sage, 1986).

71. Yunfeng Lu, *Religious Economy and Chinese Sects* (Lanham, MD: Lexington Books, 2008).

72. Paul Froese, "Hungary for Religion: Supply-side Interpretation of the Hungarian Religious Revival," *Journal for the Scientific Study of Religion* 40 (2001): 251; Paul Froese.

"After Atheism: Religious Monopolies in the Post-Communist World," *Sociology of Religion* 65 (2004): 57.

73. Allen D. Hertzke, *Freeing God's Children: The Unlikely Alliance for Global Human Right* (Lanham, MD: Rowman & Littlefield, 2004), 69.

74. See Article 18 and Article 2 of the United Nations' *Universal Declaration of Human Rights* (adopted December 10, 1948).

75. The data collection was supervised by Brian J. Grim and completed by Jaime Harris, Catherine Meyers, Julie VanEerden, and Daniel McKendrick. To view the data online, go the "National Profiles" of the Association of Religion Data Archives (ARDA): www.theARDA.com. Data files for this complete collection can also be downloaded from the ARDA: http://www.thearda.com/Archive/CrossNational.asp.

76. Brian J. Grim and Roger Finke, "International Religion Indexes: Government Regulation, Government Favoritism, and Social Regulation of Religion," *Interdisciplinary Journal of Research on Religion,* 2 (2006) Article 1: www.religjournal.com (2006).

77. Brian J. Grim and Roger Finke, "Religious Persecution in Cross-National Context: Clashing Civilizations or Regulated Religious Economies?" *American Sociological Review* 72 (2007): 633.

78. We rely most heavily on peer reviewed research, the *International Religious Freedom Reports,* and UN reports. But there are many advocacy groups (e.g., Forum 18, Voice of the Martyrs, Open Doors, and Christian Persecution) that provide information on the religious freedoms denied and multiple minority religions (e.g., Ahmadiyya Muslims, Baháís, and Jehovah's Witnesses) that offer detailed descriptions of the restrictions they face.

79. Jahangir, Asma, "2007 Report of the Special Rapporteur on freedom of religion or belief." United Nations' Human Rights Council, Fourth Session, Item 2. http://www.ohchr.org/english/issues/religion/annual.htm (2007), 16.

80. She also noted that Egypt, Eritrea, Kyrgyzstan, Turkmenistan, and Uzbekistan failed to offer a requested invitation in 2006. The 2007 report included Cuba, Ethiopia, India, Lao People's Democratic Republic, Malaysia, Mauritania, Pakistan, Saudi Arabia, Serbia and Montenegro, and Yemen as not responding to her requests for an invitation. See Jahangir, Asma. "2006 Report of the Special Rapporteur on freedom of religion or belief." United Nations' Commission on Human Rights, 62nd session, Item 11. http://www.ohchr.org/english/issues/religion/annual.htm (2006), 9.

81. Brian J. Grim and I are now completing a book tentatively titled *The Price of Freedoms Denied: The Social Consequences of Regulating Religion.*

82. For an example of recent research in this area, see: Jonathan Fox, *A World Survey of Religion and the State* (Cambridge, UK: Cambridge University Press, 2008); Forum 18 (http://www.forum18.org/) is one of many organizations documenting the restrictions faced by religious minorities.

83. For an early example, see: R. Laurence Moore, *Religious Outsiders and the Making of Americans* (New York: Oxford University Press, 1986).

84. For specific examples see: Jay P. Dolan, *The American Catholic Experience: A History From Colonial Times to the Present* (Garden City, NY: Image Books, 1985); R. Stephen Warner, "The Place of the Congregation in the Contemporary American Religious Configuration," in *American Congregations,* eds. James P. Wind and James W. Lewis, *vol. 2* (Chicago: University of Chicago Press, 1994); Helen Rose Ebaugh and Janet Saltzman Chafetz, *Religion and the New Immigrants: Continuities and Adaptations in Immigrant Congregations* (Walnut Creek, CA: AltaMira Press, 2000); Fenggang Yang and Helen Rose Ebaugh, "Transformation in new Immigrant Religions and Their Global

Implications," *American Sociological Review* 66 (2001): 269.

85. C. Eric Lincoln and Lawrence H. Mamiya, *The Black Church in the African American Experience* (Durham, NC: Duke University Press, 1990).

86. Even the famous German theologian and historian Ernst Troeltsch, who held that the religious teachings of sects were "primitive," "naive," "non-reflective," and could only appeal to the lower classes, freely acknowledged that sects "do the really creative work, forming communities on a genuine religious basis" and that they provided the foundation for all great religious movements. See Ernst Troeltsch, *The Social Teaching of the Christian Churches,* 2 Vols. (New York: Macmillan, [1911] 1931).

87. Supporting the principle of religious free exercise is far easier when minority religious groups, often zealous about their faith, are not living next door.

88. To view tables and a press release on the surveys, go to the First Amendment Center: http://www.firstamendmentcenter.org/news.aspx?Ibid=19031. To download the surveys or to view the complete survey instrument, go to the Association of Religion Data Archives: http://www.thearda.com/.

BIBLIOGRAPHY

Books

Baird, Robert. *Religion in America; or, An Account of the Origin, Progress, Relation to the State, and Present Condition of the Evangelical Churches in the United States. With Notices of the Unevangelical Denominations.* Glasgow: Blackie and Co., 1844.

Beckford, James A. *Cult Controversies: The Societal Response to New Religious Movements.* London: Tavistock Publications, 1985.

Cartwright, Peter. *Autobiography of Peter Cartwright, The Backwoods Preacher,* W.P. Strickland, ed. Cincinnati, OH: Cranston and Curts, 1856.

Chesnut, R. Andrew. *Competitive Spirits: Latin America's New Religious Economy.* Oxford, UK: Oxford University Press, 2003.

Currie, Robert, Alan Gilbert, and Lee Horsley. *Churches and Churchgoers: Patterns of Church Growth in the British Isles Since 1700.* Oxford, UK: Clarendon Press, 1977.

Dolan, Jay P. *Catholic Revivalism: The American Experience, 1830–1900.* Notre Dame: University of Notre Dame Press, 1978.

Dolan, Jay P. *The American Catholic Experience: A History from Colonial Times to the Present.* Garden City, NY: Image Books, 1985.

Ebaugh, Helen Rose and Janet Saltzman Chafetz. *Religion and the New Immigrants: Continuities and Adaptations in Immigrant Congregations* (Walnut Creek, CA: AltaMira Press, 2000).

Finke, Roger and Rodney Stark. *The Churching of America, 1776–1990.* New Brunswick, NJ: Rutgers University Press, 1992).

Fox, Jonathan. *A World Survey of Religion and the State.* Cambridge, UK: Cambridge University Press, 2008.

Gill, Anthony. *Rendering Unto Caesar: The Catholic Church and the State in Latin America.* Chicago: University of Chicago Press, 1994.

Gill, Anthony. *The Political Origins of Religious Liberty.* New York: Cambridge University Press, 2008.

Grim, Brian J. and Roger Finke. *The Price of Freedom Denied: Religious Persecution and Violence.* New York: Cambridge University Press, 2010.

Hardacre, Helen. *Shinto and the State, 1868–1988.* Princeton, NJ: Princeton University Press, 1989.

Hatch, Nathan O. *The Democratization of American Christianity.* New Haven, CT: Yale University Press, 1989.

Hempton, David. *Methodism and Politics in British Society, 1750–1850.* Stanford, CT: Stanford University Press, 1984.

Hertzke, Allen D. *Freeing God's Children: The Unlikely Alliance for Global Human Right,* (Lanham, MD: Rowman & Littlefield, 2004).

Jelen, Ted G. and Clyde Wilcox. *Public Attitudes Toward Church and State.* Armonk, NY: M.E. Sharpe, 1995.

Lambert, Frank. *The Founding Fathers and the Place of Religion in America* (Princeton, NJ: Princeton University Press, 2003).

Lambert, Frank. "Pedlar in Divinity": George Whitefield and the Transatlantic Revivals, 1737–1770 (Princeton, NJ: Princeton University Press, 1994).

Lincoln, C. Eric and Lawrence H. Mamiya. *The Black Church in the African American Experience* (Durham, NC: Duke University Press, 1990).

Lu, Yunfeng. *Religious Economy and Chinese Sects* (Lanham, MD: Lexington Books, 2008).

McFarland, H. Neill. *The Rush Hour of the Gods: A Study of New Religious Movements in Japan* (New York, NY: Macmillan, 1967).

McLoughlin, William G. *New England Dissent, 1630–1833,* 2 Vols. (Cambridge, UK: Harvard University Press, 1971).

McLoughlin, William G. *Revivals, Awakenings, and Reform* (Chicago: The University of Chicago Press, 1978).

Mead, Sidney E. *The Lively Experiment: The Shaping of Christianity in America* (New York: Harper & Row, 1976 [1963]).

Minutes of the Annual Conferences of the Methodist Episcopal Church, 1773–1828 (New York: T. Mason and G. Lane, 1840).

Moore, R. Laurence. *Religious Outsiders and the Making of Americans* (New York: Oxford University Press, 1986).

Reed, Andrew and James Matheson. *A Narrative of the Visit to the American Churches,* Vol. II. (London: Jackson and Walford, 1835).

Richardson, James T., ed. *Regulating Religion: Case Studies from Around the Globe* (New York: Kluwer Academic/Plenum Publishers, 2004).

Schaff, Philip. *America: A Sketch of Its Political, Social, and Religious Character.* (Cambridge: The Belknap Press, 1855).

Scheitle, Christopher P. *Beyond the Congregation: Christian Nonprofits in the United States* (New York: Oxford University Press, 2010).

Stark, Rodney and Roger Finke. *Acts of Faith: Explaining the Human Side of Religion* (Berkeley, CA: University of California Press, 2000).

Stark, Rodney and William Sims Bainbridge. *The Future of Religion: Secularization, Revival, and Cult Formation* (Berkeley, CA: University of California Press, 1985).

The Testimony of the President, Professors, Tutors and Hebrew Instructor of Harvard College in Cambridge, against the Reverend Mr. George Whitefield and His Conduct (Boston, N.E.: T. Fleet, 1744).

The Testimony of an Association of Ministers Convened at Marlborough, January 22, 1744, against the Reverend George Whitefield and His Conduct (Boston, N.E.: T. Fleet, 1745).

The Testimony of a Number of Ministers in the County of Bristol against Mr. Whitefield (Boston, N.E.: T. Fleet, 1745).

Tocqueville, Alexis de. *Democracy in America* (New York: Vintage Books, 1945 [1835]).

Troeltsch, Ernst. *The Social Teaching of the Christian Churches,* 2 Vols. (New York: Macmillan, [1911] 1931).

Tweed, Thomas A. *Retelling U.S. Religious History* (Berkeley, CA: University of California Press, 1997).

Wigger, John H. *Taking Heaven by Storm: Methodism and the Rise of Popular Christianity in America* (Urbana, IL: University of Illinois Press, 1998).

Wilson, John F., ed. *Church and State in American History* (Boston: D.C. Heath and Company, 1965).

Wyneken, Friedrich Conrad Dietrich. *The Distress of the German Lutherans in North America,* translated by S. Edgar Schmidt and edited by R.F. Rehmer (Fort Wayne, IN: Concordia Theological Seminary Press, [1843] 1982).

Articles/Chapters

Adamczyk, Amy, John Wybraniec, and Roger Finke. "Religious Regulation and the Courts: Documenting the Effects of *Smith* and RFRA," *Journal of Church and State* 46 (2004): 237.

Choi, Syn-Duk. "A Comparative Study of Two New Religious Movements in the Republic of Korea." in *New Religious Movements and Rapid Social Change*, eds. James A. Beckford (Beverly Hills, CA: Sage, 1986).

Drinan, Robert F. "Reflections on the Demise of the Religious Freedom Restoration Act," 89 *Georgetwon Law Journal* (1997): 101.

Finke, Roger. "Religious Deregulation: Origins and Consequences" *Journal of Church and State* 32 (1990): 609.

Finke, Roger. "Supply-side Explanations for Religious Change," In Lawrence A. Young, *Rational Choice Theory and Religion: Summary and Assessment* (1997).

Finke, Roger. "Innovative Returns to Tradition: Using Core Beliefs as the Foundation for Innovative Accommodation." *Journal for the Scientific Study of Religion* 43 (2004): 19.

Finke, Roger and Laurence R. Iannaccone. "Supply-Side Explanations for Religious Change," *The Annals of the American Academy of Political and Social Science* 527 (1993): 27.

Finke, Roger and Rodney Stark. "Turning Pews into People: Estimating Nineteenth Century Church Membership," *Journal for the Scientific Study of Religion* 25 (1986): 180.

Froese, Paul. "Hungary for Religion: Supply-side Interpretation of the Hungarian Religious Revival," *Journal for the Scientific Study of Religion* 40 (2001): 251.

Froese, Paul. "After Atheism: Religious Monopolies in the Post-Communist World," *Sociology of Religion* 65 (2004): 57.

Grim, Brian J. and Roger Finke. "International Religion Indexes: Government Regulation, Government Favoritism, and Social Regulation of Religion," *Interdisciplinary Journal of Research on Religion,* 2 (2006) Article 1: www.religjournal.com (2006).

Grim, Brian J. and Roger Finke. "Religious Persecution in Cross-National Context: Clashing Civilizations or Regulated Religious Economies?" *American Sociological Review* 72 (2007): 633.

Grund, Francis. *The Americans in Their Moral, Social, and Political Relations* (1837) as excerpted in Milton B. Powell, ed., *The Voluntary Church: Religious Life, 1740–1860, Seen Through the Eyes of European Visitors* (New York: Macmillan, 1967).

Hempton, David. "Methodism and the Law, 1740–1820," in *Sects and New Religious Movements*, A. Dyson and E. Barker (eds.), *Bulletin of the John Rylands Library* 70 (1988): 94.

Iannaccone, Laurence, Roger Finke, and Rodney Stark. "Deregulating Religion," *Economic Inquiry* 35 (1997): 350.

Jahangir, Asma. "2006 Report of the Special Rapporteur on freedom of religion or belief." United Nations' Commission on Human Rights, 62nd session, Item 11. http://www.ohchr.org/english/issues/religion/annual.htm (2006), 9.

Jahangir, Asma. "2007 Report of the Special Rapporteur on freedom of religion or belief." United Nations' Human Rights Council, Fourth Session, Item 2. http://www.ohchr.org/english/issues/religion/annual.htm (2007), 16.

Lambert, Frank. "Pedlar in Divinity': George Whitefield and the Great Awakening, 1737–1745," *Journal of American History* 77 (1990): 812.

Lupu, Ira C., "The Failure of RFRA," *University of Arkansas Little Rock Law Journal* 20 (1998): 589.

McConnell, Michael W. "Free Exercise Revisionism and the Smith Decision," *Chicago Law Review* 57 (1990): 1109.

McConnell, Michael W. and Richard A. Posner. "An Economic Approach to Issues of Religious Freedom," 56 *Chicago Law Review* 1 (1989): 14.

Mead, Sidney E., "From Coercion to Persuasion: Another Look at the Rise of Religious Liberty and the Emergence of Denominationalism," *Church History* 25 (1956): 317.

Miller, Perry G. "The Contribution of the Protestant Churches to Religious Liberty in Colonial America," *Church History* 4 (1935): 57.

Nakano, Tsuyoshi. "The American Occupation and Reform of Japan's Religious System: A Few Notes on the Secularization Process in Postwar Japan," *The Journal of Oriental Studies* 26 (1987): 124.

Robbins, Thomas and James A. Beckford. "Religious Movements and Church-State Issues," in *Handbook of Cults and Sects,* eds. David Bromley and Jeffrey Hadden (Greenwich, CT: JAI Press, 1993).

Ryan, James E. "Smith and the Religious Freedom Restoration Act: An Iconoclastic Assessment," *Virginia Law Review* 78 (1992): 1417.

Stark, Rodney and Roger Finke. "American Religion in 1776: A Statistical Portrait," *Sociological Analysis* 49 (1988): 39.

Stark, Rodney and Laurence Iannaccone. "A Supply-Side Reinterpretation of the 'Secularization' of Europe,'" *Journal for the Scientific Study of Religion* 33 (1994): 230.

Warner, R. Stephen. "Work in Progress Toward a New Paradigm for the Sociological Study of Religion in the United States," *American Journal of Sociology* 98 (1993): 1044.

Warner, R. Stephen. "The Place of the Congregation in the Contemporary American Religious Configuration." In *American Congregations,* eds. James P. Wind and James W. Lewis. *Vol.* 2 (Chicago: University of Chicago Press, 1994).

Way, Frank and Barbara J. Burt. "Religious Marginality and the Free Exercise Clause." *American Political Science Review* 77 (1983): 652.

Wybraniec, John and Roger Finke. "Religious Regulation and the Courts: The Judiciary's Changing Role in Protecting Minority Religions from Majoritarian Rule," *Journal for the Scientific Study of Religion* 40 (2001): 427.

Yang, Fenggang and Helen Rose Ebaugh, "Transformation in new Immigrant Religions and Their Global Implications," *American Sociological Review* 66 (2001): 269.

CHAPTER 18

PEEKING THROUGH JEFFERSON'S RELOCATED WALL: A SOCIOLOGICAL ASSESSMENT OF U.S. CHURCH–STATE RELATIONS

N.J. DEMERATH III

GOVERNMENTS are like patients who benefit from periodic check-ups, especially as they approach geriatric status. Every now and then it is worth assessing the relationship between what a state apparatus *should be* according to its founding and sustaining ideals, what a state apparatus *has come to be* as reflected in its recent and current practices, and what *it is likely to be* in the future. Of course, where religion is concerned, the primary document is the first sentence of the U.S. Constitution's First Amendment, "Congress shall make no law respecting an establishment of religion, or prohibiting the free exercise thereof," which most readers of this volume can now recite blindfolded. As Samuel Huntington demonstrated some time ago,[1] American history follows a series of struggles between our ideas and our institutional realities. Although the church–state area was not one of his featured examples, it might well have been. Here, as elsewhere, the sentiments are noble, but there is increasing concern that day-to-day policies on the ground do not always measure up to the lofty constitutional principles that float above them. Moreover, it is conceivable that the problems are growing worse rather than better because of developments within the government and within the country at large.

But first a confession: I am not a lawyer, legal historian, or political scientist. Instead, among my many sins, I am a sociologist who specializes in religion and politics at home and abroad. Perhaps understandably, my approach to the First Amendment differs somewhat from those in other disciplines, and although many of the facts that follow will be familiar, the frames surrounding them may be less so. This chapter begins by placing the U.S. "experiment" in global perspective. It goes on to assess our own church–state relations under four rubrics: first, issues of establishment vs. free exercise; second, cultural vs. structural exceptions; third, separation in politics vs. the state; and fourth, politics within the state. It concludes by describing recent developments concerning the definition of religion that may change the character of future American church–state relations.

Religion and the State in Global Perspective

Mention "American religion" around the world to scholars and school children alike and the response is likely to involve one or both of two seemingly inconsistent mantras. On the one hand, for many the United States quickly calls to mind religious freedom and the religious veneration of the state often referred to as "civil religion."[2] On the other hand, the United States is sometimes reflexively known for its "separation of church and state" and the way religion and the government are kept at arm's length.

There is truth in both stereotypes when the United States is compared with other countries.[3] Surveys of developed countries from Europe to Asia show that the United States consistently ranks at the top in religious participation and belief,[4] although there are also factors that exaggerate America's high level of religiosity. For example, recent studies reveal inflated respondent recollections of church attendance the previous Sunday that may account for as much as one half of the generally accepted weekly attendance rates of 40% or more in the United States;[5] other religions put much less emphasis on such quantifiable participation, and surveyers of religious belief know how much results depend on question wording and the faith tradition at issue.[6]

However, insofar as religious "free exercise" may be measured by the absence of government involvement and interference in religion, recent cross-national studies using extensive measures show the United States consistently at the top of the freedom scale. Consider, for example, Jonathan Fox's summary of the results from his extensive data set compiled for some 175 governments: "149 of 175 states (85.1%) either support some religions over others, place restrictions on some religions that are not placed on others, or both. . . ."[7] However, although other countries share at least the constitutional ideal of religious free exercise with the United States, the United States is especially distinctive regarding the nonestablishment of religion. It is even absent in the United Nation's 1948 Universal Declaration of Human Rights Charter, in which Article 18 is eloquent on the freedom of religion for individuals, but mute on anything akin to an antiestablishment provision. Again Fox's data for his 175 nations are pertinent:

> Of the 148 states for which there is sufficient information on the content of their constitutions, 133 promise some form of freedom of worship, 92 promise no discrimination on the basis of religion or equality for all religions, and 52 declare the state secular or prohibit the establishment of religion. Yet, all but 44 of the 175 states . . . engage in at least some religious discrimination and *all but one* enact at least some religious legislation.[8] (italics added)

Not surprisingly, that "one" is the United States.[9] As such global comparisons indicate, constitutional pledges of religious freedom are one thing, governmental implementation of such pledges is quite another, and the absence of some form of religious establishment is something yet again.[10]

This point is made especially clear for other societies around the world where religious violence is common and the phrase "culture war" is a tragic reality, as opposed to the inflamed rhetoric it generally amounts to in the United States notwithstanding the alarms sounded by a few scholarly Cassandras.[11] Of course, the degree to which a culture war exists anywhere is a variable, not an absolute. There is little question that culture conflict has recently increased in the United States, owing in large part to disputes between the religious right and the religious (and nonreligious) left, and the way political activists and movement entrepreneurs have poured kerosene rather than water on the sparks that have emerged. Nevertheless, as shown, for example, by my recent cross-national comparative research in some 14 societies around the world,[12] religion has been a bone of contention in one way or another in every one in which sustained violence has been chronic or endemic, including China, Egypt, Guatemala, India, Indonesia, Israel, Northern Ireland, Pakistan, Thailand, or Guatemala. Moreover, in every case in which religion has been a source of major political conflict and societal violence, the one shared characteristic is religion's actual or potential involvement in the contest over state power and government control.

In some countries this contest involves a conflict between two major faith traditions, such as Hinduism versus Islam in India or Judaism versus Islam in Israel. A more common strain involves competition between two different branches of the same major tradition, such as Protestant vs. Catholic Christians in Northern Ireland, or Sunni versus Shiite Muslims in Pakistan (as well as Iraq). Still other cases may pit extremist against more moderate or secular versions of the same tradition against each other, most notably Islam in Egypt, Turkey, and Pakistan (not to mention Afghanistan). Not surprisingly, minority vs. majority religions are often in conflict where there is an official religion. However, it is worth noting that "state religions" (in which the state controls religion, as in China, Thailand, and

Turkey) are far more common than "religious states," in which religion controls the state, as is most closely approximated by Iran.[13] Again, the larger point in all of this is that when government power is up for grabs and religion is in play, conflict and violence are likely to ensue. Of course, this has become painfully clear in Afghanistan and Iraq, both of whose recent constitutions give a nod to religious freedom, but understandably duck the issue of religious establishment as officially Islamic nations.

The relationship between religion and politics may be likened to the frequently fatal flight of a moth around a flame. The image works both ways. Religious moths often see the political flame as the point around which their moral and ethical preaching can be realized; political moths frequently see the religious flame as providing the sort of legitimacy that every politician craves. Alas, in each case there is the risk of flying too close to the flame, as evidenced by religious moths such as Martin Luther King, Jr., Malcolm X, and very nearly Pope John Paul II, plus political leaders such as Mahatma Gandhi, the unrelated Indira Gandhi, and her son Rajiv in India, as well as Egypt's Sadat and Israel's Rabin, to name only a few.

Four Common Sources of Misinterpretation and Misbehavior in the First Amendment

Since the U.S. Constitution's First Amendment was adopted in 1791, its religion clauses have been given prominence by a nation of willing believers, a battalion of legal specialists,[14] and a militia of authors who place the amendment in the broader warp of the founders' politics and philosophy.[15] Nor have these interpretive communities always agreed. The general populace has often either ignored or distorted the conclusions of experts. For example, in a survey of residents in Springfield, Massachusetts, 84% agreed that "The separation of church and state is a good idea," although only 37% agreed strongly, and some 29% only agreed "somewhat" or actually disagreed to some extent. Moreover, when asked whether they agreed or disagreed with 11 well-known court decisions in the area, on average 35% disagreed with the court decisions and another 20% answered "not sure."[16]

Overall, however, Americans are proud of their constitutional heritage, and many have treated the amendment and Mr. Jefferson's wall as both more unique and more impregnable than the facts warrant. Although many of the obstreperous facts are widely known to those who peer over, around, or through the wall, it is worth beginning with four basic areas in which colloquial interpretations and quotidian implementations have been wanting.

ESTABLISHMENT EXCEPTIONALISM

As noted, constitutionally provided religious freedom is the most commonly applauded attribute of American religion around the world and at home by citizens and scholars alike.[17] And yet the "Free Exercise Clause" actually follows the "Establishment Clause" in calling for what most people consider "religious freedom." The ordering may not have been intended to suggest their relative importance at the time, but it has become prescient in the years since. Those who summarize the First Amendment solely or even primarily in terms of its Free Exercise Clause do a gross injustice to the amendment's more "exceptional" and arguably most important prohibition of religious establishments.

In all of this, it is hard to know what was originally intended. For example, although the records of the founders' debates over the First Amendment are at best incomplete, it is at least plausible that the Establishment Clause meant something very different at its founding than it does now.[18] The founders knew that the new federal ship of state could founder on the shoals of states' rights regarding either slavery or religious establishment, and they were determined to steer clear of both. All but four of the original 13 colonies had established religions at the time of the revolution, and although four more disestablished religion during the late 1770s mid 1780s, quasi-establishments continued in Anglican Maryland and South Carolina, and official Congregationalism continued to prevail in powerful Connecticut, Massachusetts, New Hampshire, and Vermont. By the time of the First Congress in 1789, it was clear that any attempt to federally disestablish state religions would produce major opposition.[19]

Read in this context, the phrase "Congress shall enact no law respecting an establishment of religion" makes very different sense today. However, the phrase was also amenable to a slight change in interpretation that allayed another major concern at the time; namely, protecting the fledgling federal government from religious control and insuring that bullying religious majorities could not use new federal power to make life difficult for religious minorities. Because this is precisely what a slightly different reading of the clause would have prevented,[20] it was this latter interpretation that prevailed, especially after Massachusetts became the last state to undergo religious disestablishment in 1833.

Over time and over the recumbent bodies of any number of strict constitutional "originalists" (as opposed to the more historically adaptive "separationists" and the more religiously inclined "accommodationists"), the Establishment Clause has become the most distinctive part of our First Amendment—one that is still rare in other nations around the globe. Once the clause was extended from the federal government to the states in 1947,[21] it became the key to some of America's most important church–state litigation of the last half-century. Here the complaining plaintiffs have not been those seeking freedom *for* religion but those seeking freedom *from* religion and their concern to limit state religious endorsement or state-supported religious practices in public venues. These include several cases barring the display of the Ten Commandments in public schoolrooms and in courthouses,[22] and banning featured Christmas crèches on government property such as municipal squares.[23]

The most controversial U.S. Supreme Court cases have involved the ban on public school prayer and religious observances in *Engel v. Vitale* in 1962 and *Abington Township School District v. Schempp* in 1963. These decisions have been sustained in numerous court decisions since; for example, in *Wallace v. Jaffree* (1985) the Supreme Court rejected a "moment of silence" on the grounds that its primary intent was not secular but rather religiously based silent prayer. Despite these school religion decisions, a study of parent and teacher estimates of school religious observances make it at least plausible that as many of one fourth of the nation's public classrooms continue to engage in some form of silent or spoken prayer.[24] This is a reminder that courts have no monitoring system of their own and little power over violations, which are, after all, generally treated as civil rather than criminal matters.

Meanwhile, a second controversial area involves the 1973 *Roe v. Wade* decision allowing abortion up through the second trimester of a pregnancy. Contrary to popular lore, religion was not the reason given for this Supreme Court decision. It was based primarily on the Fourteenth Amendment's guarantee of individual privacy. However, religiously motivated groups such as the "Pro-Life Movement" have nevertheless made abortions difficult for many to obtain.

Clearly the definition of an offending religious establishment has evolved.[25] The establishment threat comes not just from large denominations preying on small religious groups, but from perceived state support for the idea of religion in general as opposed to nonreligion. It was President Dwight Eisenhower who allegedly defined the limits of American religious tolerance when he said he didn't care which God a citizen believed in as long as he had one. If translated into actual policy, this would have been an establishment violation because it amounted to a state official supporting religion in general. However, one can also imagine establishment violations that involve the opposite, that is, government endorsement of or support for nonreligion. Indeed, religious protagonists have sometimes conjured up an image of "secular humanism," as if to refer to a codified body of beliefs and a formal organization devoted to irreligion, neither of which exists. Nevertheless, government departures from neutrality on either side of the religious fence have been judged rightly as constitutionally offensive.

However, there are some accepted exceptions. Matters concerning the free exercise of religion often have explicit or implicit contingencies concerning the national or civic interest. In the United States, there are well-established precedents for denying free exercise to practices that endanger the health and welfare of innocent victims, including the children of Christian Scientists, who are protected from their parents' decisions to withhold critical medical care. There are also precedents for allowing church–state relationships that might otherwise suggest an "establishment." Basically, religious organizations may receive government funds to operate day care centers, hospitals, relief programs, etc. as long as both the intent and the consequences are secular. As the government's social missions have expanded, churches and other religious organizations are often indispensable allies in service provision. This has resulted in not a few winks and nudges over relationships that satisfy the needs of both church and state. For example, Bruce Nichols' excellent book on church–state relations concerning refugee and relief services abroad was almost guaranteed not to sell well because neither the churches who benefited from the funding nor the government that provided it were anxious to promote the book and its evidence that, in many cases, the supplies were distributed with proselytizing zeal and religious conditions attached.[26]

In fact, there has always been an uneasy relation between the "establishment" and "free exercise" clauses. From a strict legal standpoint, the first decision to be made concerning any potential church–state case is often which of the two clauses is most pertinent, because arguments from the two perspectives can be the converse of each other. One can imagine the ultimate church–state case in which each clause is charged with violating the other. Such a case has never actually materialized, but it is not hard to hypothesize. As we shall see later, a state guarantee of religious free exercise may itself be an establishment violation by singling out religion for special standing and special dispensations compared with the free exercise of other possible sacred beliefs and commitments. On the other hand, placing limits on any religion's effort to become the nation's established faith may be seen as an unconstitutional constraint on the religion's free exercise. If a religious denomination is strong enough to marshal control over a governmental unit, is it not a denial of its religious rights to set limits on this control?

Not long ago a prominent attorney who is periodically mentioned as a possible Supreme Court nominee was asked in an informal after-dinner gathering what would happen if, say, the Mormons grew to such an extent that they were able to attain a majority of Congress and then wanted to make the nation officially Mormon. "Well," he said, "This is a democracy after all, and the majority rules." We would hope, however, that this principle would not be true for the judicial branch. This is where the Constitution prevails, minorities are protected, and the Supreme Court trumps the Congress—at least in principle.

Cultural versus Structural Separation

In large part because of the heralded "separation of church and state," the American nation might seem a bastion of secularism. After all, any nation that keeps religion separate from its government must be one in which religion has little influence to begin with. Moreover, should not a secular state necessarily lead to a secular society? Of course, both assumptions are off the mark. The reality is that religion has thrived in the United States, and in large part because of its separation from the state, rather than in spite of it. Lacking any one established religion, all religions may compete and thrive on a level playing field.[27] The rise of different denominations and the competition among them became a defining quality of American Protestantism and American pluralism.[28]

However, another resolution of the American religious paradox involves a concept discussed earlier; namely, its "civil religion" as a form of national faith—and faith in the nation—that is anchored in the common denominator of the country's Judeo-Christian heritage.[29] It is true that some scholarly observers follow Robert Wuthnow[30] in detecting two civil religions—one liberal and another conservative—although this would seem to contradict the unifying essence of having only one civil religion. Others have suggested that a secularized version of civil religion is rising whereby what is civil becomes religious rather than vice versa.[31] Still others point to the varieties of civil religion and civil religious dynamics around the world, including some that are religious in name only.[32] Nevertheless, there is no question that American religion is alive and well overall. Insofar as there continues to be a conflict between a civil religion that melds the nation, and a church–state tradition of separation, some sort of accommodation would seem necessary. In fact, three possibilities emerged in a study of religion and politics in a medium-sized New England city.[33]

A *first* resolution involves a tendency to give public privileges to the religious mainstream, but not to controversial religious minorities. Thus, majoritarian prayers at public events are acceptable, whereas minority rituals are not. Prayers at the beginning of each day in the U.S. Congress (and virtually all state legislatures) are led by rotating Protestant, Catholic, and Jewish clergy, but sect and cult leaders are rarely among them. Prayers at major public events are also countenanced.

A *second* rapprochement makes separationism and civil religion mutually contingent. Thus, the country can endorse religion's separation from the state because religion is free to function elsewhere in the nation's cultural rounds, including its churches, temples, and mosques. Conversely, it is because religion flowers so luxuriantly in the society at large that separation is needed to protect the state and governance process from it. Put more pithily, having rich religious traditions, we need church–state separation; having church–state separation, we need other gardens for cultivating religion and can well afford them.

Finally, a *third* reconciliation of the conflict involves structural versus cultural interpretations of separation. Many citizens would apply the rigorous canon of church–state separation to concrete structural matters of actual state policy and its implementation, although applying far less strict controls to religion's cultural expressions. In fact, the latter category includes many of the most commonly cited breaches of a high Jeffersonian wall. These include the aforementioned prayers in Congress and state legislatures (after all, the Court reasoned, the framers of the First Amendment began their own assemblies with prayers) and such "merely" cultural practices as the various symbolic pieties adopted in the 1950s as a counter to godless communism: for example, inscribing "In God We Trust" on the nation's money and adding "one nation under God" to the Pledge of Allegiance.

Christian symbols are allowed as part of a wider display of symbols from different religions or secular icons appropriate to the holiday season (e.g., a Christian creche, Jewish Hanukkah candles, Santa, and Rudolph). Similarly, the courts have allowed the Ten Commandments on government property only when they are part of a historical and cultural display that also includes secular symbols. Prayers in public primary and secondary schools, and football games (cf. *Santa Fe v. Doe*, 2002) are prohibited because of their possible effects on impressionable young students, but they are not banned in more adult public ceremonies such as public university commencements, July Fourth festivities, presidential inaugurations, or swearing in court witnesses. Public opinion supports such cultural expressions of religion even as it rejects religion as the basis of actual state laws and regulations—whether these involve "blue law" restrictions on Sunday shopping or religious-based amendments to prohibit abortion.

Of course, there are those who even take issue with allowing the merely cultural exceptions even where they have been given judicial blessings. "Mere culture" is not as insignificant as the phrase suggests, because culture often wields power that can lead to structural outcomes. However, it takes both a thick wallet and a thick skin to file a lawsuit against culturally ensconced practices accepted by most of one's fellow citizens. In one case, the Sacramento, California physician, Michael Newdow, who filed the suit against the phrase "One Nation under God" has been subject to hate mail and threats. For the most part, the courts have honored cultural displays of religion despite plaintiff protests, and local community sentiment is generally a better guide to what is practiced than is national jurisprudence.

RELIGION AND ELECTORAL POLITICS

Over the past two decades, religion around the world has been increasingly involved in culture wars and state subversion with rising violence. Not surprisingly, there has been a corresponding increase in calls to ban religion from politics. In addition to scholarly testimony,[34] the argument has become a commonplace of media punditry and political talk shows, and it is a frequent weapon used by one political party against another that seems to be deriving too much warmth from the religious flame; and one can certainly imagine its appeal. If there is any truth to the cliché that religion and power are a potentially lethal combination, the solution seems obvious. Not surprisingly, keeping religion out of politics is a position embraced by an increasing percentage of national survey respondents. According to recent Pew polls, it rose in public support from 44% in 2004 to 52% in 2008.[35]

However, keeping religion out of politics is no more feasible than a complete "separation of church and state." It is one thing to bar religion from state hegemony and quite another to bar religion from political involvement by banning religious candidates from running for office, barring religious organizations from participating in electoral campaigns, or indeed prohibiting religious voters from voting their convictions. Although many assume both are central to the First Amendment, the single sentence refers only to "Congress," once elected, not to politics on the stump. In fact, the one religiously pertinent clause in the original Constitution of 1787 as opposed to the First Amendment of 1791 states that ". . . no religious test shall ever be required as Qualification to any office or public Trust under the United States" (Article VI). By implication, of course, the prohibition also extends to any test for *non*-religion.

The only real penalty for American religious organizations that participate in politics is a loss of tax exemption—a penalty that the Internal Revenue Service applies to all cultural institutions that would otherwise be exempt. However, the measure is rarely enforced, perhaps because this sanction itself could be construed as an infringement on free exercise, with the prospect of litigation to follow. The most prominent recent case involved the Christian Coalition under the aggressive leadership of Pentecostal leader and 1988 Republican presidential candidate, Pat Robertson, and his subsequently resigned political lieutenant, Ralph Reed. The Coalition's application for tax-exempt status moldered for some 10 years in an IRS seemingly reluctant to create martyrs to bureaucratic religious infringement. When the matter was finally decided in 1999, the Coalition's tax-exempt status was rescinded, but quietly and with more of a wrist slap than a body blow.

American politics are replete with religious candidates and office-holders of virtually every denominational stripe—clergy as well as laity, elected as well as defeated. Although there are periodic complaints that religion is not welcome in politics,[36] these charges generally refer to political mood not political rules, and they often amount to complaints that a particular type of religion has not been politically successful. It is true that over the nation's history, some denominations such as the Episcopalians have been more successful in gaining high office; but this is more a function of the denomination's higher social class and its attendant political capital than religion *per se*. It is also true that historically evangelicals, including fundamentalists and Pentecostals, have shied away from worldly politics, whereas pursuing other-worldly salvation, although this changed dramatically in 1979 with the advent of the Rev. Jerry Falwell's Moral Majority.

Certainly there is little doubt that George W. Bush used religion and his ability to relate to and mobilize religious fundamentalism as an effective political tool. Some say this began with his conversion from the bottle to the Bible, whereas others date it from his assignment to get out the evangelical vote for his father's 1988 presidential campaign. Today both the United States and the world at large seem to be teeming with fundamentalism, and Bush during his presidential term seems to have benefited particularly from its American Christian variety while castigating its Middle Eastern Muslim version. As is well known, fundamentalism originally described a return to the "fundamentals" of Protestantism in the first two decades of the twentieth century. More broadly, it connotes a form of "aggressive regression" within any faith tradition. In fact, the syndrome characterizes very few major figures on the world stage today. The best approximations of fundamentalism may not be Islamic visionaries such as Iran's Ayatollah Khoumeini, the Al Qaeda leader Osama Bin Laden, or Iraq's Shiite leader, Ayatollah Al Sistani—all of whom have pressed forward into the future of their faith at least as much as they have retreated into its past. Bush, at least during his term of office, was often portrayed as the one leader who came closest to being a fundamentalist's fundamentalist.[37]

In fact, Bush's presidential campaigns were especially brilliant in deploying religion. Nevertheless, under the guidance of Karl Rove, Bush actually went light on religion in his widely watched TV debates and his addresses to the nation at large. After all, American politicians have erred both in being not religious enough and being too religious, as evidenced by Jimmy Carter's controversial public confession of sexual lust just after his election in 1976.

Bush was particularly deft in juggling two basic constituencies. The *first* involved many working-class and lower-middle-class evangelicals, whom he miraculously persuaded to set aside their economic woes in favor of more cultural concerns;[38] the *second* was the more traditional Republican base among corporate managers and elites—those Bush referred to affectionately as the "haves and have mores." Whereas the former could be best reached through religion, the latter cared little about faith but a great deal about tax cuts—tax cuts that came at the expense of the first group and were to be returned to the White House in the form of campaign contributions. Part of Bush's success involved the skillful use of encoded evangelical rhetoric to reach out to the religious right even when the rest of his audience was unaware of the contact. However, another part came from using new forms of retail politics and boutique campaigning to carefully selected audiences behind closed doors. This allowed him to fulfill every politician's dream of being very different things to very different voting blocs.

Yet there are some lingering misinterpretations of religion's role in Bush's victories, and for that matter, the role of these victories in changing American religion. In the immediate aftermath of his 2004 re-election, many pundits proclaimed that he won because of religion and that somewhat mystifying residual category of "moral values." In the poll most often cited to this effect, the question at issue gave Democrats a series of more compelling alternative answers that resonated with the Democratic campaign, whereas moral values were one of the few resonant choices available to Republicans. Overall, moral values ranked only third in influencing voters. The single most important factor was, in a word, war; i.e., 9/11, Bush's "war on terror," and the war in Iraq; the economy ranked second. There is little evidence that issues such as gay marriage and abortion made much of a difference. In states in which gay marriage referenda had made this a major issue, Republicans were heading for an overwhelmingly win anyway.

It is true that Bush snared the vast majority of voters who might be termed the most religious; namely, the evangelical right-wing. It is also true that Republicans made substantial inroads among traditional Catholics who had long been primarily Democratic. On the other hand, although Kerry did particularly well in 2004 among the religiously unaffiliated, he also had his own religious constituency comprising mostly mainline Protestants and liberal Catholics, not to mention the small number of Jews and other religious groups on the liberal left. Because church attendance tends to be higher among religious conservatives who voted dispropor- tionately but by no means exclusively Republican, this contributed to the misleading claims that it was basically an election in which the churchgoers beat the Sunday stay-at-homes.[39]

The Republicans lost ground in the 2008 election, however. Barack Obama won a landslide victory, largely on the strength of the younger generation of voters. The religious right crossed over to some degree to the Democratic side, but the Republican base largely voted for its nominee, John McCain. The issues that had brought victory to George Bush—abortion, homosexuality, and general "moral values"—seemed not to make much difference. The American people were fatigued by the war in Iraq and a rapidly declining economy.

As the founders understood, because both religion and politics involve com- peting moral guidelines and ethical priorities, it is only natural that the two should inform—and occasionally inflame—each other. Religious visions can become political agendas, and vice versa. Even American public opinion reflects an in- creasing grasp of the point.[41] Neither the constitution nor this analysis demands that religion *should* be involved in politics, because there are other issues to animate the political zoo. Yet when religion does press for involvement, it is far better to allow it in than to try to keep it out. Banning religious considerations and religious leaders from politics is simply unrealistic. Moreover, the attempt to do so is apt to backfire. When religion is denied a place at the political table, it is likely to create more problems—either as an outraged victim of a repressive political system or as an unmonitored force operating in the political shadows.

In short, a politics that excludes religion is no more defensible than a state that establishes religion. It is true that mixing religion and politics can lead to a kind of cultural warfare. However, this is rare except when religion's state power hangs in the political balance. A political system that generally observes the kind of religious restraints imposed by the U.S. Constitution and its First Amendment is quite dif- ferent from a politics of winner-take-all, including the right to redefine the state rather than merely play a role within it. When the latter occurs even in putative "democracies" such as Egypt, Algeria, or the Republic of Georgia, both religion and the state can be the losers.

RELIGION AND THE POLITICS OF STATECRAFT

As illustrated, it is tempting for any hard-core First Amendment devotee to draw an absolute distinction between politics and the state and insist that all elected and appointed officials transform themselves chameleon-like from politicians to states- men upon being sworn in. It is precisely at the point that an office-seeker becomes an office-holder that the First Amendment becomes a major constraint to acting on

behalf of one's religion—or irreligion. There is little doubt that the founders understood politics as a necessary process of airing competing interests and ideologies. By
contrast, the state is a structure of government within which successful politicians
serve as temporary office-holders under the rules of the Constitution and under the
sufferance of the electorate. In fact, leaving politics open to religion while keeping
the state closed involves one of the less remarked upon of the celebrated "checks
and balances" in the American constitutional system. Each practice tends to be contingent on the other, much like the relationship between separationism overall and
civil religion described earlier. Religion can be active in politics precisely because we
are protected from its state hegemony; conversely, religion need not have a position
within the state because it can air its positions politically. Religious advocates on
every side of an issue should be welcome participants in the political contest; but
the state's primary obligation is to insure that the rules of the contest are fair to
everyone.

However, it is clear that politics finds its way into the state and into government
operations beyond the hustings. Even when matters of actual state policy are not
involved, government is a stage for political office-holders with a perpetual eye on
the problematics of political support and re-election.[42] Here too George W. Bush
provides a case in point because he is the most recent presidential example, not
necessarily the most flagrant.[43]

At one level, every decision made by a political office-holder is political.
Following an election, the victor's first task is to plot re-election, and this quickly
leads to a second because staffing the government is both an opportunity and a
responsibility. Although campaigning politicians often boast that they are open to
candidates from the opposing party, actually choosing them is as rare as those who
happen to be chosen. In this most political of all orgies, appointments generally
reflect political indebtedness and/or the need for political axe-wielders and spear
throwers, and in some administrations religion is a prime criterion. The Justice
Department during Bush's first term represents a clear example, where the new
administration's ties to the religious right were manifest in the uncommon number
of young lawyers from evangelical law schools who were brought in by the Pentecostal Attorney General, John Ashcroft. Also, although religion *per se* was not an
obvious standard for Supreme Court nominees, there was little doubt that Chief
Justice John Roberts and Associate Justice Samuel Alito were selected to concur
with religiously informed positions on matters such as abortion.

Bush also used his "bully pulpit" to preach conservative religious positions on
a wide variety of religiously infected issues, although in most cases, he and his staff
showed enough political savvy to avoid major entanglements. For example, because
Americans little know nor care about pregnancies abroad, he won plaudits from
those who favor a foreign policy that supports only sexual abstinence as opposed to
contraception or abortions without risking wide alienation on the part of those
who disagree.

Because Bush adopted the fall-back position of favoring civil unions, his
opposition to gay marriage was not as risky as it might have been despite his strong

affirmation of the 1996 "Defense of Marriage Act," which defined marriage as "only a legal union between one man and one woman as husband and wife" and his support for a Federal Marriage Amendment (Marriage Protection Amendment) to the Constitution. In fact, marriage was originally a religious concept and the term appears nowhere in the Constitution. If any amendment on this issue has merit, it would be one that strips the religious term and conception of "marriage" from all government statutes in favor of "civil unions." Thus, all couples—gay, straight, or otherwise—would be eligible to form and benefit from civil unions—and only civil unions—through government enactment at any level—federal, state, or local. Beyond such civil unions, marriages may be secured as the private sacred embellishment of a couple's choice, religious or otherwise.

Finally, consider the Bush administration's funding of "faith-based initiatives" in the nation's churches as a response to social problems. Here too the president had political cover, because the program first surfaced in President Clinton's Charitable Choice program as a rider to the 1996 Welfare Reform Act that was inserted by then-Senator Ashcroft and his religious allies. What was new in 1996 and emphasized even more in Bush's proposals was a relaxation of the proviso that eligible church programs must have a secular purpose and an effort to help churches for their own sake in the process. When the legislation sputtered then stalled in Congress, the Bush White House continued full speed ahead to establish the Office of Faith-Based and Community Initiatives. According to the office's own figures, 6,652 grants were funded at a cost of $5.3 billion from 2003 to 2005, and a conservative extrapolation suggests more than 12,000 federal and state grants, for a total of some $20 billion. This may be a record for Executive branch disbursements following a failed attempt to secure Congressional approval. Obama has promised to reform Bush's faith-based initiatives project, but exactly haw that reform will take place remains uncertain.

As a growing body of research indicates,[44] there are at least three grounds on which to evaluate these faith-based initiatives: pragmatic, political, and constitutional. *Pragmatically,* very few churches have the kind of experience with major social problems that the program assumed. Moreover, just because religious congregations are located in a neighborhood, being responsive to that neighborhood is much more the exception than the rule. *Politically,* traditional black congregations are the only real bloc of churches eager to take government money for the purposes proposed. In addition to those churches already in the social service business that have little need for federal funding, there were many others that were distrustful of its terms. Ironically, in this instance a Republican ideology seemed to work against a Republican program in that many conservative churches were wary of big government looking over their shoulders and monitoring their activities. This became especially troubling when they learned that federal support could limit taking religion into account in making staff decisions, limit the degree to which religion could be a basis for client selection and retention, and limit the extent to which religious faith itself was a part of the cures offered. Not surprisingly, a *third* reason is constitutional. Because the Establishment Clause's one clear and enduring message is that the state simply cannot provide support or sponsorship for anything that is manifestly "faith-based," skeptics might be forgiven for imagining that the very phrase "faith-based initiatives" was intended as a stick in the eye of Bush's more constitutionally sensitive opponents. As noted, the courts have long approved government funding for churches that are providing non-faith services to the needy; but the insistence that religious interventions themselves be funded—and indeed promoted—by the government is a cardinal sin in the Church of the First Amendment.[45]

Another example of religious politics in the halls of state also predates George W. Bush's administration, although it too gained momentum under the Bush regime. The International Religious Freedom Act (IRFA) was passed in 1998. It was originally conceived by a liberal Jewish group eager to monitor the abuse of religions around the world and provide annual reports to the U.S. State Department for appropriate action. However, the idea was then adopted by a group of conservative Democratic Congressmen from the Bible buckle of the Southwest, who saw it as an opportunity to protect proselytizing conservative American Christian groups when they encountered problems with host governments around the globe. Although data gathered as a result of the first objective has been a boon to several scholars,[46] the pressures applied in pursuing the second objective has been a bane to several countries affected; for example, Germany, France, Russia, and India.[47]

Finally, religious organizations and their representatives are hardly innocent in infusing faith into government. Virtually every major religious body has lobbyists in Washington and many state capitals.[48] Virtually every political issue mentioned in this chapter has been subject to their efforts. But although there is nothing wrong with lobbying in its own right, there are those who feel that this form of lobbying is wrong for bringing religious politics into the workings of the state. This is not the first evidence that subverting the First Amendment can be a cooperative enterprise.

FROM THE LAKE OF RELIGION TO THE OCEAN OF THE SACRED

Most assessments of American church–state relations compare past standards with the extent to which the present has cleaved to them; certainly this chapter has done its share. However, this last section marks a departure in charting the rise and spread of a wholly new set of standards that threaten to change the entire thrust of the First Amendment. Although the changes began with a "free exercise" decision, they point toward a radical extension of the Establishment Clause that may ultimately involve nothing less than a definitional tsunami.

The seminal case was *Employment Division v. Smith* (1990), a narrow 6-3 Supreme Court ruling that allowed the state of Oregon to deny Native Americans the religious right to use illegal peyote—an illegal psychotropic plant that had long standing in their rituals. In a majority opinion written by Justice Scalia, the court held that government did not have to show a "compelling interest" to deny religious freedom that violated the law. A veritable firestorm ensued, and a broad phalanx of religious denominations and organizations pressured Congress to restore the religious freedom that had been eclipsed. The result was the Religious Freedom Restoration Act of 1993. "RFRA" reopened the door to free exercise and stipulated that "The term 'exercise of religion' means the exercise of religion under the First Amendment to the Constitution." Yet religion itself was not defined there, nor has it been defined since. In fact, the absence of a definition has left the door far more open than the First Amendment itself might have intended.

However, there is precedent for a broad conception of religion in the absence of a specific definition. During the Vietnam War, religious rights were extended to those who had no formal religious commitments but held religious-like convictions. In the two decisions of *U.S. v. Seeger* (1965) and *Welsh v. U.S.* (1970), the Supreme Court extended conscientious objector status to persons who objected to that particular war for reasons that were avowedly not religious but held beliefs that—in the words of the latter case—occupied "in the life of that individual a 'place parallel to that filled by God' in traditional religious persons." This radical allowance represented the nose of the more secular yet still sacred camel in the religious tent. Because its legal implications were so daunting, it is not surprising that the Court has seldom touched on it since;[49] but others have.

Consider two seemingly trivial examples from Massachusetts that bear on the definitional quandary. First, on December 18, 1992 two Catholic women employed at a greyhound race track announced that they were taking Christmas day off to celebrate with their families. The track fired them on the grounds that they had been told in advance that this was its busiest day of the year, their work was indispensable, and two other persons would have to be hired in their place. The two women secured a lawyer and filed for state compensation because their religious freedom had been violated. This may seem a straightforward free exercise case. However, in keeping with similar earlier employment cases in which the courts held that the track did not deny religious free exercise, but rather denied a special religious exemption and dispensation, the Massachusetts Supreme Judicial Court[50] rejected the plaintiff's case, holding that, had the state granted the women a religious day off as part of one particular faith (in this case, Catholic and Christian) compared with all other possible faiths, it would amount to a state "establishment" of that one religion. Subsequently, the case found its way into politics, and not surprisingly during an election year, the dominantly Catholic legislature took action. Mindful of the establishment problem, it passed a bill[51] guaranteeing all employees one day off annually for their own "sincerely held religious beliefs," however they might define them. This case has yet to find its way to a court decision.

A second situation involved a female clerk in a large franchise home supply store who was fired for refusing to remove a small gold ring in her eyebrow so as to comply with a new employee regulation banning any form of facial adornment. She then hired a lawyer and sued for damages because of a violation of her religious free exercise as a member of the Church of Body Modification. Although the CBM has no link to a traditional faith, no supernatural deity, and no conventional religious ritual, it does have codified sacred beliefs reinforced by shared rituals within a faith community. Both the Federal District Court and the 1st Circuit Court of Appeals made a point of granting the woman "religious" standing, although they granted the defense's request for summary judgment on other grounds.

Meanwhile, on the strength of RFRA, courts across the country received many and varied petitions requesting special dispensations justified on the basis of personal religious practices. These included prison inmates who petitioned for everything from drug use to conjugal visits as privately important religious rituals. Finally, RFRA was struck down in a 1997 case involving a Catholic Church's claim that its religious freedom carried exemption from a local zoning ordinance in a Texas community (cf. *City of Boerne v. Flores*). The decision was not based on religion, but rather on the grounds that Congress cannot arrogate to itself powers limited to the judiciary as specified by the Fourteenth Amendment. At this point, Congress tried again and passed the current law of the land in this area; namely, the Religious Land Use and Institutionalized Persons Act (RLUIPA) of 2000, including its rather vague specification that "The term 'religious exercise' includes any exercise of religion, whether or not compelled by, or central to, a system of religious belief."

This sort of definition should keep jurisprudential interpreters and second-guessers busy for decades. However, several things already seem clear. First, here is another instance in which the religion clauses of the First Amendment seem to be in conflict. If the Establishment Clause denies the courts a clear conception of religion, it is not at all clear whose and what free exercise they must grant. Second, if we have indeed been lifted from a religious lake whose shores and boundaries are well in sight and dropped into a sacred ocean of indefinite breadth and depth, the risks of drowning seem considerably increased. The relation between religion and other sacred cultural tenets, rites, and associations will surely haunt strict constructionists of either law or religion. To the extent that religion is restricted to its conventional forms (Buddhist, Catholic, Hindu, Jewish, Muslim, Protestant), this comes close to requiring an establishment of organized religion through state certification of only recognized churches, sects, and faiths.

However, some legal scholars would want to make it clear that organized religion is anything but an unalloyed good.[52] To the extent that religion is left to the definition of each individual, this involves such wide latitude as to stretch "religion" beyond the point of credibility. Even scholars who might welcome such a stretch do so on different grounds. Some might embrace a more "implicit religion";[53] others argue that the central issues all along are reducible to matters of conscience[54] or of free speech and assembly writ large rather than religion writ small.[55] Finally for

George Freeman,[56] the search for any single constitutional definition is "misguided." He lists nine possible criteria, only five of which ("belief in a supreme being," "belief in a transcendent reality," "a world view accounting for people's role in the universe," "worship," and "prayer") may cleave close enough to traditional religion to pose possible establishment violations, whereas four others are consistent with the broad sociological sense of the sacred that is at issue here ("a moral code," "sacred rituals," "a sacred text," and "membership in a social organization").

Much of what has been at work involves a broadening from the narrowly religious to the broad domain of culture. Certainly culture has its sacred claims that are not to be trivialized. A major trend in judicial separationism has involved widening the scope of what is at issue. Initially the First Amendment focused on actual churches and denominations. Gradually decisions concerning free exercise expanded to include religious beliefs and practices sometimes only loosely tied to specific institutions; for example, the right to provide religious home schooling to one's children. Then there were the aforementioned efforts to include any culturally prescribed belief or behavior that is equivalent to religion or leaves the definition of religion to the individual involved, as with conscientious objector status during the Vietnam War. Perhaps the next step will involve at least a loosely bonded but tightly bounded faith community as in the case of the Church of Body Modification. This would at least move beyond those private individual choices of convenience that have been so common among petitioners of late. All truly sacred commitments involve a sacred community of some sort, whether small or large, real or imagined, religious or otherwise. As the great French sociologist, Emile Durkheim, put it while capping his capstone work:

> What basic difference is there between Christians' celebrating the principal dates of Christ's life . . . and a citizen's meeting commemorating the advent of a new charter or some other great event of national life?. . . If today we have some difficulty imagining what the feasts and ceremonies of the future will be, it is because we are going through a period of transition and moral mediocrity. . . . But that state of uncertainty and confused anxiety cannot last forever. A day will come when our societies once again will know hours of creative effervescence during which new ideals will again spring forth and new formulas to guide humanity for a time.[57]

Free exercise adjudication has shifted from churches to religion and then to the broadly but vaguely sacred. Can the same shift be far behind for the Establishment Clause? If there is a danger that the state may become controlled or controlling on behalf of a dominant religious interest, does not the same danger exist for other cultural interests? At first blush, this may resemble extending the sublime to the ridiculous. After all, a government without a culture suggests a nation without a soul. Yet there is ample precedent for trying to keep the state separate from establishments based on gender, ethnicity, or social class. There has been a good deal of opposition mounted against a tendency for government to reflect the interests of wealthy white males. The idea is not to expunge culture from the individual consciences of state officeholders, but rather to avoid established entanglements between the state apparatus and specific cultures and interest groups, however these are defined. This is especially important in a society undergoing increased religious and cultural pluralism and greater political polarization.

CONCLUSION

This chapter has offered an unabashedly sociological account of the First Amendment's religious clauses' past, present, and future. It has pointed to problems with conceptions of how it is perceived at home and abroad, where it stands in comparison with similar documents and practices in other countries, what it intended, how it has been implemented, and where it is heading. Although there is no question that the First Amendment ranks as one of the great constitutional triumphs of world history, questions remain concerning the gap between its rhetoric and its still evolving reality. Although both its *establishment* and *free exercise* clauses deserve great respect, the former is the real feather in the United States' cap, and the real reason why we are not all wearing helmets.

The chapter's nonexhaustive list of the amendment's various misinterpretations, conflicts, inconsistencies, and errors of omission and commission should be enough to caution anyone from taking its clauses for granted. Proffered explanations give special emphasis to the distinction between cultural and structural shortcomings, problems of politics outside and inside of government, and problems of defining religion itself, whereby escaping a religious establishment has opened the Pandora's box of sacred free exercise. Over the years, the religious clauses of the First Amendment have undergone both secularization and sacralization, withering criticism and undeserved veneration. But at the risk of engaging in such veneration myself, these clauses remain the gold standard in a field strewn with pyrite.

ENDNOTES

1. Samuel P. Huntington, *American Politics: The Promise of Disharmony* (Cambridge, MA: Belknap Press, 1981).
2. For the classic statement regarding the U.S., see Robert N. Bellah, "Civil Religion in America," *Daedalus* 96 (1967): 1–21.
3. Cf. Ted G. Jelen, *Public Attitudes toward Church and State* (Armonk, NY: M.E. Sharpe, 1995).
4. See Pippa Norris and Ronald Inglehart, *Sacred and Secular Religion: Religion and Politics Worldwide* (New York: Cambridge University Press, 2004).

5. C. Kirk Hadaway, Penny Long Marler, and Mark Chaves, "What the Polls Don't Show: A Closer Look at U.S. Church Attendance," *American Sociological Review* 58/6 (December, 1993): 741–752. The findings of this original article have been often and variously replicated in the United Kingdom as well as the United States.

6. For more discussion, see N.J. Demerath III, *Crossing the Gods: World Religions and Worldly Politics* (Piscataway, NJ: Rutgers Universtiy Press, 2001), 220–234.

7. Jonathan Fox, *A World Survey of Religion and the State* (New York: Cambridge University Press, 2008), 353.

8. Ibid., 360.

9. As always, definitions are important. If by "religious legislation," Fox means any legislation mentioning or implicating religion in any way, there are abundant examples in the United States, e.g., the 1694 Civil Rights Bill prohibiting discrimination based on religion, or as will be shown shortly, the more recent bills known as RFRA and RLUIPA. However, he is correct if he means any legislation that favors one religion in particular or religion in general.

10. Cf. John F. Wilson, ed., *Church and State in America: A Bibliographic Guide,* 2 Vols. (Westport, CT: Greenwood Press, 1987); Samuel Krislov, "Alternatives to Separation of Church and State in Countries Outside the United States," in *Religion and the State,* ed. James E. Wood, Jr. (Waco, TX: Baylor U. Press, 1985), 421–440; and Hen C. Van Moorseven and Ger Van der Tan, *Written Constitutions: A Comparative Study* (Dobbs Ferry, NY: Oceana Publishers, 1978).

11. See the different assessments of a putative American "culture war" represented in James D. Hunter, *Culture Wars: The Struggle to Define America* (New York: Basic Books, 1991); Rhys H. Williams, ed., *Culture Wars in American Politics: Critical Views of a Popular Thesis* (Chicago: Aldine de Gruyter, 1997); and N.J. Demerath III. "The Battle Over a U.S. Culture War: Inflated Rhetoric vs. Inflamed Reality," The Forum (Berkeley, CA: Electronic Press), Vol. 3, no. 2 (July 2005).

12. Cf. Demerath, *Crossing the Gods.*

13. This is elaborated in Ibid., 184–214.

14. Anson Phelps Stokes and Leo Pfeffer, *Church and State in the United States* (Westport, CT: Greenwood Press, 1964), and James E. Wood, Jr., *Religion and the State: Essays in Honor of Leo Pfeffer* (Waco, TX: Baylor University Press, 1985).

15. See, for example, Frank Lambert, *The Founding Fathers and the Place of Religion in America* (Princeton, NJ: Princeton University Press, 2003) and *Religion in American Politics: A Short History* (Princeton, NJ: Princeton University Press, 2008); Isaac Krammick and R. Laurence Moore, *The Godless Constitution: A Moral Defense of the Secular State* (New York: W.W. Norton, 2005); Gary Wills, *Head and Heart: American Christianities* (New York: Penguin, 2007); Martha Nussbaum, *Liberty of Conscience: In Defense of America's Tradition of Religious Equality* (New York: Basic Books, 2008); and Steven Waldman, *Founding Faith, Providence, Politics, and the Birth of Religious Freedom in America* (New York: Random House, 2008).

16. N.J. Demerath III and Rhys H. Williams, *A Bridging of Faiths: Religion and Politics in a New England City* (Princeton, NJ: Princeton University Press, 1992).

17. Cf. Arlin Adams and Charles Emmerich, *A Nation Dedicated to Religious Liberty: The Constitutional Heritage of the Religious Clauses* (Philadelphia: University of Pennsylvania Press, 1990); John T. Noonan, *The Luster of Our Country: The American Experience of Religious Freedom* (Berkeley, CA: University of California Press, 1998).

18. This point is elaborated in a forthcoming work by John F. Wilson as related in a personal communication.

19. See, for example, James Reichley, *Religion in American Public Life* (Washington, DC: The Brookings Institution, 1985); and Kenneth D. Wald, *Religion and Politics in the United States* (New York: St. Martin's Press, 1987).

20. Cf. Edwin S. Gaustad, *Faith of Our Fathers: Religion and the New Nation* (San Francisco: Harper & Row, 1987); and Mark Noll, ed., *Religion and American Politics: From the Colonial Period to 1980* (New York: Oxford University Press, 1990).

21. *Everson v. Board of Education*, 330 U.S. 1 (1947).

22. *Stone v. Graham*, 449 U.S. 39 (1980).

23. *Lynch v. Donnelly*, 465 U.S. 668 (1984).

24. See Demerath and Williams, *A Bridging of Faiths*, 109–117.

25. For a lengthy discussion of this evolution, see Donald L. Drakeman, *Church–state Constitutional Issues: Making Sense of the Establishment Clause* (New York: Greenwood Press, 1991).

26. J. Bruce Nichols, *The Uneasy Alliance* (New York: Oxford University Press, 1988).

27. Reichley, *Religion in American Public Life.*

28. See the line of analysis extending from H. Richard Niebuhr, *The Social Sources of Denominationalism* (New York: Henry Holt, 1928) through Talcott Parsons, *Structure and Process in Modern Societies* (Glencoe, NY: The Free Press, 1960) to the more disputatious Roger Finke and Rodney Stark, *The Churching of America, 1776–1990* (Piscataway, NJ: Rutgers University Press, 2005).

29. Marcela Cristi, *From Civil to Political Religion* (Waterloo, Ontario: Wilfrid Laurier University Press, 2001); and Cristi and Lorne L. Dawson, "Civil Religion in America and in Global Context," in *Handbook of the Sociology of Religion,* eds. James A. Beckford and N.J. Demerath III. (London: Sage Publications, 2007), 267–291.

30. Robert Wuthnow, *The Restructuring of American Religion* (Princeton, NJ: Princeton University Press, 1988), 241–267.

31. See Demerath, *Crossing the Gods,* 234–240, for a more extended discussion. .

32. Cf. Robert N. Bellah and Phillip E. Hammond, eds., *Varieties of Civil Religion* (San Francisco: Harper & Row, 1988).

33. Rhys H. Williams and N.J. Demerath III, "Religion and Political Process in an American City," *American Sociological Review* 56 (1992): 417–431.

34. For example, Ronald F. Thiemann, *Religion in American Public Life* (Washington, DC: Georgetown University Press, 1996).

35. Pew Research Center for the People and the Press, August, 2008.

36. See Richard John Neuhaus, *The Naked Public Square: Religion and Democracy in America* (Grand Rapids, MI: Erdmans Publishing, 1984); and Steven L. Carter, *Culture of Disbelief* (New York: Basic Books, 1992).

37. Cf. Kevin Phillips, *American Dynasty: Aristocracy, Fortunes, and the Politics of Deceit* (New York: Viking Press, 2004); and J. Micklewaith and A. Woolridge, *The Right Nation: Conservative Power in America* (New York: Penguin Press, 2004).

38 See Thomas Frank, *What's the Matter with Kansas?* (New York: Henry Holt Publishing, 2004).

39 See John C. Green, L.A. Kellstedt, C. E. Smidt, and J.L. Guth, "How the Faithful Voted: Religious Communities and the Presidential Vote," in *A Matter of Faith: Religion in the 2004 Presidential Election,* ed. Donald E. Campbell (Washington, DC: Brookings Institution Press, 2007).

40. See Michael Hout, and Claude Fischer, "Why More Americans Have No Religious Preference: Politics and Generations," *American Sociological Review* 68 (2002): 314–341; and Barry Kosmin and Ariela Keysar, *American Religious Identification Survey,*

Institute for the Study of Secularism in Society and Culture, Trinity College, Hartford, CT, 2009.

41. Ted Jelen, *Public Attitudes toward Church and State;* and Ted Jelen and Clyde Wilcox, eds., *Religion and Politics in Comparative Perspective* (New York: Cambridge University Press, 2002).

42. Robert Booth Fowler, Allen D. Hertzke and Laura R. Olson, eds., *Religion and Politics in America: Faith, Culture, and Strategic Choice,* 2nd ed. (Boulder, CO: Westview Press, 2004).

43. For an elaboration of this discussion, see N.J. Demerath III, "Dear President Bush: An Assessment of Religion and Politics in Your Administration for 'Posteriority,'" *Sociology of Religion* (Spring, 2007), 5–23.

44. See Mark Chaves, "Religious Congregations and Welfare Reform: Who Will Take Advantage of Charitable Choice?" *American Sociological Review* 64 (1999): 836–846; Arthur E. Farnsley II, *Rising Expectations: Urban Congregations, Welfare Reform and Community Life* (Bloomington, IN: Indiana University Press, 2003); and Farnsley, "Faith-Based Initiatives," in Beckford and Demerath, eds., *Handbook of the Sociology of Religion,* 345–357.

45. In *Walz v. Tax Commission,* 397 U.S. 644 (1970), the Supreme Court upheld property tax exemptions for churches because they were "neither the advancement nor the inhibition of religion" and the practice was applied generally and not specifically to any particular religion.

46. See Bryan J. Grim and Roger Finke, "International Religion Indexes: Government Regulation, Government Favoritism, and Social Regulation of Religion," *Interdisciplinary Journal of Research on Religion* 2 (2006).

47. Pauline Cote and Jeremy Gunn, *The New Religious Question: State Regulation or State Interference?* (New York: Peter Lang, 2006).

48. Daniel J.B. Hofrenning, *In Washington but Not of It: The Prophetic Politics of Washington Lobbyists* (Philadelphia: Temple University Press, 1995); and Carin Larson, James Madland, and Clyde Wilcox, "Religious Lobbying in Virginia," in *Representing God at the Statehouse,* eds. Edward Cleary and Allen Hertzke (Lanham, MD: Rowman and Littlefield, 2006).

49. In *Gillette v. U.S.,* 401 U.S. 437 (1971), the Supreme Court denied conscientious objector status to those who objected to only one "conflict" rather than to war generally, although it did not rescind the broad definition of religion used in the *Seeger* and *Welsh* decisions of 1965 and 1970, respectively.

50. *Pialech v. Massasoit Greyhound, Inc.* (1992).

51. Massachusetts General Laws, ch. 151 B and 4 (1A) (Supp.1997).

52. See Marci A Hamilton, *God vs. the Gavel: Religion and the Rule of Law* (New York: Cambridge University Press, 2005).

53. Edward Bailey, ed., *The Secular Quest for Meaning in Life: Denton Papers in Implicit Religion* (Lampeter, Wales: Edwin Mellen, 2002).

54. Phillip E. Hammond, David W. Machacek and Eric M. Mazur, *Religion on Trial: How Supreme Court Trends Threaten Freedom of Conscience in America* (Walnut Creek, CA: Alta Mira Press, 2004).

55. See, for example, Norman Dorsen, ed., *The Evolving Constitution: Essays on the Bill of Rights and the U.S. Supreme Court* (Middletown, CT: Wesleyan University Press, 1986).

56. George Freeman, "The Misguided Search for the Constitutional Definition of 'Religion,'" *Georgetown Law Journal* 71 (1983): 1519–1556.

57. Emile Durkheim, *The Elementary Forms of the Religious Life* (New York: Free Press, 1912/1995), 429.

BIBLIOGRAPHY

Books

Adams, Arlin, and Charles Emmerich. *A Nation Dedicated to Religious Liberty: The Constitutional Heritage of the Religious Clauses.* Philadelphia: University of Pennsylvania Press, 1990.

Bailey, Edward, ed. *The Secular Quest for Meaning in Life: Denton Papers in Implicit Religion.* Lampeter, Wales: Edwin Mellen, 2002.

Bellah, Robert N. and Phillip E. Hammond, eds. *Varieties of Civil Religion.* San Francisco: Harper & Row, 1980.

Carter, Stephen L. *The Culture of Unbelief.* New York: Basic Books, 1992.

Church, Forest. *So Help Me God: The Founding Fathers and the First Great Battle Over Church and State.* New York: Harcourt, 2007.

Cote, Pauline and Jeremy Gunn. *The New Religious Question: State Regulation or State Interference?* New York: Peter Lang, 2006.

Cristi, Marcela. *From Civil to Political Religion.* Waterloo, Ontario: Wilfrid Laurier University Press, 2001.

Davis, Derek H., ed. *The Separation of Church and State Defended: Essays in Honor of James E. Wood, Jr.* Waco, TX: J.W. Dawson Institute of Church–state Studies, 1995.

Demerath, N.J. III. *Crossing the Gods: World Religions and Worldly Politics.* Piscataway, NJ: Rutgers University Press, 2001.

Demerath, N.J. III and Rhys H. Williams. *A Bridging of Faiths: Religion and Politics in a New England City.* Princeton, NJ: Princeton University Press, 1992.

Drakeman, Donald L. *Church–state Constitutional Issues: Making Sense of the Establishment Clause.* New York: Greenwood Press, 1991.

Farnsley, Arthur E. II. *Rising Expectations: Urban Congregations, Welfare Reform and Community Life.* Bloomington, IN: Indiana University Press, 2003.

Farnsley, Arthur E. II, N.J. Demerath III, Etan Diamond, Mary Mapes, and Elfriede Wedam. *Sacred Circles/Public Squares: The Multicentering of American Religion.* Bloomington, IN: Indiana University Press, 2004.

Finke, Roger and Rodney Stark. *The Churching of America, 1776–1990.* Piscataway, NJ: Rutgers University Press, 2005.

Fowler, Robert Booth, Allen D. Hertzke, and Laura R. Olson, eds. *Religion and Politics in America: Faith, Culture, and Strategic Choices,* 2nd ed. Boulder, CO: Westview Press, 2004.

Fox, Jonathan. *A World Survey of Religion and the State.* New York: Cambridge University Press, 2008.

Frank, Thomas. *What's the Matter with Kansas?* New York: Henry Holt Publishing, 2004.

Gaustad, Edwin S. *Faith of Our Fathers: Religion and the New Nation.* San Francisco: Harper & Row, 1987.

Greeley, Andrew and Michael Hout. *The Truth about Conservative Christians.* Chicago: University of Chicago Press, 2006.

Hofrenning, Daniel J.B. *In Washington but Not Of It: The Prophetic Politics of Washington Lobbyists*. Philadelphia: Temple University Press, 1995.

Hamilton, Marci A. *God vs. the Gavel: Religion and the Rule of Law*. New York: Cambridge University Press, 2005.

Hammond, Phillip E., David W. Machacek, and Eric M. Mazur. *Religion on Trial: How Supreme Court Trends Threaten Freedom of Conscience in America*. Walnut Creek, CA: Alta Mira Press, 2004.

Hunter, James D. *Culture Wars: The Struggle to Define America*. New York: Basic Books, 1991.

Huntington, Samuel P. *American Politics: The Promise of Disharmony*. Cambridge, MA: Belknap Press, 1981.

Jelen, Ted G. *Public Attitudes toward Church and State*. Armonk, NY: M.E. Sharpe, 1995.

Jelen, Ted G. and Clyde Wilcox, eds. *Religion and Politics in Comparative Perspective*. New York: Cambridge University Press, 2002.

Krammick, Isaac and R. Laurence Moore. *The Godless Constitution: A Moral Defense of the Secular State*. New York: W.W. Norton, 2005.

Lambert, Frank. *The Founding Fathers and the Place of Religion in America*. Princeton, NJ: Princeton University Press, 2003.

———. *Religion in American Politics: A Short History*. Princeton, NJ: Princeton University Press, 2008.

Micklewait, J. and A. Woolridge. *The Right Nation: Conservative Power in America*. New York: Penguin Press, 2004.

Neuhaus, Richard John. *The Naked Public Square: Religion and Democracy in America*. Grand Rapids, MI: Erdmans Publishing, 1984.

Nichols, J. Bruce. *The Uneasy Alliance*. New York: Oxford University Press, 1988.

Niebuhr, H. Richard. *The Social Sources of Denominationalism*. New York: Henry Holt, 1928.

Noll, Mark, ed. *Religion and American Politics: From the Colonial Period to 1980*. New York: Oxford University Press, 1990.

Noonan, John T. *The Luster of Our Country: The American Experience of Religious Freedom*. Berkeley, CA: University of California Press, 1998.

Norris, P. and R. Inglehart. *Sacred and Secular Religion: Religion and Politics Worldwide*. New York: Cambridge University Press, 2004.

Nussbaum, Martha. Liberty of Conscience: *In Defense of America's Tradition of Religious Equality*. New York: Basic Books, 2008.

Parsons, Talcott. *Structure and Process in Modern Societies*. Glencoe, NY: The Free Press, 1960.

Kevin, Phillips. *American Dynasty: Aristocracy, Fortunes, and the Politics of Deceit*. New York: Viking Press, 2004.

Reichley, James. *Religion in American Public Life*. Washington, DC: The Brookings Institution, 1985.

Stokes, Anson Phelps and Leo Pfeffer. *Church and State in the United States*. Westport, CT: Greenwood Press, 1964.

Thiemann, Ronald F. *Religion in American Public Life*. Washington, DC: Georgetown University Press, 1996.

Van Moorseven, Hen C. and Ger Van der Tan. *Written Constitutions: A Comparative Study*. Dobbs Ferry, NY: Oceana Publishers, 1978.

Wald, Kenneth D. *Religion and Politics in the United States*. New York: St. Martin's Press, 1987.

Waldman, Steven. *Founding Faith, Providence, Politics, and the Birth of Religious Freedom in America.* New York: Random House, 2008.

Williams, Rhys H. ed. *Culture Wars in American Politics: Critical Views of a Popular Thesis.* Chicago: Aldine de Gruyter, 1997.

Wills, Gary. *Head and Heart: American Christianities.* New York, Penguin, 2007.

Wilson, John F. ed. *Church and State in America: A Bibliographic Guide.* 2 Vols. Westport, CT: Greenwood Press, 1987.

Wilson, John F. and Donald Drakeman. *The Church and State in American History,* 3rd ed. Boulder, CO: Westview Press, 2003.

Witte, John Jr. *Religion and the American Constitutional Experiment.* Boulder, CO: Westview Press, 2000.

Wood, James E. Jr. *Religion and the State: Essays in Honor of Leo Pfeffer.* Waco, TX: Baylor University Press, 1985.

Wuthnow, Robert. *The Restructuring of American Religion.* Princeton, NJ: Princeton University Press, 1988.

Articles/Chapters

Bellah, Robert N. "Civil Religion in America," *Daedalus* 96 (1967): 1.

Chaves, Mark. "Religious Congregations and Welfare Reform: Who Will Take Advantage of Charitable Choice?" *American Sociological Review* 64 (1999): 836.

Cristi, Marcela and Lorne L. Dawson. "Civil Religion in America and in Global Context," in *Handbook of the Sociology of Religion.* eds. James A. Beckford and N.J. Demerath III. London: Sage Publications, 2007): 267.

———. "Faith-Based Initiatives," in *Handbook of the Sociology of Religion,* eds. James A. Beckford and N.J. Demerath III. London: Sage Publications, 2007): 345–357.

Green, John C., L.A. Kellstedt, C. E. Smidt, and J.L. Guth. "How the Faithful Voted: Religious Communities and the Presidential Vote," in *A Matter of Faith: Religion in the 2004 Presidential Election,* ed. Donald E. Campbell. Washington, DC: Brookings Institution Press, 2007.

Hadaway, C. Kirk, Penny Long Marler, and Mark Chaves. "What the Polls Don't Show: A Closer Look at U.S. Church Attendance." *American Sociological Review* 58/6 (December, 1993): 741.

Hout, Michael and Claude Fischer. "Why More Americans Have No Religious Preference: Politics and Generations." *American Sociological Review* 68 (2002): 314.

Krislov, Samuel. "Alternatives to Separation of Church and State in Countries Outside the United States," in *Religion and the State,* ed. James E. Wood, Jr. Waco, TX: Baylor Universoty Press, 1985): 421.

Larson, Carin, James Madland, and Clyde Wilcox. "Religious Lobbying in Virginia," in *Representing God at the Statehouse,* eds. Edward Cleary and Allen Hertzke. Lanham, MD: Rowman and Littlefield, 2006.

Larson, Carin, James Madland, Clyde Wilcox, and N.J. Demerath III. "Religion and Political Process in an American City." *American Sociological Review* 56 (1992): 417.

CHAPTER 19

....

THE ROLE OF CIVIL RELIGION IN AMERICAN SOCIETY

....

RICHARD V. PIERARD

RELIGION is a distinctive feature of political life in the United States. Americans are unquestionably the most religious people of all industrialized nations. According to recent surveys, 63% of the population holds membership in a specific faith community—a church, synagogue, or mosque—and about 40% attend religious services on an average weekend. Most of those categorized as unchurched claim to believe in "God," however loosely that may be defined. According to one poll, only 7% profess atheism, agnosticism, or no religious preference at all. The polls also indicate that a majority of Americans feel religion should have a greater influence in the nation's life.[1] At the same time, however, the U.S. Constitution mandates a clear separation between the organized religious bodies and civil society. No religion may be "established" or given preferential treatment, and U.S. citizens have the right to practice their beliefs without interference from the state, principles that are set forth in Article VI ("no religious test" for holding public office) and the "establishment" and "free exercise" clauses of the First Amendment. Nevertheless, religiosity seems to be all-pervasive in American civic institutions, a situation that has drawn the attention of scholars throughout the twentieth century, and in recent years they have given this phenomenon the label of "civil religion."

WHAT IS CIVIL RELIGION?

Such terms as *civic, public, political, or societal religion, public piety, civic faith, public theology, religion-in-general, the religion of the republic,* and even *American Shinto* and *the American Democratic Faith* have been used to describe such vague and elusive expressions of public religiosity, but since the appearance in 1967 of sociologist Robert N. Bellah's defining essay, "Civil Religion in America," the phrase *civil religion* has become the favored label for this curious phenomenon. Bellah's essay opens with the striking line: "There actually exists alongside of and rather clearly differentiated from the churches an elaborate and well-institutionalized civil religion in America." This religion—or perhaps better, religious dimension, as he puts it—"has its own seriousness and integrity and requires the same care in understanding that any other religion does."[2] His article set off a long and complex debate as to what the American civic faith is and how it is manifested. Various scholars have even endeavored to pinpoint the appearance of the phenomenon in other societies in the world, with widely varying levels of success.[3]

Essentially, civil religion refers to the widely held body of beliefs that are tied to the nation's history and destiny. Although it possesses no formal creed, it is a kind of generic faith that relates the political society as well as the individual citizen to the realm of ultimate meaning and existence. In turn, it enables the people to view their polity in a special manner, thereby contributing to national integration, and its functions as social glue. It is the operative religion of a political community—the system of rituals, symbols, values, norms, and allegiances that determines its life, invests it with meaning and a destiny, and provides it with an overarching sense of spiritual unity that transcends all internal conflicts and differences.

It is a consensus of religious sentiments, concepts, and symbols that the state uses—either directly or indirectly, consciously or unconsciously—for its own political purposes. This general religious faith encompasses the entire society, but it does not necessarily compete with the particular faiths of sectarian or denominational groups that claim the allegiance of only a part of the populace. The latter, in fact, read into the civil faith whatever meaning they choose and peacefully coexist with it. Civil religion functions as a cluster of phenomena on the boundary between politics and religion. In the U.S. context this is illustrated by the use of religious language in public documents and political speech, the presence of religious symbols in public places—the Ten Commandments and religious quotations on public monuments—and civic rituals with a religious dimension, such as the observance of national holidays like Memorial Day, Independence Day, and Martin Luther King's birthday, the presidential inauguration and other swearing-in ceremonies, pledging allegiance to the nation's flag, and communal singing of the national anthem and various patriotic songs. It is also evident in the efforts to write U.S. history in a manner that provides evidence of divine chosen-ness and national exceptionalism.

Defenders of civil religion view it as a benign and positive force, and maintain that no political society can survive for long without it. Critics, however, feel it may attempt to force group identity and legitimate the authority of the existing order by injecting a transcendental dimension or religious gloss on the justification for rule. In this way it would be coercive and divisive and serve as a political tool.[4]

Various efforts have been made to categorize the many varieties of civil religiosity and the nuances therein. Some spokespeople emphasize the deity, whereas others see the nation itself as the reference point of highest loyalty and final judgment. Still others view civil religion in functional terms—prophetic and priestly. The prophet stands before the people and speaks to them the necessary (and sometimes unpleasant) words from God, whereas the priest stands before God and speaks on behalf of the people. The prophet focuses on judgment and repentance, whereas the priest pronounces words of comfort, praise, and celebration.

In 1974 Russell Richey and Donald Jones categorized the contrasting positions on civil religion into five closely connected and often overlapping typologies of meaning.[5]

1. Civil religion as *folk religion.* This is the common religion of Americans that emerges from the ethos and history of the "folk," or people. By empirically examining American religious behavior one arrives at the conclusion that civil religion is "the American War of Life," the "common faith" of American society. As Will Herberg, a major exponent of this approach, puts it:

   It is an organic structure of ideas, values, and beliefs that constitutes a faith common to Americans and genuinely operative in their lives, a faith that markedly influences and is influenced by the "official" religions of America society. Sociologically, anthropologically, if one pleases, it is the characteristic American religion, undergirding American life and overarching American society. . . . Americanism may be taken as the civic religion of the American people.[6]

   Civil religion in this sense is an "idolatrous" faith that competes with the particularistic faiths in American society and transcends the common life of the people.

2. Civil religion as the *transcendent universal religion of the nation.* This is the position of Bellah who, in his aforementioned essay, analyzed the religious content of several presidential addresses and the Declaration of Independence and related this to the testing of the national character that was then occurring as a result of the Vietnam War. He carried his reasoning forward in a subsequent book, *The Broken Covenant,*[7] and numerous articles. Another is Sidney Mead, who argued in *The Nation with the Soul of a Church,*[8] that the "religion of the republic" is a cosmopolitan and prophetic faith. It is a normative one that stands in judgment over the ideals and aspirations of the people and is a corrective against idolatrous

tendencies found in some forms of Christianity. He vigorously denied that it is either the deification of the nation or the American way of life. The state is not God and its citizens must not act in a lawless manner toward other peoples.

3. Civil religion as *religious nationalism.* The nation *per se* is not the church of national religion, but rather the object of adoration and glorification. It takes on a sovereign and self-transcendent character. Faith is patriotic and politics a matter of ultimate concern, but it is not necessarily incompatible with particularistic religious beliefs held by the populace. The malicious quality manifested by civil religion does not result from people using it improperly, but is inherent in its very nature. By relating God's sovereignty to American politics people open themselves to national pride and idolatry. The institutional church cannot have an autonomous existence outside the realm of the state's sovereignty, and thus it may not exercise prophetic oversight. Whether expressed positively or negatively, this is the most common position and is espoused by a host of scholars.

4. Civil religion as the *democratic faith.* Writers holding this view see it as the democratic egalitarian faith; that is, a more positive form of the previous category. The humane values of equality, freedom, and justice can exist and be affirmed without depending on a transcendent deity or a spiritualized nation. The American creed of Gunnar Myrdal, the common faith John Dewey expressed in his many works, the vision of America in Progressive Era historiography, and the democracy-as-religion of J. Paul Williams[9] are all examples of this nontheistic or deistic approach.

5. Civil religion as *Protestant civic piety.* Numerous American historians who deal with the nineteenth century have focused on "Protestant nationalism" and how this fusion colored the American ethos. They have singled out such qualities as Protestant moralism, individualism, activism, pragmatism, the work ethic, and the worldwide spread of Christianity and American values through missionary work. Also included here are Protestant theories of race and religiously embedded notions of national destiny and American exceptionalism.

A slightly different variant is that of Martin E. Marty who maintains there are "two kinds of two kinds of civil religion."[10] One kind sees the nation "under God"—a transcendent deity is somehow involved in the political process. The other stresses "national self-transcendence;" that is, because people left to themselves do not automatically engage in self-worship, the nation must somehow assume that role. In both forms references to the deity either disappear entirely or the concept of "God" is drained of the meanings people once held. Either way, God appears terminologically only out of customary reference, not purposeful faith. Within each of these are two kinds of approaches, as mentioned. The "priestly" will normally be celebrative, affirmative, and culture-building, whereas the "prophetic" tends to be dialectical in its approach to civil religion, but with a predisposition toward the judgmental. The two often interact; that is, the priest may judge and a prophet may integrate people into a system of meaning, but the priest is alert to the occasions when such integration can occur and the prophet is sensitive that he may have to be critical of existing modes of such integration.

His example of the priestly mode is the "nation under God," whereby the deity gives identity, meaning, and purpose to the nation. It is a fusion of historic faith (as in Jewish or Christian traditions) with autochthonous national sentiment. The prophetic voices include Jonathan Edwards, Abraham Lincoln, and Reinhold Niebuhr, who employed biblical motifs over against national pretensions. They talk about the promise to America from the standpoint of a transcendent deity. As for national self-transcendence, the priestly variety stresses patriotism, and sees democracy as an object of religious dedication and the promise of American life as a religious ultimate. The prophetic form is tolerant of particular faiths and pluralism, sensitive to the danger of national idolatry, and quite aware of America's place in the wider world of nations.

Richard Pierard and Robert Linder bring out that the U.S. president provides the crucial leadership in the American civil religion.[11] He presides over the nation's rituals and reaffirms its creeds. People take for granted that he is a man of faith, as Gary Smith shows in his definitive study of presidential religion.[12] All 44 presidents—from George Washington to Barack Obama—have been friendly toward organized religion. Thirty-three were actually church members, all of them attended worship on occasions, and they considered themselves to be Christians. In their inaugural addresses they acknowledged God and invoked his blessing on the nation, and they regularly used religious language and imagery in their speeches and public documents to express their heartfelt convictions, inspire the citizenry, and help legitimate their policies.

At various times he has functioned as a national pastor, priest, or even prophet, following Marty's schema. In the prophetic mode, such presidents as Abraham Lincoln, John F. Kennedy, and Jimmy Carter assessed the nation's actions in relation to transcendent values. They called upon citizens to make sacrifices in times of crisis and repent of corporate sins (failings) when their behavior fell short of the national ideals. As national pastors, Franklin D. Roosevelt and Dwight D. Eisenhower provided spiritual inspiration to the people by upholding American core values and urging them to do likewise. Assuming the priestly role, such presidents as Richard M. Nixon, Ronald Reagan, and George Bush (father and son) made America itself the ultimate reference point. They affirmed and celebrated the nation, whereas at the same time stroking and praising their political flock.

In short, American civil religion is essentially an alliance between politics and religion at the national level. It rests on a politicized ideological base consisting of four principles: (1) there is a God; (2) the deity's will can be known and fulfilled through democratic procedures; (3) America has been his primary agent in modern history; and (4) the nation is the chief source of identity for Americans in both a political and religious sense.

THE HISTORICAL BACKGROUND OF
CIVIL RELIGION

The phenomenon had an important prototype in the ancient Greek city-states. Each *polis* had a patron deity, such as Athena in Athens, who looked over the city but did not rule it, and Plato and Aristotle wrote at length about the importance of civic piety. Democracy was a gift from Athena, and as long as the citizens did not play god, invoke gods in their decisions, and cross the line into hubris, they lived in harmony with the gods. The Romans developed a quasi-religious polity cemented by a common allegiance to a deified emperor. He was revered as a manifest god and savior in the imperial state cult, which doubled as the civil religion of the realm. Alongside it existed the other religions whose adherents could practice their faith as enthusiastically as they wished, just so long as they nominally accepted the official one. The early Christians were persecuted because they stubbornly refused to cooperate with those rulers who wanted to establish a viable public faith. Their God was a jealous one who would not allow rivals, and they refused to sacrifice to Caesar as the state cult required. They were seen as seditious enemies of the state and treated accordingly. Constantine and many of his successors realized that co-opting Christianity would actually strengthen the civil religion. Giving up their status as a god, these emperors functioned as a religious figure, the *Pontifex Maximus,* under the highest God of all.[13] After the fall of Rome this role passed to the pope.

Another early example of civil religion could be seen in the history of Israel, especially the late Judaic kingdom and the exile. The temple occupied a central place and the reforms of Josiah eliminated false worship as well as reconstructed the covenant with Yahweh. However, this situation did not last. Jeremiah then condemned the religious leaders of his day and called them to repentance. In short, they saw him as unpatriotic even as he challenged their civil religion as inadequate.[14] Many other examples can be found in the medieval and early modern eras, and especially in Puritan England, from whence came many of the motifs in American civil religion.

The person actually responsible for coining the term itself was the controversial French Enlightenment figure Jean-Jacques Rousseau. Writing in *The Social Contract* (1772), the most radical political work of the eighteenth century, he argued that humans were naturally good and their social institutions were what corrupted them. He sought to harmonize individual freedom with membership in a social group ruled by law through a general civic faith. In a well-known passage in the chapter entitled "Civil Religion" Rousseau wrote:

> There is therefore a pure civil profession of faith of which the Sovereign [the political ruler] should fix the articles, not exactly as religious dogmas, but as social sentiment without which a man cannot be a good citizen or a faithful subject. . . . The dogmas of civil religion ought to be few, simple, and exactly worded, without explanation or comment. The existence of a mighty, intelligent, and beneficent Divinity, possessed of foresight and providence; the life to come,

the happiness of the just, the punishment of the wicked; the sanctity of the social contract and the laws: these are its positive dogmas.[15]

This "civil religion" would provide the moral glue for the political order that the social contract created. It would be the "general will" of the people expressed religiously in the life of the state with a benign but watchful Supreme Being to preside over the keeping of the public faith. Civil society was the focus of the deity's work on earth, the way to the new heaven and earth. It was the center of humankind's religious and political loyalty, as well as the place in which people found security and freedom and expressed themselves morally and rationally. Particular religions and cults could exist as long as they did not interfere with the overarching devotion to the state. The civil religion had no transcendental reference point by which the nation could be judged, nor did it stand under a higher law. "Reason" enabled each member of the civil society to read the revelation of Nature's God in the creation. The state encompassed everything that matters, and there was no law or loyalty higher than the state.

Writing well over a century later, French Sociologist Émile Durkheim agreed that a common, overarching civil religion was a vital part of the constitution of every civil society. The vast majority of the people could identify with the general public faith and affirmed it at regular intervals by means of collective ideas and ceremonials. It gave moral coherence to the state and served as social cement, just as Rousseau expected civil religion to do. The political order was also tolerant of people who adhered to other faiths as long as they accepted the simple dogmas of the civic faith.[16]

CIVIL RELIGION IN THE AMERICAN CONTEXT[17]

American civil religion's roots lay in the colonial era. From Anglican and Puritan thought in England came the idea of *chosen-ness* and *covenant*. After the turmoil of the Reformation many Englanders came to feel that their country was divinely appointed to lead in the cosmic struggle between God and Satan, and the idea was popularized in John Foxe's enormously popular *Book of Martyrs* (1st ed., 1563). Those in the Puritan wing of the Church of England saw themselves as a covenant people—like ancient Israel. Just as God's covenant with Israel was conditional, so too was his covenant with England. Both were a chosen nation and a covenant people; each stood under God's judgment and was ultimately accountable to him.

The resolute folk who settled in New England transported the idea across the Atlantic. The Pilgrims, actually a separatist group, adopted a solemn pledge aboard their ship before landing at Plymouth in 1620. Known as the Mayflower Compact, it stated the purpose of their colony was to establish a "civil body politic" that would honor God and advance the Christian faith. The Puritans, who arrived in Massachusetts a decade later, carried the theological–political concept of divine chosen-ness even further. John Winthrop, the person elected as their first governor, declared in his famous tract written during the Atlantic crossing, *A Model of Christian Charity* (1629), that they enjoyed a special covenant relationship with God through Jesus Christ and that he expected unique behavior from his people. If they would covenant with one another to form a polity based on true godliness and biblical principles, they would enjoy peace and prosperity. Winthrop said that they had a commission from God: "We must consider that we shall be a city upon a hill. The eyes of all are upon us." He was drawing upon Jesus' words in the Sermon on the Mount (Matthew 5:15) to argue that they could complete the Protestant Reformation in America. Their outpost in the wilderness would be a moral and political example to the entire world, and out of their Zion light and wisdom would radiate in all directions for the good of humanity and the glory of God.

During the ensuing century the Puritan idea waned, whereas the scattered colonies along the Atlantic seaboard prospered in population and wealth. Then the inhabitants grew closer to one another as a result of the first "national" movement, a revival known as the Great Awakening. The more limited notion of the chosen people bearing witness to all nations and leading them to turn to Christ morphed into *civil millennialism,* the idea that the activity of the American people themselves was the hope of the future. America was the new seat of liberty, and it would win out over the arch enemies of liberty, both civil and religion, beginning first with France and then England.

Gradually, the nation itself emerged as the primary agent of God's activity in history, and the founding documents of the revolutionary era and afterward were the new covenants that bound the populace together and secured for them God's blessing and summons to carry out their historic task. This theme was an integral part of the experience of the American Revolution, in which the patriots saw Europe as Egypt, America as the Promised Land, and God's directing hand as they established a "new order in the world," as the seal on the one dollar bill reads. George Washington was the American Moses who led his people to fulfill their historic assignment.

The idea of *national mission* flourished in the nineteenth century with the "manifest destiny" of America being, as journalist John L. O'Sullivan wrote in 1845: "to overspread and possess the whole of the continent which Providence has given us for the development of the great experiment of liberty and federative self government entrusted to us." America was the "redeemer nation," which had a mission to save the world by creating a new humanity based on evangelical Protestantism and ennobling democratic institutions. The Civil War with its themes of sacrifice and rebirth and Abraham Lincoln as a Christ figure further contributed to this missionary understanding, Woodrow Wilson proclaimed America's task was to make the world "safe for democracy," and Ronald Reagan confidently affirmed in 1983 that a "divine plan" had put the American continent here between the two oceans, where people who "had a special love for freedom" could come and create "something new in all the history of mankind—a country where man is not beholden to government; government is beholden to man."[18]

An important contribution to the civil religion was made by nineteenth-century evangelicalism. The revival movement in the early years of the new century, commonly known as the Second Great Awakening, gave the United States its basically evangelical cast. As historian William G. McLoughlin put it, during the years 1800 to 1900 evangelical religion:

> made Americans the most religious people in the world, molded them into a unified, pietistic-perfectionistic nation, and spurred them on to those heights of social reform, missionary endeavor, and imperialistic expansionism which constitute the moving forces of our history in that century.[19]

A broad evangelicalism provided the religious glue for the republic, established the ethical norms that stood above parties, creeds, and denominations, and informed the consciences and molded the lifestyles of most Americans. In America, nationalism was integrated into civil religion through a marriage of evangelical Christianity and liberal democracy. America was God's chosen instrument to spread both Christianity and democracy. There was no conflict in rendering loyalty to God and his chosen nation.

Historian Ralph H. Gabriel labeled this fusion of evangelical religion and national interests the "American Democratic Faith." Various churches and sects contributed to the evangelical religion of the land, which flowed in the same channel as romantic democracy. They assented to common ideas: a basic moral law, the necessity of constitutional government to restrain evil, the doctrine of the free individual, the philosophy of progress, and the mission of America to save the world from autocracy and satanic governance.[20] Possibly the most significant force in inculcating these ideas in the populace was *McGuffey's Eclectic Readers,* a textbook series that was both a civil catechism and elementary school reader and that sold an estimated 120 million copies between 1836 and 1920. The books upheld the ideal of the Puritans as the creators of the civil faith and moral heroes of the republic, the place of orators and preachers in celebrating the nation's history, and the norms of evangelical Christianity as the ethical dimension—individual responsibility and rectitude, sound literary tastes based on the Bible, hard work, piety (love of God), kindness (love of neighbor), and patriotism (love of country). These elements reinforced the conviction that the United States was God's new Israel and the hope of the world.

A final contribution to civil religion in America is that of *deism.* The nation's Founders for the most part subscribed to some form of rationalism, but their social ideals were in harmony with the prevailing religious temper. The Protestant leaders in turn identified with the political philosophy of the intellectual elite. They agreed that humans possessed a natural ability to grasp the truth about the world and morality without the absolute need for divine grace and revelation. The light of natural reason could reveal the eternal principles of God's law to any right-thinking individual. At the same time, the American Enlightenment was far more flexible in its attitude toward organized religion than was its European counterpart because the existing regime was not upheld by or upholding an established faith.

The intellectuals saw the natural law as the primary expression of the divine will, whereas evangelical Christians regarded the moral law as the expression of God's will—and both recognized the Creator God as the source of the law. Christians saw true liberty as coming from the release from sin by Christ, whereas the intellectuals upheld the idea of the free individual. Accordingly, both groups subscribed to the democratic faith within the context of the new Israel and its sense of divine mission.

As time passed, evangelical Christianity gradually lost its spiritual vitality as it identified with the prosperity and sentimentality of Victorian America. Then, in the wake of the new immigration and the stresses of industrialization and urbanization came the challenges of new ideas—biblical criticism, theological liberalism (modernism), Darwinian evolution, and Marxist socialism. The evangelical consensus hardened into the Protestant Establishment, which cohabited with corporate capitalism. In the burgeoning cities Protestantism soon became a minority faith as it competed with the Roman Catholicism, Eastern Orthodoxy, and Judaism that the immigrants brought with them. This inexorably resulted in a transformation of the civil religion. The chosen nation theme now smacked of superiority and condescension, the mission of American democracy turned into strident nationalism and even imperialism, and the belief in progress was transformed into materialism.

Even as civil religion became increasingly an expression of American tribal identity, pressures mounted to make it more inclusive and accommodating to the newcomers. Emerging out of World War I was the recognition of the "three great faiths"—Protestant, Catholic, Jewish—and with it the "Judeo-Christian" tradition. Figures such as John Dewey proposed a revision of the civil faith to meet the needs of the post-Protestant era. They felt that the new values of liberal humanism and the common good of an increasingly pluralistic society should replace those of the old *McGuffey Readers* and be inculcated in the nation's school children. A civil religion based on the three faiths and "brotherhood" carried the nation through the agonies of World War II, but then it faced another challenge—the Soviet Union and global communism.

National leaders had to respond to the threat of Soviet aggression as well as new problems that went beyond religious and cultural pluralism, such as racial unrest, the assertion of ethnic pluralism, alienation of the youth, the women's movement, the repudiation of traditional personal values and sexual mores, and an ill-conceived and unpopular war in Vietnam. During the course of American history the umbrella of civil religion had grown from evangelical consensus to Protestantism-in-general, to Christianity-in-general, to the Judeo-Christian tradition-in-general, and finally to deism-in-general. Many evangelical Christians were unwilling to accept this broadening of the public faith and stood against the changes that were taking place. Their resistance during the fundamentalist-modernist controversy of the 1920s had had no impact, but they were not prepared to lose again.

The late twentieth century came to be marked by increasingly bitter "culture wars," as traditionalist Protestants, eventually joined by many Roman Catholics, fought bitterly to reverse the tide. All too frequently, what the public regarded as merely "church–state" issues were in reality conflicts arising over matters of the civil faith. Because other contributors to this volume deal with these in depth, the last section only briefly mentions some questions that particularly relate to civil religion concerns.

Recent Issues with Significant Civil Religion Ramifications

Public prayers have been a topic of great controversy, and there has been no consistent pattern of judicial or legislative response. Congressional, state legislative, and even some city council sessions are opened with public prayers, whether by appointed chaplains, invited clergymen, or lawmakers themselves. The practice of formal prayer at the presidential inaugural ceremony was initiated by Franklin D. Roosevelt in 1937, with prayers being offered by both a Protestant and a Catholic clergyman. Harry S. Truman included a Jewish rabbi in 1949 and Dwight D. Eisenhower used a Greek Orthodox cleric in 1957. Richard Nixon's hour-long inauguration in 1969 was a veritable worship service, with prayers by five clergymen, one from each major tradition and an African American churchman. In the stenographic text in the *Congressional Record,* the prayers took up more space than the president's inaugural address. Those who give inaugural prayers are carefully selected to woo various religious constituencies, for example, Billy Graham's repeated appearances. However, at times this can become controversial, such as Barack Obama's choice of the evangelical megachurch pastor Rick Warren in 2009. Dwight D. Eisenhower in 1953 and George H.W. Bush in 1989 actually included a prayer they composed as part of their inaugural addresses.

Prayer was a noteworthy aspect of Cold War civil religiosity. In April 1952 Congress adopted a resolution mandating the president to "set aside and proclaim" a National Day of Prayer in which the citizenry "may turn to God in prayer and meditation at churches in groups, and as individuals," and every chief executive since has dutifully carried out this charge. The actual event is coordinated by a private foundation, which may be managed by evangelicals. In 1953 the first Presidential Prayer Breakfast, also organized by a private foundation, took place to affirm the national faith in the face of godless communism, and it became an annual event. It was renamed the National Prayer Breakfast in 1974 because Richard Nixon, in a fit of pique about a speech at the previous year's breakfast criticizing the Vietnam War, refused to attend if it was associated with the presidency per se. It continues to be one of the major civil religion events on the Washington social calendar.

Prayer in the public schools is quite another matter. The traditional practice that the civil authority could mandate the practice of devotional reading from the

Bible (usually the King James version) and the reciting of prescribed prayers, did not sit well with some people, especially Catholic parents. Many schools, above all in urban areas, had ceased doing so by the middle of the twentieth century, and when the Supreme Court in the 1962 to 1963 prayer and Bible reading cases ruled that the practice violated the Establishment Clause of the First Amendment, it simply acknowledged what many already recognized. However, a vehement storm of protest swept the country and the Court was accused of expelling God from the schools. Defenders of the decisions pointed out that students were free to pray in their homes and churches and they could attend private schools, where prayers were part of the curriculum. Accordingly, many southerners who linked the action with school desegregation started private schools where their children could continue to pray as well as not be in the same classroom with African Americans.

The real issue, however, was that of civil religion. The rulings challenged what essentially was a civic rite, a practice that had become a part of the American way of life, and they occurred at a time when civil religion was a weapon in the national arsenal against Soviet communism. Although congressional efforts to pass a "prayer amendment" overturning the decisions have repeatedly failed, many politicians continue to pay lip service to the "restoration of school prayer," and conservatives to this day have been unrelenting in their attacks on the judicial prayer rulings.

Two actions in the 1950s illustrate the important role civil religion played in the Cold War struggles. The first was adding the words *under God* to the flag salute; the other was the adoption of *In God We Trust* as the national motto.[21] The Pledge of Allegiance was an innocuous patriotic exercise that a Baptist minister and journalist in Boston had composed for school children to recite during the 400th anniversary celebration of Columbus' discovery of America in 1892. Over the next years it rapidly caught on as a public ritual; in 1942 it was included in the codification of existing practices pertaining to the use and display of the flag; and in 1945 Congress recognized it as the official Pledge of Allegiance. There was, however, growing sentiment for inclusion of a reference to the deity by adding two words from Lincoln's Gettysburg Address so that it would read "one nation *under God,* indivisible, with liberty and justice for all." This became a hot issue in 1954 when a Presbyterian minister in Washington declared in a Lincoln Day sermon with Eisenhower in the congregation that belief in God was the "definitive factor in American life." As the Pledge now stood, "Muscovite" children could just as easily recite it, because the Soviet Union claimed to be indivisible and to stand for liberty and justice for all.

Congress immediately responded to the groundswell of public enthusiasm that followed and rushed a measure through modifying the Pledge in time for President Eisenhower to sign it on Flag Day, June 14, 1954. An American Legion honor guard brought a flag to the Capitol, and it was raised in the presence of the congressional leaders with the two authors of the bill reciting the Pledge while a bugler played "Onward Christian Soldiers." At the signing ceremony in the White House, the president declared that our children everywhere will daily proclaim "the dedication of our Nation and our people to the Almighty." He went on to say:

In this way we are reaffirming the transcendence of religious faith in America's heritage and future; in this way we shall constantly strengthen those spiritual weapons which forever will be our country's most powerful resource, in peace or in war.[22]

The modified Pledge of Allegiance gave recognition to the deity, but it was the god of civil religion, not historic Christianity. This deity was equally acceptable to Christians and Jews and was a valuable ally in the struggle against communism. Yet, all efforts in the subsequent years to remove the two words and return to the earlier version have been overwhelmingly rejected by the Congress and the judiciary. The power of civil religion trumps that of atheists who resent the phrase.

Now that America had acknowledged its position before the Almighty, the next logical action was a formal declaration of faith. This was accomplished by choosing a national motto to supplement the *e pluribus unum* on the Great Seal of the United States. The other phrase on the seal, *annuit coeptis* ([Providence] favors our undertaking), was too vague. However, in the fourth verse of "The Star-Spangled Banner," since 1931 the official national anthem, were these lines:

> Then conquer we must, when our cause it is just,
> And this be our motto,—"In God is our trust."

Legislation adopted in 1864 to bolster support for the Union cause in the Civil War provided for placing "In God We Trust" on an American two-cent coin, and an act in 1865 allowed the Director of the Mint to include it on gold and larger silver coins as he saw fit. When a flap arose in 1907 over the omission of the motto from a new gold coin, Congress mandated that it should be placed on all coins when new designs were adopted. The matter lay dormant until the 1950s when a campaign was mounted to place it on stamps and currency. An executive order in 1955 followed by congressional legislation provided for the motto to be placed on U.S. currency. When it was discovered that the great seal phrase had never been officially adopted as the national motto, legislation was introduced into Congress declaring that it would "of great spiritual and psychological values to our country to have a clearly designated national motto of inspirational quality in plain, popularly accepted English." The measure easily passed and on July 30, 1956 "In God We Trust" became the official motto.

In 1962 the House of Representatives voted to inscribe the national motto in gold above the Speaker's chair as a way of showing its disagreement with the Supreme Court ruling in the 1962 school prayer case, *Engel v. Vitale*. During the congressional hearings in 1964 over a prayer amendment, several testified that this motto proved that America was a religious nation. A nation that trusted in God obviously must permit the devotional reading of the Bible and the recitation of prayers by public school children or it could not longer claim to be object of divine favor. Civil religion thus was becoming the substitute for the personal religion practiced in homes, churches, and synagogues across the land.

Another matter with serious civil religion implications is that of *flag desecration*.[23] Veterans' groups at the turn of the twentieth century launched a campaign to give the national flag a kind of special status as a way of stifling political dissent, and the flag soon attained a sacred status. The unwillingness of Jehovah's Witnesses to salute it evoked widespread anger in the early 1940s, although the Supreme Court belatedly came to recognize the right of this unpopular minority to do so. Actually defacing the national symbol came to be labeled flag "desecration," an obviously religious term. When those dissatisfied with the policies of the dominant political leadership, whether in the early twentieth century, the Vietnam War era, and the late 1980s to early 1990s, protested by destroying the flag, the outpouring of national indignation was instantaneous. Flag burning incidents were universally condemned and measures to "protect the flag" were adopted, even though no evidence of actual harm ever could be shown. When the Supreme Court overturned the convictions of those who had burned flags, Congress reacted by trying to pass a constitutional amendment to "prohibit the physical desecration" of the flag, but it was unsuccessful. If such an amendment ever is sent out to the states for ratification, there is little doubt that it would pass. The flag is *the* symbol of America and the religious content imputed to it is far greater than that which Christians give to the cross.

CONCLUSION

Even though the Religious Right has made ample use of civil religion issues to mobilize support for its programs, and its spokespeople have made religious matters out of what were essentially political ones, there are occasions when the public religion has its positive side. It served to unite the country after the attacks of September 11, 2001, as exemplified by the Prayer Service at Washington's National Cathedral 3 days later, in which representatives of the Protestant Catholic, Jewish, and Muslim faiths spoke, another service at New York's Yankee Stadium, and services in churches across the land. Patriotic hymns and speeches do recognize that Americans are a religious people and their feelings genuine. Still, the difference between particular, personal religious faith and the generalized civil religion is not a clear one, often resulting in church–state issues being politicized in a way that one might not expect. We need a clearer understanding of the differences and their political implications.

ENDNOTES

1. Data from various polling agencies cited in Gary Scott Smith, *Faith and the Presidency: from George Washington to George W. Bush* (New York: Oxford University Press, 2006), v.

2. *Daedalus* 96 (Winter 1967), 1–21, and frequently reprinted in anthologies.

3. For a brief overview of this see Richard V. Pierard, "Civil Religion," in *The Encyclopedia of Christianity* (Grand Rapids, MI: Eerdmans, 1999), 1: 585–587.

4. This argument is made by Marcele Cristi, *From Civil to Political Religion: the Intersection of Culture, Religion and Politics* (Waterloo, Ontario: Wilfrid Laurier University Press, 2001).

5. Russell E. Richey and Donald G. Jones, eds., *American Civil Religion* (New York: Harper & Row, 1974), 14–18.

6. Will Herberg, *Protestant-Catholic-Jew,* rev. ed. (Garden City, NY: Doubleday, 1960), 77, 263.

7. Robert N. Bellah, *The Broken Covenant: American Civil Religion in a Time of Trial.* 2nd ed. (New York: Seabury Press, 1992).

8. Sidney E. Mead, *The Nation with the Soul of a Church* (New York: Harper & Row, 1975).

9. J. Paul Williams, *What Americans Believe and How They Worship* (New York: Harper & Row, 1962).

10. Martin E. Marty, "Two Kinds of Two Kinds of Civil Religion," in *American Civil Religion,* eds. Richey and Jones, 139–157.

11. This is the central argument of Richard V. Pierard and Robert D. Linder, *Civil Religion and the Presidency* (Grand Rapids, MI: Zondervan, 1988).

12. Smith, *Faith and the Presidency,* 5.

13. Pierard and Linder, *Civil Religion,* 36–40.

14. Paul L. Redditt, "When Faith Demands Treason: Civil Religion and the Prophet Jeremiah," *Review and Expositor* 10 (Spring 2004): 227–246.

15. Jean-Jacques Rousseau, *The Social Contract and Discourses*, ed. G. D. H. Cole (New York: Dutton, 1959), 139.

16. Émile Durkheim, *The Elementary Forms of Religious Life* (New York: Macmillan, 1915), 415–447.

17. The literature on the topic is so vast and readily accessible that it is not necessary to footnote all references.

18. *Public Papers of the Presidents of the United States. Ronald Reagan* (Washington, DC: Government Printing Office), 1983: 152.

19. William G. McLoughlin, *The American Evangelicals, 1800–1900* (New York: Harper & Row, 1974), 1.

20. Ralph H. Gabriel, *The Course of American Democratic Thought.* 2nd ed. (New York: Ronald Press, 1956), chap. 3.

21. The story has been told many times. This account is drawn from Richard V. Pierard, "One Nation under God: Judgment or Jingoism," in *Christian Social Ethics,* ed. Perry C. Cotham (Grand Rapids, MI: Baker, 1979), 81–103.

22. *Public Papers of the Presidents. Dwight D. Eisenhower,* 1954: 563.

23. A useful treatment of the entire issue is Robert Justin Goldstein, *Saving Old Glory: The History of the American Flag Desecration Controversy* (Boulder, CO: Westview Press, 1996).

BIBLIOGRAPHY

Books

Adams, David L. and Ken Schurb, eds. *The Anonymous God: The Church Confronts Civil Religion And American Society.* St. Louis: Concordia, 2005.

Balmer, Randall. *God in the White House: How Faith Shaped the Presidency from John F. Kennedy to George W. Bush.* New York: HarperOne, 2008.

Bellah, Robert N. *The Broken Covenant: American Civil Religion in a Time of Trial*, rev. ed. New York: Seabury Press, 1992.

Bellah, Robert N. and Phillp E. Hammond. *Varieties of Civil Religion*. San Francisco: Harper & Row, 1980.

Cristi, Marcela. *From Civil to Political Religion: the Intersection of Culture, Religion and Politics*. Waterloo, Ontario: Wilfrid Laurier University Press, 2001.

Durkheim, Émile. *The Elementary Forms of Religious Life*. New York: MacMillan, 1915.

Forney, Craig A. *The Holy Trinity of American Sports: Civil Religion in Football, Baseball, and Basketball (Sports and Religion)*. Macon, GA: Mercer University Press, 2007.

Gabriel, Ralph H. *The Course of American Democratic Thought*. 2nd ed. New York: Ronald Press, 1956.

Goldstein, Robert Justin. *Saving Old Glory: the History of the American Flag Desecration Controversy*. Boulder, CO: Westview Press, 1996.

Herberg, Will. *Protestant-Catholic-Jew*. rev. ed. Garden City, NY: Doubleday, 1960.

Kessler, Sanford. *Tocqueville's Civil Religion: American Christianity and the Prospects for Freedom*. Albany, NY: State University of New York Press, 1994.

Lipset, Seymour Martin. *American Exceptionalism: A Double-Edged Sword*. New York: Norton, 1997.

Marty, Martin E. *A Nation of Behavers*. Chicago: University of Chicago Press, 1976.

McGraw, Barbara. *Rediscovering America's Sacred Ground: Public Religion and Pursuit of the Good in a Pluralistic America*. Albany, NY: State University of New York Press, 2003.

McLoughlin, William G. *The American Evangelicals, 1800–1900*. New York: Harper & Row, 1974.

Meacham, Jon. *American Gospel: God, the Founding Fathers, and the Making of a Nation*. New York: Random House, 2007.

Mead, Sidney E. *The Nation with the Soul of a Church*. New York: Harper & Row, 1975.

Muller-Fahrenholz, Geiko, and Donald W. Shriver, Jr. *America's Battle for God: A European Christian Looks at Civil Religion*. Grand Rapids, MI: Eerdmans, 2007.

Parsons, Gerald. *Perspectives on Civil Religion (Religion Today: Tradition, Modernity and Change)*. London: Ashgate, 2002.

Phillips, Kevin. *American Theocracy: The Peril and Politics of Radical Religion, Oil, and Borrowed Money in the 21st Century*. New York: Viking, 2006.

Pierard, Richard V. and Robert D. Linder. *Civil Religion and the Presidency*. Grand Rapids, MI: Zondervan, 1988.

Pottenger, John R. *Reaping the Whirlwind: Liberal Democracy and the Religious Axis*. Washington, DC: Georgetown University Press, 2007.

Public Papers of the Presidents of the United States. Washington, DC: U.S. Government Printing Office. An annual volume has been issued for each president and is identified by name and year.

Richey, Russell E. and Donald G. Jones, eds. *American Civil Religion*. New York: Harper & Row, 1974.

Rousseau, Jean-Jacques. *The Social Contract and Discourses*, ed. G.D.H. Cole. New York: Dutton, 1959.

Shanks, Andrew. *Civil Society, Civil Religion*. New York: Wiley-Blackwell, 1995.

Smith, Gary Scott. *Faith and the Presidency: From George Washington to George W. Bush*. New York: Oxford University Press, 2006.

Tuveson, Ernest L. *Redeemer Nation: The Idea of America's Millennial Role*. Chicago: University of Chicago Press, 1968.

Waldman, Steven. *Founding Faith: Providence, Politics, and the Birth of Religious Freedom in America.* New York: Random House, 2008.

Williams, J. Paul. *What Americans Believe and How They Worship.* New York: Harper & Row, 1962.

Wuthnow, Robert. *American Mythos: Why Our Best Efforts to Be a Better Nation Fall Short.* Princeton, NJ: Princeton University Press, 2008.

———. *The Restructuring of American Religion: Society and Faith since World War II.* Princeton: Princeton University Press, 1988.

Articles/Chapters

Angrosino, Michael. "Civil Religion Redux." *Anthropological Quarterly* 75 (Spring 2002): 239.

Bellah, Robert N. "Civil Religion in America." *Daedalus* 96 (Winter 1967): 1.

Canipe, Lee. "Under God and Anti-communist: How the Pledge of Allegiance Got Religion in Cold-War America." *Journal of Church and State* 45 (Spring 2003): 305.

Cloud, Matthew W. "'One Nation, Under God': Tolerable Acknowledgement of Religion or Unconstitutional Cold War Propaganda Cloaked in American Civil Religion." *Journal of Church and State* 46 (Spring 2004): 311.

Coles, Roberta L. "Manifest Destinies Adapted for 1990's War Discourse: Mission and Destiny Intertwined." *Sociology of Religion* 63/4 (2002): 403.

Davis, Derek H. "God and the Pursuit of America's Self-Understanding: Toward a Synthesis of American Historiography." *Journal of Church and State* 46 (Summer 2004): 461.

———. "Law, Morals, and Civil Religion in America." *Journal of Church and State* 39 (Summer 1997): 411.

——— and Matthew McMearty. "America's 'Forsaken Roots': The Use and Abuse of Founders' Quotations." *Journal of Church and State* 47 (Summer 2005): 449.

Kao, Grace Y. and Jerome E. Copulsky. "The Pledge of Allegiance and the Meanings and Limits of Civil Religion." *Journal of the American Academy of Religion* 75 (March 2007): 121.

Linder, Robert D. "Universal Pastor: President Bill Clinton's Civil Religion." *Journal of Church and State* 38 (Autumn 1996): 733.

——— and Richard V. Pierard. "The President and Civil Religion." In *Encyclopedia of the American Presidency*, ed. Leonard W. Levy (New York: Simon and Schuster, 1994): 1: 203.

———. "Ronald Reagan, Civil Religion, and the New Religious Right in America." *Fides et History* 23 (Fall 1991): 57.

Marvin, Carolyn, and David W. Ingle. "Blood Sacrifice and the National: Revisiting Civil Religion." *Journal of the American Academy of Religion* 64 (Winter 1996): 767.

Mathisen, James A. "Twenty Years after Bellah: Whatever Happened to American Civil Religion?" *Sociological Analysis* 50/2 (1989): 29.

McDermott, Gerald Robert. "Civil Religion in the American Revolutionary Period: An Historiographic Analysis." *Christian Scholars Review* 18 (June 1989): 346.

McKenna, Joseph H. "Civil Society, Civil Religion." *Theological Studies* 58 (June 1997): 380.

Meizel, Katherine. "A Singing Citizenry: Popular Music and Civil Religion in America." *Journal for the Scientific Study of Religion* 45/4 (2006): 497.

Mirsky, Yehudah. "Civil Religion and the Establishment Clause." *Yale Law Journal* 95 (May 1986): 1237.

Pierard, Richard V. "Civil Religion." In *The Encyclopedia of Christianity*, ed. Edwin
    Fehlbusch et al. (Grand Rapids, MI: Eerdmans, 1999): 1: 585.
———. "Civil Religion: Parallel Development or Replacement for Traditional
    Christianity." In *Christianity in the Post Secular West,* eds. John Stenhouse and Brett
    Knowles (Adelaide, Australia: ATF Press, 2007): 163.
———. "'In God We Trust. . . . All Others Pay Cash': Reflections on Civil Religion."
    Stimulus: The New Zealand Journal of Christian Thought and Practice 10 (August
    2002): 11.
———. "One Nation under God: Judgment or Jingoism." In *Christian Social Ethics,* ed.
    Perry C. Cotham (Grand Rapids, MI: Baker, 1979): 81.
Reddit, Paul L. "When Faith Demands Treason: Civil Religion and the Prophet Jeremiah."
    Review and Expositor 101 (Spring 2004): 227.
Stackhouse, Max L. "Civil Religion, Political Theology and Public Theology: What's the
    Difference?" *Political Theology* 5/3 (2004): 275.
Stookey, Stephen M. "In God We Trust?: Evangelical Historiography and the Quest for
    a Christian America." *Southwestern Journal of Theology* 41/2–3 (Spring–Summer
    1999): 43.
Woodrum, Eric and Arnold Bell. "Race, Politics, and Religion in Civil Religion among
    Blacks." *Sociological Analysis* 49/4 (1989): 353.

PART VI

CONCLUSION

....

CHAPTER 20

THE INTERPLAY OF LAW, RELIGION, AND POLITICS IN THE UNITED STATES

....

DEREK H. DAVIS

ANY discussion of law, religion, and politics in the American system must be understood in context. The system embraces four distinct yet interrelated sets of rules: *separation* of church and state, *cooperation* between sacred and secular, *integration* of religion and politics, and *accommodation* of civil religion. Each of these four categories is important to the overall American public philosophy, and each category is part of a nuanced, albeit sometimes confusing, interconnected system that has as its goal the Good Society. The whole system cannot be understood without understanding each component of the system; thus this chapter examines successively each component while describing its function in the larger system.

The rules that comprise the American interplay of law, religion, and politics—rules dictated mostly by judicial interpretations of the First Amendment's religion clauses, but also embracing sacred traditions that the U.S. Supreme Court deems inviolable—are voluminous and contradictory at times, even to the most ripened experts. Apparent inconsistencies abound. How is it, for example, that students in public schools cannot have vocal prayers in their classrooms[1] or at their football games,[2] but the U.S. Congress can have its own chaplains to lead it daily in prayer? Why is it that the Ten Commandments cannot be regularly posted in public school

Portions of this chapter are taken from Derek H. Davis, "Explaining the Complexities of Religion and State in the United States: Separation, Integration, and Accommodation," in David Odell Scott, ed., *Democracy: Free Exercise and Diverse Visions and Religion* (Kent, OH: Kent State University Press), 2004.

classrooms, yet the U.S. Supreme Court building in Washington, DC, both inside and out, features several displays of the Ten Commandments?[3] How can a nation committed to the separation of church and state adopt a national motto that proclaims to the world, "In God We Trust?" On their face, these seemingly contradictory rules and practices might appear to be bizarre; but understood in the broader, elaborate American framework in which religion, law, and politics interact, these apparent consistencies can be understood, and even justified.

Separation of Church and State

It is often said of the United States that its system is one of strict separation between church and state. Although true in some respects, this depiction can only be described as a colossal overstatement; nevertheless "separation of church and state" has become the customary way of describing the relationship between religion and state in the American system.[4] Yet the phrase is too broad to accurately describe the whole system, because in many respects there clearly is no "separation." How can a system that proclaims "In God We Trust" as its national motto, invokes the names of God in its pledge of allegiance, observes a national day of prayer, and sanctions government-paid legislative chaplains be said to have a commitment to the separation of church and state? Obviously, the American tradition of separation of church and state does not mean that a separation of religion from government is required in all cases. Therefore, although the phrase is too broad to embrace the whole system, it does accurately describe an important part of the system.

The U.S. Supreme Court has frequently resorted to an examination of the eighteenth-century Founding Fathers' writings to ascertain the relationship between religion and state that was intended to undergird the American social and political order. The Court has tended to rely extensively on Thomas Jefferson, the author of the Declaration of Independence and the nation's third president, to determine much of the Founders' "original intent." In fact, the phrase "wall of separation between church and state" was first used in America by President Jefferson in 1802 as a shorthand explanation of the meaning he assigned to the religion clauses. This well-known phrase was enlisted by the U.S. Supreme Court in 1947 as a useful metaphor in adjudicating religion clause disputes.[5] The Court thus acknowledges that separating church and state was fundamental to the Founders' project, and one scholar has offered recently a fresh and insightful analysis of how the Founders and their immediate successors, under Jeffersonian influence, implemented the separation of church and state in the early national period.

Legal historian Mark McGarvie carefully documents how Jeffersonian liberals led the way in moving early America from a communitarian society in which private institutions, including churches, functioned as semipublic institutions under government nurture and control to educate the young, care for the poor and elderly, and shape the society's moral values, to a more individualistically grounded society that freed private institutions to operate independently of government control and influence. The process was complex and controversial, but accomplished primarily through the disestablishment process in which the states, one by one, cut their formal ties with religion and stopped supporting one or more churches to the detriment of others. The end result, largely achieved by the advent of the Andrew Jackson era in the early nineteenth century, separated church and state, enhanced religious liberty, deepened religious pluralism, and secularized the public domain. McGarvie finds these developments to be marks of progress, not setbacks, in shaping the character of the new nation.

In the disestablishment process, newly emerging conceptions of corporate law were instrumental. In colonial days, McGarvie argues, corporate charters were granted to individuals who agreed to use their grants of power to perform public tasks and meet public needs. This policy applied to business and commercial ventures, but also to churches and institutions of higher learning. Thus, charters were awarded only to churches and colleges that furthered the colony's religious and educational goals, which were interrelated. Dissenting groups that wanted to incorporate their churches or schools were out of luck. A cultural transformation took place in the first 50 years of nationhood, a legal and ideological transformation led by rationalistic Jeffersonian liberals that sought to enfranchise, in the interest of diversity and competition, private organizations in business, religion, education, social welfare, public health, and other areas of American life. McGarvie's is one of the finest scholarly accounts to come along in years arguing effectively for the separation of church and state as part of the founders' "original intent."[6] His account counters other recent works that minimize "separation" as one of the Founders' principal goals.[7]

"Separation of church and state" is therefore a legitimate concept in America, but it describes more of an *institutional* separation than a *strict* separation. In other words, the Constitution requires that the *institutions* of church and state in American society not be interconnected, dependent upon, or functionally related to each other. The purpose of this requirement is to achieve mutual independence and autonomy for these institutions, based on the belief that they will function best if neither has authority over the other. Affected are the institutional bodies of religion, i.e., churches, mosques, temples, synagogues, and other bodies of organized religion, and the institutional bodies of governmental authority—state and federal governments, but also small local bodies such as school districts, police departments, city councils, utility districts, municipal courts, county commissions, and the like. Consequently, churches and other houses of worship receive no direct governmental funding, nor are they required to pay income or property taxes. Government officials appoint no clergy; conversely, religious bodies appoint no government officials. Governments, and even courts, are not allowed to settle church disputes that involve doctrinal issues.[8] Religious bodies, unlike the Catholic Church in the Middle Ages, have no authority to dictate law or public policy, although they might try because they are not excluded as participants in political discourse.

One of the most fundamental meanings of the separation of church and state is that the state is prohibited from shaping, directing, or framing the religious beliefs of the individual citizen. Although persons might believe that which is untrue, and even be duped into believing that which is false, the Supreme Court has said repeatedly that it is not the province of the state to protect one from "bad" religions, even those that "might seem incredible, if not preposterous to most people."[9] As Justice William O. Douglas noted in *U.S. v. Ballard:*

> The Fathers of the Constitution were not unaware of the varied and extreme views of religious sects, of the violence of disagreement among them, and of the lack of any one religious creed on which all men would agree. They fashioned a charter of government which envisaged the widest possible of toleration of conflicting views. Man's relation to his God was made no concern to the state. He was granted the right to worship as he pleased and to answer to no man for the verity of his religious views.[10]

It is not the case, of course, that American citizens can do anything without fear of legal retribution in the name of religion. Thus sacrificing one's child, refusing blood transfusions or other medical treatment to one's child who is unable to speak for herself, intentionally defrauding parishioners, participating in snake handling practices during worship services, or delivering incompetent counseling—all acts entered into on the strength of religious belief—are practices that have occasionally been proscribed by American courts. Nevertheless, the courts remain admirably reluctant to interfere in religious acts, and continue to cite the abiding and virtually sacrosanct principle first enunciated by the Supreme Court in an 1872 case, *Watson v. Jones:*

> In this country the free right to entertain any religious belief, to practice any religious principle, and to teach any religious doctrine which does not violate the laws of morality and property, and which does not infringe personal rights, is conceded to all. The law knows no heresy, and is committed to the support of no dogma, the establishment of no sect.[11]

The institutional separation of church and state is observed most frequently, and most controversially, in judicial decisions that limit religious activity in the public schools. Court decisions limiting schools' ability to entertain vocal prayers[12] and scripture readings,[13] post the Ten Commandments and other religious texts,[14] or advance a particular religious world view[15] are intended to protect the sacred domain of religion from state interference. Courts often stress that children are highly impressionable, and that although it might be permissible for the state occasionally to accommodate religious observances in higher public education settings or legislative assemblies, it is important to leave the religious training of young children generally to parents, religious bodies, and other private organizations. Thus it might be said that a "high" wall of separation is observed in the nation's public K–12 schools. Yet it is important to remember that in the public school context, it is the precepts and practices of *institutionalized* religion that are prohibited from being embraced or proscribed. Courses that teach comparative religion, the historical or literary aspects of religion, or religion in a secular and objective way without any attempt to inculcate faith, are permitted, and even encouraged. As Justice Tom Clark wrote in *Abington v. Schempp* (1963), "one's education is not complete without a study of comparative religion or the history of religion and its relationship to the advancement of civilization. . . . study of the Bible or of religion, when presented objectively as part of a secular program of education [does not violate] the First Amendment."[16]

The institutional separation of church and state is a novel experiment in human history. Most societies throughout history have operated on the assumption that government should be a moral agent, that it must play a leading role in crafting the human being. It became customary in ancient times for governments to sponsor, even require, religious worship and instruction as the means of inculcating morality into citizens' lives. The American Founders were convinced that successful nation-building would be impossible in the absence of a moral citizenry, but they believed that moral training, insofar as it was religiously based, must derive primarily from the faith community, not government.[17] The Establishment Clause was the founders' attempt to end government's coercive role in directing the religious course of citizens' lives; the Free Exercise Clause reflected their goal of putting religion in the hands of the citizens to enable them to shape their own religious commitments. It was a bold experiment, but one that is now central to the American public philosophy. As Supreme Court Justice Wiley Rutledge once declared, "We have staked the very existence of our country on the faith that complete separation between the state and religion is best for the state and best for religion."[18] Justice Rutledge knew better than anyone that *complete* separation between church and state is impossible, but his words are a powerful reminder of how central the principle of separation is to the American way of life.

COOPERATION BETWEEN SACRED AND SECULAR

The U.S. Supreme Court has never authorized government money for churches and other houses of worship to be used strictly for religious, "nonsecular" purposes, such as payment of clergy salaries or conducting worship services. However, government funding of other religiously based institutions, especially private religious schools, has been a subject of great controversy in the United States. In the mid-twentieth century, the U.S. Supreme Court, when it began adjudicating a large number of religion cases, enunciated a "no aid" principle. Based on a strong principle of church–state separation, funding of religiously affiliated educational institutions in particular was considered beyond the scope of what the Constitution permits. This perspective advanced the idea that various forms of aid to religious institutions inevitably compromises their religious mission, causes dependence on governmental support, politicizes religion, and ultimately causes religion to lose its prophetic role as well as its ability to provide the moral foundations that the nation needs. It was in *Everson v. Board of Education* (1947) that the Court so clearly enunciated this principle, but even the *Everson* decision seemed to defy the Court's thoroughly separationist rhetoric. In *Everson,* the Court included in a litany of prohibited acts foreclosed by the Establishment Clause this notable declaration: "No tax in any amount, large or small, can be levied to support any religious activities or institutions, whatever they may be called, or whatever form they may adopt to teach or practice religion."[19] The Court then held, inexplicably to some observers, that it was not a violation of this declaration to prevent the city of Ewing, New Jersey from reimbursing parents for bus fares incurred to transport their children to Catholic schools. The decision seemed to some critics inconsistent with the Court's own pronouncement of what the Constitution requires, thus giving rise to the argument that the Court never really adopted the "no aid" approach at all.

However, occasionally the Court would make rulings that genuinely seemed to support the "no aid" approach. *Meek v. Pittenger* (1975),[20] for example, struck down an attempt by the Pennsylvania legislature to send various forms of aid to private religious schools. The Court ruled that most of the aid, which ostensibly did not advance the "religious" aspects of the educational enterprise, such as loans of instructional equipment, recorders, lab instruments, and the provision of counseling and testing services for remedial students, was divertable to religious purposes and therefore violated the Establishment Clause. The Court further noted, as it often did in "no aid" cases, that *any* aid to church-related schools, even that which was arguably "secular" in nature and thereby enabled the schools to expend their own funds on religion-specific activities, caused a breach of the Establishment Clause. The latter principle never was the majority view on the Court, however, thus opening the door to a friendly linkage between church and state that might permit certain kinds of aid to religiously based educational institutions.

Although the High Court could have stuck by its "no aid" principle and universally denied any type of government aid, direct or indirect, to church-related schools, it chose to go another route—one of *cooperation* between government and religion by which it would approve funding of "secular" components of private religious schools while denying funding for those components that might advance the "sacred." Consequently, the courts have permitted governments to purchase or provide, by way of example, textbooks,[21] computers,[22] equipment for diagnostic testing,[23] auxiliary services performed away from a sectarian campus,[24] standardized exams prepared by state officials,[25] expenses for grading state-prepared exams,[26] fees to an interpreter attending classes with a student at a religious school,[27] buildings in which only secular activities are conducted or secular subjects are taught,[28] and other miscellaneous expenditures on behalf of private religious schools because these forms of aid advance only the "secular" character of education and thus are not endorsements of religion. Programs that provide benefits that might be used for promoting or advancing religion, however, such as teacher stipends,[29] open-ended subsidies that might be used to purchase religious texts or erect religious statues,[30] reimbursements to parents sending their children to religious schools,[31] salaries for teachers to teach in a "community education" program conducted at their own parochial school campus,[32] or funds to finance field trips in which religious instruction might take place,[33] have been held unconstitutional.

The Supreme Court subsequently moved even further from its original "no aid" approach in a series of cases that highlighted the principles of "even-handed neutrality" and "private choice." An increasingly conservative Court, led by Chief Justice William Rehnquist, began formulating in the 1980s a softer approach to aid to religious educational institutions that deepened further the concept of cooperation between the sacred and the secular. The Court seized upon the idea that if government sought to benefit educational institutions in a neutral, even-handed way in which religious recipients were not favored over nonreligious recipients, then there was no advancement of religion that might violate the Establishment Clause. Thus in *Mueller v. Allen* (1983),[34] the Court approved a Minnesota statute that granted tax deductions to taxpayers for most kinds of educational expenses. The benefit was available to parents of students attending all public and private schools. It mattered not, as noted by four dissenters, that the major deduction was for private school tuition that was not enjoyed by public school parents, nor that 96% of the attendees of private schools were enrolled in sectarian schools. The structure of the benefit package was such that the deductions allowed were available to *all* parents. This "even-handed" structure provided "equal treatment" across the board and thus did not offend the Constitution. According to the Court, programs "that neutrally provide state assistance to a broad spectrum of citizens [are] not readily subject to challenge under the Establishment Clause."[35]

The Court developed further this principle in *Zobrest v. Catalina Hills*.[36] James Zobrest, a deaf student, wanted to attend a Catholic high school in Tucson, Arizona. Public school officials determined that a federal statute, the Individuals with Disabilities Educational Act, which made various kinds of aid to disabled students available no matter what kind of school the student attended, authorized payment for an interpreter for Zobrest who would attend all classes with him. The aid was challenged as an unconstitutional advancement of religion, but the Court eventually held that because Zobrest could choose any school to attend, public or private, the legislation was "even-handed" and nondiscriminatory, thus the expense for the interpreter was permissible. The Court also deemed it important that Zobrest made a "private choice" to attend a Catholic school; therefore, the legislature was not deemed to be influencing his decision or favoring or advancing religion in any way.

Advancing the same principles of even-handed neutrality and private choice, the Court subsequently held in *Mitchell v. Helms*[37] that if a state school system distributes federal funds to a range of both public and private schools that apply for the funds, the Establishment Clause is not violated because there is no predetermined outcome of how the funds will be distributed. A plurality of justices held that the expenditures must be for activities that are secular on their face without regard to potential divertibility to religious use or whether the funding was direct (to the schools rather than the students) rather than indirect. Justice Sandra Day O'Connor objected on the basis that "the plurality opinion foreshadows the approval of direct monetary subsidies to religious organizations, even when they use the money to advance their religious objectives."[38] A subsequent case, *Zelman v. Simmons-Harris*,[39] held that a state statute providing voucher funds to Cleveland, Ohio students who wished to attend a school other than their own was not a violation of the Establishment Clause because the students could choose among an array of public, private, religious, community, or charter schools. It was irrelevant that 96% of the students enrolled in sectarian, mostly Catholic, schools.

The doctrines of even-handedness and private choice now seem fairly well embedded in the Supreme Court's church–state jurisprudence. However, the decisions supporting the doctrines are relatively new, not universally accepted by all of the Court members, and controversial in a nation that traditionally has stood on the side of the separation of church and state. As Flowers, Rogers, and Green note, these decisions are certain to lead to a higher incidence of government funding of religious institutions in the near future,[40] but it is also possible that the Court will continue to search for a more nuanced balance among its disparate versions of cooperation between the secular and the sacred.

The cooperation principle affects other areas of religion–government interaction as well. In the late 1990s, the U.S. government passed a set of measures that attempted to provide government funding of churches and other religious institutions that were willing to administer social service programs—soup kitchens, drug and alcohol rehabilitation programs, clothing pantries, homeless shelters, youth anticrime programs, and the like. Theoretically, these programs advance secular ends, thus passing constitutional scrutiny. But they are a bold challenge to traditional, pre-1980 constitutional doctrine, which held that churches, temples, mosques, and other houses of worship are "pervasively sectarian," which means that their mission and purpose is so pervaded by religion that it is virtually impossible for them to ferret out the "secular" aspects of their activity.[41] This legislation, initially dubbed "Charitable Choice" because program beneficiaries under the legislation in which it was first adopted, the Welfare Reform Act of 1996, could choose either a government-funded religious or secular provider, challenged traditional "separationist" judicial interpretations of the Establishment Clause. Proponents of Charitable Choice advance the ancient fear that without government aid, religion will suffer, potential recipients of assistance will be ignored, and society will experience moral decline. Opponents counter with the argument that religion thrives best when it relies on private rather than government resources, and that morality is best fostered in a climate of self-sustaining voluntarism rather than government-sustaining inducements.[42] These are the same arguments that fueled the debate over "separation" ideals in the founding generation, but this time they were spurred by a new constitutional doctrine of "even-handed neutrality."[43]

During the administration of President George W. Bush (2000–2008), an administrative office was created exclusively to further the Charitable Choice concept. The Office of Faith-Based and Community Initiatives was created by executive order and paid for out of general appropriations, thus skirting Congressional oversight. The office created satellite offices in 12 government departments that funded various faith-based projects around the country. Although, according to one study, only 7.1% of American congregations received any funding pursuant to the initiative,[44] the program awarded contracts to faith-based institutions averaging more than $2 billion annually during the Bush years.[45] One scholar opined that the program only placed social services in the hands of entities—churches and other faith-based organizations—that had borne the weight of providing social services in the nineteenth century; but he neglected to explain that those services were financed largely by the private sector, not by government.[46] In the first month of his presidency that began in 2009, Barack Obama renamed the office: Office of Faith-Based Initiatives and Neighborhood Partnerships. He promised to make changes that would not entangle church and state, but the details of those changes were never entirely clear. What was apparent, however, was that he wanted to continue to pursue a workable arrangement that would make possible real cooperation between the sacred and the secular.

INTEGRATION OF RELIGION AND POLITICS

Separation of church and state and cooperation between the sacred and secular are indeed important to the American public philosophy, but as noted, they do not describe all aspects of the interplay between religion and state. This is readily seen in the way that the American system encourages the participation of religious voices in the political process. Were the system one of *total* separation, it would not countenance the active involvement of religious persons, faith communities, and religious organizations that vigorously enter public discourse, seeking to persuade government officials of the merits of framing law and public policy to reflect their distinctly religious outlooks.

The right of churches and other religious bodies to engage in political advocacy and make political pronouncements has never been seriously questioned throughout this nation's history, from the colonial period down to the present. In the years leading up to the American Revolution, for example, the churches assumed a leading role in the political debate on the question of whether the colonies should go to war with the mother country. In the nineteenth century, the major causes for political action among the churches and other religious groups were slavery, temperance, and nonsectarian education. In the twentieth century, the engagement of religious bodies in the body politic grew to cover a wide range of issues, including economic and social justice, war and peace, abortion, homosexuality, civil rights, and world hunger. Today virtually all of the major religious groups in America and many religious coalitions have public affairs offices in Washington, DC to lead their lobbying efforts.[47] These groups, for the most part, do not consider these offices to exist for the promotion of their own interests, but as an effective means by which they give witness in public affairs based upon their own understanding of their mission in the world.

Given the time-honored right of religious bodies to be active participants in the American political process, it is not surprising that the United States Supreme Court has not seriously challenged this basic right. The strongest affirmation of this right was given by the Court in *Walz v. Tax Commission* (1970): "Adherents of particular faiths and individual churches frequently take strong positions on public issues, including . . . vigorous advocacy of legal and constitutional positions. Of course, churches as much as secular bodies and private citizens have that right."[48] Likewise, in *McDaniel v. Paty* (1978), a case striking down the last of the state statutes prohibiting ministers from seeking state office, the Supreme Court affirmed the importance and protected status of religious ideas in public debate: "[R]eligious ideas, no less than any other, may be the subject of debate which is uninhibited, robust, and wide-open. . . . That public debate of religious ideas, like any other, may arouse emotion, may incite, may foment religious divisiveness and strife, does not rob it of its constitutional protection."[49]

Supreme Court pronouncements such as these, however, should not lead one to assume that organized religion in America enjoys an absolute right to participate in the making of public policy, free from governmental interference of any type. These groups are subject to losing their tax exemptions, for example, for "substantial" political expenditures[50] or for endorsing political candidates (lobbying).[51] Nevertheless, they enjoy essentially the same rights as secular groups to participate in the political process. The principles of democracy prevail in this instance, such that the rights of every person or group in American society, religious or secular, that wishes to contribute to democratic governance is free to do so, even encouraged to do so, even though such participation constitutes a technical violation of the principle of church–state separation. *Complete* separation would mean banning the activities of the Christian Coalition and approximately 125 other religious lobbies whose sole reason for existence is to influence lawmaking and public policy according to religiously inspired perspectives. Although many of these lobbies, unfortunately, attempt to issue dictates rather than offer advice, mandates rather than persuasive arguments, the great majority of them have learned to submit their perspectives with some degree of humility, recognizing that America is a democracy shaped by many views, not a theocracy shaped by a few.

American adherence to the integration of religion and politics also means that potential candidates and office-holders are free to speak about their religious views. They may think it prudent at times to abstain from too much "God-speak," but the Free Exercise Clause gives them the freedom to speak freely about matters of faith, even, for the most part, when acting in their official capacities. It is unlikely that a candidate for president could be elected in America without some candid talk about his or her religious views. America is diverse in its religious makeup, but it is unmistakably one of the most religious nations on the globe, and the American people generally demand to know their representatives' religious beliefs. No avowed atheist has ever been elected president, and although many of the early presidents (perhaps as many as the first seven) were deists, every president has personally participated in Protestant religious activities while in office save two: John F. Kennedy, who was a Catholic, and Richard M. Nixon, who was a Quaker.

The Constitution forbids the administration of formal religious tests for holding public office (all but six states have followed suit), but this is different from the unofficial expectation that an office-holder have at least some religious commitments. This expectation is the product of a religious culture, of a body of citizens who "are a religious people whose institutions presuppose a Supreme Being." This was the perspective of Supreme Court Justice William O. Douglas in 1954,[52] but it remains true more than a half century later.

Religion and politics in the United States are intertwined in inextricable ways. Americans for the most part accept this. This mix is a part of political/governmental life. In the making of law and public policy, there are a great many issues that need resolution. Religious issues (e.g., abortion, homosexuality, stem cell research, and war policy) often need political solutions in the same way that more strictly secular issues such as commerce, health policy, defense, and education need political solutions. Of course good people often disagree about the best resolutions, thus we have witnessed the evolution and development of political parties over the life of American history. Disagreement among citizens and political parties, therefore, is expected; healthy debate on the resolution of issues, including those that are religious in nature, is part of a vibrant, healthy democracy.

Accommodation of Civil Religion

If in the American system the Establishment Clause is relaxed in sanctioning cooperation between the sacred and secular and the integration of religion and politics, it is also somewhat relaxed in accommodating various expressions of civil religion. Simply stated, the "separation" ideal is lightly enforced when it comes to American civil religious practice. According to Robert Bellah, the most celebrated scholar on American civil religion, civil religion is about those public rituals that express the nexus of the political order to the divine reality.[53] By most accounts, civil religion is a form of religion that gives sacred meaning to national life. It is a kind of theological glue that binds a nation together by allying the political with the transcendent. Civil religion is a way for Americans to recognize the sovereignty of God over their nation without getting bogged down in theological differences.

Many Americans affirm the separation of church and state, but this does not remove their belief that the nation—as a civil entity—is still somehow obligated to God. For them, nationhood makes little sense unless it is part of a universe ruled by God; consequently, they believe that the body politic should have a religious dimension. Stated in another way, religion is not merely private; it is inescapably public, too. Bellah acknowledges this, arguing that separation of church and state does not deny the political realm a religious dimension.[54]

The form of civil religion that exists today in the United States seems to embrace ideas from two distinct theological traditions. On the one hand, American civil religion consists of ideas derived from Puritanism such as the covenanted, millennial, and chosen nation. These ideas have been, and remain, inherently religious, and implicitly particularistic and coercive. On the other hand, ideas contributed from the American Enlightenment, such as the Declaration's affirmation that "all men are created equal," and are entitled to rights of "life, liberty, and the pursuit of happiness," are clearly more secular, and implicitly universalistic and persuasive in character. Both traditions have usually sought the aid of government for their advancement, which of course has created unique problems for the propagation of the more distinctly religious Puritan ideas because of the Constitution's church–state separation principle. Nevertheless, as Richard Hughes has rightly observed, most Christian patriots during the course of our nationhood have never perceived any tension between "the god of Puritan particularism and the god of universal liberties."[55] Even Bellah fuses the two traditions in his description of that civil religion to which the nation should commit itself.

The Puritan strain of the American civil religion distinctly follows after the medieval vision of a Christian commonwealth. In the Constantinian-Justinian-Calvinistic pattern, the Christian religion is recast into a law code, for it is legislation, divinely based law, which is God's favored method for instituting the divine order on earth. The aim is the reformation of the civil order, with Christian values imposed on society through force of law. It is this Puritan tradition that conservatives mostly aggressively support and seek to implement as the American civil religion.

However, many Americans have never rested comfortably in the prospect of an official enshrinement of the Puritan tradition. It stands in stark contrast to the tradition of the American Enlightenment, which looks to "the laws of nature and of nature's God" for the securement of humankind's unalienable rights.[56] This tradition is no less committed to religious faith, but because it places all humankind on an equal footing before a deity who is equally accessible to all, it endorses persuasion, not coercion, as the means by which one is brought to embrace the object of faith. The Enlightenment tradition rejects the Constantinian union of church and state, since the union acts to compel obedience on matters that should be left, as John Locke held, "to the dictates of conscience." Liberty and equality are the tradition's creed, and universality of application its goal.

The American civil religion is a rather awkward joinder of Puritanism and the Enlightenment, of coercion and persuasion, of conformity and diversity. To its credit, it seeks to be all-inclusive by merging the two traditions; this indeed is the motivation of Bellah in praising and seeking to preserve both traditions in American civil religion. The joinder probably fails, however, because the Puritan strain represents a distinctive Christianizing of a rival tradition that is in no way hostile to Christianity, but is specifically committed to transcending all religious traditions, including Christianity. In a highly pluralistic society such as the United States, the two traditions, as an amalgam, strain to negotiate a workable compatibility.

The Enlightenment tradition, dominated as it is by its persuasive and pluralistic dimensions, likely has the greater capacity to serve as the basic framework of an American civil religion. Such a civil religion would perhaps feature commitments to freedom, justice, brotherhood, and equality. These are commitments that are not specifically religious, but are shared by most Americans. They are social values that constitute a trans-institutional symbol realm that embodies much of what the nation stands for. Moreover, these values are consistent with most religious perspectives, being located in the revealed and natural law sources of truth that characterize most religions.

It should be noted that although the church–state separation principle prohibits an official governmental endorsement of civil religion, the same principle in no way prevents the development of a cultural civil religion. It is civil religion as a *legal* institution rather than as a *cultural* institution that the Constitution prohibits. Bellah is surely correct in saying that "the fact that we have no established religion does not mean that our public life has no religious dimension or that fundamental questions of our national existence are not civil religious questions."[57] Thus the prospect that a unifying civil religion might develop in America remains intact, although the precise elements of such a common faith remain uncertain.

Civil religion is a sociological reality in every society. It manifests itself in different ways in different contexts, but French Sociologist Émile Durkheim (1858–1917) was probably correct in suggesting that every society at its deepest foundations is religious, and the sovereign must act responsibly to respect and acknowledge this, lest the society itself deteriorate and pass into oblivion.[58] For most Americans, of course, a nation that takes steps to acknowledge the sovereignty of God, even if in generic, symbolic ways, is not merely accommodating the wishes of the citizenry in the sense of filling a sociological need, but acting to affirm the divine reality. In any case, the accommodation of civil religion can be said to prevent the nation from steering too far in the direction of a secularized culture.

The U.S. Supreme Court occasionally acknowledges the evidence of civil religion in American life. Legislative prayer,[59] legislative and military chaplaincies,[60] Christmas[61] and Hanukkah[62] displays, and graduation prayers in public schools,[63] as expressions of civil religion, have all been challenged as violations of the "separation" requirements of the Establishment Clause. The Court tends to sanction those civil religious traditions that are generic, longstanding, and not likely to offend persons of tender age. Thus, in the case of legislative prayer, the Supreme Court has held that the practice is constitutional because it has a long and unbroken tradition in American political life.[64] In the public school context, however, given the impressionability of young persons, similar prayers are prohibited as violations of the institutional separation of church and state. The same contrary set of rules, applied in the respective contexts of legislative halls and public school classrooms, can be said to apply to the posting of the Ten Commandments[65] and other sacred texts. Legislative and military chaplaincies are likewise affirmed as longstanding traditions, although it is doubtful that courts would endorse the concept of public school chaplains because of the impressionability and potential for indoctrination of the students they would serve. Holiday displays have been held not to violate the Establishment Clause if their religious message is muted by surrounding secular symbols.[66] Prayer offered by a clergyman at a public school graduation ceremony, however, has been held to violate the Establishment Clause as an inappropriate government sponsorship of religion.[67]

In summary, civil religion has been for much of American history, and remains, a vital cultural force. It is manifested in our own day in prayers at presidential inaugurations, the invocation used each time the Supreme Court itself hears argument ("God save this honorable court"), Thanksgiving and National Day of Prayer proclamations, the words "under God" in the pledge of allegiance, the phrase "In God We Trust" on coins, various Scripture quotations inscribed on government buildings ("Moses the Lawgiver" is the inscription above the Supreme Court's bench), and even the ritual benediction, "God Bless America," used frequently by presidents. These civil religious expressions are not promoted exclusively by the state, or exclusively by the religious community. Rather, they are promoted by both, serving to imbed in the national civil order an unmistakable religious quality.

All of these civil religious traditions are violations of a strict notion of the separation of church and state. Yet they form a rich tradition of practices that are culturally and judicially accommodated. Undoubtedly they offend many, but they are for the most part generic practices that are not coercive in the way that, for example, audible school prayers in the public schools are. Indeed, these practices are accepted and celebrated by most Americans, and they contribute to a unique, nuanced, and sometimes contradictory set of concepts, principles, customs, beliefs, and symbols that comprise the American tradition of religion and state.[68]

CONCLUSION

Although contradictory in many respects, the principles of separation of church and state, cooperation between sacred and secular, integration of religion and politics, and accommodation of civil religion combine to provide unique but important contributions to America's public philosophy. The role of religion in American public life has been controversial since the founding and will likely remain so far into the future. But perhaps the separation-cooperation-integration-accommodation typology described in this chapter removes some of the hard edges from the controversy, because it embraces elements of both conservative and liberal thought, of competing philosophical and theological beliefs, indeed of arguments advanced by both separationists and anti-separationists. Such is the way a democracy should work—disparate elements coming together to produce that which hopefully serves everyone, that which we have come to call the common good, indeed that which we might refer to as the Good Society.

ENDNOTES

1. *Engel v. Vitale,* 370 U.S. 421 (1962) and *Abington v. Schempp,* 374 U.S. 203 (1963).

2. *Santa Fe v. Doe,* 530 U.S. 27 (2002).

3. For a discussion of the Ten Commandments in public life, see Derek H. Davis, "The Ten Commandments as Public Ritual," *Journal of Church and State* 44 (Spring 2002): 221–228.

4. Two basic views of "separation" dominate the scholarly literature. Those who see separation as requiring only the prohibition against a national church thus allowing for broader governmental advancement of religion are often called accommodationists. Those who argue for more extensive prohibitions of governmental support of religion are frequently referred to as separationists. Among the best works presenting accommodationist interpretations are Chester James Antieu, Arthur L. Downey, and Edward C. Roberts, *Freedom from Federal Establishment: Formation and Early History of the First Amendment Religions Clauses* (Milwaukee, WI: Bruce Publishing, 1964); Walter Berns, *The First Amendment and the Future of American Democracy* (New York: Basic Books, 1976); Michael J. Malbin, *Religion and Politics: The Intentions of the Authors of the First Amendment* (Washington, DC: American Enterprise Institute for Public Policy Research, 1978); Robert L. Cord, *Separation of Church and State: Historical Fact and Current Fiction* (New York: Lambeth Press, 1982); and Philip Hamburger, *Separation of Church and State* (Cambridge, MA: Harvard University Press, 2002). Among the best with separationist stances are Leo Pfeffer, *Church, State and Freedom.* 2nd ed. (Boston: Beacon Press, 1967); Leonard Levy, *The Establishment Clause: Religion and the First Amendment* (New York: Macmillan, 1986); Anson Phelps Stokes, *Church and State in the United States: Historical Development and Contemporary Problems of Religious Freedom under the Constitution,* 3 vols. (New York: Harper & Brothers, 1950); and Isaac Kramnick and R. Laurence Moore, *The Godless Constitution: The Case against Religious Correctness* (New York: Norton, 1996).

5. See *Everson v. Board of Education,* 330 U.S. 1 (1947). For disparate treatments of the origin and development of the "separation" metaphor, see Daniel Dreisbach, *Thomas Jefferson and the Separation of Church and State* (New York: NYU Press, 2002); and Derek H. Davis, "The 'Wall of Separation' Metaphor," *Christian Ethics Today* 49 (Spring 2004): 1.

6. Mark McGarvie, *One Nation Under Law: America's Early Struggles to Separate Church and State* (DeKalb, IL: Northern Illinois University Press, 2005).

7. See, for example, Dreisbach, *Thomas Jefferson and the Wall of Separation between Church and State,* and Hamburger, *Separation of Church and State.*

8. *Jones v. Wolf,* 443 U.S. 595 (1979).

9. *U.S. v. Ballard,* 322 U.S. 78 (1944), 87.

10. Ibid.

11. *Watson v. Jones,* 80 U.S. 679 (1872), 728.

12. *Engel v. Vitale, 370 U.S. 421 (1962); Lee v. Weisman, 505 U.S. 577 (1992).*

13. *Abington v. Schempp, 374 U.S. 203 (1963).*

14. *Stone v. Graham,* 449 U.S. 39 (1980).

15. *Epperson v. Arkansas,* 393 U.S. 97 (1968); *Edwards v. Aguillard,* 482 U.S. 578 (1987).

16. *Abington* v. *Schempp,* 225.

17. See Chapter 10, "Virtue and the Continental Congress, in Derek H. Davis, *Religion and the Continental Congress, 1774–1789: Contributions to Original Intent* (New York: Oxford University Press, 2000).

18. *Everson* v. *Board of Education,* 330 U.S. 1 (1947), 59.

19. *Everson*, 16.

20. *Meek v. Pittenger*, 421 U.S. 229 (1977). *Meek* has been referred to as "the 'high water mark' of no-aid separationism." See Ronald B. Flowers, Melissa Rogers, and Steven K. Green, *Religious Freedom and the Supreme Court* (Waco, TX: Baylor University Press, 2009), 569.

21. *Board of Education* v. *Allen*, 392 U.S. 236 (1968).

22. *Mitchell* v. *Helms*, 530 U.S. 793 (2000).

23. *Levitt v. Pearl*, 413 U.S. 472 (1973).

24. *Wolman v. Walter*, 433 U.S. 229 (1977).

25. *Levitt v. Pearl*.

26. *Wolman v. Walter*.

27. *Zobrest v. Catalina Hills*, 509 U.S. 1 (1993).

28. *Tilton v. Richardson*, 403 U.S. 672 (1971); *Roemer v. Board of Public Works of Maryland*, 426 U.S. 736 (1971); and *Hunt v. McNair*, 413 U.S. 734 (1973).

29. *Lemon v. Kurtzman*, 403 U.S. 602 (1971).

30. *Pearl v. Nyquist*, 413 U.S. 756 (1973).

31. *Ibid.*

32. *Grand Rapids v. Ball*, 473 U.S. 373 (1985).

33. *Wolman v. Walter*, 433 U.S. 229 (1977).

34. *Mueller v. Allen*, 463 U.S. 388 (1983).

35. Ibid. at 398–399.

36. *Zobrest v. Catalina Hills*, 509 U.S. 1 (1993).

37. *Mitchell v. Helms*, 530 U.S. 793 (2000).

38. Ibid. at 847. For further analysis of the *Helms* case, see Derek H. Davis, "The U.S. Supreme Court as Moral Physician: *Mitchell v. Helms* and the Constitutional Revolution to Reduce Restrictions on Governmental Aid to Religion," *Journal of Church and State* 43 (Spring 2001): 213–233. It is further discussed in Flowers, Rogers, and Green, *Religion and the Supreme Court*, 568–571.

39. *Zelman v. Simmons-Harris*, 536 U.S. 639 (2002).

40. Flowers, Rogers, And Green, *Religion and the Supreme Court*, 571.

41. After *Mitchell v. Helms*, the "pervasively sectarian" principle has a precarious status in Supreme Court jurisprudence.

42. On Charitable Choice legislation generally, see Derek Davis and Barry Hankins, *Welfare Reform and Faith-based Organizations* (Waco, TX: J.M. Dawson Institute of Church-State Studies, 1999); and Sheila Suess Kennedy and Wolfgang Bielefeld, *Charitable Choice at Work: Evaluation Faith-Based Job Programs in the States* (Washington DC: Georgetown University Press, 2006).

43. See Derek H. Davis, "A Commentary on the Supreme Court's 'Equal Treatment' Doctrine as the New Constitutional Paradigm for Protecting Religious Liberty," *Journal of Church and State* 46 (Autumn 2004): 717–737.

44. Ann Farris and Claire Hughes, Roundtable on Religion and Social Welfare Policy, "Durability of Bush Administration's Faith-Based Effort at Issue in 2008," January 8, 2008, www.religionandsocialpolicy.org/news/article_print.cfm?id=7551.

45. Amy E. Black, Douglas L. Koopman, and David K. Ryden, *Of Little Faith: The Politics of George W. Bush's Faith-Based Initiatives* (Washington DC: Georgetown University Press, 2004).

46. Marvin Olasky, *Compassionate Conservatism: What It Is, What It Does, and How It Can Transform America* (Glencove, NY: Free Press, 2000).

47. For excellent treatments of religious lobbying, see Ronald J. Hrebenar and Ruth K. Scott, *Interest Group Politics in America* (Englewood Cliffs, NJ: Prentice-Hall, 1982);

Jeffrey M. Berry, *The Interest Group Society* (Glenview, IL: Scott, Foresman, and Company, 1989); Allen D. Hertzke, *Representing God in Washington: The Role of Religious Lobbies in the American Polity* (Knoxville, TN: The University of Tennessee Press, 1988); Jeffrey M. Berry, *The New Liberalism: The Rising Power of Citizens Groups* (Washington, DC: Brookings Institution Press, 1999); Daniel J. B. Hofrenning, *In Washington, but Not Of It: The Prophetic Politics of Religious Lobbyists* (Philadelphia: Temple University Press, 1995); Cynthia D. Moe Lobeda, *The Public Church: For the Life of the World* (Augsburg Fortress Publishers, 2004); and Luke Eugene Ebersole, *Church Lobbying in the Nation's Capital* (New York: Macmillan, 1951).

48. *Walz* v. *Tax Commission*, 397 U.S. 664 (1970).

49. *McDaniel* v. *Paty*, 435 U.S. 618 (1978), 640.

50. Although there is no clear rule for defining "substantial," one case suggests there is a "safe harbor" if an organization's lobbying expenses do not exceed 5%. *Seasongood v. Commissioner*, 227 F.2d 907 (6th Cir. 1955). In another case, a court held that a church spending approximately 22% of its revenues on members' medical bills under a church medical plan was engaged in a "substantial nonexempt activity." *Bethel Conservative Mennonite Church v. Commissioner* 80 T.C. 352 (1983), rev'd., 746 F.2d 388 (7th Cir. 1984). Another court has held that a percentage test is inappropriate. *Haswell v. United States*, 500 F.2d 1133 (Ct. Cl. 1974), cert. denied, 419 U.S. 1107 (1975). Still, according to one source, no more than 20% of expenditures would be deemed "insubstantial." See Lynn R. Buzzard and Sherra Robinson, *I.R.S. Political Activity Restrictions on Churches and Charitable Ministries* (Diamond Bar, CA: Christian Ministries Management Association, 1990), 53–59.

51. "Lobbying" is defined in the Internal Revenue Code Section 4911 (d)(1). Various regulations, rulings, and court decisions on the meaning of "lobbying" are explained well in Lynn R. Buzzard and Sherra Robinson, *I.R.S. Political Activity Restrictions*, 42–52.

52. *Zorach* v. *Clauson*, 343 U.S. 306 (1952) at 313.

53. See generally, Robert N. Bellah, *The Broken Covenant: American Civil Religion in Time of Trial*, 2nd ed. (Chicago: University of Chicago Press, 1975), especially p. 3.

54. Ibid., 169–170.

55. Richard T. Hughes, "Civil Religion, the Theology of the Republic, and the Free Church Tradition," *Journal of Church and State* 22 (Winter 1980): 77–78.

56. Ibid.

57. Bellah, *The Broken Covenant*, 169.

58. Emile Durkheim, *The Elementary Forms of the Religious Life*, rev. ed. (New York: Free Press, 1965).

59. *Marsh* v. *Chambers*, 463 U.S. 783 (1983).

60. *Abington* v. *Schempp*, 374 U.S. 203 (1963), 296-97 (Brennan concurring).

61. *Lynch* v. *Donnelly*, 465 U.S. 668 (1984).

62. *Allegheny* v. *Pittsburgh ACLU*, 492 U.S. 573 (1989).

63. *Lee* v. *Weisman*, 505 U.S. 577 (1992).

64. *Marsh* v. *Chambers*, 463 U.S. 783 (1983).

65. *Stone* v. *Graham*, 449 U.S. 39 (1980).

66. *Lynch* v. *Donnelly*, 465 U.S. 668 (1984) (Christmas crèche paid for with public monies constitutional when surrounded by Santa Claus, reindeer, elves, and related secular Christmas decorations); *County of Allegheny* v. *A.C.L.U.*, 492 U.S. 573 (1989) (Jewish menorah displayed on public property constitutional when located next to a Christmas tree and a sign saluting liberty).

67. *Lee* v. *Weisman*, 505 U.S. 577 (1992).

68. This position is consistent with the Supreme Court's doctrine of "benevolent

neutrality," first expressed in *Walz v. Tax Commission,* 397 U.S. 664 (1970). "Benevolent neutrality" is appropriately sensitive to the institutional difference between religion and government that was intended by the framers while simultaneously allowing for some governmental expressions of religion in public life.

BIBLIOGRAPHY

Books

Antieu, Chester James, Arthur L. Downey, and Edward C. Roberts. *Freedom from Federal Establishment: Formation and Early History of the First Amendment Religions Clauses.* Milwaukee, WI: Bruce Publishing, 1964.

Bellah, Robert N. *The Broken Covenant: American Civil Religion in Time of Trial,* 2nd ed. Chicago: University of Chicago Press, 1975.

Berns, Walter. *The First Amendment and the Future of American Democracy.* New York: Basic Books, 1976.

Jeffrey M. Berry, *The Interest Group Society.* Glenview, IL: Scott, Foresman, and Company, 1989.

———. *The New Liberalism: The Rising Power of Citizens Groups.* Washington, DC: Brookings Institution Press, 1999.

Black, Amy E., Douglas L. Koopman, and David K. Ryden. *Of Little Faith: The Politics of George W. Bush's Faith-Based Initiatives.* Washington, DC: Georgetown University Press, 2004.

Buzzard, Lynn R., and Sherra Robinson. *I.R.S. Political Activity Restrictions on Churches and Charitable Ministries.* Diamond Bar, CA: Christian Ministries Management Association, 1990.

Cord, Robert L. *Separation of Church and State: Historical Fact and Current Fiction.* New York: Lambeth Press, 1982.

Davis, Derek H. *Religion and the Continental Congress, 1774–1789: Contributions to Original Intent.* New York: Oxford University Press, 2000.

Davis, Derek H., and Barry Hankins. *Welfare Reform and Faith-based Organizations.* Waco, TX: J. M. Dawson Institute of Church-State Studies, 1999.

Dreisbach, Daniel. *Thomas Jefferson and the Separation of Church and State.* New York: NYU Press, 2002.

Durkheim, Emile. *The Elementary Forms of the Religious Life,* rev. ed. New York: Free Press, 1965.

Ebersole, Luke Eugene. *Church Lobbying in the Nation's Capital.* New York: Macmillan, 1951.

Flowers, Ronald B., Melissa Rogers, and Steven K. Green. *Religious Freedom and the Supreme Court.* Waco, TX: Baylor University Press, 2009.

Hertzke, Allen D. *Representing God in Washington: The Role of Religious Lobbies in the American Polity.* Knoxville, TN: The University of Tennessee Press, 1988.

Hofrenning, Daniel J.B. *In Washington, But Not of It: The Prophetic Politics of Religious Lobbyists.* Philadelphia: Temple University Press, 1995.

Hrebenar, Ronald J., and Ruth K. Scott. *Interest Group Politics in America.* Englewood Cliffs, NJ: Prentice-Hall, 1982.

Kennedy, Sheila Suess, and Wolfgang Bielefeld. *Charitable Choice at Work: Evaluation Faith-Based Job Programs in the States.* Washington, DC: Georgetown University Press, 2006.

Kramnick, Isaac, and R. Laurence Moore. *The Godless Constitution: The Case against Religious Correctness.* New York: Norton, 1996.

Levy, Leonard. *The Establishment Clause: Religion and the First Amendment.* New York: Macmillan, 1986.

Lobeda, Cynthia D. Moe. *The Public Church: For the Life of the World.* Augsburg Fortress Publishers, 2004.

McGarvie, Mark. *One Nation Under Law: America's Early Struggles to Separate Church and State.* DeKalb, IL: Northern Illinois University Press, 2005.

Malbin, Michael J. *Religion and Politics: The Intentions of the Authors of the First Amendment.* Washington, DC: American Enterprise Institute for Public Policy Research, 1978.

Hamburger, Philip. *Separation of Church and State.* Cambridge, MA: Harvard University Press, 2002.

Olasky, Marvin. *Compassionate Conservatism: What It Is, What It Does, and How It Can Transform America.* Glenove, IL: Free Press, 2000.

Pfeffer, Leo. *Church, State and Freedom,* 2nd ed. Boston: Beacon Press, 1967.

Stokes, Anson Phelps. *Church and State in the United States: Historical Development and Contemporary Problems of Religious Freedom under the Constitution,* 3 vols. New York: Harper & Brothers, 1950.

Articles/Chapters

Davis, Derek H. "A Commentary on the Supreme Court's 'Equal Treatment' Doctrine as the New Constitutional Paradigm for Protecting Religious Liberty." *Journal of Church and State* 46 (Autumn 2004): 717.

———. "The Ten Commandments as Public Ritual." *Journal of Church and State* 44 (Spring 2002): 221.

———. "The U.S. Supreme Court as Moral Physician: *Mitchell v. Helms* and the Constitutional Revolution to Reduce Restrictions on Governmental Aid to Religion." *Journal of Church and State* 43 (Spring 2001): 213.

———. "The 'Wall of Separation' Metaphor." *Christian Ethics Today* 49 (Spring 2004): 1.

Farris, Ann, and Claire Hughes. Roundtable on Religion and Social Welfare Policy, "Durability of Bush Administration's Faith-Based Effort at Issue in 2008," January 8, 2008, www.religionandsocialpolicy.org/news/article_print.cfm?id=7551.

Hughes, Richard T. "Civil Religion, the Theology of the Republic, and the Free Church Tradition." *Journal of Church and State* 22 (Winter 1980).

Court Cases

Abington v. Schempp, 374 U.S. 203 (1963).

Allegheny v. Pittsburgh ACLU, 492 U.S. 573 (1989).

Bethel Conservative Mennonite Church v. Commissioner 80 T.C. 352 (1983), rev'd., 746 F.2d 388 (7th Cir. 1984).

Board of Education v. Allen, 392 U.S. 236 (1968).

Edwards v. Aguillard, 482 U.S. 578(1987).

Epperson v. Arkansas, 393 U.S. 97 (1968).

Engel v. Vitale, 370 U.S. 421 (1962).

Everson v. Board of Education, 330 U.S. 1 (1947).

Grand Rapids v. Ball, 473 U.S. 373 (1985).

Haswell v. United States, 500 F.2d 1133 (Ct. Cl. 1974), cert. denied, 419 U.S. 1107 (1975).

Hunt v. McNair, 413 U.S. 734 (1973).

Lee v. Weisman, 505 U.S. 577 (1992).

Lemon v. Kurtzman, 403 U.S. 602 (1971).

Levitt v. Pearl, 413 U.S. 472 (1973).

Lynch v. Donnelly, 465 U.S. 668 (1984).

McDaniel v. Paty, 435 U.S. 618 (1978).

Meek v. Pittenger, 421 U.S. 229 (1977).

Mitchell v. Helms, 530 U.S. 793 (2000).

Mueller v. Allen, 463 U.S. 388 (1983).

Pearl v. Nyquist, 413 U.S. 756 (1973).

Roemer v. Board of Public Works of Maryland, 426 U.S. 736 (1971).

Santa Fe v. Doe, 530 U.S. 27 (2002).

Seasongood v. Commissioner, 227 F.2d 907 (6th Cir. 1955).

Stone v. Graham, 449 U.S. 39 (1980).

Tilton v. Richardson, 403 U.S. 672 (1971).

U.S. v. Ballard, 322 U.S. 78 (1944).

Walz v. Tax Commission, 397 U.S. 664 (1970).

Watson v. Jones, 80 U.S. 679 (1872), 728.

Wolman v. Walter, 433 U.S. 229 (1977).

Zelman v. Simmons-Harris, 536 U.S. 639 (2002).

Zobrest v. Catalina Hills, 509 U.S. 1 (1993).

Zorach v. Clauson, 343 U.S. 306 (1952).

BIBLIOGRAPHY

CATEGORIES

HISTORICAL PERSPECTIVES

Development of Western Church–State Relations

Ahlstrom, Sydney E. *A Religious History of the American People,* 2 vols. Garden City, NY: Doubleday, 1975.

Bainton, Roland. *The Travail of Religious Liberty*. New York: Harper and Brothers, 1951.

Barraclough, Geoffrey. *The Medieval Papacy*. New York: Harcourt, Brace & World, 1968.

Bates, M. Searle. *Religious Liberty: An Inquiry*. New York: Harper and Brothers, 1945.

Benestad, J. Brian, ed. *Classical Christianity and the Political Order; Ernest Fortin: Collected Essays*. Lanham, MD: Rowman and Littlefield, 1996.

Berman, Harold J. *Faith and Order: The Reconciliation of Law and Religion*. Atlanta, GA: Lightning, Source, Inc., 1993.

Bratton, Fred Gladstone. *The Legacy of the Liberal Spirit: Men and Movements in the Makings of Modern Thought*. New York: Scribner's, 1943.

Canavan, Francis. *Edmund Burke: Perception and Providence*. Durham, NC: Carolina Academic Press, 1987.

Ehler, Sidney Z. and John B. Morrall, eds. *Church and State through the Centuries: A Collection of Historic Documents with Commentaries*. Westminster, MD: Newman Press, 1954.

Ellul, Jacques. *The Theological Foundation of Law*. trans. Marguerite Weiser. London: SCM Press, 1961.

Kamen, Henry. *The Rise of Toleration*. New York: McGraw-Hill, 1967.

Norwood, Frederick A. *Strangers and Exiles: A History of Religious Refugees*. 2 vols. Nashville, TN: Abingdon Press, 1969.

O'Donovan, Oliver and Joan Lockwood O'Donovan, eds. *From Irenaeus to Grotius: A Sourcebook in Christian Political Thought*. Grand Rapids, MI: William B. Eerdmans, 1999.

Reynolds, Noel B. and W. Cole Durham, eds. *Religious Liberty in Western Thought*. Atlanta, GA: Emory University Studies, in Law and Religion, 1996.

Skinner, Quentin. *The Foundations of Modern Political Thought*. 2 vols. New York: Cambridge University Press, 1978.

Tierney, Brian. *Religion, Law, and the Growth of Constitutional Thought, 1150–1650*. Cambridge, UK: Cambridge University Press, 1982.

————. *The Crisis of Church and State, 1050–1300*. Toronto: University of Toronto Press, 1988.

Sagorin, Perez. *How the Idea of Religious Toleration Came to the West*. Princeton, NJ: Princeton University Press, 2003.

Colonial Era

Ahlstrom, Sydney E. *A Religious History of the American People*. 2 vols. Garden City, NY: Doubleday, 1975.

Backus, Isaac. *Appeal to the Public for Religious Liberty Against the Oppressions of the Present Day*. 1773.

Bonomi, Patricia U. *Under the Cope of Heaven: Religion, Society and Politics in Colonial America*. New York: Oxford University Press, 1986.

Bridenbaugh, Carl. *Mitre and Sceptre: Transatlantic Faiths, Ideas, Personalities and Politics, 1689–1775*. London: Oxford University Press, 1962.

Balmer, Randall. *A Perfect Babel of Confusion: Dutch Religion and English Culture in the Middle Colonies*. New York: Oxford University Press, 1989.

Bloch, Ruth H. *Visionary Republic: Millennial Themes in American Thought, 1756–80*. Cambridge, UK: Cambridge University Press, 1985.

Bodo, John R. *The Protestant Clergy and Public Issues, 1812–1848*. Princeton, NJ: Princeton University Press, 1954.

Boles, John B. *The Great Revival, 1787–1805.* Lexington, KY: University Press of Kentucky, 1972.

Bonomi, Patricia U. *Under the Cope of Heaven: Religion, Society, and Politics in Colonial America.* New York: Oxford University Press, 1986.

Brauer, Jerald C., Sidney E. Mead, and Robert N. Bellah. *Religion and the American Revolution.* Philadelphia: Fortress Press, 1976.

———. *The Great Awakening: Documents on the Revival of Religion, 1740–1745.* New York: Atheneum Publishers, 1969.

Butler, Jon. *Awash in a Sea of Faith: Christianizing the American People.* Cambridge, MA: Harvard University Press, 1990.

Cobb, Sanford H. *The Rise of Religious Liberty in America.* New York: Macmillan, 1902.

Cousins, Norman, ed. *"In God We Trust:" The Religious Beliefs and Ideas of American Founding Fathers.* New York: Harper, 1958.

Coyle, Wallace, *Roger Williams: A Reference Guide.* Boston: G.K. Hall, 1977.

Curry, Thomas J. *The First Freedoms: Church and State Relations to the Passage of the First Amendment.* New York: Oxford University Press, 1986.

Dargo, George. "Toleration and its Limits in Early America." *Northern Illinois University Law Review* 16 (Spring 1996): 341.

Davidson, Elizabeth H. *The Establishment of the English Church in Continental American Colonies.* Durham, NC: Duke University Press, 1936.

Davis, Derek H. *Religion and the Continental Congress, 1774–1789: Contributions to Original Intent.* New York: Oxford University Press, 2000.

———. "The Enduring Legacy of Roger Williams: Consulting America's First Church-State Expert on Today's Controversies." *Journal of Church and State* 41 (Spring 1999): 201.

Dunn, Mary. *William Penn: Politics and Conscience.* Princeton, NJ: Princeton University Press, 1967.

Eckenrode, H.J. *Separation of Church and State in Virginia: A Study in the Development of the Revolution.* Richmond, VA: Virginia Historical Society, 1910.

Ellis, John T. *Catholics in Colonial America.* Baltimore: Helicon, 1965.

Frost, William J., *A Perfect Freedom: Religious Liberty in Pennsylvania.* Cambridge, UK: Cambridge University Press, 1993.

Gaustad, Edwin S., ed. *A Documentary History of Religion in America to the Civil War.* Grand Rapids, MI: Eerdmans, 1986.

———. "Colonial Religion and Liberty of Conscience." In *The Virginia Statute for Religious Freedom: Its Evolution and Consequences,* eds. Merrill D. Peterson and Robert Vaughan. New York: Cambridge University Press, 1988.

———. *Liberty of Conscience: Roger Williams in America.* Grand Rapids, MI: Eerdmans, 1991.

———. *Neither King nor Prelate.* Grand Rapids, MI: Eerdmans, 1993.

Greene, Louise M. *The Development of Religious Liberty in Connecticut.* Cambridge, MA: The Riverside Press, 1905.

Hall, David. *Worlds of Wonder, Days of Judgement: Popular Religious Belief in Early New England.* Cambridge, MA: Harvard University Press, 1990.

Hall, Timothy L. *Separating Church and State: Roger Williams and Religious Liberty.* Urbana, IL: University of Illinois Press, 1998.

Handy, Robert T. *A Christian America: Protestant Hopes and Historical Realities.* 2nd rev. ed. New York: Oxford University Press, 1984.

Haskins, G.L. *Law and Authority in Early Massachusetts.* Totowa, NJ: Rowman and Littlefield, 1960.

Heimert, Alan E. *Religion in the American Mind: From the Great Awakening to the Revolution.* Cambridge, MA: Harvard University Press, 1966.

Howe, Mark D. *The Garden and the Wilderness: Religion and Government in American Constitutional History.* Chicago: University of Chicago Press, 1965.

Humphrey, Edward F. *Nationalism and Religion in America, 1774–1789.* New York: Russell & Russell, 1965.

Isaac, Rhys. *The Transformation of Virginia, 1740–1790.* Williamsburg, VA: University of North Carolina Press, 1982.

Johnson, Curtis D. *Islands of Holiness: Rural Religion in Upstate New York, 1790–1860.* Ithaca, NY: Cornell University Press, 1989.

Kinney, Charles B., Jr. *Church and State: The Struggle for Separation in New Hampshire, 1630–1900.* New York: Teachers College, Columbia University, 1955.

Levy, Leonard. *The Establishment Clause: Religion and the First Amendment.* New York: Macmillan, 1986.

Love, William DeLoss, Jr. *The Fast and Thanksgiving Days of New England.* Boston: Houghton Mifflin, 1895.

Lutz, Donald S., ed. *Colonial Origins of the American Constitution: A Documentary History.* Indianapolis, IN: Liberty Fund, 1998.

Marcus, Jacob R. *The Colonial American Jew, 1492–1776.* Detroit, MI: Wayne State University Press, 1970.

Mathews, Donald G. *Religion in the Old South.* Chicago: University of Chicago Press, 1977.

McGarvie, Mark Douglas. *One Nation Under Law: America's Early National Struggles to Separate Church and State.* Dekalb, IL: Northern Illinois Press, 2005.

McLoughlin, William G. *New England Dissent, 1630–1833.* 2 vols. Cambridge, MA: Harvard University Press, 1971.

Meyer, Jacob C. *Church and State in Massachusetts, 1750–1833.* Cleveland, OH: Western Reserve Press, 1930.

Miller, Perry. *Roger Williams: His Contribution to the American Tradition.* Indianapolis, IN: Bobbs-Merrill, 1953; reprinted New York: Atheneum, 1962.

———. *The New England Mind,* vol. l: "The Seventeenth Century." New York: Oxford University Press, 1939; and vol. 2: "From Colony to Province." Cambridge, MA: Harvard University Press, 1963.

Miller, William Lee. *The First Liberty: Religion and the American Republic.* New York: Alfred A. Knopf, 1986.

Moore, Leroy. "Religious Liberty: Roger Williams and the Revolutionary Era." *Church History* 34 (March 1965): 57–76.

Morgan, Edmund S. *Roger Williams: Church and State.* New York: Harcourt, Brace & World, 1967.

Norwood, Frederick A. *Strangers and Exiles: A History of Religious Refugees.* 2 vols. Nashville, TN: Abingdon Press, 1969.

Palm, Daniel C. *On Faith and Free Government.* Lanham, MD: Rowman and Littlefield, 1997.

Penn, William. *The Great Case of Liberty of Conscience.* London, 1670.

Peterson, Merrill and Robert C. Vaughan. *The Virginia Statute for Religious Freedom: Its Evolution and Consequences.* New York: Cambridge University Press, 1988.

Stout, Harry S. *The New England Soul: Preaching and Religious Culture in Colonial New England.* 1986.

Strout, Cushing. *The New Heavens and the New Earth: Political Religion in America.* New York: Harper & Row, 1974.

Ward, Harry M. *"Unite or Die": Intercolony Relations, 1690–1763.* Port Washington, NY: Lefert's Press, 1971.

Williams, George Hunston. "The Chaplaincy in the Armed Forces of the United States of America in Historical and Ecclesiastical Perspective." In *Military Chaplains: From a Religion Military to a Military Religion,* ed. Harvey G. Cox, Jr. New York: American Report Press, 1972.

Williams, Roger. *The Bloudy Tenet, of Persecution, for Cause of Conscience.* London, 1644. In *The Complete Writings of Roger Williams.* 7 vols. Boston: Russell & Russell, Inc., 1963.

Wilson, John F. and Donald Drakeman. *The Church and State in American History.* 3rd ed. Boulder, CO: Westview Press, 2003.

Puritan Thought

Bercovitch, Sacvan. *The Puritan Origins of the American Self.* New Haven, CT: Yale University Press, 1975.

Brauer, Jerald C. "Puritanism, Revivalism, and the Revolution." In *Religion and the American Revolution,* Jerald C. Brauer. Philadelphia: Fortress Press, 1976.

Breen, T.H. *The Character of the Good Ruler: A Study of Puritan Political Ideas in New England, 1630–1730.* New Haven, CT: Yale University Press, 1970.

Bushman, Richard L. *From Puritan to Yankee: Character and the Social Order in Connecticut, 1690–1765.* Cambridge, MA: Harvard University Press, 1967.

Cohn, Charles Lloyd. *God's Caress: The Psychology of Puritan Religious Experience.* New York: Oxford University Press, 1986.

Holstun, James. *A Rational Millennium: Puritan Utopias of Seventeenth-Century England and America.* New York: Oxford University Press, 1987.

Morgan, Edmund S. *Puritan Political Ideas, 1558–1794.* Indianapolis, IN: Bobbs-Merrill, 1965.

———. *The Puritan Dilemma: The Story of John Winthrop.* Boston: Little, Brown, 1958.

———. "The Puritan Ethic and the American Revolution." *The William and Mary Quarterly* 24 (January 1967): 3.

———. *Visible Saints: A History of a Puritan Idea.* Ithaca, NY: Cornell University Press, 1974.

Holifield, Brooks E. *The Covenant Sealed: The Development of Puritan Sacramental Theology in Old and New England,* 1974.

Winthrop, John. "Speech to the General Court." In *The Puritans: A Sourcebook of Their Writings,* eds. Perry Miller and Thomas H. Johnson. New York: Harper & Row, 1963.

Revolutionary Era

Bailyn, Bernard, ed. *Pamphlets of the American Revolution 1750–1776.* Cambridge, MA: Harvard University Press, 1965.

Bailyn, Bernard. *The Ideological Origins of the American Revolution.* Cambridge, MA: Harvard University Press, 1967.

Buckley, Thomas E. *Church and State in Revolutionary Virginia, 1776–1787.* Charlottesville, VA: University of Virginia Press, 1977.

Carroll, Peter N., ed. *Religion and the Coming of the American Revolution.* Waltham, MA: Ginn-Blaisdell, 1970.

Chauncy, Charles. "A Discourse on the Good News from a Far Country." (1766). In *The Pulpit of the American Revolution,* ed. John Thornton. New York: Da Capo Press, 1970.

Davis, Derek H. "Religious Dimensions of the Declaration of Independence: Fact and Fiction." *Journal of Church and State* 36 (Summer 1994): 469–482.

———. "Religion and the American Revolution." *Journal of Church and State* 36 (Autumn 1994): 709–724.

Fay, Bernard. *Revolution and Freemasonry, 1680–1800.* Boston: Little, Brown, 1935.

Gilpin, Thomas. *Exiles in Virginia: With Observations on the Society of Friends During the Revolutionary War.* Philadelphia: C. Sherman, 1848.

Hatch, Nathan O. "In Pursuit of Religious Freedom: Church, State, and People in the New Republic." In *The American Revolution: Its Character and Limits*, ed. Jack P. Greene. New York: New York University Press, 1987.

Hatch, Nathan O. *The Sacred Cause of Liberty: Republican Thought and the Millennium in Revolutionary New England.* New Haven, CT: Yale University Press, 1977.

Hogue, William M. "The Religious Conspiracy Theory of the American Revolution: Anglican Motive." *Church History* 45 (1976): 277.

Henderson, H. James. "The Structure of Politics in the Continental Congress." In *Essays on the American Revolution*, eds. Stephen G. Kurtz and James H. Hutson. Chapel Hill, NC: University of North Carolina Press, 1973.

Hoffman, Ronald, and Peter J. Albert, eds. *Religion in a Revolutionary Age.* Charlottesville, VA: NC/London, 1994.

Joyce, Lester Douglas. *Church Clergy in the American Revolution.* New York: Exposition Press, 1966.

Katz, Stanley N. "The Legal and Religious Context of Natural Rights Theory: A Comment." In *Party and Political Opposition in Revolutionary America*, ed. Patricia U. Bonomi. Tarrytown, NY: Sleepy Hollow Press, 1980.

McLoughlin, William G. "The Role of Religion in the Revolution." In *Essays on the American Revolution*, eds. Stephen G. Kurtz and James H. Hutson. Chapel Hill, NC: University of North Carolina Press, 1973.

Mead, Sidney E. "American Protestantism during the Revolutionary Epoch." *Church History* 22 (December 1953): 279.

Moore, Frank, ed. *The Patriot Preachers of the American Revolution.* New York: Charles T. Evans, 1862.

Noll, Mark A. *Christians in the American Revolution.* Washington, DC: Christian University Press, 1985.

Otis, James. *The Rights of the British Colonies Asserted and Proved. Boston, 1764.* In *Pamphlets of the American Revolution, 1750–1776*, ed. Bernard Bailyn. Cambridge, MA: Harvard University Press, 1965.

Prowell, George Reeser. *Continental Congress at York, Pennsylvania and York County in the Revolution.* York, PA: York Printing Co., 1914.

Singer, C. Gregg. "Theological Aspects of the Revolution." *Christianity Today* 3 (22 June 1959): 5.

Thornton, John Wingate. *The Pulpit of the American Revolution.* 1860; reprinted, New York: Da Capo Press, 1970.

White, Morton. *The Philosophy of the American Revolution.* New York: Oxford University Press, 1978.

Wood, Gordon S. *The Creation of the American Republic, 1776–1787.* Chapel Hill, NC: University of North Carolina Press, 1969.

———. *The Radicalism of the American Revolution.* New York: Random House, 1991.

Wright, Esmond, ed. *Causes and Consequences of the American Revolution.* Chicago: Quadrangle Books, 1966.

Founding Era

Allen, Brooke. *Moral Minority: Our Skeptical Founding Fathers.* Chicago: Ivan R. Dee, 2006.

Alley, Robert, ed. *James Madison: A Free Conscience in a Secular Republic.* Buffalo, NY: Prometheus books, 1985.

Baker, John S. "James Madison and Religious Freedom." *Benchmark* 3 (January–April 1987): 71.

Banning, Lance. "James Madison, the Statute for Religious Freedom, and the Crisis of Republican Convictions." In *The Virginia Statute for Religious Freedom,* eds. Merrill D. Peterson and Robert D. Vaughan. Cambridge, UK: Cambridge University Press, 1988.

Becker, Carl. *The Declaration of Independence: A Study in the History of Political Ideas.* New York: Vintage Books, 1958.

Beeman, Richard, Stephen Botein, and Edward C. Carter II, eds. *Beyond Confederation: Origins of the American Constitution and American National Identity.* Chapel Hill, NC: University of North Carolina Press, 1987.

Boller, Paul F., Jr. *George Washington and Religion.* Dallas, TX: Southern Methodist University Press, 1963.

Borden, Morton. "Federalists, Anti-Federalists, and Religious Freedom." *Journal of Church and State* 21 (1979): 469.

Botein, Stephen. "Religious Dimensions of the Early American State." In *Beyond Confederation: Origins of the American Constitution and American National Identity,* eds. Richard Beeman, Stephen Botein, and Edward C. Carter II. Chapel Hill, NC: University of North Carolina Press, 1987

Buckley, Thomas E. "The Political Theology of Thomas Jefferson." In *The Virginia Statute for Religious Freedom: Its Evolution and Consequences in American History,* ed. Merrill D. Peterson and Robert C. Vaughan. Cambridge, UK: Cambridge University Press, 1988.

Burnett, Edmund C. *The Continental Congress: A Definitive History of the Continental Congress from its Inception in 1774 to March, 1789.* New York: Macmillan, 1941.

Burnett, Edmund C., ed. *Letters of Members of the Continental Congress.* 8 vols. Washington, DC: The Carnegie Institution, 1921–1936.

Castro, William. "Oliver Ellsworth's Calvinism: A Biographical Essay on Religion and Political Psychology in the Early Republic." *Journal of Church and State* 36 (1994): 507.

Church, Forest. *So Help Me God: The Founding Fathers and the First Great Battle Over Church and State.* New York: Harcourt, 2007.

Cobb, Sanford. *The Rise of Religious Liberty in America: A History.* New York: Macmillan, 1902.

Cole, Franklin P., ed. *They Preached Liberty.* Indianapolis, IN: Liberty Press, 1976.

Cousins, Norman, ed. *In God We Trust: The Religious Beliefs and Ideas of the American Founding Fathers.* New York: Harper & Brothers, 1958.

Cox, Harvey G., Jr., ed. *Military Chaplains: From a Religion Military to a Military Religion.* New York: American Report Press, 1972.

Curry, Thomas J. *The First Freedoms: Church and State in America to the Passage of the First Amendment.* New York: Oxford University Press, 1986.

Davis, Derek H. *Religion and the Continental Congress, 1774–89: Contributions to Original Intent.* New York: Oxford University Press, 2000.

DePauw, Linda Grant, ed. *Documentary History of the First Federal Congress of the United States of America.* 3 vols. Baltimore: Johns Hopkins University Press, 1971.

Donovan, Frank. *Mr. Jefferson's Declaration: The Story Behind the Declaration of Independence.* New York: Dodd, Mead and Co., 1968.

Dreisbach, Daniel. "The Constitution's Forgotten Religion Clause: Reflections on the Article VI Religious Test Ban." *Journal of Church and State* 38 (Spring 1996): 267.

———. *Thomas Jefferson and the Separation between Church and State.* New York: NYU Press, 2002.

Dreisbach, Daniel L. and Mark David Hall, eds. *The Sacred Rights of Conscience: Selected Readings on Religious Liberty and Church-State Relations in the American Founding.* Indianapolis, IN: Liberty Fund, 2009.

Dumbald, Edward. *The Declaration of Independence and What It Means Today.* Norman, OK: University of Oklahoma Press, 1950.

Dunn, Mary Maples. *William Penn: Politics and Conscience.* Princeton, NJ: Princeton University Press, 1967.

Edwards, Jonathan. *Some Thoughts Concerning the Revival of Religion in New England.* In *The Works of Jonathan Edwards,* ed. C.C. Goen. New Haven, CT: Yale University Press, 1972.

Elliot, Jonathan, ed. *The Debates of the Several State Conventions on the Adoption of the Federal Constitution* (collected and revised by John Elliot, 1836), cited in the edition issued by J.B. Lippincott Co., Philadelphia, 1901.

Fleet, Elizabeth, ed. "Madison's Detached Memoranda." *William and Mary Quarterly* 3 (October 1946): 554.

Ford, Worthington C., ed. *The Washington-Duche Letters.* Brooklyn, NY: Cole Printing Co., 1890.

———, et al., eds. *Journals of the Continental Congress.* 34 vols. Washington, DC: 1904–1937.

Gaines, William H. "The Continental Congress Considers the Publication of a Bible, 1777." *Studies in Bibliography* 3 (1950–1951): 274.

Gaustad, Ed. *Faith of Our Fathers: Religion and the New Nation.* San Francisco: Harper & Row, 1987.

Humphrey, Edward Frank. *Nationalism and Religion in America, 1774–1789.* Boston: Chipman Law Publishing Company, 1924.

Hutson, James. *Church and State in America: The First Two Centuries.* New York: Cambridge University Press, 2008.

———. *Forgotten Features of the Founding: The Recovery of Religious Themes in the Early American Republic.* Lanham, MD: Lexington Books, 2003.

———. *Religion and the Founding of the American Republic.* Washington, DC: Library of Congress, 1998.

———. "Thomas Jefferson's Letter to the Danbury Baptists: A Controversy Rejoined." *William and Mary Quarterly,* 3d ser., 56, no. 4 (1999): 775.

Hutson, James H., ed. *Religion and the New Republic: Faith in the Founding of America.* Lanham, MD: Rowman and Littlefield, 2000.

Hyneman, Charles S. and Donald S. Lutz, eds. *American Political Writings During the Founding Era, 1760–1805.* Indianapolis, IN: Liberty Press, 1983.

Isaac, Rhys. *The Transformation of Virginia, 1740–1790.* Chapel Hill, NC: University of North Carolina Press, 1982.

Kurland, Philip B. and Ralph Lerner, eds. *The Founders' Constitution,* 5 vols. Chicago: University of Chicago Press, 1987.

Madison, James. *Notes of Debates in the Federal Convention of 1787.* Adrienne Koch, ed. Athens, OH: Ohio University Press, 1966.

Henton, Ronald E. *Masonic Membership of the Founding Fathers.* Silver Spring, MD: Masonic Service Association, 1965.

Hills, Margaret T. "The First American Bible, as Published by Robert Aitken." *Bible Society Record* 113 (January 1968): 1.

Hofstadter, Richard. "The Founding Fathers: An Age of Realism." In *The Moral Foundations of the American Republic*, ed. Robert Horwitz. Charlottesville, VA: University of Virginia Press, 1986.

Horwitz, RobertH.,ed. *The Moral Foundations of the American Republic.* 3rd ed. Charlottesville, VA: University Press of Virginia, 1986.

Kramnick, Isaac, ed. *The Federalist Papers.* New York: Penguin Books, 1987.

Labunski, Richard. *James Madison and the Struggle for the Bill of Rights.* New York: Oxford University Press, 2006.

Lambert, Frank. *The Founding Fathers and the Place of Religion in America.* Princeton, NJ: Princeton University Press, 2003.

Malbin, Michael. *Religion and Politics: The Intentions of the Authors of the First Amendment.* Washington, DC: American Enterprise Institute, 1978.

McConnell, Michael W. "Establishment and Disestablishment at the Founding, Part I: Establishment of Religion." 44 *William and Mary Law Review* (1992): 2105.

McGarvie, Mark. *One Nation Under Law: America's Early Struggles to Separate Church and State.* DeKalb, IL: Northern Illinois University Press, 2005.

Meacham, Jon. *American Gospel: God, the Founding Fathers, and the Making of a Nation.* New York: Random House, 2006.

Mead, Sidney E. "Neither Church nor State: Reflections on James Madison's 'Line of Separation.'" *Journal of Church and State* 10 (1968): 349.

Munoz, Vincent Phillip. "James Madison's Principles of Religious Liberty." *American Political Science Review* 97 (February 2003): 17.

Pearson, Samuel C., Jr. "Nature's God: A Reassessment of the Religion of the Founding Fathers." *Religion in Life* 46 (Summer 1977): 152.

Peters, Thomas Nathan. "Religion, Establishment, and the Northwest Ordinance: A Closer Look at an Accommodation Argument." 89 *Kentucky Law Journal* (2000–2001): 743.

Sandoz, Ellis. "Religious Liberty and Religion in the American Founding Revisited." In *Religious Liberty in Western Thought*, eds. Noel B. Reynolds and W. Cole Durham. Grand Rapids, MI: Scholars Press, 1996.

Sandoz, Ellis, ed. *Political Sermons of the American Founding Era, 1730–1805.* Indianapolis, IN: Liberty Press, 1991.

Schlissel, Lillian. *Conscience in America: A Documentary History of Conscientious Objection in America, 1757–1967.* New York: E.P. Dutton & Co., 1968.

Sheldon, Garrett W. and Daniel L. Dreisbach, eds. *Religion and Political Culture in Jefferson's Virginia.* Totowa, NJ: Rowman and Littlefield, 2000.

Stevens, William Perry. *The Faith of the Signers of the Declaration of Independence.* New Haven, CT: Yale University Press, 1926.

Tocqueville, Alexis De. *Democracy in America.* J.P. Mayers and Max Lerner, eds. George Lawrence, trans. New York: Harper & Row, 1969.

Vetterli, Richard and Gary Bryner. *In Search of the Republic.* Totowa, NJ: Rowman and Littlefield, 1987.

Waldman, Steven. *Founding Faith, Providence, Politics, and the Birth of Religious Freedom in America.* New York: Random House, 2008.

West, John G., Jr. *The Politics of Revelation and Reason: Religion and Civic Life in the New Nation.* Lawrence, KS: University Press of Kansas, 1996.

Wood, Gordon S. *The Creation of the American Republic 1776–1787*. Chapel Hill, NC: University of North Carolina Press, 1969.

Enlightenment Thought

Davis, Derek H. "Jesus vs. the Watchmaker: Which Ideas Energized the American Revolution—Those of Evangelical Christianity or Enlightened Deism?" *Christian History* 15 (No. 2, 1996): 35.

May, Henry F. *The Enlightenment in America*. New York: Oxford University Press, 1976.

Cranston, Maurice William. *Philosophers and Pamphleteers: Political Theorists of the Enlightenment*. New York: Oxford University Press, 1986.

Gavin, Frank. *Seven Centuries of the Problem of Church and State*. New York: Hawood Fertig, 1971. Originally published in 1938 by Princeton University Press

Gavin, Frank. *The Enlightenment: An Interpretation*. 2 vols. New York: Knopf, 1966–1999.

Hampson, Norman. *The Enlightenment: An Evaluation of its Assumptions, Attitudes, and Values*. 1968. Reprint, New York: Penguin Books, 1986.

Koch, Adolf. *Religion of the American Enlightenment*. New York: Thomas Y. Crowell and Co., 1968.

Nicholls, David. *God and Government in an Age of Reason*. London: Routledge, 1995.

CONSTITUTIONAL PERSPECTIVES

Religion Clauses

Antieu, Chester James, Arthur L. Downey, and Edward C. Roberts. *Freedom from Federal Establishment: Formation and Early History of the First Amendment Religions Clauses*. Milwaukee, WI: Bruce Publishing, 1964.

Berg, Thomas C. "Religion Clause Anti-Theories." *Notre Dame Law Review* 72 (1997): 693.

Berman, Harold. "Religion and Law: The First Amendment in Historical Perspective." *Emory Law Journal* 35 (1986): 777.

Berns, Walter. *The First Amendment and the Future of American Democracy*. New York: Basic Books, 1976.

Bradley, Gerald v. "The No Religious Test Clause and the Constitution of Religious Liberty: A Mahine That Has Gone of Itself." *Case Western Reserve Law Review* 37 (1987): 674.

Brownstein, Alan. "Protecting Religious Liberty: The False Messiahs of the Free Speech Doctrine and Formal Neutrality." *Journal of Law and Policy* 18 (2002): 119.

Carmella, Angela C. "State Constitutional Protection of Religious Exercise: An Emerging Post Smith Jurisprudence." *Brigham Young University Law Review* (1993): 275.

Choper, Jesse H. "The Religion Clauses of the First Amendment: Reconciling the Conflict." *University of Pittsburgh Law Review* 41 (Spring 1980): 673.

Cookson, Catherine. *Regulating Religion: The Courts and Free Exercise*. New York: Oxford University Press, 2001.

Curtis, Michael Kent. "Conceived in Liberty: The Fourteenth Amendment and the Bill of Rights." *North Carolina Law Review* 65 (1987): 889.

Dreisbach, Daniel L. "The Constitution's Forgotten Religion Clause: Reflections on the Article VI Religious Test Ban," *Journal of Church and State* 38 (1996): 263.

Esbeck, Carl H. "The Establishment Clause as a Structural Restraint on Governmental Power." *Iowa Law Review* 84 (1998):1.

Evans, Bette Novit. *Interpreting the Free Exercise of Religion.* Chapel Hill, NC: University of North Carolina Press, 1997.

Feldman, Noah. "The Intellectual Origins of the Establishment Clause." *New York University Law Review* 77 (2002): 346.

Freedman Howard. "Rethinking Free Exercise: Rediscovering Religious Community and Ritual." *Seton Hall Law Review* 24 (1994): 1800.

Garfield, Alan E. "A Positive Rights Interpretation of the Establishment Clause." *Temple Law Review* 76 (2003): 281.

Gedicks, Frederick Mark. "Toward a Defensible Free Exercise Doctrine." *George Washington Law Review* 68 (2000): 925.

Glendon, Mary Ann and Raul F. Yanes. "Structural Free Exercise," *Michigan Law Review* 90 (1991): 477

Glenn, Gary D. "Forgotten Purposes of the First Amendment Religion Clauses." *Review of Politics* 49 (1987): 340.

Greenawalt, Kent. "Quo Vadis: The Status and Prospects of 'Tests' under the Religion Clauses." *1995 Supreme Court Review* (1995): 323.

Hunter, James D. and Os Guinness, eds. *Articles of Faith, Articles of Peace: The Religious Liberty Clauses and the American Public Philosophy.* Washington, DC: Brookings Institution Press, 1990.

Jeffries, John C., Jr., and James E. Ryan. "A Political History of the Establishment Clause." *Michigan Law Review* 100 (2001): 279.

Katz, Wilbur. "Radiations from Church Tax Exemption." *Supreme Court Review,* 1970.

Kurland, Philip B. "The Origins of the Religion Clauses of the Constitution." *William and Mary Law Review* 27 (Special Issue, 1985–1986): 839.

Lash, Kurt T. "The Second Adoption of the Free Exercise Clause: Religious Exemptions under the Fourteenth Amendment." *Northwestern University Law Review* 88 (1994): 1106.

———. "The Second Adoption of the Establishment Clause: The Rise of the Nonestablishment Principle." *Arizona State Law Journal* 27 (1995): 1085.

Laycock, Douglas. "Formal, Substantive, and Disaggregated Neutrality Toward Religion," *DePaul Law Review* 39 (1990): 993.

———. "Non-Coercive' Support for Religion: Another False Claim About the Establishment Clause." *Valparaiso University Law Review* 26 (1991): 37.

———. "Text, Intent, and the Religion Clauses," *Notre Dame Journal of Law Ethics and Public Policy* 4 (1990): 683.

———. "Toward A General Theory of the Religion Clauses: The Case of Church Labor Relations and the Right to Church Autonomy," *Columbia Law Review* 81 (1981): 1378.

———. "The Benefits of the Establishment Clause," *DePaul Law Review* 42 (1992): 373.

———. "The Remnants of Free Exercise," *Supreme Court Review* (1991): 1.

———. "Toward a General Theory of the Religion Clauses: The Case of Church Labor Relations and the Right to Church Autonomy," *Columbia Law Review* 81 (1981): 1373.

Lee, Francis Graham. *All Imaginable Liberty: The Religious Liberty Clauses of the First Amendment.* Lanham, MD: University Press of America 1995.

Levy, Leonard W. *The Establishment Clause: Religion and the First Amendment.* New York: Macmillan, 1986.

———. *Original Intent and the Framers' Constitution.* New York: Macmillan, 1988.

———. "The Original Meaning of the Establishment Clause of the First Amendment." In
    Religion and the State: Essays in Honor of Leo Pfeffer, ed. James E. Wood, Jr. Waco, TX:
    Baylor University Press, 1985.

Lupu, Ira C. "Reconstructing the Establishment Clause: The Case Against
    Discretionary Accommodation of Religion." *University of Pennsylvania Law Review*
    140 (1991): 555.

——— "Where Rights Begin: The Problem of Burdens on the Free Exercise of Religion,"
    Harvard Law Review 102 (1989): 933.

Marnell, William H. *The First Amendment: The History of Religious Freedom in America.*
    Garden City, NY: Doubleday, 1964.

Marshall, William P. "Solving the Free Exercise Dilemma: Free Exercise as Expression."
    Minnesota Law Review 67 (1983): 545.

McConnell, Michael W. "Free Exercise Revisionism and the *Smith* Decision." *University of
    Chicago Law Review* 57 (1990): 1109.

——— "Accommodation of Religion." *Supreme Court Review,* 1985.

———. "Neutrality Under the Religion Clauses." *Northwestern Law Review* 81
    (1986): 146.

———. "The Origins and Historical Understanding of the Free Exercise of Religion."
    Harvard Law Review 103 (1990): 1409.

———. "The Origins and Historical Understanding of Free Exercise of Religion." *Harvard
    Law Review* 111 (1997): 153.

Moehlman, Conrad H. *The Wall of Separation between Church and State: An Historical
    Study of Recent Criticism of the Religious Clauses of the First Amendment.* Boston:
    Beacon Press, 1951.

Moore, John Norton. "The Supreme Court and the Relationship between the
    'Establishment' and 'Free Exercise' Clauses." *Texas Law Review* 42 (1963): 149.

Poppel, Stuart D. "Federalism, Fundamental Fairness, and the Religion Clauses."
    Cumberland Law Review 25 (1995): 247.

Reynolds, Laurie. "Zoning the Church: The Police Power Versus the First Amendment."
    Boston University Law Review 64 (1985): 767.

Schwarz, Alan. "No Imposition of Religion: The Establishment Clause Value." *Yale Law
    Journal* 77 (1968): 692.

Serr, Brian J. "A Not-so-Neutral 'Neutrality': An Essay on the State of the Religion Clauses
    on the Brink of the Third Millennium." *Baylor Law Review* 51 (1999): 319.

Simson, Gary J. "The Establishment Clause in the Supreme Court: Rethinking the Court's
    Approach." *Cornell Law Review* 72 (1987): 905.

Tushnet, Mark. "The Origins of the Establishment Clause." *Georgetown Law Journal* 75
    (April 1987): 1509.

———. "The Redundant Free Exercise Clause." *Loyola University Chicago Law Journal* 33
    (2001): 71.

Van Patten, Jonathan K. "In the End Is the Beginning: An Inquiry Into the Meaning of the
    Religion Clauses." *Saint Louis University Law Journal* 27 (February 1983): 1.

Wallace, J. Clifford. "The Framers' Establishment Clause: How High the Wall?" *Brigham
    Young University Law Review* (2001): 755.

Way, Frank and Barbara Burt. "Religious Marginality and the Free Exercise Clause."
    American Political Science Review 77 (1983): 654.

Wood, James E., Jr. "'No Religious Test Shall Ever Be Required': Reflections on
    the Bicentennial of the U.S. Constitution." *Journal of Church and State* 29 (Spring
    1987): 199.

General Works

Adams, Arlin and Charles Emmerich. *A Nation Dedicated to Religious Liberty: The Constitutional Heritage of the Religious Clauses.* Philadelphia: University of Pennsylvania Press, 1990.

Alley, Robert, ed. *The Constitution and Religion: Leading Cases on Church and State.* Amherst, NY: Prometheus Books, 1999.

Ariens, Michael S. and Robert A. Destro. *Religious Liberty in a Pluralistic Society.* Durham, NC: Carolina Academic Press, 1996.

Bassett, William. *Religious Organizations and the Law.* 2 vols. St. Paul, MN: West Publishing Co., 1997–2007.

Berg, Thomas C. "The Constitutional Future of Religious Freedom Legislation." *University of Arkansas Law Journal* 20 (1998): 715.

Beth, Loren P. *The American Theory of Church and State.* Gainesville, FL: University of Florida Press, 1958.

Blakely, William Addison. *American State Papers on Freedom of Religion.* 3rd rev. ed. Washington, DC: Review and Herald, 1943.

Blakeman, John. *The Bible in the Park: Federal District Courts, Religious Speech, and the Public Forum.* Akron, OH: The University of Akron Press, 2005.

Bradley, Gerard *v. Church-State Relationships in America.* Westport, CT: Greenwood Press, 1987.

Carmella, Angela. "A Theological Critique of Free Exercise Jurisprudence." *George Washington Law Review* 60 (1992): 782.

———. "Houses of Worship and Religious Liberty: Constitutional Limits on Landmark Preservation and Architectural Review." *Villanova Law Review* 36 (1991): 401.

Carter, Stephen L. "Reflections on the Separation of Church and State." *Arizona Law Review* 44 (2002): 293.

——— "The Resurrection of Religious Freedom?" *Harvard Law Review* 107 (1993): 118.

Choper, Jesse H. "A Century of Religious Freedom." *California Law Review* 88 (December 2000): 1709.

———. *Securing Religious Liberty.* Chicago: University of Chicago Press, 1995.

Chopko, Mark. "Religious Access to Public Programs and Governmental Funding." *George Washington Law Review* 60 (1992): 645.

Clinton, Robert Lowry. *God & Man in the Law: The Foundations of Anglo-American Constitutionalism.* Lawrence, KS: University of Kansas Press, 1997.

Conkle, Daniel O. "Congressional Alternatives in the Wake of City of *Boerne v. Flores:* The (Limited) Role of Congress in Protecting Religious Freedom from State and Local Infringement." *University of Arkansas Law Journal* 20 (1998): 633.

Cookson, Catharine, ed. *Encyclopedia of Religious Freedom.* New York: Routledge, 2003.

Curry, Thomas J. *Farewell to Christendom: The Future of Church and State in America.* New York: Oxford University Press, 2001.

Davis, Derek H. "A Commentary on the Supreme Court's 'Equal Treatment' Doctrine as the New Constitutional Paradigm for Protecting Religious Liberty." *Journal of Church and State* 46 (Autumn 2004): 717.

———. "Completing the Constitution: Enforcing the Religion Clauses under the Fourteenth Amendment," *Journal of Church and State* 42 (Summer 2000): 437.

———. "*Mitchell v. Helms* and the Modern Cultural Assault on the Separation of Church and State," *Boston College Law Review*, Volume XLIII, No. 5, September 2002, pp. 1035.

————. *Religion and the Continental Congress, 1774–1789: Contributions to Original Intent.* New York, NY: Oxford University Press, 2000.

————. "The Supreme Court and the Constitutional Definition of Religion: A History and Critique." In *The Role of Government in Monitoring and Regulating Religion in Public Life,* eds. James E. Wood, Jr. and Derek Davis. Waco, TX: J.M. Dawson Institute of Church-State Studies, 1992.

————. "Resolving Not to Resolve the Tension between the Establishment and Free Exercise Clauses." *Journal of Church and State* 38 (Spring 1996): 245.

————. *Original Intent: Chief Justice Rehnquist and the Course of American Church/State Relations.* Buffalo, NY: Prometheus Books, 1991.

————. "The Dark Side to a Just War: The USA Patriot Act and Counterterrorism's Potential Threat to Religious Freedom," *Journal of Church and State* 44 (Winter 2002): 5.

————. "Thomas Jefferson and the 'Wall of Separation' Metaphor," *Journal of Church and State* 44 (Winter 2003): 5.

Davis, Derek H., ed. *The Separation of Church and State Defended: Essays in Honor of James E. Wood, Jr.* Waco, TX: J.W. Dawson Institute of Church-State Studies, 1995.

Dawson, Joseph M. *America's Way in Church, State, and Society.* Westport, CT: Greenwood Press, 1953.

Destro, Robert A. "By What Right?: The Sources and Limits of Federal Court and Congressional Jurisdiction over Matters 'Touching Religion.'" *Indiana Law Review* 29 (1995): 1.

Drakeman, Donald L. *Church-State Constitutional Issues: Making Sense of the Establishment Clause.* New York: Greenwood Press, 1991.

Dreisbach, Daniel L. *Real Threat and Mere Shadow: Religious Liberty and the First Amendment.* Westchester, IL: Crossway Books, 1997.

————. "Thomas Jefferson and the Danbury Baptists Revisited." *William and Mary Quarterly,* 3d series, 56, no. 4 (1999): 805.

Drinan, Robert F. "Reflections on the Demise of the Religious Freedom Restoration Act." *George Washington Law Journal* 89 (1997): 101.

————. *Can God & Caesar Coexist? Balancing Religious Freedom and International Law.* New Haven, CT: Yale University Press, 2004.

Duncan, Ann W. and Steven L. Jones, eds. *Church-State Issues in America.* Westport, CT: Greenwood Publishing Co., 2008.

Eastland, Terry. *Religious Liberty in the Supreme Court: The Cases That Define the Debate over Church and State.* Grand Rapids, MI: Eerdmans, 1993.

Eisgruber, Christopher L. "Why the Religious Freedom Restoration Act is Unconstitutional." *New York University Law Review* 69 (1994): 437.

Eisgruber, Christopher and Lawrence Sager. *Religious Freedom and the Constitution.* Cambridge, MA: Harvard University Press, 2007.

Eisgruber Christopher L. and Lawrence G. Sager. "The Vulnerability of Conscience: The Constitutional Basis for Protecting Religious Conduct." *University of Chicago Law Review* 61 (1994): 1245.

Epps, Garrett. *To an Unknown God: Religious Freedom on Trial.* New York: St. Martin's Press. 2001.

Epstein, Steven B. "Rethinking the Constitutionality of Ceremonial Deism." *Columbia Law Review* 96 (1996): 2083.

Esbeck, Carl H. "Church Autonomy and Establishments of Religion." *Brigham Young University Law Review* (2004): 1385.

————. "Five Views of Church-State Relations in Contemporary American Thought."
    Brigham Young University Law Review 86 (1986): 371.

Estep, W. R. *Religious Liberty: Heritage and Responsibility.* North Newton, KS: Bethel
    College, 1988.

Feldman, Noah. *Divided by God.* New York: Farrar, Straus and Giroux, 2005.

Feldman, Stephen M. *Please Don't Wish Me a Merry Christmas: A Critical History
    of Separation of Church and State.* New York: New York University Press,
    1997.

Flowers, Ronald B. *That Godless Court? Supreme Court Decisions on Church-State
    Relationships.* 2nd ed. Louisville, KY: Westminster/John Knox Press, 2005.

————. *To Defend the Constitution: Religion, Conscientious Objection, Naturalization, and
    the Supreme Court.* Lanham, MD: Scarecrow Press, 2003.

Flowers, Ronald B., Melissa Rogers, and Steven K. Green. *Religious Freedom and the
    Supreme Court.* Waco, TX: Baylor University Press, 2008.

Frankel, Marvin E. *Faith and Freedom: Religious Liberty in America.* New York: Hill and
    Wang. 1995.

Freman, George C. "The Misguided Search for a Constitutional Definition of Religion."
    Georgetown Law Journal 71 (1983): 1519.

Gaffney, Edward M. "Governmental Definition of Religion: The Rise and Fall of the IRS
    Regulations of an Integrated Auxiliary of a Church." *Valparaiso University Law
    Review* 25 (1991): 203.

Garry, Patrick M. *Wrestling with God: The Courts' Tortuous Treatment of Religion.*
    Washington, DC: The Catholic University of America Press, 2006.

Gaustad, Edwin S. *Proclaim Liberty Throughout All the Land: A History of Church and State
    in America.* New York: Oxford University Press, 2003.

Gedicks, Frederick Mark. "Public Life and Hostility to Religion." *Virginia Law Review* 78
    (1992): 671.

————. *The Rhetoric of Church and State: A Critical Analysis of Religion Clause
    Jurisprudence.* Durham, NC: Duke University Press, 1995.

Gey, Steven G. "Why is Religion Special: Reconsidering the Accommodation of Religion
    under the Religion Clauses of the First Amendment." *University of Pittsburgh Law
    Review* 52 (1990): 75.

Gregory, David L. "The Role of Religion in the Secular Workplace." *Notre Dame Journal
    of Law, Ethics, and Public Policy* 4 (1990): 65.

Gedicks, Frederick Mark. "Religions, Fragmentations, and Doctrinal Limits." *The William
    and Mary Bill of Rights Journal* 15 (Oct. 2006): 25.

————. "Religious Exemptions, Formal Neutrality, and *Laicite*." *Indiana Journal of Global
    Legislative Studies* 13 (Summer, 2006): 473.

————. "Toward a Constitutional Jurisprudence of Religious Group Rights." *Wisconsin
    Law Review* 1989 (1989): 99.

Gamwell, Franklin. *The Meaning of Religious Freedom.* Albany, NY: SUNY Press, 1995.

Glendon, Mary Ann. "Law, Communities, and the Religious Freedom Language of the
    Constitution." *George Washington Law Review* 60 (1992): 672.

Goldwin, Robert A. and Art Kaufman, eds. *How Does the Constitution Protect Religious
    Freedom?* Washington, DC: American Enterprise Institute, 1987.

Green, Steven K. *The Second Disestablishment: Church and State in the Nineteenth Century.*
    New York: Oxford University Press, 2009.

Greenawalt, Kent. *Religion and the Constitution.* 2 vols. Princeton, NJ: Princeton University
    Press, 2006–2008.

———. "History as Ideology: Phillip Hamburger's Separation of Church and State." *California Law Review* 93 (2005): 367.

———. "Religion as a Concept in Constitutional Law." *California Law Review* 72 (1982): 753.

———. *Religious Convictions and Political Choice.* Oxford University Press, 1991.

Gregory, David L. "The Role of Religion in the Secular Workplace." *Notre Dame Journal of Law, Ethics and Public Policy* 4 (1990): 749.

Gunn, Jeremy T. *A Standard for Repair: The Establishment Clause, Equality, and Natural Rights.* New York: Garland Publishing, 1992.

Hall, Timothy L. "Religion, Equality, and Difference." *Temple Law Review* 65 (1992): 1.

Hamburger, Philip A. "A Constitutional Right of Religious Exemption: An Historical Perspective." *George Washington Law Review* 60 (1992): 915.

Hamburger, Philip A. *Separation of Church and State.* Cambridge, MA: Harvard University Press, 2002.

Hamilton, Marci. *God vs. Gavel: Religion and the Rule of Law.* Cambridge, UK: Cambridge University Press, 2005.

———. "Law and Morality: Constitutional Law: Moral and Religious Convictions as Categories for Special Treatment: The Exemption Strategy." *William and Mary Law Review* 48 (April, 2007): 1605.

———. "Objections in Conscience to Medical Procedures: Does Religion Make a Difference?" *University of Illinois Law Review* (2006): 799.

———. "The Belief/Conduct Paradigm in the Supreme Court's Free Exercise Jurisprudence: A Theological Account of the Failure to Protect Religious Conduct." *Ohio State Law Journal* 54 (1993): 713.

———. "The Religious Freedom Restoration Act: Letting the Fox into the Henhouse Under Cover of Section 5 of the Fourteenth Amendment." *Cardozo Law Review* 16 (1994): 357.

Hammar, Richard R. *Pastor, Church & Law.* Springfield, MO: Gospel Publishing House, 1983.

Hammond, Phillip. *With Liberty for all: Freedom of Religion in the United States.* Louisville, KY: Westminster John Knox Press, 1998.

Hammond, Phillip E., David W. Machacek, and Eric M. Mazur. *Religion on Trial: How Supreme Court Trends Threaten Freedom of Conscience in America.* Walnut Creek, CA: Alta Mira Press, 2004.

Handy, Robert T. *Undermined Establishment: Church-State Relations in America, 1880–1920.* Princeton, NJ: Princeton University Press, 1991.*Undermined Establishment: Church-State Relations in America, 1880–1920.* Princeton, NJ: Princeton University Press, 1991.

Houtman, Roxanne. "Rebuilding the Wall between Church and State." *Syracuse Law Review* 55 (2005): 395.

Howe, Mark DeWolfe. *Cases on Church and State in the United States.* Cambridge, UK: Cambridge University Press, 1952.

———. *The Garden and the Wilderness: Religion and Government in American Constitutional History.* Chicago: University of Chicago Press, 1965.

Idleman, Scott C. "The Religious Freedom Restoration Act: Pushing the Limits of Legislative Power." *Texas Law Review* 73 (1994): 247.

"James R. Browning Symposium for 1994: The Religious Freedom Restoration Act." *Montana Law Review* 56 (1995): 1–324.

Johnson, Alvin N. and F.H. Yost. *Separation of Church and State in the United States.* Minneapolis, MN: University of Minnesota Press, 1948.

Jones, Richard H. "Accommodationist and Separatist Ideals in Supreme Court Establishment Clause Decisions." *Journal of Church and State* 28 (1986): 193.

Katz, Wilber G. "Freedom of Religion and State Neutrality." *University of Chicago Law Review* 20 (1953): 426.

Kauper, Paul G. "The Constitutionality of Tax Exemptions for Religious Activities." in *The Wall Between Church and State,* ed. Dallin H. Oaks. Chicago: University of Chicago Press, 1963.

Kelsay, John, and Sumner B. Twiss, eds. *Religion and Human Rights.* New York: The Project on Religion and Human Rights, 1994.

Kramnick, Isaac and R. Laurence Moore. *The Godless Constitution: The Case against Religious Correctness.* New York: Norton, 1996.

Kurland, Philip. *Religion and the Law: Of Church and State and the Supreme Court.* Chicago: Aldine, 1962.

Laycock, Douglas. "Formal, Substantive, and Disaggregated Neutrality Toward Religion." *DePaul Law Review* 39 (1990): 993.

———. "Freedom of Speech That Is Both Religious and Political." *University of California Davis Law Review* 29 (1996): 793.

———. "'Nonpreferential' Aid to Religion: A False Claim About Original Intent." *William and Mary Law Review* 27 (Special Issue 1985–1986): 875.

———. "Religious Liberty as Liberty." *Journal of Contemporary Legal Studies* 7 (1996): 313.

———. "Summary and Synthesis: The Crisis in Religious Liberty." George *Washington Law Review* 60 (1992): 841.

Lupu, Ira C. "The Failure of RFRA." *University of Arkansas Little Rock Law Journal* 20 (1998): 589.

———. "The Trouble with Accommodation." *George Washington Law Review* (1992): 743.

Marshall, Bill. "The Constitution Under Clinton: A Critical Assessment: The Culture of Belief and the Politics of Religion." *Law & Contemporary Problems* 63 (2000): 453.

McConnell, Michael. "Accommodation of Religion." *Supreme Court Review* (1985): 1.

———. "Religious Freedom at a Crossroads." *University of Chicago Law Review* 59 (1992): 115.

———. "Why Is Religious Freedom the 'First Freedom'?" *Cardozo Law Review* 21 (2000): 1243.

McConnell, Michael, John Garvey, and Thomas Berg. *Religion and the Constitution*, 2nd ed. New York: Aspen, 2006.

McConnell, Michael W. and Richard A. Posner. "An Economic Approach to Issues of Religious Freedom." *Chicago Law Review* 56 (1989): 1.

Miller, William Lee. *The First Liberty: Religion and the American Republic.* New York: Alfred A. Knopf, 1986.

Monsma, Stephen v. *Positive Neutrality: Letting Religious Freedom Ring.* Westport, CT: Greenwood Press, 1993.

Monsma, Steven V., ed. *Church-State Relations in Crisis: Debating Neutrality.* Lanham, MD: Rowman and Littlefield, 2002.

Monsma, Steven *v.* and Christopher Soper, eds. *Equal Treatment of Religion in a Pluralistic Society.* Grand Rapids, MI: Eerdmans, 1998.

Morgan, Edmund S. *The Church and the State.* New York: Harcourt, Brace and World, 1967.

Morgan, Richard E. *The Politics of Religious Conflict: Church and State in America.* New York: Pegasus, 1968.

———. *The Supreme Court and Religion.* New York: Free Press, 1972.

Murray, Bruce T. *Religious Liberty in America: Navigating the First Amendment in the newsroom and Beyond.* Pasadena, CA: Foundation for American Communications, 2005.

Neuhaus, Richard John. "Contending for the Future: Overcoming the Pfefferian Inversion." *Journal of Law and Religion* 8 (1990): 115.

Noonan, John. "How Sincere Do You Have to Be to Be Religious?" 1988 *University of Illinois Law Review* (1988): 1.

Noonan, John T. *The Lustre of Our County: The American Experience of Religious Freedom.* Berkeley, CA: University of California Press 1998.

O'Dell-Scott, David, ed. *Democracy and Religion: Free Exercise and Diverse Visions.* Kent, OH: Kent State University Press, 2004.

O'Neill, James M. "Nonpreferential Aid to Religion is not an Establishment of Religion." *Buffalo Law Review* 2 (1952): 242.

Paulsen, Mike. "*Lemon* Is Dead." *Case Western Law Review* 43 (1993): 795.

Pepper, Stephen. "*Reynolds, Yoder,* and Beyond: Alternatives for the Free Exercise Clause." *Utah Law Review* (1981): 309.

Picarello, Anthony, Jr. and Roman Storzer. "The Religious Land Use and Institutionalized Persons Act of 2000: A Constitutional Response to Unconstitutional Zoning Practices." *George Mason Law Review* 929 9 (2001): 32.

Pfeffer, Leo. *Church, State and Freedom,* 2nd ed. Boston: Beacon Press, 1967.

———. *Religion, State, and the Burger Court.* Buffalo, NY: Prometheus Books, 1984.

Powell, H. Jefferson. "The Original Understanding of Original Intent." *Harvard Law Review* 98 (March 1985): 1317.

Rogers, Melissa. "Federal Funding and Religion-Based Employment Decisions." In *Sanctioning Religion? Politics, Law, and Faith-Based Social Services,* eds. David K. Ryden and Jeffrey Polet. Boulder, CO: Lynn Rienner Publishers, 2005.

Sandel, Michael. "Religious Liberty: Freedom of Conscience or Freedom of Choice." 1989 *Utah Law Review* (1989): 597.

Sandoz, Ellis. *A Government of Laws: Political Theory, Religion, and the American Founding.* Baton Rouge, LA: Louisiana State University Press, 1991.

Smith, Michael E. "The Special Place of Religion in the Constitution." *Supreme Court Review* (1983): 83.

Smith, Rodney K. *Public Prayer and the Constitution: A Case Study in Constitutional Interpretation.* Wilmington, DE: Scholarly Resources, 1987.

Smith, Steven D. *Foreordained Failure: The Quest for a Constitutional Principle of Religious Freedom.* New York: Oxford University Press, 1995.

———. "The Rise and Fall of Religious Freedom in Constitutional Discourse." *University of Pennsylvania Law Review* 140 (1991): 149.

Steinberg, David E. "Religious Exemptions as Affirmative Action." *Emory Law Journal* 40 (Winter 1991): 77.

Stokes, Anson Phelps. *Church and State in the United States: Historical Development and Contemporary Problems of Religious Freedom under the Constitution.* 3 vols. New York: Harper & Brothers, 1950.

Sullivan, Winnifred Fallers. *Paying the Words Extra: Religious Discourse in the Supreme Court of the United States.* Cambridge, MA: Harvard University Press, 1994.

———. *The Impossibility of Religious Freedom.* Princeton, NJ: Princeton University Press, 2005.

Swomley, John M. *Religious Liberty and the Secular State.* Buffalo, NY: Prometheus Books, 1985.

Urofsky, Melvin I. *Religious Freedom: Rights and Liberties under the Law.* Goleta, CA: ABC Clio, 2002.

Van Alstyne, William. "The Failure of the Religious Freedom Restoration Act Under Section 5 of the Fourteenth Amendment." *Duke Law Journal* 46 (1996): 291.

Waldman, Steven. *Founding Faith: How Our Founding Fathers Forged a Radical New Approach to Religious Liberty.* New York: Random House, 2008.

Walker, J. Brent. *Church-State Matters: Fighting for Religious Liberty in Our Nation's Capital.* Macon, GA: Mercer University Press, 2008.

Wilcox, Clyde. "Public Attitudes Toward Church-State Issues: Elite-Mass Differences." *Journal of Church and State* 34 (Spring 1992): 259.

Wilson, John F. ed. *Church and State in America: A Bibliographic Guide.* 2 vols. Westport, CT: Greenwood Press, 1987.

Wilson, John F. and Donald L. Drakeman, eds. *Church and State in American History.* 3rd ed. Boulder, CO: Westview Press, 2003.

Witte, John Jr. *Religion and the American Constitution.* 2nd ed. Boulder, CO: Westview Press, 2005.

———. "Facts and Fictions About the History of Separation of Church and State." *Journal of Church and State* 48 (2006): 15.

———. "That Serpentine Wall of Separation." *Michigan Law Review* 101 (2003): 1869.

Wood, James. E. Jr. "The Secular State." *Journal of Church and State* 7 (Spring 1965): 169.

Wood, James E. Jr., ed. *Readings on Church and State.* Waco, TX: James M. Dawson Institute of Church State Studies, Baylor University, 1989.

———. *Religion and the State: Essays in Honor of Leo Pfeffer.* Waco, TX: Baylor University Press, 1985.

———. *The First Freedom: Religion and the Bill of Rights.* Waco, TX: Baylor University Press, 1990.

Zollman, Carl. "Religious Liberty in the American Law." *Michigan Law Review* 17 (1919): 355.

THE STATES AND RELIGIOUS FREEDOM

Adams, Willi Paul. *The First American Constitutions*, trans. Rita and Robert Kimber. Chapel Hill, NC: University of North Carolina Press, 1980.

Antieu, Chester James, P.M. Carroll, and T.C. Burke. *Religion under the State Constitutions.* Washington, DC: Georgetown University Press, 1965.

DeForrest, Mark Edward. "An Overview and Evaluation of State Blaine Amendments: Origins, Scope, and First Amendment Concerns." *Harvard Journal of Law & Public Policy* 26 (Spring 2003): 551.

Green, Steven K. "'Blaming Blaine': Understanding the Blaine Amendment and the 'No-Funding' Principle. *First Amendment Law Review* 2 (2003): 107.

———. "The Blaine Amendment Reconsidered." *Journal of Legal History* 36 (1992): 38.

———. "The Insignificance of the Blaine Amendment." *B.Y.U. Law Review* (2008): 295.

Laycock, Douglas. "State RFRAs and Land Use Regulation." *University of California Davis Law Review* 32 (1999): 755.

Maffly-Kipp, Laurie F. *Religion and Society in Frontier California.* New Haven, CT: Yale University Press, 1994.

Milne, Elijah L. "Blaine Amendments and Polygamy Laws: The Constitutionality of Anti-Polygamy Laws Targeting Religion." *Western New England Law Review* 28 (Winter 2006): 257.

O'Brien, F. William. "The Blaine Amendment: 1875–76." *University of Detroit Law Journal* 41(1963): 137.

———. "The States and 'No Establishment': Proposed Amendments to the Constitution Since 1789." *Washburn Law Journal* 4 (1965): 183.

Patel, Eboo. "Religious Pluralism in the Public Square." In *Debating the Divine: Religion in 21st Century American Democracy,* ed. Sally Steenland. Washington, DC: Center for American Democracy, 2008.

Pratt, John Webb. *Religion, Politics, and Diversity: Church-State Themes in New York History.* Ithaca, NY: Cornell University Press, 1967.

Smith, Steven A. "Prelude to Article VI: The Ordeal of Religious Test Oaths in Pennsylvania." In Dale A. Herbeck, ed., *1992 Free Speech Yearbook.* Carbondale, IL: Southern Illinois Press, 1992.

Sorauf, Frank J. *The Wall of Separation: The Constitutional Politics of Church and State.* Princeton, NJ: Princeton University Press, 1976.

Tarr, Alan G. "Church and State in the States." *Washington Law Review* 64 (1989): 73.

Thorpe, Francis Newton, ed. *The Federal and State Constitutions, Colonial Charters, and Other Organic Laws.* 7 vols. Washington, DC: n.p., 1909.

Wilson, John K. "Religion under the State Constitutions, 1776–1800." *Journal of Church and State* 32 (Autumn 1990): 764.

THEOLOGICAL AND PHILOSOPHICAL PERSPECTIVES

Christianity

Dams, David K. and Cornelis A Van Minnen, eds. *Religious and Secular Reform in America: Ideas, Beliefs, and Social Change.* New York: NYU Press, 1997.

Bates, Ernest Sutherland. *American Faith: Its Religious, Political and Economic Foundations.* New York: W.W. North & Co., 1940.

Bennett, John C. *Christians and the State.* New York: Charles Scribner's Sons, 1958.

Berkhofer, Robert F., Jr. *Salvation and the Savage: An Analysis of Protestant Missions and American Indian Response, 1787–1862.* Lexington, KY: University of Kentucky Press, 1965.

Billington, Ray Allen. *The Protestant Crusade, 1800-1860, A Study of the Origins of American Nativism.* New York: Macmillan, 1938.

Banner, Stuart. "When Christianity Was Part of the Common Law." *Law and History Review* 16 (1998): 27.

Butler, Jon. *Awash in a Sea of Faith: Christianizing the American People.* Cambridge, MA: Harvard University Press, 1992.

Cort, John. *Christian Socialism.* New York: Orbis, 1988.

Davis, Derek H. "From Engagement to Retrenchment: An Examination of First Amendment Activism by America's Mainline Churches, 1980–2000." In *The Public Role of Mainline Protestantism in Late 20th-Century America,* ed. Robert Wuthnow. Princeton, NJ: Princeton University Press, 2001.

————. "Christian Faith and Political Involvement in Today's Culture War." *Journal of Church and State* 38 (Summer 1996): 473.

————. "Equal Treatment: A Christian Separationist Perspective." In *Equal Treatment of Religion in a Pluralistic Society,* eds. Steven Monsma and Christopher Soper. Grand Rapids, MI: Eerdmans, 1998.

————. "Kingdom Living in Today's Culture War." In *Empowering Believers: Christian Citizenship Through the Culture Wars.* Nashville, TN: Baptist Center for Ethics, 1996.

————. "Thoughts on the Possible Realignment of the Christian Right in Twenty-first Century America," *Journal of Church and State* 41(Summer 1999): 433.

Green, John. "Finding a Place." In *Toward an Evangelical Public Policy: Political Strategies for the Health of the Nation*, eds. Ron J. Sider and Diane Knippers. Grand Rapids, MI: Baker Books, 2005.

Handy, Robert T. "The Protestant Quest for a Christian America, 1830–1930." *Church History* 22 (1953): 8.

Helfman, Harold M. "The Cincinnati 'Bible War,' 1869–1870." *Ohio State Archaeological and Hitorical Quarterly* 60 (1951): 369.

Hillerbrand, Hans J. "An Early Anabaptist Treatise on the Christian and the State." *Mennonite Quarterly Review* 32 (1958): 28.

Johnson, Lorenzo D. *Chaplains of the General Government.* New York: Buford Press, 1856.

Kalthoff, Albert. *The Rise of Christianity.* Translated by Joseph McCabe. London: Watts & Co., 1907.

Hatch, Nathan O. *The Democratization of American Christianity.* New Haven, CT: Yale University Press, 1989.

Kautsky, Karl. *The Foundations of Christianity.* New York: International Publishers, 1925; reprint ed. New York: Monthly Review Press, 1980.

Marty, Martin E. "Living With Establishment and Disestablishment in Nineteenth-Century Anglo-America." *Journal of Church and State* 18 (Winter 1976): 61.

————. *Religion and Republic: The Christian Circumstance.* Boston: Beacon Press, 1987.

Mead, Sidney. *The Lively Experiment: The Shaping of Christianity in America.* 1963.

Miller, Perry G. "The Contribution of the Protestant Churches to Religious Liberty in Colonial America." *Church History* 4 (1935): 57.

Morris, Benjamin F. *Christian Life and Character of the Civil Institutions of the United States.* Philadelphia: George W. Childs, 1864.

Mott, Stephen Charles. *Biblical Ethics and Social Change.* New York: Oxford University Press, 1982.

Niebuhr, Richard H. *Introduction to The Social Teaching of the Christian Churches.* trans. Olive Wyon. New York: Macmillan 1931; reprint. Chicago: University of Chicago Press, 1981.

Noll, Mark. *One Nation Under God? Christian Faith and Political Action in America.* New York: Harper & Row, 1988.

Noll, Mark, Nathan O. Hatch and George M. Marsden. *The Search for Christian America.* Westchester, IL: Crossway Books, 1983.

Oaks, Dallin H., ed. *The Wall Between Church and State.* Chicago: University of Chicago Press, 1963.

Sanders, Thomas G. *Protestant Concepts of Church and State.* New York: Holt, Rinehart, and Winston, 1964.

Sandoz, Ellis. *A Government of Laws.* Baton Rouge: Louisiana State University Press, 1991.

————. "Power and Spirit in the Founding." *This World* 9 (Fall 1984): 66.

Schaff, Philip. "Church and State in the United States." In *Papers of the American Historical Association*. New York: Knickerbocker Press, 1890.

Shain, Barry. *A Theological Interpretation of American History*. Nutley, NJ: Craig Press, 1964.

Shain, Barry Alan, ed. *The Nature of Rights at the American Founding and Beyond*. Charlottesville, VA: University of Virginia Press, 2007.

Tinder, Glenn. *The Political Meaning of Christianity: An Interpretation*. Baton Rouge, LA: Louisiana State University Press, 1988.

Tocqueville, Alexis de. *Democracy in America*. eds. J.P. Mayers and Max Lerner. trans. George Lawrence. New York: Harper & Row, 1969.

Todd, Jonathan. *Civil Rulers the Ministers of God*. New London, CT: Timothy Green, 1749.

Waldron, Jeremy. *God, Locke, and Equality: Christian Foundations in Locke's Political Thought*. Cambridge, UK: Cambridge University Press, 2002.

Whitman, Walker K. *A Christian History of the American Republic*. Boston: Green Leaf Press, 1948.

Whitney, Josiah. *The Essential Requisites to Form the Good Ruler's Character*. Hartford, CT: Elisha Babcock, 1788.

Wills, Garry. *Head and Heart: American Christianities*. New York, Penguin, 2007.

Wood, James E., E. Bruce Thompson, and Robert T. Miller. *Church and State in Scripture, History, and Constitutional Law*. Waco, TX: Baylor University Press, 1958.

Denominational Perspectives

Baker, James T. "Baptists in Early America and the Separation of Church and State." In *Religion and American Law: An Encyclopedia*. ed. Paul Finkelman. New York: Garland Publishing, 2000.

Blanshard, Paul. *American Freedom and Catholic Power*. Boston: Beacon Press, 1949.

Bodo, John R. *The Protestant Clergy and Public Issues: 1812–1848*. Princeton, NJ: Princeton University Press, 1954.

Curran, Francis X. *Catholics in Colonial Law*. Chicago: Loyola Press, 1963.

Davis, Derek H., ed. *The Baptist Tradition of Religious Liberty: Essays by Edwin S. Gaustad*. Waco, TX: J.M. Dawson Institute of Church-State Studies, 1995.

———. "Baptist Approaches to Presidential Politics and Church-State Issues." *Baptist History and Heritage* 32 (January 1997): 28.

———. "Staking Out America's Sacred Ground: Baptists and the Tradition of Religious Liberty." In *Finding America's Sacred Ground*, eds. Barbara McGraw and Jo Formicola. Waco, TX: Baylor University Press, 2005.

———. "The Baptist Tradition of Religious Liberty." *Perspectives in Religious Studies* 33 (Spring 2006): 41.

Driggs, Kenneth. "After the Manifesto: Modern Polygamy and Fundamentalist Mormons." *Journal of Church and State* 32 (1990): 367.

Ellis, John T. *Catholics in Colonial America*. Baltimore: Helicon, 1965.

Gordon, Sarah B. *The Mormon Question: Polygamy and Constitutional Conflict in Nineteenth Century America*. Chapel Hill, NC: University of North Carolina Press, 2002.

Greven, Philip. *The Protestant Temperament: Patterns of Child-Rearing, Religious Experience, and the Self in Early America*. New York: New American Library, 1977.

Harrell, David Edwin, Jr. *Quest for a Christian America, 1800–1865: A Social History of the Disciples of Christ*. Nashville, TN: Disciples of Christ Historical Society, 1966.

Herberg, Will. *Protestant-Catholic-Jew: An Essay in American Religious Sociology*. Chicago: University of Chicago Press, 1955.

Ivers, Gregg. *To Build a Wall: American Jews and the Separation of Church and State*. Charlottesville, VA: University Press of Virginia, 1995.

Kerwin, Jerome G. *The Catholic Viewpoint on Church and State*. Garden City, NY: Doubleday, 1960.

Leonard, Bill J. *Baptist Ways: A History*. Valley Forge, PA: Judson Press, 2003.

Lincoln, C. Eric and Lawrence H. Mamiya. *The Black Church in the African American Experience*. Durham, NC: Duke University Press, 1990.

McLoughlin, William G. *New England Dissent, 1630–1833: The Baptists and the Separation of Church and State, 2 vols*. Cambridge, MA: Harvard University Press, 1971.

———. *Soul Liberty: The Baptists' Struggle in New England, 1630–1833*. Hanover, NH: University Press of New England, 1991.

Mead, Sidney E. "From Coercion to Persuasion: Another Look at the Rise of Religious Liberty and the Emergence of Denominationalism." *Church History* 25 (1956): 317.

Murray, John Courtney. *We Hold These Truths: Catholic Reflections on the American Proposition*. New York: Sheed and Ward, 1960.

Niebuhr, H. Richard. *The Social Sources of Denominationalism*. New York: Henry Holt, 1928.

Schaff, Philip. *Church and State in the United States*. New York: Arno Press, 1972

Thomas, David. *The Virginian Baptist; or, A View and Defence of the Christian Religion as It Is Professed by the Baptists of Virginia*. Baltimore: Enoch Story, 1774.

Miscellaneous Religions

Arrington, Leonard J., and Davis Bitton. *The Mormon Experience: A History of the Latter-day Saints*. New York: Vintage Books, 1979.

Bailey, Edward, ed. *The Secular Quest for Meaning in Life: Denton Papers in Implicit Religion*. Lampeter, Wales: Edwin Mellen, 2002.

Baird, Robert. *Religion in the United States of America*. Glasgow: Blackie & Son, 1844.

Beaver, R. Pierce. *Church, State, and the American Indians*. St. Louis, MO: Concordia Publishing House, 1966.

Bowden, Henry Warner. *American Indians and Christian Missions*. Chicago: University of Chicago Press, 1981.

Carter, Stephen L. *The Culture of Unbelief*. New York: Basic Books, 1992.

Davis, Derek H. "Is Atheism a Religion? New Judicial Perspectives on the Constitutional Meaning of 'Religion'," *Journal of Church and State* 47 (Autumn 2005).

Dawkins, Richard. *The God Delusion*. New York: Bantam Press, 2006.

Durham, Cole W. "Treatment of Religious Minorities in the United States." In *The Legal Status of Religious Minorities in the Countries of the European Union*. European Consortium for Church-State Research. Thessaloniki, Greece: Sakkoulas Publications, 1994.

Feldman, Stephen M. "Religious Minorities and the First Amendment: The History, the Doctrine, and the Future." *University of Pennsylvania Journal of Constitutional Law* 6 (November 2003): 222.

Fenton, John. *Transplanting Religious Traditions: Asian Indians in America*. New York: Praeger, 1988.

Firmage, Edwin Brown and Richard Collin Mangrum. *Zion in the Courts: A Legal History of the Church of Jesus Christ of Latter-day Saints, 1830–1900.* Urbana, IL: University of Illinois Press, 1988.

Garry, Patrick M. "The Democratic Aspect of the Establishment Clause: A Refutation of the Argument that the Clause Serves to Protect Religious or Nonreligious Minorities." *Mercer Law Review* 59 (Winter 2008): 595.

Gaustad, Edwin S. *Dissent in American Religion.* Chicago: University of Chicago Press, 1973.

Gibson, John. *The War on Christmas.* New York: Sentinel, 2005.

Gordon, Sarah Barringer. *The Mormon Question: Polygamy and Constitutional Conflict in Nineteenth-Century America.* Chapel Hill, NC: The University of North Carolina Press, 2002.

Harris, Sam. *The End of Faith: Religion, Terror, and the Future of Reason.* New York: W.W. Norton & Company, 2005.

Hitchens, Christopher. *God Is Not Great: How Religion Poisons Everything.* New York: Twelve/Warner Books, 2007.

John, Richard R. "Taking Sabbatarianism Seriously: The Postal System, the Sabbath, and the Transformation of American Political Culture." *Journal of the Early Republic* 10 (Winter 1990): 517.

Kidwell, Clara Sue, Homer Nolan, and George E. "Tink" Tinker. *A Native American Theology.* Maryknoll, NY: Orbis Books, 2001.

Kramnick, Isaac and R. Laurence Moore. *The Godless Constitution: The Case Against Religious Correctness.* New York: W.W. Norton and Co., 1996.

Levine, Samuel J. "Toward a Religious Minority Voice: A Look at Free Exercise Law through a Religious Minority Perspective." *William & Mary Bill of Rights Journal* 5 (Winter 1996): 153.

Linford, Orma. "The Mormons and the Law: The Polygamy Cases, Part I." *Utah Law Review* 9 (1964): 308.

Long, Carolyn. *Religious Freedom and Indian Rights: The Case of Oregon v. Smith.* Lawrence, KS: University of Kansas Press, 2001.

McConnell, Michael. "Freedom From Persecution or Protection of the Rights of Conscience? A Critique of Justice Scalia's Historical Arguments in *City of Boerne v. Flores.*" *William & Mary Law Review* 39 (February 1998): 819.

McDonald, Forrest. *Novus Ordo Seclorum.* Lawrence, KS: University Press of Kansas, 1985.

Melton, Gordon, ed. *The Encyclopedia of American Religions.* 3rd ed. Detroit, MI: Gale Research, Inc., 1989.

Moore, R. Laurence. *Religious Outsiders and the Making of Americans.* New York: Oxford University Press, 1987.

Peters, Shawn Francis. *Judging Jehovah's Witnesses: Religious Persecution and the Dawn of the Rights Revolution.* Lawrence, KS: University Press of Kansas, 2000.

Piar, Daniel F. "Majority Rights, Minority Freedoms: Protestant Culture, Personal Autonomy, and Civil Liberties in Nineteenth-Century America." *The William and Mary Bill of Rights Journal* 14 (February 2006): 987.

Prucha, Francis Paul. *American Indian Policy in Crisis: Christian Reformers and the Indian, 1865–1900.* Norman, OK: University of Oklahoma Press, 1976.

———. *American Indian Policy in the Formative Years.* Cambridge, MA: Harvard University Press, 1962.

Sherry, Suzanna. "Religion and the Public Square: Making Democracy Safe for Religious Minorities." *DePaul Law Review* 47 (Spring 1998): 499.

Smith, Gary Scott. *The Seeds of Secularization: Calvinism, Culture, and Pluralism in America 1870–1915*. Grand Rapids, MI: Christian University Press, 1985.

Turner, James. *Without God, Without Creed: The Origins of Unbelief in America*. Baltimore: The Johns Hopkins University Press, 1985.

Wildenthal, Bryan H. and Patrick M. O'Neil. "Native American Religious Rights." In *Religion and American Law: An Encyclopedia*. ed. Paul Finkelman. New York: Garland Publishing, 2000.

RELIGIOUS PLURALISM

Beaman, Lori G. "The Myth of Pluralism, Diversity and Vigor: The Constitutional Privilege of Protestantism in the United States and Canada." *Journal for the Scientific Study of Religion* 42 (September 2003): 3.

Beyer, Peter. "Constitutional Privilege and Constituting Pluralism: Religious Freedom in National, Global and Legal Contexts." *Journal for the Scientific Study of Religion* 42 (September 2003): 3.

Berg, Thomas C. *Minority Religions and the Religion Clauses*. St. Louis: School of Law, Washington University, 2004.

Demerath, N.J. III. *Crossing the Gods: World Religions and Worldly Politics*. Piscataway, NJ: Rutgers University Press, 2001.

DiIulio, John J. Jr. *Godly Republic: A Centrist Blueprint for America's Faith Based-Future*. Berkeley, CA: University of California Press, 2007.

Eck, Diane. *A New Religious America: How a "Christian Country" Has Become the World's Most Religiously Diverse Nation*. San Francisco: Harper, 2002.

Farnsley, Arthur E. II, N.J. Demerath III, Etan Diamond, Mary Mapes, and Wedam Elfriede. *Sacred Circles/Public Squares: The Multicentering of American Religion*. Bloomington, IN: Indiana University Press, 2004.

Gaustad, Edwin S. *A Religious History of America*. New York: Harper & Row, 1966.

Gvosdev, Nikolas K. "Tolerance versus Pluralism: The Eurasian Dilemma." *Analysis of Current Events* 12 (December 2000): 7.

Littell, Franklin H. *From State Church to Pluralism: A Protestant Interpretation of Religion in American History*. New York: Macmillan, 1971.

Machacek, David W. "The Problem of Pluralism." *Sociology of Religion* 64 (2003): 24.

Mazur, Eric Michael. *The Americanization of Religious Minorities: Confronting the Constitutional Order*. Baltimore: Johns Hopkins University Press, 1999.

McGraw, Barbara. *Rediscovering America's Sacred Ground: Public Religion and Pursuit of the Good in a Pluralistic America*. Albany, NY: State University of New York Press, 2003.

Miller, Randall M. *Immigrants and Religion in Urban America*. Philadelphia: Temple University Press, 1977.

Monsma, Steven *v*. and Christopher Soper, eds. *The Challenge of Pluralism: Church and State in Five Democracies*. Lanham, MD: Rowman & Littlefield, 1997.

North, Gary. *Political Polytheism: The Myth of Pluralism*. Tyler, TX: Institute for Christian Economics, 1989.

Mary Segers, ed. *Piety, Politics, and Pluralism: Religion, the Courts, and the 2000 Election*. Lanham, MD: Rowman and Littlefield, 2002.

Viteritti, Joseph P. "Reading Zelman: The Triumph of Pluralism, and Its Effects on Liberty, Equality, and Choice." *Southern California Law Review* 76 (2003): 1105.

Warner, R. Stephen and Judith G. Wittner, eds. *Gatherings in Diaspora: Religious Communities and the New Immigration*. Philadelphia: Temple University Press, 1998.

Wentz, Richard E. *The Culture of Religious Pluralism*. Boulder, CO: Westview Press, 1998.

ETHICS AND VALUES

Adams, G.D. "Abortion: Evidence of an Issue Evolution." *American Journal of Political Science* 41 (1997): 718.

Al-Hibri, Azizah Y., Jean Bethke Elshtain, and Charles H. Haynes. *Religion in American Public Life: Living with our Deepest Differences*. New York: W.W. Norton & Co., 2001.

Audi, Robert. *Religious Commitment and Secular Reason*. New York: Cambridge University Press, 2000.

Baird, Robert M. and Stuart E. Rosenbaum, eds. *Same-Sex Marriage: The Moral and Legal Debate*. New York: Prometheus Books, 1997.

Ball, Carlos A. "The Positive in the Fundamental Right to Marry: Same-Sex Marriage in the Aftermath of *Lawrence v. Texas*." *Minnesota Law Review* 88 (2004): 1184.

Bellah, Robert N., Richard Madsen, William M. Sullivan, Ann Swidler, and Steven M. Tipton. *Habits of the Heart: Individualism and Commitment in American Life*. Berkeley, CA: University of California Press, 1985.

Beneke, Chris. *Beyond Toleration: The Religious Roots of American Pluralism*. New York: Oxford University Press, 2006.

Brenner, Lenni, ed. *Jefferson & Madison on Separation of Church and State: Writings on Religion and Secularism*. Fort Lee, NJ: Barracade Books, 2004.

Carmella, Angela C. "Mary Ann Glendon on Religious Liberty: The Social Nature of the Person and the Public Nature of Religion." *Notre Dame Law Review* 73 (1998): 1191.

Davis, Derek H. "God and the Pursuit of America's Self-Understanding: Toward a Synthesis of American Historiography." *Journal of Church and State* 46 (Summer 2004): 461.

———. "The Pledge of Allegiance and American Values." *Journal of Church and State* 44 (Autumn 2003):

———. "Religion and State in the United States: Separation, Integration, and Accommodation." In *Democracy: Free Exercise and Diverse Visions and Religion*, ed. David Odell Scott. Kent, OH: Kent State University Press, 2004.

———. "Preserving the Moral Integrity of the Constitution: An Examination of Deconstruction and Other Hermeneutical Theories." In *Problems and Conflicts Between Law and Morality in a Free Society*, eds. James E. Wood, Jr. and Derek Davis. Waco, TX: J.M. Dawson Institute of Church-State Studies, 1994.

———. "Reflections on Moral Decline in America: Consulting the Founding Fathers' Views on the Roles of Church and State in Crafting the Good Society." *Journal of Church and State* 42 (Spring 2000): 237.

———. "Religion and the Abuse of Judicial Power." *Journal of Church and State* 39 (Spring 1997): 203.

———. "The Ten Commandments as Public Ritual." *Journal of Church and State* 44 (Spring 2002): 221.

Davis, Derek and Barry Hankins, eds. *New Religious Movements and Religious Liberty in America*. J.M. Dawson Institute of Church-State Studies, 2001.

Davis, James Calvin. The *Moral Theology of Roger Williams: Christian Conviction and Public Ethics*. Louisville, KY: Westminster John Knox Press, 2004.

Dent, George W. Jr. "The Defense of Traditional Marriage." *The Journal of Law and Politics* 15 (Fall 1999): 581.

Dreisbach, Daniel L. "In Search of a Christian Commonwealth: An Examination of Selected Nineteenth-Century Commentaries on References to God and the Christian Religion in the United States Constitution." *Baylor Law Review* 48 (1996): 927.

Eberle, Christopher. *Religious Conviction in Liberal Politics.* Cambridge, UK: Cambridge University Press, 2002.

Feldman, Noah. *Divided by God: America's Church-State Problem—and What We Should Do About It.* New York: Farrar, Straus & Giroux, 2005.

Finkelman, Paul. "The Ten Commandments on the Courthouse Lawn and Elsewhere." *Fordham Law Review* 73 (2005): 1477.

Garber, Marjorie and Rebecca L. Walkowitz, eds. *One Nation Under God? Religion and American Culture.* New York: Routledge, 1999.

George, Robert P. *The Clash of Orthodoxies: Law, Religion, and Morality in Crisis.* Wilmington, DE: ISI, 2001.

Gerstmann, Evan. *Same-Sex Marriage and the Constitution.* Cambridge, UK: Cambridge University Press, 2008.

Horwitz, Robert H., ed. *The Moral Foundations of the American Republic.* 3rd ed. Charlottesville, VA: University Press of Virginia, 1986.

Kemeny, Paul C., ed. *Church, State and Public Justice: Five Views.* Downers Grove, IL: Inter Varsity Press, 2007.

McConnell, Michael W., and Richard A. Posner. "An Economic Approach to Issues of Religious Freedom." *University of Chicago Law Review* 56 (1989): 1.

McGreevy, John. *Catholicism and American Freedom: A History.* New York: Norton, 2004.

Murphy, Andrew R. *Conscience and Community: Revisiting Toleration and Religious Dissent in Early Modern England and America.* University Park, PA: Penn State University Press, 2001.

Nichols, J. Bruce. *The Uneasy Alliance.* New York: Oxford University Press, 1988.

Noonan, John T. *The Luster of Our Country: The American Experience of Religious Freedom.* Berkeley, CA: University of California Press, 1998.

Nussbaum, Martha. *Liberty of Conscience: In Defense of America's Tradition of Religious Equality.* New York: Basic Books, 2008.

Powell, Jefferson H. *The Moral Tradition of American Constitutionalism: A Theological Interpretation.* Durham, NC: Duke University Press, 1993.

Rawls, John. *Political Liberalism.* New York: Columbia University Press, 1993.

Reid, Eric. "Assessing and Responding to Same-Sex 'Marriage' in Light of Natural Law." *Georgetown Journal of Law & Public Policy* 3 (2005): 523.

Richards, David A.J. *Toleration and the Constitution.* New York: Oxford University Press, 1986.

Schlitz, Patrick. "The Impact of Sexual Clergy Misconduct Litigation on Religious Liberty." *Boston College Law Review* 44 (2003): 949.

Schwartz, Sally A. *"A Mixed Multitude": The Struggle for Toleration in Colonial Pennsylvania.* New York: New York University Press, 1988.

Sharlet, Jeff. *The Family: The Secret Fundamentalism at the Heart of American Power.* New York: Harpers, 2008.

Skeels, Heather Rae. "Patient Autonomy versus Religious Freedom: Should State Legislatures Require Catholic Hospitals to Provide Emergency Contraception to Rape Victims?" *Washington and Lee Law Review* 60 (2003): 1007.

Spaht, Katherine Shaw. "Revolution and Counter-Revolution: the Future of Marriage in the Law." *Loyola Law Review* 49 (2003): 1.

Sweet, William W. *Religion in the Development of American Culture, 1765-1840*. New York: Charles Scribner's Sons, 1952.

Wallis, Jim. *God's Politics: Why the Right Get It Wrong and Why the Left Doesn't Get It.* San Francisco: Harper San Francisco, 2005.

———. *The Soul of Politics: A Practical and Prophetic Vision for Change.* New York: The New Press and Orbis Books, 1994.

Weber, Timothy P. *On the Road to Armageddon: How Evangelicals Became Israel's Best Friend.* Chicago: Baker Academic, 2004.

Weinrib, Lloyd. *Natural Law and Justice.* Cambridge, MA: Harvard University Press, 1987.

POLITICAL PERSPECTIVES

Religion and Politics

Adams, Jasper. *The Relation of Christianity to Civil Government in the United States.* Charleston, SC: A.E. Miller, 1833.

Berry, Jeffrey M. *The Interest Group Society.* Glenview, IL: Scott, Foresman, and Company, 1989.

———. *The New Liberalism: The Rising Power of Citizens Groups.* Washington, DC: Brookings Institution Press, 1999.

Blanshard, Paul. *God and Man in Washington.* Boston: Beacon Press, 1960.

Buzzard, Lynn R., and Sherra Robinson. *I.R.S. Political Activity Restrictions on Churches and Charitable Ministries.* Diamond Bar, CA: Christian Ministries Management Association, 1990.

Campbell, Donald E., ed. *A Matter of Faith: Religion in the 2004 Presidential Election.* Washington, DC: Brookings Institution Press, 2007.

Carter, Stephen. *God's Name in Vain: The Wrongs and Rights of Religion in Politics.* New York: Basic Books, 2000.

Carwardine, Richard J. *Evangelicals and Politics in Antebellum America.* New Haven, CT: Yale University Press, 1993.

Cochran, Clarke. *Religion in Public and Private Life.* New York: Routledge, 1991.

Crawford, Sue E.S., and Laura R. Olson, eds. *Christian Clergy in American Politics.* Baltimore: Johns Hopkins University Press, 2001.

Dreisbach, Daniel L. *Religion and Politics in the Early Republic.* Lexington, KY: University of Kentucky Press, 1996.

Demerath, N.J. III and Rhys H. Williams. *A Bridging of Faiths: Religion and Politics in a New England City.* Princeton, NJ: Princeton University Press, 1992.

Fackre, Gabriel. *Judgment Day at the White House: A Critical Declaration Exploring Moral Issues and the Political Use and Abuse of Religion.* Grand Rapids, MI: William B. Eerdmans, 1999.

Fowler, Robert Booth, Allen D. Hertzke, and Laura R. Olson, eds. *Religion and Politics in America: Faith, Culture, and Strategic Choices.* 2nd ed. Boulder, CO: Westview Press, 2004.

Gill, Anthony. *The Political Origins of Religious Liberty.* New York: Cambridge University Press, 2008.

Glendon, Mary Ann. *Rights Talk.* New York: Free Press, 1991.

Greenawalt, Kent. *Religious Convictions and Political Choice.* New York: Oxford University Press, 1988.

Guth, James L. and John C. Green. *The Bible and the Ballot Box: Religion and Politics in the 1988 Election*. Boulder, CO: Westview Press, 1991.

Hadaway, C. Kirk, Penny Long Marler, and Mark Chaves. "What the Polls Don't Show: A Closer Look at U.S. Church Attendance." *American Sociological Review* 58/6 (December, 1993): 741.

Hout, Michael and Claude Fischer. "Why More Americans Have No Religious Preference: Politics and Generations." *American Sociological Review* 68 (2002): 314.

Huntington, Samuel P. *American Politics: The Promise of Disharmony*. Cambridge, MA: Belknap Press, 1981.

Jelen, Ted G. and Clyde Wilcox, eds. *Religion and Politics in Comparative Perspective*. New York: Cambridge University Press, 2002.

Jelen, Ted G. *The Political Mobilization of Religious Beliefs*. Westport, CT: Praeger, 1991.

———. *The Political World of the Clergy*. Westport, CT: Praeger, 1993.

Kelley, Dean M. *Why Churches Should Not be Taxed*. New York: Harper & Row, 1977.

Kelly, George Armstrong. *Politics and Religious Consciousness in America*. New Brunswick, NJ: Transaction, Inc., 1984.

Kengor, Paul. *God and Ronald Reagan: A Spiritual Life*. New York: HarperCollins, 2004.

Lambert, Frank. *Religion in American Politics: A Short History*. Princeton, NJ: Princeton University Press, 2008.

Larson, Carin, James Madland, Clyde Wilcox, and N.J. Demerath III. "Religion and Political Process in an American City." *American Sociological Review* 56 (1992): 417.

Malbin, Michael J. *Religion and Politics: The Intentions of the Authors of the First Amendment*. Washington, DC: American Enterprise Institute for Public Policy Research, 1978.

McBrien, Richard P. *Caesar's Coin: Religion and Politics in America*. New York: Macmillan, 1987.

Micklewaith, J. and A. Woolridge. *The Right Nation: Conservative Power in America*. New York: Penguin Press, 2004.

Mittleman, Alan, Jonathan D. Sarna, and Robert Licht, eds. *Jewish Polity and American Civil Society: Communal Agencies and Religious Movements in the American Public Square*. Lanham, MD: Rowman and Littlefield, 2002.

Neuhaus, Richard John. *The Naked Public Square: Religion and Democracy in America*. Grand Rapids, MI: Erdmans, 1984.

Noll, Mark A. *Religion and American Politics: From the Colonial Period to the 1980s*. New York: Oxford University Press, 1990.

Northcott, Michael. *An Angel Directs the Storm: Apocalyptic Religion & American Empire*. New York: I.B. Tauris, 2004.

Perry, Michael J. *Religion and Politics: Constitutional and Moral Perspectives*. New York: Oxford University Press, 1997.

Phillips, Kevin. *American Dynasty: Aristocracy, Fortunes, and the Politics of Deceit*. New York: Viking Press, 2004.

Rawls, John. *Political Liberalism*. New York: Columbia University Press, 1993.

Segers, Mary C. and Ted G. Jelen. *Wall of Separation: Debating the Public Role of Religion*. Lanham, MD: Rowman and Littlefield, 1997.

Strout, Cushing. *The New Heavens and New Earth: Political Religion in America*. New York: Harper & Row, 1974.

Thiemann, Ronald F. *Religion in American Public Life*. Washington, DC: Georgetown University Press, 1996.

Wald, Kenneth and Allison Calhoun-Brown. *Religion and Politics in the United States*. 5th ed. Lanham, MD: Rowman and Littlefield, 2007.

Williams, Rhys H., ed. *Culture Wars in American Politics: Critical Views of a Popular Thesis.* Chicago: Aldine de Gruyter, 1997.

Wills, Garry. *Under God: Religion and American Politics.* New York: Simon and Schuster, 1994.

Thiemann, Ronald. *Religion in Public Life: A Dilemma for Democracy.* Washington, DC: Georgetown University Press, 1996.

The Christian Right in Politics

Aikman, D. *A Man of Faith: The Spiritual Journey of George W. Bush.* Nashville, TN: W. Publishing Group, 2004.

Appleton, A.M. and D. Francis. "Washington: Mobilizing for Victory." In *God at the Grassroots 1996: The Christian Right in the 1996 Elections,* eds. M.J. Rozell and C. Wilcox. Lanham, MD: Rowman and Littlefield, 1997.

Bates, S. *Battleground: One Mother's Crusade, the Religious Right, and the Struggle for Control of Our Classrooms.* New York: Poseidon Press, 1993.

Boston, R. *Close Encounters with the Religious Right: Journeys into the Twilight Zone of Religion and Politics.* Amherst, NY: Prometheus Books, 2000.

———. *The Most Dangerous Man in America? Pat Robertson and the Rise of the Christian Coalition.* Amherst, NY: Prometheus Books, 1996.

Brown, Steven P. *Trumping Religion: The New Christian Right, the Free Speech Clause, and the Courts.* Tuscaloosa, AL: University of Alabama Press, 2004.

Bruce, S. *The Rise and Fall of the New Christian Right.* Oxford, UK: Clarendon Press, 1988.

Deckman, M.M. *School Board Battles: The Christian Right in Local Politics.* Washington, DC: Georgetown University Press, 2004.

Gilbert, C.P. and Peterson, D.A. "Minnesota: Christians and Quistians in the GOP." In *God at the Grassroots: The Christian Right in the 1994 Elections,* eds. M.J. Rozell and C. Wilcox. Lanham, MD: Rowman and Littlefield, 1997.

Green, J.C., J.L Guth, C.E. Smidt, and L.A. Kellstedt. *Religion and the Culture Wars: Dispatches from the Front.* Lanham, MD: Rowman and Littlefield, 1996.

Green, J.C., M.J. Rozell, and C. Wilcox. *Prayers in the Precincts: The Christian Right in the 1998 Elections.* Washington, DC: Georgetown University Press, 2000.

———. *The Christian Right in American Politics: Marching to the Millennium.* Washington, DC: Georgetown University Press, 2003.

———. "The Christian Right's Long March." In *The Christian Right in American Elections: Marching to the Millennium,* eds. J.C. Green, M.J. Rozell, and C. Wilcox. Washington, DC: Georgetown University Press, 2003.

Guth, J.L., Kellstedt, L.A., Green, J.C., and Smidt, C.E. "Getting the Spirit? Religious and Partisan Mobilization in the 2004 Elections." In *Interest Group Politics.* 7th ed. eds. A.J. Cigler and B.A. Loomis. Washington, DC: CQ Press, 2007.

Hacker, H.J. *The Culture of Conservative Christian Litigation.* Lanham, MD: Rowman and Littlefield, 2003.

Hertzke, A.D. *Echoes of Discontent: Jesse Jackson, Pat Robertson, and the Resurgence of Populism.* Washington, DC: CQ Press, 1993.

Jelen, Ted G. "Political Esperanto: Rhetorical Resources and Limitations of the Christian Right in the United States." *Sociology of Religion* 66 (2005): 303.

———. *The Political Mobilization of Religious Belief.* Westport, CT: Praeger, 1991.

Larson, C., D. Madland, and C. Wilcox. "Religious Lobbying in Virginia: How Institutions Can Quiet Prophetic Voices." In *Representing God in the Statehouse: Religion and*

Politics in the American States, eds. E. Cleary and A. Hertzke. Lanham, MD: Rowman and Littlefield, 2005.

Lunch, W.M. "Oregon: Identity Politics in the Northeast." In *God at the Grassroots: The Christian Right in the 1994 Election,* eds. M.J. Rozell and C. Wilcox. Lanham, MD: Rowman and Littlefield, 1995.

Martin, William. *With God on Our Side: The Rise of the Religious Right in America.* New York: Broadway Books, 1996.

Moen, Matthew. C. *The Christian Right and Congress.* Tuscaloosa, AL: University of Alabama Press, 1989.

———. "The Evolving Politics of the Christian Right." *Political Science and Politics* 29 (1996): 461.

Rausch, David A. and Douglas E. Chismar. "The New Puritans and Their Theonomic Paradise." *Christian Century,* 3 August 1983, 713.

Reed, Ralph. *After the Revolution.* Dallas, TX: Word Publishers, 1994.

———. *Politically Incorrect: the Emerging Faith Factor in American Politics.* Dallas, TX: Word Publishing, 1994.

Rozell, Mark J. and Wilcox, Clyde. "Second Coming: The Strategies of the New Christian Right." *Political Science Quarterly* 111 (1996): 271.

———. *Second Coming: The New Christian Right in Virginia Politics.* Baltimore: Johns Hopkins University Press, 1996.

Rozell, Mark J., Clyde Wilcox, and J.C. Green. "Religious Constituencies and Support for the Christian Right in the 1990's." *Social Science Quarterly* 79 (1998): 815.

Rushdoony, Rousas J. *The Institutes of Biblical Law.* Philadelphia: The Presbyterian and Reformed Publishing Co., 1984.

Schaeffer, F.A. *A Christian Manifesto.* Rev. ed. Westchester, IL: Crossway Books, published in association with Nims Communications, 1982.

Shields, J.A. "Between Passion and Deliberation: The Christian Right and Democratic Ideals." *Political Science Quarterly* 12 (2007): 89.

Shupe, Anson. "The Reconstructionist Movement on the New Christian Right." *Christian Century,* 4 October 1989, 881.

Smidt, C.E. and J.M. Penning. *Sojourners in the Wilderness: The Christian Right in Comparative Perpsective.* Lanham, MD: Rowman and Littlefield, 1999.

Viteritti, J.P. *The Last Freedom: Religion from the Public School to the Public Square.* Princeton, NJ: Princeton University Press, 2007.

Watson, Justin. *The Christian Coalition: Dreams of Restoration, Demands for Recognition.* New York: St. Martin's Griffin, 1997.

Wilcox, Clyde. *God's Warriors: The Christian Right in Twentieth Century America.* Baltimore: Johns Hopkins University Press, 1992.

———. *Onward Christian Soldiers? The Religious Right in American Politics.* 2nd ed. Washington, DC: Georgetown University Press, 2000.

———. "Premillenialists at the Millenium: Some Reflections on the Christian Right in the Twenty-first Century." *Sociology of Religion* 55 (1994): 243.

Wilcox, C. and C. Larson. *Onward Christian Soldiers: The Christian Right in American Politics.* 3rd ed. Boulder, CO: Westview Press, 2006.

Wilcox, Clyde and C. Robinson. "The Faith of George W. Bush: The Personal, Practical, and Political." In *Religion and American Presidents,* eds. M.J. Rozell and G. Whitney. New York: Palmgrave/Macmillan, 2007.

Wilcox, Clyde and L. Sigelman. "Political Mobilization in the Pews: Religious Contacting and Electoral Turnout." *Social Science Quarterly* 83 (2001): 524.

Religious Lobbies

Benson, Peter L. and Dorothy L. Williams. *Religion on Capitol Hill: Myths and Realities.* San Francisco: Harper & Row, 1982.

Cleary, Edward and Allen Hertzke, eds. *Representing God at the Statehouse.* Lanham, MD: Rowman and Littlefield, 2006.

Ebersole, Luke Eugene. *Church Lobbying in the Nation's Capital.* New York: Macmillan, 1951.

Hertzke, Allen D. *Representing God in Washington: The Role of Religious Lobbies in the American Polity.* Knoxville, TN: The University of Tennessee Press, 1988.

Hofrenning, Daniel J.B. *In Washington, But Not of It: The Prophetic Politics of Religious Lobbyists.* Philadelphia: Temple University Press, 1995.

Hrebenar, Ronald J. and Ruth K. Scott. *Interest Group Politics in America.* Englewood Cliffs, NJ: Prentice-Hall, 1982.

Lobeda, Cynthia D. Moe. *The Public Church: For the Life of the World.* Augsburg Fortress Publishers, 2004.

Reichley, James A. *Religion in American Public Life.* Washington, DC: The Brookings Institute, 1985.

Church–State and Education

Alley, Robert S. *School Prayer: The Court, the Congress, and the First Amendment.* Buffalo, NY: Prometheus Books, 1994.

Bailyn, Bernard. *Education and the Forming of American Society.* New York: Vintage Books, 1960.

Beckwith, Francis J. *Law, Darwinism, and Public Education: The Establishment Clause and the Challenge of Intelligent Design.* Lanham, MD: Rowman and Littlefield, 2003.

Boles, Donald E. *The Bible, Religion, and the Public Schools.* 2d ed. Ames, IA: Iowa State University Press, 1963.

Bower, William. *Church and State in Education.* Chicago: University of Chicago Press, 1944.

Brown, Steven and Cynthia Bowling. "Public Schools and Religious Expression: The Diversity of School Districts' Policies Regarding Religious Expression." *Journal of Church and State* 45 (Spring 2003): 259.

Carper, James C. "Pluralism to Establishment to Dissent: The Religious and Educational Context of Home Schooling." *Peabody Journal of Education* 75 (2000): 8.

Carper, James, C. and Thomas C. Hunt. *The Praeger Handbook of Religion and Education in the United States.* 2 vols. Westport, CT: Praeger, 2009.

Clifford, Geraldine. "Home and School in 19th Century America: Some Personal-History Reports from the United States." *History of Education Quarterly* 18 (1978): 3.

Cremin, Lawrence A. *American Education: The Colonial Experience, 1607–1783.* New York: Harper & Row, 1970.

Culver, Raymond B. *Horace Mann and Religion in the Massachusetts Public Schools.* New Haven, CT: Yale University Press, 1929.

Cutler, William. "Cathedral of Culture: The Schoolhouse in American Educational Thought and Practice since 1820." *History of Education Quarterly* 29 (1989): 1.

Cutler, William. *Parents and Schools: The 150-year Struggle for Control in American Education.* Chicago: University of Chicago Press, 2000.

Davis, Derek H. "Character Education in America's Public Schools," *Journal of Church and State* 48 (Winter 2006): 1.

————. "Moments of Silence in America's Public Schools: Constitutional and Ethical Considerations." *Journal of Church and State* 44 (Summer 2003): 465.

————. "Reacting to France's Ban: Headscarves and other Religious Attire in American Public Schools." *Journal of Church and State* 46 (Spring 2004): 221.

————. "Kansas Versus Darwin: Examining the History and Future of the Creationism-Evolution Controversy in America's Public Schools." *Kansas Journal of Law and Public Policy* 9 (Winter 1999): 205.

Davis, Derek H. and Robert Haener. "Church-State Curriculum in American Higher Education." *Journal of Church and State* 38 (Winter 1996): 155.

Dent, George W. "Of God and Caesar: The Free Exercise Rights of Public School Students." *Case Western Law Review* 43 (1993): 707.

Dierenfield, Bruce J. *The Battle over School Prayer: How* Engel v. Vitale *Changed America.* Lawrence, KS: University of Kansas Press, 2007.

Dolbeare, Kenneth M. and Philip E. Hammond. *The School Prayer Decisions: From Court Policy to Local Practice.* Chicago: University of Chicago Press, 1971.

Formicola, Jo Renee and Hubert Morken, eds. *Everson Revisited: Religion, Education, and Law at the Crossroads.* Lanham, MD: Rowman & Littlefield, 1997.

Glenn, Charles L. *The Myth of the Common School.* Amherst, MA: The University of Massachusetts Press, 1988.

Glenn, Charles L. *The Ambiguous Embrace: Government and Faith-Based Schools and Social Agencies.* Princeton, NJ: Princeton University Press, 2000.

Good, Harry Gehman and James D. Teller. *A History of American Education.* New York: Macmillan, 1973.

Greenawalt, Kent. *Does God Belong in Public Schools?* Princeton, NJ: Princeton University Press, 2005.

Hyneman, Charles S. and Donald S. Lutz, eds. *Political Writing During the Founding Era, 1760–1805.* Indianapolis, IN: Liberty Fund, Inc., 1983.

Jackson, Jerome K. and Constance F. Malmberg. *Religious Education and the State.* Garden City, NY: Doubleday, Doran & Co., 1928.

Jorgenson, Lloyd. *The State and the Non-Public School, 1825–1925.* Columbia, MO: University of Missouri Press, 1987.

Kaestle, Carl F. *Pillars of the Republic, Common Schools and American Society, 1780–1860.* New York: Hill and Wang, 1983.

Kovalchick, Anthony T. "Educational Aid Programs under the Establishment Clause: The Need for the U.S. Supreme Court to Adopt the Rule Proposed by the Mitchell Plurality." *Southern California Law Review* 30 (2003): 117.

Larson, Edward J. *Summer for the Gods: The Scopes Trial and America's Continuing Debate Over Science and Religion.* Cambridge, MA: Harvard University Press, 1997.

Locke, John. *The Educational Writings of John Locke.* ed. James Axtell. New York: Cambridge University Press, 1968.

Mawdsley, Ralph D. "Leveling the Field for Religious Clubs: The Interface of the Equal Access Act, Free Speech, and the Establishment Clause." *Education Law Reporter* 174 (2003): 809.

McAfee, Ward M. *Religion, Race, and Reconstruction: The Public School in the Politics of the 1870s.* Albany, NY: State University of New York Press, 1998.

McCloskey, Robert G., ed. *The Bible in the Public Schools—Arguments in the Case of John D. Minor, et al., versus The Board of Education of the City of Cincinnati, et al.* New York: Da Capo Press Reprint, 1967.

McCarthy, Rockne, et al. *Society, State, & Schools: A Case for Structural and Confessional Pluralism.* Grand Rapids, MI: Eerdmans, 1981.

Michaelson, Robert. *Piety in the Public School: Trends and Issues in Relationship between Religion and the Public Schools in the United States.* New York: Macmillan, 1970.

Moore, R. Laurence. "Bible Reading and Nonsectarian Schooling: The Failure of Religious Instruction in Nineteenth-Century Public Education." *Journal of American History* 86 (2000): 1581.

Muir, William K., Jr. *Prayer in the Public Schools: Law and Attitude Change.* Chicago: University of Chicago Press, 1967.

Myers, Richard S. "Reflections on the Teaching of Civic Virtue in the Public Schools." *University of Detroit Mercy Law Review* 74 (1996): 63.

Neuhaus, Richard John, ed. *Democracy and the Renewal of Public Education.* Grand Rapids, MI: Eerdmans, 1987.

O'Neill, J.M. *Religion and Education under the Constitution.* New York: Harper & Row, 1949.

Peters, Shawn Frances. *The Yoder Case: Religious Freedom, Education, and Parental Rights.* Lawrence, KS: University Press of Kansas, 2003

Ravitch, Diane. *The Great School Wars, New York City, 1805–1973: A History of the New York City Schools as a Battlefield of Social Change.* New York: Basic Books, 1974.

Ravitch, Frank S. *School Prayer and Discrimination: The Civil Rights of Religious Minorities and Dissenters.* Boston: Northeastern University Press, 1999.

Russo, Charles. "Prayer at Public School Graduation Ceremonies." *Brigham Young University Education and Law Journal* (1999): 1.

Sizer, Theodore, ed. *Religion and Public Education.* Washington, DC: University Press of America, 1967.

Shipton, Clifford. "Secondary Education in Puritan Colonies." *The New England Quarterly* 7 (1934): 646.

Sky, Theodore. "The Establishment Clause, the Congress, and the Schools: An Historical Perspective." *Virginia Law Review* 52 (1966): 1395.

Smith, Timothy. "Protestant Schooling and American Nationality, 1800–1850." *The Journal of American History* 53 (1967): 679.

Teaford, Jon. "The Transformation of Massachusetts Education, 1670–1780." *History of Education Quarterly* 10 (1970): 287.

Tyack, David. *Law and the Shaping of Public Education, 1785–1954.* Madison, WI: University of Wisconsin Press, 1987.

———. *Tinkering Toward Utopia: A Century of Public School Reform.* Cambridge, MA: Harvard University Press, 1995.

Wood, James E. Jr. "Religion and Public Education in Historical Perspective." *Journal of Church and State* 14 (Autumn 1972): 397.

Wood, James E. Jr, ed. *Religion, the State, and Education.* Waco, TX: Baylor University Press, 1984.

Regulation of Religion

Adamczyk, Amy, John Wybraniec, and Roger Finke. "Religious Regulation and the Courts: Documenting the Effects of *Smith* and RFRA." *Journal of Church and State* 46 (2004): 237.

Cote, Pauline and Jeremy Gunn. *The New Religious Question: State Regulation or State Interference?* New York: Peter Lang, 2006.

Finke, Roger. "Religious Deregulation: Origins and Consequences." *Journal of Church and State* 32 (1990): 609.

Fisher, Louis. *Religious Liberty in America: Political Safeguards.* Lawrence, KS: University Press of Kansas, 2002.

Formicola, Jo Renee, Mary C. Segers, and Paul Weber. *Faith Based Initiatives and the Bush Administration: The Good, the Bad, and the Ugly.* Lanham, MD: Rowman and Littlefield, 2003.

Iannaccone, Laurence, Roger Finke, and Rodney Stark. "Deregulating Religion." *Economic Inquiry* 35 (1997): 350.

Kelley, Dean. *Government Intervention in Religious Affairs.* New York: Pilgrim Press, 1982.

Richardson, James T. "Apostates, Whistleblowers, Law, and Social Control." In *The Politics of Religious Apostasy.* ed. David Bromley. Westport, CT: Praeger, 1998.

Richardson, James T. and John DeWitt. "Christian Science Spiritual Healing, Public Opinion, and the Law." *Journal of Church and State* 34 (1992): 549.

Wood, James E., Jr. and Derek H. Davis, eds. *The Role of Religion in the Making of Public Policy.* Waco, TX: J.M. Dawson Institute of Church-State Studies, 1991.

———. *The Role of Government in Monitoring and Regulating Religion in Public Life.* Waco, TX: J.M. Dawson Institute of Church-State Studies, 1993.

———. *Problems and Conflicts between Law and Morality in a Free Society.* Waco, TX: J.M. Dawson Institute of Church-State Studies, 1994.

———. *New Religious Movements and Religious Liberty in America.* 2nd ed. Waco, TX: Baylor University Press. 2007.

Stuart Wright, ed. *Armageddon in Waco.* Chicago: University of Chicago Press, 1995.

Wybraniec, John and Roger Finke. "Religious Regulation and the Courts: The Judiciary's Changing Role in Protecting Minority Religions from Majoritarian Rule." *Journal for the Scientific Study of Religion* 40 (2001): 427.

Faith-Based Initiatives; Charitable Choice

Black, Amy E., Douglas L. Koopman, and David K. Ryden. *Of Little Faith: The Politics of George W. Bush's Faith-Based Initiatives.* Washington, DC: Georgetown University Press, 2004.

Davis, Derek H. "The Church-State Implications of the New Welfare Reform Law." *Journal of Church and State* 38 (Autumn 1996): 217.

Davis, Derek H., and Barry Hankins. *Welfare Reform and Faith-based Organizations.* Waco, TX: J.M. Dawson Institute of Church-State Studies, 1999.

Farnsley, Arthur E. II. *Rising Expectations: Urban Congregations, Welfare Reform and Community Life.* Bloomington, IN: Indiana University Press, 2003.

Dionne, E.J. and John DiIulio, eds. *What's God Got to Do with the American Experiment.* Washington, DC: Brookings Institution, 2000.

Dionne, E.J. and Ming Hsu Chen. *Sacred Places, Civic Purposes: Should Government Help Faith-Based Charity?* Washington, DC: Brookings Institution Press, 2001.

Glennon, Fred. "Blessed Be the Ties that Bind? The Challenge of Charitable Choice to Moral Obligation." *Journal of Church and State* 42 (2000): 825.

Kennedy, Sheila Suess, and Wolfgang Bielefeld. *Charitable Choice at Work: Evaluation Faith-Based Job Programs in the States.* Washington, DC: Georgetown University Press, 2006.

Monsma, Stephen *v. When Sacred and Secular Mix: Religious Nonprofit Organizations and Public Money.* Lanham, MD: Rowman & Littlefield Publishers, 1996.

Olasky, Marvin. *Compassionate Conservatism: What It Is, What It Does, and How It Can Transform America.* New York: The Free Press, 2000.

Solomon, Lewis D. *In God We Trust? Faith-Based Organizations and the Quest to Solve America's Social Ills.* New York: Lanham Books, 2003.

Unruh, Heidi Rolland, and Ronald J. Sider. "Evangelism and Church-State Partnerships." *Journal of Church and State* 43 (2001): 401.

Chaves, Mark. "Religious Congregations and Welfare Reform: Who Will Take Advantage of Charitable Choice?" *American Sociological Review 64* (1999): 836.

SOCIOLOGICAL PERSPECTIVES

Civil Religion

Adams, David L. and Ken Schurb, eds. *The Anonymous God: The Church Confronts Civil Religion And American Society.* St. Louis, MO: Concordia, 2005.

Albanese, Catherine. *Sons of the Fathers: The Civil Religion of the American Revolution.* Philadelphia: Temple University Press, 1976.

Angrosino, Michael. "Civil Religion Redux." *Anthropological Quarterly* 75 (Spring 2002): 239.

Balmer, Randall. *God in the White House: How Faith Shaped the Presidency from John F. Kennedy to George W. Bush.* New York: HarperOne, 2008.

Bellah, Robert N. "Civil Religion in America," *Daedalus* 96 (1967): 1.

Bellah, Robert N. *The Broken Covenant: American Civil Religion in Time of Trial.* 2nd ed. Chicago: University of Chicago Press, 1975.

———. "Religion and the Legitimization of the American Republic." In *America, Christian or Secular: Readings in American Christian History and Civil Religion,* ed. Jerry S. Herbert. Portland, OR: Multnomah Press, 1984.

Bellah, Robert N. and Phillip E. Hammond, eds. *Varieties of Civil Religion.* San Francisco: Harper & Row, 1980.

Canipe, Lee. "Under God and Anti-communist: How the Pledge of Allegiance Got Religion in Cold-War America." *Journal of Church and State* 45 (Spring 2003): 305.

Cloud, Matthew W. "'One Nation, Under God': Tolerable Acknowledgement of Religion or Unconstitutional Cold War Propaganda Cloaked in American Civil Religion." *Journal of Church and State* 46 (Spring 2004): 311.

Coles, Roberta L. "Manifest Destinies Adapted for 1990's War Discourse: Mission and Destiny Intertwined." *Sociology of Religion* 63/4 (2002): 403.

Coleman, John A. "Civil Religion." *Sociological Analysis* 31 (1970): 67.

Cristi, Marcela. *From Civil to Political Religion: the Intersection of Culture, Religion and Politics.* Waterloo, Ontario: Wilfrid Laurier University Press, 2001.

Cristi, Marcela and Lorne L. Dawson. "Civil Religion in America and in Global Context," in *Handbook of the Sociology of Religion,* eds. James A. Beckford and N.J. Demerath III. London: Sage Publications, 2007.

Davis, Derek H. "God and the Pursuit of America's Self-Understanding: Toward a Synthesis of American Historiography." *Journal of Church and State* 46 (Summer 2004): 461.

———. "Law, Morals, and Civil Religion in America." *Journal of Church and State* 39 (Summer 1997): 411.

———. "Thoughts on a Civil Religion Solution to Religion Clause Jurisprudence." In *Chronos, Kairos, Christos II: Essays in Honor of Ray Summers.* ed. Jerry Vardaman. Macon, GA: Mercer University Press, 1998.

———. "Civil Religion as a Judicial Doctrine." *Journal of Church and State* 40 (Winter 1998): 7.

———. "Competing Notions of Law in American Civil Religion." *Law/Text/Culture* 5, No. 1 (2000): 265.

Deloria, Vine, Jr. "Secularism, Civil Religion, and the Religious Freedom of American Indians." *American Indian Culture and Research Journal* 16 (1992): 9.

Durkheim, Emile. *The Elementary Forms of the Religious Life*. rev. ed. New York: Free Press, 1965.

Forney, Craig A. *The Holy Trinity of American Sports: Civil Religion in Football, Baseball, and Basketball (Sports and Religion)*. Macon, GA: Mercer University Press, 2007.

Goldstein, Robert Justin. *Saving Old Glory: The History of the American Flag Desecration Controversy*. Boulder, CO: Westview Press, 1996.

Gunn, T. Jeremy. *Spiritual Weapons: The Cold War and the Forging of an American National Religion*. Westport, CT: Praeger, 2009

Herbert, Jerry S., ed. *America, Christian or Secular? Readings in American Christian History and Civil Religion*. Portland, OR: Multnomah Press, 1984.

Hudson, Winthrop, ed. *Nationalism and Religion in America: Concepts of American Identity and Mission*. New York: Harper & Row, 1970.

Hughes, Richard T. "Civil Religion, the Theology of the Republic, and the Free Church Tradition." *Journal of Church and State* 22 (Winter 1980): 78.

Jolicoeur, Pamela M. and Louis L. Knowles. "Fraternal Associations and Civil Religion: Scottish Rite Freemasonry." *Review of Religious Research* 20 (Fall 1978): 3.

Kao, Grace Y. and Jerome E. Copulsky. "The Pledge of Allegiance and the Meanings and Limits of Civil Religion." *Journal of the American Academy of Religion* 75 (March 2007): 121.

Kessler, Sanford. *Tocqueville's Civil Religion: American Christianity and the Prospects for Freedom*. Albany, NY: State University of New York Press, 1994.

Linder, Robert. "Civil Religion in Historical Perspective: The Reality that Underlies the Concept." *Journal of Church and State* 17 (Autumn 1975): 399.

———. "Universal Pastor: President Bill Clinton's Civil Religion." *Journal of Church and State* 38 (Autumn 1996): 733.

——— and Richard v. Pierard. "The President and Civil Religion." In *Encyclopedia of the American Presidency*, ed. Leonard W. Levy. New York: Simon and Schuster, 1994.

———. "Ronald Reagan, Civil Religion, and the New Religious Right in America." *Fides et History* 23 (Fall 1991): 57.

Little, David. "The Origins of Perplexity: Civil Religion and Moral Belief in the Thought of Thomas Jefferson." In *American Civil Religion*, eds. Russell E. Richey and Donald D. Jonesy. New York: Harper & Row, 1974.

Lippy, Charles H. "The 1780 Massachusetts Constitution: Religious Establishment or Civil Religion?" *Journal of Church and State* 20 (Autumn 1978): 533.

Lipset, Seymour Martin. *American Exceptionalism: A Double-Edged Sword*. New York: Norton, 1997.

Marty, Martin. "A Nation of Behavers." *Worldview* 17 (May 1974): 11.

Marvin, Carolyn and David W. Ingle. "Blood Sacrifice and the National: Revisiting Civil Religion." *Journal of the American Academy of Religion* 64 (Winter 1996): 767.

Mathisen, James A. "Twenty Years After Bellah: Whatever Happened to American Civil Religion?" *Sociological Analysis* 50/2 (1989): 29.

McDermott, Gerald Robert. "Civil Religion in the American Revolutionary Period: An Historiographic Analysis." *Christian Scholars Review* 18 (June 1989): 346.

http://www.amazon.com/Civil-Society-Religion-Theological-Studies/dp/B00097N0BU/ref=sr_1_73?ie=UTF8&s=books&qid=1243219305&sr=1–73.

McKenna, Joseph H. "Civil Society, Civil Religion." *Theological Studies* 58 (June 1997): 380.

Meacham, Jon. *American Gospel: God, the Founding Fathers, and the Making of a Nation.* New York: Random House, 2007.

Mead, Sidney E. *The Nation with the Soul of a Church.* New York: Harper & Row, 1975.

Meizel, Katherine. "A Singing Citizenry: Popular Music and Civil Religion in America." *Journal for the Scientific Study of Religion* 45/4 (2006): 497.

Mirsky, Yehudah. "Civil Religion and the Establishment Clause." *Yale Law Journal* 95 (1986): 1237.

Muller-Fahrenholz, Geiko and Donald W. Shriver Jr. *America's Battle for God: A European Christian Looks at Civil Religion.* Grand Rapids, MI: Eerdmans, 2007.

Parsons, Gerald. *Perspectives on Civil Religion (Religion Today: Tradition, Modernity and Change).* London: Ashgate, 2002.

Phillips, Kevin. *American Theocracy: The Peril and Politics of Radical Religion, Oil, and Borrowed Money in the 21ˢᵗ Century.* New York: Viking, 2006.

Pierard, Richard V., and Robert D. Linder. *Civil Religion and the Presidency.* Grand Rapids, MI: Zondervan, 1988.

———. "Civil Religion: Parallel Development or Replacement for Traditional Christianity." In *Christianity in the Post Secular West.* eds. John Stenhouse and Brett Knowles. Adelaide, Australia: ATF Press, 2007.

———. "One Nation under God: Judgment or Jingoism." In *Christian Social Ethics.* ed. Perry C. Cotham. Grand Rapids, MI: Baker, 1979.

Reddit, Paul L. "When Faith Demands Treason: Civil Religion and the Prophet Jeremiah." *Review and Expositor* 101 (Spring 2004): 227.

Richey, Russell E. and Donald G. Jones, eds. *American Civil Religion.* New York: Harper & Row, 1974.

Rouner, Leroy S., ed. *Civil Religion and Political Theology.* Notre Dame, IN: University of Notre Dame Press, 1986.

Smith, Gary Scott. *Faith and the Presidency: From George Washington to George W. Bush.* New York: Oxford University Press, 2006.

Stackhouse, Max L. "Civil Religion, Political Theology and Public Theology: What's the Difference?" *Political Theology* 5/3 (2004): 275.

Stookey, Stephen M. "In God We Trust? Evangelical Historiography and the Quest for a Christian America." *Southwestern Journal of Theology* 41/2–3 (Spring–Summer 1999): 43.

Tuveson, Ernest L. *Redeemer Nation: The Idea of America's Millennial Role.* Chicago: University of Chicago Press, 1968.

Waldman, Steven. *Founding Faith: Providence, Politics, and the Birth of Religious Freedom in America.* New York: Random House, 2008.

Woodrum, Eric and Arnold Bell. "Race, Politics, and Religion in Civil Religion among Blacks." *Sociological Analysis* 49/4 (1989): 353.

Wood, James E. Jr. "Public Religion vis a vis the Prophetic Role of Religion." *Journal of Church and State* 41 (Winter 1999): 62.

Wuthnow, Robert. *American Mythos: Why Our Best Efforts to Be a Better Nation Fall Short.* Princeton, NJ: Princeton University Press, 2008.

American Culture

Baird, Robert. *Religion in America; or, An Account of the Origin, Progress, Relation to the State, and Present Condition of the Evangelical Churches in the United States. With Notices of the Unevangelical Denominations*. Glasgow: Blackie and Co., 1844.

Berger, Peter. *The Sacred Canopy: Elements of a Sociological Theory of Religion*. New York: Doubleday, 1967.

Cherry, Conrad and Rowland A. Sherrill, eds. *Religion, the Independent Sector, and American Culture*. Atlanta, GA: Scholars Press, 1992.

Finke, Roger and Rodney Stark. *The Churching of America, 1776–2005*. New Brunswick, NJ: Rutgers University Press, 2005)

Frank, Thomas. *What's the Matter with Kansas?* New York: Henry Holt Publishing, 2004.

Greeley, Andrew and Michael Hout. *The Truth about Conservative Christians*. Chicago: University of Chicago Press, 2006.

Heclo, Hugh and Wilfred McClay, eds. *Religion Returns to the Public Square*. Baltimore: Johns Hopkins University Press, 2003.

Hunter, James D. *Culture Wars: The Struggle to Define America*. New York: Basic Books, 1991.

Jelen, Ted G. and Clyde Wilcox. *Public Attit udes toward Church and State*. Armonk, NY: M.E. Sharpe, 1995.

Kosmin, Barry A. and Seymour P. Lachman. *One Nation Under God: Religion in Contemporary Society*. New York: Harmony books, 1993.

McDonald, Forest. *Revivals, Awakening, and Reform: Religion and Social Change in America, 1607–1977*. Chicago: University of Chicago Press, 1978.

Rauschenbush, Paul, ed. *Christianity and the Social Crisis in the 21ˢᵗ Century*. New York: HarperCollins, 2007.

Schaff Philip. *America: A Sketch of Its Political, Social, and Religious Character*. Cambridge, MA: The Belknap Press, 1855.

Sweet, William Warren. *Religion in the Development of American Culture, 1765–1840*. New York: Charles Scribner's Sons, 1952.

Thomas, John L. *Religion and the American People*. Westminster, MD: The Newman Press, 1963.

Wilson, John F. *Public Religion in American Culture*. Philadelphia: Temple University Press, 1979.

Wuthnow, Robert. *The Restructuring of American Religion: Society and Faith Since World War II*. Princeton, NJ: Princeton U. Press, 1988.

New Religious Movements

Beckford, James A. *Cult Controversies: The Societal Response to New Religious Movements*. London: Tavistock Publications, 1985.

Belknap, Michal and Cathy Shipe. "Cults and the Law." In *Religion and American Law: An Encyclopedia*, ed. Paul Finkelman. New York: Garland Publishing, 2000.

Best, Joel. *Threatened Children*. Chicago: University of Chicago Press, 1990.

Bromley, David and James T. Richardson. *The Brainwashing/Deprogramming Debate*. New York: Edwin Mellen, 1983.

Bromley, David. *The Politics of Religious Apostasy*. Westport, CT: Praeger, 1998.

Hempton, David. "Methodism and the Law, 1740–1820." In *Sects and New Religious Movements*, eds. A. Dyson and E. Barker. *Bulletin of the John Rylands Library* 70 (1988): 94.

Palmer, Susan and C. Hardman, eds. *Children in New Religions.* New Brunswick, NJ:
    Rutgers University Press, 1999.
Richardson, James T. *Money and Power in the New Religions.* New York: Edwin Mellen,
    1998.
Robbins, Thomas and James A. Beckford. "Religious Movements and Church-State
    Issues." In *Handbook of Cults and Sects.* eds. D. Bromley and J. Hadden. Greenwich,
    CT: JAI Press, 1993.
Ryan, James E. "Smith and the Religious Freedom Restoration Act: An Iconoclastic
    Assessment." *Virginia Law Review* 78 (1992): 1417.
Shupe, Anson. *Spoils of the Kingdom: Clergy Misconduct and Religious Community.* Urbana,
    IL: University of Illinois Press, 2007.*Virginia Law Review* 78 (1992): 1417.
Williams, Cynthia Norman. "America's Opposition to New Religious Movements:
    Limiting the Freedom of Religion." *Law and Psychology Review* 27 (Spring 2003): 171.
Yang, Fenggang and Helen Rose Ebaugh. "Transformation in New Immigrant Religions
    and Their Global Implications." *American Sociological Review* 66 (2001): 269.

TABLE OF CASES

Abingdon School District v. Schempp, 374 U.S. 203 (1963).
ACLU v. Florissant, 186 F.3d 1095 (8th Cir. 1999).
ACLU of Ohio v. Capitol Square Review and Advisory Board, 243 F.3d 289 (6th Cir. 2001).
ACLU v. Schundler, 168 F.3d 92 (3d Cir. 1999).
Africa v. Pennsylvania, 662 F.2d 1025 (3d Cir. 1981) *cert.* denied 456 U.S. 908 (1983).
Agostini v. Felton, 521 U.S. 203 (1997).
Aguilar v. Felton, 105 S. Ct. 3232 (1985).
Allegheny County v. Greater Pittsburgh ACLU, 492 U.S. 573 (1989).
American Jewish Congress v. City of Beverly Hills, 90 F.3d 379 (9th Cir. 1996).
Ansonia Board of Education v. Philbrook, 479 U.S. 60 (1986).
Aronov v. United States, 432 F.2d 242 (9th Cir. 1970).
Arver v. United States, 245 U.S. 366 (1918).
Ashcroft v. O Centro Espirita Beneficento Uniao Do Vegetal, 546 U.S. 418 (2006).
Ashwander v. TVA, 297 U.S. 288 (1936).
Att'y Gen. v. Desilets, 636 N.E.2d 233 (Mass. 1994).
Baker v. Nachtrieb, 19 Howard, 60 U.S. 126 (1856).
Bethel Conservative Mennonite Church v. Commissioner, 80 T.C. 352 (1983), rev'd., 746 F.2d
    388 (7th Cir. 1984).
Board of Education v. Allen, 392 U.S. 236 (1968).
Bob Jones University v. United States, 461 U.S. 574 (1983).
Bd. of Educ. of Kiryas Joel Village Sch. Dist. v. Grumet, 512 U.S. 687 (1994).
Bd. of Educ. v. Minor, 23 Ohio St. 211 (1873).
Bob Jones University v. United States, 461 U.S. 574 (1983).
Boerne v. Archbishop Flores, 521 U.S. 507 (1997).
Bowen v. Roy, 476 U.S. 693 (1986).
Bowers v. Hardwick, 478 U.S. 186 (1986).
Bradfield v. Roberts, 175 U.S. 291 (1899).
Braunfeld v. Brown, 366 U.S. 599 (1961).
Burton v. United States, 196 U.S. 283 (1905).

Cantwell v. Connecticut, 310 U.S. 296 (1940).

Capitol Square Review & Advisory Bd. v. Pinette, 515 U.S. 753 (1995).

Catholic Charities of Sacramento v Superior Court, No. SO99822 (SC CA, 2004).

Chaplinsky v. New Hampshire, 315 U.S. 568 (1942).

Church of the Holy Trinity v. United States, 143 U.S. 457 (1893).

Church of the Lukumi abalu Aye, Inc. and Ernesto Pichado v. City of Hialeah, 508 U.S. 520
    (1993).

City Chapel Evangelical Free Inc. v. City of South Bend, 744 N.E.2d 443 (Ind. 2001).

Cochran v. Louisiana Board of Education, 281 U.S. 370 (1930).

Coleman v. City of Griffin, 302 U.S. 636 (1937).

Colorado River Water Conservation District v. United States, 424 U.S. 800 (1976).

Committee for Public Education & Religious Liberty v. Nyquist, 413 U.S. 756 (1973).

Congregation Lubavitch v. City of Cincinnati, 997 F.2d 1160 (6th Cir. 1993).

Cornelius v. NAACP Legal Defense & Educational Fund, Inc., 473 U.S. 788 (1985).

Corporation of the Presiding Bishop of the Church of Jesus Christ of Latter-Day Saints v.
    Amos, 438 U.S. 327 (1987).

County of Allegheny v. ACLU of Greater Pittsburgh, 492 U.S. 573 (1989).

Cox v. New Hampshire, 312 U.S. 569 (1941).

Crowell v. Benson, 285 U.S. 22 (1932).

Cruz v. Beto, 405 U.S. 319 (1972).

Cutter v. Wilkinson, 544 U.S. 709 (2005).

Davis v. Beason, 133 U.S. 333, 342 (1890).

DeJong v. Commissioner, 36 T.C. 896 (1961).

Douglas v. City of Jeanette, 319 U.S. 157 (1943).

Edwards v. Aguillard, 482 U.S. 578(1987).

Eisenstadt v. Baird, 405 U.S. 438 (1972).

Elewski v. Syracuse, 123 F.3d 51 (2d Cir. 1997).

Elk Grove Unified School District v. Newdow, 542 U.S. 1 (2004).

Employment Division, Department of Human Resources of Oregon v. Smith, 495 U.S. 872
    (1990).

Engel v. Vitale, 370 U.S. 421 (1962).

Epperson v. Arkansas, 393 U.S. 97 (1968).

Estate of Thornton v. Caldor, 472 U.S. 703 (1985).

Estep v. United States, 327 U.S. 114 (1946).

Everson v. Board of Education, 330 U.S. 1 (1947).

Falbo v. United States, 320 U.S. 549 (1944).

Fiscal Court v. Brady, 885 S.W.2d 681 (Ky. 1994).

Flast v. Cohen, 392 U.S. 83 (1968).

Florey v. Sioux Falls, 619 F.2d 1311 (8th Cir. 1980).

Follett v. Town of McCormick, 321 U.S. 573 (1944).

Fortin v. Roman Catholic Bishop of Portland, 871 A.2d 1208 (Me. 2005).

Founding Church of Scientology of Washington DC v. United States, 409 F.2d 1146 (D.C.
    Cir.) cert. denied 296 U.S. 963 (1969).

Fowler v. Rhode Island, 345 U.S. 67 (1953).

Fraternal Order of Police Newark Lodge No. 12 v. City of Newark, 170 F.3d 359 (3rd Cir.
    1999).

Frazee v. Illinois Department of Employment Security, 489 U.S. 829 (1989).

Freethought Society of Greater Philadelphia v. Chester County, 334 F.3d 247 (3d. Cir. 2003).

Frothingham v. Mellon, 262 U.S. 447 (1923).

Gallagher v. Crown Kosher Super Market of Mass., Inc., 366 U.S. 617 (1961).

Gaylor v. United States, 74 F.3d 214 (10th Cir. 1996).

Gillette v. United States, 401 U.S. 437 (1971).

Girouard v. United States, 328 U.S. 61 (1946).

Goesele v. Bimeler, 55 U.S. 589 (1853).

Goldman v Weinberger, 475 U.S. 503 (1986).

Gonzales v. Archbishop, 280 U.S. 1 (1929).

Gonzales v. O Centro Espirita Beneficente Uniao Do Vegetal, 546 U.S. 418 (2006).

Good News Club v. Milford Central School, 533 U.S. 98 (2001).

Grand Rapids School District v. Ball, 473 U.S. 373 (1985).

Griswold v. Connecticut, 381 U.S. 479 (1965).

Grossbau v. Indianapolis, 100 F.3d 1287 (7th Cir. 1996).

Hamilton v. Regents of the University of California, 293 U.S. 245 (1934).

Hasan and Chaush v. Bulgaria, App. No. 309985/96, Eur. Ct. H.R. Decision of 26 Oct. 2000.

Haswell v. United States, 500 F.2d 1133 (Ct. Cl. 1974), cert. denied, 419 U.S. 1107 (1975).

Heffron v. International Society for Krishna Consciousness (ISKCON), 452 U.S. 640 (1981).

Hein v. Freedom from Religion Foundation, 551 U.S. 587 (2007).

Hernandez v. Commissioner of Internal Revenue, 490 U.S. 680 (1989).

Hobbie v. Unemployment Appeals Commission, 480 U.S. 136 (1987).

Holy Trinity Church v. United States, 143 U.S. 457 (1892).

Horen v. Commonwealth, 479 S.E.2d 553 (Va. Ct. App. 1997).

Humphrey v. Lane, 728 N.E.2d 1039 (Ohio 2000).

Hunt v. Hunt, 648 A.2d 843 (Vt. 1994).

Hunt v. McNair, 413 U.S. 734 (1973).

Illinois ex rel. McCollum v. Bd. of Educ. of Sch. Dist. No. 71, 333 U.S. 203 (1948).

In re Browning, 476 S.E.2d 465 (N.C. Ct. App. 1996).

International Society for Krishna Consciousness (ISKCON) v. Lee, 505 U.S. 672 (1992).

Jamison v. Texas, 318 U.S. 413 (1943).

Jimmy Swaggart Ministries v. Board of Equalization of California, 493 U.S. 378 (1990).

Joki v. Board of Educ. of Schuylerville Cent. School Dist., 745 F. Supp 823 (N.D.N.Y., 1990).

Jones v. City of Opelika, 316 U.S. 584 (1942).

Kedroff v. St. Nicholas Cathedral of the RU.S.sian Orthodox Church, 344 U.S. 94 (1952).

Knights of Columbus v. Lexington, 272 F.3d 25 (1st Cir. 2001).

Koenick v. Felton, 190 F.3d 259 (4th Cir. 1999).

Kreisner v. San Diego, 1 F.3d 775 (9th Cir. 1993).

Lamb's Chapel v. Center Moriches Union Free School District, 508 U.S. 384 (1993).

Largent v. Texas, 318 U.S. 418 (1943).

Larson v. Cooper, 90 P.3d 125 (Alaska 2004).

Lawrence v. Texas, 539 U.S. 558 (2003).

Lee v. Weisman, 505 U.S. 577 (1992).

Lemon v. Kurtzman, 403 U.S. 602 (1971).

Levitt v. Pearl, 413 U.S. 472 (1973).

Light v. United States, 220 U.S. 523 (1911).

Liverpool, NY: & P.S.S. Co. v. Emigration Commissioners, 113 U.S. 33 (1885).

Lovell v. City of Griffin, 303 U.S. 444 (1938).

Lynch v. Donnelly, 465 U.S. 668 (1984).

Lyng v. Northwest Indian Cemetery Protective Association, 485 U.S. 439 (1988).

Malnak v Yogi, 592 F.2d 197 (3d Cir. 1979).

Marsh v. Alabama, 326 U.S. 501 (1946).

Marsh v. Chambers, 463 U.S. 783 (1983).

McCollum v. Board of Education, 333 U.S. 203 (1948).

McCready v. Hoffius, 586 N.W.2d 723 (Mich. 1998).

McCreary County v. ACLU of Kentucky, 545 U.S. 844 (2005).

McDaniel v. Paty, 435 U.S. 618 (1978).

Meek v. Pittenger, 421 U.S. 229 (1977).

Metropolitan Church of Bessarabia v. Moldova, App. No. 45701/99, Eur. Ct. H.R., Decision of 13 Dec. 2001.

Metzl v. Leininger, 57 F.3d 618 (7th Cir. 1995).

Minersville School District v. Gobitis, 310 U.S. 586 (1940).

Mitchell v. Helms, 530 U.S. 793 (2000).

Modrovich v. Allegheny County, 385 F.3d 397 (3d Cir. 2004).

Mueller v. Allen, 463 U.S. 388 (1983).

Murray v. The Charming Betsey, 6 U.S. 64 (1804).

National Labor Relations Board v. Catholic Bishop of Chicago, 440 U.S. 490 (1973).

Niemotko v. Maryland, 340 U.S. 268 (1951).

O'Lone v. Estate of Shabazz, 482 U.S. 342 (1987).

Open Door Baptist Church v. Clark County, 995 P.2d 33 (Wash. 2000).

Order of St. Benedict v. Steinhauser, 234 U.S. 640 (1914).

Palko v. Connecticut, 302 U. S. (1937).

Pearl v. Nyquist, 413 U.S. 756 (1973).

Perry Educ. Ass'n v. Perry Local Educators' Ass'n, 460 U.S. 37 (1983).

Pierce v. Society of Sisters, 268 U.S. 510 (1925).

Poulos v. New Hampshire, 345 U.S. 395 (1953).

O'Lone v. Estate of Shabazz, 482 U.S. 342 (1987).

Open Door Baptist Church v. Clark County, 995 P.2d 33 (Wash. 2000).

Reynolds v. United States, 98 U.S. 145 (1878).

Roe v. Wade, 410 U.S. 113 (1973).

Roemer v. Board of Public Works of Maryland, 426 U.S. 736 (1971).

Romer v. Evans, 517 U.S. 620 (1996).

Rosenberger v. Rector & Visitors of Univ. of Va., 515 U.S. 819 (1995).

Rourke v. NY: State Dep't of Corr. Servs., 603 N.Y.S.2d 647 (NY: Sup. Ct. 1993).

Saia v. New York, 334 U.S. 558 (1948).

Santa Fe v. Doe, 530 U.S. 27 (2002).

Schneider v. New Jersey, 308 U.S. 147 (1939).

Seasongood v. Commissioner, 227 F.2d 907 (6th Cir. 1955).

Serbian Eastern Orthodox Diocese v. Milivojevich, 426 U.S. 696 (1975).

Serif v. Greece, App. No. 38178/97, Eur. Ct. H.R., Decision of 14 Dec. 1999.

Sherbert v. Verner, 374 U.S. 398 (1963).

Sherman v. Community Consolidated School District, 980 F.2d 437(7th Cir. 1992), 445 cert. denied, 508 U.S. 950 (1993).

Sicurella v. United States, 348 U.S. 385 (1955).

Siler v. Louisville & Nashville Railway Co., 213 U.S. 175 (1909).

Skoros v. New York, 437 F.3d 1 (2d Cir. 2006).

Smith v. Board of Commissioners of Mobile County, 655 F. Supp. 939 (S. Dist. Ala 937) (1986).

Spector Motor Service v. McLaughlin, 323 U.S. 101 (1944).

State ex rel. Heitkamp v. Family Life Servs., 560 N.W.2d 526 (N.D. 1997).

State v. Evans, 796 P.2d 178 (Kan. App. 1990).

State v. Hershberger, 462 N.W.2d 393 (Minn. 1990).

State v. Miller, 549 N.W.2d 235, 238-42 (Wis. 1996).

Stein v. Plainwell Community Schools, 822 F.2d 1406 (6th Cir. 1987).

St. John's Lutheran Church v. State Comp. Ins. Fund, 830 P.2d 1271 (Mont. 1992).

Stone v. Graham, 449 U.S. 39 (1980).

Sultaana Lakiana Myke Freeman v. State of Florida, 924 So.2d 48 (Fla. App. 5 Dist. 2006).

Thomas v. Review Board of the Indiana Employment Security Division, 450 U.S. 707 (1981).

Thornton v. Caldor, 472 U.S. 703 (1985).

Tilton v. Richardson, 403 U.S. 672 (1971).

Torcaso v. Watkins, 367 U.S. 488 (1961).

Trans World Airlines v. Hardison, 432 U.S. 63 (1977).

Tucker v. Texas, 326 U.S. 517 (1946).

United States v Ballard, 322 U.S. 78 (1944).

United States v. Bland, 283 U.S. 636 (1931).

United States v. Kauten, 133 F. 2d 703, 708 (2d Cir. 1943).

United States v. Lee, 455 U.S. 252 (1982).

United States v. Macintosh, 283 U.S. 605 (1931).

United States v. Meyers, 906 F. Sup 1494 (D. Wyo., 1995).

United States v. Schwimmer, 279 U.S. 644 (1929).

United States v. Seeger, 380 U.S. 163 (1965).

United States v Welsh, 398 U.S. 333 (1972).

Valley Forge Christian College v. Americans United for Separation of Church and State, 454 U.S. 464 (1982).

Van Orden v. Perry, 545 U.S. 677 (2005).

Vidal v. Girard's Executors, 43 U.S. 127 (1844).

Wallace v. Jaffree, 472 U.S. 38 (1985).

Walz v. Tax Commissioner, 397 U.S. 664 (1970).

Walz v. Tax Commissioner, 397 U.S. 664 (1970).

Ware v. Hylton, 3 U.S. 19 (1796).

Warner v. City of Boca Raton, 64 F. Supp. 2d 1272 (1999), 267 F.3d 1223, 1227 (2001); 887 S.2d 1023 (Fla. 2004).

Warren v. Fairfax County, 196 F.3d 186 (4th Cir. 1999).

Washegesic v. Bloomingdale Public Schools, 33 F.3d 679 (6th Cir. 1994).

Watson v. Jones, 80 U.S. 679 (1872).

Wells v. Denver, 257 F.3d 1132 (10th Cir. 2001).

West Virginia State Board of Education v. Barnette, 319 U.S. 624 (1943).

Widmar v. Vincent, 454 U.S. 263 (1981).

Wisconsin v. Yoder, 406 U.S. 205 (1972).

Wolman v. Walter, 433 U.S. 229 (1977).

Warner v. City of Boca Raton, 64 F. Supp. 2d 1272 (1999), 267 F.3d 1223, 1227 (2001); 887 S.2d 1023 (Fla. 2004).

Watson v. Jones, 80 U.S. 679 (1872), 728.

Welsh v. United States, 398 U.S. 333 (1970).

Wolman v. Walter, 433 U.S. 229 (1977).

Wisconsin v. Yoder, 406 U.S. 205 (1972).

Zelman v. Simmons-Harris, 536 U.S. 639 (2002).

Zobrest v. Catalina Hills, 509 U.S. 1 (1993).

Zorach v. Clauson, 343 U.S. 306 (1952).

INDEX